SLAPSTICK DIVAS

THE WOMEN OF SILENT COMEDY

BY STEVE MASSA

Slapstick Divas: The Women of Silent Comedy
© 2017. Steve Massa. All rights reserved.

All illustrations/photographs are copyright of their respective owners, and are also reproduced here in the spirit of publicity. Whilst we have made every effort to acknowledge specific credits whenever possible, we apologize for any omissions, and will undertake every effort to make any appropriate changes in future editions of this book if necessary.

No part of this book may be reproduced in any form or by any means, electronic, mechanical, digital, photocopying or recording, except for the inclusion in a review, without permission in writing from the publisher.

Published in the USA by:
BearManor Media
P O Box 71426
Albany, Georgia 31708
www.bearmanormedia.com

Printed in the United States of America
ISBN   978-1-62933-132-4 (paperback)

Book & cover design and layout by Darlene Swanson • www.van-garde.com

Thelma Hill (far left) and a bevy of unknown beauties pose in front of the Fred Balshofer Studio circa 1920. Courtesy of Sam Gill.

To the scores of women who were involved in silent comedy – named and unnamed, in front of and behind the camera – who worked hard and did their part in turning an unappreciated and often considered low-class genre into an art form.

And to the generosity and camaraderie of Robert S. Birchard, Cole Johnson, and Charles Silver. Thanks so much guys.

CONTENTS

	Introduction and Acknowledgements	vii
Chapter One:	Film Comedy's Eves	1
Chapter Two:	"The Sugar on the Keystone Grapefruit"	25
Chapter Three:	Starring Clowns	69
Chapter Four:	Leading Ladies of the Teens	109
Chapter Five:	Leading Ladies of the Twenties	179
Chapter Six:	Behind the Camera	210
Chapter Seven:	Supporting Characters	295
Chapter Eight:	Bathing Beauties and Love Interests	349
Chapter Nine:	Distaff Duos	406
Part Two:	Selected Biographies	420
	Bibliography	615
	About the Author	619
	Index	621

Universal Weekly caricature of their diminutive comedy star Baby Peggy.

INTRODUCTION AND ACKNOWLEDGMENTS

"Dying is easy....comedy is hard."

The above is the famous deathbed quote that has been attributed to illustrious actors such as Edmund Kean, Sir Donald Wolfit, and Edmund Gwenn. Doesn't matter who actually said it – the sentiment accurately sums up the common view of performing comedy as a "roll up your sleeves" type of hard labor. Among comedians, images of battle are even frequent ranging from stand-up comics who talk about "killing their audiences," to the war scars borne by veteran performers like Lupino Lane and his brother Wallace Lupino from years of mistimed bits of business. So when it comes to women and comedy, the prevailing attitude has always been, "It's a tough business, so the soft and pretty need not apply."

American silent comedy in particular has come to be regarded as man's work, as if only men were brave (or foolhardy) enough to hang off a building or pratfall down a flight of stairs in the name of entertainment. Film historians and critics have rhapsodized over and devoted volumes to the talents of Chaplin, Keaton, Lloyd, and Laurel & Hardy, but outside of the usual references to Mabel Normand or Marie Dressler, perhaps a photo of Louise Fazenda in pigtails, or a kind word about Anita Garvin falling on the pie at the end of *The Battle of the Century* (1927), there's been very little said about the ladies who took bumps and bruises alongside the guys in the Teens and Twenties.

Even as astute a critic as Walter Kerr overlooks the women. The same kind of neglect occurs in his seminal 1975 book *The Silent Clowns*. Not until chapter 30 does Kerr get around to discussing the women, and in two paragraphs comes to the conclusion that "No comedienne ever became a truly important silent film clown," basically because he feels that it was impossible for an actress to be funny and pretty at the same time. That said, he hightails it back to the boys.

I'm not sure what exactly denotes a "truly important silent film clown," but if popularity is a criterion, Mabel Normand was the first comic to move from shorts to an ongoing series of silent features, beating Arbuckle, Chaplin, Lloyd, and the others to the punch, and was soon followed by Bebe Daniels, Dorothy Gish, and Marie Prevost. Some of the biggest stars of the 1920s were Colleen Moore, Marion Davies, and Clara Bow. In shorts, Alice Howell, Gale Henry, Fay Tincher, Polly Moran, Dorothy Devore, and Alice Day had been part of comedy ensembles and were moved into their own starring series of shorts designed to showcase and exploit their unique talents because audiences liked them and wanted to see more of them.

As far as reappraisals go, the silent comedy "boys club" seems to have started in earnest with James Agee's 1947 *Life* magazine article "Comedy's Greatest Era." As far as the ladies there are only passing mentions of the Mack Sennett Bathing Beauties and Louise

Fazenda, while the main thrust of Agee's piece is establishing the hierarchy of Chaplin-Keaton-Lloyd-Langdon. Since then most of the discussion of the women comics has been in the shadow of the male clowns – as support to people like Laurel & Hardy or Harold Lloyd. In contrast to the mini-industry of biographies on Chaplin and Keaton, it's been very sporadic on the ladies – a couple on Marie Dressler, one on Mabel Normand, the autobiographies of Colleen Moore and Marion Davies, with the best of this slender output being David Stenn's excellent *Clara Bow: Runnin' Wild* (Doubleday, 1988).

Whatever the reasons, there's no doubt that the women have been neglected, but I'll leave it to the sociologists to detail all the whys and wherefores. I'd like to go ahead and try to bring some attention to their careers and work. It may seem odd and presumptuous for a man to be writing this book, but in my defense this work originally grew out of my love for two particular comediennes – Alice Howell and Gale Henry. Researching their films and careers caused it to really sink in to me just how many funny women there were in silent comedy, and to formulate the obvious question—"Why aren't they better known?"

As always in an endeavor like this, that's taken years from inception to fruition, there are many, many people to thank. First off, I'd like to acknowledge the inspiration, encouragement, and guidance I've received from Eileen Bowser, Robert S. Birchard, Serge Bromberg, Sam Gill, Elif Rongen-Kaynacki, Dave Kehr, Ron Magliozzi, Mike Mashon, Ben Model, David Robinson, Rob Stone, and Brent Walker.

For sharing research, photos, films, and other materials I'll always be in the debt of Robert Arkus, Peter Bagrov, John Bengtson, Robert S. Birchard, Eileen Bowser, Serge Bromberg, Bruce Calvert, Michael Campino, Philip Carli, Stefan Drossler, Rob Farr, Frank Flood, Sam Gill, Michael J. Hayde, Cole Johnson, Elif Rongen-Kaynakci, Dave Kehr, Jim Kerkhoff, Robert James Kiss, Richard Koszarski, Crystal Kui, Bruce Lawton, James Layton, Marianne Lewinsky, Ron Magliozzi, Mike Mashon, Bruno Mestdagh, Ben Model, Rachel Parker, Tom Reeder, Steve Rydzewski, Charles Silver, Richard Simonton, Marilyn Slater, Larry Smith, David Stenn, Rob Stone, Ashley Swinnerton, Brent Walker, Jay Weissberg, and George Willeman.

I've also been incredibly lucky to have special help from two very talented people – Robert Arkus and Marlene Weissman Abadi. As he had on *Lame Brains and Lunatics*, Rob supervised the transferal and tweaking of this book's images, as well as providing photos from his own collection. His untiring work, superb eye, and great ideas were an invaluable contribution and support. Marlene designed this fantastic cover – in fact, designed *four* covers that were all wonderful and very hard to choose between. She has the knack for always coming up with an image that's striking and interesting on its own, but at the same time is evocative of the silent era.

In addition to everyone mentioned above there are the friends, fellow researchers, and comedy lovers Mike Abadi, Joe Adamson, Mana Allen, Norbert Aping, Alice Artzt, Lisa Bradberry, Neil Brand, Geoff Brown, Rick De Croix, Louie Despres, Dennis Doros, David Eickemeyer, Richard Finegan, Valerio Greco, Bob Greenberg, Geraldine

Hawkins, Mark Heller, Tommie Hicks, Lisa Stein Haven, Laura Horak, Nelson Hughes, Mark Johnson, Rob King, Annette D'Agostino Lloyd, Hooman Mehran, Jon Mirsalis, Molly Model, Joe Moore, Jack Roth, Jeni Rymer, Uli Ruedel, Frank Schiede, David Schwartz, Linda Shah, David Shepard, Andrew Sholl, Randy Skretvedt, Melinda Solan, Yair Solan, Tommy Stathes, Dave Stevenson, Cathy Surowiec, Karl Tiedemann, Kim Tomadjolou, Lorenzo Tremarelli, Lee Tsiantis, Ed Watz, Bill Weber, Steven Winer, Joseph Yranski, Steve Zalusky, and Henry Zorn, plus a nod to mentors William K. Everson and Jay Leyda.

As far as archives, libraries, and research facilities I must first thank my colleagues in the Billy Rose Theatre Collection at the New York Public Library for the Performing Arts at Lincoln Center, and especially Ton Lisanti, Jeremy MeGraw, David Callahan, Doug Reside, and Charlie Morrow. I also want to give big thanks to:

The Museum of Modern Art Department of Film: Dave Kehr, James Layton, Ron Magliozzi, Anne Morra, Rajendra Roy, Josh Siegel, Charles Silver, Ashley Swinnerton, Katie Trainor, and Peter Williamson.

The Library of Congress: Rob Stone, Mike Mashon, Madeline Matz, Rosemary Hanes, Rachel Parker, Jenny Paxson, Zoran Sinobad, Larry Smith, and George Willeman.

EYE Filmmuseum, Netherlands: Elif Rongen-Kaynacki, Catherine Cormon, Mark Paul Meyer, Rixt Jonkman, Marlene Labst, Dorrette Schootemeijer, and Frederique Urlings.

George Eastman House: Anthony L'Abbate, Jared Case, and Nancy Kaufman.

Thank you to Ben Ohmart, Annette D'Aogostino, Darlene Swanson, and everyone else at BearManor Media for the opportunity to make this volume a reality.

My most important thank you goes to my very patient wife and son, who have put up with and encouraged my silent comedy obsession. Without their love and support, this study wouldn't have been possible.

Stage star May Irwin is credited with providing the first onscreen pucker in *The Kiss* (1896). Author's collection.

Chapter 1

FILM COMEDY'S EVES

When the cinema first began, everything was a short subject – little actualities showing the electrocution of an elephant, or re-enactments of historical events featuring toy boats fighting the Battle of Manila Bay. Filmed snippets of stage acts were also a staple, and this is how the first funny women appeared on the screen. The year 1896 saw two well-known comediennes, May Irwin and Cissy Fitzgerald, each stick a toe in the early cinematic waters for the Edison Company. *The Kiss* captured the kissing scene between Ms. Irwin and John C. Rice from their hit Broadway comedy play *The Widow Jones*. On screen it lasted less than a minute and wasn't funny, but it did create a sensation and brought up the first censorship issues for the infant industry. Never giving the cinema a serious thought, May Irwin remained on stage, only making one other movie appearance in the feature *Mrs. Black is Back* (1914), again based on one of her stage hits.

Cissy Fitzgerald, on the other hand, became a film comedy regular. Famous for her skirt dances and "the winking song" – so much so that for decades she was known as "the girl with the wink" – her first film, *Cissy Fitzgerald* (1896), captured her dancing and wink, and along with *The Kiss* was shown in some of the first Edison exhibitions. In 1927, thirty-one years later, she recalled for *Photoplay* magazine the experience of going out to East Orange, New Jersey on a very cold winter's day:

> Mr. Edison was in his laboratory. At one end of the room was this little black box with a handle. It stood on a tripod, in just the way it does today. He commenced to crank. It sounded like a Gatling gun. The noise was terrific for such a small black box. It clattered and spluttered and I danced my 'Gayety Girl' dance. Back and forth I dipped and curtsied. I sang snatches of my little song…

After a large gap, Ms. Fitzgerald returned to movies with a vengeance in 1914 to work for Vitagraph in comedy shorts such as *How Sissy Made Good* and *The Win(k)some Widow*. Moving over to George Kleine Productions, Mutual's Casino Comedies, and Producers Security Corporation, she continued making shorts like *Zablitzky's Waterloo* (1915), *Leave It to Cissy* (1916), and *Cissy's Saucy Stockings* (1921) through 1921. No longer the saucy young thing, she transitioned to an older character actress and was in demand as support in features. Some of the many silent and sound films she appeared in before her death in 1941 include *Babbitt* (1924), *McFadden's Flats* (1927), *Two Flaming Youths* (1927) with W.C. Fields and Chester Conklin, *Only Yesterday* (1933), and *The Masquerader* (1933).

Dancer and comedienne Cissy Fitzgerald in action. Billy Rose Theatre Division, the New York Public Library for the Performing Arts.

The comedies that were produced immediately after 1900 were simple one-joke situations. Focus was on the brief story and the performers were anonymous and almost superfluous. This began to change around 1910 as filmmaking techniques became more sophisticated – in particular the camera moved closer to the actors so now humor could come from their performances. Film comediennes began turning up in Europe, and a number of them became popular and entertained audiences with regular cinematic misadventures. Women's roles in the earlier European slapstick, especially domineering mothers-in law or hideous prospective brides, were played by men in drag. Always popular on the stage for comic effect, the early cinema adopted it right away particularly when a female character was due to take a lot of physical punishment during the ensuing knockabout action. But after 1910 there were a number of hardy actresses who weren't afraid of taking punishment in the line of slapstick duty.

In France, roly-poly Sarah Duhamel had been a child actress on the stage from the age of three. Extremely prolific, she starred in her own *Rosalie* comedies for Pathé, as well as *Petronille* for Éclair. In these entries she was frequently a large and excitable maid or cook who left a good deal of destruction in her wake. She also co-starred as the rotund love interest for the stunted Maurice Schwartz in the *Little Moritz* series, and was paired opposite Lucien Bataille in his *Casimir* comedies. After marrying actor Edouard Louis Schmit she retired in 1916, but made one final appearance in *Les mysteries of Paris* (1924).

Known as "La Farfalletta," Valentina Frascaroli appeared in dramas as well as slapstick comedies. Authors collection.

The Italian-born Valentina Frascaroli was the wife and partner of the French comedy star Andre Deed, and appeared with him in his misadventures such as *La fete de Boireau* (*Boireau's Celebration*, 1912) and *Une extraordinaire aventure de Boireau* (*Boireau's Extraordinary Adventure*, 1914). Also supporting Deed when he defected to the Itala Company of Turin where he was renamed Crettinetti, after the couple returned to France she starred in her own brief series of five *Gribouillette* comedies in 1914. Little and childlike, she was known as "La Farfalletta" (Little Butterfly), and besides her work with Deed she also appeared in *L'emigrant* (1915) and Giovanni Pastrone's *Tigre reale* (1916). One of Deed and Frascaroli's later films was the comedy/sci fi feature *L'Uomo Meccanico* (*The Mechanical Man* 1921). "La Farfalletta" left the screen in 1923, and passed away in the late 1950s.

Two other early French comediennes were popular but their names are unknown

Gigetta Morano was a popular star of Italy's Ambrosio Company. Author's collection.

today. Leontine was a bratty and destructive little girl in a series for Comica, the subsidiary of Pathé. Twenty-one titles were made from 1909 to 1912, and included entries such as *La bate au de leontine* (*Leontine's Toy Boat*, 1911) where left alone she floods an entire townhouse in order to play with a new toy boat. The other anonymous performer is the actress who played the oafish servant Cunegonde in twenty-five shorts for the Lux Company from 1911 to 1913. Ruddy-faced and awkward, a good example of the series is *Cunegonde de aime son maître* (*Cunegonde in Love with her Master*, 1912) where the lady of the house wants a maid that her amorous husband won't flirt with, so she hires the ugly Cunegonde. She, of course, falls in love with the master and drives him crazy with her unwanted attentions. Although both have been forgotten, they left their mark on film comedy, as well as on the skulls of some of their co-stars.

The first lady of the early Italian cinema was Gigetta Morano, who was a popular star of the Ambrosio Company of Turin, and appeared in over one hundred and forty films for the studio from 1909 to 1920. Her output ranged from slapstick epics such as *Robinet troppo amato de sua moglie* (*Robinet Too Much Loved by His Wife*, 1912) and *Robinet ina moratodi una chantuse* (*Robinet Loves a Cabaret Singer*, 1911) where she supported Marcel Fabre, to more sly and sophisticated comedies like *Acque Miracolose* (*Miracle Waters*, 1912) where the healing waters of a spa are the cover for an extra-marital affair that "cures" the infertility problems of a childless couple. Directed by and co-starring her real-life partner Eleuterio Rodolfi, the pair made numerous films like *Gigetta e gelosa* (*Gigetta* is Jealous, 1914), *Amor pacifico* (*Peaceful Love*, 1915), and *Gigetta l'avventuriera* (*Gigetta the Adventuress*, 1916) through 1916. On the strength of dramas such as *Mam'selle Nitouche* (1912) she was also able to appear in serious films as well. Her career ended in 1921, but she occasionally turned up in bit parts, most notably in Federico Fellini's *I Vitelloni* (1953). Born in 1887, she made it close to her centenary when she died in 1986.

Lea Giunchi was another popular Italian funny lady who came from circuses and vaudeville where she had teamed up with Natale Guillame, and formed an act along with his brother Ferdinand. When the brothers entered films for the Cines company, with Ferdinand becoming very well-known as Tontolini (and later Polidor), Lea joined them as support in 1910, and in 1911 started her own series of *Lea* comedies. Making around thirty-five *Leas* until 1916, she also found the time to work with the comics Kri-Kri, Checco, and the child Cinessino (her son Eraldo Guillame). Besides the comedies she also acted in epics like *Quo Vadis* (1912), fantasies such as *Pinocchio* (1910), westerns on the order of *A Sister's Ordeal* (1912), and even suspense pictures like *The Unknown Hands* (1913). After Natale Guillame was killed performing a stunt in 1917, Giunchi married, and retired from the screen in 1919.

Mathilde Comont with Stan Laurel in *The Handy Man* (1923). Courtesy of Cole Johnson.

There were also two female Euro-clowns who came to the U.S. and continued their careers in American comedies, making them two of the very few direct links in the genre. Mathilde Comont was a tubby French actress who began her career in comedies for Pathé with the likes of Charles Prince. In addition to American and London stage work, her first American film appearances were in two of Max Linder's 1917 two-reelers for Essanay – *Max Wants a Divorce* and *Max in a Taxi*. From that beginning she went to L-Ko to star in shorts such as *A Bad Little Good Man* (197) and *Eddie Get the Mop* (1918), and she was soon all over the silent comedy map – working in shorts with comics like Stan Laurel, not to mention numerous features like *Rosita* (1923), *The Thief of Bagdad* (1924), *La Boheme* (1926), and *What Price Glory?* (1926). She continued appearing as European characters in sounds films such as *Freaks* (1932), *Design for Living* (1933), and *Poor Little Rich Girl* (1936) until her death in 1938.

Nilde Baracchi models the latest for screen partner Marcel Perez. Author's collection.

The other Franco-American comedienne was Nilde (Leonilda) Baracchi who co-starred as Robinette in the Italian Ambrosio-made Robinet Comedies of her partner Marcel Perez (as Marcel Fabre). Beautiful and statuesque, the Italian-born Baracchi had appeared on stage in Italian music hall and dramas, and in 1911 became a great screen foil for Perez. Besides her work opposite Perez she also starred in a few solo Robinette shorts such as *La Nuova Cameriera E Troppo Bella* (*The New Maid is Too Much of a Flirt*, 1912) and *Robinetta Presa per Nikilistra* (*Robinette is a Nihilist*, 1913). In 1915 the pair came to the United States because of World War I, and she continued to work with Perez in his comedies for the Eagle Film Company and Jester Comedies like *The Near Sighted Auto-Pedist* (1916), *This is the Life* (1918), and *Camouflage* (1918). Her last known American film is *The Tenderfoot* (1919) before the pair separated and Baracchi returned to Europe.

While the above mentioned lady clowns were cavorting in Europe, a few film comediennes were emerging back in America. Heretofore, the actors in U.S. films were never credited but audiences took it upon themselves to identify their favorites and create names for them. Biograph actress Gladys Smith was dubbed "Little Mary" by her public, and took that name when she re-christened herself Mary Pickford. After 1910 the names of the players began to be issued by the studios, but these would often vary from country to country. In the U.K. for instance Mabel Normand was known as Muriel Fortesque, Mack Sennett was Walter Terry, but the best moniker was saved for Fred Mace – Sydney Pinkhurst. Two of the first group of comic actresses taking hold in America appeared together in some early films, shared the first name of Florence, and even had similar trajectories in their careers.

Florence Turner is sometimes referred to as the first movie star as she joined the Vitagraph Company in 1907, and became so popular with audiences that they named her "The Vitagraph Girl." Although she appeared in all types of films she had a true gift for comedy, and like Marion Davies years later she was an inspired mimic, imitating her peers and contemporaries on stage and film. Born in 1887 to a theatrical family in New York City, she made her stage debut at age three. During this time she was known as Eugenie Florence and besides appearing with heavyweights such as Robert Mantell and Sir Henry Irving, she also toured vaudeville with impersonations of Fay Templeton and Marie Dressler. Joining Vitagraph in 1907 Florence remembered:

> Our work was new to us as to the public, and so we went about making pictures as children play games, throwing ourselves into what we were doing at the moment with the most unbounded enthusiasm. I remember my first picture. It was a slapstick comedy (all we made was slapstick). I'll always believe that I was afterwards starred because I could run faster than anyone else. Anyway, that first picture was called *How to Cure a Cold*. We began it at ten one morning and finished it in time for lunch!

Said to be the first American film actress to be signed to a contract, her duties in those early days also included being paymaster, accountant, and wardrobe woman. But as movies became more and more popular the stock of its performers rose and brought the creation of the star system. Often teamed with Vitagraph's

Florence Turner portrait from the time of *The Chinese Parrott* (1927). Courtesy of The Museum of Modern Art.

matinee idol Maurice Costello, Turner was extremely versatile – in addition to comedy she played in historical dramas such as *Francesca di Rimini* (1908), Shakespearian opuses on the order of *The Merchant of Venice* (1908), *A Midsummer Night's Dream* (1909), and *Twelfth Night* (1910), plain old melodramas like *Romance of a War Nurse* (1908), plus the literary adaptations *A Tale of Two Cities* (1911) and *Uncle Tom's Cabin* (1910) where she was Topsy.

Florence Turner demonstrates her comic prowess for a 1912 issue of *Moving Picture Magazine*. Billy Rose Theatre Division, the New York Public Library for the Performing Arts.

But it was her ability at comedy that really set her apart from the regular run of dramatic actresses, sadly many of the films are lost today, but a few survivors are available for appraisal. In *She Cried* (1912) Turner plays a slow girl on her first day of a new job at a busy box making plant. Slowing up the progress of the well-oiled assembly-line she breaks into tears at any criticism or word from a boss or co-worker. Because of her crying the supervisors throw up their hands and pass her from department to department until she finally arrives at the toughest boss in the company, Red Grogan. After she completely collapses into tears when he barks at her, everyone's surprised when he goes out of his way to comfort her. The next day everyone wonders where Grogan is until a telegram arrives saying he's taken the day off to get married. The last scene shows Turner and Grogan riding in a horse cart after their wedding with her sobbing for joy and he muttering "Oh shut up."

Up and Down the Ladder (1913) concerns a book-loving crusty bachelor who decides to hire a housekeeper after his butler breaks a valuable bust. Wanting no empty-headed young thing he puts an ad out for ladies forty-five and older. Turner plays a young woman who is desperately in need of a job, so she makes up as an old woman and applies. Acting the old lady she lands the job and begins her work, but of course the bachelor ultimately discovers that she's young and pretty. Having already fallen for her, he proposes, and the film ends with the ex-curmudgeon now an adoring father to a group of children. Other Turner comedies on the survivor's list from the Vitagraph days include *A Tin-Type Romance* (1910), *Jean the Match-Maker* (1910), *The New Stenographer* (1911), *When Persistancy and Obstinacy Meet* (1912), *Everybody's Doing It* (1913), and *Stenographer Troubles* (1913).

Turner's extreme popularity was aided by her personal appearances. Thanks to her vaudeville experience she was one of the first movie performers to perform for her audiences in the flesh. A good description of her basic act appeared in the March 22, 1913 issue of the *Moving Picture World*:

> Just before she appears for her turn, a Vitagraph reel is run in which Miss Turner plays the leading role. This scheme is doubly effective. First, because if by any chance there should be a person in the house who had never seen her it would be a preparation for the young lady's appearance; and secondly, because it heightens the effect of wonder to see a person acting a picture and a moment later see that person stepping out upon the stage in person. Miss Turner's act consists of impersonations. Her first one is that of a little girl singing a song, which is capital. Her next is that of a boy in the gallery following every move of the villain, the hero and the heroine. It is a remarkable character study. Perhaps her best piece of work is The Village Gossip; a character sketch of an old woman done without make-up and entirely by facial control. As a finish Miss Turner gives an imitation of a saleslady in a 5 and 10 cents store, which is funny and only too true.

Despite being off the screen for seven months in 1912 due to health problems related to exhaustion, she was at the peak of her fame in 1913 when she made a decision that would affect the rest of her career. In the spring of that year Turner and her frequent director Lawrence Trimble moved to England and formed the Turner Film Company. Setting up production at the Hepworth Studio at Walton-on-Thames, the pair made big four and five reels features such as *The Murdoch Case* (1914) and *Far From the Madding Crowd* (1916), but their most successful was *My Old Dutch* (1915) in which she co-starred with well-known British comedian and singer Albert Chevalier and was based on his popular song. In addition to these prestigious features the company turned out one and two-reel comedies, and *Daisy Doodad's Dial* (1914) is one of Turner's best surviving films.

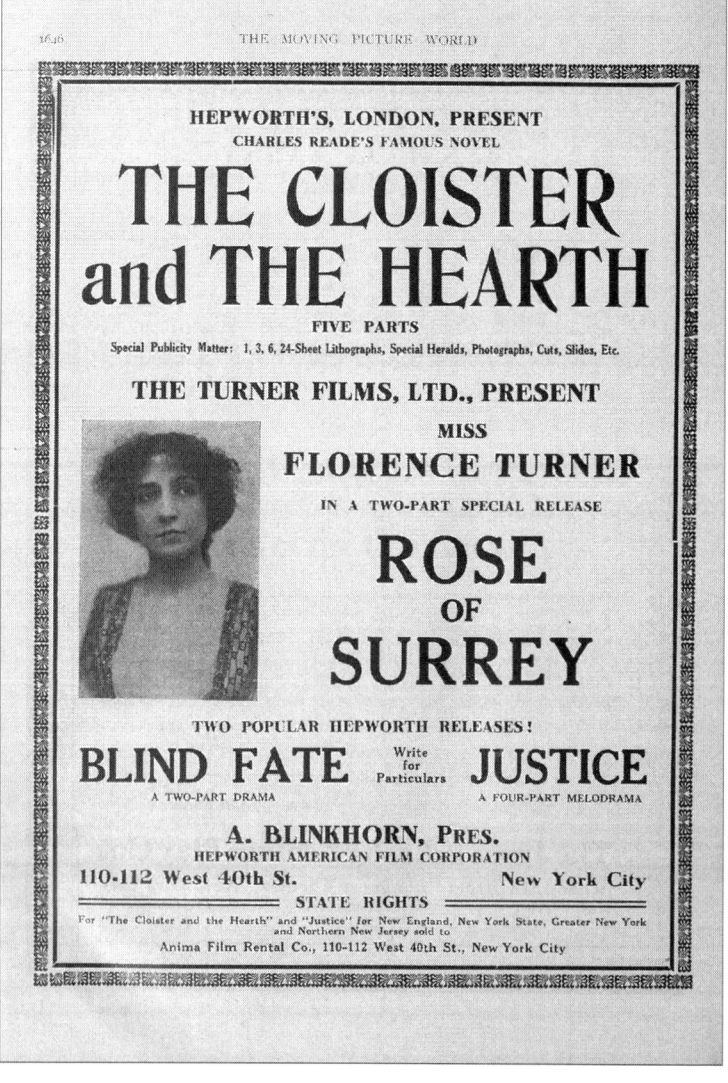

A husband (played by director Lawrence Trimble) and wife read about an upcoming face making contest and decide to enter. Due to a toothache wifie isn't able to enter so hubby easily wins first prize. When another contest is announced she decides to go all out, and continually practices her various faces on the train and in the streets, finally causing her to be arrested as potentially crazy and for disturbing the peace. Hubby has to come and bail her out of lock-up, but she accuses him of arranging the arrest so she couldn't win the contest. Back at home with her husband banished from the bedroom Daisy has a nightmare where she's haunted by all her various faces. The film ends with an extreme close-up of Turner doing her "mugs" directly into the camera.

While in England Turner toured theatres extensively with her stage act, and another of her comedy shorts is a particularly sad loss as it was based on it. At the moment all we have of the one-reel *Florence Turner Impersonates Film Favorites* (1915) are descriptions from trade publications like this from the November 20, 1915 *Moving Picture World*:

> The curtain rises on her as a slavey in a kitchen. The slavey is film crazy and soon has a dream in which we see sketches, first of a scene in a French Pathé picture. This is followed by her idea of Ford Sterling, which made this reviewer ball right out with laughter, although it is not so compellingly funny as her idea of the early Biograph method; at this we had to wipe tears from our cheeks. Her impersonations of Broncho Billy is also good and her Mabel Normand will more than pass muster. She closes the picture with the last scene in Sarah Bernhardt's "Queen Elizabeth," when she falls on some piled up cushions and bounces up from them to a more comfortable position. Then she wakes up in the kitchen.
>
> It is a picture that ought not to be missed. It is rich and the spectators will count it as a privilege to see it. We have told the whole story, though it is worthy of a much more extended space than we can give it.

Although her British-made features were distributed in America by Mutual, and some of the shorts picked up by smaller companies such as Min A, there was a long lag where she was off U.S. screens. The outbreak of World War I caused production problems in England and Europe and by 1916 Turner Films was no more. Both Trimble and Turner returned to America, but her moment of stardom seemed to have passed. Back in the States she was able to get a few roles in independent productions such as *Fool's Gold* (1919) and *The Brand of Lopez* (1920) with Sessue Hayakawa.

It was announced that she would be directing and starring in comedy one-reelers for Universal, but only one, *Oh, It's E.Z.* (1919), appears to have come to fruition. This was followed by other shorts for the independent Radin Pictures' *Zip Comedies*:

> The announcement of the acquisition by Radin Pictures of the Turner Comedies was greeted by inquiries from the states rights buyers from all parts

of the country – an indication of the regard in which Miss Turner's efforts are held. Miss Turner was formerly one of the screen's most popular stars and her admirers are still legion. (*Moving Picture World*, April 3, 1920)

One of Turner's later starring shorts, possibly *Old Dials for New* (1920). Authors collection.

In a short life span Radin produced dramas and a comedy feature with *Ziegfeld Follies* star Johnny Dooley. The series of *Zip Comedies* were to number twelve – six to star character comic Christian Rub (later the voice of Geppetto in Disney's 1940 *Pinocchio*) and six with Turner. At this writing not much is known about the films and only two Turner titles can be confirmed – *Old Dials for New,* which had a plot similar to Charley Chase's later *Mighty Like a Moose* (1926) where a husband and wife have their faces remodeled, and *Stenographers First* (both 1920).

Despite signing with Metro to be in their stock company of supporting players, she was unhappy with her prospects in America and returned to Britain, but a post-war recession had hampered their film industry. Outside of some work in pictures and touring with her stage act, she was said to have been in dire straits when Marion Davies brought her back home to appear in *Janice Meredith* (1924). Trying to hit the comeback trail she even wrote a movie star-based horoscope column in *Pictures and Picturegoers* magazine in 1924 entitled *Their Planets and Yours* and more importantly had featured roles in quality pictures such as *Flame of the Argentine* (1926), *Stranded*, and *The Chinese Parrott* (both 1927). Today her most often seen film is from this period – Buster Keaton's *College* (1927) where she plays the comedian's mother early in the production. With the changeover to sound her roles became smaller and uncredited. She kept working, and put together a new stage presentation titled *Pioneer Film Days*. In 1937 she went on contract as a stock extra at MGM, but in the early 1940s entered the Motion Picture Country Home where she died on August 28, 1946.

The second Florence to be discussed began her film career at Edison and also spent time at Vitagraph before moving to Biograph where she became known as "The Biograph Girl." Born Florence Anne Bridgwood in Hamilton, Ontario, Canada on January 2, 1886, her mother Charlotte Dunn was an actress who, after separating from carriage builder George Bridgwood when her daughter was four, took a new last name from the dramatic company she was touring with, and so Florence Bridgwood became Florence Lawrence. Like Ms. Turner she appeared on stage as a child, singing, dancing, and mimicking her mother's performances as "Baby Flo, the Child Wonder."

After touring across the country for a few years the family settled in Buffalo, New York, and in 1906

Turner captures the essence of Larry Semon in one of her stage performances. Courtesy of The Museum of Modern Art.

Florence and her mother came to Manhattan. Outside of a little work as an artist's model employment was scarce, but Florence and her mother found themselves in the 1907 Edison production *Daniel Boone*. Although not happy with her final performance, and in spite of her mother's objections that film work would tarnish their stage reputations, Lawrence decided on being a screen actress – "My mind was made up. I liked the work, and I positively did not feel that motion picture play was beneath me." Haunting the New York studios she landed more work at Vitagraph, but to appease her mother she went on tour as the lead in *The Seminary Girl*. When the tour ended in 1908, she returned to the "Big V" and became a member of their stock company where she learned the film ropes from well-seasoned veterans like William Shea, Ralph Ince, and Florence Turner.

A playful Florence Lawrence. Courtesy of The Museum of Modern Art.

At Vitagraph, Florence became friendly with an extra named Harry Solter, who soon left the company and joined Biograph where his friend D.W. Griffith was the top director. In the middle of 1908 Biograph's leading lady Marion Leonard left their employ to do a stage show, and Griffith sent Solter to Brooklyn to approach Florence Turner about joining Biograph. Waiting outside the Vitagraph Studio Solter found that he had missed Turner, but saw Ms. Lawrence and talked her up to Griffith. Soon she was at Biograph with a ten dollar raise appearing in dramas like *Betrayed By a Handprint* and *The Heart of O Yama* (both 1908), but she was also cast in *A Smoked Husband* (1908) opposite the overlooked comic John Cumpson—this led to a series of *Jones Family Comedies*.

Lawrence later told *Photoplay*;

When we undertook the first picture there was no intention of making a series of comedy productions, but when the exchanges started asking for more and more "Jonsesy" pictures, we kept it up until I left the Biograph Company. Mr. Cumpson was the most serious comedian I have ever known. Nothing was ever funny to him, and he never tried to be funny. When all the rest of the cast would laugh at something he had said or done he would become indignant, thinking we were making fun of him. What turned out to be the first of the "Jonesy" pictures was called "A Smoked Husband," a play in which groundless jealousy gets its just deserts. Instead of being called "Jones," Mr. Cumpson was called "Benjamin Bibbs," and how the public ever came to calling him "Jonesy" is more than I know.

One of the first comedy series, lasting from 1908 until Florence left Biograph in 1909, the focus was on the misadventures of a long-time married couple and encompassed titles such as *Mr. Jones at the Ball* (1908), *Mr. Jones Has a Card Party, Her First Biscuits, His Wife's Mother*, and *Mrs. Jones' Love, or, "I Want My Hat"* (all 1909). Besides these domestic entries Lawrence appeared in other comedies like *The Christmas Burglars* (1908), *A Wreath in Time, The Curtain Pole*, and *The Politician's Love Story* (all 1909), plus numerous dramas on the order of *The Mended Lute, The Way of Man*, and *What Drink Did* (all 1909). The difficulty in taking a fresh look at Florence's career is that her Biograph films make up almost ninety-seven per cent of her surviving films. This is due to D.W. Griffith's importance and his enduring popularity, but the other three per cent of her work that does exist, just a handful of her later films for Imp, Lubin, Victor, etc., are scattered around the world at various archives and extremely difficult to see.

Florence and Harry Solter had gotten more than friendly and were married in August 1908. Not happy under Griffith's domination, the pair made overtures to other studios, but when Griffith got wind of this they were fired. At the end of 1909 they took up residence at Carl Laemmle's new Independent Motion Picture Company of America, better known as Imp, with Solter directing and Florence acting opposite King Baggot and Owen Moore. Laemmle had set up Imp in direct competition with the studios that were part of the Motion Pictures Patent Trust, so not only did the company have to deal with starting from scratch they also had to watch out for interference from the Trust. Florence recalled:

> Our studio was inadequately equipped and new pieces of property could not be built and painted with the speed of today. We borrowed furniture and the like from stores and factories and made out as best we could with our very limited means. Mr. Laemmle was engaged in a bitter fight with the Motion Picture Patents Company and at times it looked as though he would lose every dollar. This legal battle prevented him from tying up any great amounts of money in Imp productions until they began to become popular with the public. It was just a

matter of time, however, and pretty soon there were two producing directors constantly at work – one producing farce comedy and the other producing dramas.

Florence as a Universal star. Author's collection.

Florence did both, and it was at this time that her name became known to the public as the charming leading lady of Imp comedies like *The Widow, The Winning Punch,*

Never Again, The Coquette's Suitors, His Sick Friend, The Miser's Heart (all 1910), and even a re-teaming with her old Jones Family co-star John Cumpson in *The Nichols on Vacation* (1910). Another way that her name became known was as part of the first movie publicity stunt where Laemmle sent a story to the press in February 1910 that Ms. Lawrence had been killed in a car accident, which led to a series of personal appearances for her to demonstrate that she was very much alive. By the end of the year though she and Solter decided to move on, and this time it was to a year-long stay with the Lubin Company of Philadelphia.

Again under Solter's direction Florence was paired with Arthur V. Johnson, a colleague from her days at Biograph. A great deal of their output were romantic comedies such as *His Friend, the Burglar, Her Artistic Temperament, The Bachelor,* and *An American Girl* (all 1911), which led the March 1913 issue of *Motography* to later comment; "Take those recent Lubin comedies with Florence Lawrence in the cast: aren't they perfectly delightful? Nothing clownish or exaggerated – just downright human nature bubbling over with fun." Although the films were popular, Lawrence and Solter's stay at Lubin was brief. A pattern of them moving from studio to studio had developed suggesting they were difficult to work with. The pair were also having marital problems, the anxiety leading to health problems for Florence. "I left the Lubin Company to take a long rest. My work had been very arduous and trying, and I was extremely nervous. So much so that I could not work to my own satisfaction. I wanted to get away from motion pictures and motion picture studios for a while."

After a long tour of Europe the Solters hooked up with producer Pat Powers in early 1912 and together formed the Victor Film Company. Over the next three years, although Florence was "retired" for most of 1913, the pair turned out a large spate of

Florence with Owen Moore in a scene from *Not Like Other Girls* (1912). Billy Rose Theatre Division, the New York Public Library for the Performing Arts.

films. Teamed again with Owen Moore and also his brother Matt, Florence starred in many comedies such as *Not Like Other Girls, Her Cousin Fred, Betty's Nightmare* (all 1912), *The Honeymooners, A Singular Cynic,* and *A Disenchantment* (all 1914). Distributed by her old employer Carl Laemmle for his Universal Film Company, this was the peak of Lawrence's career. A typical review is this one for *Her Ragged Knight* (1914) from the October 15, 1914 issue of *The Bioscope*:

> Miss Florence Lawrence is perfectly delightful in every part in which she appears, and particularly charming is she as an unruly girl whose manners are the despair of a staid old aunt and also of her male guardian, who, however, speedily falls a victim to her charms, though in a most unorthodox way.

But while Victor ads enthused "with all the sunshine and sparkle and jubilant joy in captivity laughing in her eyes and shouting their happiness in every gesture and jesture," all wasn't so happy behind the scenes. Not only were their difficulties between the Solters and Universal, but between the Solters themselves. Ending their Victor series in 1914 Florence was off screen until the unsuccessful 1916 Universal feature *Elusive Isabel,* not long after which she filed for divorce.

**Lawrence outside her short-lived cosmetics store.
Courtesy of The Museum of Modern Art.**

The rest of Florence Lawrence's life and career were frustrating attempts to regain her early film fame and find some kind of personal stability. Although she and Harry Solter never actually divorced they remained separated until he died from a stroke in 1920. Two brief marriages followed, and an attempt to establish herself as a businesswoman with a store called Hollywood Cosmetics failed. Her last starring role was in the independent feature *The Unfoldment* (1922), but after a few supporting roles in films such as *Lucretia Lombard* (1923) and *Gambling Wives* (1924) the rest of her film work was in uncredited bits. Some of her fame as "The Biograph Girl" continued to follow her and led to an occasional publicity interview, where she generally blamed her absence from current films to an "accident" that occurred during her days at Victor. The 1930s were particularly unkind, offering only extra work, sometimes alongside Florence Turner, and declining health. In 1933 she was given a contract to be a stock extra at MGM, where she worked until her physical problems made it impossible and she killed herself in December 1938. Obituaries talked about her role as "the first movie star" and blamed her eclipse on the rapid changes that occurred in the infant film industry.

Two other important early comediennes, Dot Farley and Mary Pickford, were also both very active behind the scenes and will be discussed in Chapter Six. That leaves the talented and supremely skinny Flora Finch to finish out this chapter. Finch was the ideal surname for her as there was something very bird-like in the combination of her sharp, hawkish features and stork-thin length. Her specific type of looks led her to specialize in spinsters and domineering wives, particularly when working with her frequent co-star John Bunny. Born in Surrey in 1867, Finch began doing impersonations while still in English boarding school, and started her onstage career working for famous impresario Ben Greet in Shakespeare productions such as *A Midsummer Night's Dream*. After coming to the U.S. she worked to establish herself on the American stage in the productions *The Worst Woman in London, The Missourians,* and Marie Cahill's *The Boys and Betty*, in addition to vaudeville.

Debuting at Biograph in 1908 she caught the attention of D.W. Griffith, and made an impression in the *Jones Family* shorts and other comedies. *Those Awful Hats* (1909) is about women wearing ridiculously large and adorned hats to movies and obstructing the view of the other cinema goers. A giant claw descends from the ceiling and snatches the offending headwear. Ms. Finch has a prominent role as the final woman to enter the theatre with the largest hat yet, but when the claw comes this time it clamps on Flora herself and drags her skyward, much to the approval of the rest of the audience. After more shorts such as *Muggsy's First Sweetheart* and *All on Account of the Milk*

Flora Finch shows a dual personality for Vitagraph publicity. Author's collection.

(both 1910) the actress left Biograph to relocate to the Vitagraph Studio in Brooklyn. There in February 1911 she first worked with John Bunny, and the combination of the severe Finch with the expansive Bunny was a match made in comedy heaven. There was an instant combative chemistry (which may have been helped by the fact that they're said to have had an active mutual dislike for each other), and their films together, called "Bunnyfinches" by fans, were hugely popular with many moviegoers assuming they were married in real life.

Flora and hubby John Bunny square off against neighbors Josie Sadler, Sidney Drew, and Paul Kelly in *The Feudists* (1913). Billy Rose Theatre Division, the New York Public Library for the Performing Arts.

The Subduing of Mrs. Nag (1911) finds Flora as the henpecker of the title who objects to pretty Mabel Normand as her spouse Bunny's business secretary. No matter how Mabel tries to homely herself up Mrs. Nag is still not satisfied, so finally the secretary pretends to be a man in her brother's clothing and gets the old lady to flirt with "him." Husband Bunny is in on the scheme, and catching the missus in the flirtation now has the upper hand to order her to keep her nose out of his business office. In the famous *A Cure for Pokeritis* (1912) Bunny has sworn off poker playing to Flora, but is actually still indulging one night a week under the guise of it being a "Sons of the Morning" social club meeting. Flora gets suspicious when Bunny re-enacts the poker games in his sleep, and contacts her effeminate cousin Freddie. Following Bunny on his next evening out Freddie confirms the truth and conspires with Flora to have his bible class masquerade as cops and "raid" the next game. The following week the scheme goes through as planned and when Freddie and company are dragging the gamblers off to the hoosegow their wives conveniently show up and get them off the hook, leaving the miscreants in their custody and debt.

A later pairing, *Bunny Backslides* (1914), has Flora as a widow who's engaged to Bunny but after attending a lecture on eugenics decides that he's too fat and she's too thin. They agree to attend Dr. Sweatem's Sanitarium together. While there Bunny is frustrated by the fact that despite all the strenuous exercise and dieting he's done - he does nothing but gain weight, and meets a flirtatious fat woman. Finally fed up with Flora and her demands, Bunny and the fat woman decide to be fat together and elope, leaving Flora to end up in the arms of Dr. Sweatem himself. Although the outings with Bunny were some of her most popular, Flora did plenty at Vitagraph on her own, and while limited in her roles by her distinctive appearance, she still managed to find variation in her characters and never played stock harridans or shrews.

The Hand Bag (1912) stars Flora as an old spinster who drops her hand bag on the street while out shopping. Pretty Rosemary Theby finds it and takes it with her on a streetcar where she attracts the attention of Frank Bennett. Jumping off the car in a hurry she leaves the bag, which Bennett finds and assumes is hers. Looking in the bag he finds the name and address, and thinking it's the beautiful Ms. Theby he sends a romantic note praising her beauty and proposing a date so he can return the item. A meeting is set, and Flora, excited by the note, is busy kissing it and primping for the date. Bennett, needless to say, is very surprised on meeting the flirty Flora, and knocks over a good deal of her furniture trying to get out of her grasp. In *Cutey and the Chorus Girls* (1913) Ms. Finch plays an unattractive chorus girl (named Flora Scrawny) who becomes smitten with "stage door Johnny" Cutey (Wally Van), who can't stand her and is himself smitten with Lillian Walker. To teach Cutey a lesson two of his buddies hire a gigantic sign sandwich man to pose as Flora's brother and demand that he "make good" in his attentions to his injured sister.

At the end of 1914 John Bunny stopped appearing in films (and died in April 1915) and besides her solo films Flora worked with Jay Dwiggens, a Bunny substitute hired and introduced by Vitagraph in *Bunny's Little Brother* (1914), for films like *Fixing Their Dads, The Rocky Road of Love, A Strand of Blonde Hair* (all 1914), *The Smoking Out of Bella Butts, Whose Husband?, Strictly Neutral*, and *A Mistake in Typesetting* (all 1915). Flora also joined Kate Price, Hughey Mack, and William Shea to make "The Big Comedy Four" for Vitagraph titles such as *A Pair of Queens, Some Duel* (both 1915), *When Hooligan and Dooligan Ran for Mayor* (1916), and especially the hilarious *Sweeney's Christmas Bird* (1914). This short chronicles the Sweeneys and Clancys who live in the same boarding house. Mrs. Sweeney (Flora) is mourning the death of her beloved pet parrot Caesar, and forces her husband (Mack) to take him out and give him a proper burial. On the way to bury the bird Mack stops in for a drink where he meets Mr. Clancy (Shea) who has just bought his family's Christmas dinner turkey. After several drinks the men mix up their packages, so that Mack buries the turkey and Shea brings home the dead parrot for his wife to cook. Mrs. Clancy (Kate Price) gives him hell, and the rest of the film details the switching back and forth of the parrot carcass with Mack's newly purchased dinner turkey.

Flora headlining for her own Flora Finch Corporation.

In spite of her continued popularity at Vitagraph, which included the feature *A Night Out* (1916), not to mention variations on her name in film titles like *The Misses Finch and their Nephew Billy* (1911), *The Starring of Flora Finchurch* (1915), and even *The Fates of Flora Fourflush* (1914), a melodrama spoof series that starred Clara Kimball Young, Ms. Finch moved on. The end of 1916 saw the formation of The Flora Finch Comedy Company, an independent outfit designed to put out Finch-starring two reelers on the state's rights market (a system of releasing films through independent distributors who represented different territories around the country. Each territory was generally made up of one or two states). Despite a slate of films announced – *The Vampir-r-r-e!, Flora the School Teacher, Flora the Manicure Girl, Flora the Life-Saver, Flora the International Spy, Flora the Dressmaker,* and *Flora in the Movies* – only two titles were finally released.

Flora and her daughter Veronica Marsh during the shooting of 1924's *Monsieur Beaucaire*. Courtesy of The Museum of Modern Art.

The first short was *War Prides* (1917), a spoof of Nazimova's recent feature *War Brides* (1916), which starred Flora as Mlle. Noximova, a patriotic biscuit-baker who rejects the hand and crown of the widower king of the empire to remain at the dough-pile and do her "bit" for the boys at war. The next and last release was *Guess What* (1917) another spoof, this time a parody of the Stanford White – Evelyn Nesbit murder case, that had Flora as an artist's model posing as Cupid who becomes involved in a battle with the artist's wife. This leads to a dagger fight in which Flora kills the wife, which, as everyone knows, entitles her to headline in vaudeville. Sadly these releases were coolly received by critics and audiences, leading to a quick demise for the enterprise.

Despite this failure Flora kept busy playing a succession of aunts and spinsters in New York-made features such as *Prudence the Pirate* (1916) for Thanhouser, the Alice Guy produced and directed *The Great Adventure* (1918), *Oh Boy* (1919), and her old boss J. Stuart Blackton's *Dawn* (1919). In 1920 another independent concern was set up. The Film Frolics Pictures Corporation announced that Flora was under a three-year contract to star in no less than six comedies a year. Although the title *His Better Half* was publicized, *The She-Male Sleuth* was the only short to materialize from this deal. Ultimately released by the Reelcraft Pictures Corporation as part of their Royal Comedies series it's a woefully unfunny and low-budget endeavor that spelled the end of any other starring films for Flora.

From here she went back to the supporting ranks where she was in demand for C.C. Burr Productions. Not only did she turn up in a few of their *All Star Comedy* and *Torchy* shorts, but she had nice parts in their Johnny Hines features *Luck* (1923), *The Early Bird*, *The Live Wire* (both 1925), and *The Brown Derby* (1926). Other pictures included juicy roles in Constance Talmadge's *Lessons in Love* (1921) and *Monsieur Beaucaire* (1924) with Rudolph Valentino, in addition to some of the *Carrie of the Chorus* two-reelers, the only live-action series done by Max and Dave Fleischer of Betty Boop and Popeye fame. Flora appeared in entries such as *The Berth Mark* and *'Morning Judge* (both 1926) where she supported star Peggy Shaw and a young Ray Bolger.

Up to this point all of Flora's film career had taken place on the East Coast. In the beginning of 1927 the actress settled in California, which may have been due to the death of her daughter Veronica Marsh in late 1924. Veronica had appeared with her mother in many films and was only nineteen at the time of her death. The move west was a good one as Flora ended up with excellent parts in big pictures like *Captain Salvation*, *Quality Street* (both 1927), *The Haunted House* (1928), and especially *The Cat and the Canary* (1927). It looked like better roles were coming her way, but the changeover to sound surprisingly demoted her to smaller bit appearances. After her years on stage her voice and acting were fine, but it may be that she was unconsciously overlooked because she represented an earlier era of filmmaking. Like the Florences' Turner and Lawrence she ended up on salary as a stock extra at MGM, but still had a few memorable moments such as the society lady presenting the statue in Charlie Chaplin's *City Lights* (1931), the village gossip in *The Scarlet Letter* (1934), and her funny cameo as a plain prairie wife at the opening of Laurel & Hardy's *Way Out West* (1937). Remaining a trouper to the end, her last known appearance was in *The Women* (1939), and she died from a streptococcus infection in 1940.

Thanks to the popularity of players like Florence Turner, Florence Lawrence, and Flora Finch by 1911 the star system was firmly entrenched in the film industry and with the public, setting the stage for the emergence of the most influential woman in the history of film comedy.

Chapter 2

"THE SUGAR ON THE KEYSTONE GRAPEFRUIT"

Most of the silent comics came from the stage or circuses, but Mabel Normand had been a teenage model for photographers and popular artists such as James Montgomery Flagg, Charles Dana Gibson, and J.C. Leyendecker. Born on Staten Island in 1892, Mabel also posed for commercial ads, lantern-slides, and photo postcards which gave her much experience in front of a camera, and being in New York with the fledgling movie industry all around her it was just a matter of time before she ended up in films. In 1918 Mabel told the *New York Morning Telegraph* that it had been fellow model and recent moving picture actress Alice Joyce who got her started:

> She (Joyce) was then working at the Kalem Studio on Twenty-Third Street, but she still had the habit of running into Eddow's at lunch time to see the rest of us. She tried to get me over to the Biograph, where D.W. Griffith was working at that time. I didn't want to go at first. I was fairly satisfied with $3 a day for posing with an occasional extra $5 or $10 at the Fashion Camera studio. Besides I wanted to be an illustrator. I could draw a little and I kept my eyes and ears open to pick up everything I could in the artist's studios.

> But the next day Mr. Gibson had to be at Collier's office again, so I had a free day. I met Alice Joyce again, and the result was I went over to the Biograph studio. Griffith put me to work at once. I forget the name of the picture, but Florence Lawrence, and Marion Leonard, and Del Henderson and Henry Walthall were the principals. They gave me a pair of tights and a page's costume which terrified me almost out of my wits. I had never worn tights before and it seemed to me that everybody around the place had nothing to do but stare at my legs. What was more they kept me there until 12:30 and I didn't get home to Staten Island until nearly 2. So I did not get back next day and they were furious. I met Mack Sennett on the street a few days later and he said: "That was a terrible thing you did to Griffith not going back." I didn't understand that I was to be in another scene or what it meant.

> But eventually Griffith sent for me and I worked regularly for Biograph until they went to the coast for the winter. Then I went to the Vitagraph and got $20 a week, working with John Bunny, Flora Finch, Ralph Ince and others. I remember Anita Stewart was an extra girl at the time.

**Mabel Normand sketched by James Montgomery Flagg.
Courtesy of Marilyn Slater.**

One of her first Biographs was *Wilful Peggy* (1910), and although she can't be spotted on screen she's listed in the company records. Her first known appearance with Vitagraph was in *The Indiscretions of Betty* (March 29, 1910), a drama about a young wife who gets in debt trying to make an impression in society circles. While Mabel had no formal experience as an actress, she was spontaneous and spunky, and the camera loved her. Vitagraph quickly picked up on this and began showcasing her in comedies like *Betty Becomes a Maid*, *When a Man's Married His Troubles Begin*, *Two Overcoats*, and *The Subduing of Mrs. Nag* (all 1911). *Troublesome Secretaries* (March 21, 1911) is the only one readily available today, and co-stars Mabel with John Bunny and Ralph Ince. The plot has Bunny's personal secretary and his daughter Mabel in love, but so much so that the young man neglects his duties while mooning over her and Bunny fires him. A new secretary is promptly hired, but she is a school chum of Mabel's and they've hatched a plot for her to irritate the old man with her fawning and flirtatious ways. Finally father decides to go with a male secretary over sixty, and the boyfriend dons whiskers and old age make-up to beat out a slew of codgers for the job.

Mabel showing a little ankle in a 1910 photo card. Courtesy of Marilyn Slater.

Troublesome Secretaries shows that the extremely young Mabel could have easily become one of Vitagraph's comedy stars as she works in perfect rapport with Bunny, and her irreverence and impish charm are already well in place. After more than a year of working steadily and becoming popular at Vitagraph, Mabel switched to Biograph in August 1911 with two starring comedies – *The Diving Girl* and *The Baron*. Mack Sennett had recently gotten his own directorial unit, and a professional and personal relationship led to Mabel becoming his leading lady. *The Diving Girl* is the prototype for Sennett's later "Bathing Girl" films, and features Mabel in a racy bathing suit (for that day) showing off her diving and swimming skills as well as her figure.

Del Henderson is the star of *The Baron*, which has a soon-to-be standard Keystone plot, but without the outrageous slapstick. It concerns a German waiter who has everyone convinced in his rooming house that he's a titled baron. Despite the fact that he continually borrows money from them they buy his pretense, and Mabel is offered as a reluctant bride by her awestruck mother. While the wedding is taking place Henderson's old waiter pal turns up and spills the beans, and although it's too late to stop the ceremony Mabel is saved because a mix-up at the license bureau left "the Baron" with a dog license.

At this point Mabel spent a couple of months under the tutelage of D.W. Griffith appearing in dramas such as *The Squaw's Love, Italian Blood, Her Awakening,* and *The Unveiling* (all 1911), and although she had previously worked for him in bit roles it seems that the master may have taken more notice of her in the Sennett shorts and decided to see what she could do. In *The Squaw's Love* she's an Indian maid who loves a brave that her father doesn't approve of, but after he helps thwart an attack by a gang of renegades all ends happily. Instead of his usual ethereal heroine, Griffith makes good use of Mabel's athletic prowess – having her dive from a rock ridge into a lake and swim under water to sabotage the enemy canoes.

**Early Mabel publicity post card.
Courtesy of Jim Kerkhoff.**

Her Awakening is standard Griffith fare about a young woman who is embarrassed by her old and shabby mother. When she gets a new beau she even pretends to not recognize the old woman on the street so that her young man won't see her, but when the mother is accidently killed Mabel realizes how badly she treated her. Although perfectly fine in these dramatic roles Griffith must have determined that Mabel's true talents were in comedy. Never interested in comedy, Griffith was also involved in the first films of Fay Tincher, Max Davidson, and Douglas Fairbanks but was happy to let them go and develop their comic styles on their own. Outside of appearances in *The Eternal Mother* and *The Mender of Nets* (both 1912), where she played the dark other woman to blonde Blanche Sweet, Mabel was returned to the Sennett unit.

**Mabel and her crepe-haired beau Ford Sterling
in an unidentified short.**

With Sennett Mabel created something new in comedy heroines – pretty and sweet per regulation but with an independence and feistiness that enabled her to give back as good as she got in any slapstick proceedings. 1912 saw them turning out about nineteen comedies together for Biograph and highlights include *Katchem Kate* where Mabel decides to become a detective, and while still taking her sleuthing classes she rounds up a gang of anarchists. *Tomboy Bessie* stars her as the overactive younger sister of Kate Toncray, who makes like difficult for Kate's bashful swain Mack, and in the famous *A Dash through the Clouds* Mabel flies through the air with pilot Philip Parmalee to come to the aid of boyfriend Fred Mace. Certain films were also Keystone forerunners such as *Help! Help!*, a spoof on Griffith melodramas like *The Lonely Villa* (1909) with their last minute rescues, and *Helen's Marriage* where a fake movie wedding turns into the real thing with the addition of an actual minister. Both subjects would be developed further in *Mabel and Fatty's Married Life* and *Hash House Mashers* (both 1915).

Easy to see who was the main draw on the Keystone program.

Sennett incorporated the Keystone Film Company on August 3, 1912 with himself, Ford Sterling, Fred Mace, and Mabel as the stars. Surprised by the developments, Mabel remembered:

> When Mack Sennett first came to me and said:" How would you like to make $100 a week?" I said, "Stop making fun of me – don't be ridiculous." And when he took me to see Kessell and Bauman they said, they liked my looks. I asked if they intended to pay me $100 a week and they said, "Well, call it $125."

> You may believe me or not, but when I got that contract in my hands I walked in a daze from Union Square to Times Square and back. Every five blocks I would read it again. I couldn't believe it. I took it to Alice Joyce in the Park Avenue Hotel and showed it to her. We both decided that it meant $25 a week and that the figure 1 was a fake.

Even before the official incorporation Sennett had already started shooting comedies in New York in July and early August. Only a handful of these initial eastern Keystones survive – three starring Mabel. *The Water Nymph* (September 23, 1912) was the first release (sharing the bill with *Cohen Collects a Debt*) and reprises *The Diving Girl* with Mabel at the beach again, this time with Sterling and Sennett vying for her attentions. *At Coney Island* (October 28, 1912) is exactly that – a valentine to Luna Park with Mabel, Mack, and Sterling frolicking on the Steeplechase, spinning discs, and other famous Coney attractions. We get a nice look at the park's main promenade, cafes, elephants, and even the same boat ride that Roscoe Arbuckle gets thrown from in his later *Coney Island* (1918). The newly-found *The Duel* was held back and released a bit later (December 30, 1912) and is a split-reel about a count and a duke fighting a duel for Mabel's affections.

> At first it was a hard struggle. Money was scarce, and it was a long time before we were sure of our paycheck at the end of the week. Our first picture was produced right here in Fort Lee, but we soon went west.

By the time the first comedies were released in September 1912 the fledgling unit was already settled in California, where they had been joined by Fred Mace. Although the Keystones were a hit, the company had to scramble and shoot non-stop to turn out new product every week (an early ad line was "Comedy Reel Every Monday"). Sadly the majority of these early releases are missing. Titles like *Mabel's Adventures, A Temperamental Husband* (both 1912), *Professor Bean's Removal, The Mistaken Masher,* and *Foiling Fickle Father* (all 1913) are intriguing. The sporadic survivors include *Mabel's Stratagem* (1912), a re-working of Mabel's earlier Vitagraph short *The Subduing of Mrs. Nag* (1910) where Fred Mace's wife Alice Davenport objects to his flirty ways with his secretaries and has them all canned. Only allowing him to hire males, Mabel shows up in drag and the wife takes a shine to the "boy" – coquettishly fussing over him and even taking him to lunch where she has a couple of drinks and gets very randy. When hubby Mace presents his missus with divorce papers Mabel reveals her subterfuge.

Barney Oldfield's Race for a Life (1913) has Mabel abducted and tied to the railroad tracks by Ford Sterling in a spoof of melodramatic pennydreadfuls which ends with country oaf Sennett enlisting auto-racer Barney Oldfield to speed to the last-minute rescue. Movie-making and the Keystone Studio itself play large roles in *Mabel's Dramatic Career* (1913). Jilted by her country beau Mack, Mabel goes to the city and gets work at

Keystone where she becomes a star. After mistaking the images on the screen for reality, Mack tracks her down and finds that she's happily married to the actor who plays the villain in her pictures. *A Muddy Romance* (1913) is exactly that – to the Nth degree. To get away from rejected suitor Ford Sterling, Mabel and Charles Inslee decide to get married in a rowboat in the lake at Echo Park. To get even Sterling drains the lake leaving the lovers and the Keystone Cops to wade through waist-high mud.

Mack and Mabel under the evil eye of Ford Sterling in *Barney Oldfield's Race for a Life* (1913). Author's collection.

Mabel commented on this film, and her slapstick trials and tribulations in general, in 1916 to the *Los Angeles Times*:

> There are many drawbacks and at the same time there are many compensations attached to my profession. In one picture we used a lake in Los Angeles at a time when it was just being drained. We knew of this event a few weeks ahead and a comedy was prepared by Mack Sennett in which the lake was the locality and emptying the principal situation. In the picture I went for a boat ride. While my escort was rowing his rival was at the mechanism that operates the outlet, opening the flood gates. The water lowered and finally we were left marooned in mud. A rope was thrown and we were dragged through the slimy mud to the bank. It was awful. We were covered from head to foot and before we could drive back to the studio the mud had commenced to dry and harden.

That night I sat at dinner with a friend from Denver, whom I had not seen in several years. An elaborate bath and the attentions of a maid had removed all traces of my strenuous afternoon. My friend remarked in the course of our conversation "I suppose the hardships of motion picture actresses are very much overestimated." I agreed with her. I was too tired from my rescue from the lake to argue or explain. I told her that it was an exceedingly monotonous life. Poor dear – I hope she will never have any personal experience to disillusion her.

I have had to dive and swim in rough ocean scenes. I have fought with bears, fallen out of a rapidly moving automobile, jumped off a second story roof into a flower bed and risked life, limb and peace of mind in innumerable ways – and all to make people laugh. Some work days I have gone home and cried with ache in body and heart and at the very moment of my misery thousands of theatre-goers were rocking in their seats with laughter at some few scenes in which I had worked a few weeks before.

Through it all Mabel appears to have been a total trouper. Sennett praised her and told the press:

Miss Normand is such a wonderful success even more on account of her head than her good looks. She is quick as a flash and just naturally funny. She is funny to talk to. She seems to think in sparks.

Co-star Fred Mace chimed in with:

We worked together in Biograph films and went to Keystone at the same time and are still the best of friends. All of us in Keystone worked fine together, and Mabel Normand is one of the best little actresses I know. The only trouble I had with her were the times she'd start giggling and couldn't stop; she's a wonderful giggler.

In addition to her usual strenuous stunts, Sennett kept Mabel returning to the beach as shorts such as *The Diving Girl* and *The Water Nymph* had made a huge impression:

Mabel Normand, called by some the "Divine Diver," formerly of the Vitagraph and Biograph companies, is now diving for the Keystone Company.

Appropriately mixed in with her diving is that same winsome smile, pretty pout and vivacious action.

Mabel's Lovers (1912), *Mabel's New Hero* (1913), and *The Sea Nymphs* (1914) are some of her other seaside titles, and eventually Mack created his Bathing Beauties and devoted a whole sub-series for their appearances. A big event occurred at the end of 1913.

After almost three years of working hard being on the giving and receiving end of all kinds of slapstick roughhouse, Mabel finally began calling the shots. Starting with the production of *The Champion* (December 27, 1913):

> Mabel Normand, leading woman with the Keystone, will hereafter direct every picture in which she appears. Madame Blache has been the only woman director for some time, but now she will have a rival in Mabel who will both act and direct. (*Motion Picture News*, December 13, 1913)

**Mabel puts a run in Fred Mace's hose in *Those Good Old Days* (1912).
Courtesy of The Museum of Modern Art.**

At this point Sennett was getting busier and busier dealing with studio business and administrative duties, so he began curtailing his on-screen appearances and began giving his star comics the opportunity to supervise their own films. Although he soon offered the same opportunity to Sterling, Arbuckle and Chaplin, Mabel's appointment to director is significant, not only because she was the first, but because it made her one of the extremely few women who directed silent comedy.

Today it's hard to discern a strong directorial style in the shorts she helmed as more than half of them are missing. The earliest surviving example is the recently rediscovered *Won in a Closet* (a.k.a. *Won in a Cupboard,* January 22, 1914). Mabel is the local beauty that all the country boobs unsuccessfully try to win while she only has eyes for her little

Romeo, Charles Avery. At the same time Mabel's father, the rural constable, is making a play for Charles' mother. Both couples have clandestine meetings, but when Mabel and Charles return too soon the older folks hide in the kitchen cupboard because they don't want their children to see them together. Mabel and Charles realize that someone's in the cupboard and assume it's the tramp that was seen in the vicinity. All the neighbors and the constable's squad are called for help and after the cupboard is dragged outside, chopped with an axe, and flooded with a hose, the much worse-for-wear parents are discovered. Following the standard Keystone recipe very well, Mabel gets in all the required knockabout, but there is one striking sequence that shows unusual directorial imagination. Mabel and her beau meet and are drawn to each other like magnets – first in long sustained close-ups, and then finally in a creative double-exposure shot where the pair are on either side of the screen and traveling closer and closer together.

Glamor pose for Keystone Comedies. Billy Rose Theatre Division, the New York Public Library for the Performing Arts.

Three others – *Mabel's Strange Predicament*, *Mabel at the Wheel*, and *Caught in a Cabaret* – survive, most likely thanks to Charlie Chaplin's presence in the casts. *Mabel's Strange Predicament* is another comedy built around Mabel's sex appeal, this time a risqué farce that has Mabel getting innocently locked out of her hotel room clad only in pajamas and her misadventures avoiding people in the halls and hiding under the bed of the older couple next door. Of course the wife blames her husband, as does Mabel's boyfriend Harry McCoy. An interesting aspect of the film is longer takes than the norm, giving the performers a bit more leisure to partake and react to what's happening around them. Chaplin plays an annoying drunk at the hotel, and the short's main claim to fame is that it was the first film shot with him in his make-up and costume of the little tramp. His next short, *Kid Auto Races at Venice*, was shot during this production but beat it into the theatres.

In *Mabel at the Wheel* her sweetheart Harry McCoy is an auto racer, and when they have a spat she encourages the attentions of Charlie Chaplin (dressed as a cross between his sharpie character from his first film *Making a Living* (1914) and Ford Sterling) to make him jealous. This ends quickly after she falls off the back of his motorbike into a mud puddle, where she's rescued by Harry and they make up. For revenge Charlie decides to sabotage Harry's chances in the big race, in addition to making himself generally obnoxious in the stands. Chaplin has his henchmen Dave Anderson and Grover Ligon tie Harry up, and when he can't be found to start the race Mabel takes his place in the car. Although Charlie does his worst to thwart her efforts Mabel drives to victory. Director Normand keeps the film clipping along at a nice pace with Chaplin enjoying himself immensely spoofing the stock melodrama villains. On location during shooting Mabel and Charlie had a disagreement over a gag, with Charlie refusing to work. Returning to the studio Chaplin had to face Sennett's wrath, but luckily he had just been told how popular Chaplin's films were becoming so he stopped short of giving him the gate.

Everything had been patched up by the time *Caught in a Cabaret* was made, with Mabel generously taking a back seat and giving Charlie a star vehicle. Chaplin is a waiter in a very seedy cabaret, and Mabel a society belle. While out on his lunch break Charlie recues Mabel from a thug and tells her that he's a baron. She invites him to the society party she's throwing that evening, but in the meantime her spurned boyfriend Harry McCoy follows Charlie back to the dive and discovers the truth. At the party Mabel and her guests make a fuss over the supposed baron, as Harry fumes on the sidelines. After Charlie leaves, Harry gets even by taking all the society swells to the cabaret where of course Charlie is discovered and all hell breaks loose in usual Keystone style. In her next to last directorial effort Mabel gets a lot of atmosphere in the cabaret scenes, with much detailed character work coming from Minta Durfee, Hank Mann, Chester Conklin, Phyllis Allen, Edgar Kennedy, Glen Cavender, and Mack Swain as its denizens. Also a long two-shot during the party where Charlie and Mabel sing to the music provided by a small band gives Mabel the opportunity for some funny reactions to Charlie's repeated belching and hiccupping.

It appears that Mabel stopped directing after *Mabel's Nerve* (May 16, 1914), and years later in the 1920s she was asked about her directorial work. She responded that filmmaking was so simple in 1913 and 1914 that you really couldn't call it directing by modern standards. So with typical modesty she dismissed her work as America's first woman slapstick comedy director.

Mabel's best known 1914 films had her co-starred with Chaplin such as *Mabel's Married Life*, *His Trysting Place*, and *Getting Acquainted*, but there are a couple of survivors with her on her own. *Hello Mabel* follows her misadventures as a telephone operator at a hotel where she and her boyfriend Harry McCoy get mixed up with a flirting Mack Swain and his wife Alice Davenport, not to mention various run-ins with the other hotel guests. In *Mabel's Blunder* she's engaged to Harry, but her boss, Harry's father, is sweet on her as well. Mabel gets suspicious when Harry makes a big fuss over a strange woman who shows up at the office, and through the keyhole she can see them kissing and hugging in the other room. When they go out to a restaurant Mabel disguises herself and becomes their chauffeur. While spying on the pair she gets mixed-up in a spat between another couple and in the resulting pandemonium it's revealed that Harry's other woman is, of course, his sister. Although the plot is predictable, Mabel gives an understated and very effective performance.

**Mabel, Fatty, and dolly makes three.
Courtesy of The Museum of Modern Art.**

The year culminated with the release of Sennett's first feature-length film *Tillie's Punctured Romance* (December 21, 1914). Famous today as the film debut of stage star Marie Dressler, it was Mabel and Charlie Chaplin's first feature appearances and a huge hit that added extra prestige to both their careers. Dressler, used to playing to the back row from her barnstorming days, gives a broadly stylized performance that has to be seen to believed, and Chaplin also pulls out the stops to keep up with her. Mabel, on the other hand, gives an understated and sly performance as Chaplin's paramour and partner in crime, and really walks off with the acting honors in the midst of all the mugging and flailing around of the rest of the ensemble.

1915 saw almost all of Mabel's output in partnership with Roscoe "Fatty" Arbuckle. The duo were great friends and had worked together frequently since Arbuckle's arrival on the lot in 1913, but starting with *Mabel and Fatty's Wash Day* (January 14, 1915) the teamwork became official, leading to outings such as *Mabel, Fatty and the Law*, *Wished on Mabel*, *Mabel's Willful Way*, and more. Two of the best are *Mabel and Fatty's Married Life* (February 11, 1915) and *That Little Band of Gold* (March 15, 1915). Both films include more character detail and delineation than the usual Keystone, and while having action and slapstick sequences the films are more leisurely paced and never frenetic.

Mabel and Fatty's Married Life presents Mabel as a spouse who's influenced by the exciting books that she reads. After an incident in the park with an organ grinder and his monkey, Mabel gets nervous by herself at home when Roscoe goes out on business. Reading about neighborhood thieves in the newspaper makes her take out her gun for protection, and she practically turns Roscoe into a Swiss cheese firing at him when he returns home unexpectedly. After he leaves she spots the organ grinder and a friend prowling around outside. Trying to stay calm and concentrate on some sewing doesn't work as there's something moving behind the drapes. In a long sustained sequence Mabel goes through a myriad of emotions as the drapes keep moving – with a hat that practically flies straight up in the air with fright. In a panic she calls Roscoe's office, who in turn call the Keystone Cops. Roscoe ends up at home at the same time as the Cops, and the something behind the drapes turns out to be the monkey the organ grinder was looking for.

This short has the pair more comfortably middle-class than the usual Keystone riff-raff, and *That Little Band of Gold* even ups the ante by making them well-to-do. The film starts out with Mabel and Fatty as a shy and awkward couple who marry at City Hall. Things jump ahead a few years to show Roscoe taking Mabel for granted – stumbling home after having had a few snorts, flirting with the maid, and having a tussle with mother-in-law Alice Davenport. Dragged to the opera by his spouse, Roscoe runs into Ford Sterling and hooks up with him and his two lady companions for drinks. The woman that Sterling favors takes a shine to Roscoe, so Sterling calls Mabel and gives her an anonymous tip that her husband is stepping out. Mabel and mother show up at the restaurant and catch him in the act, and the next scene is back at City Hall, but this time getting a divorce. Outside afterwards they patch things up and run back in to re-marry.

Mabel gives essentially a dramatic performance as the neglected and disappointed wife, and Arbuckle brings out unlikeable aspects in his character – generally brusque and grumpy – even reprimanding Mabel when she slips and falls instead of helping her up. Both of these shorts were slapstick versions of the situational comedies of Mr. and Mrs. Sidney Drew as, despite generous helpings of knockabout, director Arbuckle still managed to include sly digs and satirical observations on marriage and male-female relationships.

Mabel and stage star Raymond Hitchcock in the Sennett four-reeler *My Valet* (1914). Courtesy of The Museum of Modern Art.

Outside of her appearances with Arbuckle, Mabel shot footage with Sennett, Ford Sterling, and Owen Moore for a five-reel feature that would not be released until 1922 (more on this later), and she finished 1915 working with stage star Raymond Hitchcock in two films – *My Valet* and *Stolen Magic*. Sennett had recently joined D.W. Griffith and Thomas Ince as a third of the Triangle Film Corporation. Engineered by producer Harry Aitken to align three of the biggest names in Hollywood, for additional prestige Aitken acquired famous stage names to star in Triangle pictures. Sennett got Weber and Fields, Sam Bernard, William Collier Sr., and Raymond Hitchcock. A star comic who had first appeared on Broadway in 1898, Hitchcock was a writer and producer as well and appeared in his annual *Hitchy-Koo* revues.

My Valet (November 7, 1915) was Sennett's first release for Triangle, and part of the inaugural Triangle program at the Knickerbocker Theatre in New York on September 18, 1915. Sennett himself came out of semi-retirement to play the title character in this prestigious four-reel production where Hitchcock plays a wealthy fellow who goes on a trip to the west coast with his valet Mack. After rescuing Mabel from a runaway horse, Hitchcock is contacted by the parents of the woman he's been betrothed to since childhood, which is of course Mabel but he doesn't know it. Since he's already smitten with Mabel, in order to avoid this marriage he has Mack take his place and Hitchcock pretends to be the valet. Since this is a farce complications ensue but ultimately Hitchcock again rescues Mabel, this time from a French count who tries to drown her, and all ends happily.

At the moment the film survives in fragmentary form, with segments at the Danish Film Institute, Library of Congress, and UCLA. Sennett pulled out all the stops for his first Triangle effort and the film was well received:

> Hitchcock not only makes good as a screen comedian, but he dominates most of the scenes in which he appears, but he has a dangerous rival for first honors in the shapely Mabel Normand. Mabel is too great a favorite to be lost in any crowd. Her fine training as a swimmer equipped her for the strenuous movement of athletic comedy, and she has a personality that wins without effort. When she is tied to a rock in the ocean by Fred Mace, a "heavy" in many senses of the word, she is a veritable Aphrodite, "foam-born and sweet to the eye," that she stimulates admiration as well as laughter. She and Hitchcock make a fine comedy team, well deserving of further united opportunity. (*Moving Picture World*, October 9, 1915)

Mabel told *Motography* magazine that working with Hitchcock was "the most fun she ever had in pictures," and she became great friends with the comic and his wife Flora Zabelle. She also told *Motography*:

> Working with Raymond Hitchcock in "My Valet" made up for all the hardships. I think I laughed straight through the "water stuff." Fred Mace was the villain. He took me out to a rock and tied me there. But he was so afraid of the water that he was in terror the whole time I believe. And at last the current was so strong it swept him away, and we all had to turn in and rescued the frightened "villyan."

When *My Valet* was in general release Mabel was recovering from an accident that had a lasting effect on the rest of her life and career. Having recently started the shooting of *Fatty and Mabel Adrift* (1916) she sustained a major head injury and was hospitalized for a time in very serious condition. The often told version of the story has Mabel catching boyfriend Mack Sennett having a tryst with her friend Mae Busch. In the confrontation and confusion Mae is said to have picked up a vase and hit Mabel over the head with it. Whether or not this is true, she was hospitalized with reports that she was dangerously ill, and her condition was touch and go for several days. According to the October 9, 1915 *Moving Picture World* she was:

Courtesy of Robert Arkus.

> suffering with a concussion of the brain. For several days she remained semi-conscious and developed a high fever which made her recovery a matter of doubt. At the time of this writing her condition has improved and, unless new complications arise, she will soon be out of danger.

The studio put out the cover story that she was hurt shooting a burlesque wedding scene with Roscoe Arbuckle – that a boot that was thrown along with rice and shoes knocked her unconscious. Mabel's version for interviewers had a more comic spin – that Arbuckle accidentally sat on her head while they were shooting a scene.

As soon as Mabel was well enough filming resumed on *Fatty and Mabel Adrift*, which was finished right before the holidays on December 17, 1915. At three reels it was a "Mabel and Fatty" special, and is generally considered the best of their films together. The simple plot has the pair as a young farm couple who marry. The bride's parents give them a seaside bungalow as a wedding gift. Rejected suitor Al St John has sworn vengeance, and on a rainy and stormy night he and his cohorts set the cottage adrift in the ocean. Fatty and Mabel wake up to find their love nest rapidly filling with water, so their dog Luke is dispatched with a message to get help – which comes in the form of Mabel's folks and the Keystone Cops.

Excellently directed by Arbuckle, the film has immense charm with many clever and human touches. It opens with tableaus of the leads framed in heart-shaped cut-outs (of course Al's gets broken), and Cupid shoots an arrow that unites Fatty and Mabel's. There's also a touching moment where Roscoe's shadow gives Mabel a goodnight kiss, a realistically played funny scene about Mabel's first attempt at making biscuits, and a slam-bang action climax with everyone mobilizing to the rescue.

While Mabel had been recuperating in October *Variety* announced:

Mabel Normand Coming East. As soon as she recovers from her accident, Mabel Normand is coming east to locate permanently. She will be assigned to Keystone's Fort Lee studio and work with Roscoe Arbuckle.

From this point on any personal relationship she had had with Sennett was over, and she seemed determined to put as much physical distance between them as possible. To that end, she, the Arbuckles, and Al St. John, headed to the East Coast. A *Chicago Post* reporter had this description of Mabel as they stopped there:

Pretty Miss Normand is just recovering from a severe illness, so very severe in fact, that she has lost her "pep." Tipping the scales at just ninety pounds, one couldn't imagine in her the sprightly Mabel whose antics with Fatty have made the Keystones what they are. In her smart seal coat with trimmings of blue fox and her close-fitting turban she looked not unlike the Mabel we know on the screen, but the deep shadows beneath her eyes told of her weeks of suffering. "But," said Mrs. Arbuckle, "she has picked up wonderfully in these four days out of Los Angeles, and we feel sure that three months in the East will restore the vim that is sadly missing." (December 30, 1915)

The group arrived in New York the next day and soon got to work at the Willatt Studio in Fort Lee, New Jersey. Her illness and break with Sennett led her to focus more on her career and how she wanted it to move ahead. When asked by the *New York Morning Telegraph* in February 1916 if it was difficult to be funny and beautiful she replied:

Most pretty girls who go into comedy work are content to be merely pretty. The great difference is to put character into acting without either distorting your face or using comedy make-up. Anyone who photographs well can walk on a scene and flirt with the comedian which is all that most good looking girls are required to do in comedies. It takes very little ability on their part for all they have to do is follow direction. (And here Miss Normand gave an imitation of a comedy coquette flirting according to the commands of her director). But to make a farce heroine more than a mere doll, you must think out the situation yourself and above all you must pay great attention to every little detail in the scene. The little bits of business that seem insignificant are what make good comedy.

Mabel and a canine friend. Author's collection.

Away from Sennett's supervision director Arbuckle did very strong work during this stay on the East Coast. Films such as *The Waiter's Ball*, *His Wife's Mistake* (both 1916), and *A Reckless Romeo* (shot in 1916 but released in 1917), while continuing with plenty of slapstick action, were more cleverly choreographed and motivated, plus stronger plot and character development was added. Mabel appeared with Roscoe in the first two Eastern productions – *He Did and He Didn't* (January 30, 1916), and *The Bright Lights* (February 20, 1916). Sadly the latter is not known to exist today, but without a doubt the most unusual film made on the trip was *He Did and He Didn't*.

Roscoe plays a well-to-do doctor, and the picture opens with Roscoe and Mabel in their very posh home dressing for dinner. He, of course, is having trouble with his collar button, but when Mabel tries to help he is grumpy and bad-tempered. Right before dinner Mabel's old school chum and former sweetheart William Jefferson comes for a surprise visit, making Roscoe jealous. While the trio dines on lobsters, a couple of burglars case the house. When one of them pretends to need the doctor's care, Roscoe catches on immediately and tosses him out. Returning to the dinner table Roscoe's jealousy gets the best of him and he has a scene with Mabel. One of the crooks phones to get Roscoe out of the house on a fake emergency. While he's gone Mabel and Jefferson catch Al St John under her bed and chase him around the house. Before Al flees he throttles Mabel, and Jefferson helps her into bed.

Roscoe returns to find him there, and thinking the worst throws him out the window and strangles Mabel. Not dead, she finds Roscoe's pistol and kills him. At this point Roscoe and Jefferson both awake from a mutual bad dream that was caused by their lobster dinner, and laugh it all off to become friends. With its combination of dramatic feature lighting and adult situations *He Did and He Didn't* has a sophistication rarely seen in a slapstick comedy short. After their years of working together, Arbuckle and Mabel have a remarkable ease in their domestic scenes and are completely convincing as a longtime married couple, and while the settings and camerawork are more sophisticated Roscoe still gets in plenty of well-choreographed knockabout, particularly in the sequence of St John getting chased through the house (Arbuckle would remake the film in 1924 as *One Night It Rained*).

After these two eastern shorts Mabel's contract with Keystone was expiring and she entertained other offers. Comedy films were changing and she was very aware of what was needed to move forward:

> I make it a part of my daily work" she told me, "to attend theatres where they show Keystone pictures. I listen eagerly for criticisms among the audience and many times get good ideas in this way. But I do not confine myself to my own pictures either. I see everybody's. That is the only way I can keep in touch.
>
> The comedy of four or five years ago was a very different affair from those made today, but I think there is still plenty of room for improvement, and the next few years will witness as great a development.

Triangle was determined to keep her, but it wasn't certain whether she would be working for Sennett or Thomas Ince:

Mabel Normand in Wider Field. As frequently rumored within the last few months, Mabel Normand, the "Keystone Girl," is to have a wider field of motion picture activity. This is the announcement from the offices of the Triangle Film Corporation, with which she has recently signed a new contract. She is to be a star in comedy drama. A director all her own will select plays for her, and it is said that the first will follow the line of "Peggy," in which Billie Burke made her film debut – under the direction of Thomas Ince.

Whether Miss Normand will make her first picture in this brand new field in the East or on the Coast has not yet been determined. She is now in New York resting after strenuous Keystone activities. (*Moving Picture World*, April 8, 1916)

Finally, Sennett won out by doubling her salary and setting her up in her own studio to make starring features (something he had been promising for some time). May 1, 1916 saw the formation of the Mabel Normand Feature Film Company, which was separate from Triangle, and gave Mabel story and director approval. Production began in mid-May on *Mickey* with James Young in the director's chair. Young (more on him in Chapter Six) was a former stage actor who came to prominence in the early teens directing his wife Clara Kimball Young in many Vitagraph films, and on paper seemed like the perfect choice for Mabel's inaugural production as he had been helming dramatic and comedy features such as *Marrying Money, Over Night* (both 1915), and *The Thousand Dollar Husband* (1916) for Kimball Young, Vivian Martin, Mae Murray, and Blanche Sweet. The scenario was by John Gerald Hawks, who had spent the last few years writing Thomas Ince-produced shorts and features for the likes of William S. Hart and Sessue Hayakawa. Originally titled *Pat*, production difficulties began almost immediately after shooting started, as by mid-June:

James Young is no longer the director of Mabel Normand. Mr. Young directed a few scenes for the former Keystoner and it seemed impossible for the two to get along, so Mr. Young, like the courteous gentleman he is, withdrew. He has been succeeded by J. Farrell MacDonald, late of the American Women Film Company, and for a long time with the Biograph Company. He will be assisted by A. Gillstrom of the Keystone forces, and Mr. Sennett will continue as the general supervising director. Miss Normand's initial comedy-dramatic picture under her own name will be released about the first of August. (*New York Morning Telegraph*, June 18, 1916)

This last sentence was more than wishful thinking. In July J. Farrell MacDonald was replaced by F. Richard Jones, an up-and-coming Sennett writer and director. But the delays continued for various reasons, and the shooting of the picture was not completed until April 1917. As if this wasn't bad enough Sennett then sat on the film for more than a year, not releasing it until August 1918. Although a second picture, an adaptation of J.M. Barrie's *The Little Minister,* had been talked about Mabel severed her connection with the company that bore her name and signed a contract with Goldwyn Pictures.

Things didn't exactly start smoothly with Mabel and the Goldwyn Company either. It appears she signed her contract during the shooting of *Mickey,* and its various stoppages pushed back her starting for Goldwyn. In July 1917 they finally took out an injunction to stop her from working for any other concern. It's hard to say how many of these detours and delays were caused by Mabel, but the erratic behavior that would plague the rest of her life begins at this time. While often used as an example of her alleged drug use, it's possible that it may have been a result of her recent head injuries. Finally, by September 1917 she was at work at the Goldwyn Studios in Fort Lee.

Work is perhaps too mild a word, as Mabel would have seven Goldwyn features come out in 1918 alone. In three years she would make a total of sixteen full-length films for the producer in addition to a Liberty Bond short, a number rivaled by Will Rogers who turned out thirteen Goldwyn features during the same time. Goldwyn had an assembly line going, and now Mabel wasn't just a comedienne she was a Goldwyn leading lady – along with prestigious types such as Mae Marsh, Madge Kennedy, Jane Cowl, Mary Garden, and Maxine Elliot – although it was Mabel's comedies that brought in the money.

Mabel began shooting *Joan of Plattsburg* in September, but it proved difficult and was shelved so *Dodging a Million* (January 27, 1918) was her initial Goldwyn release. This made her the first slapstick shorts star to graduate to longer films, which had her beating the likes of Arbuckle, Chaplin, and Lloyd to the punch by a few years. Sadly out of

Joan of Plattsburg (1918) was started as Mabel's first Goldwyn production, but ended up being released fourth.

these sixteen features only four are known to exist today. Her second release, *The Floor Below* (March 10, 1918), is the earliest of her Goldwyn pictures that can be viewed.

Mabel is Patricia O'Rourke who works as a "copy girl" in a newspaper office, although she seems to spend more time rolling dice with an elderly messenger boy and keeping the rest of the staff laughing. When she's going to be fired by the head editor for causing trouble, a reporter talks him into letting her assist him in getting a story. She pretends to be a crook in order to get the scoop on a settlement house that's being funded by a millionaire. Turns out the millionaire's crooked secretary is using the house as a way to pass information to thieves about the homes belonging to the friends of the young benefactor. Mabel gets a place in the millionaire's home as a young woman that he's going to reform, and besides falling for him she manages to expose the secretary and his cohorts. All ends well with Mabel getting her millionaire.

A dramatic scene from the surviving *The Floor Below* (1918). Courtesy of Marilyn Slater.

It seems that from out of the gate Goldwyn used a basic "Cinderella" type of plot about a poor working class girl who always wins her wealthy Prince Charming by the end of the picture. The plot of *The Floor Below* is a bit overly complicated, with sidebars that include a conniving fiancé for the millionaire, and the millionaire's bet with his uncle that Patricia can't be reformed, which leads to Mabel spending most of her screen time dancing around the plot and adding all kinds of little character bits to liven up the proceedings.

After her fifth Goldwyn picture, *Back to the Woods* (July 28, 1918), Mack Sennett re-entered the picture. Although he'd been putting out publicity for the long-shelved *Mickey* for more than a year ownership issues had kept it unreleased, but it finally came out through the Aitken's Brothers W.H. Productions in August 1918 and was an immense hit. The story of the film has Mickey as a tomboy who has grown up in the wild, reared by miner Joe Meadows and his Indian housemaid Minnie. Although Joe loves her he wants her to grow up to be a lady, so she's sent to live with her rich aunt Mrs. Drake. Actually the aunt and her family are strapped for cash, and think that Mickey is an heiress. When they find out that she's the opposite they put her to work as a housemaid. Mrs. Drake's only hope for solvency is having her daughter marry the wealthy Herbert Thornhill, a mining engineer who Mickey has already charmed when he was doing some surveying near her cabin.

Mickey (1918) sees Mabel in hot water with George Nichols in spite of Princess Minnie's attempts to hide her. Courtesy of The Museum of Modern Art.

When the aunt finds out that Thornhill is more interested in Mickey than her daughter, she's sent packing back to Joe and the mine, but just as she leaves a telegram arrives with the info that the mine has come in and she's worth a million. She's brought back and of course is now well-treated. Thornhill is told by a business associate that he's broke, so the Drakes are quickly done with him. Reggie, Mrs. Drake's son, jealous that Mickey loves Thornhill, gets Thornhill to bet five thousand on his horse in an upcoming race as a way to recoup his loses. But Reggie wants to ruin Thornhill. He plots with his jockey to throw the race. Mickey overhears the planning, and takes the place of the jockey and almost wins the race, but she and the horse take a terrible spill before the finish line.

After recuperating Mickey goes riding with Reggie who comes on to her and chases her to an empty house. To get away from him she climbs out on the roof, but in true cliffhanger style Thornhill arrives in the nick of time to thrash Reggie and eventually rescue Mickey as she's hanging for dear life. The ending has Mickey and Thornhill wed and leaving for their honeymoon back at the cabin where they first met. After the train pulls out of the station a telegram arrives from the business associate saying that the "business loss" was just a trick to get Thornhill out of the engagement with the Drakes, and everything ends happily.

Given its protracted production history *Mickey* is more cohesive than one would expect, but like most of the Mack Sennett features the film's plot structure is fairly rocky, particularly having the unnecessary cliff-hanging sequence after what should have been the climactic horserace finish. Mabel gives a wonderful performance, and is surrounded by excellent players like George Nichols, Minnie Ha-Ha, Laura La Varnie, Minta Durfee, and the always creepy Lew Cody (more on him later). Wheeler Oakman is a satisfactory hero, and the setting and production values are good, but all the different elements revolve around Mabel. A sensation at the box office, Sennett claimed that it earned $18 million, although it's unclear exactly how much he finally pocketed thanks to ownership issues.

After this blast from her Sennett past, Mabel signed a new contract with Goldwyn and the features continued being released at a rapid pace. Out of the eleven films that followed – *Peck's Bad Girl* (1918), *A Perfect 36*, *Sis Hopkins*, *Upstairs*, *Jinx* (all 1919), *Pinto*, *The Slim Princess* (both 1920), etc. – only three are known to exist. *When Doctor's Disagree* (1919), although it survives the only known print is at the Cinematheque Royale in Brussels and has only been available on its premises. According to reviews Mabel plays a small town girl named Millie who is the terror of her village, spending her time breaking up the May party that she wasn't invited to. Much of the action takes place in a sanitarium where, thanks to complications, Millie must try to avoid operations that she doesn't need. As a May 1919 *Exhibitors Herald* advised:

> There is nothing to distract the attention from the wholesome antics of the star. There is no jerking of the mood from the comic to the serious. The whole is just a series of incidents bordering closely upon the slapstick and funny in the style of Mabel Normand's always popular Keystone efforts. Advertised with reference to the old Keystone days and the recent "Mickey" the attendance should be satisfactory.

For decades *What Happened to Rosa?* (1920) was the only one of her Goldwyn pictures to be available. It's an overly complicated story of a little shopgirl that gets carried away with the romantic concept that she is the reincarnation of a Spanish dancer, Rose Alvaro. Obsessed with her other identity Mabel's Mayme Ladd is more than a little schizophrenic, and much of her screen time is spent trying to break an arm or hand so that she has a reason to go to the doctor she's fallen in love with. An unsettling aspect of this film is Mabel's physical appearance – looking gaunt and somewhat pop-eyed. She also seems listless and furtive as she goes through her scenes.

Mabel disguises herself as a boy in *What Happened to Rosa* (1920) to get close to the doctor she fancies. Courtesy of Cole Johnson.

Rumors and stories of Mabel's drug use have freely circulated since she was alive. Although no real details are available – perhaps it started from overwork, her respiratory problems, or even her 1915 head injury – the peak of her drug use seems to have been 1919 and 1920. Reviewers and commentators noted her changing and often haggard appearance. Mabel's health and erratic behavior were only part of Samuel Goldwyn's problems. Issues with his partners and overproduction led to him selling off his shares in the company and starting up a new Goldwyn Productions in 1923. The earlier Goldwyn assets were acquired by Marcus Lowe in 1924 and merged with his Metro Pictures, and eventually Louis B. Mayer Productions, to become Metro-Goldwyn–Mayer. That's how MGM ended up with its famous lion logo – it had originally been Goldwyn's.

Thanks to Goldwyn's up and downs, *Head Over Heels*, Mabel's last film for the producer, was shot in the summer of 1920 but not released until the spring of 1922. After that it promptly disappeared with the bulk of her Goldwyn pictures, but in 2001 it was found in the basement of a family in Massachusetts, and restored by the American Film Institute. Quite a lucky find, as at the moment it's the best of her handful of Goldwyn survivors. Mabel plays Tina, the star of an Italian acrobatic company that's hired by a theatrical producer to come to America. When she arrives she's homely, ill clad, and maltreats the English language, which causes the producer to immediately lose interest and foist her on his partner. In the meantime her guardian and head of the troupe, Papa Bambinetti, falls under the influences of press agent Pepper who puts over a deal where Tina will become a motion picture actress.

Mabel's not sure about the statuary in Head Over Heels *(1922). Courtesy of Marilyn Slater.*

To this end she is dragged to a beauty make-over from which she emerges a real beauty. Lawson, the partner put in charge of her, falls in love with her and wants her to give up show business and become his wife. Tina is happy about this and cancels her movie contract, but the disgruntled movie producer tells her that her fiancée Lawson is carrying on with a well-known actress. Tina tracks them to a busy restaurant while they are actually having an innocent business meeting, and beats the living daylights out of the star. When the real truth is revealed she's sure that she's lost Lawson, so she and Papa Bambinetti pack up to return to Italy, but Lawson finds her at the last minute and persuades her to stay.

The bare bones of the plot don't do justice to the film which is entirely dependent on Mabel's performance for its laughs and entertainment value. It seems likely that the Goldwyn people finally realized that they shouldn't hem their star in with too much plot, as *Head Over Heel*'s loose structure gives her plenty of room for funny physical gags and personality business. Instead of a typical ingénue, the role of Tina is more of a character part to which Mabel plays to maximum comedic effect. Hugh Thompson makes a rather mournful love interest, but this actually works well and gives the comedienne much to play off of. She also has excellent support from Raymond Hatton as the scheming press agent, Russ Powell's bombastic Papa Bambinetti, an unbilled Laura La Varnie as the doubtful beauty expert hired to do her best on Tina, plus the presence of Adolphe Menjou and Lionel Belmore. Sadly, in keeping with the film's belated release it was hardly noticed and disappeared quickly.

At the beginning of 1921 Mabel had finished with her Goldwyn contract, and went away for what was called in the press "a rest." On January 15, columnist Louella Parsons reported:

> **Taking the Milk Cure.** That winsome young person, Mabel Normand, gave all her friends a terrible shock when she grew thinner by the hour, a few months ago. I saw her at the theatre, and was haunted by her white face, and her eyes with their deep shadows. Mabel's eyes are so big and deep, when she looks badly they seem to cover her whole face.
>
> After meeting her, I heard she had gone to the country and was drinking gallons of milk. Then I didn't see her for weeks, until we met at the auction of Olive Thomas's things. She has put on ten pounds, and is as round and pink as when she used to make everyone laugh in her famous comedies with Fatty Arbuckle.
>
> "I'm just resting," she said, "and I refuse to make another picture until I can get a story I want, and the sort of director I need."

Photoplay also picked up the story and summarized in their February 1921 issue:

> Mabel Normand has been taking a vacation. On an up-state farm. Only comes into Manhattan once in a while. Leading the simple life. Reason? Mabel wanted to gain ten pounds. Doesn't know when she'll come back to work. "Wanta good story first," she says. She looks perter and prettier than she ever did.

Seven months later writer Adela Rogers St Johns practically "outed" Mabel's drug experiences in a thinly veiled piece titled *Hello Mabel* that appeared in the August 1921 issue of *Photoplay*. First she describes Mabel's "illness:"

When I saw her about a year and a half ago just before she went to New York, it did not seem possible that she could be the same girl whose arresting prettiness had made us gasp at Al Levy's that night.

She was sitting in her car on the Goldwyn lot.

She looked ill. She looked unhappy. But more than that, she looked harassed, eaten up inside by something that was bitter to her spiritual digestion.

Smiling – yes, but we all know that Mabel will go to meet St. Peter with a smile on her face, no matter what road she goes.

Her face was sunken so that her eyes looked uncannily large and dark. Her cheeks were the gray-white of a sea fog. Within her rich clothes she seemed wasted away, their gorgeousness hung loose about her thin frame.

She haunted me. It hurt to see her – as it hurts to see a gorgeous, fragrant budding Jacqueminot rose suddenly cut from a bush and flung carelessly on the ground, helpless, fading, bruised by sun and wind.

There were constant stories as to her failing health, her fading beauty. There were rumors that she was photographing very badly, and that Goldwyn – paying her an enormous salary – was most unhappy.

St Johns goes on to mention Mabel's head injury (here disguised as a car accident), and then charts the progress of her "illness," recent recovery, and cheers her on:

Four years ago, Mabel was in a very serious automobile accident. For months her life hung in the balance. For weeks she was not expected to live.

But the doctors had failed to count on Mabel Normand's heart – on that courage which she rates so highly.

Somehow she won that fight with death. Gamely, smilingly, wide-eyed and unafraid, not particularly because she wanted to live, but because she did not think it courageous to die.

She won – but that was the beginning of all that followed. For several years, Mabel's health – not even cared for as it should have been because Mabel would not care for it – sank steadily.

And then, Mabel Normand disappeared. The Goldwyn lot, where she was working, knew her no more.

But in the rock-ribbed hills of a New England state, in a small village and in surroundings without comforts or indulgences of any kind, a girl was beginning a real fight for life.

For six months, Mabel "rested." With that smiling courage of hers, she took up the steady, soul-grinding task of building up a wrecked nervous system, of recuperating a weak and neglected body.

She made good. She has come back. The whispers and the words have all changed now. It is – "Doesn't Mabel Normand look wonderful?"

There is hardly a gathering in Hollywood where her return to health and beauty is not discussed. Her quiet, systematic way of living is talked of now.

Coincidentally, Mabel is back on the Mack Sennett lot where she made her first pictures, and where for years she was starred to advantage. Comedy queens and bathing beauties may come and go, but there is only one Mabel Normand. They could not replace her. So when you go over to the same old lot, and see the same old Mabel, it seems as though the hands of the clock had been turned back.

Publicity shot during the making of *Molly 'O* (1921). Courtesy of Robert S. Birchard.

As St Johns mentioned Mabel was already back at work with Sennett, which had happened at the beginning of the year:

> **Mabel Normand Re-Engaged by Mack Sennett**. After weeks of negotiations Mabel Normand has been signed up by Mack Sennett, and the Goldwyn star becomes once more the Sennett star. Under the terms of the now existing agreement, Miss Normand's services have been engaged on a long-term contract, and her first work will be as star of "Molly O," a big romantic comedy soon to be put in rehearsal at the Sennett studio. To satisfy the Goldwyn interests and entice the celebrated star to the signing of a long-term contract involved a sum of approximately $1,000,000. It is known that this is not the first time that ne-

gotiations have been opened between Sennett and his former star, but the need for her services were never felt before so keenly as when casting of "Molly O" was undertaken. In the opinion of those who have read the finished scenario and studied the completed continuity, there was but one artist to portray the title role. That one was Mabel Normand. (*Los Angeles Record*, February 3, 1921)

Since the wild success of Mickey, Sennett had been concentrating on feature comedies such as *Yankee Doodle in Berlin* (1919), *Down on the Farm, Married Life, Love, Honor and Behave* (all 1920), *A Small Town Idol*, and *Home Talent* (both 1921). Shorts had always paid the bills, but features were more prestigious as far as the film industry was concerned. Although he later claimed that he hadn't known the full extent of her "problems" when he re-hired Mabel, re-gaining the star of his biggest hit must have looked like a sure bet to Mack, and he may also have had a guilty conscience or even hoped to re-kindle their previous relationship. Whatever his true reasons – a,b,c, or all of the above – *Molly O* was filmed in four weeks in May and June of 1921.

Molly O'Dair is a perky working-class girl, whose mother takes in washing and whose honest, hard-working father is a ditch-digger. Pop wants Molly to settle down with his digging partner Danny Smith, but she has her own ideas on a perfect beau. She daydreams about the handsome Dr. James Bryant, after she reads about his philanthropic good deeds in the newspaper. She happens to meet her doctor when he treats a neighbor's sick baby, and they become friendly. Dr. Bryant is engaged to a snobby woman who's after him for his money and social prestige, and when Molly O has to deliver some laundry to Bryant's house, she's insulted by the fiancée but defended by the doctor (Molly also managed to help herself to some teacakes while waiting in the kitchen).

When the doctor has a charity ball he invites Molly, but her father, thinking that the wealthy doctor is just toying with her, refuses to allow her to go. She sneaks out with the help of her mother, and at the ball all sorts of complications occur which throw her together with the doctor. Going home she's assaulted by Danny, and is rescued by Bryant, but her father, not understanding the compromising look of the situation, banishes her from the house. Changing his mind the old man goes to Bryant's home the next day and when he finds Molly there he tries to shoot Bryant until they tell him that they are married.

Now that Molly is a society wife the rejected fiancée and her brother get Molly's brother in debt. The ex-fiancée's brother has Molly meet him at an airfield and bring money to cover her brother's debts, but while there he abducts her in a zeppelin. Dr. Bryant, having been put wise to the situation, comes to the rescue in a seaplane and rescues Molly in the big action climax. Despite the chaotic structure, *Molly O* is perhaps the best of Mabel's, and Sennett's, feature films. Although again using the basic "Cinderella" plot this time the characters are more complex, and while the picture starts out as out and out comedy it believably moves to romance and family melodrama. Mabel has never been funnier or better in the dramatic scenes, and she has excellent support in George Nichols and Anna Hernandez as her ultimately loving parents, Jack Mulhall makes a believable and personable hero, and the rest of the cast – Eddie Gribbon, Lowell Sherman, Jacqueline Logan, and Albert Hackett – are very good.

Like *Mickey* the film has a tacked on action climax that's detrimental – this time with baddie Lowell Sherman trying to have his way with Mabel on a dirigible. Well shot, and better than the thrill sequence in *Mickey*, it still is unnecessary and takes the film in an arbitrary direction. The film turned into a solid hit, although there was some concern and a slight delay in the release as actor Lowell Sherman was a participant in Roscoe Arbuckle's infamous Labor Day party which resulted in a huge scandal. A few months after *Molly O* was released on November 19, 1921 another scandal affected the film – this time with Mabel as one of the main players.

Popular movie director William Desmond Taylor was murdered on February 1, 1922. Mabel was involved with Taylor and was the last person to see him alive (besides his murderer). It's not known definitely if they were romantically involved, but it appears that Taylor was the person who organized Mabel being sent away on her "milk cure." While she was never in any way implicated in the murder, her career was seriously damaged by the rumors and stories that blazed all over the newspapers. Taylor was a big force in trying to run drugs out of the movie industry, and it seems likely that he was murdered by the drug sellers whose toes he was stepping on. While the press was having a field day Mabel was in production on *Suzanna*, another Sennett feature. It wouldn't come out until a year later on February 15, 1923.

In the meantime 1922 saw the belated release of two earlier-made Normand pictures. One was the aforementioned *Head Over Heels* for Goldwyn, and the other *Oh! Mabel Behave!* – made up of seven-year old footage that had been shot in 1915 during the early days of Triangle. Released on the states' rights market (system of distributing films territorially instead of nationwide) at the very end of 1921 by Photocraft Productions, Inc., it seems an odd choice for Sennett to release, but as it came out right before the Taylor controversy it would at least be a test to see how the scandal affected her box-office drawing powers. The film also headlined a younger Ford Sterling, Owen Moore, and Sennett himself, and was for many years considered lost but was found and restored by the Cinematheque Francaise in 2002.

The sketchy plot is set in the 1800s and has Sterling as the local squire who uses the mortgage he holds on the widowed innkeeper's property to try and win her pretty daughter (Mabel). But the daughter loves the young and dashing Randolph Roanoke, so the squire and his dopey henchman decide to cause trouble for Roanoke by challenging him to a duel, etc. Although only five reels in length the film meanders terribly and is full of aimless improvisation between Sterling and his goofy sidekick Sennett. Mabel, looking very young and pretty, is barely in the picture, which shows tell-tale signs of its being cobbled together years later when a double (with his back to the camera) fills in for Owen Moore. Exhibitors were confused by the obviously elderly footage so disclaimers appeared in the trade magazines:

"Oh, Mabel Behave!" Not a Reissue. A number of exhibitors and several buyers appear to be under the impression that "Oh, Mabel Behave!" the five-reel Mack Sennett comedy starring Mabel Normand, Own Moore, Mack Sennett and Ford Sterling being offered by Photocraft Productions, Inc., is a reissue.

Nathan Hirsh, president of Photocraft, announces it is an absolutely original picture and not a single scene of it was ever shown before in this country or in any other; that he realized its value as a box office attraction and found in it an excellent vehicle for his newly established firm, and before purchasing the negative he made a thorough investigation as to the picture's originality. (*Moving Picture World*, December 24, 1921)

Mabel flummoxed by Ford Sterling and Mack Sennett's heavy mugging in *Oh, Mabel Behave* (1922). Courtesy of Robert Arkus.

The William Desmond Taylor murder case continued to rage in the newspapers for months with fuel added to the fire by the January 1923 death of actor Wallace Reid due to morphine addiction. After the Fatty Arbuckle trials and the murder of Taylor, this was the third major Hollywood scandal and helped reinforce the image of the filmmaking community as a sin city and focused the microscope of the media on it. Right before the Taylor murder Mack Sennett spoke about his plans for Mabel:

Miss Normand's next vehicle, a period play by the working titles of "Suzanna" to be directed by Mr. Jones, has passed through the preliminary stages, has been cast and production started. In this, as in "Mickey" and "Molly O," Miss Normand will be different but only in character. That youthful roguishness and fascinating personality will predominate – the personality which refuses to be hidden by costume or makeup. I am giving my promise to make "Suzanna" a legitimate successor to Miss Normand's previous screen success. (*Moving Picture World*, December 31, 1921)

George Nichols and Mabel have a stand-off in *Suzanna* (1923). Courtesy of Cole Johnson.

Suzanna had been completed in April 1922 and because of all the to-do wasn't released until almost a year later in February 1923. Set in old California, Suzanna is an excitable peasant girl who is loved by the son of a wealthy rancho owner, but his father disapproves of their relationship. Padre has arranged a wedding for the son with the daughter of another wealthy rancher, and another complication is a toreador who courts Suzanna to try to get to the wealthy daughter. Finally the son stands up to his dictatorial father, and a swordfight between the young men is the big climax of the film.

Three of the film's five reels still exist today. *Suzanna* was a departure for the Sennett studio – it was more drama with incidental comedy. There's no slapstick, and it's the most lavishly produced of the Sennett features, with elaborate settings and costumes. Mabel is very good, and George Nichols turns in his usual solid work, not to mention Minnie Ha-Ha being back as Mabel's protector and surrogate mother.

After *Suzanna* the next film Sennett was developing for Mabel was *Mary Anne*, a story about the adopted daughter of a San Francisco policeman who has to choose between a working-class Irish cab driver and a wealthy architect. Of course complications ensue involving class structure and the usual last-minute kidnapping climax, with the story sounding like a rehash of the previous Sennett/Mabel features, especially *Molly O.* But at the same time Sennett was developing *Millie of the Movies*, a feature to star former bathing girl Phyllis Haver. Eventually titled *The Extra Girl*, the production started with Haver but when she abruptly left the studio Mabel and director F. Richard Jones inherited the project. They shot the film from April through July of 1923.

In *The Extra Girl* (1923) Mabel plays Sue Graham, a small-town girl who's crazy to be in the movies. Her parents and their chosen suitor for her, the town druggist, are convinced that her movie aspirations are a waste of time. Dave Giddings is her childhood sweetheart who supports her dreams, and when she wins a movie contest (by mistake) he helps her to run out on her wedding to the druggist and catch a train to Hollywood. When she gets to the studio the error of her winning the contest is discovered, but she's given a job in the wardrobe department where's she's under the thumb of virago Louise Carver.

Besides her comic adventures at the studio, there's a dramatic side plot where her parents sell their business, move to Hollywood, and invest all their money with a crooked conman. Her sweetheart Dave has also joined her in Hollywood and gets a job at the studio. Dave takes care of the conman and gets the money back, and finally convinces Sue to give up her movie dreams and marry him.

Mabel's most accessible feature is unfortunately her weakest. The overall dramatic plot is tired and predictable, cobbled together from the star's previous films. The funniest comedy sequences are at the studio where she has a disastrous screen test and mistakes a real lion for Teddy the dog made up as a lion. The supporting performances are very strong – as always George Nichols and Anna Hernandez are excellent as her parents, as is Vernon Dent as the rejected druggist. Ralph Graves is a very good love interest, plus Louise Carver and Max Davidson turn in their usual spot-on comedy work. Sadly Mabel is the weak link – giving a listless and routine performance. She's also oddly clothed in formless, sack-like dresses, and resembles a plump Bette Davis – overweight, tired, and slightly pop-eyed.

By the summer of 1923 the fallout from the Taylor murder had finally started to calm down, and Sennett was ready to continue making Mabel Normand features:

Mack Sennett Closes With Associated Exhibitors For Series of Mabel Normand Features. Mack Sennett and Arthur S. Kane, president of Associated Exhibitors, have just closed one of the biggest and most important deals of the year in signing a contract calling for the distribution of Associated of a series of features starring the popular comedienne, Mabel Normand.

Two, but never to exceed three, productions a year, are to be made, the contract calling for pictures of a super-type, exclusively. It is understood that under the terms of the contract, the production cost of each is to be between $350,000 and $500,000. And president Kane added in summation:

It is a pleasure for Associated to add Mabel Normand to the list of stars whose features we are to distribute. Miss Normand occupies a unique place among screen artistes, and now that Mr. Sennett has cast her in pictures of the type of "The Extra Girl," a yet more brilliant future is assured her. I am more than glad, too, to enter into this close business association with Mack Sennett. (*Weekly Film Review*, August 11, 1923)

Mabel and Ralph Graves in *The Extra Girl* (1923). Courtesy of Cole Johnson.

All was well when the film was released on October 23, 1923, but on January 1, 1924 Mabel was involved in another scandal that ended up plastered all over the newspapers. During a long New Year's Day celebration at the apartment of oil millionaire Courtland Dines with Mabel, Edna Purviance, and Dines, the millionaire was shot after an altercation with Mabel's chauffeur. It appears that Ms. Purviance and Dines were dating, and Mabel came over to visit them. Heavy drinking seems to have been going on and the events leading up to the shooting by the driver were never fully explained in the subsequent hearings. This event, that generated headlines such as "Playmate of Mabel

Normand is Shot," gave new fuel to the Taylor murder controversy, with religious groups calling for bans on the films of Mabel and Edna Purviance. The media field day went on for months, and by July *Variety* reported:

> **Will Miss Normand Be Left Flat On The Lot?** Mabel Normand's contract with Mack Sennett is completed and has not been renewed. It looks like a permanent business split between the film star and the comedy producer.
>
> A further prospective is that Miss Normand's future film career is uncertain. Recognized producers are somewhat wary of the comedienne as a result of the publicity she has obtained during the past few years.
>
> The two shootings, in which Miss Normand was named, the Taylor killing and the more recent Dines affair, are said to have cost Sennett extra expenditures for the overcoming of the notoriety, while Miss Normand's last release necessitated a special publicity staff, by itself, to offset the Dines odor.

Although Sennett issued a few half-hearted denials of the situation, the scheduled *Mary Anne* never came to fruition, and Mack and Mabel never worked together again.

Cut loose from film work, Mabel traveled abroad, and in the fall had more bad press when she was named a co-respondent in a divorce suit against millionaire Norman Church. In 1925 the press floated items of Mabel returning to films – that she was under negotiations with Tiffany-Truart Pictures for a feature to be entitled *Shelia*, also for a picture to be produced by the Chadwick Company that would be directed by comic Larry Semon – but Mabel said that while she had a number of offers she wasn't ready to accept any of them. Although she had never appeared on the professional stage, what she finally decided to do was a play.

> **Film Star Signs for New Play**. Another star has been lured from the screen to the stage, reversing the usual order of procedure. A.H. Woods, famous New York producer, announced yesterday that he had signed Mabel Normand under a five-year contract to appear in a new comedy on the speaking stage. The play, as yet unnamed, is being written by Otto Harbach, author of the three greatest musical comedy hits of the past season, "Kid Boots," "Rose Marie," and "No, No, Nanette," and will open at the Ritz Theatre, New York City, August 27, next. (*Los Angeles Times*, June 9, 1925)

A.H. Woods was a well-known Broadway producer, with a forty-year career that lasted from 1903 to 1943, during which his popular shows included *Potash and Perlmutter* (1913), *Parlor, Bedroom and Bath* (1917-1918), *Getting Gertie's Garter* (1921), and *Her Cardboard Lover* (1927). The play that was picked for Mabel was *The Little Mouse*, and it was anything but a "new comedy." It originally came from a German source, but a French version was attributed to an Alphonse Poiret. It was adapted and re-written a few times in America by playwrights such as Walter De Leon and Martin Brown, under titles like *Lonely Wives*, *Naughty Diana*, and *Loose Moments*. Producer Wood had already presented a couple of these versions but seems to have been determined to not give up on the property, and commissioned the aforementioned Otto Harbach to do yet another re-write, now titled *The Little Mouse*. The September 15, 1925 *Brooklyn Eagle* gave this description of the plot:

Stamford : Theatre
EMILY WAKEMAN HARTLEY, Manager   Phone 2800

Friday and Saturday, August 28 and 29, 1925
A. H. WOODS Presents

MABEL NORMAND
(In Person)
in
A New Comedy Entitled

"THE LITTLE MOUSE"
A New Farce by Otto Harbach
Staged by Norman Houston

CAST
(In the Order of their First Appearance)

Kitty Hayden	Marie Adels
Andrews	Spencer Charters
Mrs. Mantell	Alice Hegeman
Musette	Gaby Fleury
Richard Smith	Russell Mack
Molly O'Dare	MABEL NORMAND
Felix Farrell (Zero)	Byron Hawkins
Madeline Smith	Alyn King
A Taxi-driver	William McFadden

Synopsis of Scenes
ACT I.—At Richard Smith's. After Dinner.
ACT II.—Same as Act I. Before Breakfast.
ACT III.—Same as Act I. After Breakfast.
Settings designed by P. Dodd Ackerman

PIANO FROM FURER'S MUSIC SHOP
VARUNA SPRING WATER SERVED TO OUR PATRONS

Stage bill for *The Little Mouse*, 1925.

"The Little Mouse" is a play in which Ilse Marvenga appeared several years ago at the same theatre. It was called "Naughty Diana" then. Dual identities provide the hilarity of the plot. Richard Smith, a lawyer, played by Russell Mack, is mimicked by Byron Hawkins, who takes the part of a vaudeville impersonator. Smith is a male vampire, endowed with sufficient masculinity to allow him to be a perfectly natural husband, hires the impersonator to take his place in his home while he gallivants about town out of sight of his mother-in-law, with his stenographer and the "little mouse" (Mabel Normand), who is the wife of the impersonator. The unexpected return of the lawyer's wife (Allyn King), places the impersonator in a comical predicament that evolves into mirth that causes the audience to wriggle delightfully in their chairs and enables the play to be justly dubbed "naughty."

In August the company embarked on an out of town tour that started in Stamford, Connecticut and hit Brooklyn, Philadelphia, Washington, and Baltimore. Sadly not a success – the critical response to Mabel's stage debut was very mixed:

Mabel Normand seems to put a rather tentative foot upon the stage. Not that her work is not very good, but that there's rather little of it. About ten minutes to each act seems to be the limit of Miss Mabel's appearances. And only in the second act, is she given the opportunity to cut loose with what might be regarded as the typical "Normand stuff," when she does a brief and very alcoholic war dance on an overly stuffed divan. Her appearances in the first and last acts are absolutely devitalized and conventional bits. The Normand speaking voice, which we have all been wondering about, is pretty and a little throaty, but not very flexible which is hardly to be wondered at. (*Washington Times*, September 9, 1925)

Miss Normand adds little but her name to the play. (*Brooklyn Eagle*, September 15, 1925)

The capitalization of Miss Normand's name on the program leads to the conclusion that her role is to be considered the stellar one. There is nothing to bear out this conclusion, however. Yet we owe her thanks for added proof of what has so often been asserted – that there is a vast gulf between motion picture work and acting. (*Advocate*, August 29, 1925)

It closed early in the fall in Providence, Rhode Island. *Variety* reported on September 30, 1925:

Mabel Normand Disappointed by failure of "The Little Mouse." A woman reached New York Sunday about as disappointed as one ever could be over the flop of a show that failed to reach Broadway. That was Mabel Normand, film comedienne, who had been out on a preliminary road tour in "The Little

Mouse. " Miss Normand is said to have blamed the show for its failure to click. A check-up of the writers on the different papers during the four weeks and two days the show was out told a different story.

In almost every town where the show opened, the first night was noticeably off in receipts, a fact which surprised the A.H. Wood office, which produced the Normand play. The factors in that New York sanctum felt reasonably sure that Miss Normand, by reason of her picture popularity would prove a draw.

It is understood that Woods is not planning to place Miss Normand in another show as the prime figure although if remaining under his managerial wing she may be assigned to some show that has regularly ascribed legitimate "names."

After this brave attempt to do something different Mabel was ready to return to California. There had been some changes while she had been busy on the East Coast. Most important for her was that her favorite director, F. Richard Jones, had left the Sennett organization in the fall of 1925 and become the director-general of the Hal Roach Studio. At the time Mabel was coming back to Hollywood Hal Roach had embarked on a plan of hiring established feature film stars to appear in, and thereby give class to, a series of two-reel "All Star" Comedies. This was similar to a scheme used by Harry Aitken back in 1915 when he sought out big stage stars for Triangle Films.

Mabel, Carl Miller, and a stunned Max Davidson in *Raggedy Rose* (1926).
Courtesy of Cole Johnson.

Of course the only feature stars that Roach could get a hold of were past their prime. Many of the performers used – Theda Bara, Priscilla Dean, Lionel Barrymore, Agnes Ayres, and Herbert Rawlinson – were all dramatic performers with no experience in sight gag comedy. Roach's solution to this was to have the bulk of the physical business fall to his regular crew of clowns such as James Finlayson, Oliver Hardy, Stan Laurel, etc., or as he told the *Motion Picture News*: "People asked me why I tried to make Theda Bara a comedienne. The answer is: I didn't. I surrounded her with a comedy and her name appeared in electric lights." Of course this wasn't necessary with a tried and true comedy veteran like Mabel. It wasn't long before the studio announced:

Normand Signs With Hal Roach

Mabel Normand back!

Hal Roach has signed Miss Normand to make one short comedy feature for his series of "Star Comedies," the previous ones of which feature Theda Bara, Lionel Barrymore, Claude Gillingwater, Ethel Clayton, and other notable players.

March 5 has been set as the tentative production starting date. (*Los Angeles Times*, February 23, 1926)

Mid-March saw Mabel report in on the Roach lot in Culver City and begin to shoot *Raggedy Rose*. She was put in the hands of Richard Wallace, who directed in collaboration with Stan Laurel:

Mabel Normand Keeps Two Directors Busy. Mabel Normand's troupe at the Hal Roach Studios has divided itself into two units, working within 50 feet of each other on adjoining sets. Richard Wallace is handling the scenes directly involving Miss Normand, while his director Stan Laurel is taking scenes with Carl Minner, Alta Allen, Laura La Varnie, Max Davidson and others nearby. Miss Normand has signed a new contract.

The story was prepared by Jones' staff under his personal supervision after wires were received from New York announcing the completion of negotiations with Miss Normand (*Exhibitors Herald*, May 1, 1926)

Raggedy Rose continues the basic "Cinderella" plot of most of Mabel's features. This time she's a little waif who works for ragman Max Davidson. While out one night collecting shoes that are thrown at a couple of prop screeching cats, she gets clobbered by a shoe thrown by the hero and is immediately smitten with him. Millionaire Carl Miller is taken with her too, but as in *Mickey* a gold-digging society girl (Anita Garvin) and her scheming mother already have their hooks in him. Mabel gets his undivided attention, and into his house, by pretending to be run over by a car, and during the evening works her wiles and vanquishes her rival. The Roach staff prepared a two-reel and a five-reel version of the film for Pathé's approval. Pathé declined the longer version, which led to retakes and much indecision on how long the film should be. Finally a three-reel version was released in America, but what has survived and circulated via 16mm prints is the longer cut which has a good deal of padding and rocky continuity.

**Mabel doing her best Harry Langdon in *Anything Once* (1927).
Courtesy of Robert Arkus.**

    Nevertheless, Mabel is very funny, particularly in the early parts of the film where she works very well with Max Davidson. Now thirty-four years old she's gotten a tad long in the tooth for the little waif persona, and relies a bit too much on clown-white make-up. The combination of the make-up with her battered hat and baggy sweater makes her at times resemble Harry Langdon. But also like Langdon, Mabel was such a consummate film comic that she's able to say volumes with a small look or gesture. The response to *Raggedy Rose* paved the way for more Roach films – four more shorts were shot in steady succession from June through September. Of the ensuing comedies *The Nickel Hopper* (1926) and *Anything Once* (1927) continued with the poor girl getting the wealthy hero theme, but the still lost *One Hour Married* (1927 – shot second but released last) changed things by having Mabel as a new bride whose soldier husband is sent overseas right after the ceremony. To be near him she dresses as a private and stows away with the troops to Europe.

    Very different *is Should Men Walk Home?* (1927). Teamed with the great Leo McCarey as director the film dispenses with the usual plot and puts her in a crook comedy that makes excellent use of her gift for small, intimate comedy moments, in addition to surrounding her with pros like Oliver Hardy, Creighton Hale, and Eugene Pallette. McCarey showed that Mabel could have continued on into screwball comedy if her health hadn't given out. Overall her Roach films are a worthy coda and swansong for her rich career in film comedy.

In September 1926, near the end of her Roach work, she married actor Lew Cody. According to Hollywood lore the wedding was spur-of-the-moment, sometimes recounted as a joke that went too far, where Cody proposed during a party and the participants carried it through to waking up a judge at 3 a.m. Mabel told the press:

> The unexpected elopement and marriage of two of its best known principals took the film colony completely by surprise. They were known to have been good friends for years, but the idea of marriage had seldom been associated with them.
>
> But Miss Normand in her statement disclosed that their romance was of four year's duration, having its inception at the time Cody appeared as leading man in one of her best-known pictures, "Mickey."
>
> "He had proposed before," she said in her statement, "the first time, I believe, on the night of the opening of the Beverly Hills Theater. At that time I hesitated, believing it possibly some passing infatuation. But time proved our love was more substantial, so now I'm Mrs. Lew Cody." (*Los Angeles Times*, September 18, 1926)

Comedienne Anita Garvin, who had played with Mabel in *Raggedy Rose* and had amazing recall, remembered Cody on the set when the film was shot about six months before the wedding in March and April:

> She was married to Lew Cody, and he was an angel. He would always be standing by on the set for her. She was losing her mind about that time – or having some kind of problems, and he was absolutely wonderful! (Interview with William Thomas Sherman)

Mabel's health was rapidly deteriorating and this brought about the end of her being able to work. Garvin also remembered:

> Mabel was hard to work with. She would move away – which would confuse you if you were working with her. She kept you jumping, you didn't know what to expect. One thing I remember that she didn't do perfect was that she couldn't find her spot. She would get a little wild and not stay within camera range where she was supposed to be, if you know what I mean. But you must realize that this happened in her later days. She was trying to make a comeback at that time (1926), but it didn't work out.

Mabel and husband Lew Cody. Courtesy of Marilyn Slater.

This jibes with some of the scenes in her Roach comedies where she suddenly seems confused and gets a flickering look of panic on her face – almost as if for a moment she didn't know where she was or what she was doing. The completion of her Roach contract was the end of her career, and sadly the rest of her life was spent in and out of hospitals, mostly due to her escalating respiratory problems. For the next three years the newspapers were full of updates on her health issues – with headlines such as "Mabel Normand Very Ill," "Mabel Normand Worse," "Mabel Normand's Condition Remains Unchanged," and finally "Mabel Normand Is Now Out of Danger." This coincided with Lew Cody's illnesses which were connected to his heavy drinking. He continued working though, at the time he was a popular star at MGM, and in 1928 did a vaudeville publicity tour in Europe. Cody being away led to Mabel's last appearance before a moving picture camera:

> **Wife Makes Own Picture For Lew Cody**. For the first time since her retirement from the screen months ago, Mabel Normand, once-popular actress, appeared last week before a camera for the making of a motion picture.
>
> The film she made was a production which she personally directed and penned herself. It is going to be a Christmas present for her husband Lew Cody, who sailed yesterday for Europe for a vaudeville tour in England and France.

Lew and Mabel will be separated over the holidays, so she took a camera man, George Nogel, at the Metro-Goldwyn-Mayer Studio into her confidence and shot her "little play."

The story is a secret known only to herself and the cameraman. She will ship the film so that it will reach Cody before Christmas with a seal on it "Do not open until Christmas." (*Los Angeles Times*, December 17, 1928)

Mabel making her last film appearance in a little Christmas film for her touring husband Lew Cody. Courtesy of Marilyn Slater.

The incident was even documented with photos, one of which appeared in the May 1930 issue of *Motion Picture Classic* a few months after Mabel's passing. By October 1929 the newspapers were reporting Mabel's imminent death, which came at 2:30 a.m. on February 23, 1930 at the Pottenger Sanitorium in Monrovia, California. At her bedside was her secretary Julia Benson and a night nurse. Husband Lew Cody found out about her death later that morning at the end of an all-night party at actor Norman Kerry's house. He didn't outlive his spouse by very long – dying of heart disease at fifty in 1934. Her obituaries dredged up all the details from the William Desmond Taylor murder and Courtland Dines shooting.

Although today Mabel Normand is still the most famous female name in silent comedy, her films are rarely screened and her talents have been taken for granted. Like her friend and co-star Roscoe Arbuckle, she's often better remembered for the scandals to which she was linked to than for the joy that she brought to movie audiences. In a career that lasted seventeen years she was a comedienne, athlete, screen beauty, and film director. Both clown and leading lady, Mabel is truly the acorn from which all the ensuing star comediennes sprang.

Chapter 3
STARRING CLOWNS

Quickly following on Mabel Normand's heels in the teens was a small group of ladies who ventured into the "men's terrain" of roughhouse physical comedy and developed comic characters that weren't tied to romantic plots. Taking spills and hard knocks like the men, these women starred in comedies that were produced expressly to showcase and exploit their talents and the characterizations that they had made popular. Marie Dressler, Gale Henry, and Fay Tincher are comics who would normally be in this chapter, but as all three had their own production companies they will be discussed with the other woman who worked behind the scenes in Chapter Six.

The next physical comedienne after Mabel to make a big impact on the screen was Josie Sadler – big in size as well as stage reputation. Although forgotten today the small and round Josie Sadler was discovered by stage impresario Tony Pastor at age nine, and in shows such as *Prince Pro Tem* (1899), *The Silver Slipper* (1902), and *Peggy from Paris* (1903) she became one of the best-loved comediennes at the beginning of the 20th Century. Specializing in naïve immigrant girls, she ran the gamut from Cockney, French, Dutch, German, and Swedish, and wrote many of her own musical numbers, some of which she recorded for Victor. Her co-stars were the Who's Who of the American Theater – Weber & Fields, Eddie Foy, Bert Williams, Leon Errol, Fay Templeton, Fred Mace, and a couple of her future Vitagraph cohorts Sidney Drew and Harry Davenport.

Sadler joined the Vitagraph Company in 1913 and her first appearance was supporting Norma Talmadge in *Omens and Oracles*. She was soon working with John Bunny, Sidney Drew, and Hughie Mack, and before long the studio began tailoring films to her stage fame and characters. *The Coming of Gretchen* (1913) and *The Maid from Sweden* (1914) were about the misadventures of immigrant women. A month after the latter film her own "Josie" series was launched. *The Arrival of Josie* (July 15, 1914) told the story of an orphaned German household drudge who chucks it all and comes to America. The rest of the film details her seasickness on the boat over, confusion concerning the big city and American customs, and a budding romance with a goofy grocery boy named Hank. Over the next three months, in five episodes, Josie would work for a variety of employers, have a raucous time with Hank at Coney Island, become obsessed with romantic novels, and in the last installment get saddled with two kids from a deceased aunt.

After her Josie shorts, Sadler did one last film for Vitagraph, the surviving *Bunny Backslides* (October 30, 1914), and after leaving the company slowed down the pace of her working to make occasional stage appearances, and only two more films, one of which, the William A. Brady feature *What Happened to Jones?* (1915) teamed her with

Fred Mace. She retired in 1920 to run the electrical business of her late husband and died in 1927. Part of the huge list of overlooked silent comediennes, although her film work was only a fraction of her total career, her immigrant servant girl persona was a forerunner for ladies like Louise Fazenda and Jane Bernoudy who would soon follow.

A despondent Josie Sadler and Billy Quirk in Josie's *Declaration of Independence* (1914). Billy Rose Theatre Division, the New York Public Library for the Performing Arts.

Sadler's success (as well as Marie Dressler's in the 1914 feature *Tillie's Punctured Romance*), brought another well-known stage performer to the screen. Rose Melville was a longtime dramatic and musical comedy actress who near the turn of the 20th century created a character named Sis Hopkins that took the country by storm. Originating in a traveling play titled *Zed*, the character became so popular that Melville created a vaudeville skit, *Sis Hopkin's Visit*, which led to the play *Sis Hopkins*. Sis was a plain-Jane country imp with pigtails that defied gravity by sticking out horizontally on either side of her head. She dressed in the most outrageously patterned gingham dresses or aprons possible, topped off with striped socks and clodhopper shoes. She was basically a female version of the prototype rube character Toby, a long-time audience favorite in traveling tent shows across America. Sis, although unschooled and backward, had a knack for dispensing common sense in her own simple way. In fact at the height of Melville's fame her homespun sayings were collected in *Sis Hopkin's Library of Fun*, and sold along with Sis Hopkin aprons, hair ribbons, and dolls. Sis became Melville's career, and she's said to have played the character more than five thousand times during an eighteen year run on the stage.

At the end of 1915 the Kalem Company announced that it was bringing Melville to the screen in a series of one-reel Sis Hopkins Comedies. They

As Sis Hopkins, Rose Melville demonstrates gravity with her pinwheel while her pigtails defy it. Author's collection.

were made at Kalem's Jacksonville, Florida studio, and Frank Minzey, Melville's husband, was brought along to repeat his stage role as her long-time foil. All the films were directed by Robert Ellis and the supporting stock company was made up of Kalem players that included Arthur Albertson, Richard Purdon, Olive West, and Henry Murdock. Sadly it's impossible to judge Melville's film work first hand today as none of the shorts are known to exist or circulate, but contemporary reviews give an idea of Sis' progress from stage to screen:

> *A Leap Year Wooing* – The first of the 'Sis Hopkins' one-reel comedies does not give Rose Melville , the creator of the role, the same opportunities which she enjoyed on the stage, principally the reason that her quaint manner of expressing herself is practically lost inasmuch as the subtitles may be made to assist. Her opportunities for effective work are also somewhat curtailed in the film. 'Sis Hopkins' will at the same time always be interesting. She is there with her pig-tails, gingham apron, etc. (*Moving Picture World*, March 25, 1916).

But as her ad tag-line "Making Folks Laff is My Bizness! What's Yours?" promised, later reviews suggest that after an initial period of awkwardness Melville and the series hit a stride:

> **When Things Go Wrong** (Kalem) March 24 – The material in this one-reel "Sis Hopkins" comedy fulfills its mission, and Rose Melville shows that she is rapidly learning to make the most of every bit of business that comes her way. (*Moving Picture World*, April 8, 1916).

and:

> Another strong feature of this day will be "Juggling Justice" of the Sis Hopkins series. These Kalem comedies always "get over" and "Juggling Justice" will be no exception. (*Moving Picture World*, June 10, 1916).

Despite the growing favorable response the series only lasted through twenty shorts, and Kalem itself went out of business in 1917. Although her film career was brief, Melville's influence on the female film clowns was considerable. On stage and screen her character was a well-known icon, and, apart from Mabel Normand's portrayal in the feature *Sis Hopkins* (1919), many aspects of Sis can be seen in characters adopted by Alice Howell, Gale Henry, and Polly Moran.

A direct descendant of Sis Hopkins was the naïve bumpkin persona made famous by Louise Fazenda in Mack Sennett comedies. Fazenda, born in Lafayette, Indiana in 1889, spent a brief time on stage before starting at Universal as an extra in 1913. There she ended up in one-reel Joker comedies where she was taught the rudiments of film acting by Joker star Max Asher, and

Wallace Beery lightens Louise Fazenda's load in *Maggie's First False Step* (1917). Courtesy of Robert Arkus.

played a variety of roles – young ingénue, household drudge, eccentric servants – that brought her attention:

> My own stage experience was too limited to speak about and three years ago I started with the Universal Company as an extra. I kept my eyes open, tried to do my work differently yet naturally, and was offered every encouragement by directors and finally landed as leading comedienne with the best company of them all – Keystone. (*Motion Picture Magazine*, December 1916)

After joining Keystone in 1915 she was used for quite a while as an all-purpose support for the male leads, appearing in many entries of Mack Swain's "Ambrose" series, and also in character roles such as Cecile Arnold's overbearing mother in *A Bear Affair* and the gum-chewing cashier in *A Hash House Fraud* (both 1915). A February 5, 1916 *Moving Picture World* article, *Young Keystoners*, took special notice of her versatility:

> In particular Miss Louise Fazenda has developed quite a new line of eccentric comedy characters which has stamped her as a comer in the film world. In "A Game Old Knight" she played the ugly princess with a rare sense of humor. Then in "The Great Vacuum Robbery" she was the lady crook at the other extreme of looks from the ugly maid, extremely knowing and fascinating. Now in "His Hereafter," a burlesque of the Western type of story, she is fittingly described as a "sweet character in a faro frame," being the daughter of Harry Booker, who has the role of a gambling house proprietor. Her versatility has proven equal to each of these parts and she will no doubt get the lead in a forthcoming play.

She did indeed, and soon her regular comedy persona began to solidify in films such as *The Feathered Nest* (1916), *Her Fame and Shame*, and *Her Torpedoed Love* (both 1917) where Louise is a gawky kitchen slavey or country girl who falls in love with cads like Charlie Murray or Ford Sterling. Of course these rogues are only stringing her along to get at her inheritance money (real or imagined), and she luckily always has a goofy but steadfast boyfriend, often played by Wayland Trask, to save the day and win her in the end.

Triangle publicity portrait.
Author's collection.

To play this role Fazenda made herself looks as plain as possible, pulling her hair severely back into a bun or little side pigtails, later adopting a big spit curl on her forehead which became a trademark. She wore little make-up except for a light base that made her look pale and drab, but allowed all kinds of subtle emotions to shift across her luminous and expressive face. The character's work clothes consisted of mind-bogglingly loud checkered dresses, and when she spruced up it was circa 1880 in a long-sleeved formal blouse with a high collar, corseted sides, and balloon shoulders. This was complimented with a matching long skirt (which had tendency to fall down at inappropriate moments), clunky shoes, and a short-brimmed pillbox hat with a few meager flowers on top. Her pantomime style was delicate and demure, and she carried out her slapstick antics in a very realistic way yet with great aplomb. She played this girl very sincerely, with much emotion in her big saucer eyes. Shy, but at the same time flirty, she was always hopeful for romance or a new beau.

**Fazenda at the peak of her stardom for Mack Sennett.
Courtesy The Museum of Modern Art.**

Seeing Louise in her other roles or in out of character photos it's obvious that she was really an attractive and well-endowed young woman, but she played this slavey so believably and well that she's often described today as having been a plain and homely woman. Fazenda was aware of the sacrifice for her art and in 1918 told *Photoplay*:

> I think that all women like attractive surroundings and pretty clothes and hate to be laughed at. After three years of this work, I'm still extremely sensitive to ridicule….Of course I don't mind my friends and my relatives going to see my pictures, but I wouldn't have them come to the studio and watch me for anything on Earth!

From 1917 to 1921 Fazenda was a full-fledged Mack Sennett star with films like *The Kitchen Lady* (1918) and *The Gingham Girl* (1920) built around her portrayal and style of comedy, and her character was even made a little more attractive. Many of the Sennett shorts from this period, which were distributed by Paramount, are missing. *Hearts and Flowers* (1919) does circulate and has Louise as an awkward cigarette girl at a hotel with a yen for egotistical orchestra leader Ford Sterling. Tricked into thinking that she's an heiress Ford goes out of his way to woo her. Probably the funniest scene is Sterling's pre-wedding meeting with Louise's family where her large ex-con brothers, Edgar Kennedy, Bert Roach, and Kalla Pasha, literally pick him up and pass him around as they check him out. An excellent showcase for Fazenda's talent and charm, the short surrounds her with a top-notch supporting cast that also includes Phyllis Haver, Billy Armstrong, Eva Thatcher, and little Jack Ackroyd.

In mid-1921 Louise left the Sennett fold and played her established character in two different series of starring shorts distributed by Educational Pictures. The first was three Punch Comedies produced by the California Producers Corporation, where she was supported by comedy pros like Chester Conklin, Neely Edwards, Charlotte Merriam, Eddie Baker, Jack Duffy, John Henry Jr., and her old Sennett buddy Teddy the Great Dane. Twelve were announced, but only *The Love Egg* (1921), *Country Chickens*, and *A Rural Cinderella* (both 1922) were released, and none are known to exist. From here she moved over to Jack White Comedies. White, the boy wonder of silent comedy, began his career at Keystone as an office boy, then learned editing at L-Ko, and was directing at Fox by age nineteen. After creating a partnership with comic Lloyd Hamilton he became a full-fledged producer at twenty-one, and in June 1922 announced that:

> With Lloyd Hamilton, Louise Fazenda, famous comedy actress of the kinky curls, will be one of the bright lights.

> Miss Fazenda was signed up by Mr. White shortly after his arrival in New York and she is now on the coast and will work in the first picture of the new Mermaid Comedy series.

Producer Jack White, Louise Fazenda, Educational Pictures head
E.W. Hammons, and director Fred Hibbard (a.k.a. Fred Fishback) during
the shooting of *Dizzy Daisy* (1924). Courtesy of Cole Johnson.

Like the Punch Comedies this series was warmly received by the press and again only three were made, but this time one of the shorts still exists. *Dizzy Daisy* was released June 29, 1924, almost a year after *Pest of the Storm Country* and *Cold Chills* (both 1923), and is a breezy short that presents Louise as her usual spacey young thing. Her father (John Rand), who's so tough that his spitting disassembles their front porch, gives her a want ad from the newspaper for "A maid. Not too bright," and adds, "That job was made for you." She applies and is hired by crooks Lee Moran, Cliff Bowes, Dick Sutherland, and Bobby Burns, who kidnap a visiting dignitary and force him to help them throw a fake society party so they can relieve the guests of their jewelry. Louise finally catches on to the situation and steals the jewels back from the crooks. This results in a major chase with the crooks after Louise, and the society guests and cops after them in hot pursuit on land and sea. It's a shame that Fazenda's stay with the White unit was so brief, as this is an extremely fast-paced short that's brimming with great sight gags and action.

While with Sennett Louise had starred in the feature *Down on the Farm* (1920) and appeared in *Married Life* (1920) and *A Small Town Idol* (1921). She continued in big films like *Quincy Adams Sawyer* (1922) and after the demise of her shorts series concentrated on supporting roles in features. Sometimes she would play a variation of her old comedy character, like the scared servant in *The Bat* (1926), but for the most part she returned to the versatility of her earlier career in parts as varied as a fiery Latin dancer in *The Night Club* (1925) to the sweet German beer hall waitress of *Riley, the Cop* (1928). In the late twenties she signed with Warner Brothers for a series of features, some teamed with comic Clyde Cook like *A Sailor's Sweetheart* (1927) and *Pay as You Enter* (1928). One of the survivors, *Footloose Widows* (1926), is an excellent comedy where Louise gives a performance that's a forerunner of the character that Joan Blondell would make famous in early talkies, as one of a pair of goldiggers pretending to be royalty at an exclusive resort to hook a rich bachelor.

An elegant Louise Fazenda in *Grounds for Divorce* (1925) with Gene Morgan behind her and Olive Borden on the far right. Author's collection.

When sound arrived Fazenda continued as an in demand character actress in features such as *Wonder Bar* (1934) and *Swing Your Lady* (1938), and even did some shorts for Al Christie and RKO. Married to producer Hal Wallis (referred to by Hollywood insiders as "The Prisoner of Fazenda"), she retired in 1939 and devoted herself to charity work until her death in 1962.

Another unsung woman who worked a good deal at Universal was Alice Howell. Headlining in shorts for L-Ko, Century, and Reelcraft, she was an extremely talented and hardworking young woman who climbed her way through periods of adversity to become a respected and ultimately wealthy performer.

Born Alice Florence Clark in New York City on May 20, 1886, although on later legal documents she would give her name as Alice Florence McGinnis, she began her performing career in 1907, spending seven years on the stage. After a brief first marriage, which produced her daughter Yvonne (herself a silent comedy ingénue), she met her second husband Dick Smith in a 1910 DeWolf Hopper musical comedy and the couple toured the country in a vaudeville comedy/eccentric dancing act. Their stage careers ended when Smith was diagnosed with tuberculosis and the family went to California for his recuperation. Alice became the sole wage earner as an extra at Mack Sennett's Keystone Studio:

Rube Miller uses Alice Howell for an armrest in the 1914 Keystone *Bombs and Bangs*. Author's collection.

I came to California because the health of one of the members of my family demanded it. I've tried my best to make good. It was a pretty hard struggle for me to get along at first. When I started with the Keystone there were times when rainy weather kept my salary down to as low as six and nine dollars a week. That wasn't very much to live on, was it? Thank goodness that period is over. (*Moving Picture World*, March 2, 1918)

It's rumored that Smith and Howell may have known Mack Sennett in New York, but nevertheless she started in the background. She had her own ways of getting noticed:

It started about five years ago at the Mack Sennett Studio. I was one of the mob in a police raid. Suddenly I threw myself into the thick of the fray. The other women drew back. We all had on evening gowns and the girls didn't want to spoil them. I fell downstairs and literally wiped the floor with my gown. Mack Sennett was impressed and decided to give me a chance. (*Moving Picture World*, June 26, 1920)

In no time she worked her way up to featured parts in shorts such as *Lover's Luck*, *Cursed by his Beauty*, and Chaplin's *Laughing Gas* (all 1914). Becoming known as "the Keystone scrub lady," Alice starred in at least one short, *Shot in the Excitement* (1914), where she's the sweetheart of Al St John. When a jealous rival shows up, complications ensue and the film ends with Alice, Al, the rival, Alice's father, and a couple of cops all being chased by flying cannonballs. This one-reeler shows that her timing and soon-to-be trademark penguin-waddle walk are already in place, as is her ability to take punishment. During the course of the film she slips down stairs, gets soaked with water, is chased by cannonballs, and has a rock bounced off her head.

Alice Howell gives Charlie Murray the what-for in *He Loved the Ladies* (1914). Courtesy of The Museum of Modern Art.

Despite making progress at Keystone, Alice took an offer at Sennett's former collaborator Henry "Pathé" Lehrman's new L-Ko Comedies to provide support for stars Billie Ritchie and Hank Mann. Her first known L-Ko appearance, *Father was a Loafer*

(February 10, 1915), has recently been preserved by Library of Congress. It is a good example of her initial work for the studio. Alice and Ritchie have four children and as the picture opens she gives birth to triplets. Seven offspring are just too much for Ritchie to bear so he takes a powder. Soon he comes to the rescue of young heiress Gertrude Selby, who falls for Billie and a wedding date is set. Abandoned wife Alice happens to see an announcement of the nuptials in the newspaper society pages and crashes the ceremony with her unruly brood in tow. The wedding party is dispersed and the would-be bigamist is lambasted and hauled home.

While supporting the studio's headliners she was also starring in one-reelers like *Cupid and the Scrublady* and *From Beanery to Billions* (both 1915) which made her popular and brought her screen persona to full fruition. The character she developed was a slightly addled working-class girl – maid, beanery waitress, charwoman – anything that fell under the term "slavey." Although attractive, her comic get-up emphasized the eccentric. A round Kewpie-doll face with large eyes and bee-stung lips was topped off with a mountain of frizzy hair piled high on her head that resembled smoke billowing from an active volcano. To compliment her look of having just kissed an electric light socket, she wore old-fashioned plaid or checkered blouses, long print skirts, and big clod-hopper shoes. Her physical movements were as clean and precise as Keaton and Chaplin's and she could match tumbles and falls with Al St John and Billie Ritchie. A stiff-backed penguin-waddle walk and her pile of hair became her signature trademarks.

As her popularity grew Alice was no longer used to back up other comics and had people such as Raymond Griffith, Fatty Voss, and Dick Smith, whose health had improved, supporting her. "Pathé" Lehrman and Billie Ritchie left L-Ko in the fall of 1916 making Alice the biggest fish in the pond. The studio was taken over by Carl Laemmle's brothers-in-law Abe and Julius Stern, and Alice's popularity was so great that the Sterns set up a separate company for her releases:

> **Alice Howell in New Comedies**. Julius Stern, President of L-Ko Comedies and J.G. Blystone, general director, have determined that Alice Howell has so firmly established herself as a favorite, through her appearances in L-Ko's, that the time has come to recognize her talents and encourage and reward her energies. They will therefore present her hereafter in a new brand of mirth makers to be called Howl Comedies. Three productions are ready for distribution and Director Blystone has others now contemplated or in active production. (*Moving Picture World*, May 19, 1917)

Howl Comedies became Century Comedies, and although originally set up on the independent state's rights market Universal picked up the series at the beginning of 1918. One of the few survivors, *Hey Doctor* (1918), has Alice as a receptionist in a doctor's office that is seriously short of patients. To get more, she walks down the street dropping banana peels on the sidewalk. As the pedestrians begin slipping and falling Alice distributes business cards for the doctor. The second half of the film details her misadventures at a fancy soiree where she is completely out of place and causes much embarrassment.

Although considered "one of the screen's leading exponents of the rough-and-ready in comedy work," Alice maintained a realistic and understated pantomimic style that was based on her experiences of life and her down-to-earth personality. In 1917 she told the *New Jersey Tribune*:

> The days are not so far in retrospection when I was glad to do any kind of work and I have not forgotten how it feels to stand in line waiting for a chance to do extra work. I wanted the money so badly that I offered to wear any eccentric sort of make-up or take any chance so long as there was a pay check at the end of the week.

I often felt then like the down-trodden, put upon, much abused slavies that I struggle to portray humorously today. Most of my scenes are broad farce, of course, but when I get an opportunity I try to register faithfully the character of such a girl.

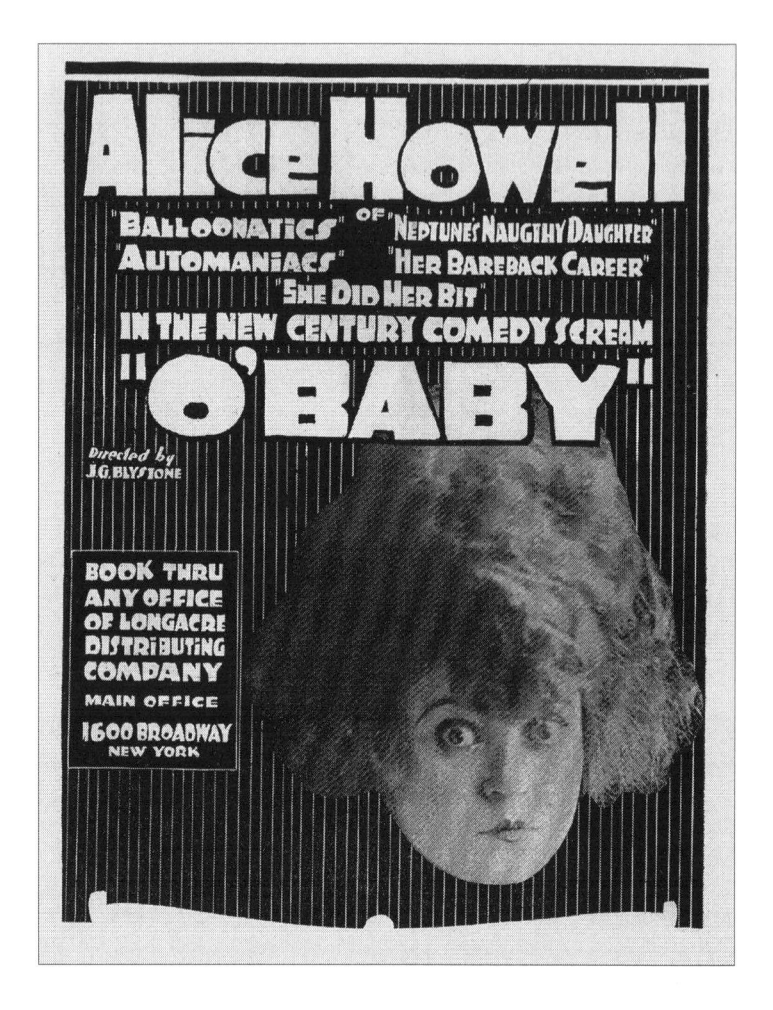

During the two and a half years Alice spent with Century her popularity continued to build, helped by support from veterans like Billy Armstrong, Neal Burns, Jimmy Finlayson, Eddie Barry, and Hughie Mack, but when she realized that the Stern Brothers were more interested in promoting shorts with Joe Martin the orangutan and Brownie the Wonder Dog, she left. In October 1919, the *Moving Picture World* announced:

> **Alice Howell Joins Emerald**. Alice Howell has been added to the list of Emerald comedy stars. This was announced yesterday by Frederick J. Ireland, president of the Emerald Motion Picture Company.

Mr. Ireland is now preparing a series of comedies especially for Miss Howell.

Emerald was based in Chicago and had just secured the talents of Chaplin imitator Billy West, who had left Bulls Eye to join them. Dick Smith came along as Alice's main support. Smith alternated as director with President Ireland, a former song and dance man who was Chicago's answer to George M. Cohan. Soon after production began in Chicago the company merged with the Bulls Eye Film Co., the Bee Hive Film Exchange, and the Interstate Film Co. of New York to form the Reelcraft Pictures Corporation. Organized to produce and distribute short subjects for the state's rights market, Reelcraft also handled comedies with Gale Henry, Billy West, Milburn Moranti, and Billy Franey.

Seven of the ten Howell Reelcrafts survive, and three of them are perhaps the best existing examples of her work. In *Cinderella Cinders* (1920) she plays a waitress/cook at a crummy diner who gets fired and ends up as a maid for a wealthy family. For a society party, Alice and butler Dick Smith are enlisted to pose as the Count and Countess De Bunco, who are actually crooks. Of course, everything ends in confusion with Alice saving the day. Alice is really the whole show and is hilarious as she primps and flirts with the customers in the diner, at one point putting up a musical chart and conducting their loud soup slurpings. Other highlights include a rollicking chase where she races to get a position on foot, bicycle, and finally roller skates pulled along by a bull dog to beat a horde of out-of-work maids from getting there first, and a fruity, fancy dance exhibition, where their spoofs of ballroom dancing probably dates back to their vaudeville act.

Alice Howell has Phil Dunham (left) and Frank J. Coleman (right) at her feet in her Reelcraft Comedy *Goodnight, Nurse* (1920). Billy Rose Theatre Division, the New York Public Library for the Performing Arts.

A Convict's Happy Bride (1920) is a domestic melodrama spoof where evil iceman Frank J. Coleman frames Alice's husband Phil Dunham for attempted murder so he can make time with Alice while hubby's in jail. Turns out that the prison is just across the street and the inmates are on an honor system where they're allowed to go home for lunch. To make hubby feel more at home Alice and the baby wear stripes and have decorated the entire house in the same pattern. Not giving up the villain takes Alice out riding and attacks her. Hubby sees this from his jail cell and escapes in the nick of time to save her, and although caught again by the prison guards the baby saves the day by exposing the iceman and freeing his father. This outing is less character driven and concentrates on the melodrama spoof as well as surreal, non-sequitur gags with midgets, difficult Murphy beds, biscuits with too much baking powder that float around the room like balloons, and a tin lizzie that runs amok on bootleg hooch.

The origins of *Distilled Love* (1920) are something of a mystery. Although released by Reelcraft, it appears to be an unused film from her days at L-Ko or Century due to the California locations, the presence of Oliver Hardy, Billy Bevan and Fay Holderness, and the co-direction of Vin Moore. Alice plays a farm girl who's framed as the mother of a baby by evil bootlegger Hardy. Forced to leave the farm, she goes to the big city with the baby and works for Hardy doing her eccentric dancing in the streets. The climax takes place at another big society party which Alice makes a shambles of, but all ends happily with the arrival of her former farm lover Dick Smith.

Chock-full of gags, which are executed with snap and precision by the cast of comedy pros, the highlights include Alice performing the gag made famous by Mary Pickford where she wants to eat some pie but sees a placard of "Thou Shalt Not Steal" on the wall, which stops her until she sees a second that says "The Lord Helps Those That Help Themselves." Another is when Alice arrives in the big city with the hungry baby and spots a milk truck driving by. In a great traveling shot, she runs behind the truck, opens the back door, and produces a hose, one end of which she sticks in a can of milk and the other in the baby's mouth so he can siphon down lunch as they trot along. Bits at the society party include riding from room to room on the long train of Fay Holderness' gown – even transferring to someone else's gown – and a flirtation with a rich old goat (a white-haired Billy Bevan) that ends in a tit for tat slap fest. Again, Alice uses an underplayed pantomimic style and has some effective moments of pathos, especially when she's driven off the farm during a raging storm, though a bolt of lightning that just happens to strike her in the rear end brings the pathos to an abrupt end.

After six months and six shorts in Chicago, Alice and Smith moved back to California, where they made three more comedies and ended their relationship with Reelcraft:

Celebrated Players Secures United States Rights To Sunkist Comedies With Alice Howell As Star. J.L. Friedman, president of Celebrated Players

Film Co., has closed with George B. West, general manager of Sunkist Comedy Co., for the entire United States rights to the new series of Alice Howell comedies. These comedies have met the highest praise. They were directed by Dick Smith and presented the comedienne in roles in which she excels and unadulterated slapstick. The Sunkist Company is making a series of 52 single reel comedies. The first to be released with Miss Howell starring will be "Boulevard Profiteers." This will be followed by "Who Chose Your Wife?" (*Moving Picture World*, December 4, 1920)

Alice Howell literally pulling Victor Potel's leg in *The Elite of Hollywood* (1923). Billy Rose Theatre Division, the New York Public Library for the Performing Arts.

George B. West was the brother of comedian Billy West, and outside of a few more trade magazine items and ads there's no definite info on this venture. In fact, the next three years of Alice's career are very cloudy with only a few scraps of information. It's recently come to light that Dick Smith directed the fabled lost Marx Brothers silent short *Humor Risk* in the spring of 1921. Shot in the New York area, the film was never released, and it was announced a few months later that Smith would direct a group of Pearl Sheppard comedies for Reelcraft. At that time the Reelcraft product was being made by Schiller Productions at the Mittenthal Studio in Yonkers, NY. Nothing seems to have come of this series, but when all of this was happening on the East Coast it seems like Alice was with Smith and perhaps taking a well-earned vacation.

She did appear as comic relief in two features, *Love is an Awful Thing* (1922) and *Wandering Daughters* (1923), plus a couple of films that were produced and directed by

Fred Caldwell for the *Hollywood Comedies* series. This was a low-budget series and it's definite that Alice appeared in *The Elite of Hollywood* (1923) and another that's turned up in an unidentified print at UCLA titled *Oil Well Comedy*. She returned to Universal in 1924 for her last starring series of comedies. This new group teamed her with Neely Edwards and Bert Roach, and was about a married couple (Alice & Neely) and their goofy butler (Roach). Alice's character was still addled and had her trademark hair and walk, but had graduated to a comfortable, middle-class status. No longer the young slavey, she takes care of the nice house while hubby works and traded in her old mismatched costume for more up-to-date attire. Similar in tone to the earlier films of Mr. & Mrs. Sidney Drew and Mr. & Mrs. Carter De Haven, the series still managed to work in generous helpings of slapstick and, at one-reel, were short and sweet.

Of the three entries of the series that still exist the best is *Under a Spell* (1925). Alice suspects Neely of sneaking a woman into the house and hires "Professor Svengoolash A.T.C. M.V." to hypnotize hubby and get to the truth. Svengoolash makes Neely think he's a monkey, but then gets knocked out. Neely escapes and his ape antics, along with Alice and butler Roach's attempts to lure him back home, provide the film's funniest moments. After Svengoolash revives and cancels his monkey spell, it's revealed that Alice's suspected other woman is actually "the Bobbed Hair Bandit," a burglar who robs houses in drag, which gets Neely off the hook for a happy ending. Director Dick Smith keeps the pace moving and the absurdities building for a very entertaining ten minutes.

The trio continued their misadventures until late 1925 (with Billy Bletcher and Harold

Austin occasionally standing in for Neely Edwards), after which Alice slowed down the pace of her work. Her last known films are a couple of Fox Comedy shorts: the very funny *Madame Dynamite* (1926), which has Alice as a pesky mother-in-law, and *A Society Architect* (February 13, 1927), one of the *Van Bibber in Society* two-reelers. By this time, Dick Smith had stopped acting, but continued directing Universal shorts with comics such as Charles Puffy, Slim Summerville, and Neely Edwards. Her daughter Yvonne began acting and appeared as an ingénue in many shorts such as Charley Bower's *Hop Off* (1928) and a few features. Yvonne's career was brief, as it ended in 1930 when she married Hal Roach cameraman (and soon to be famous director) George Stevens. Alice's grandchild George Stevens Jr., born in 1932, became head of the American Film Institute.

After the changeover to sound, silent films were looked on as ancient history or curios. Many former favorites who weren't currently visible in talkies were forgotten. Stevens Jr. has said that he didn't know that his grandmother had been in films and that "she seemed to me to be a loving, red-haired grandmother business-woman with a lively sense of humor." Having invested her movie earnings well in California real estate, Alice lived comfortably managing her investments and enjoying her family until her death on April 11, 1961.

Another neglected lady clown, whose starring films for Kalem and Fox have almost all vanished without a trace, is Ethel Teare. Born in Arizona in 1894, she went on the stage at fourteen and had an extensive six year career during which she was in vaudeville on the Orpheum Time with B.A. Raffle's act *College Girls*, toured in stock companies, appeared with Dave Lewis in *Don't Lie to your Wife*, did Mort Singer's shows in Chicago, then finally went back to vaudeville with her sister and played at Harlow's Café in Los Angeles. She and her sister Betty started at Kalem in the fall of 1914 and first worked as support to the studio's forgotten comedy star John E. Brennan. Ethel seems to have hit the ground running as she's very funny as the female lead in her second film appearance *The No-Account Count* (October 27, 1914).

Teare plays the ugly daughter of rich Mr. Hardup, who finds it impossible to get a husband for her. Finding out that the famous Count De Bluffe

Portrait of Ethel Teare. Author's collection.

is coming to America, he invites him to their home and sets his sights on him as a son-in-law. Ethel is promptly sent off to a beauty doctor to have her face renovated for the meeting. It happens that the Count is broke and looking for a wealthy girl to marry. On his way to meet the family a tramp ends up with the Count's clothes and is mistaken for his nobleness. He proposes to Ethel but then the real Count finally arrives and claims her for himself. The tramp is shown the door, but gets his revenge at the wedding where he pops in and pulls off Ethel's wig to reveal her bald head.

Ethel first shows up in the film at her father's office with her face all covered with warts and various knobs. When she's sent to the beauty doctor for her sand-blasting it's revealed that she also wears a wig and has just a few transparent wisps of hair on her shiny dome. Not afraid to go to extremes in make-up and costume in the name of comedy, Teare was statuesque and quite a beauty but had a natural comic bent. Besides an earnestness and a sweetness, which led her to take a low-key approach to gags and seriously play her characters, she had a toothy smile that was just a hair too large, and a slightly bow-legged walk with her rear sticking out.

In another surviving Kalem from this period, *Through the Keyhole* (December 18, 1914), Ethel is allowed to be attractive this time as another wealthy daughter. An impoverished mother and son find out that the rich father and daughter Millionbucks are stopping at their hotel and concoct a scheme to snare them. The old woman easily wins Millionbucks' heart, and refuses to marry him unless Ethel marries her son. In the meantime Ethel has fallen in love with Freddy, the son of the hotel proprietress. Algy, her would-be-suitor, refuses to give up his designs on Miss Millionbucks despite being manhandled by Freddy. The old couple is in the next room and Father Millionbucks takes up a post at the keyhole to see what's happening, but is eventually squirted in the eye with ammonia for his troubles. Finally father attacks Algy, thinking its Freddy, and is getting a thrashing when rescued by Freddy and his daughter. In gratitude he finally consents to their marriage.

1915 saw her working with William Wolbert, Phil Dunham, and Merta Sterling, appearing in comedies directed by Marshall Neilan, and becoming the lucky girl to be the love interest for those scuzzy bums Ham and Bud. Lloyd Hamilton and Bud Duncan played this undynamic duo in more than one hundred one-reelers from late 1914 to 1917, with Ethel as their frequent leading lady. Some of her early shorts with them include *The Spook Raisers* and *The Winning Wash* (both 1915), and her character seems to be a young woman who's taken leave of her senses as she's usually ready to flirt with and even smooch either or both of these unsavory tramps. In *Ham at the Fair* (1915) the buddies visit the Panama-Pacific Exposition in San Diego. Ham starts a flirtation with the pretty Ethel but when he kisses her she starts crying for help and won't stop until he gives her all his money. Ham then sets Bud up to meet her and the same thing happens to him. Finally they decide to set up a third fellow and are ready to enjoy the show, but Ethel likes his kiss and gives him all her money. Turns out he's her accomplice in the scam.

Ethel seems interested in tramp Lloyd Hamilton in *The Winning Wash* (1915). Courtesy of Robert S. Birchard.

When star Lloyd Hamilton was sidetracked for months with a broken leg Ethel continued working with Bud Duncan, and along with Rube Miller and David Morris made a solid comedy quartet. *Whitewashing William* (October 5, 1915) survives and concerns rivals Duncan and Morris fighting over the fair Ethel while she and father John Rand try to whitewash a fence. A remake of the Keystone comedy *Shot in the Excitement* (1914), which Rube Miller directed and played the rival suitor, this new version was again directed by Miller and ends differently, this time with the rivals battling while canoeing. Duncan thinks that Ethel has drowned, but she and Morris have taken the opportunity of the confusion to run off and get married.

In February 1916 Kalem announced that Ethel was going to headline in her own series of one-reelers. Starting with *A Molar Mix-Up* (February 16, 1916) these shorts were more situational than the rough and ready Ham and Bud offerings, and Teare had regular support from players like Gus Leonard, Jack MacDermott, and Victor Rottman. *Trapping the Bachelor*, *Fashion and Fury*, and *Not What the Doctor Ordered* (all 1916) are a few of the titles, sadly none of which are available today, but the reviews were very positive and praised Ethel's work.

ETHEL TEARE IN WHEN HUBBY FORGOT. Vivacious Ethel Teare, who has been made a full-fledged star through the new Kalem Wednesday Ethel Teare Comedies, is given a role that fully befits her in "When Hubby Forgot," a single reel issue scheduled for March 8th. When it is considered that Ethel Teare's rise to stardom has occurred in the space of a year, the strength of her captivating personality is clearly apparent. Ethel charms through a naïve manner, without self-consciousness, and a spirit bubbling over with joyous delight in her work. The ability to wear bewitching gowns in a natural and graceful manner is another Ethel Teare asset. (*Moving Picture World*, March 4, 1916).

But by July 1916 she was back with Ham and Bud, replacing Norma Nichols who had replaced her, and stayed with them into early 1917 through shorts such as *The Love Magnet*, *A Sauerkraut Symphony* (both 1916), *The Safety Pin Smugglers*, and *Bulls and Bullets* (both 1917). Kalem was ailing financially, but before it collapsed Ethel's good work had been noted and she moved on to greener pastures:

ETHEL TEARE JOINS KEYSTONE. A number of new people have been added to the stock of Keystone Company during the past few days by general manager Mack Sennett. Included in this list is Ethel Teare, who for the past two years has played leads in Kalem comedies, a greater portion of the time opposite Lloyd Hamilton and Bud Duncan in the Ham comedies, and for a time being the head of her own company (*Motion Picture News*, March 10, 1917)

A nice move to the top comedy company in Hollywood. Spending a chunk of 1917 and 1918 with "the King of Comedy," Ethel developed the persona of an innocent and somewhat slow-on-the-uptake country girl in shorts such as *Thirst* and *Lost: A Cook* (both 1917) where she's taken advantage of (in a tongue-in-cheek way) by cads like Mack Swain and Cliff Bowes. Ethel also incurs the wrath of Polly Moran's Sheriff Nell when she shows up as former flame Ben Turpin's mail order bride in *Roping Her Romeo* (1917), and in *An International Sneak* (1917) plays a wily female detective hot on the trail of foreign spies Chester Conklin and Billy Armstrong as they try to obtain Erle C. Kenton's secret explosive formula. Besides her work on screen, Teare was featured in studio publicity that oddly had her fishing and hunting, and much was made about her investment in an oil well:

There is Ethel Teare, whose spiffy little automobile bustles out of Los Angeles toward one of the suburbs every day when the sun gets too dim for studio work. Her destination is a place thickly forested by oil derricks. Miss Teare is the owner of a hunk of an oil well, not to mention being manager of the same. She knows more about oil sand than the average girl does about the newest style in tailor-mades.

Despite being kept busy at Sennett her stay was brief. It's possible that there was too much overlap in Ethel and Louise Fazenda's personas and styles for Teare to really be used to her full advantage on the Sennett lot. By the spring of 1918 it was announced:

ETHEL TEARE TO SUPPORT "HAM." After three years Lloyd V. Hamilton, or "Ham" as he is known wherever pictures are shown, has his leading woman back with him once more – Ethel Teare, who used to play with "Ham" in the old Kalem comedies, which were so popular on the General Film program. When "Ham" joined the Sunshine Comedies, which William Fox releases, he tried to get Ethel Teare for his leading woman, but she was tied up under contract. That has now expired. (*Moving Picture World*, May 4, 1918)

Ethel doing some angling with Maude Wayne and Vera Reynolds in the Sennett promo film *Keystone Girls Open Trout Season* (1917). Courtesy of Sam Gill.

Her debut short for Fox was *Wild Women and Tame Lions* (1918) and her early appearances were as leading lady for the likes of Hamilton, Billie Ritchie, and Mack Swain in *A Tight Squeeze*, *The Fatal Marriage* (both 1918), and *Oh, What a Knight* (1919). This changed with *Her First Kiss* (1919) which took advantage of her gawky and innocent country girl character. At the moment this is the only survivor of her starring Fox shorts and gives us a rare look at Teare at the peak of her career. Ethel stars as Minnie Spuds, a farm girl whose affections are manipulated by a villainous summer boarder played by

Slim Summerville. Suspected by her parents of compromising herself with Slim she's banned from the farm, and being rejected by Summerville she heads to the city. In the meantime Slim and her parents find out that a rich uncle has left Ethel a prosperous department store in the city. Ethel ends up, of course, working as a slavey in her own store, and after Slim tries to frame her as a shoplifter the climax of the film involves speeding automobiles and flying missiles careening through the store.

The film is a wonderful showcase for Teare's character – sort of a mix between Alice Howell and Louise Fazenda. Outfitted in loud checkered dresses, with her hair in little buns on either side of her head, the use of white-face make-up gave her an innocent look, and the highlighting of her full lips gives her a resemblance to Lucille Ball. A gallumping walk, slightly bow-legged with her rear sticking out, was complimented with hesitant gestures, and a low-keyed and matter-of-fact handling of the most outrageous gags. Despite all the adversity that her character faces she mostly retains a cheerful and hopeful air with a big-toothed smile that had just a trace of an overbite.

Ethel Teare threatens Tom Kennedy and Lois Scott with a limp cat in
Mary's Little Lobster (1920). Courtesy of Robert S. Birchard.

Sadly the rest of her starring Fox shorts such as *The Roaming Bathtub, Monkey Business, The Jazz Bandits, Ten Nights Without a Barroom, Pretty Lady* (all 1920), and *The Baby* (1921) are missing and we have to rely on trade magazine items such as "Miss Teare is rapidly forging to the front as a comedienne to be reckoned with" to chart her progress. Hopefully more of these films will be found and recovered so that additional focus can be given to Ethel's talents and career.

Her last Fox comedies were in 1921, and culminated with the release of the six-reel Sunshine feature *Skirts* (April 10, 1921) which also starred half the comedians in Hollywood – Clyde Cook, Chester Conklin, Polly Moran, Slim Summerville, Harry McCoy, Bobby Dunn, Jack Cooper, Billy Armstrong, Edgar Kennedy, Glen Cavender, Tom Kennedy, Billy Franey, Alice Davenport, Harry Booker, and the Singer Midgets. The plot seems to have loosely been about a circus handyman (Clyde Cook), son of the bearded lady, who tries to acquire his rightful inheritance from the estate of his late millionaire father. Something of a slapstick spectacular, the August 14, 1920 *Exhibitors Herald* gave a rundown of the aspects involved in its making:

> Hampton Del Ruth, in charge of production, was assisted by five well-known directors, Roy Del Ruth, Eddie Cline, Jack Blystone, Delmar (Del) Lord, and K.C. Maclean.
>
> Sixteen principals used in the production are all recognized artists with a personal following, who have been starred in their own right from time to time.
>
> One thousand girls, comprising the chorus in the spectacle, represent types of beauty from every nationality selected with great care from every large city in the United States.
>
> The Singer Midgets, the world famous troupe of tiny folks, and their midget menagerie, were hired in a body to assist in the production.
>
> Thrills include the washing away of a palatial home by a flood, a train plunging through a burning bridge, a submarine rescue at sea, a 2,000 foot parachute drop from an airship, an explosion which blew up a three-story set, and the rescue of the heroine from the roof of a speeding train by an airplane.

Although lost today, the surviving reviews and descriptions like the one above make *Skirts* sound like a regular Sunshine short suffering from a glandular condition.

Also in 1921 Ethel appeared as support in the Eileen Percy feature *The Tomboy*, in an entry of Chester Comedies Snooky the human-zee series *Snooky's Twin Troubles*, and even returned to Sennett for what was basically a cameo at the end of the Billy Bevan short *Be Reasonable*. The beginning of the next year saw her teamed with comic Bert Roach for the Universal one-reelers *Westward Whoa*, *Fur Coats and Pants*, and *Almost a Rancher* (all 1922) before a break in her film work. During her days at Kalem it was often noted in the trades that she was turning down offers to return to vaudeville, but *Variety* reported in June 1922:

Ethel Teare, who appeared in the movies in the Sunshine comedies, is an added attraction at the Terrace Gardens, Chicago. Miss Teare does singing and dancing.

A few months later she was still working in Chicago, and the October 1922 *Variety* reports that she was appearing with the Marx Brothers in their *Twentieth Century Revue*:

Ethel Teare, who plays the ingénue in the Marx Bros. mezzanine floor hotel bit, comes from pictures, where she had worked until six months ago.

The routine mentioned was variously known as *On the Mezzanine Floor, On the Mezzanine*, and *On the Balcony*. It's not know how long she worked with the Marxes but in 1924 she made a brief return to the screen. Besides a supporting role in the feature *A Woman who Sinned*, she did one last return to the Sennett lot to play Alberta Vaughn's best friend in the Harry Langdon short *Picking Peaches*, and made her last known film appearances in *Columbus and Isabella*, and *Anthony and Cleopatra* (both 1924), two of Universal's Hysterical History comedies. Directed by Brian Foy and written by Monte Brice, the series was a take-off on famous historical or literary figures such as Benjamin Franklin and Robinson Crusoe with performers on the order of Ethel, Slim Summerville, Billy Franey, Merta Sterling, Phil Dunham, and Leo White. While all the entries are considered lost today the synopsis for Ethel's *Anthony and Cleopatra* gives a good indication of what the shorts were like:

Cleo's nose, stung by a bee concealed in a bouquet given her by Julius Caesar, swells up and has to be fixed by her beauty doctor, who tries out several shapes before he finds one that appeals to the historical vamp. Anthony arrives on the scene, cuts Caesar out with Cleo, and runs away with her down the Nile in his two-oared galley.

Caesar sics his pet alligator on the fleeing couple, the boat breaks in half, and Mark manages to capture the reptile. As the two rivals gamble for Cleo's hand, she runs off with Rameses in his Ford chariot, but the machine breaks down and Cleo, like many other girls since, has to walk home.

During 1924 she married Frank F. Risso, vice-president of the Bank of America,

A young and almost unrecognizable Polly Moran. Courtesy of The Museum of Modern Art.

and after sixteen years in show business she retired, raised a family, and lived in San Mateo, California until her death in 1959.

About a year after Ethel Teare made her screen debut for Kalem, Polly Moran took up residence at Mack Sennett's Keystone Studio. Moran specialized in broad and outrageous physical comedy and, unlike someone like Fay Tincher, seems to have reveled in rough slapstick and never gave even a second's thought that there could be such a thing as "serious acting." Born in 1884 in Chicago, her parents were seasoned stage performers and Polly made her debut at the age of eight in *Uncle Tom's Cabin*. By the turn of the century Pauline Moran was singing and clowning in London, Paris, Berlin, Rome, and even Antwerp. She straddled vaudeville and burlesque, touring with companies like *Maurice Kraus' Twentieth Century Maids* or *The Imperial Burlesquers*, and eventually found a home on the Orpheum Circuit. Even at this early stage of her career she appears to have been ready to do anything to entertain her audience, eliciting reviewer comments like:

> The burlesque had to do with the completion of the Panama Canal, and of course, it was a woman who accomplished the tremendous task of building the great waterway. Pauline Moran was the heroine and she certainly looked as though she could build canals or houses or railroads or any old thing without becoming flustered. (*Philadelphia Record*, August 20, 1907)

and:

> In appearance and manner she seemed like a moving and talking cartoon. (*Rochester Democrat*)

Singing, dancing, and mugging her way through a repertoire that included *In Dear Old Tennessee, Bright Eyes Tell Me True,* and *I'd Rather Two-Step Than Waltz, Bill*, her stage presence was well captured in this October 8, 1911 review from the *Denver Times*:

> By the singing of an Irish "rag" Miss Moran introduces herself to the audience. She hasn't a shred of beauty beyond a set of teeth which gave her the appearance of being lined with ivory; she has no more voice than the edge of a saw evokes from a log, and, according to her own gleeful admission, she is "fat." But she is alive and sparkling; she catches the flow of feelings and ebbs with it – on the audience. She has the charm of the unexpected about her, like the colors of a blatant sunset, and she wins hands down over all the others by being just what she is – a personality, crude, rough, half-refined maybe, but definite, vivid.

Her first brush with the movies occurred while she was on tour out west in 1912-1913, and might have been enough to scare off a less hardy performer:

> **Orpheum Star Just Recovering From Knife Wound Inflicted Before A "Movies" Camera.** After beholding the vivacious, rollicking Pauline

Moran cavort about the Orpheum stage this week in the midst of her lively, character songs and excruciatingly funny parodies on "Ragtime Violin" and other popular hits, one would be slow to believe that she is just recovering from a serious knife wound accidentally received while participating two weeks ago in one of the realistic Wild West productions for a moving picture company at Santa Monica Canon, California. (*Denver Times*, September 26, 1912)

Although the name of the film or the production company isn't given, it may happened during the making of the Powers short *When Joe Went West* (1913), her earliest known film. The article goes on to recount how Polly got stabbed during a big battle scene, and includes a photo of her on horseback with the Sioux Indian actors Sky Eagle, Good Boy, and Kill-and-Thunder (the accidental stabber).

Polly Moran in full comic uniform for her early Keystone appearances. Courtesy of The Museum of Modern Art.

Two years later Polly's stage fame paved the way for her entry at the top of the film comedy heap when it was announced on July 5, 1915 – "**Noted Stage Favorite Joins Keystone Forces**" and added:

> Miss Moran, it was announced by Director Sennett, will play opposite popular Charles Murray in a series of laugh-provoking photoplays that have been prepared for her.

> "This is the most beautiful spot I have ever seen," the young comedienne de-

clared with enthusiasm, after a trip through Inceville and adjacent territory, "and I know I am going to like it immensely. It has been my ambition for some time to appear in motion picture work, and when Mr. Sennett offered me a position with him, I quickly accepted the offer."

Teamed with Irish comic Charlie Murray, known for his popular "Hogan" character, Polly's initial Sennett releases presented a very broad and grotesque portrayal of a shanty Irish working-class couple. The first film, *Caught in the Act* (March 27, 1915), opens with the title "The Janitor's Happy Home" only to show Murray and his slattern wife Polly battling it out in their kitchen. After he's called upstairs to clean the studio of artist Eddie Cline, Murray gets the bright idea to pose as the artist's helper so he can flirt with all the cute models that come to pose at the studio. Eventually elevator boy Slim Summerville apprises Polly of what's going on, and when she finds Murray's trousers in the dumbwaiter that's the last straw. She rides the dumbwaiter up to the studio and surprises Murray just at the same time that artist Cline returns and all hell breaks loose. Polly, broom in hand, spins around and around like a demented top and attacks everything in sight as Murray runs from room to room. When Cline pulls out a pistol the chase goes out the window and on to the rooftops, with Murray, Cline, Summerville, and Polly leaping from building to building. Finally Polly lays waste to Cline and Summerville with her broom, and makes up with Murray in time for the iris out.

The screen character and style of comedy that Polly would use from these beginning Sennett days to her final film appearances emerges full-blown in *Caught in the Act*. Not bothering with the subtlety of Alice Howell or Louise Fazenda, Polly would confront a laugh opportunity head on and wrestle it to the ground until it cried "uncle." The hallmark of her character was a complete lack of class, which made her capable of doing things that mannered and cultured people would never do, and also made her stick out like a sore thumb in any kind of nice society or fancy event. Making no bones about her stout figure Polly made herself shapeless and blowsy in a baggy checkered top, large long skirt, and a filthy apron. She had a prominent nose, teeth, and chin, which were often the only thing that could be seen through her rat's nest of hair, although on one occasion she combs her hair back with the same brush that she's scrubbing the floor with. All her emotions are large and volcanic and seem to erupt out of her – she cries frequently (usually blowing her nose on her skirt), is always ready for a fight, and her large eyes are often almost popping out of her head in big takes of umbrage or surprise.

The battling continues in all her films with Murray, whether as janitors again in *Those College Girls* (1915), or after they come into money in *Their Social Splash* (1915). *Her Painted Hero* (1915) is slightly different. It gives Polly the role usually played by Louise Fazenda as the daughter of Harry Booker, and has Murray and Slim Summerville fighting for her favor. After five or six comedies with Murray, Polly spent a period of time as the sort of "all-purpose-eccentric" of the Sennett lot and popped up all over – as a local widow who marries tramp Eddie Foy in *A Favorite Fool* (1915) and then surprises him with a tribe of kids (the Seven Little Foys), as an overzealous member of a movie audience in *A Movie Star* (1916), and as Mack Swain's country lover in *His Naughty Thought* (1917).

In mid-1917 Polly emerged in a new character, Sheriff Nell, a rough and tumble lady marshal, which provided amble opportunity for turning gender roles on their head and plenty of room for western parody:

> Miss Moran and Ben Turpin share honors in the burlesque of the wild and wooly west, but it's the daring little policewoman of the mountains who provides the thrills. Polly takes her pony hurdling across a mountain waterfall – an abyss of alarming proportions – and performs other matinee idol stunts with magnificent bravado. Her courage in fact knows no end for doesn't she clean out the village saloon? She drives all the wild element of the community to church, reforming the town by strength of example and her sure fire shooting. (*Los Angeles Examiner*, January 17, 1918)

The wild and western cowgirl Sheriff Nell. Author's collection.

Wearing her cowboy hat and six-shooters in shorts like *Cactus Nell*, *Roping Her Romeo* (both 1917), and *Sheriff Nell's Tussle* (1918), the character became very popular and a perfect vehicle for Polly's over-the-top approach to comedy, although this time, her usual gung-ho work attitude caught up with her:

> After stopping stove lids, runaway flivvers, rabid motorcycles and fire engines with various parts of her anatomy for two years without even sustaining a bruise, Polly Moran, Keystone comedienne, has finally reached the hospital. It was nothing more exciting than the stumbling of her horse, the fair Pauline

being precipitated to the ground, and incurring in the process one broken arm, a sprained ankle, and severe contusions. (*Photoplay*, January, 1917)

Book Them Now!

Polly Moran Two Reel Comedies

"Illiterate Digest" Novelty Weekly by Will Rogers

"Smiling Bill" Jones One Reel Comedies

Grace Cunard Two Reel Westerns

for State Rights wire

MARION H. KOHN PRODUCTIONS, *Inc.*
1600 Broadway   Joe Brandt Gen. Rep.   New York

Despite the success of Sheriff Nell, Polly left Sennett and in 1919 moved over to Fox Sunshine Comedies. Sunshine Comedies had begun in 1917 under the supervision of Henry "Pathé" Lehrman, and when Lehrman was bounced in 1919 Hampton Del Ruth, former assistant manager of production for Mack Sennett, was brought in as director-general. From the start Sunshine had raided the Sennett talent roster, and with Del Ruth's arrival the ranks swelled and included Polly, Slim Summerville, Chester Conklin, Alice Davenport, Harry Booker, Laure La Varnie, Glen Cavender, Edgar and Tom Kennedy, plus directors Frank Griffin and Eddie Cline. Today very few of the Sunshines exist, but the survivors are wild and surreal with elaborate slapstick sequences performed on big sets on what look to have been huge budgets. Besides appearing in regular Sunshine two-reelers like *A Schoolhouse Scandal* (1919) and *Training for Husbands* (1920), Polly brought Sheriff Nell with her for *Sheriff Nell's Comeback* (1920), and was also one of the sixteen stars in the afore mentioned feature *Skirts* (1921).

Like her film career, Polly's private life was undergoing changes as well. Having been married to vaudevillian Bob Sandberg since 1911 *Photoplay* reported:

> Polly Moran, the "sheriff girl" in Mack Sennett comedies, has been granted a divorce from Robert Sandberg. Sandberg is an actor, but he won't work at it says Polly. "He would go out in the yard, pull a few weeds, then come in the house and take a bath. Then he would pull a few more weeds and take another bath." She says she couldn't induce him to go to work. (*Photoplay*, July 1918)

It was also reported that Polly invested her earnings in a pig farm near L.A., and in 1918 she adopted a baby, a war orphan named John Michael Joseph Moran. In her usual subdued and tasteful way Polly offered this description of John Michael:

> "He's part wop and part Irish," explains Polly, "he was born with a stiletto in one small fist, and an Irish shillelagh in the other, and he is going to be able to fight his own battles. (*Photoplay*, January 1919)

Between picture work she returned to the stage:

> **Polly Moran Back In Vaudeville: The Screen Has Yielded Back To Vaudeville Another Of The Recruits – Polly Moran**. Miss Moran, prominent in vaudeville several years ago, has been on the Pacific Coast in the interim, starring in motion picture productions as a sort of female Charlie Chaplin. After appearing successfully in many pictures, she is turning her attention to vaudeville again. She is at present in New York awaiting the completion of a new sketch being written for her.

Polly continued her live appearances for a number of years as she reached a somewhat rocky period in her film career. She left Sunshine Comedies after a short stay to star in her own series for the states' rights market:

> **Polly Moran Comedies Will Be Two Reelers**. The Polly Moran comedies will be released as two-reelers instead of single reelers as originally planned announced Marion H. Kohn Productions. Miss Moran is at work on the new series of "Sheriff Nell" pictures, and the first, "Sheriff Nell Surrounded," has been completed.

Produced by Marion H. Kohn and released by C.B.C. Film Sales Corp. as *Carnival Comedies*, this series ran from 1920 into early 1922. Initially directed by Ward Hayes, with photography by Bert Glennon, titles included *The Society Bug* (1920), *Nell's Busted*

Romance, and *Look Before You Sleep* (both 1922). Other *Carnival Comedies* starred Smiling Billy Jones and Earl Montgomery, but with none of Polly's Carnivals in circulation and reviews scarce, it's difficult to judge the series or gauge how it was received. C.B.C., formed by Harry and Jack Cohen and eventually mutating into Columbia Pictures, also produced the very popular *Hallroom Boys* Comedies and Polly appeared as support in many of them such as *A Close Shave* (1920) and *In Bad Again* (1921). In addition she turned up in the features *The Affairs of Anatol* and *Two Weeks with Pay* (both 1921), but after *Luck* (1923) with Johnny Hines she was off the screen for four years, probably concentrating on her live performances.

Polly Moran, nonplussed as usual, with Gertrude Olmstead and Grant Withers in *Bringing Up Father* (1928). Courtesy of Sam Gill.

Polly returned to Hollywood in 1927 on contract to MGM as their resident zany, and as such played a succession of comic maids, landladies, and frumps in the dramatic pictures of Lillian Gish, Lon Chaney, and Greta Garbo. She also turned up in some Hal Roach shorts such as *Are Brunettes Safe?* (1927), and *That Night* (1928). Occasionally she'd star in a comedy feature like *The Callahans and the Murphys* (1927) or *Bringing Up Father* (1928), which returned her to the lower class Irish roots of her Sennett shorts and began her association with Marie Dressler (more on this in Chapter Nine). Most of

Polly's early sound work was with Dressler, and after Marie's death in 1934 Polly's direct and earthy style of comedy kept her popular with depression audiences. Continuing her antics in pictures such as *Hollywood Party, Down to their Last Yacht* (both 1934), and *Sailor Maid* (1937), Polly began turning up less frequently and retired in 1941 after more than twenty years on the screen. Near the end of her life she suffered from heart trouble but came back to MGM and did bits in *Adams' Rib* (1949) and *The Yellow Cab Man* (1950), and died at the age of sixty-eight on January 1, 1952.

As if it weren't enough that men dominated slapstick films in general there were a few male comics who specialized in drag and often played female characters. Before moving on to our last starring lady clown of the 1920s I'd like to briefly mention some of the men who were the most active. Drag was a common and usually sure-fire laugh getter and almost every comedian, male and female, took advantage of it at some point, like both Sidney Drew and Edith Storey in *A Florida Enchantment* (1914), but in the teens and twenties a number of the guys spent a lot of time in women's clothing and strayed into the ladies' territory.

John Bunny was one of the first globally-known movie comedians. Rotund, bulbous, and red-faced, he looked like Shakespeare's Falstaff and Sir Toby Belch come to life. Remembered for playing harassed husbands, Bunny started his movie career in 1910 and it wasn't long after that he started turning up in crinoline and lace. *A Queen for a Day* (February 4, 1911) stars the comic as Bridget McSweeney, an Irish cook who has come into an inheritance. Now that she has dough her old working-class boyfriend is no longer good enough for her, and she decides to marry nobility to get a title. Other examples include *Kitty and the Cowboys* (1911) where the comedian appears as his sister to trick a group of ranch hands, *Doctor Bridget* (1912) which has Bunny as another cook who this time decides that the way to cure the sickly pampered son of her employers is to get rid of the fancy doctors and medicines and put him to good old-fashioned work, and *Bunny's Honeymoon* (1913) where to teach wastrel Wally Van a lesson the comic poses as the wife that Van can't remember marrying on a drunken spree. The prospect of Bunny as his bride sobers Wally up pretty quickly.

Another heavyweight clown with great skill in cross-dressing was Roscoe "Fatty" Arbuckle. Becoming popular at Mack Sennett's Keystone comedies in 1913, Arbuckle was an out and out slapstick practitioner as opposed to the more situational John Bunny. When Arbuckle played ladies in shorts like *Rebecca's Wedding Day* (1914) and particularly *Miss Fatty's Seaside Lovers* (1915) he took and gave out a great deal of physical punishment, usually as a fat heiress surrounded by fortune-hunting swains whose courtships consisted of slaps, kicks, and tremendous pratfalls. In other films such as *Coney Island* (1917) the comedian used women's clothes as a disguise to get away from an overbearing wife.

Both Bunny and Arbuckle were fairly convincing in drag, but much more grotesque and outrageous were Wallace Beery and Frank Hayes. Wallace Beery is remembered today for 1930s MGM classics such as *The Champ* (1931) and *Grand Hotel* (1932), but the earliest part of his film career was spent in silent slapstick. Coming from a background of circuses and the stage in 1913 he began working for the Essanay Company in Chicago, and besides appearing in some of their *George Ade Fables* he made his first movie mark starring as a big lummox Swedish girl in the studios *Sweedie Comedies*. In 1914 and 1915 about twenty-nine episodes of Sweedie's misadventures were filmed, with Beery directing as well as starring. Survivors such as *Sweedie Learns to Swim*, *She Landed a Big One*, *Sweedie the Laundress*, and *Topsy Turvy Sweedie* (all 1914) have a burly Beery, who towers above everyone else in the cast, playing a coy, flirtatious, and extremely fickle maiden whose love play consists of slapping and punching, and who always takes a good deal of physical punishment in the big action windups. From here Beery moved on to Sennett and Universal, and eventually used his comedy skills to break into features as a busy character actor.

An artist's rendition of Wallace Beery as Sweedie. Author's collection.

Frank Hayes was a string bean who often performed without his teeth in numerous Mack Sennett comedies from 1914 on. Besides playing the occasional chief of the Keystone Cops and various fathers and farmers, Hayes specialized in comic spinsters for a wide variety of producers. In the Fox comedy *Who's your Father?* (1918) he's an old crone who spreads a rumor that a foundling is actually the love-child of herself and hunky sheriff Tom Mix, and for the Mermaid Comedy *Sunless Sunday* (1921) he's the blue-nosed leader of a temperance organization that wants all spirits outlawed. Hayes played girl's school headmistresses for Larry Semon, flirty old maids opposite Al St John, and love-sick nurses with Billy West until his premature death in 1923.

The cross-dressing tradition of these four would be continued in the 1920s by Syd Chaplin. As the older brother of Charlie Chaplin, Syd had the same English music hall background and training. When Charlie hit pay dirt with Sennett and was moving on to Essanay at the end of 1914 he brought his brother in to replace him at Keystone. After a few years overseeing Charlie's business dealings and supporting him on screen, Syd scored a big hit in Al Christie's 1925 filming of *Charley's Aunt*, a popular farce about an English lord pretending to be his own aunt. Now in demand for features, Syd signed with Warner Brothers for starring comedies and many of them, such as *The Man on the Box* (1925) and *Oh, What a Nurse!* (1926) worked in extended drag sequences. Syd's female characters were generally older types – aunts, maids or nurses – and were sometimes flirty or other times officious, busy putting the other male characters in their place.

Frank Hayes in all his gummy glory from *Who's Your Father?* (1918). Courtesy of the Library of Congress.

Stan Laurel, sharing a background in the English music hall with the Chaplin brothers, was also very proficient in drag and used it in his solo film *The Sleuth* (1925), and most memorably in the 1929 Laurel & Hardy short *That's My Wife*, where Stan is pressed to fill in for Hardy's absent spouse to fool a rich uncle. The other comedy drag performer of the 1920s was the overlooked Fred Kovert (a.k.a. Frederick Ko Vert). A female impersonator and dancer in vaudeville, in addition to gracing sheet music cover photos, Kovert made his film debut in *An Adventuress* (1920, a.k.a. *The Isle of Love*) where he appeared opposite the most famous female impersonator of the day Julian Eltinge (more on him in a minute). Although Kovert originally appeared in dramatic films he quickly moved into silent comedies such as Ben Turpin's *The Reel Virginian* (1924), *Starvation Blues* (1925), and the Bert Lytell feature *The First Night* (1927).

His largest role was probably in *Chasing the Chaser* (1926), a Stan Laurel-directed Hal Roach short where Kovert is teamed with James Finlayson. As a detective who's undercover in drag, Kovert is hired by Finlayson's wife to catch her philandering hubby in action, and the bulk of the film has Kovert leading Finlayson on and getting him comically hot under the collar. For Larry Semon's *The Wizard of Oz* (1925) Kovert not only does a bizarre turn as "The Phantom of the Basket," but designed all the costumes as well. After his movie days he opened a photography studio and became "Kovert of Hollywood," a pioneer in male physique photography. Said to have had much trouble with the LAPD's vice squad, Kovert shot and killed himself in 1949.

Julian Eltinge confers with himself in a 1917 publicity shot for his Paramount Comedies. Billy Rose Theatre Division, the New York Public Library for the Performing Arts.

But the "King (or Queen) of the Cross-Dressers" was Julian Eltinge. A huge star on the stage, in addition to a few cameos as himself, Eltinge crossed over to headline in a few screen comedies. In the teens he did three for producer Jesse L. Lasky – *The Countess*

Charming, *The Clever Mrs. Carfax* (both 1917), and *The Widow's Mite* (1918). These titles did not have him actually playing a woman, but presented him as a young man who has to take on the impersonation of a female character because of plot demands. Having begun his career at the turn of the century, by 1917 Eltinge had gotten fairly stocky, and his female portrayal at this time was more matron than ingénue. After *An Adventuress* (1920), a dramatic intrigue picture, Eltinge made one more silent comedy feature, the Al Christie-produced *Madame Behave* (1925). Again doing a dual role, he had solid support from Ann Pennington, Jack Duffy, Tom Wilson, and director Scott Sidney. Eltinge would make one low-budget sound picture, *Maid to Order* in 1931, but mostly stuck to the stage, where he continued working until 1940.

When the 1920s rolled around the wave of leading ladies took dominance in film comedy over the vaudeville-based pure clown female performers, reflecting the rise of independent young women in post-World War I American society. The already established female clowns continued in shorts for a while, but for the most part moved into supporting comic relief roles in features. One exception to this trend, and the last woman covered in this chapter, is the film debut of the stage clown Beatrice Lillie.

Beatrice Lillie is a slave to her art and Franklin Pangborn (sitting center) in *Exit Smiling* (1926). Author's collection.

In the early 1920s Beatrice Lillie was the toast of the London and New York stage. Her dry comic style and deadpan ridiculousness kept audiences wanting more for fifty years. Born on May 29, 1894 to an Irish family that had settled in Toronto, Canada, she made her professional debut as part of the Lillie Trio – a singing group that included her mother and sister Muriel. Muriel showed so much promise as a pianist and composer that she was sent to London to study, and young Bea tagged along. Although originally wanting to be a serious singer, Bea ended up a comedienne after being discovered by theatrical producer Andre Charlot.

Appearing nonstop in revue after revue, she refined her skills for sophisticated comedy and musical parody working with the likes of Noel Coward, Gertrude Lawrence, Jack Hulbert, and Jack Buchanan. First coming to America in *Andre Charlot's Revue of 1924*, she was an immediate hit. Bea's next U.S. appearance was *The Charlot Revue of 1926*, which was also warmly received, and the tour of this took her to California where she was spotted and signed by MGM to star in a film.

Under the tight control of its head producers Louis B. Mayer and Irving Thalberg, MGM specialized in high gloss melodramas and star vehicles showcasing big name talent like John Gilbert, Norma Shearer, and their new discovery Greta Garbo. Although not known for their comedies the studio wisely put together a solid unit to create Bea's film, headed by writer Marc Connolly and director Sam Taylor. Taylor in particular had much experience in feature sight gag comedies as a long-time collaborator with Harold Lloyd.

Like many stage veterans before her, Bea had to get used to the stony silence of working before a camera, and shooting scenes out of sequence. In her autobiography *Every Other Inch a Lady* she says:

> Sweet reason had no part in making movies, and there was no audience to learn from – only the grips and gaffers and the rest of the nice people who made up the tribe of strangely named apostles of the faith.
>
> I'd try to introduce a fitful note of humor before we started to roll 'em. "Now boys, be careful to get all my nose in this scene."
>
> After the first laugh, nobody paid much attention. I was used to working for months to perfect a gesture or a piece of business. Here, we were due to finish in five weeks, and it was hard to believe that these disconnected scenes could possibly be patched together to make a movie with any kind of plot.

Despite her misgivings *Exit Smiling* (1926) is a delight. Bea plays Violet, a girl of all trades (seamstress, prompter, cook, etc.) for a low-rent theatrical company touring the Midwest with a fragrant production titled *Flaming Women*, and gets to run the gamut from filling in on stage in drag for the missing villain, to playing a femme fatale to detain a crook blackmailing hero Jack Pickford. While there's plenty of broad burlesque of the theatrical life, Bea turns in a wonderfully modulated and sincere dramatic performance when her character falls in love with Pickford. The sad ending even predates Chaplin's *City Lights* (1931), as Bea let's Pickford go off with his fiancée without telling him that it was she who got the information that cleared his name. Physically her character of the company slavey harkens back to Alice Howell and Louise Fazenda in her working clothes – a smock, apron, and a single bow in her hair. She's also very tomboyish, slim and slender with bobbed hair. Her face is long, and there's a hint of a female Stan Laurel. She gives an impressive performance and has solid support from comedy pros like Harry Myers, Franklin Pangborn, William Gillespie, and Dorothea Wolbert.

Beatrice Lillie makes like a vamp to delay Harry Myers in *Exit Smiling* (1926). Courtesy of Cole Johnson.

After *Exit Smiling*, for all its flaws, the people at MGM had a three-year option on my services. But making more movies would have meant that I had to live indefinitely in Hollywood and I had engagements to fulfill on the stage.

Although unimpressed with her moviemaking experience, Bea returned periodically to stick a toe in the cinematic waters. In 1929, when sound hit the industry, she appeared in *Your Show of Shows* (1929) and *Are You There?* (1930), and later made similar forays for *Dr. Rhythm* (1938) and *Thoroughly Modern Millie* (1967), but the only films that captured some of the scope of her talents were *Exit Smiling* and the British *On Approval* (1943). Content on the stage, she continued entertaining audiences until ill health forced her to stop. She died in her nineties in 1989.

In the talking film era the lady knockabout silent clowns seemed for the most part to be forgotten as the screwball comedy heroines quickly took their place. But remnants of the style and spirit of these ladies survived not only in the 1930s films of Marie Dressler and Polly Moran and the Hal Roach teaming of Thelma Todd with Zasu Pitts and Patsy Kelly, but also into the 1940s with the starring comedies of Martha Raye, Joan Davis, Vera Vague, and Judy Canova.

Chapter Four
LEADING LADIES OF THE TEENS

While the teens were the heyday of the female clowns there were also a number of popular leading ladies – heroines and everywomen –whose characters and misadventures were similar to the girls sitting in the audience. Florence Turner and Florence Lawrence had been the first, but others followed quickly.

Victoria Forde was only fifteen when she began her film career in 1910, but she'd had years of experience on stage. Born in New York in 1896, as the daughter of actress Eugenie Forde (nee Parker) and actor/stage manager Arthur Forde she first went on stage at the age of three:

> It was called "A Desperate Chance," and really I think we took a desperate chance every time we played it. Mother was in the play, and I always stood in the wings and watched another child play the baby part. One day the little one was bitten by a dog, and I was given the part. (*Picture Play*, January 1922)

From here she appeared with John Drew in *His House in Order*, and worked with other famous actors such as Chauncey Olcott, Maxine Elliott, and Blanche Walsh, before touring in vaudeville with her mother Eugenie (see appendix) in a sketch called *Mrs. Danforth's Experience*:

> Afterward, mother took me off the stage and put me in a convent. It was when I was fifteen, and had played one or two parts, that mother lost her voice, which caused her to go into pictures. In those days that was thought an awful comedown, and mother felt very bad, though glad and grateful for the work at the same time.

After the convent she had the lead in the play *Polly of the Circus*, and in 1910 began working in pictures like her mother.

Nestor publicity photo of Victoria Forde. Author's collection.

Her first stop was New York's Biograph Studio and her earliest known film is the Frank

Powell-directed comedy *Love in Quarantine* (1910). The next year she joined the Nestor Company, appearing mostly in New Jersey-shot westerns, and moved with them when they re-located to California to have access to real western locations. 1912 and 1913 saw her switching between various outfits, with her first stop Mack Sennett's Keystone Studio.

Vicky appeared as an ingénue in some of the earliest California-made Keystone releases – shorts like *The Beating He Needed, Pedro's Dilemma, His Only Son, Stolen Glory,* and *The Ambitious Butler* (all 1912). She also spent time at Biograph working for D.W. Griffith, not to mention Bison, Selig, and Balboa. A stop at the St Louis Motion Picture Company had her working in Frontier Comedies like *A Hasty Jilting,* and *When Roaring Gulch Got And Suffrage,* plus she was teamed with comic Dot Farley for three "Frontier Twins" shorts (see Chapter Nine) – *The Frontier Twins Start Something* and *The Frontier Twins Heroism* (all 1913).

Eddie Lyons and Victoria Forde get on the bad side of Lee Moran in *His Egyptian Affinity* (1915). Courtesy of Cole Johnson.

Early in 1914 she re-joined Nestor and became their starring comedienne under the direction of Al Christie, giving her the distinction of being the very first "Christie Girl." Her characters were usually simply named Victoria, and she hit the ground running with *She Was Only a Working Girl* (March 4, 1914). Over the next year and a half she appeared in almost seventy-five comedies along with Eddie Lyons, Lee Moran, Stella Adams, Harry Rattenberry, Neal Burns, and Billie Rhodes. Most were centered on romantic mix-ups, with Vicky as the sweetheart or young newlywed wife, others were parodies of melodramas or movie genres.

"Sophie of the Films" New Nestor Series. When Al E. Christie, director of the Nestor Comedy Company, devised a working script for a one-reel comedy entitled "Sophie of the Films," he planned better than he knew. General Manager Isidore Bernstein, of the Universal West Coast studios, heard of Christie's plans and promptly instructed the latter to make the one-reel comedy into a series of four, each picture to be complete in itself.

The first reel of the "Sophie" series will show her as a student in the "movie class" of the Bunkem Dramatic School. She secures her "diploma" and seeks a job as a leading lady and in the process spoils a scene which is being staged. Sophie overcomes obstacles and finally lands a leading woman. The "villain" promptly falls in love with her, and Sophie's strenuous existence commences. The leading man also falls in love with her and becomes her protector. Between the two of them they make Sophie's existence a blood-curdling nightmare. Victoria Forde will play the part of "Sophie," Eddie Lyons that of the leading man and rescuer, and Lee Moran will be the "director" and "villain" of the company in which "Sophie" is leading lady. (*Universal Weekly*, May 9, 1914)

The Sophie films spoofed acting schools, working with animals, doing stunts like jumping from burning buildings, and shooting on location. Through it all Sophie ruins take after take, and eventually:

When they finally arrive at the studio, poor Sophie is fired. She returns to the old homestead. Her sorrowed is lessened, however, when she is given her old job in a laundry. It is said that forever after she never grew weary of recalling the days when she was a leading lady. (*Universal Weekly*, June 20, 1914)

For a leading lady Forde wasn't exactly pretty – in fact she was wall-eyed, which is very apparent in surviving films and photos. Normally this would be a detriment for an actress, but it didn't seem to hold her back in the least. She was small and basically attractive, but her thinness and slightly off-kilter eyes gave a touch of Gale Henry to her appearance which may have made her more of a natural for comic roles. *Lizzie's Dizzy Career* (February 5, 1915) is one of her few available Nestor comedies, and stars her as a singer whose voice is the pride of the country village. The local banker is so enthused that he pays for her to go to the big city to develop her voice. Of course things don't go well in the city where villains try to take advantage of her naïveté, and eventually she returns home with her country beau.

Tom Mix and his cowboy rival about to take ten paces for Victoria's favor in *Some Duel* (1916). Courtesy of Robert S. Birchard.

What ended her starring string of Nestor comedies was Tom Mix. Introduced to the cowboy by her mother, who was working in his shorts for the Selig Company, a romance developed and it wasn't long before she joined his unit in Las Vegas, New Mexico as leading lady in the mostly light-hearted westerns he was producing and directing. Thanks to her plentiful experience in Nestor and Bison westerns she was an excellent horsewoman and fit right into the company. Many of the comedies such as *How Weary Went Wooing* (1915) and *An Angelic Attitude* (1916) used the bashful Tom's attempts to woo Victoria for their comic material. In *A Bear of a Story* (1916) Vicky has a friend who has a tame bear for a pet, and tells her boyfriend Tom that what she wants more than anything else is a pet bear of her own. Determined to impress her, Tom and his buddy go out to capture a bruin, and get themselves nearly killed in the process. In the meantime Vicky's playing with her friend's bear, which snaps at her and scares her off the idea of having her own. Tom returns the victor with his furry offering, but it's less than happily received by Vicky.

Although busy cranking out the Mix films at a steady pace, Forde found the time to write and direct a Selig comedy of her own:

> **When Cupid Slipped**. Victoria Forde, the clever little leading lady, who plays opposite Tom Mix in many Selig western plays, recently wrote, directed and played the lead in a Selig comedy. This comedy is entitled "When Cupid Slipped"

and will be released Saturday Nov. 11th in General Film Service. Miss Forde assumes an entirely new role that of a simple-minded cook in a cheap restaurant. She brings to her part much versatility and talent and it is predicted that she will make a decided hit in this comedy. (Unidentified, October 23, 1916)

Vicky is immune to Tom's charms in *Hearts and Saddles* (1918). Courtesy of Robert S. Birchard.

In 1917 the pair transferred their western comedies to the Fox Studio, making Foxfilm two-reelers such as *Hearts and Saddles*, *A Soft Tenderfoot*, and *Tom and Jerry* (all 1917). On her own she made appearances at Universal in *In Again, Out Again* and *Please*

Be My Wife (both 1917). When Mix obtained a divorce from Olive Stokes he and Victoria were married in 1918, and appeared together in the feature *Western Blood* (1918). Her last film before retiring into married life was back at Nestor for the short *She Wasn't Hungry – But* (1919) where she plays a young working girl that has no appetite but spends the short eating everything in sight. Tom Mix became one of the biggest stars of the 1920s and Victoria was a popular Hollywood wife, said to have the second largest jewelry collection in the community after Mrs. Cecil B. DeMille. The pair eventually divorced in 1932, but Vicky remained in Hollywood until her death in 1964.

Today Victoria Forde and her work are forgotten, but the name Pearl White is still remembered. Renowned as the original "Queen of the Serials" – it's generally overlooked that she first made her name in comedy. Born in Green Ridge, Missouri in 1889, her early years were spent on the stage playing child roles like Little Eva in *Uncle Tom's Cabin*. She's even said to have been a circus equestrienne, but an injury ended that. As a teenager she acted with the local Diemer Theatre, and later left school to tour with the Trousdale Stock Company. By 1910 she was in New York and got her first film work with the Powers Picture Play Company, appearing in mostly westerns and dramas with an occasional comedy.

Pearl had never seen herself on screen, and in her 1919 autobiography *Just Me* she had this to say about the experience:

> I had gone on about three weeks before I saw my first picture on the screen. Oh, what a sensation that is! Up until that time I had a mental picture of myself that was quite good looking, but when I got a flash of myself as I was and as others saw me, I nearly died. I was so disheartened that I walked out of the studio and disappeared for three or four days. If it hadn't been that I was in the middle of a picture and they wanted me to finish it, that would probably have been my last appearance on the screen. Anyway, they needed me for finishing scenes, so they discovered my whereabouts and lured me back to the studio, said that with a little making over they were sure I would turn out all right. I soon disposed of my small waist and big pompadour and changed my entire scheme of dressing to more simple styles.

Her Powers short *The Woman Hater* (1910) has recently resurfaced, giving us a look at one of her earliest appearances. The story is about a rich man who's just been jilted by his fiancée and goes out west to visit a rancher friend to get away from women. At the same time the rancher's pretty niece (Pearl) shows up for a visit. The woman-hater acts very coldly to Pearl, who likes him anyway, and follows him when he goes out riding. While he's out an Indian tries to steal his horse and in the ensuing struggle he stabs the thief leading the other Indians to take him prisoner. Pearl, who was following, takes all this in and rides back to her uncle's cabin for help with an Indian at her heels. Thanks to Pearl the cowboys head to the rescue, and get there as the Indians have started to toast our feminine-impaired hero. They save him in the nick of time. Pearl oversees his convalescence, and he gets over his woman-hating to give her a closing snuggle.

Although largely a western melodrama the comedy elements are fully developed, and the result is an easygoing and charming little film. Pearl is cute and warm, shows off her expert horse-riding skills, and although she's remembered as a blonde, here she has her natural brunette hair color. In 1911 she spent a brief time at Lubin:

Early shot of Pearl White surrounded by feathers. Courtesy of Cole Johnson.

At that time Florence Lawrence and Arthur Johnson were the stars of the Lubin Company, in fact, I think they were about the first people to reach stardom in the entire picture business. I was to play secondary parts. I don't know what it was, whether I was too good or too bad – anyway, Miss Lawrence refused to work with me, so that they put me in other pictures in which I played leading parts. However, I didn't get on well there and only lasted about two months. I came back to New York, drifted over to the Pathé Freres in Jersey City.

Pearl made a slew of shorts for Pathé – mostly westerns such as *The Heart of an Indian Maid* (1911), where, as the title character, she sacrifices herself for the white man that she's fallen in love with. The fall of 1912 saw her career go in an entirely different direction:

We got along so well that I was sorry to leave Pathé for a better offer. However, the Crystal Moving Picture Company came along and offered me so much more money that my Jewish instinct forced me to pack up my things and leave behind the emotional and dramatic parts that I had been playing in Jersey.

I became chief pie-slinger in the Crystal slapstick comedies. I don't know why, but all through my career I have had to change my line of parts in every company that I have worked for. Be that as it may. I was getting a very good salary and also was being advertised enough that I began to become known to the public. It was then that I began to receive letters from the fans asking for photographs, etc.

The Crystal Moving Picture Company was a small outfit that released through Universal. The creative person behind the camera on the split-reel and one-reel comedies was writer and director Phillips Smalley, who was well-known as the partner and husband of Lois Weber. Pearl was teamed with young actor Chester Barnett for the series, and although she describes herself as "chief pie-slinger" in the films, there's no pastry in sight in surviving examples. There's not much slapstick either, so Pearl's reminisces appear to be more the common attitude of comedies being on the "low end" of the entertainment totem pole as opposed to the higher place of drama. The Crystals were more of the domestic and situational variety of comedies that had much in common with the later films of Mr. and Mrs. Sidney Drew and Mr. and Mrs. Carter De Haven. Pearl and Chester were usually young lovers or newlyweds who had to deal with quarrelsome bosses or in-laws.

Her Dress Makers Bills (1912) concern's Pearl not being able to resist buying new gowns, much to Chester's dismay as he's getting all the bills when the dressmakers show up at his office for payment. To teach Pearl a lesson he dresses up as a sheriff and hires a couple of thugs to go with him to the house and confront Pearl. Just before they arrive Chester's newly-cleaned suit is delivered. As the sheriff Chester bursts in demanding money from his wife and when she can't pay has his "deputies" gather up all the gowns and the box with his suit in it. After leaving he pays the men off and tells them they can do whatever they want with the gowns. Coming home he plays innocent as Pearl tells him what happened. He's enjoying himself mightily until he finds out that his suit was part of the "confiscated" items.

Pearl and Chester are a butler and maid in *A Night on the Town* (1913), and when their wealthy employers go on an overnight trip the pair throw a party and dress in their bosses clothing. During the festivities the employer's old uncle shows up for a visit and mistakes Pearl for his niece-in-law. They play along to keep him happy, but uncle begins flirting big time with Pearl which causes Chester to confront him and throw him out of the window. Uncle lands on a cop and gets sent to the hoosegow with a black eye. He comes back the next morning to find his real nephew and niece have returned. The jig is up for Pearl and Chester.

CRYSTAL FILMS

PEARL WHITE
AMERICA'S LEADING PHOTOPLAY ARTIST
WILL APPEAR ONLY IN
CRYSTAL FILMS

SPLIT REEL EVERY SUNDAY

Consisting of Two Rip-Roaring Comedies

Miss Pearl White.

FIRST RELEASE SUNDAY, OCTOBER SIXTH

THE GIRL IN THE NEXT ROOM
THE MAN FROM THE NORTH POLE

EXHIBITORS SEND US THE NAME OF YOUR THEATER FOR SPECIAL ADVERTISING MATTER THAT WILL INCREASE YOUR BUSINESS.

ADDRESS — **Crystal Films** Wendover and Park Avenues, New York
Released by
Universal Film Mfg. Co.

CRYSTAL FILMS

FIRST RELEASE — SUNDAY, OCTOBER 6TH
UNIVERSAL PROGRAMME

FIRST RELEASE — SUNDAY, OCTOBER 6TH
UNIVERSAL PROGRAMME

The Hallroom Girls (1913) examines the dating problems of lower income characters. Pearl lives in a boarding house and between her roommate and snoopy landlady she has difficulty getting any privacy when her beau Chester comes to call. Chester has the same problems at his boarding house, and on a night when they're all going to a big ball Pearl pretends to have a toothache so when her roommate goes out to get her medicine she can "borrow" her new dress. At the same time Chester "borrows" his roomies' fancy suit and sets out to pick up Pearl, but when he gets there the roommates catch up with them. A fight breaks out and the landlady runs for the police. The boys end up in jail and the girls have a massive pillow fight. Joseph "Baldy" Belmont was their main character support and eventually got his own comedies, while Vivian Prescott and Charles deForrest headlined in other Crystal series.

Pearl and Chester's Crystal's were a comedy series, but an occasional drama was thrown in for variety. *Lost in the Night* (1913) stayed this side of comedy but almost became a tragedy. Pearl and Chester have a guest coming to stay who brings some valuable jewelry with him, which Chester puts securely in their safe. Pearl is very fond of the necklace, and at night she sleepwalks to the safe and takes it, hiding it outside in a hollow of an old tree. In the morning they find the necklace missing and panic ensues. A detective is called and the innocent housemaid is grilled, but Chester ultimately accepts financial responsibility for his friend's loss, mortgaging their home to do so. A year later the mortgage is due and things look dire, but luckily Pearl walks in her sleep again and goes outside and retrieves the jewelry for the happy ending. Turning out an amazing over one hundred and fifty shorts, the overall series is well described by this *Motion Picture News* review of *Bella's Beau* (1912):

> Pearl White has a large following among picture fans and deserves to have. This brisk little comedy gets across delightfully on her charm and skill, but she is well supported by four or five men, two of whom, strongly contrasted, are her beaus. It is very humanly played and without artificiality. Surely it is good entertainment.

In the midst of her 1914 Crystals Pearl made the celebrated *Perils of Pauline* for the Pathé Company. Making a huge impression as an action heroine, this was followed up by the Wharton Company's *Elaine* trilogy – *The Exploits of Elaine* (1914), *The New Exploits of Elaine*, and *The Romance of Elaine* (both 1915), and she was off doing more serials for Astra and Edward Jose Productions like *The Iron Claw* (1916), *The Fatal Ring* (1917), and *The House of Hate* (1918). Although this is the type of productions that she is remembered for, she also tried to do dramas and

Classic shot of Pearl White after she became everyone's favorite serial queen. Courtesy of Cole Johnson.

romances like *Mayblossom* (1917) and *Any Wife* (1922), and even returned to comedy shorts. In 1918 with support from Don Barclay, Charles Hutchinson, Estelle Deland, and William Browning, Pearl headlined in a series of Crystal Comedies (familiar name) one-reelers with titles like *What She Did to Her Husband, What's in the Trunk?, The Lady Detective,* and *Her Necklace.*

She ended her American career in features for Fox and the George B. Seitz serial *Plunder* (1923), made her last film *Terreur* (*Terror,* 1924) in France, and afterward retired. Following her film work she made stage appearances in France and England, and having invested well lived a life of luxury, but died at forty-nine from cirrhosis of the liver.

While Pearl White's comedies were of the sophisticated brand our next leading lady was part of some of the most outrageous slapstick comedies of the period from L-Ko and Fox. Born in Philadelphia in 1896, Gertrude Selby was raised in New York City and went on the stage at a young age:

> She told me that she had never been in pictures before joining the L-Ko Company, but had been on the stage for three years from the time she was fifteen until she reached the exciting age of eighteen. For two seasons musical stock was her pastime, after which she was with Gus Edwards. This was followed by an engagement in vaudeville touring the country. (*Universal Weekly,* April 24, 1915)

During her stage years she had danced with Gertrude Hoffman, spent a year in Gus Edward's *School Days,* and played with the Hackett-Morgan Stock Company. She was "discovered" for films by Henry "Pathé" Lehrman. Although generally overlooked today, Lehrman was one of the most important Hollywood comedy pioneers of the teens who started his career at Biograph, and became Mack Sennett's right hand man there and in the formation of Keystone, where Lehrman was influential in creating the studio's style and maintaining the output. In 1914 he left Sennett for a brief sojourn directing Ford Sterling at Sterling Comedies, which were released through Universal. While there Lehrman se-

L-Ko publicity photo of Gertrude Selby. Author's collection.

cured a deal with Universal's head Carl Laemmle for his own company L-Ko (Lehrman Knockout Comedies). Organized in the summer of 1914, the three principals were Billie Ritchie, Henry Bergman, and Gertrude. It's said that Lehrman tried hard to lure Mabel Normand away from Keystone but she remained true to Sennett. Gertrude bears some superficial resemblance to Normand – she was small, dark-haired, and spunky. Rotund Henry Bergman was the main support, invaluable at playing authority figures which he had been doing for Pathé comedies and would soon do for Charlie Chaplin.

Star comic Billie Ritchie came from a similar music hall background as Chaplin, both were graduates of the Fred Karno Company and had played the drunken toff in the popular sketch *Mumming Birds*. Producer Lehrman went out of his way to draw attention to the similarities since Lehrman had been Chaplin's first director at Keystone. But while Ritchie and Chaplin shared a common background and comic vocabulary they were very different, and while the little tramp was essentially playful Ritchie's screen persona was a borderline psychopath – possibly the most low-down, despicable, and unlikeable character ever seen on the screen. This set the tone for the L-Kos, which were down and dirty, anything-for-a-laugh slap-fests.

The first release, *Love and Surgery* (October 25, 1914) starts out like many Lehrman comedies with love intrigue in a park. Hobo Billie begins a flirtation with Gertrude which she enjoys until her hubby Bergman catches them. He pulls out a gun and all hell breaks loose. The second reel takes place in a hospital where the injured Ritchie was taken and it just so happens that the supervising doctor is Bergman, who recognizes Ritchie and has him strapped to an operating table while he prepares to probe Billie with some heavy industrial instruments. Ritchie gets loose, all the other patients join in the melee, and the L-Ko police force arrives for the wind-up of the studio's maiden offering.

The trade magazine description of another early L-Ko, *The Fatal Marriage* (1914), gives a precise distillation of the ethos of the series in a nutshell:

> The marriage was, indeed, fatal. Autos were overturned, lives were risked, property was destroyed in this mad, wild round of fun and laughter. The best slap-bang bunch of fun in a long time.

Gertie was the catalyst that would set Richie off on his reign of terror. In *Father Was a Loafer* (1915) Billie's wife Alice Howell has just presented him with triplets to add to their already four children. The strain determines Ritchie to leave home. When he starts out, he has the opportunity to rescue Miss Rocks (Gertie) a multi-millionairess whose horses have gone out of control. Gertie's grateful father bestows her hand and her money on Billie. He is just about to seal the deal at the wedding when wife Alice shows up with their seven progeny in tow. The usual riot breaks loose, and Alice eventually hauls Billie home for repairs. Gertrude is almost always the obscure object of desire for Ritchie, whether it's as another heiress in *After Her Millions* (1915), or as the pretty cashier that he and Bergman fight over in *Bill's New Pal* (1915).

Selby makes a funny heroine, very expressive and natural, who seems to have been unafraid to join in the slapstick action. After these initial entries with Ritchie she was busy in a string of action comedies like *Rough but Romantic, Gertie's Joy Ride, Greed and Gasoline* (all 1915), *Gertie's Busy Day, Sea Dogs and Land Rats*, and *Gertie's Awful Fix* (all 1916). According to the May 1916 issue of *Picture Play*:

> Gertrude Selby, also in Universal comedies, recently went flying off a high dock in a motor car for a scene in "Gertie's Joy Ride." She was not doubled by a professional dare-devil, for I saw the scene taken myself. It was with difficulty that a rescue was achieved. The following week, she jumped from a fifth-story window of a burning building into a net. This seems commonplace for an actress, but most people in real fires prefer other means of escape.
>
> One of Miss Selby's best thrillers was when she and an actor rode in a large racing automobile at a fast rate of speed, in front of an onrushing train. Both the locomotive and her car were started a goodly distance from a cross-road, because the director wanted to get a long-range view of the thriller, to make it more impressive. This made it harder to gauge the time and distance, and, as a result, three retakes were necessary before the car was missed narrowly enough – that is, to suit the director – Miss Selby thought that the huge engine came entirely close enough the first time.

The surviving *Gaby's Gasoline Glide* (1916) is a melodramatic spoof with Gertie and her two suitors – Billy Armstrong and Phil Dunham. Billy has a motorcycle and Phil a Model T flivver, and while Gertie clearly favors Phil when his car breaks down she rides off with Billy. Eventually they are sparking in the park when Phil catches up to them and a tug of war with Gertie in the middle ensues. After their battle and slap-fest Gertie goes off with Phil to get married. When it turns out that Phil doesn't have the two bucks for the ceremony disappointed Gertie goes outside. There she sees Billy, borrows the money from him and returns inside

Author's collection.

to marry Phil. This drives Billy mad, so he tricks the pair into his car and vows to drive them to their deaths. The last part of the film is an all-out chase with the police in pursuit – the highlight of which is the cars and various motorcycles bursting through a hospital – sending splinters and patients flying. They finally all drive off a pier into the drink.

In autumn 1916 Lehrman was ousted from L-Ko, and Universal's head Carl Laemmle's brothers-in-law Abe and Julius Stern took over the company. At this point Gertrude stopped working for the outfit and instead moved over to Universal itself:

> "Desperate Medicine" is the title given the subject by director Charles Bartlett. This features Gertrude Selby in her first dramatic subject, she having played in L-Ko comedies since her screen debut. (*Motion Picture News*, September 2, 1916)

Dave Morris (right) working to make hamburger out of Fatty Voss' hand as Gertie stands by in *Dirty Work in a Beanery* (1916). Courtesy of Robert Arkus.

Probably finishing out her contract with "Big U" she starred in a number of intrigue melodramas such as *The Sign of the Poppy, A Child of Mystery* (both 1916), and *The Double Room Mystery* (1917), some of them five reels in length. After his boot from Universal Henry Lehrman landed at Fox and initiated a new brand of Fox Sunshine Comedies, with Gertrude and Billie Ritchie joining him there.

The first Lehrman-made Fox comedy has been given the title "The House of Terrible Scandals" and is now on the way to New York for release January 22. The studio employees laugh every time they think of it, for it offers Billie Ritchie the best man, Gertrude Selby the bride, and Dot Farley the mistress of ceremonies. A greater portion of the film shows the nightmares of the wedding party following a pre-nuptial celebration (*Motion Picture News*, January 27, 1917)

Other Fox comedies she appeared in include *His Smashing Career* (1917), *Damaged – No Goods*, *Who's Your Father?*, *Son of a Hun* (all 1918), and *Money Talks* (1919). Unfortunately she doesn't turn up in the surviving footage of *The House of Terrible Scandals*, which appears to be from the first reel and has Ritchie and Henry Lehrman suffering from the ill-effects from a wild bachelor party, but she is in the existing *Who's Your Father?* (1918). Tom Mix stars as the local cowboy hero, and Gertie is the daughter of Jimmie Adams, owner of the town's general store, who's being forced to marry corrupt sheriff Henie Conklin because he owns the mortgage on her dad's store.

Gertie and Tom are in love. Our hero gets the money to pay the mortgage and wins Gert. Complications arise when Tom finds an abandoned baby and the sheriff starts a rumor that the baby is Tom's with the town's ugly spinster (Frank Hayes in drag). A trial is held and the spinster tells a tale of how Tom seduced her, but the wrong baby is produced (a black one) so she and the sheriff are caught in their lies. Desperate, the sheriff and his deputy knock out Tom and kidnap Gertie, who gives them a hard time on her own as Tom and the cowboys chase their runaway car. Gertie is rescued and the villains comically captured. As with most Fox Sunshines the action and gags are fast and furious, and Tom Mix fits gamely into the slapstick, although most of the physical bits are handled by Gertie, Henie Conklin, Victor Potel, Frank Hayes, and Tom Wilson.

Lehrman didn't stay long at Fox and neither did Gertie. Although it was announced in mid-1919 that she was going to star in some of Lehrman's upcoming independent specials for First National release, she never did. In the midst of her working for Fox she also headlined in a series of shorts with Neal Burns:

> **Gertrude Selby and Neal Burns Co-Star**. New Brand of Weekly One-Reelers to Be Produced by Horsley and Douglas. From the David Horsley Studios comes the announcement that production has begun on a series of one-reel parlor comedies featuring Gertrude Selby and Neal Burns, directed by Horace Davey. The distribution will be one picture per week. The new venture is a result of a combination between David Horsley and W.A.S. Douglas.
>
> As a picture comedienne Miss Selby holds an assured place in the front rank. Although only twenty years old, her stage and screen experience covers a period of six years. Beginning as a dancer in the Gertrude Hoffman Revue she

was quickly singled out by managers for her exceptional work, and at the age of fifteen was starring as a vaudeville single act.

Miss Selby's entrance into pictures came over two years ago, when she joined the L-Ko company as principal comedienne. Her series of feature comedies, including "Gertie's Gasoline Gallop," and "Gertie's Joy Ride," assured her future in picture work. Leaving the L-Ko company she joined Universal, co-starring with Hobart Henley in Bluebird Productions. Last year Miss Selby came under the Fox banner, this time again as a comedienne and left there to take up her new work. (*Moving Picture World*, June 23, 1017)

Gertie, Neal Burns, and an elephant friend in an exhibitor ad for Selburn Comedies.

Producer David Horsley had started the Nestor Company in 1909 on the East Coast, where he gave Al Christie his first important film work, and eventually took the company to Hollywood in 1911. Horsley sold his interest in Nestor to Universal, and later formed MinA and then Cub Comedies. Horace Davy would be the director of this new series, and had started his career with Nestor back East, later directing for Al Christie. His career ended in 1920, although he lived until 1970. This new series was called Selburn Comedies (a combination of Selby and Burns) and titles included *An Interrupted Vacation, Too Much Elephant, Hubby's Holiday* (all 1917), *Wedding Bells and Lunatics*, and *His College Proxy* (both 1918). Presented by the Piedmont Pictures Corporation none of the films are known to exist, but trade magazine descriptions give us an idea:

> **Wedding Bells and Lunatics** – This a clean, up-to-date and novel one-reel subject in which the two principals are involved in the blundering net of their playful friends while on their way to the church for their wedding. While one group of friends kidnap the bride, another sets out to find the groom, but they make the mistake of capturing an escaped lunatic. The belated appearance of Neal with the ring prevents the wedding ceremony from degrading into a riot. (*Moving Picture World,* January 26, 1918)

> **His College Proxy** – Highly amusing complications are said to ensue when Neal persuades the chauffeur to take his place in college while he accepts a position as butler in order that he may be near Gertrude. Neal's proxy proves too good a spender and both masqueraders are exposed (*Motion Picture News*)

Short-lived, the series seems to have ended in 1918, and Gertrude began breaking into feature comedies, appearing as support to light comedian Bryant Washburn in his features *Twenty-One* and *Kidder and Ko* (both 1918). This continued with Bert Lytell in *Easy to Make Money* (1919), but her final film work was two series of shorts:

> **Engages Gertrude Selby**. The Macdon Pictures Corporation announces that it has signed Gertrude Selby star of Fox Sunshine Comedies, L-KO, and Sennett Comedies for a series of eighteen pictures a year which are expected to start at once at a local studio which the company has leased. Frank P. Donovan will direct and William H. MacNulty will have charge of production, it is stated. (*Motion Picture News*, February 23, 1919)

Selby, like performers such as Buster Keaton and Fay Tincher, often got Mack Sennett listed in her credits although she never worked for him. Macdon pulled together a solid team behind her:

> Supporting Miss Selby is Bobby Connelly who recently made an outstanding hit in "The Unpardonable Sin." This child, it will be remembered, was starred

in a series of pictures called "Sonny Boy." Patsy De Forest also appears in these comedies. She has been connected with a number of the best known comedy organizations in the country. Lew Marks who started his career as a comedian in Keystone comedies appears to advantage in support of Miss Selby. (*Moving Picture World*, May 3, 1919)

Three shorts – *Neptune's Stepdaughter*, *Hubby's Mistake*, and *Pardon Me*, appear to have been made at the Thanhouser Studio in New Rochelle – and after a delay of many months were finally released as Jolly Comedies on the States rights market by the Film Specials organization. None of the shorts are known to exist, but for *Neptune's Stepdaughter* the company boasted:

> The comedy is the first to be produced entirely under water, with spectacular sets and specifically constructed properties designed by William B. MacNulty with Albert Fowler, late technical and art director for Clara Kimball Young, acting in the same capacity for the Macdon Comedies. The picture is said to offer something new in the line of farce comedy. (*Exhibitors Herald and Motography*, 1919)

After this venture in the East Gertrude returned to California and joined the cast of the Al Christie-produced Strand Comedies. As with most of the Christie product these were domestic comedies, mostly directed by Scott Sidney, that were short and sweet at the one-reel length. Selby's co-star was Harry Depp, who was almost a dead ringer for Bobby Vernon and saw his career eclipsed by the popular Vernon, with support from Katherine Lewis, Teddy Sampson, and James Liddy. Two titles with Gertie have been verified *Betty and the Boys,* and the surviving *Betty's Back Again* (both 1919).

A group of three buddies are all excited as they heard that the cute Betty is back in town. They're all rushing around trying to be the first to see her, and they bring more and more elaborate gifts. Harry makes a hit giving her a puppy and becomes her favorite. The other two boys decide to do Harry in by arranging to have everyone come up to him and ask him what's the matter or say that he looks terrible. The powers of suggestion work as Harry thinks he's dying and the world is spinning around him. The plan blows up in the boys' faces through as Gertie cancels the party trip she had invited them on to devote herself to nursing Harry. A doctor tells Harry that he's the victim of a joke, and at this point Gertrude and Harry get involved with helping the doctor avoid a subpoena server. This gives him an idea for revenge on his rivals. Now that he's well the party trip is put back on, and when the two boys are waiting to go Harry comes disguised as a cop and serves them with subpoenas saying that they have to be in court in an hour – hence no party trip. The boys decide to risk jail to make time with Gertrude, but Harry returns as the cop and chases them off. Now he has Gertie to himself, so he takes off his disguise mustache and they kiss.

At the very end of 1919 it was announced that Gertie was going to leave the cast of the Strand Comedies for another Christie brand – a series of Supreme Comedy two-reelers distributed by the Robertson-Cole Company – but it doesn't look like she ultimately appeared in any. Instead she married Chicago millionaire Townsend Netcher and retired from films. Although she and Netcher would divorce in 1928 (he next married Constance Talmadge) she never returned to movies, and lived the life of a socialite, eventually remarrying and spending much of her time in Europe before her death in 1975.

The next comedy heroine was born, raised, and began her film career in Brooklyn. Lillian Walker, originally Lillian Wolke, was born in 1888. After the death of her father she became the support of her family and besides modeling did many other jobs:

> "I was born in Brooklyn, and educated in the public schools here," she said. "Yes, I graduated, but I just got thru by the skin of my teeth. Then I was a telephone girl, a typewriter, various kinds of office assistant. Finally, I needed to make more money, and I saw an ad in the newspaper – Gus Edwards was looking for young girls for his vaudeville act, "School Boys and Girls." I went to see him and he shook his head at first. "You don't want to go on the stage," he said, "you'll lose your rosy cheeks." However, he took me on, and I played first with his school boys and girls; then I was one of his "Blonde Typewriters." After that I went with a melodrama "The Little Organ Grinder." Maurice Costello was in it, too. (*Motion Picture Magazine*, July 1913)

Lillian Walker Vitagraph star. Author's collection.

After touring she returned to New York, appeared in the *Follies* of 1910, and because she had what was called a "light voice" – difficult to project in a large theatre, she returned to modeling. A founder of a New York studio saw her photos and:

Mr. J. Stuart Blackton, of the Vitagraph company, gave me my first opportunity to appear on the screen; but I had to win my spurs – there was no royal road to fame. I played bit parts first; then small parts; then larger ones were entrusted to me; and today I am proud to be known as a Vitagraph star. (*Motion Pictures*, February 1916)

At first she was used as an all-purpose ingénue, often as John Bunny's daughter. In *An Elephant on Their Hands* (1912) she's the daughter of old drunkard George Ober, who while out on a spree buys a baby elephant and brings it home (into the house and up the stairs to be exact). Lillian, his wife Kate Price, and sister Flora Finch, are terrified and give the old man the what for once the little pachyderm is taken care of. *Mr. Bolter's Infatuation* (1912) gives her a more character part as a saucy actress who leads on romantically-inclined old bachelor John Bunny. Having seen her in a burlesque show he goes backstage to ask her out, and she tells him to call on her the next day at the Hotel des Imbeciles. Bunny spends the following morning having a terrible time trying to find his Hotel des Imbeciles until he realizes that the joke is on him.

Wally Van and Lillian Walker flirt in *Doctor Polly* (1914) as old family detainers Josie Sadler and William Shea look on. Billy Rose Theatre Division, the New York Public Library for the Performing Arts.

Other early survivors include *Stenographers Wanted* (1912) where the firm of Brown and Jones has advertised for a new stenographer. A bunch of girls show up – Brown (Bunny) likes a tall brunette, but Jones (Charles Eldridge) prefers Lillian. First they try out the brunette but she's frightened away by their fighting, and next they bring in Lillian who gets the job. That is until Mrs. Brown and Mrs. Jones show up and decide that she's entirely too pretty. Firing her they hire the ugly and bad-tempered Flora Finch to do the job. The last scene has Brown and Jones suffering with Flora, and giving each other the high-sign that they need to go out for a drink. Lillian is also one of the title characters in *The Lovesick Maidens of Cuddleton* (1912), where the old village doctor has retired and is replaced by a young and handsome physician. Mysteriously all the young village women get sick and need the attentions of the young doctor.

> I do a new picture-play every week, on the average," continues this attractive young actress, "so that stepping into and out of all sorts of queer characters becomes almost second nature to me. It is just one change after another, all day long. They are doing at least half-a-dozen different plays at this moment – a wild west drama in the back yonder, and a Boer War scene and the Bible story of Daniel out in the yard. And as a film-play has at least ten times as many scenes as a regular stage drama, you may imagine how busy and complicated our day is. To an outsider, it is a mad world, indeed. But, really, system and order are the key to it all. I like the excitement of it, and I could never be as happy at any other kind of stage work. (*Everybody's*, November 1913)

The size of her roles were increasing. In addition to working with Bunny she was frequently paired with Wally Van. A former civil engineer who worked as part of the engine crew on studio founder J. Stuart Blackton's racing boat, Wall Van (Nostrand) became a popular star, and also directed his own series of *Cutey* comedies. Walker spent a good deal of 1913 and 1914 as a romantic team with Van. *The Feudists* (1913) is a Vitagraph slapstick version of Romeo and Juliet as Lillian and Wally are lovers whose quarreling parents live next door to each other and erect a huge wall between their two yards. Beehives and dead cats are exchanged over the wall in combat, but the children finally trick their parents into a reconciliation so they can be married. This short was actually a "special feature in two parts" and had an all-star cast that included Bunny, Sidney Drew, Flora Finch, and Josie Sadler in addition to Van and Walker.

Other shorts from this period include *Bunny's Dilemma* (1913) where the old comic's rich Aunt Eliza, whom he's never met, is coming to visit and is bringing along her cousin who she wants him to marry. Happy in his bachelor life, Bunny gets his pal Wally to pose as Bunny, while the old comic gets in drag and masquerades as the cook. Aunt Eliza arrives and the cousin is the beautiful Lillian, who Bunny falls for immediately but doesn't want to blow his cover as the cook. When he tries to set up a clandestine meeting the heavily veiled woman who shows up turns out to be Aunt Eliza, so Bunny has to stand by and see Lillian successfully wooed by Wally. *Which Way Did He Go?* (1913) has Lillian and Wally as lovers again. This time their obstacle is Lillian's domineering mother Flora Finch, who hates Wally and has someone else for Lillian to marry. Pa Bunny sympathizes with Lillian and decides to help the couple elope. On the evening of the intrigue Lillian and Wally go off, but Pa is snagged on the ladder to Lillian's window by a nail, and is caught between irate Flora at the top of the ladder and the rival's bulldog at the bottom.

Lillian Walker and Wally Van have brought their parents John Bunny, Sidney Drew, Josie Sadler, and Flora Finch together in *The Feudists* (1913). Billy Rose Theatre Division, the New York Public Library for the Performing.

Continuing to work with Van in titles that include *Cutey's Vacation, Art for a Heart, The Boys of the I.O.U.*, and perhaps their most popular, *Love, Luck and Gasoline* (all 1914), Lillian's apprenticeship was over, and her smiling and sunny personality became the pride of the studio:

> Throughout the civilized world Miss Walker's nickname is "Dimples." She is an excellent swimmer, a good rider and has made many trips in aeroplanes. In the fall of 1913 she was elected Queen of the Coney Island (N.Y.) Mardi Gras, her fellow ruler being the late John Bunny, who was selected as the king. (*Vitagraph Life Portrayal*, February 1916)

Having played "Miss Tomboy" in *Love, Luck and Gasoline*, her series became unofficially known as the *Miss Tomboy* comedies with shorts such as *Fanny's Melodrama, Lillian's Dilemma*, and *Miss Tomboy and Freckles* (all 1914).

Although Miss Walker had won popularity in general comedy parts, it is in the Miss Tomboy series that she has gained the most favor. These pictures not only give her an opportunity to display her athletic talents, but also show her frolicsome nature. In fact, some of the best of them have been merely elaborations of practical jokes of her own devising and which she never intended for the films. Included in these stories are numerous forms of miscellaneous athletics, such as climbing down from upper windows of houses, jumping from moving surface cars and other feats regarded by most actresses as decidedly extracurriculum. (*New York Tribune,* April 19, 1914)

When Lillian became a full-fledged Vitagraph star in late 1914, the studio split up the team of Lillian and Wally Van (making two popular series instead of one). Van ended up with Nitra Frazer (see appendix) for his leading lady, and Lillian worked with light leading men like Billy Quirk, Darwin Karr, Arthur Ashey, and most frequently, Ewart Overton. "Dimples" became her popular character name, and was often used in the titles of her films such as *Dimples and the Ring* (1915), *Dimples the Diplomat,* and *Dimple's Baby* (both 1917). *Dimples, the Auto Salesgirl* (1915) concerns Dimples falling in love with "flivver" salesman Billy Quirk. When Billy asks for Dimples hand in marriage her father says no since "no man can make a living for my daughter selling "Flivver" cars." Dimples announces that she can sell "flivvers," and does using her feminine wiles to get wealthy old gentlemen, and everyone in their entire families, to buy them. Despite all the sales her father still proves obstinate, so the lovers take off in one of the "flivvers' with father following in his big car. The large auto is no match for the little "flivver" so the pair gets to the minister's home with plenty of time to spare.

The surviving *The Honeymoon Pact* (1915) has Lillian and Evart Overton returning home from their honeymoon trip and vowing to always continue their honeymoon – to have "no girl friends, no club friends – only their two selves – always together." This is great for a while, but eventually they both have strong desires to have good long chats with old friends. When their maid suddenly leaves to get married, Lillian gets an old school chum to replace her so they can catch up. At the same Evart does the same thing – putting an old buddy in as his chauffeur. The "maid" and

Vitagraph publicity photo for Walker's *Dimples* series. Courtesy of The Museum of Modern Art.

"chauffeur" fall for each other and elope. Lillian and Evart feel guilty as they are worried how the aristocratic families of each of their friends will react to them marrying "servants." When the pair confesses to each other their mutual breaking of the "honeymoon pact' – they're happy to find they've actually brought two of their friends together.

By 1916 most of Walker's long-time co-stars at Vitagraph – John Bunny, Flora Finch, Florence Turner, Wally Van, Mr. & Mrs. Sidney Drew – had left or were in the process of leaving the studio, but Lillian remained one of the company's big draws and was moved into longer pictures. Numerous four and five reel productions, some comedy and some drama, made her a feature star. *Green Stockings* (January 17, 1916) was the first with Lillian as the eldest daughter of a family who is treated like a servant. To stop her family's bad treatment she creates a fiancé, Colonel Smith, who's going to come and marry her. When she makes a big production about writing to him her sister mails it. Later, tiring of the pretense, she tells the family that her fiancé has died, but a real Colonel Smith, who had received the mailed letter, shows up and eventually marries her. According to the January 8, 1916 *Dramatic Mirror*:

> Although not a hilarious comedy, this play is highly amusing, and, moreover, it is continuously funny, not only the situations, but the plot itself. The comedy is of a quality seldom used in long plots, and what is more remarkable, the original qualities of the story are carried out faithfully on the screen. A more realistic comedy has seldom been produced, and there is not the least bit of artificiality. The characters are exceptionally true to life and a more creditable cast would be hard to pick. Lillian Walker is seen in an unusual role during the first part, that of an unmarriagable girl; but her engagement changes everything, and we again see her as her own vivacious self. Robert Travar is excellent in his portrayal of the English politician, and Adele de Garde shows marked talent in her portrayal of the aunt. The settings are very elaborate and the photography is exceptionally clear and distinct.

Titles such as *Mrs. Dane's Danger*, *Hesper of the Mountains*, *The Kid*, and *Kitty MacKay* (all 1916) followed which had Lillian portraying plucky girl reporters, eastern woman surviving out west, and spunky Scottish girls, in addition to utilizing her sex appeal:

> In her latest Vitagraph release "Indiscretion," Lillian Walker reveals considerably more of her physical charms than her usual fascinating dimples. In the opening scenes she is in a one-piece bathing suit, known in France as a "myo" (I'm not sure the spelling is correct, but you know what I mean). And Lillian has some figure. The visualization is as alluring as anything perpetrated by the daring Audrey Munson in her various nude revealments. Later on in the picture Miss Walker wears a most unbecoming evening gown. Of the two, it is safe to say most picture fans prefer the "myo." (*Variety*, February 2, 1917)

After a few early 1917 three-reelers such as *Dimples Baby, Dimples the Diplomat*, and *Sally in a Hurry*, she left Vitagraph, which had been her start in films and her home for six years. She was now breaking out on her own in the larger film industry and trying to embrace more serious films. Her first project was two features – *The Lust of the Ages* (1917) and *The Grain of Dust* (1918) – for the Ogden Pictures Corporation, a states' rights organization based in Utah. Besides Lillian as star, both features were directed by Harry Revier, who for many years would be on the edge of the exploitation industry with serials such as *The Lost City* (1935) and the infamous *Child Bride* (1938).

The supporting company is being organized by Lester Park, vice-president and general manager of the Ogden Pictures Corporation. A studio is ready at

Ogden, Utah, and plans are completed for starting the first picture within a few weeks. Albert Scowcroft, a leading Utah business man and a pioneer in the film business is president (*Motography*, April 21, 1917)

Both films were moralistic dramas. *The Grain of Dust* was about a woman who lures a successful businessman, and *The Lust of Ages* chronicled the lust for wealth in three different eras, and:

> presents Miss Walker in one of her few serious dramas. It is a propaganda play and afforded her, she said, opportunity to apply her talents before the camera to a more serious vein of the drama. "There are bits of comedy contained," said Miss Walker, "but only to relieve the more serious element of an essentially strong drama." (*Motion Picture News*, 1917)

Following these dramas, August 1918 saw the formation of the Lillian Walker Pictures Corporation, and ads announced:

The Most Refreshing Personality on the Screen – Lillian Walker – In a Series of Eight Happy Pictures

Production started at the Thanhouser Studio in New Rochelle, New York with former Biograph and Fine Arts director Edward Dillon in charge (see Fay Tincher section of Chapter Six). Lester Parks from Ogden Pictures was again president and general manager. Eddie Dillon appears to have only worked on the first release *The Embarrassment of Riches* (1918), and then the company moved to California to make the second *The Love Hunger* (1919). Out of the eight pictures announced only two appear to have been made. Both are lost, but the *Moving Picture World* described *The Love Hunger* when it was still being called *Fixing It*:

> Lillian Walker plays the role of a girl who has been brought up in the circus, but decides she wants a real home and love that is rightfully hers. In the town of Littleberg she appears before Hamilton Gregory, an exhorter, and demands a home, but finds that in the bosom of the righteous is not always to be found the truest religion. A child of nature, the girl's simplicity and faith eventually bring happiness to others. The part is light comedy, with some splendid dramatic moments, and Miss Walker is given every opportunity to display her versatility. (February 8, 1919)

During production of the two films she told Beulah Livingston in the November 1918 *Photo-Play Journal* of her plans for the series:

> I am always best on the screen when I am just myself, and it is for that reason, you see, that I have formed my own company. Now I can choose my own stories and they will all be happy pictures. I am planning to make eight five-reel

comedies a year. Perhaps later on, I will also make some two-reelers, as I feel that there is a splendid market for short comedies on joint programs. Neither sex problem nor stories of the underworld will play any part in my own productions. It has ever been my contention that a story need be none the less interesting just because it happens to be clean and pleasant. I am old-fashioned enough to like best the kind of pictures in which the hero and the heroine are close in each other's arms at the finish. I like to see all of their obstacles overcome, even at the expense of plausibility if necessary. I think the picture where the guttersnipe becomes the heiress in the end is fine. I prefer modern pictures to costume or period films because I adore everything up-to-date. That feeling of being current with your times always thrills me, particularly such as we are now experiencing when a new history is being written every day.

After the dissolving of her company she appeared as a leading lady for J. Warren Kerrigan, worked as support in features such as *The Better Wife* (1919), *A Woman of No Importance*, and *The Woman God Changed* (both 1921), and even starred in the Ithaca, New York-made serial *The $1,000,000 Reward* (1920 and it's re-cut feature version *The Evil Dead* in 1922). Her last film before a seven-year hiatus was the British-made *Love's Boomerang* (1922). When sound hit the industry she attempted to return to work, but was only able to get roles in the Robert Florey-directed short *The Pusher In-the-Face* (1929) and the exploitation feature *Enlighten Your Daughters* (1934). In 1932 she had appeared as herself in one of Educational Pictures' *Broadway Gossip* one-reelers, a series that *Film Daily* described as:

> The inside stories of various celebs who were once in the money but are now more or less in the discard are presented with a very human and interesting slant. Good diversity of subject matter, with a running commentary that explains each individual past and present, with remarks by the subject in question.

Lillian was interviewed by columnist Leo Donnelly and described her struggle to make a living on a small farm in New York State. According to an undated clipping in a scrapbook kept by her old co-star Wally Van, at about this time she was suing a secret husband, whom she had married in 1910, for divorce and an alimony settlement. Lillian claimed that she and Charles E. Hanson had only lived together as man and wife for a week in 1910 before he moved out and set up separate living quarters, declining her pleadings for him to return. Over the years he had borrowed money from her, and at the time of the divorce suit he was a wealthy New York real estate operator.

The last bit of information available on the actress is that she died in 1975 at age eighty-eight in Trinidad, so she may have won her alimony and taken the money and moved out of the country many years after she and her film career were forgotten.

The next two ladies – Billie Rhodes and Betty Compson – carried on the tradition started by Victoria Forde as a "Christie Girl." Billie Rhodes was born Levita Axelrod in San Francisco in 1894, and began her career on stage there on the Orpheum Circuit. She told accompanist/writer Stuart Oderman in 1968:

I started singing there when I was eleven. I was a single, which means I worked alone. The act was six minutes. Two songs separated by a dance and that was it. I could pass for sixteen and I dressed "old" if you know what I mean. But I never travelled alone. My older sister was my chaperone.

Billie Rhodes. Courtesy of Jim Kerkhoff.

Wanting to do more than sing in vaudeville, she got a job in dramatic stock with the Morrison Stock Company so she could learn to act:

An agent by the name of William Menzel helped me get a job with a 10-20-30 drama rep group. It was headed by an actress named Laura Hudson. I appeared in Three Weeks written by Elinor Glynn and I also did a play called The Devil. Both of those plays were pretty strong stuff. I was a maid, a French maid in Three Weeks and I was a tart in The Devil. I was about thirteen when I did these roles.

The big show that really made people aware of me was Victor Herbert's Babes in Toyland. The girl couldn't finish the run in San Francisco and the show had four weeks to play in Los Angeles.

After the run of *Babes in Toyland* she was back in San Francisco, and began singing in cafes along the pier in Santa Monica. At a café named Brinks she was seen by George Melford, who was scouting new talent for the Kalem Film Company. Melford, who would later become a director and helm Rudolph Valentino in *The Sheik* (1921) and make the Spanish version of Universal's *Dracula* (1931), was impressed and thought she was perfect for some upcoming films:

One of their staff people, Jimmy Haine, had just completed writing six scenarios and there were parts for a young girl.

The Kalem Studio used a lot of natural sunlight in their movies" says Billie. "Their sets had no ceilings and if they had to shoot the inside of a living room for a domestic scene or society party, they would readjust the canvas covers they stretched over the rollers. That was the way they were able to control the light.

We acted on platform stages and yes, we did have scripts. That is, we knew what the story was about and what the intention of each scene was. And we knew where we supposed to stand and walk.

We made pictures pretty quickly. A reel a week and sometimes more. We used local people for crowd scenes and that made the films seem more natural. A three reeler took a month to film and that was considered a feature.

They filmed stories about everything, even Indian life. They had an authentic Indian star, Mona Darkfeather, who both acted and served as technical advisor.

It was a nice company, but nobody stayed there very long. My leading men were Carlyle Blackwell and Paul Hurst. Mr. Blackwell was a very handsome leading man. Dashing and rugged, if you know what I mean. We made Perils of the Sea together.

Billie spent 1913 working for Kalem. In addition to *Perils of the Sea* she also appeared in action and western pictures such as *A Daughter of the Underworld*, *The Chinese Death Thorn*, *Indian Fate*, and *The Vengeance of the Vaquero*. She was still singing in clubs and was seen by Al Christie, who was turning out comedies for the Nestor Company:

I made my debut in 1914 when Nestor studios were very new. The second company headed by Mr. Christie liked my face and the way I performed. Other studios had girls: the Biograph girl, etc., so I was the Nestor Girl.

Mr. Christie was a nice man. He had a very good approach to comedy. By that, I mean he wanted comedy to grow out of the situation. He didn't like a string of sight gags that did nothing for the story. He used to tell the actor, "Act. Act. Don't stand there making funny faces." He hated slapstick comedy. He thought slapstick was vulgar and crude.

Mr. Christie didn't want to be a Sennett imitator and turn out an imitation Sennett product. He didn't think Sennett comedies were all that funny. The people at Sennett's place always seemed to be throwing pies at each other or chasing up and down hills or playing in mud. Mr. Christie didn't want a troupe of actors to play in mud. He wanted a more refined comedy.

It was a nice company to work with: Lee Moran, Jay Belasco, Eddie Lyons, Victoria Forde. We were a little rep company. Mr. Christie thought of us as an ensemble and we knew how to play off each other when the cameras were rolling.

Small (5ft), petite, and dark-haired with huge eyes, Billie did have a resemblance to Mabel Normand, although she felt "the kind of comedy I did was light comedy, not the knockabout comedy that Sennett did." Nestor released their one-reelers through Universal and were often turned out twice a week. Billie was always the young girl, the heroine, the ingénue. Her first film for the company was *A Maid by Proxy* (1915) where Billie plays a young lady who meets a famous novelist in an art gallery. They become friendly, but Billie's aunt warns her that men like him are not to be trusted so they decide to put him to a test. The author is invited to a party at their home where Billie pretends to be a maid. He likes her anyway, so Billie and the aunt put him through more hoops until he eventually figures out the deceptions and all comes together for a happy ending.

His Wife's Husband (1915) is another of her early Nestor's where she's paired with her frequent co-star Jack Dillon:

> Jack and Billie are secretly married and start house-keeping. Jack's college chum comes to visit them. Everything is happy until word is received from Jack's parents that they are coming to visit him, bringing with them the girl they expect him to marry.
>
> To save his inheritance, Jack persuades his chum to pose as the husband of his own bride. Many amusing complications ensue. Finally the college chum secretly weds the girl whom Jack's parents have brought with them.
>
> The dilemma is finally straightened out and the two married couples receive the blessings of the old people. (*Universal Weekly*, March 6, 1915)

In July 1915 Universal noted that Billie was transferred from the second Nestor comedy company, where she was

Billie makes a model bride for Christie Comedies. Author's collection.

mostly directed by Horace Davy, to the first company under Christie's personal supervision. The studio also noted "Miss Rhodes has been with the Universal western forces the greater part of a year and during that time has earned for herself an enviable reputation as a screen actress."

Continuing on with their non-stop output, *Her Hero Maid* (1916) concerns Lee Moran as the leading man of a theatre company and at the last performance of the season he notices a "peach" sitting in the audience. The "peach" is Billie, and he meets her the next day when she's down town to put in an advertisement for a maid. Lee decides to pose as the maid to be near Billie, and ingratiates "herself" in the household. A rich young man is a persistent caller of Billie's, who detests him, but her mother favors him as he's rich. When he shows up and gets overly affectionate Lee clocks him, and the rest of the staff admires the maid's strength. Eventually he is caught changing into the maid, but it all works out happily as the aunt decides that Lee has true devotion because he was willing to do the duties of a maid.

His Wooden Leg (1916) has Billie and Ray Gallagher as newlyweds. Hubby's old wooden-legged uncle, a major who served in battles, is coming to live with them. The old man is difficult but the newlyweds try to please him as he's said to be wealthy. He becomes unjustly angry at them and leaves. Several months later they get news that uncle has passed away and have left them his most treasured possession – his wooden leg. Unnerved by the leg they try many ways to get rid of it but it always is retuned to them. The last time Ray is so disgusted that he slams the leg down on the sidewalk and it breaks. Turns out it is filled with money, so besides gathering up the money Billie and Ray keep the remnants of the wooden leg as a remembrance of uncle.

In September 1916 the trade magazines announced:

Christie Comedies Will Be Placed on the Open Market. Al E. Christie, one of the best directors of light comedy in the business, has announced the placing of his entire output on the open market. During the past three months since Mr. Christie severed his connections with Universal, he has steadily been producing one-reel comedies with the result that at the present time he has about ten subjects ready to distribute to the independent exchanges when he is ready to start releasing (*Motion Picture News*, September 9, 1916)

After many years in the business Christie and his brother Charles decided to incorporate, and create the Christie Film Company, their own outfit. Most of his regular players went with him, and they were kept busy by two units – one led by Horace Davy and the other by Christie. Billie remembered:

I left with Mr. Christie. It was around 1916. Other Nestor people left. Mr. Christie wanted to start his own studio, work with people he had developed and continue to turn out the type of comedy he believed people wanted to see.

I had a 52 picture contract. Fifty-two pictures a year. A reel a week. I was signed at $250 a week.

Mr. Christie wasn't a very good business man once he had his own place to run. They found themselves in bad financial trouble and a lot of his people were without jobs. I managed to get my salary and I stayed around, but when contact renewal came up, I told him I wanted to leave.

Many of the independent Christies' came out under the Cub Comedies banner and were distributed by Mutual. Billie starred in many of these such as *Catching that Burglar, Oh! For a Caveman, Won by a Fowl,* and *His Blushing Bride* (all 1916). She was a co-ed in *Their College Capers* (1916) who decides to go with the boys to an off-limits prize fight. The girls dress as boys and go, followed by one of the professors, but the fight is raided and the whole group is rounded up and taken to jail.

Billie and her frequent co-star Jay Belasco in an unidentified Strand Comedy. Courtesy of The Museum of Modern Art.

When Christie had some financial problems Billie took a break to take some stage offers and visit her family:

> When Mr. Christie had capital to work with, I rejoined the studio. Mr. Christie was going to release his films through the Mutual Corporation. I was in their first Strand Comedy, Her Hero. I also did Beware of Blondes with Cullen Landis as my co-star and I did several films with Jay Belasco. They were a lot of fun to make. They were very popular and I received quite a lot of fan mail.

Fifty-Two One Reel Comedies For Mutual To Feature Billie Rhodes: "Her Hero," First, Comes April 11. Billie Rhodes, the well-known comedienne, will be featured in a series of fifty-two one-reel comedies to be published through Mutual under the general title of Strand Comedies.

Miss Rhodes will be assisted by Jay Belasco of the noted Belasco family and well-known for his work in juvenile leads on the stage, vaudeville and the screen.

The production of the Strand Comedies will be under the direction of Al Christie.

John R. Freuler, present of the Mutual Film Corporation, has signed a contract with H.B. Caulfield of the Caulfield Photoplay Company for this series of comedies. These comedies will be scheduled for publication through Mutual on Wednesday of each week, starting April 11: the first three films will be "Her Hero," April 11; "When Mary Took the Count," April 18; "And in Walked Uncle," April 25.

"The Strand Comedies," says Mr. Freuler, "will give the exhibitor just the class of picture which will please everybody in the audience. Utterly devoid of any element of slapstick, the Strand Comedies are filled with clean, wholesome fun. They are built around the love affairs, quarrels and adventures of young people, and depict laughable incidents of everyday life." (*Exhibitors Herald*, March 31, 1917)

Billie appeared in over fifty of the Strands, and a few of them are still around to be viewed today. In *Somebody's Widow* (1918) Billie and her girlfriends are at the beach. Cullen Landis is a young writer who comes to the beach hotel to finish a serial story. When taking a break on the beach he ignores the girls, and Billie bets her friends that she can get his attention. She dresses in black with a veil pretending to be a widow, and positions herself so he's sure to see her weeping. He definitely notices her, and stunned by her beauty tries to comfort her. Billie goes back and gloats to her friends, so one of the girls decides to trick her and tells Cullen's secretary the truth. The secretary passes along the information that she is not a widow, so Cullen gets the secretary to dress up as Billie's "husband" and accuse her of being unfaithful, etc. It all ends up in a chase around the hotel, and when Billie appeals to Cullen for help he reveals the joke. Everyone has a good laugh as Billie and Cullen walk together on the beach.

Her Rustic Romeo (1918) has Billie as an actress whose director is going to star her in a rural drama so he sends her to a farm to study types and acquire a "good Rube dialect." On the farm she falls for Cullen, the new hired man. Tildy the neighbor girl falls for Cullen too, much to the jealousy of Si, the farmer's son. Billie finds out that Cullen is an actor also sent by the director to study, and when Tildy is upset because he won't pay attention to her, Billie advises her to throw herself at him. She does, and Cullen ends up hightailing it back to the city. When Billie returns for the first day of rehearsals for the rural play, she surprises Cullen and has a good laugh at his expense.

In *Waltzing Around* (1918) Billie's girlfriend loves to dance but her husband has two left feet. Billie volunteers to teach him the latest steps so he can surprise his wife at the next club dance. The plot thickens when the wife gets wind that her hubby's made an appointment to meet another woman, and not knowing it's Billie, thinks the worst. Billie's boyfriend also gets suspicious, and the situation comes to a climax when both parties trail Billie and hubby to one of their dancing lessons and come in upon them while Billie's demonstrating *The Honolulu Wiggle*.

> But things got a little tough. When I had rejoined Mr. Christie and had started making more films, I met Billy Parsons who wanted me to do two comedies for his company, National Film Company. I would do these films on approval, which means I wouldn't get a contract unless the New York office liked them. So, for a while, I had a busy schedule, working for Mr. Christie and then doubling and doing two films for National Film Company.

> Mr. Christie heard what I had done and he was quite upset. He'd yell and make all kinds of threats. "I found you and I developed your character and your style of acting and now you're going to walk out on me' and you can imagine the rest. The New York people liked the two films I did and they were going to sign me up at a good salary, much better than Mr. Christie. They seemed more reliable than Mr. Christie. Mr. Christie was always making salary adjustments. Half salary, then no salary, then back to full salary, when things got better. He was a very nice man, but you can't keep people dangling all their careers.

William Parsons, a.k.a. "Smiling Bill" Parsons, was a former M.D. and insurance salesman who set up his National Film Corporation in 1915. Acquiring the old Oz Film Studio he began producing shorts starring himself and other comics, distributing them through General Film. He temporarily cut back his performing to concentrate on producing, and had a tremendous success with his 1918 feature adaptation of *Tarzan of the Apes*. Parsons returned to the screen in 1918, and was very popular with his everyman persona – bald and overweight – and was perfect as henpecked husbands or crotchety bachelors. He also produced other series with the teams of Mr. and Mrs. Carter De Haven and Ned Flannigan & Neely Edwards, and scored distribution through Samuel Goldwyn. Billie had supported Parsons in a few shorts like *Bill's Baby* (1918) as her tryout for the New York people.

> I took the offer from Mr. Parsons which was three hundred a week for the first year, five hundred for the second year, and seven hundred and fifty for the third year. It was a three year contract. I did six six-reel features.

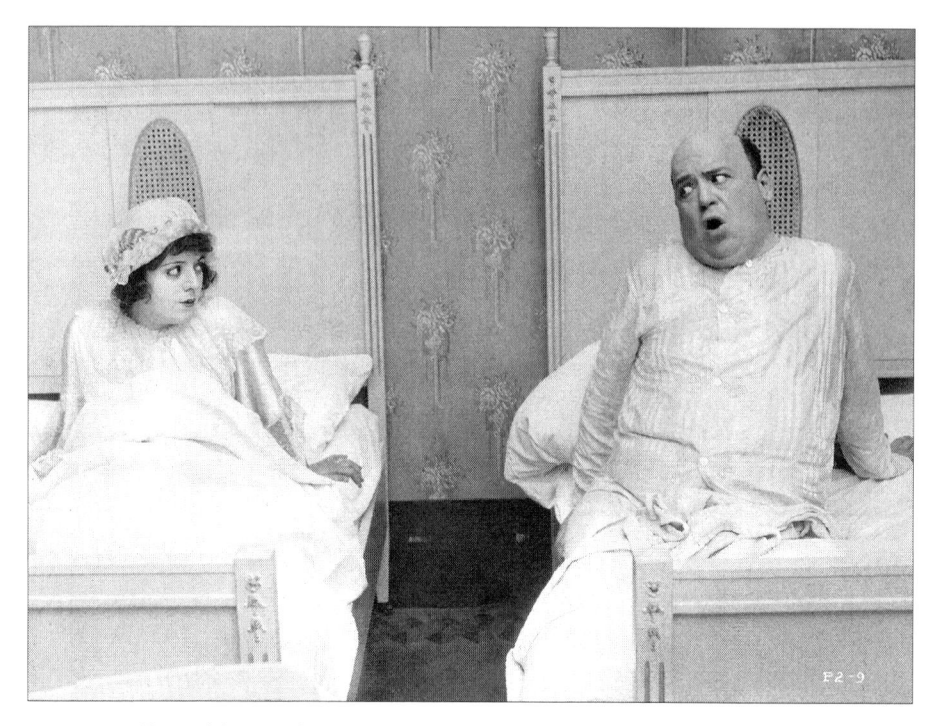

Billie with her producer and soon to be husband "Smiling Bill" Parsons in *Bill's Predicament* (1918). Courtesy of Robert S. Birchard.

Eight features were planned by Mr. Parsons, of which Billie did seven and married Parsons to boot. It's generally overlooked that she starred in features, in part because most of them are missing. *The Girl of My Dreams* (1918), *The Lamb and the Lion*, *The Love Call*, *In Search of Arcady*, and *Miss Nobody* (all 1919) are lost with only *Hoop-La* and *The Blue Bonnet* (both 1919) known to survive. Parsons was managing her career and the plan was to make her a dramatic star. Most of these features were light comedies with dramatic moments such as *The Lamb and the Lion* in which she was a waif who was raised by a gang of crooks and ends up married into a wealthy family. Mr. Parsons produced them through his National Film Corporation with distribution by the W.W. Hodkinson Corporation.

> They were quite elaborate. Louis Chaudet directed one of them, Hoopla a circus story and he also directed The Blue Bonnet. We shot these films in New York City. The Blue Bonnet is a Salvation Army story and they made the clothes I wear in the film.

What stopped the trajectory of her feature career was Mr. Parsons' death at age forty-one on September 28, 1919. Only married for about a year, his death was caused by pneumonia, which according to *Photoplay* was aggravated by:

The effects of an accident which happened in the studio about a year ago. Parsons was doing a comedy scene at the time, in which large blocks of ice were used, and a heavy cake fell on his chest causing a hemorrhage.

Suddenly a widow, Billie spent some time in seclusion. The January 1920 issue of *Photoplay* reported:

Billie Rhodes, widow of "Smiling Bill" Parsons, has announced her retirement from the screen, owning to the death of her husband. She has even declined to go ahead with "Hearts and Masks," the Harold McGrath story, and will be replaced by Elinor Field.

But she soon went back to work and tried to continue with features. *His Pajama Girl* (1920) was an independent production that had the involvement of a lot of her old Christie work mates – the story was co-written by Scott Darling, and the supporting cast comprised of Harry Hamm, Eddie Barry, Harry Rattenberry, and George French – but the result, according to the *Moving Picture World* was: "…a somewhat confusing combination. It starts off as a melodrama, wherein the ruler of Mexico is abducted by crooks and then switches into a rough and tumble comedy with chases over roofs, down fire escapes, etc., making it somewhat difficult for the spectator to adjust his viewpoint."

> I did a lot of independent films in those days," Billie remembers." His Pajama Girl was a one-picture deal. At least, that was the way it turned out. I did the film for C.B. Price, an independent distributor. I don't know how the film did. I never saw very much of it except maybe a few rushes at the end of the day. I don't know if the film had any bookings. The company fell apart after the film was completed.

She did other features such as *The Star Reporter* (1921) and *Daddy's Love* (1922), and made a return to comedy shorts. This time though she wasn't the star, but the supporting leading lady for the male comics Billy West and Joe Rock. She did at least two shorts, *Don't Be Foolish* and *You'd Be Surprised* (both 1922), as part of Billy West's CBC Sunrise Comedies series, and numerous two-reelers with Joe Rock. Having made his name as part of the Vitagraph duo of Montgomery and Rock, Joe Rock went solo at the end of 1920, and began producing his own starring comedies. Billie joined him in 1922 for titles such as *Little Red Robin Hood*, *Ali Baba* (both 1922), *The Cold Homestead*, *Too Much Dutch*, *Laughing Gas* (all 1923), and *It's a Bear* (1924) that were distributed by Grand Asher and Federated.

In *Chop Suey Louie* (1923) Joe is a sailor whose ship is in port in China, and Billie is a young American whom the Chinese ganglord (Shy Won Lung) has set his sights on. Joe rescues her from Lung's kidnapping attempt, but the thugs got a rare watch that her father had given her. Father says he'd give anything to get the watch back so Joe gets him to agree to let him marry Billie if he retrieves the ticker. Joe gets the watch, and the bulk of the film is his eluding the ganglord's minions so he can deliver it to father. Once Joe returns it Billie is kidnapped again, and the rest of the short is another rescue. Although just as charming as usual Billie doesn't get much of an opportunity to do more than stand around and be pretty in her surviving Rock shorts. Unfortunately there was no way she could return to the Christie organization. Not only were there his hard feelings about her leaving him to go with Billy Parsons, but in 1919 she "was awarded a judgement for nearly a thousand dollars said to be due her by Al Christie for unpaid salaries."

Two more features followed in 1924. *Leave It to Gerry* was a six reel Ben Wilson production that was distributed by Grand-Asher and was another comedy-drama that starred Billie as a tomboyish girl who is separated from her mother and is taken East to live with wealthy relatives. While she's away her mother is dispossessed by the mortgageholder and oilman and sent to a poorhouse, as they're trying to get ahold of her property. Oil has been discovered on it. Billie returns from the East and puts everything right. This surviving film had solid direction from Arvid E. Gillstrom, and support from comedy regulars on the order of Blanche Payson, Glen Cavender, and Ena Gregory. The available facts are very vague about the other feature, *Fires of Youth*. It may never have been released. Billie remembered:

> I came in after they started making the picture. A middle-aged couple starred in the film and I played their youngster. They never had any real shooting script and as the filming progressed, my part got bigger. I never heard anything more about it. I left after my work was done and they were still shooting.

**Billie gets a call from a delayed Joe Rock in *Laughing Gas* (1924).
Courtesy of EYE Filmmuseum, Netherlands.**

Her last film was the Joe Rock-produced Ton of Fun two-reeler *Three Wise Goofs* (1925). Frank Alexander, Hilliard Karr, and Kewpie Ross are up to their usual extra-large antics, this time with Billie as their sister, and while she seems to be having a good time and enjoying their antics, she again doesn't have much to do.

My sister was living in Chicago and I went there in 1926 to spend some time with her, frankly, just to get out of Hollywood. I think the truth is I wanted a change. A complete change.

I never gave a thought to talkies. By the time they were here, I was singing in nightclubs in Chicago.

I was never a wild party girl and I never lived beyond my means. I saved my money and one day I woke up and said, "I've had it." And I just stopped working. I was able to get out gracefully. Oh sure, I had good times and it was fun, but it was fun only when I said to myself that it was time to get out.

She kept busy, doing what she liked, until her death at ninety-three in 1988.

The third major female Christie star of the teens was Betty Compson, although she's better remembered today for her later dramatic turns in *The Miracle Man* (1919) and *The Docks of New York* (1928), as well as being the wife of director James Cruze. Born Eleanor Luicime Compson in Beaver City, Utah in 1897, her father was a ne'er-do-well who left the family for the gold fields of Alaska when Luicime (the Betty came later) was just a few months old. Her mother worked for several years as a domestic before her father returned with $25,000, which sadly was almost immediately lost in the stock market. The family moved to Salt Lake City where her father opened a grocery store, but he contracted tuberculosis and died in 1912. Mrs. Compson went back to work while Luicime attended high school. Studying music, she played the violin, which came in handy for extra money:

My music teacher, George E. Skelton, finally found me a job as a violinist at the Mission Theatre. Vaudeville – two or three short motion pictures of the vintage of 1912 – and that was my first contact with the screen. Picture my playing a soft accompaniment to Earle William's love-making and imaging myself his leading lady. (*Sunday Mirror Magazine Section*, 1933)

She made $15 a week, and when one of the acts went on a drinking binge she was asked to fill in with her violin. Not having any fancy clothes she went on barefoot and in ragged clothes as a street urchin:

I became an actress very suddenly. One night an act that had gone alcoholic failed to appear. I was put on stage to play a violin solo. My friends applauded – and that was how it happened that I quit my job, joined a small new company under an amateur promoter. We played a skit at Ogden, went to San Francisco – and disbanded. I had to find work, and did, playing cheap theatres in and around San Francisco, from the Barbary Coast to San Jose. My mother joined me and we went gloriously broke, ending the summer by working as domestics in the home of the wealthy John J. Haviside, and after that at a summer resort in Inverness. But I never ceased to think of myself as an actress.

And when Margaret Whitney, a Salt Lake woman, organized an act called "The Wrong Bird," which was booked over the Pantages circuit, I got a job at $25 a week. I played the violin. This act succeeded and "The Shadow Girl" followed it.

Hollywood legend and Christie publicity told the story that Al Christie "discovered" her after seeing her perform at the Pantages Theatre in Los Angeles, but Betty said that story wasn't true. Her version has her on tour in Alberta, Canada when:

Betty Compson and "Smiling" Billy Mason in *Cupid's Camouflage* (1917). Courtesy of Cole Johnson.

I ran into an old actor Robert Bradbury, and told him I had screen ambitions. He said:

"It's easy, Luicime. You're a pretty girl. You'd be great in pictures. I'll tell you what – when you get down there on this trip, call Al McQuarrie, who plays character roles at Universal City. I know a photographer in Portland who'll make some pictures for you and let you pay him a little each week.

The act reached Los Angeles. I telephoned McQuarrie, who said: "If you've got half the stuff Bob Bradbury says you have, you'll be a sensation!" Through him I was finally introduced to Al Christie, who was associated with his brother, Charles Christie, in making short comedies. I had a screen test, with the usual noncommittal "I'll let you know." Hundreds of girls had been turned away with the same soothing promise. But I didn't know that. I wrote my mother that I'd been "signed."

The tour over, I returned to Salt Lake to find a letter from Al Christie calling me to work.

Christie was working for the Nestor Company, producing and directing one-reelers. He told Luicime to report to Universal City:

Christie was brief. He wanted me at $40 a week, to play as leading lady opposite Eddie Lyons and Lee Moran. Of course I accepted. Then he studied me and said:

"Luicime…..sounds like a vegetable. The exhibitors wouldn't be able to spell it – say – Betty. Betty Compson. Swell! Report to work at 9 tomorrow morning, Betty.

Her first film was *Wanted: A Leading Lady* (1915), which she said was a fictionalized version of her coming to the studio. Making an extremely positive impression, she was set, and was busy making shorts:

Up at six, at work at seven, so the director might use all the sunshine. The sets had no roofs, for we depended entirely on the sun. Gertrude Astor, a leading woman, showed me how to put on make-up. Eddie Lyons and Lee Moran welcomed me as their leading lady with genial smiles.

I was young, had plenty of fun and ambition in me, had lots of hard experience and didn't mind the aching work. Those Christie comedy roles demanded plenty of trick falls, punchings, slappings, rough-houses in which they hurled bric-a-brac. Sometimes they worked in the rain, soaked to the skin. For some reason directors always chose the coldest winter days for making scenes in which we had to fall into swimming pools, tanks or the ocean.

When we weren't making pictures – imagine this today – Al Christie would call me into the office to help write advertising copy for the motion picture trade journals! One of my masterpieces showed a poker-hand with three kings and two queens, with insert pictures of Lyons, Moran, Neal Burns, Billie Rhodes, and myself and the line above: "Draw a Full House."

Betty's second film was *Their Quiet Honeymoon* (1915) that has Eddie and Lee as star members of the Bachelor's Club. As they're the only two bachelors left in the organization they make a bet that the first to marry will pay the other $500. Of course they go out and each marry immediately, and spend the rest of the film trying to keep the marriages a secret from each other as neither wants to pay the money. After many misadventures that include hiding in various rooms, running up and down fire escapes, and suspicious hotel detectives, the boys declare it a tie and call the bet off.

Not many of Betty's Nestor shorts survive. One of the rarities is *The Deacon's Waterloo* (1916). Betty and Eddie Lyons are young lovers who are both in the church choir. It turns out that Deacon Squibbs (Lee Moran), the leader of the choir, is also sweet on her. The Deacon sees Betty and Eddie together and decides to take action. At the end of rehearsal it's pouring rain, and since the Deacon brought his umbrella he gets to take Betty home. The next day he comes back to her house to ask for her hand, but having been put wise by Betty, Eddie determines to put the Deacon out of the way. The Deacon arrives in a buggy, and leaves the horse outside. Eddie and his friends steal a life-sized wooden horse used as an advertisement for a livery stable, and exchange it with the Deacon's horse. They then send word that the Deacon is wanted for an emergency at the church, and he rushes out without popping the question to Betty. Hurriedly jumping into the buggy the Deacon furiously tries to get the horse to go, and doesn't realize the switch until the livery owner and a cop show up. The Deacon is arrested and taken to jail, which Betty is enjoying from her vantage point in the house. With the Deacon out of the way Eddie talks to Betty's father and gets his consent. The film ends with Betty and Eddie having a good laugh over the Deacon's Waterloo.

Betty said that her favorite of the series was playing a princess in *Where the Heather Blooms* (1915), but her other Nestors included *Cupid Trims his Lordship* (1916) in which Betty's title-crazy parents try to hook her up with the wealthy Lord Cheestowers Cranberry, who is a phoney. Eddie is a traveling salesman but truly in love with Betty and does his best to expose Cranberry. Eddie clears things up just in the nick of time, and is able to win Betty's hand. Less than a year after Betty joined Nestor Al Christie decided to leave the firm and set up his own company. Two production units were set up, with Billie Rhodes and Betty the stars of each. Christie ballyhooed to the press:

> The stars and support under the Christie banner deserve mention. Billie Rhodes, leading lady, is one of the most popular of comediennes, bright, vivacious and skilled in her work. Betty Compson, who plays with the other company, is also gaining popularity with each new release. She is undoubtedly one of the prettiest girls on the screen today and her presence adds much to the value of any picture. Dave Morris and Eddie Barry have a great appreciation for eccentric parts, while Neal Burns and Harry Ham handle straight roles adequately, the former sometimes appearing in character as well.
>
> In support of these players there are Harry Rattenberry, Stella Adams, Gus Alexander, Ethel Lynne, Jane Waller, Nolan Leary and others, most of them people whose faces are familiar to picture audiences throughout the country.

Like Billie Rhodes, Betty appeared in the regular Christies and his Cub Comedies. One of her surviving Cubs is *Inoculating Hubby* (1916). Betty and Neal Burns are newlyweds who get an announcement from Betty's mother that she's coming to teach the young couple how to run their house. The idea doesn't appeal to Neal who consults with his friend the doctor who offers sympathy. Mother arrives and disrupts the household and Neal, unable to stand it, comes home only after the old lady has retired. Disgruntled by Neal, mother sees an ad in the paper for a serum by a Professor Pill that makes wayward husbands gentle and home-loving. When mother goes to see Professor Pill about giving a shot of his serum to Neal, his doctor friend overhears the conversation and substitutes water for the serum. The doctor then puts Neal wise to the plot, so when the old lady jabs him with the hypo he begins acting like a cat – purring, meowing, licking himself, and lapping cream from a saucer. Mother calls Pill to reverse the serum and restore Neal, and Betty and the doctor upbraid her so terribly that she packs up and heads for home. Getting the result that he wanted, Neal is cured of his "feline-itis."

Another that came out as part of the regular Christie brand was *Those Primitive Days* (1916), which is exactly what the title suggests with Betty, Neal Burns, and David Morris as cavepeople at the dawn of civilization. Betty is Heela Hoola the belle of the primitive community. Of course she has various suitors such as Stony Kone, Hairy Hand, and Little Big Club, fighting for her hand. After a terrific battle Betty ends up with her favorite, Willy Walla, and together they go to Willie's cave in great happiness.

Other titles include *Sauce for the Goose, Crazy by Proxy, Love and Locksmiths* (all 1917), *Somebody's Baby*, and *Betty's Adventure* (both 1918). Betty appeared in more than fifty Christie Comedies in the two years from 1916 to 1918, but in late 1918 she left the company. Multiple reasons have been given for the split – one version has the producer firing her for refusing to make a personal appearance, another cites Christie's perennial money problems. Betty later said that she wanted to do more than slapstick:

**Adolph Menjou uses his charms on Betty in *The Fast Set* (1924).
Courtesy of Bruce Calvert.**

For one thing my increasing knowledge of Hollywood's ways told me that I was committing the most deadly of all mistakes. I was allowing myself to become "typed."

A girl who stayed too long as a comedy girl, or a serial queen, or a western heroine, was thought of by the producers as a comedy girl, a serial queen, or western girl – and that was that. The particular grade I wanted to make was to break away from type and get into a full-length feature picture. Once you do that, and succeed, you were accepted as a versatile actress. Then you'd get chances to do any kind of role.

On her own she moved around – doing a short, *The Sheriff* (1918) opposite Roscoe "Fatty" Arbuckle, the western serial *The Terror of the Range* (1919) with daredevil George Larkin for Pathé, in addition to some features. She was a leading lady in the westerns *Border Raiders* (1918), *The Prodigal Liar,* and *The Devil's Trail* (both 1919), was support for Baby Marie Osborne in *The Little Diplomat* (1919), and had a solid dramatic starring role as an alcoholic who is redeemed by an act of heroism in *Light of Victory* (1919). What set her feature career on course and really made her a star was *The Miracle Man* (1919).

A melodrama based on a play by George M. Cohan about a gang of crooks and their plot to bilk a community with a fake faith healer, the picture was expertly directed by George Loane Tucker and a huge hit that made stars out of Betty, Thomas Meighan, and Lon Chaney. On the strength of this film Betty set up her own production company with Mr. Tucker as the artistic supervisor. He directed her again in *Ladies Must Live* (1921) but died that year of cancer at age forty-one. After *The Little Minister* (1922) her company was dissolved, and Betty appeared in various undistinguished films, even working in England for titles such as *The Royal Oak* (1923) and *The White Shadow* (1924). Becoming known as the "Queen of Poverty Row," these quickly-made features added little to the luster of her name. One exception to this trend, and one of Betty's best films, was the 1925 Paramount comedy *Paths to Paradise*.

A sly and elegant crook comedy, deftly played with split-second comic timing by an expert ensemble, *Paths to Paradise* was directed by Clarence Badger, one of the top comedy directors of the 1920s, and teamed Betty with one of the overlooked masters of silent comedy - Raymond Griffith. Her next film, *The Pony Express* (1925), was noteworthy as it was a collaboration with her husband James Cruze, but the peak of her career was 1928 with the dramas *The Docks of New York* and *The Barker*. Although *The Barker* was finished as a silent, talking sequences were added, which gave Betty a solid transition to the new sound medium and garnered her an Oscar nomination.

Outside of *The Great Gabbo* (1929), where she was again directed by James Cruze and supported Erich von Stroheim, the bulk of her starring sound films were routine, and by the mid-1930s she was playing supporting roles. She retired from films in 1948. Besides a few stage appearances, she ran a cosmetics business and also started Ashtrays Unlimited, which supplied personalized ashtrays to hotels and restaurants. She died in 1974.

Betty and Raymond Griffith are very well matched in *Paths to Paradise* (1925). Courtesy of Bruce Calvert.

Film producers were always on the look-out for stage personalities that might make good movie stars, and two that were brought to the screen in the teens were Olive Thomas and Madge Kennedy. Today Olive Thomas is remembered for her marriage to Mary Pickford's brother Jack and her tragic death. She was a movie natural – a great beauty and a clever comedienne – although it was the beauty that first brought her to prominence.

Her short life had all the "rags to riches" of a Hollywood movie story. She was born Olive Elaine Duffy (sometimes Oliva or Oliveretta) in the industrial town of Charleroi, Pennsylvania, not far from Pittsburgh. Her father worked in a steel mill and died in a work-related accident, causing Olive to leave school at fifteen to become a sales clerk selling gingham:

> "I am a good judge of ginghams to this day," she said. "No one can put anything over on me in that line." Indeed, you get the impression that anyone who tries to put anything over on her in any line is in for defeat. "My ideal of those days," she went on, "was Miss Milligan, the head of the ginghams. She was small and cute, and to be like her was the hope of my childhood." (*Motion Picture*, June 1919)

In 1911 at age sixteen she married Bernard Krug Thomas and continued working as a salesgirl. Unhappy with her marriage she filed for divorce two years later, and moved in with family in New York City. There she went to work in department stores. Her life was changed by a newspaper ad for a contest, The Most Beautiful Girl in New York City, run by noted commercial artist Howard Chandler Christy. Olive entered and won, becoming a commercial model like Mabel Normand before her:

> "It was not long before I began posing for photographic studies and later for artists. It was wonderful pay for me – fifty cents an hour." She has posed for Harrison Fisher ("You can say I ADORE him," teasingly), Penrhyn Stanlaws, Haskell Coffin and other famous painters.

Having appeared on the cover of the *Saturday Evening Post* she set her sights on show business. She came to the attention of impresario Florenz Ziegfeld Jr. – some sources say he spotted her or had a recommendation, but Olive said she had her own approach:

"How," I asked, "did you get started with Ziegfeld?"

"I just went up there and asked for a job," she answered.

"No letters of introduction or anything?"

"NO; I just went up and asked for a job and got it. I didn't do much at first – just posed around, standing in boxes and frames while some one sang songs at me."

She made her debut in the *Ziegfeld Follies* in June 1915, and quickly becoming extremely popular she found a featured place in his risqué roof garden revue *The Midnight Frolic*. The February 5, 1916 *Dramatic Mirror* reported:

Luring us last Tuesday night to his latest revel atop the New Amsterdam Theatre, Mr. Ziegfeld showed us convincingly the futility of war, the utter uselessness of general staffs, white papers, treaties, and all the other properties of Mars. We defy the most bellicosely-inclined to resist the pacificatory influences of Olive Thomas's superlative beauty.

Said to have been the favorite of wealthy business men, and even the

Olive Thomas. Author's collection.

mistress of Mr. Ziegfeld, she's rumored to have received a $10,000 string of pearls from German Ambassador Albrecht von Bernstorff. With all this attention it was just a matter of time before the movies came calling:

> Olive Thomas, of the Ziegfeld "Midnight Frolic," has joined the International Film Company forces as leading woman for Harry Fox in comedies. (*Motography*, July 1, 1916)

What Harry Fox was appearing in for the International Film Company was the 1916 serial *Beatrice Fairfax*, where he was co-starred with Grace Darling. Fox and Darling played reporters investigating various cases – some humorous, others full of intrigue and action – in fifteen episodes shot in Ithaca, New York by brothers Leopold and Theodore Wharton.

Olive made her first appearance in the surviving episode ten, *Play Ball*, where she plays the girlfriend of Giants pitcher Bert Kerrigan, who crooked gamblers are plotting to kidnap to ruin a ballgame. The crooks use Olive as bait for Kerrigan, getting her to come to a deserted house and getting him to follow. Not working out as the crooks plan, Kerrigan ends up rescuing the tied-up Olive. In her first appearance before the movie camera Olive is absolutely beautiful, although her acting is a bit rocky in scenes where she has to register dismay after reading a disturbing letter, and it's easy to spot in this novice appearance that she's responding to the off-camera orders of her director telling her what to do. This is not surprising as she had no acting background, but she would quickly learn by doing as she had with dancing.

Her next work was a supporting role in the Irene Fenwick and Owen Moore starring Famous Players/Paramount vehicle *A Girl Like That* (1917), and it was soon announced in the April 14, 1917 *Motography*:

Olive makes her first screen appearance with pitcher Bert Kerrigan in the 1916 serial *Beatrice Fairfax*. Author's collection.

Follies Girl with Ince. Thomas H. Ince has engaged Olive Thomas, the popular young star of the Ziegfeld Midnight Frolic and featured beauty of a late edition of the Follies, to create important roles in forthcoming Kay-Bee productions. Miss Thomas is now in California, and has already been assigned the lead in one of the first plays that Ince will do under his new arrangement with Triangle.

Reporting to Ince's Culver City Studio, Olive was put through her paces in the swiftly moving farce comedy *Madcap Marge* (1917):

> The "Flower" family is made up of a father of the hardy variety; a mother of the climbing variety; an elder daughter who threatens to be a "perennial," and a young bold, Madge, aptly named "Madcap."
>
> The scene opens in a Young Ladies Finishing School where they put the final polish on future social timber, where Madge is shown to shapely advantage in a gymnasium suit and exercises. Later she is the moving spirit in a pajama party where the lady principal is appropriately caricatured by a calf borrowed from a nearby farmhouse.
>
> Expelled from the school, Madge becomes a refugee to the family gathering at Palm Beach. There the maternal Flower is endeavoring to secure for the "perennial" an English Lord traveling incognito in this country. A hotel arrival with similar initials to the Earl of Larlsdale is surrounded by the Flower family and succumbs to the bait shrewdly displayed.
>
> To increase the matrimonial chances of the older sister, Madge is relegated to long curls and short skirts, to her exasperation and chagrin.
>
> There follows several episodes of the effervescing "Madcap," delightfully culminating in her meteoric entrance to a masque ball on roller skates. The social situation is further complicated by three of the guests appearing in the same costume as Mephistopheles.
>
> The elder sister procures a matrimonial prize, who is not an Earl. Madge captivates an Earl, but only by sur-name. However, as he happens to be the Junior Partner in a firm holding her father's financial obligations, the paternal Flower assures him that he is more welcome as a son-in-law than any other Earl in the world. The real Earl, a disconsolate, elderly, globe trotter disappears in disgust. (*Catalogue of Pathéscope Deluxe Special Features*, 1922)

From the sounds of a 1917 newspaper item describing her experiences making *Madcap Madge*, Olive got a crash course in silent comedy filmmaking. All in a day's work for an Alice Howell or Gale Henry, but tough for a Follies Girl:

The initiation of Olive Thomas, that cunning thing from the Ziegfeld shows, was certainly something to make even the most enthusiastic actress sit down and cogitate. Here's what happened to her: Three days in a Gymnasium and a whole day in the rain sitting under an automobile. Then nearly a week on roller skates and riding on the back of a calf, whose back, Miss Thomas declares, "was just like a broom handle."

**Olive gets the draw on some cowboy extras on the Triangle lot.
Courtesy of The Museum of Modern Art.**

Before the end of the year she turned out three more features in rapid succession – *An Even Break*, *Broadway Arizona*, and *Indiscreet Corinne* (all 1917). Many of her Triangle films presented her as a sweet and backward girl who comes to the city. In *Limousine Life* (1918) she's Minnie, a shy country girl who turns the tables on a big city roue. Later she was an innocent Quaker girl in *Prudence on Broadway* (1919), whose father sends her to a fashionable New York school so that she'll learn how to battle the wicked world. Other roles include the little social butterfly in *Indiscreet Corinne* (1917) who does her best to live down the fact that the family is too respectable with nary a scandal, a sin, or a past, and the more dramatic *Toton the Apache* (1919) where she played two parts – a Parisienne model who marries a wealthy American painter, and her daughter Toton, who is raised by a street Apache as a pickpocket who dresses as a boy.

With her movie stardom Olive was taking care of her family – getting her brothers started in the film business – and in her early days at Triangle she began a romance with Jack Pickford. Famous as the younger brother of Mary Pickford, Jack had begun his own film career as a child with the Biograph Company playing small parts, and eventually became popular in light male ingénue roles in films such as *Seventeen* (1916), *Freckles*, and *Tom Sawyer* (both 1917).

Her first meeting with Jack Pickford was at a dance in a beach café founded by the late Nat Goodwin.

> "Jack," she said, "is a beautiful dancer. He danced his way into my heart. We knew each other for eight months before our marriage, and most of that time we gave to dancing. We got along so well on the dance floor that we just naturally decided that we would be able to get along together for the remainder of our lives." (*Motion Picture*, June 1919)

In addition to being a good dancer Jack was known as a carouser, and was fast and loose with women, alcohol, drugs and gambling. Being Mary's brother helped him out of many scrapes and assured him a place in the film industry. It's a bit sketchy as far as when the couple actually married. It was announced to the press in 1917, but they may have been secretly married slightly earlier, but other records suggest that they may not have officially tied the knot until 1918. At any rate Olive continued working, as for a while Pickford was doing a World War I stint in the navy (which didn't work out well as he was accused of taking bribes from rich men to help them stay out of real action). In 1919 Olive left Ince and Triangle for a new company:

> Only a few years ago she was a "Follies" coryene. Now she is one of the highest salaried actresses in motion pictures. Olive Thomas passed through Chicago yesterday for California to take up her new duties as an independent star under the managerial wing of Myron T. Selznick, who bids fair to outrival his father in business sagacity.
>
> Miss Thomas consented to an association with young Selznick after turning up her pretty nose to the magnanimous offers of several film magnates ranging from $2,500 to $4,000 per week. She believes with her youthful sponsor that she will surpass these figures once her productions emerge for public inspection. She has met with some success since she left Mr. Ziegfeld, first as a member of the famous Players company and more recently under the Triangle management.
>
> Mr. Selznick acquired "Upstairs and Down" for her purposes from the Hattons with the consent of Grace Valentine, who was to do the play in pictures according to previous plans. Miss Thomas will render the role of the "baby vampire,"

the play having been rewritten to emphasize this character (Unidentified clipping, January 16, 1919)

Myron Selznick was the son of Lewis J. Selznick, a pioneer film producer who had been involved with Equitable, World, and Famous Players, later setting up Selznick-Select Pictures. This is the organization that put out Olive's pictures. Lewis J. would go bankrupt in 1923, and Myron and his brother David O. Selznick spent most of their careers refurbishing the family name. David became a legendary producer and Myron eventually one of the most powerful agents in Hollywood. In 1919 Olive was one of the Selznick Company's biggest names and turned out pictures like *Upstairs and Down*, *The Spite Bride* (both 1919), and *Youthful Folly* (1920) where she essayed the role of the "baby vampire." This character finally became "the flapper" and was the title of her most famous film. About half of Olive's features are known to survive - roughly eleven out of twenty-one - but as they're spread out at various archives they're difficult to see. Her most accessible picture, and the only one to have a home video release, is 1920's *The Flapper*.

The film opens in the sleepy berg of Orange Springs where "a church social was a social event." Olive plays Ginger King who's bored to death, and after trying to liven things up she gets in trouble with her father and stern housekeeper. She's sent off to Miss Paddles Boarding School outside New York. Ginger has a young beau at a nearby military academy but she's dissatisfied with him and instead idolizes an older man, Theodore Westman Jr., who rides by the school every day on his horse. She meets him when he comes to her aid after she's thrown out of a horse sleigh into the snow, which leads to him asking her to a country club dance. Ginger, of course sneaks out of the school and has a great time at the dance, until Miss Paddles, informed of the date by one of the other girls, shows up during the fun to inform Westman that his date is only sixteen and drag her back to school.

The second half of the film has Ginger innocently getting involved with crooks who've stolen the contents of the school's safe. During a school break in Manhattan the crooks get Ginger to hold the stolen goods, and she takes the opportunity to act sophisticated when she sees Theodore Westman at the Hotel's café. Returning home to Orange Springs she's decked out and arrives as a "fallen woman" for the benefit of startled family and neighbors. She soon decides to give this up and sends the stolen jewels to the Chief of Police in New York. The problem is she did her act too well, so no one believes it was an act. New York detectives show up at her home during a confrontation with her father and Westman. Luckily the crooks show up in Orange Springs to reclaim their loot and arrive at her house just in time to get nabbed by the detectives and clear everything up for the happy ending. Now after her brush with sophistication Ginger is happy just to hold hands with her military school beau.

The film has clever titles by Frances Marion. One example has Ginger's military school boyfriend bragging about being an expert horseman – "Ever since I was six years old I've been an EXPERT" – which fades into a shot of a little boy on a rocking horse. In addition to lots of footage of the girls clowning around at school and playing in the snow, *The Flapper* gives full reign to Olive's impish humor, plus allows her to be her usual sweet self as well as do parody versions of sophisticated and "fallen women."

After *The Flapper* Olive had two more films – *Darling Mine*, and *Everybody's Sweetheart* (both 1920). In September 1920 she and Jack Pickford went on a second honeymoon to Paris, but during the trip a tragedy occurred:

> Olive Thomas, movie star, died on Thursday in Paris from mercurial poisoning. She swallowed the potion accidentally, according to a statement issued by her physician Dr. Joseph Choate, of Los Angles, Cal. Dr. Choate, formerly was Mary Pickford's physician.
>
> Dr. Choate stated that on Sept. 5, Miss Thomas drank a bichloride preparation containing 10 grains of mercury. She had swallowed about eight grains when she realized her mistake and called her husband, Jack Pickford. He kept her alive by first aid, pouring water down her throat.
>
> The effect of the poison came on with unusual rapidity.

The incident is said to have occurred in the bathroom of their flat after a night of heavy drinking. Although the police investigations came to the conclusion that she drank the solution by accident, rumors were rife that she committed suicide due to despondency over marital problems with Pickford, or because she had contracted syphilis from him. Other stories circulated that Jack had murdered her, but the accidental ingestion seems the most likely, with the solution being either a cleaning fluid or a topical treatment for Pickford's syphilis sores.

After taking the corrosive she lingered in the hospital for five days before ultimately dying of kidney failure just a month shy of

The original incarnation of the flapper.

her twenty-sixth birthday. Often regarded as the first major Hollywood scandal, it was one of a series of tragic filmland deaths – coming along with Bobby Harron's from a bullet wound, Clarine Seymour's from a vague abdominal problem, pilot Omar Locklear being killed doing a flying stunt for a film, Wallace Reid dying due to his morphine addiction, Virginia's Rappe's burst bladder, and the shooting of director William Desmond Taylor.

Olive's screen image was the personification of youth, so it's hard to say how her career would have developed had she lived and continued working as she got older. She raised the issue herself in a January 6, 1920 *Exhibitors Trade Review* interview:

> "But I want to create a certain role," she explained. "You see Mary is the kid in pictures; Norma does drama; Constance is the flippant, flighty wife; Dorothy the hoyden; Nazimova is exotic and steeped in mystery, my Jack does boys, while I – I – why don't you see, I'm just nothing at all."

> She grew quite excited as she pursued the subject. "I have no fixed position. I don't mean a DEFINITE thing to anybody. Now you see if a fan wants to enjoy a comedy he knows he can pick Charles Ray, or Dorothy Gish and get what he's looking for. If a fan is looking for a picture of youth he can walk in to see Mary Pickford or my Jack and find it. For a frothy affair of sophisticated humor - - there is "Connie" Talmadge. If it's a drama that's wanted – well, drop in to see Norma. But how - - I ask you – how can a fan know what he's getting when he pays his money to see me? He or she is likely to find me weeping through five reels because I haven't a child, or tripping the light fantastic as a chorus girl of questionable reputation. I grow to womanhood and am tossed back to the flapper type. I am nothing in particular. Don't you see?"

Jack Pickford continued his acting career until the mid-1920s, as well as his carousing. He married two other Ziegfeld Girls, but his lifestyle caught up with him, and he died of his unnatural causes at age thirty-seven in 1933. Not long after her death stagehands at the New Amsterdam Theatre thought they saw Olive, dressed in one of her Follies gowns and carrying a blue bottle, backstage and on the roof. The sightings continue to this day. Since the theatre was renovated and reopened in the late 1990s, night watchmen and stagehands have been reported to have even had conversations with her restless spirit.

Olive Thomas' career, combining her Ziegfeld days and movies, lasted only nine years. On the flip side, our other stage transplant Madge Kennedy worked for over sixty-five years in theatre, film, and television. Born in Chicago in 1891, Kennedy grew up in California before her family moved to New York when she was in her teens. Interested in being an artist, she enrolled in the Arts Students League, with the idea of becoming an illustrator:

"I was what was called a promising pupil at the League," she continues. "I had a certain flare – I made an effective drawing. My teachers would say, "If you would only work – if you would only interest yourself in construction and drawing." But I couldn't. I only liked it all because I could make a splurge with it."

Another student at the League was Roy Webb, who with his brother Kenneth was a songwriter and playwright. Madge joined the Webbs for the summer at the theatrical community at Siansconset, Nantucket Island, and they asked her to be part of an amateur charity performance. In the audience was Henry Woodruff, who offered Madge the female lead in his 1910 touring production of *The Genius*, a comedy about an artist's model and the three artists interested in her. While on tour in Cincinnati she was seen by Grace George, wife of producer William A. Brady, who recommended that her husband put Kennedy under contract. Shows such as *Over Night* followed before she made her New York debut in *Little Miss Brown* in 1912.

Goldwyn star Madge Kennedy. Courtesy of Cole Johnson.

This all led to two major Broadway hits for the actress, *Twin Beds* in 1914, and *Fair and Warmer* in 1916. Both were innocent bedroom farces full of jealous husbands, bored married couples experimenting with twin beds, people hiding in linen closets, and much running around in night clothes. Madge mentioned to the November 1915 *Green Book Magazine*:

> During the last few seasons I have been cast rather frequently in what you might call negligee parts, so I feel that I can talk freely. In spite of the Grecian simplicity of some of my costumes, kind critics have clothed me with praise. They have called me innocently devilish, unsophisticatedly sophisticated, and one said – hold hard; we're going around a curve! – that I wore a nightie as if it were more respectable than an evening gown – which it actually is, if you ask me. There's only an hour or so's difference anyway.

These are real compliments, both to my ability and to my breeding and upbringing. I have done some real awake-at-night worrying over these parts – I was afraid there might be such a thing as my being cast in a nightgown or pajamas for the rest of my natural stage career.

Reviewers cited that Ms. Kennedy's delicacy of performance, combined with her youth and beauty, kept the plays only slightly risqué and free from any kind of vulgarity. Both huge hits, movies came calling and soon:

Kennedy and Rockcliffe Fellows in *Friend Husband* (1918). Courtesy of Bruce Calvert.

Madge Kennedy Becomes Star for Goldwyn Corp. Will Report to Studio at Fort Lee Following Expiration of her "Fair and Warmer" Contract – Lasky heads Insured. – And so it goes the Goldwyn Corporation has robbed the stage of another favorite by signing Madge Kennedy to appear in a series of motion pictures. This has been perpetrated right on top of the acquisition of Jane Cowl and Maxine Elliott. It will be Miss Kennedy's first appearance before the camera, but she is already widely known for her chief participation in three great successes of the last few years – "Over Night," "Twin Beds," and "Fair and Warmer." She was the discovery of Grace George and under the Selwyn management became one of the youngest stars of the stage. (*New York Telegram*, January 25, 1917)

Her inaugural production for Goldwyn was *Baby Mine*, an adaptation of the 1910 stage farce by Margaret Mayo about a frivolous young wife whose husband leaves her. To get him back she pretends to have had a baby, but of course the plan doesn't progress smoothly – the husband comes back too soon leaving her to scramble to find a baby, ending up with too many kids so she has to tell hubby that she had twins, and even triplets, and the parents of the "borrowed" babies showing up to reclaim their offspring. With this ideally chosen property Ms. Kennedy made a smooth transition to the screen:

> Miss Kennedy in "Baby Mine" should prove a gold mine in the motion picture business. The pretty comedienne made her debut on the screen yesterday at the Strand Theatre. "Baby Mine," a picturization by the Goldwyn Pictures Corporation of the very funny play of the same name by Miss Margaret Mayo, displayed an astonishing amount of life and humor.
>
> Miss Kennedy takes to the screen like a fly to fly paper, and practically none of her ingenuous and at the same time highly ingenious comedy is lost. It is all done with much cleverness on the part of actors and directors. The spectators were laughing constantly. (*New York Herald*, September 24, 1917)

Movie audiences immediately took to the dark-haired, slender and big-eyed Kennedy and Goldwyn kept her busy turning out similar romantic comedies such as *Nearly Married* (1917), *Our Little Wife, Friend Husband* (both 1918), *Leave It to Susan, Strictly Confidential* (both 1919), *Dollars and Sense, Help Yourself* (both 1920), *The Girl with the Jazz Heart*, and *Oh Mary Be Careful* (both 1921). She made a total of twenty-one features in three years, beating fellow Goldwyn comedy stars Mabel Normand (sixteen features) and Will Rogers (a mere fourteen). The Goldwyn Company was a humming factory, and its films were first shot in Fort Lee, New Jersey at Alice Guy Blache's old Solax Studio. Later the company shifted to the Universal Studio on Main Street, the largest glass-enclosed studio in the U.S., before finally moving out west to Culver City in November 1918. Getting her movie experience on the fly, like Beatrice Lillie in the 1920s, Kennedy found out that there was quite a difference in being a farceur for the screen:

> Before a camera, I have found, a laugh is a hypothetical equation. It is not necessary – indeed, it would be fatal – to wait for it. It is generally assumed upon the screen to be funny when a gentleman in a dress suit is hit with a pie. After he is so wounded upon the screen he either begins a hot pursuit or a speech. He couldn't do this under the same circumstances in the spoken drama. If he began a pursuit he would spoil a good laugh, always assuming that there is something funny about a pie, and if he started to speak he couldn't be heard. On the spoken stage he would sit quietly and remove the pie from his ears until the audience had ceased to laugh.

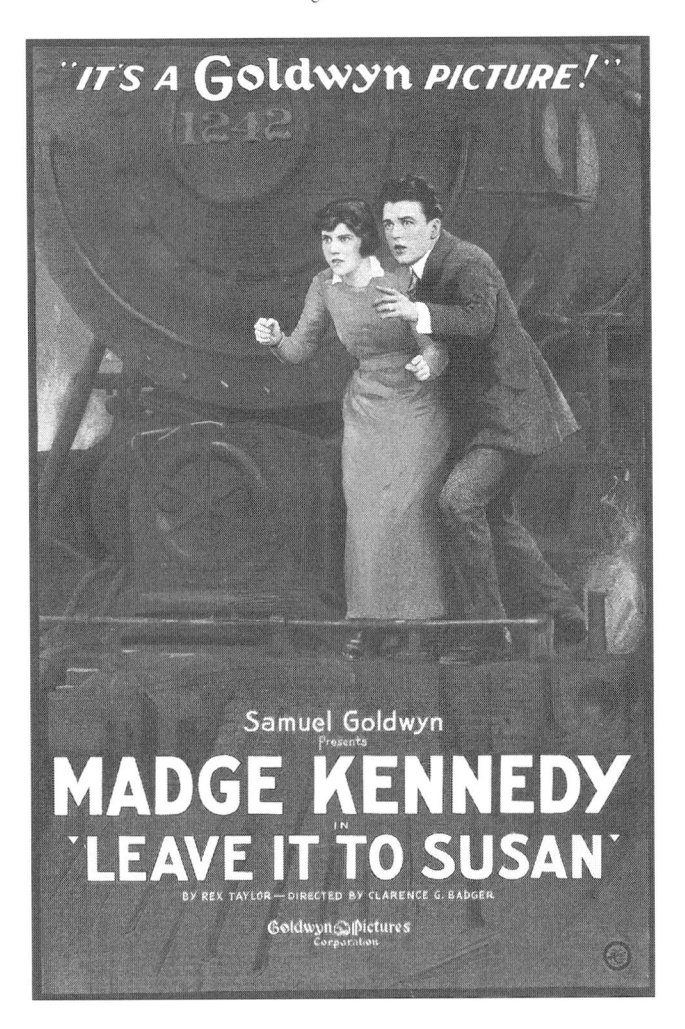

In one scene of a certain play upon the stage I was forced to come to a full stop a dozen times because of laughter. I became used to playing this scene in staccato. This same action before the camera was accomplished without a single halt. No one smiled. The cameraman was downright sad about it, and the director seemed more interested in his continuity sheet than he was in me. I felt embarrassed. Lines were spoken that had never failed to carry a laugh and there was an accompanying action which I had been assured was extremely funny. The director was a sober as a pall-bearer.

"Perhaps I'd better try it again," I said.

"What for?" asked the director.

"It didn't seem to go," I answered.

"Go!" he contradicted, "I don't know how it could have been funnier. Now in the next scene when you enter with –"

It dawned upon me that a cameraman and director are too busy manufacturing laughter to indulge in it themselves." (Unidentified clipping, June 23, 1917)

Sadly practically all of her Goldwyn comedies are unavailable. This original Goldwyn Company went bankrupt in 1923 (its name was bought on paper and became part of MGM), and all its pictures became orphan films, left to survive catch-as-catch-can. Only a handful of the huge amount made with the likes of Mabel Normand, Will Rogers, Mary Garden, and Kennedy survive today. A reconstruction of Kennedy's *The Danger Game* (1918) was produced by film historian Richard Koszarski and Glenn Edridge at the Rutgers University Media Center, from a Spanish version preserved by the Filmteca de la Generalitat Valenciana.

The script by Roy Somerville casts Kennedy as Clytie Rogers, the pampered daughter of a rich businessman, who fancies herself a "serious writer" and surrounds herself with sponging Bohemian types. She also has a clinging suitor who's really after her money. Her first novel, published by dear old dad, is meant to be a serious portrayal of crime and lower class criminals, but since she has no experience of this life the critics as well as her parent's influential friends laugh her book off as ludicrous. Hurt by their derision, she decides to leave home and prove that a girl like herself could manage a life of crime. As soon as she gets set up in a cheap boarding house, she goes out and spotting an open window sees it as an invitation to start with burglary. Since the gentleman of the house is home, things take a different turn than she expected and she's shuttled off to the police station.

The Sherlocks at the station mistake her for "Powder-Nose Annie," a wanted feminine felon. Jimmy Gilpin, who just happens to be the critic who panned her book, is at the station and recognizes who she really is. After telling his cop friends her true identity, he convinces them to let her "escape," with him pretending to be a two-bit hood who's helping her so that she'll pull a big caper with him. Gilpin shows her that there's nothing romantic in crime and the sordid side of life, but falls for her while doing it. Madge comes across her former suitor who makes a new play for her, but ultimately she gets the truth on him, sends him packing, and returns home to the mansion sadder but wiser. When the critic James Gilpin requests a meeting she agrees to see him, but finds that he was "Jimmy" all along.

The bare bones of the plot really don't give an inkling of what a charming and funny film this is. Much of the credit must go to Ms. Kennedy, whose deft playing and sincerity of feeling really bring Clytie to life and makes her believable. Small and slight, she has huge dark eyes that dart back and forth as she takes in the novel situations opening up in front of her. Despite her success on stage, her work here is in miniature with little gestures and touches that add humor and feeling. She has excellent support from Tom

Moore, and supporting character players like Leroy Hunter, Ned Burton, Kate Blancke, Lincoln Plummer, and Max Asher (who appears to be moonlighting on the East Coast). All in all a smart and entertaining film, that really makes one wish that the rest of her pictures were readily available.

Madge Kennedy and Mary Garden in a publicity shot on the set of The Splendid Sinner (1918). Courtesy of Bruce Calvert.

When Kennedy's three-year contract with Goldwyn was over she went back to the stage with the drama *Cornered* in 1920. Her biggest stage hit of the 1920's was *Poppy* in 1923, in which she starred in the title role opposite W.C. Fields. Not completely abandoning films, Ms. Kennedy and her husband Harold Bolster, former business manager for Vitagraph, set up their own production company, the Kenma Corporation, and made two films shot at Paramount's Astoria Studios – *The Purple Highway* (1923) and *Three Miles Out* (1924). Neither film was well-received and the company was short-lived, and it's said that although they owned the screen rights to *Dorothy Vernon of Haddon Hall*, Kenma wasn't able to raise the funds to make the historical epic and sold the rights to Mary Pickford.

She did four more independent features in the 1920s, the most comedic being *Oh, Baby!* (1926) about a midget prize fighter who pretends to be a little girl with Madge posing as Little Billy's "mother." After a Paramount sound short with Roland Young, *Walls Tell Tales* (1928), Kennedy was away from films for thirty-four years.

Brought back in 1952 by Ruth Gordon, Garson Kanin, and George Cukor for *The Marrying Kind*, she then spent the next twenty-four years extremely busy in films such as *The Catered Affair, Lust for Life* (both 1956), *North by Northwest* (1959), *They Shoot Horses Don't They?* (1969), and *The Day of the Locust* (1975), in addition to tons of television. Over the years she showed up on *The Ford Television Theatre, Goodyear Theatre, Wyatt Earp, Alfred Hitchcock Presents, The Twilight Zone, Julia, The Odd Couple*, and played Aunt Martha from 1957 to 1963 on *Leave It to Beaver*. Her last film was *Marathon Man* (1976) and she passed away at age ninety-six in 1987.

During this period the American cinema was flourishing. This was due in part to the disruption of production in Europe at the outbreak of World War I. Europe had some of the first female comics and now it produced two notable ladies in the latter teens. Asta Nielsen was a great dramatic diva of the European cinema, renown internationally for films such as *Afgrunden* (*The Abyss*, 1910) and *Hamlet* (1921), but she was equally at home in comedy.

A popular stage star, in 1910 she was brought to the screen and her best-known film comedies are *Die Filmprimadonna* (*The Film Prima Donna*, 1913), *Engelein* (*Little Angel*, 1914), *Das Liebes-ABC* (*The ABC of Love*, 1916), and *Das Eskimobaby* (*The Eskimo Baby*, 1918). *The Film Prima Donna* is just as the title suggests, where *Engelien* is about a sixteen year-old girl who has to pose as twelve to fool a rich American uncle. Definitely the blueprint for Billy Wilder's later *The Major and the Minor* (1942), the film is full of split-second changes from one age to the other, and mix-ups as she forgets she is smoking a cigarette, etc.

Das Liebes-ABC concerns her family wanting her to marry Philip, in whom she's disappointed because his upbringing by two aunts has made him a prissy wimp. She decides to educate him, and spends much time in drag as a man-about-town and a clumsy waiter in her quest to make a man of him. *Das Eskimobaby* is her best regarded comedy, where she stars as a backward Greenland native set loose in civilization under the charge of a sophisticated Copenhagen family. Nielsen continued her film work until 1927, although she did make one sound film, *Crown of Thorns* (1932), and acted on the German stage until 1936. Returning to Copenhagen, she acted on stage there, and died at ninety in 1972.

In contrast to the sometimes dark and dour Ms. Nielsen, the German comedienne Ossi Oswalda was blonde and bubbly. She was working as a model and dancer at the Berliner Theatre where she was spotted by the writer Hans Kraly and brought to the attention of comedian and director Ernst Lubitsch. She made her film debut with a small part in his starring comedy *Schuhpalast Pinkus* (*Shoe Store Pinkus*, 1916), and worked almost entirely for him in outings like *Des Fidele Gefangis* (*The Merry Jail*, 1917) and *Meyer aus Berlin* (*Meyer in Berlin*, 1919).

**Ossi Oswalda in *Ich Mocht Kein Mann Sein (I Don't Want to be a Man,* 1919).
Courtesy of Cole Johnson.**

Her career peak came at the end of the decade starting with 1919's *Ich Mocht Kein Mann Sein* (*I Don't Want to be a Man*). Oswalda plays a wild young woman who won't listen to her stern governess in her pursuit of fun. Her father appoints a male guardian, who's ready to have a good time when he's on his own. To avoid all the supervision Ossi dresses in a top hat and tails and goes off to a dance where she meets her guardian. They carouse around as buddies, but eventually Ossi falls in love with him and decides that she no longer wants to be a boy and goes back to being a girl.

Her other main films are both from 1919 - *Die Austernprinzessin* (*The Oyster Princess*) and *Die Puppe* (*The Doll*). *Die Austernprizessin* is a parody of Americans and their wealthy ways with Ossi as a hyperactive daughter of a millionaire businessman who wants to marry into German royalty. *Die Puppe* is a fantasy where a timid young man is forced to marry to preserve the family line by his uncle the Baron. When the young man hides in a monastery to escape from marrying, the monks suggest he marry a mechanical doll made by the local doll maker. When the doll gets broken the assistant convinces Ossi to take its place. She does, and eventually the timid Lancelot falls for the windup "doll." By this time she was known as the "German Mary Pickford," and continued making comedies through the 1920s such as *Colibri* (1924) and *Schatz, Mach Kasse* (1926) for her own production company and for UFA, but her popularity sharply declined and her career was over in the early days of sound. She spent the latter part of her life in poverty living in Prague before her death at fifty in 1948.

Back in the United States, our last comedy heroine of the teens to be profiled is the youngest – Baby Marie Osborne – arguably the first American child film star who paved the way for Jackie Coogan, Baby Peggy, and Shirley Temple. Born Helen Alice Myres on November 5, 1911 in Denver, Colorado, at eleven days old she was taken to the Colorado State Home for Dependent Children. Three months later she was given to the care of Leon and Edyth Osborne. Although the Osbornes never legally adopted Baby Marie, or a younger child named Gloria, the adult Marie said that they were always kind and loving parents. The Osbornes were in show business – Mr. Osborne operated a theatre in Trinidad, Colorado and Mrs. Osborne was an experienced variety actress. In 1914 they sold their theatre, packed up themselves, their daughters Marie and Gloria, in addition to an animal show, and moved to Long Beach, California to try movies.

Making the rounds of the studios, the Osbornes were signed to stock contracts at the Balboa Amusement Producing Company were they played supporting roles for leading players such as Ruth Roland, Cullen Landis, Marguerite Nichols (later Mrs. Hal Roach), and Lew Cody. Marie and Gloria were taken to the studio while their parents were working, and would play occasional child parts if needed. Director Henry King needed a boy for his picture *Maid of the Wild* (1915). There were no boys to be found, but "I had a Dutch bob," said Marie, "and when they put little boy's clothes on me, I was the little boy they needed." King, a mainstay at the studio as a director and star, was impressed and urged the studio to tailor a script for her. This became *Little Mary Sunshine* (1916) which made her a star.

> **Helen Marie Osborn.** Balboa claims to have the youngest leading lady before the public today in Helen Marie Osborn. Only recently she celebrated her third birthday anniversary and on that occasion she was elevated to stellar honors, playing opposite no less a screen favorite than Henry King.
>
> Until this event, the little lady was known about the Balboa Studio as "Baby Marie," but now she takes exception to such address and out of respect to her position she is called Miss Osborn. She comports herself with unspoiled dignity, is childishly frolicsome, and withal ladylike.
>
> Helen Marie Osborn is a native of Denver, Colo. Her parents are both professionals. As "Babe" St Clair, her mother is known to many people of the stage. Leon T. Osborn is the father. Both are members of the Balboa playing force. But since Helen Marie is doing leads she has become the most important member of the family. Mother is acting in the capacity of maid to her daughter; while father serves as manager. (*Moving Picture World*, October 30, 1915)

Her starring features for Balboa, mostly directed and co-starring King, were melodramas brightened by occasional humorous sequences and by Baby Marie's bubbly personality. *Joy and the Dragon* (1916) has Marie survive a shipwreck and now an orphan, ends up controlled by a gang of crooks, which she escapes from and puts behind bars with the help of Henry King. *Twin Kiddies* (1917) is a bit of a modern version of *The Prince and the Pauper* about a poor child and a rich one who change places, and in *Sunshine and Gold* (1917) Marie is kidnapped by gypsies.

Quickly becoming extremely popular her parents decided not to renew Marie's contract with Balboa and create their own company. 1917 saw the formation of the Lasalida Film Company to make Marie's films, and three features were made – *Captain Kiddo, Tears and Smiles*, and *When Baby Forgot* (all 1917) – before the outfit was re-organized into the Diando Film Company. Leon Osborne and W.A.S. Douglas were the founders (the "D" and "O") and they took over the old Kalem Studio in Glendale to make the films, with Pathé as their distributor:

Baby Marie Osborne poses with a stuffed leopard. Author's collection.

> **Complete First Pathé Baby Osborne Subject**. The first Baby Marie Osborne subject for the Pathé Company made by the newly-organized Diando Company, of which W.A.S. Douglas is president and general manager, was completed during the past week, and has been shipped to the Eastern laboratories. This has been titled "Little Patriot," and besides Baby Marie, the important roles are taken by Herbert Standing, Marion Warner, John Connelly and Frank Lanning. (*Motion Picture News*, November 3, 1917)

The move from Balboa to her own company saw the film's comedy quota make a leap. This was due in large part to the addition of a regular partner in crime for Marie's antics. Starting with *Captain Kiddo* (1917) Ernest Frederick Morrison, the son of a chef and born in 1912, became her sidekick and gathered a good amount of attention for himself, eventually becoming known as "Sunshine Sammy" Morrison and becoming a regular at the Hal Roach Studio. Although an important ingredient in Marie's films at first the black child was never mentioned in the official cast lists, but reviewers and publicity articles singled him out:

> **Baby Marie Osborne** is announced in the five part Gold Rooster Play
>
> ## Captain Kiddo
>
> Produced by Lasalida
>
> Baby Osborne ranks with almost any star in the business as a box office attraction. This is what the Manager of one of Omaha's very best theatres says of her:
>
> "Last night we played 'Sunshine and Shadow' with Baby Osborne and it was a record breaking attraction for us. Baby Osborne, Pearl White and Gladys Hulette are all very popular stars with the Dundee patrons."—C. H. Schofield, Dundee Theatre, Omaha, Neb.

BABY MARIE OSBORNE

There is a little darky in the cast who is full of fun and his little comedy touches furnish much of the entertainment. (*Daddy's Girl* review, *Exhibitors Herald*, March 16, 1918)

A tiny negro boy whose name is not mentioned in the cast is the most spontaneous note in the whole production, and he pretty nearly usurps all of the honors and attention. His sunny smile, ingenuous acting and comical appearance win for him an immediate position of importance among real entertainers. (*Daughter of the West* review, *Exhibitors Trade Review*, May 25, 1918)

Unfortunately he's also frequently referred to as "Sambo" or "Chocolate Drop," and a 1918 exhibitor ad had the jaw-dropping line:

If there are any persons in your audience who do not like children, they'll LOVE them when they see Baby Marie Osborn and the funny little coon in the Pathé photoplay A Daughter of the West.

Despite the prejudice the films took advantage of Morrison's talents and he and Marie became an excellent team in pictures such as *The Little Diplomat* (1919):

Emma Bell Clifton in writing this story for "Little Mary Sunshine" makes an appeal to the heart by casting her little heroine as a French orphan rendered homeless and parentless by the ravages of the Great War. The locale, however, is strictly American, and the story has nothing whatever to do with the war or the European battlefields in any way.

Baby Marie is seen as a carefree child rejoicing in her new-found liberty under the banner of Old Glory, romping with Little Sambo, whom she says "has not been colored – he was born that way!" Incidentally, these two prove somewhat of a trial to the studious husband of the kind-hearted woman who has adopted Marie, but that kindness is amply repaid in service by the wee French girl when the opportunity arises.

A great deal of fun is caused throughout the course of the picture by the various stunts performed by Marie and her colored playmate, Little Sambo, who as "George Washington Jones Jr.," leads the French child into considerable mischief – although she is by no means backward herself at suggesting pranks. (*Moving Picture World*, June 21, 1919)

Baby Marie and Sunshine Sammy in a hard to believe ad for *A Daughter of the West* (1918).

Marie's films included *Cupid by Proxy, Winning Grandma, Dolly's Vacation* (all 1918), *The Old Maid's Baby*, and *The Sawdust Doll* (both 1919). By this time she was older and understood that she was acting, but later said "making movies was fun for me, there were other children, so it was like play. It all came so natural to me. There was no forcing of emotions." The spontaneous and natural aspects of her personality were written about by Edward Weitzel when he visited her at the Diando Studio and viewed *Dolly's Vacation* (1919) with her:

"Shall I start the picture now?" called the operator from the booth.

The little star sat up straight and clapped her hands:

"Oh, goody!" she exclaimed; "they going to show my picture!"

The opening scenes of Marie's latest release shows the youthful heroine looking at her colored nurse and performing a feat of contortion at the same time. Her position is somewhat startling, and the impersonator of Dolly gave a little chuckle and then burst into a hearty laugh.

"Guess you didn't 'spect anything like that!" she announced with pride.

As the story progressed and the pranks of Dolly with her nurse, who is big and fat but determined to maintain her dignity, grew more uproarious, the real cause of the trouble gave a practical illustration of how to enjoy the movies. She followed every movement with the keenest interest and unconsciously acting over again the scene before her. Marie Osborne's talent is inborn. The child lives the part she is playing and has inherited a personality that is a perfect instrument for the expression of her emotions.

When a comedy scene was over and the dramatic portion of the story was being carried on without her aid, Marie explained what was going to happen in a dramatic whisper that was very impressive.

"There's going to be a strike at my father's mill, so he sends me and mammy and Ernest into the country. Wait til you see what Ernest does now – he's fine – Here he comes."

The little colored boy who has played in so many of Marie's pictures and helped her so often to land a big laugh, was seen crawling up behind the leader of the strikers. Reaching between the man's legs, Ernest seized an incriminating note dropped by the conspirator, and backed quickly away on all fours.

Once more Marie gave a squeal of delight and clapped her hands.

"Wasn't Ernest splendid?" she asked.

A moment later her laughter and applause were heard again.

"That's Tiny! He used to be my dog, but I gave him to Ernest. And here's my big dog. Wait till I take hold of his rope and you see how he pulls me along! Now, there's going to be some more about the strikers."

"I'd rather watch you."

"So would I. Wait till Ernest and I get lost in the woods hunting for Tiny. We have lots of fun at the farm. We nail Pete's shoes to the doorstep and make a swing down in the cellar and the tap comes out of the barrel and Ernest steals a jar of soft soap because he thinks it's preserves, but the funniest thing he does is when he locks his mammy in the chicken coop."

And so it went, all through the picture. For every good word for her own work Marie had three for her brother artist. Professional jealousy has no place in the nature of little Miss Osborne. (*Moving Picture World*, January 11, 1919)

Despite her popularity Diando was in financial trouble and Marie's last films for the company – *Baby Marie's Round-Up*, *Daddy Number Two*, and *Miss Gingersnap* (all 1919) – were two-reelers. The studio closed and Marie spent the next three years traveling the country on a personal appearance tour. A few of her earlier successes such as *Daughter of the West* and *Cupid by Proxy* were re-released in 1922 in cut-down three-reel versions, but these did nothing to jump-start her film career, as at this time she was growing up and no longer the cute little girl of her movies. During her heyday she had reportedly been earning $1,000 a week with much of it being put into a trust fund. But the financial problems with the demise of Diando wiped that out, and Marie settled into life as an average teenager.

Around the time of the end of her public appearance tours Marie's parents divorced,

Publicity shot of an older Baby Marie. Author's collection.

and she and her sister Gloria spent time alternating living with each parent. In 1931 she married and two years later found out that the Osbornes weren't her actual parents. A newspaper story was published saying that her natural father was looking for her. Marie contacted the Colorado State Home for Dependent and Neglected Children and found that they had been looking for her for five years. At this time the Home tried to contact the man who claimed to be her father, H.L. Shiver, but weren't able to locate him again. Nothing more ever came of the incident. In 1931 she decided to return to the movie business, and through her original mentor Henry King she was able to start working as an extra, and began as a regular stand-in for Ginger Rogers and Deanna Durbin.

Eventually tiring of always looking for more acting work, she became an apprentice at the Western Costume Company, and in the next few years she worked her way up to costume supervisor on big films such as *Guys and Dolls* (1955), *Spartacus* (1960), *The Killing of Sister George* (1968), *The Way We Were* (1973), and *The Godfather; Part 2* (1974). After she retired in 1976 she lived with her daughter and would take part in film events until her death in 2010 at age ninety-nine.

Like Madge Kennedy, virtually nothing of Baby Marie's silent film work is readily available to today's silent film aficionados. The titles that do exist - *Baby Marie's Round Up* (1919), *Daddy Number Two* (1919), *The Old Maid's Baby* (1919), *Little Mary Sunshine* (1916), and eleven others – all in varying states of completeness – are scattered at archives around the globe.

Chapter 5

LEADING LADIES OF THE TWENTIES

As the 1920s rolled around a new wave of leading ladies took dominance in film comedy which reflected the rise of independent young women in post-World War I American society. Many of their forerunners of the teens, such as Victoria Forde and Billie Rhodes, saw their careers end or wind down, while others like Pearl White, Lillian Walker, and Betty Compson moved from comedy into serials or drama. The common aspect shared between these two generations of comedy ladies is that they were always attractive, as romance was a very important plot element in their films. Some, such as Colleen Moore and Marion Davies, alternated dramas with their comedies. Most of these ladies were some of the biggest stars of their day, and are still some of the best remembered women in this book.

Dorothy Gish embodying the phrase "look out below" in *Flying Pat* (1920). Billy Rose Theatre Division, the New York Public Library for the Performing Arts.

Two transitional leading ladies from the teens to the twenties were Dorothy Gish and Constance Talmadge. Both had begun their careers in the teens, but didn't realize their full potential until the twenties. Thanks to the loss of almost ninety-eight per cent of her films Dorothy Gish's career has been overwhelmed by the enduring fame of her sister Lillian. Most of her surviving appearances are in D.W. Griffith dramas such as

Orphans of the Storm (1922), which show her at a disadvantage as her natural talents were for comedy (never a Griffith strong point). Like her sister, Dorothy had her own starring features and was a popular favorite throughout the silent era.

After early years on the stage the Gish girls began their film career as five dollar a day extras at the Biograph Company in 1912. Lillian's career progressed much faster there as she was the ethereal type that Griffith doted on, while Dorothy was more of a tomboy, but she was kept busy getting valuable screen time and experience in shorts such as *Almost a Wild Man* (1913) and *Liberty Belles* (1914). Her lot improved when the Griffith unit joined the Reliance/Majestic Company in 1914. Although she wasn't a part of his epics *The Birth of a Nation* (1915) or *Intolerance* (1916), she was starred in a series of comedies on the order of *How Hazel Got Even* and *Minerva's Mission* (both 1915) that began to showcase her fresh and spunky personality.

This continued with Triangle/Fine Arts releases such as the charming *Gretchen the Greenhorn* and *Atta Boy's Last Race* (both 1916), and reached a peak with her role as "the Little Disturber" in Griffith's World War I saga *Hearts of the World* (1918). Dorothy was a hit as the much needed comic relief, and this success led to her starring in a series of feature comedies for Paramount release. Although supervised by Griffith the direction was by Elmer Clifton, and titles on the order of *Peppy Polly* (1919), *Little Miss Rebellion*, and *Flying Pat* (both 1920) chronicled Dorothy's misadventures as a young woman about town who gets involved in aviation, newspaper reporting, and a revolution in a mythical kingdom. Sister Lillian even directed her in the marital comedy *Remodeling Her Husband* (1920), and while these early 1920s efforts are sadly missing, surviving reviews are unanimous in their opinion of Dorothy's skills:

> Played as "straight" comedy the picture would reveal many amusing features, but it is the rapidly and thoroughly developed gift for farce-acting possessed by Dorothy Gish that makes the entire performance an unbroken string of spontaneous laughs. Every incident of which she is a part is tricked out and adorned by bits of byplay that are so quickly and so accurately done they rival the best efforts of the masters of pantomime. The art of knowing just how far to go in everything connected with her class of acting is shown to perfection by Dorothy Gish. (*Moving Picture World*, May 31, 1919)

Despite some dramas opposite Richard Barthelmess like *Fury*, *The Bright Shawl* (both 1923), and *The Beautiful City* (1925), she kept busy in comedies such as *The Ghost in the Garrett* (1921), *The Country Flapper* (1922), *Night Life of New York*, and *Clothes Make the Pirate* (both 1925). In 1926 she relocated to England, and there made her best surviving film – the light-hearted, historical bio *Nell Gwyn* (1926), which gives her plenty of room for madcap comedy bits within a strong dramatic story. While neither of the Gish girls are remembered for being particularly sexy, Dorothy certainly is in *Nell Gwyn* – wearing extremely low-cut outfits and trading on her sexuality for favors, which is historically faithful to Gwyn's rise from courtesan to famous actress. While in Britain Gish also did the comedy *Tip Toes* (1927) which teamed her with Will Rogers, as well as made her sound debut with the unsuccessful *Wolves* (1930). From here she mostly left films, and outside of a few featured appearances in *Our Hearts Were Young and Gay* (1944), *Centennial Summer* (1946), and *The Cardinal* (1963), the remainder of her career was spent on stage and television until her death in 1968.

Nelson Keys, Dorothy Gish, and Will Rogers play out of work vaudevillians in *Tip Toes* (1927). Billy Rose Theater Division, the New York Public Library for the Performing Arts.

Constance Talmadge, who like Dorothy also had a dramatic older sister and was starring in her own feature vehicles by the end of the teens, started her career in 1913 at the Vitagraph Studio as the tag-along younger sister of rising star Norma Talmadge:

One thing I surely do think about myself is that I am darned lucky in being Norma's sister. She was the little trail-breaker for the whole family. Back in the old Vitagraph days, after Norma took the initiative and broke in and then went ahead through hard work and kept graduating to better and better parts, she used to take me along sometimes, to hook up her dresses, or be generally useful. I always say the first role I ever played was that of a maid!

Well, in no time she managed to work me in as an extra, and so the way was paved for me, whereas she had had all the initial hard work. (*Pantomime*, March 18, 1922)

It's said that Connie was always clowning around on the sets, which was noted by the powers in charge and transferred to the screen. After spending some time supporting Norma in items like *The Peacemaker* (1914) and playing opposite Billy Quirk in one-reelers such as *The Egyptian Mummy* (1914) and *Billy the Bear Tamer* (1915), the sisters moved from Brooklyn to California.

There Connie made a few Min A brand comedies with "Smiling Billy" Parsons, and both sisters joined D.W. Griffith's Fine Arts Company. Connie fared better there than Norma, for not only did she appear in *The Matrimaniac* (1916) with Douglas Fairbanks and headline in her own vehicles like *Betsy's Burglar* (1917), but also played the spunky mountain girl in the Babylonian story of Griffith's mammoth *Intolerance* (1916). From there she made sixteen romantic comedies for Louis J. Selznick's Select Pictures such *Sauce for the Goose* (1918), and *Experimental Marriage* (1919). Meanwhile, her sister Norma had married producer Joseph M. Schenck who oversaw her films, in addition to the wildly popular two-reelers of Roscoe "Fatty" Arbuckle. After 1919 Schenck took over the production of Connie's films as well.

Constance Talmadge is the center of attention in her last film, the French-made *Venus* (1929). Author's collection.

I like comedies of manners," says Miss Talmadge, "comedies that are, what sounds like a paradox when I say, subtle burlesque, comedies that are funny because they delight one's sense of what is ridiculously human in the way of little, every-day, common-place foibles and frailties, not comedies of the slapstick variety. (*Motion Picture News*, December 27, 1919)

The beginning of 1920 saw Talmadge become one most popular stars of the day. The first thing Schenck had done when taking over her pictures was to hire the team of John Emerson and Anita Loos to write and supervise the series, which led to hits on the order of *Polly of the Follies* (1922) and *Dulcy* (1923). In the mid-1920s director Sidney Franklin and writer Hans Kraly became her regular collaborators, resulting in sly and sophisticated films such as *Her Night of Romance* (1924), *Her Sister from Paris* (1925) and *The Duchess of Buffalo* (1926). Her last feature was the French-made *Venus* (1929) and she retired with the coming of sound, without even trying a talking film. By this time she and her sisters were very well off, and Connie settled into a comfortable private life. At the time of her death in 1973 most of her films were considered lost, leading to an eclipse in her reputation. Happily in recent years many of her films have been found and restored, and are making their way into the hands of film scholars and fans, giving her a new opportunity to charm and amuse.

Eden Gray (left) and Bebe Daniels (right) in the 1925 feature *Lovers in Quarantine*. Author's collection.

Another actress who started in the teens was Bebe Daniels, who first made a name for herself in Harold Lloyd's series of one and two-reel comedies, but Virginia Daniels (nicknamed Bebe) had a fifty-year career that encompassed stage, silent and sound films, radio, and television. Bebe was "born in a trunk," as her father was a theatre manager and her mother an actress. She began appearing on stage as a child, starring in *The Prince Chap* in San Francisco at age four, in addition to playing in all kinds of stock companies. Early movies beckoned at age eight, and she worked for Selig, Pathé, Bison, and Vitagraph before settling in at the Hal Roach Studio at age fourteen. Joining the company in 1915 as Harold's leading lady, Daniels wasn't a conventional shrinking and demure heroine – but instead a scrappy tomboy who gave back as good as she got in shorts like *Lonesome Luke, Messenger* (1917), *All Aboard* (1918), and *Take a Chance* (1919). She stayed at Roach through Lloyd's transition from Lonesome Luke to his wildly popular "glasses character," and after four years went out on her own following the short *Captain Kidd's Kids* (1919).

Her reason for leaving Roach was an offer from Cecil B. DeMille, for whom she played the "other woman" in films such as *Male and Female* (1919), *Why Change Your Wife?* (1920), and *The Affairs of Anatol* (1921), and at the same time starred in breezy comedies like *Ducks and Drakes* (1921), and *A Game Chicken* (1922) for Paramount's subsidiary Realart. The peak of her comedy career was from 1924 through 1928 when the studio put her in a series of fast-paced "modern everywoman comedies" such as *Miss Bluebeard* (1925), *The Campus Flirt* (1926), *She's a Sheik* (1927), and *Feel My Pulse* (1928), directed by top directors like Clarence Badger, Frank Tuttle, and Gregory La Cava. Most of these are missing today, so her mature comedy work is little known. When sound arrived she made an auspicious talkie debut in the musical *Rio Rita* (1929), which was a huge success. She followed it up with more musicals such as *Dixiana* (1930) and *42nd Street* (1933), plus some dramatic features including *The Maltese Falcon* (1931) and *Counselor-at-Law* (1933). In the mid-1930s she and husband Ben Lyon left Hollywood for England, where they worked on stage, and had the hit radio programs *Hi Gang!* and *Life with the Lyons*, which transferred to television, spinning off into the films *Family Affair* (1954) and *The Lyons Abroad* (1955). After a life of hard work, Bebe Daniels retired in 1961 and died ten years later at the age of seventy.

One of Universal Picture's biggest attractions of the 1920s was Laura La Plante. Although a great beauty, her popularity was based on her immense charm and a feeling of familiarity – that even though she was a knockout she didn't know it, and could conceivably be someone you knew living next door. Born in St. Louis, Laura and her mother moved to San Diego, and while visiting a cousin in Hollywood in 1918 she became an extra in Christie Comedies. She later related to author Jordan R. Young for his 1988 book *Let Me Entertain You* how sometimes easy it was for a pretty young girl to break into the movies:

> My cousin moved to a house near Gower Gulch, around the corner from Christie Studios. She said "Just walk down there and ask them if they need anybody." So I went down to the studio offices and I saw a woman in a little

cubbyhole. I said "I came to see if anybody needed anybody in a film." A man came running out and said that one of the bridesmaids didn't show up for a wedding scene.

He sent me over to wardrobe and told them to put my hair up to make me look more grown up; I was still only 14. I didn't know anything. I didn't even know where the camera was – the first thing I did was walk right through the background of a shot while they were filming.

I worked two or three days on the first picture there, at $5 a day. I kept going down to the studio and they put me in things. One day I saw Al Christie talking to a carpenter and I went over and said "Hey, how do you get in stock around here?" He said "From now on you're in it – Monday through Friday." In stock I was guaranteed five days a week.

Charles Delaney is surprised by Laura La Plante in *Home James* (1928). Author's collection.

She was also eloquent about the difference between Christie Comedies and Mack Sennett Comedies:

> Christie specialized in domestic comedies. They didn't do slapstick. Their two-reelers were quality films; they were the elite of that type of comedy. The films were broad, but not nearly as crude as Mack Sennett Comedies. They used to

have the men do a "double wings" where they'd fall down, jump up and kick their legs out – they'd say, "Do a double wings and scram."

From doing bits in shorts like *Wild and Western* (1919) she got noticed quickly, and the next year got promoted to the role of Maggie and Jigg's daughter Nora in *Jiggs and the Social Lion, Jigg's in Society,* and *Father's Close Shave* (all 1920) which were Christie's short-lived screen version of the comic strip *Bringing Up Father*. After a stint as leading lady for Bobby Vernon and Neal Burns she got attention as Charles Ray's love interest in *The Old Swimmin' Hole* (1921) and soon ended up at Universal, which would be her home for the next nine years.

At first she was used an all-purpose ingénue – doing time in westerns with Hoot Gibson and Art Accord, serials such as *Ned of the News* (1922), plus lots of comedy shorts with Roy Atwell, Bert Roach, Neely Edwards, Eddie Boland, and Harry Gribbon on the order of *Should Husbands Do Housework?* (1921), *A Bottle Baby, His Inheritance Taxi* (both 1922), and *Won't You Worry* (1923). At some point during this period she went from brunette to blonde, and in early 1924 made a huge impression in the comedy feature *Sporting Youth* opposite Reginald Denny. From here, despite an occasional drama like *Smouldering Fires* (1925) or *The Midnight Sun* (1926), she became the studio's elegant yet down-to-earth female comedy star. Further teamings with Reginald Denny were *The Fast Worker* (1924) and *Skinner's Dress Suit* (1926), both of which were directed by comedy expert William Seiter whom Ms. La Plante married in 1926. Her down-to-earth approach is also reflected in this astute summation of working in silent films:

Laura La Plante has a laugh on John Harron in 1928's *Finders Keepers*. Author's collection.

What was special about the silent films was the pantomime. You had to get the story over without words. The scripts actually had dialogue in those days. We didn't learn the lines but we got over the idea. The director gave us the situation, who said what to who, and we pretty much conveyed it.

Her string of starring comedies included *Poker Faces, Butterflies in the Rain* (both 1926), *Silk Stockings, Beware of Widows* (both 1927), *Finders Keepers,* and *Thanks for the Buggy Ride* (both 1928) where she had support from sterling farceurs like Edward Everett Horton, Bryant Washburn, T. Roy Barnes, and Glenn Tryon. By far her most famous films were the Paul Leni-directed horror/comedies *The Cat and the Canary* (1927), and *The Last Warning* (1929), where Ms. La Plante played it fairly straight as the in-peril heroine and left most of the comedy to the likes of Creighton Hale, Slim Summerville, Flora Finch, Gertrude Astor, and Bert Roach.

Heinie Conklin and Ben Turpin take notes on Marie Prevost and Tom Kennedy in *Hide and Seek, Detectives* (1918). Courtesy of Steve Rydzewski.

Her sound debut came in Universal's big-budget version of *Show Boat* (1929) where she starred and sang as Magnolia, and she did well in comedies like *The Love Trap* and *Hold Your Man* (both 1929), not to mention the studio's color musical extravaganza *King of Jazz* (1930). After leaving the "Big U" in 1931 she worked for a few more years but retired in 1935. She later worked when she felt like it, doing an occasional film or television show, or a stage production like *The White Sheep of the Family* or *Springtime for Henry* with her old friend Edward Everett Horton. She passed away at ninety-one in 1996.

An overlooked star of 1920s comedy features is Marie Prevost, who started her career in the mid-teens as a Mack Sennett Bathing Beauty:

> About four years ago, while in Los Angeles, I visited an old school chum who was playing in Mack Sennett comedies. I was struck with the glamor of life on the screen – what impressionable girl isn't? And when my girl friend asked me if I wouldn't like to work at the studio I jumped at the opportunity.
>
> At that time bathing girl comedies were reaching their greatest popularity, and I soon was promoted to major roles. Some of my best known pictures were "Love, Honor and Behave," "A Small Town Idol," "Down on the Farm," "Call a Cop," and "Uncle Tom Without the Cabin." In the last-named picture, while enacting the role of Little Eva, the wire suspending me on my trip to Heaven broke and I landed kerplunk on Uncle Tom, who was distractedly sobbing over the bed from which I had just risen. He couldn't have been very much in earnest about his grief, because his lamentations immediately changed to the sort of language that no self-respecting angel should hear. (*Motion Picture Weekly*, December 10, 1921)

As she said she worked her way up to leading roles at Sennett, and in 1921 moved to Universal where she starred as a flapper in *A Parisian Scandal* (1921) and *The Midnight Flapper* (1922), and then moved on to three prestigious Ernst Lubitsch productions – *The Marriage Circle* (1923), *Three Women* (1924), and *Kiss Me Again* (1925). This led to the peak period of her career when she appeared as an independent young woman in a series of light comedy bedroom-farce features for Producers Distributors Corp. that included *Getting Gertie's Garter*, *The Girl in the Pullman* (both 1927), *Rush Hour,* and *Blonde for a Night* (both 1928).

The arrival of sound brought the series to an end, but she made a good transition to the new medium with supporting roles in films such as *Ladies of Leisure* (1930) and *The Sin of Madelon Claudet* (1931). Sadly, roles became more difficult for her to come by, complicated by a developing weight problem. Her last prominent parts were in 1935's *Hands Across the Table* and the short *Keystone Hotel*. Her 1937 death was attributed to the combination of acute alcoholism and malnutrition, reportedly due to extreme dieting.

One of the most popular silent stars was little Colleen Moore. Born in 1902, she was movie struck at a young age, part of the first generation of people who grew up wanting to be movie stars. Thanks to her uncle Walter Hewey, the managing director of the newspaper *The Chicago American*, she got a screen test for D.W. Griffith, who signed her to a six-month contract. She arrived in Hollywood in 1916 at age fourteen. Stints for Selig,

Thomas Ince, Fox, and Universal followed, and although she was working she admitted in her 1968 autobiography *Silent Star* that she felt deficient in comedy:

Marie uses skills learned during her Sennett days in one of her late 1920's features. Author's collection.

Shortly after making my first picture with Tom Mix in 1919, I made a second picture with Charles Ray at Ince Studio called *The Egg-Crate Wallop*, a story about a prize fighter whose previous experience as a drayman handling heavy egg crates had given him a wow of a punch. In one of the scenes I was supposed to go through a trap door, fall down, and come up with a reaction that would get a laugh.

The director worked on the scene with me one entire afternoon, but – in comedy lingo – I just didn't know how to "take it."

I knew then that I needed comedy training, but I didn't do anything about it until the following year when I read an article in Photoplay in which Cecil B.

De Mille said that no girl could be a great dramatic actress unless she had comedy training. This was why he was looking to the slapstick comedy studios for his future stars.

That decided me.

Colleen Moore at the peak of her popularity in the late 1920s. Author's collection.

To this end she signed in 1920 with comedy producer Al Christie for a few two-reelers, plus the feature *So Long Letty* (1920). With that under her belt bigger parts for Marshal Neilan and Samuel Goldwyn came her way, leading to her signing with First National Pictures in 1923. Her second picture for them, *Flaming Youth* (1923), was a box-office sensation, making her a top star. A pageboy haircut, which she took from a Chinese doll, became her trademark, as did her image as a flapper.

Afraid of being permanently typecast, she convinced First National to let her make a film version of Edna Ferber's novel *So Big* (1925), and the picture's success allowed her to vary her roles. Most often she appeared in comedies, making use of Cinderella-type of stories for films such as *Irene* (1926), *Orchids and Ermine* (1927), and *Her Wild Oat* (1927), and there were echoes of Mabel Normand in her portrayals of lively working-class girls who get their Prince Charming (a.k.a. millionaire) by the end of the picture. Her best-remembered film is *Ella Cinders* (1926), which was based on a popular comic strip, and is a solidly crafted comedy-drama with a generous number of sight-gag sequences peppered throughout. Starting with her picture *Sally* (1925) a young Mervyn Leroy began contributing gags to her films, and worked on a number them before his first directorial assignment in 1928:

> Mervyn invented the gags for many of my pictures after *Sally* – invented, too, a screen credit for himself as Comedy Constructor! (And said to me one day on the set when I asked him if he thought comedy or drama was harder for an actress to do, "Comedy. An onion can make an actress cry, but the vegetable has yet to be grown that can make her funny." I agree. Both comedy and drama

are hard, but in a tragic scene you can dig down into your emotions, whereas in comedy there's no depth of experience in life to call upon. Similarly, in drama the director becomes an actresses audience and, if there is a rapport between them, the wellspring of her emotional outpourings. But in comedy you're on your own, taking only from the director's intellect.)

At her peak in the late 1920s Moore was one of the highest paid actresses of the era, and continued to turn out hits like *Twinkletoes* (1927), and *Lilac Time* (1928). The arrival of sound, plus a divorce from producer/husband John McCormick, effectively ended her career despite a couple of good talkies that included *The Power and the Glory* (1933), written by Preston Sturges. Wealthy, she retired in 1934 but was later on hand for revivals of her films, in addition to providing charming commentary for Kevin Brownlow and David Gill's 1980 *Hollywood* series. She passed away in 1988.

Marion Davies under cover in *The Cardboard Lover* (1928). Courtesy of Robert Arkus.

Fate has played a dirty trick on Marion Davies, as she is best-remembered as the mistress of newspaper tycoon William Randolph Hearst, who made her a star by financing her films and publicizing her in his papers. Often overlooked are her sizeable talents as a comedienne and wicked mimic in some very funny comedies. Chiefly responsible for this situation is *Citizen Kane* (1941), Orson Welles' thinly-veiled examination of Hearst, which portrays Kane's mistress, Susan Alexander, as an untalented singer that the magnate tries to promote as an opera star. Luckily many of Davies' pictures survive and plainly illustrate that while she did have the Hearst machine behind her, she also had the talents to warrant movie stardom.

Born Marion Cecelia Douras in Brooklyn in 1897, she followed her older sisters onto the stage as a dancer, and made her Broadway debut in 1914. Despite a life-long stutter, the *Ziegfeld Follies* and parts in popular shows like *Oh Boy* and *Very Good Eddie* followed, as did her meeting and becoming the consort of the powerful Hearst. Movies were the next step – her first was in 1917:

> I couldn't act, but the idea of silent films appealed to me, because I couldn't talk either. Silent pictures were right up my alley. (*The Times We Had,* 1975)

The next year Hearst formed the Marion Davies Film Corp. (which soon became Cosmopolitan Productions). Her early films were often light, romantic comedies such as *Getting Mary Married* (1919), and *Enchantment* (1921), but she was soon starring in a stream of lavish historical sagas such as *When Knighthood Was in Flower* (1922), *Little Old New York* (1923), and *Janice Meredith* (1924).

In 1925 Davies and Cosmopolitan moved to Hollywood and joined forces with MGM resulting in a new focus on her true strength – comedy. Her gift for mimicry was taken advantage of in films such as *The Patsy* (1928), where in long takes she breathtakingly transforms herself into Mae Murray, Lillian Gish, and Pola Negri, and spoofs them to a frazzle. In her most popular film *Show People* (1928) she not only roasts Gloria Swanson, but also all of Hollywood to boot. Other comedies such as *Quality Street* (1927), and *The Cardboard Lover* (1928), on which she is credited as executive producer, involve her creating and impersonating alternate characters to test the ardency of her love interest.

The late silent era was the peak of her career:

> I really wanted to give up when the talkies came in. I was all right in silent movies when I just had to make faces at the camera. It wasn't really work. When talkies began, I realized I had to work; I couldn't stall around anymore. (*The Times We Had,* 1975)

Although nervous because of her stammer, she made the changeover to sound very smoothly, and as a bonus the new medium gave her opportunity to use her singing and dancing abilities. Good pictures such as *Marianne* (1929), *The Floradora Girl* (1930), and *Blondie of the Follies* (1932) ensued, but by 1933 she was no longer the peppy young ingénue. For the film *Going Hollywood* (1933) she was given an ill-advised beauty makeover which gave her a slightly Madame Tussaud's Wax Museum look. Even so, her last films made by Warner Brothers, still had moments of great charm, but she called it quits with 1937's *Ever Since Eve*. In her retirement she devoted herself to charities and spending time with her family, before passing away in 1961.

On the set of *The Patsy* (1928) director King Vidor and Marion Davies work on her Pola Negri imitation. Courtesy of Cole Johnson.

Perhaps the best-remembered of the 1920s funny ladies is Clara Bow. Known as the "It Girl," in the late 20s, she was the flapper personified when she starred in a string of hits such as *It* (1927), *Red Hair* (1928), and *The Fleet's In* (1928). Like Colleen Moore, Clara was movie-struck as a child, but for her it was an escape from an abusive Brooklyn childhood with a schizophrenic mother and an absentee father. At age sixteen she entered and won a 1921 photo / talent contest where she ended up with a small part in a film that got her foot in the door of the industry. The picture in which she first garnered attention was *Down to the Sea in Ships* (1922), and she was soon signed to producer B.P. Schulberg and his Preferred Pictures Company.

Clara Bow. Courtesy of Cole Johnson.

There she became a veritable workhorse, cranking out low-budget features, but because directors like Elmer Clifton and Frank Tuttle were impressed with her natural talent, Schulberg was able to loan her out for better films such as *Black Oxen* (1923), *Helen's Babies* (1924), and best of all, Ernst Lubitsch's *Kiss Me Again* (1925). In 1925 Schulberg joined Paramount Pictures and brought his main asset, Clara, along with him. Right away the quality of her films picked up with an excellent supporting role in *Dancing Mothers* (1926) and as leading lady to Eddie Cantor in *Kid Boots* (1926). The first of her classic comedies was *Mantrap* (1926) where she's the bored wife of backwoodsman Ernest Torrence.

Pictures such as *It* (1927), *Rough House Rosie* (1927), and *Three Weekends* (1928) followed which crystallized her image of the "bad girl" – the girl who does what she wants and goes after whomever she wants - but is really a good girl at heart. She had many of the screen qualities of a jazz-age Mabel Normand – the puckish humor, the spontaneity – and audiences responded to her as they had to Mabel. Unfortunately also like Mabel her wild life style created scandals that damaged her career. The changeover to sound brought further complications. Although Bow made a smooth transition to the new medium, she hated the microphone and was never comfortable in talking films. She retired from the screen at age twenty-eight in 1933.

Taking a look at Europe in the 1920s, their favorite movie comedy heroine was England's Betty Balfour, who never made an impression in America but broadened her popularity beyond Britain with films made in France and Germany at the end of the silent era. Born in London in 1903, she made her professional stage debut at age ten in that city's West End Ambassador's Theatre as part of the C.B. Cochran revue *Odds and Ends* in 1914. Other plays, such as *From Lourain* followed, and she continued with Cochran, headlining in his revue *All Women* which toured around the country. In 1917 she appeared at the Palace in London but was hurt in a German bomb attack which left her bedridden for a few months before she returned in the hit *Medorah* in 1919.

During the war producer T.A. Welsh and director George Pearson had seen her perform, making such an impression on Pearson that he vowed "when the war was over I would find Betty Balfour and give her the opportunity of proving to the world through the screen that she was one of the greatest artists of the time." Pearson made good on his determination in 1920 after he and Welsh had set up a production company. They cast Balfour as a maid in support of Moyna MacGill (Angela Lansbury's mother) in *Nothing Else Matters* (1920). After replacing Gertrude Lawrence on stage in *The Midnight Follies* she and Pearson embarked on her starring film career with *Mary Finds the Gold* (1921). Their next production was *Squibs* (1921) which hit pay dirt and forever crystalized her screen persona. Squibs was a peppy, Cockney flower girl who worked in Piccadilly Circus, and this story of her life and adventures was so popular that it led to three sequels – *Squibs Wins the Calcutta Sweeps* (1922), *Squibs M.P.*, and *Squib's Honeymoon* (both 1923). Post-war audiences took her to their hearts:

> Betty Balfour's forte is comedy, and broad comedy at that. She can set you rocking with laughter at her antics, or even at the expressions that chase each other with such lightning swiftness across her saucy face. Also, and this is a more recent accomplishment, she can express tragedy. She can make you feel a whole lot

Betty Balfour as Squibs. Courtesy of Cole Johnson.

without facial contortions, frantic gestures, or subtitles. (*Picture and Picturegoer*, December 1924)

She was dubbed "Britain's Queen of Happiness" and the "British Mary Pickford." Between the Squib's entries, films such as *Mord Emily* and *Wee MacGregor's Sweetheart* (both 1922) continued to present her in similar tomboy roles. Although happy with her success, the star and director Pearson still wanted to explore different material. *Love, Life and Laughter* (1923) used her basic Squibs character but tried to give it more depth and dramatic moments in the story of a music hall actress. *Reveille* (1924) was very different as it showed how the war had affected a group of regular working class people. *Squibs* was released in America in 1922 as *Me and My Girl*, followed by *Love, Life and Laughter* in 1925, but interest in her never took root in the United States.

More films such as *Somebody's Darling* (1925) and *Cinders* (1926) followed in Squibs mold, but after *Blinkeyes* (1926) she had a personal and professional split with George Pearson. She headed to the continent where she made pictures in France, Germany and Sweden such as *Die Sieben Tochter der Frau Gyurkovies* (*A Sister of Six*, 1926), *Croquette* (1927), and *Le Diable au Coeur* (*Little Devil May Care*, 1928). Back in England she finished the 1920s playing opposite Syd Chaplin in his only made-in-Britain feature *A Little Bit of Fluff* (1928, released as *Skirts* in America) and the Alfred Hitchcock-directed *Champagne* (1928) where she plays a spoiled rich girl whose father tells her they're broke so that she has to make something of herself.

Her last silent film, *The Vagabond Queen* (1929), was a send-up of Ruritanian romances, particularly *The Prisoner of Zenda*, with Betty playing a dual role of work maid Sally from a run-down London boarding house and the regal Princess Xania of Botonia. She made her sound debut in *The Brat* (1930), but a talking version of *Squibs* wasn't particularly successful and her popularity diminished in the 1930s. Even working with Jessie Matthews in *Evergreen* (1934) and a musically revamp *Squibs* (1935) wasn't able to jump start her career. She made her last film appearance in 1945, and after an unsuccessful bid to return to the stage in 1952, that was followed by a suicide attempt, she retired from public life and in 1977 died at age seventy-four.

In addition to the women in features, there were a number of comediennes who got their laughs in shorts. Dorothy Devore was born Alma Inez Williams in Texas, and after moving to Los Angeles as a child she eventually sang and danced in amateur revues and at L.A. nightclubs like Al Levy's. She made her film debut in the late teen's one-reelers of Eddie Lyons and Lee Moran, who were the most popular screen comedy team before Laurel & Hardy in shorts like *House Cleaning Horrors* (1918), and *Marry My Wife* (1919). From there she went to work for producer Al Christie who starred her as a plucky girl who always gets into hot water and has to go to great lengths to get herself out.

> Al Christie was wonderful. There were two brothers, Charles and Al. Charles handled all the business; he was in the background more or less. And Al, of

course, was producing and directing; he directed many of my films. The studios were small, and, well, it was like a family, and you knew everyone. Of course, naturally, daily or at least yearly, it grew and grew and grew. But when I first started in 1919, it was just very small; it was on the corner of Gower and Sunset Boulevard, Paramount was on the other side, adjoining on Vine and Sunset.

Al Christie gives Vera Steadman and Dorothy Devore grief over their skirt lengths. Courtesy of The Museum of Modern Art.

I made a number of pictures with William Beaudine, a fine, fine man. Also his brother Harold Beaudine, he was younger, but a good director. When Al Christie would direct me, he'd say, "Let's do it once," and Bill Beaudine would start with the same thing. If I was in a scene alone, he'd always do that. He'd say, "Let's make it once now" – in other words the first take. I was so used to working with him, why he understood me and I understood him.

Another of my directors at Christie was a man that finally went to England and made some very fine pictures, Scott Sidney. He passed away when I was quite young; he was a great deal older than I was. He was one of the ones that I thoroughly enjoyed working with. (*The Silent Picture*, 1972)

Her screen adventures such as *Saving Sister Susie* (1922), *Kidding Kate, Navy Blues* (both 1923), *Stay Single,* and *Getting Gertie's Goat* (both 1924) were very popular, and her five years with Christie culminated in the feature *Hold Your Breath* (1924) where she staked her claim in Harold Lloyd territory by climbing and dangling off a tall building. During the next few years she left slapstick and starred in all types of features, such as crime dramas like *Money to Burn* (1925) or the society story of *Mountains of Manhattan* (1927), but she returned to two-reelers for Jack White Comedies:

> No one wants to see me cry," Miss Devore stated calmly, "and I don't blame them. I don't care about seeing *myself* cry. I started my career in Christie comedies, and I was trained as a comedienne. But when I went into feature pictures I was always having to be – oh, so emotional. And I just don't know how!" (*Picture Play*, February 1928)

Shorts like *Up in Arms* (1927), *Cutie* (1928), and *Auntie's Mistake* (1929) took her to the end of the silent era when she retired with the coming of sound after only a couple of talking appearances.

Snooky the chimp and Ernie Adams have a weenie tug-of-war in *Snooky's Twin Troubles* (1921). Courtesy of Sam Gill.

Monkeys were big in silent comedy, and one of the best known was Snooky the Human-Zee. Although described in Educational Pictures pressbooks as a *he*, trade magazine articles reveal that she was actually a *she,* and named Snookums, but was dressed as and played a boy (hence an animal drag performer):

"Snookie" is the charming young daughter of Napoleon the Great, and Sally, well known to stage and screen. Snookie has been working in the movies since the death of Napoleon, her father, in a laudable effort to help her widowed mother scratch along, and from all accounts she is going to be a more celebrated monk than either of her parents. (*Moving Picture World*, August 7, 1920)

Napoleon and Sally starred in a series of shorts produced by the E & R Jungle Film Company, which had been founded in 1914 by J.S. Edwards and John Rounan. Napoleon had appeared on stages around the world with an elephant named Hip, but after Hip died Napoleon and Sally were teamed in films. Snookums appears to have been born in 1916 or 1917, and first turned up on screen in 1919 shorts such as Jimmy Aubrey's *Mules and Mortgages*:

> One of the big features of the picture is the introduction of "Snookums," a performing chimpanzee, who is the offspring of "Napoleon" and "Sally," who will be remembered as the stars in the "Chimp Comedies" released some time ago. (*Motion Picture News*, April 9, 1919)

Her other early appearances include *The Star Boarder* (1919) where she gives star Larry Semon a big soul kiss on the lips, and *The Rajah* (1919) smoking cigarettes and playing cards with Harold Lloyd.

With John Rounan as her owner and trainer in 1920 she was launched in her own starring two-reel series produced by C.L. Chester, distributed by Educational Pictures, and directed by William S. Campbell. Usually supported by nine-year-old Ida Mae McKenzie, baby Arthur Nowell, and character comic Hap Ward, titles such as *Four Times Foiled*, *You'll Be Surprised* (both 1920), and *Ready to Serve* (1921) are mostly burlesques on standard melodramas with Snooky in the hero's role. There's always a baby to rescue, a race horse to ride to victory, or a mortgaged farm to save. Before the films petered out in 1923 later items like *Snooky's Covered Wagon*, and *Snooky's Treasure Island* (both 1923) became more genre parody with all-animal supporting casts. After this her appearances became less frequent. *Kids Days*, a 1924 Universal short may be her last, but after her owner Rounan was killed by a lion in 1928 she disappeared from the screen.

In 1920 producer Hal Roach was looking for talent to fill out his production schedule. He'd had success spinning Snub Pollard off from the Harold Lloyd shorts into his own series, but other series with Toto, and Dee Lampton hadn't flown. Beatrice La Plante was a young actress, who according to contemporary sources was from France, although some sources say that she really had been born in Illinois. She broke into pictures in 1919, and after playing supporting roles in a couple of dramas made an impression as leading lady to Sessue Hayakawa in his comedy feature *The Beggar Prince* (1920). Roach hired La Plante for a series of one-reelers that were in the Mabel Normand / Fay Tincher mold.

Small and petite with dark eyes and hair, she resembled both, and in surviving entries like *Merely a Maid*, *Little Miss Jazz*, and *Start the Show* (all 1920) she's cute and charming, and while adept at broader physical comedy she also shows a knack for crisply timed little intimate bits of business. Sadly, the series wasn't warmly received and died after only five entries before it could really get started. From here she had a nice supporting role in the Eddie Lyons and Lee Moran feature *Fixed by George* (1920), but after a couple more features she finished her film career back at Roach supporting Gaylord Lloyd (Harold's brother as a revived Lonesome Luke) in his shorts *Rough Seas*, and *Trolley Troubles* (both 1921). Having recently married she retired from films and passed away in 1973.

A Hal Roach publicity photo of Beatrice La Plante. Courtesy of The Museum of Modern Art.

The overlooked and vivacious Alberta Vaughn started her career in the early 1920s in Century Comedies with the likes of Harry Sweet, Lee Moran, and Brownie the wonder dog before she headed over to Fox for two-reelers such as *The Pirate* (1922), plus the five-reel *A Friendly Husband* (1923), where she was the leading lady for Lupino Lane and Clyde Cook. In 1923 she took a step up with a move to the Mack Sennett Studio for shorts like *Nip and Tuck, Down to the Sea in Shoes,* and *Skylarking* (all 1923), in addition to being Harry Langdon's first co-star in *Picking Peaches* and *Smile Please* (both 1924). After being selected as a 1924 WAMPAS Baby Star she was on the rise as a comedy star when she headlined in FBO's *The Telephone Girl* comedies (1924), which chronicled her misadventures as a flirty and street-wise telephone switchboard operator.

Alberta Vaughn looking skeptical in *The Telephone Girl* entry *The Square Sex* (1924). Courtesy of Karel Caslavsky.

This was quickly followed by similar series on the order of *The Go-Getters* (1924-1925), *The Pacemakers* (1925), and *The Adventures of Maizie* (1926), where she was supported by the team of Al Cooke and Kit Guard. Her success led to a number of starring features like *Collegiate, The Adorable Deceiver* (both 1926), *Uneasy Payments,* and *Ain't Love Funny* (both 1927), but she was back with Al Cooke for some 1928 *Racing Blood* two-reelers. She continued to work in the early days of sound in *The Record Breakers* (1930) shorts, and some increasingly low-budget features until finishing her career in some mid-1930s westerns. The erratic quality of the end of career may have been due to her drinking problems that led to run-ins with the law and numerous arrests in the 1940s. By the mid-1950s she appears to have worked out her problems and lived quietly until her death at age eighty-seven in 1992.

Century Comedies, which had been formed in 1917 by Julius and Abe Stern to exploit the talents of Alice Howell, developed three other female comedy stars in the mid-1920s. Peggy-Jean Montgomery, better known as Baby Peggy, made her film debut at nineteen months in 1920, and started at Century as support to Brownie the wonder dog. In her excellent 1996 autobiography *What Ever Happened to Baby Peggy?*, Montgomery had this to say about her days with Brownie:

> As costars, Brownie and I turned out a veritable blizzard of fast-paced two-reelers. These were true slapstick comedies which some theatre managers ran as "chasers" – screening them as one audience was exiting the house and the next coming in. Referred to on the lot as "five-day wonders," they were produced at what seemed the speed of light, at an average cost to the studio of less than three thousand dollars each, and sold to exhibitors at vastly inflated prices, earning Century enormous profits.

Baby Peggy, possibly after asking boss Julius Stern for a raise. Courtesy of Jim Kerkhoff.

Peggy also worked with Teddy and Lee Moran, and soon became the star of her own series. Tiny and cute, but in a character sort of way with a pug nose, big eyes, and bowl haircut, Montgomery became a miniature working girl in shorts such as *The Kid Reporter* (1923) or spoofed rival movie stars in *Peg O' the Movies* and *Carmen Jr.* (both 1923). Part of the fun is seeing the pint-sized Montgomery enact routines that were part of the standard repertoire of seasoned professionals such as Roscoe Arbuckle or Lloyd Hamilton.

For instance in *Peggy, Behave!* (1922) the tot has broken a window and in order to escape the wrath of her large stepmother Blanche Payson she makes a big show of "polishing" the imaginary glass, even making extra effort to get rid of an obstinate flyspeck. Peggy was also headlined in a series of loose fairy tale adaptations, like *Hansel and Gretel* (1923) and *Jack and the Beanstalk* (1924), and moved into features such as *The Darling of New York* (1923) and *Captain January* (1924). Her immense popularity had led to all kinds of Baby Peggy merchandise – dolls, cut-outs, books, etc. – but by age six she was out of films due to a disagreement between her father and producer Sol Lesser. Her Hollywood fame secured her appearances in vaudeville for a time, but she was never able to get a foothold in pictures again. Today as author Diana Serra Carey she remains a feisty presence presiding over screenings of her films and preserving film history.

Edna Marion and Charley Chase from a surviving print of *Aching Youth* (1928). Courtesy of EYE Filmmuseum, Netherlands.

Edna Marion is remembered today for her appearances at the Hal Roach Studio in support of Laurel & Hardy, and Charley Chase, but at Century she was the star of her own films. She came from vaudeville, where she worked for Gus Edwards. She entered films in some independent *Puppy Love Comedies* for Hollywood Photoplay Productions (as Edna Hannan). She headlined at Century from 1924 through 1926 as wide-eyed little girl with big ideas who usually starts something that snowballs out of her control. Surviving entries include *My Baby Doll*, *Uncle Tom's Gal* (both 1925), and *Movie Madness* (1926). On leaving Century, she made brief stops at Christie, Fox, and Jack White Comedies working with the likes of Neal Burns, George Davis, and Sid Smith, and even became a 1926 WAMPAS Baby Star (promising ingénues picked yearly by the

Western Association of Motion Picture Advertisers), before ending up on the Hal Roach lot. Although she was always winning and cute, it's too bad the studio never attempted to star her in her own shorts. She left Roach along with Viola Richard and Dorothy Coburn in a puzzling 1928 studio housecleaning move, and appeared in a few features like *Skinner Steps Out* (1929), *Romance of the West* (1930), and *Murders in the Rue Morgue* (1932) before her career sputtered out in the early days of sound.

Century's other 1920s comedy heroine was the neglected Wanda Wiley. A former dental student, this attractive, lanky brunette was launched by the studio in 1924 as a very athletic girl-about-town in a stunt-heavy series all about speed. Survivors such as *A Speedy Marriage* (1925) and *Flying Wheels* (1926), plus trade magazine descriptions, give a standard plot about a girl who usually has to get somewhere or do something by a deadline, who spends the bulk of a short in motion – involved in chases on motorcycles or hopping from one car to another. Other shorts like *The Queen of Aces* (1925) has her posing as a boy to fool her sweetheart's disapproving father, and the clever *A Thrilling Romance* (1926) chronicles her struggles as a would-be writer of romance novels who gets involved with handsome Earl McCarthy and an elusive bag of money, which at the end all turns out to be one of her unsold stories. An attractive and game performer – the trade magazines are full of items about her taking spills and getting bruised in the line of slapstick duty – sadly Wiley is forgotten due to the loss of about ninety-nine per cent of her pictures. After leaving Century in 1927, she appeared in a few of Bray's *Fistical Culture* series opposite Lewis Sargent, but soon retired from the screen.

A Driver's Ed. session gone wrong with Wanda Wiley and Eddie Baker in *Jane's Flirtation* (1927). Courtesy of Jim Kerhoff.

Mack Sennett continued to retain his title of "King of Comedy" in the 1920s despite solid competition from Hal Roach and Al Christie. While still maintaining his gag-crazy slapstick shorts with the likes of Ben Turpin and Billy Bevan, in perhaps an acknowledgement of his rivals he began exploring more polite and situational styles of comedy with a series starring leading man Ralph Graves and the domestic Smith Family two-reelers with Raymond McKee, Ruth Hiatt, and Mary Ann Jackson. Alice Day was a little ingénue who was supporting Harry Langdon that caught popular attention and was spun off into her own series. She had moved to Los Angeles from Colorado in 1922, and along with her younger sister Marceline began working as an extra at various studios. Quickly advancing to featured roles in pictures such as *Temple of Venus* (1923) and Norma Talmadge's *Secrets* (1924), she also worked at Century Comedies in items like *My Pal* (1923) before being hired by Sennett.

Alice Day and friend try to sneak past Irving Bacon in *Kitty from Killarney* (1926). Courtesy of Bruce Calvert.

She immediately was put to work with Harry Langdon. Small and demure she had some of the same quiet hesitancy as Langdon, and from a small bit in *Picking Peaches* (1924) she became his love interest in *Shanghaied Lovers* (1924) where she proved her mettle with a hilarious scene in which she poses in disguise as a male sailor to be near her recently shanghaied husband Harry. He doesn't recognize her and finds it more than peculiar that this other "sailor" is cozying up and making moon-eyes at him. From here Day and Langdon were paired in *Flickering Youth*, *The Cat's Meow*, *His New Mama*, and *The First 100 Years* (all 1924). Seeing potential in her, Sennett moved her from the Langdon shorts, where she was replaced by her sister Marceline, and teamed her with Ralph Graves for a long string of romantic comedies that included *East of the Water Plug*, *Riders of the Purple Cows* (both 1924), *The Beloved Bozo*, and *Bashful Jim* (both 1925). Finally with *Tee for Two* (August 2, 1925) she was launched in her own starring series.

Being dainty and demure gave her a natural underdog look, and her persona was that of a sensible and slightly old-fashioned girl who was often shown working in department stores or laundries in shorts like *Hotsy Totsy* and *The Soapsuds Lady* (both 1925), in addition to portraying a just off the boat immigrant from Scotland or Ireland in *Tee for Two* (1925) and *Kitty from Kilarney* (1926). Sometimes she was saddled with an annoying family and had to hold her own with scene-stealing supporting players like Sunshine Hart, Barney Hellum, Marvin Loback, and Mary Ann Jackson. She even did a version of her own story with *Hotcakes for Two* (1926) where she plays a little girl who comes from the sticks to become a Hollywood movie queen.

The Sennett publicity machine referred to her as "a lump of sugar in the cup of happiness," and advised:

> A comedienne is born, not made. She must be funny without being coarse. She must be able to appear in grotesque clothes without being repulsive. A certain almost indefinable quality of winsomeness, coupled with a delicate sense of humor makes the real comedienne, says Mr. Sennett. Under all conditions she must be ineffably charming. Cinderella's fame didn't come from the fact that she carried out the ashes, nor because she had a dainty foot. It was a combination of the two. Every comedienne, in the opinion of the famous comedy producer, must be a Cinderella in a sense.

After three years and twenty-one starring shorts she left Sennett and became active as an all-purpose light-comedy leading lady in features such as *See You in Jail*, *The Gorilla* (both 1927), *The Smart Set*, and *Phyllis of the Follies* (both 1928), not to mention a few dramas like the young Frank Capra's *The Way of the Strong* (1928), and *Drag* (1929) opposite Richard Barthelmess. Making the transition to sound she still did occasional leads, but mostly featured roles. Some of her better films were for Warner Brothers/ First National such as *Little Johnny Jones*, *The Show of Shows*, and *The Love Racket* (all 1929), but outside of a couple for Columbia most of her work came at smaller independent studios on the order of Chesterfield, Tiffany, and Peerless. Her final films were the westerns *Two-Fisted Law*, and *Gold* (both 1932) before retiring in 1932.

Producer Joe Rock brought a new comedienne to the screen in 1925, whom he prophesied "will be one of the screen sensations of the year." Alice Ardell was a young Parisian actress who Rock headlined in a series of Blue Ribbon comedies such as *Hold*

Tight, A Peaceful Riot (both 1925), *Mummy Love, Alice Blues,* and *She's a Prince* (all 1926) for a total of twelve entries. A gimmick for the series was a different well-known male comic playing opposite Ardell in each short, so the likes of Chester Conklin, Slim Summerville, Lee Moran, Sid Smith, and Joe Rock himself took turns appearing with her as well as supplying most of the laughs. Ardell was pretty, athletic, and had a pleasing screen personality – but wasn't at all funny.

The surviving shorts are funny due to the talents and guidance of old pros behind the camera such as Jay A. Howe, Marcel Perez, Percy Pembroke, and Harry Sweet, in addition to her leading men and supporting comics on screen. Ardell often comes across as a guest in her own starring films as she's barely in entries like *Alice Blues* and *Mummy Love* (both 1926) where the lion's share of the footage goes to Sid Smith and Neely Edwards respectively. Said to have been an on again – off again girlfriend of Stan Laurel's for many years, after the Blue Ribbon comedies Ardell disappears from the screen until the early 1930s when she did numerous bits, almost always as a French maid, in shorts and features until 1939.

Alice Ardell, Ella McKenzie, and Gale Henry in *A Fraternity Mixup* (1928). Courtesy of EYE Filmmuseum, Netherlands.

Two later entries in the comedy shorts field were brought to the screen by Al Christie. Anne Cornwall had been in pictures since 1918 after appearing in the choruses of Broadway musicals such as *Oh, Look!* with the Dolly Sisters. But she told *Picture Play* magazine the she "didn't like doing the same thing night after night," and preferred working in films. She first worked supporting Alice Brady in romantic comedies like *The Indestructible Wife* and *The World to Live In* (both 1919), and dramas such as Lionel Barrymore's *The Copperhead* (1920). She moved to Universal where she appeared with with Eddie Lyons and Lee Moran in their five-reel comedies *Everything But the Truth* and *La La Lucille* (both 1920). The studio also starred her in dramas like *The Path She Chose* and *The Girl in the Rain* (both 1920).

She went on to support Gloria Swanson, Richard Barthelmess, and Betty Compson, and kept popping up in comedies such as Constance Talmadge's *Dulcy* (1923), *Introduce Me* (1925) with Douglas MacLean, and Monty Bank's *Keep Smiling* (1925). Producer Al Christie began using her for support for Bobby Vernon in shorts like *Bright Lights* (1924), and *French Pastry* (1925), finally launching her in her own series of two-reelers in 1926:

Ann Cornwall hoping to get a break from editor Bill Blaisdell in *Hold Still* (1926). Courtesy of Robert S. Birchard.

The screen lacks good comediennes and the entry of Miss Cornwall into the ranks of featured players in laugh-making movies is a welcome addition. She proves that she can bring as many laughs as her male brother players who have so long monopolized screen comedies (Educational Pictures pressbook for *Cool Off*, 1926).

Teamed with "Foxy Grandpa" character comic Jack Duffy, Cornwall played his granddaughter who was always in some sort of trouble, or was trying to keep some kind of golddigger from moving in on grandpop Duffy. The series straddled Christie's releases from Educational to Paramount, and consisted of the shorts *Hold Still*, *Cool Off* (both 1926), *Chicken Feathers*, *Scared Pink* (both 1927), *Fighting Fannie*, *Half-Back Hannah*, and *Love's Young Scream* (all 1928). During this time she appeared in the best known of her films, Buster Keaton's *College* (1927), in which she is Buster's sports-positive love interest. When sound came in her Christie series had ended, but she had a good role in Laurel and Hardy's two-reel *Men O'War* (1929). After this she was unfortunately demoted to uncredited walk-on parts, which she did on and off until 1959.

Saucy Frances Lee was Al Christie's other late twenties comedienne. She had appeared as a dancer in a vaudeville act with Billy Dooley, and they were signed for pictures by Christie in 1925. Lee was installed as leading lady for Christie's biggest star Bobby Vernon, and after two years of supporting him in shorts such as *Page Me* (1926) and *Jail Birdies* (1927), plus being named a 1927 WAMPAS Baby Star, she got her own series. The *Confessions of a Chorus Girl* shorts were adapted from a group of stories by French writer Jean Arlette. The plots revolved around Lee as a free-spirited and fun-loving show dancer who inevitably finds herself in hot water and dressed in as little as possible. The first in the series was *Skating Home* (1928), and others included *Nifty Numbers*, and *Stage-Struck Susie* (both 1929). The most was made of

Glamor shot of Christie star Frances Lee. Author's collection.

her sassy personality and knock-out figure, while she was surrounded by Christie supporting players like Billy Engle, and Eddie Barry, high budgets, and technical gloss. When sound arrived Lee continued to work for Christie, and then later appeared in low-budgeted features like *Her Splendid Folly* (1933) and *These Thirty Years* (1934). She left the screen after marrying in 1935, and died in 2000.

The starring ladies of the 1920s were every bit as important and popular as their male counterparts – all headlining in vehicles that were expressly written and tailored to their talents. Their names on the marquee meant money in the studio coffers, and they all worked long and hard to make funny and enjoyable films. Most of the women detailed here had retired by the early days of sound – making way for the new crop of screwball comedy heroines that would rule the roost into the 1940s.

Chapter Six
BEHIND THE CAMERA

Even more neglected than the onscreen performers are the women who worked behind the camera in silent comedy as directors, producers and writers. Besides the already-mentioned Mabel Normand (see Chapter Two), comedies were also directed by Alice Guy-Blache, Mrs. Sidney Drew, and Ruth Stonehouse. Alice Guy-Blache is of course a bona-fide cinema pioneer, starting her career as a secretary at France's Gaumont Company in 1895, soon becoming the office manager and then directing and producing silent and early sound films (known as Chronophone Films). In 1906 she left Gaumont to come to America with her husband Herbert Blache, who was introducing the Chronophone system in the U.S. After helping Blache with his presentations and having two children, Guy-Blache formed the Solax Film Company in 1910.

> It has long been a source of wonder to me that many women have not seized upon the wonderful opportunities offered to them by the motion picture art to make their way to fame and fortune as producers of photo dramas. Of all the arts there is probably none in which they can make such splendid use of talents so much more natural to women than to a man and so necessary to its perfection. (*Moving Picture World*, July 11, 1914)

Over four years Solax turned out all types of films, including a large number of comedies for which Madame Blache had a definite flair. While in France she had directed some very funny slapstick shorts such as *Le Matelas Epileptique* (*The Drunken Mattress* 1906) and *La Femme Collante* (*The Sticky Woman* 1906), and at Solax she directed many situational comedies acted by a reg-

Study of film pioneer Alice Guy-Blache. Courtesy of The Museum of Modern Art.

ular company that included Darwin Karr, Marion Swayne, Fraunie Fraunholz, Blanche Cornwall, Billy Quirk, and Lee Beggs.

Shorts such as *When Mary was Little* (1911), *Canned Harmony* (1912), and *Burstup Holmes' Murder Case* (1913) were very similar to the comedies coming out of the Vitagraph Studio. In *Officer Henderson* (1913) two cops dress as women to nab purse snatchers, *A House Divided* (1913) has a battling husband and wife living in separate parts of their house and only communicating through notes, and *His Double* (1912) even contains a version of the "mirror routine" made famous by the Marx Brothers in *Duck Soup* (1933). After 1914 Guy-Blanche moved on to dramatic features, and ended her career in 1920, but while still at Solax she gave this opinion to the *Moving Picture World*:

> There is nothing connected with the staging of a motion picture that a woman cannot do as easily as a man, and there is no reason why she cannot completely master every technicality of the art. The technique of the drama has been mastered by so many women that it is considered as much her field as a man's and its adaptation to picture work in no way removes it from her sphere. The technique of motion picture photography, like the technique of the drama is fitted to a woman's activities.

In 1914 Lucille McVey was a young actress who had recently joined the Vitagraph Company. Born in 1890, she was a graduate of the Sedalia College of Music and the Nebraska School of Expression, and had spent six years presenting recitations on the concert stage under the auspices of the Redpath Lyceum Bureau where she was said to have been one of the foremost child dialect readers in America. Working at Vitagraph under the name of Jane Morrow, she appeared in small roles in shorts such as *Never Again* (1914) and the feature *A Florida Enchantment* (1914) which starred, and were directed by, Sidney Drew. A member of the famous Drew and Barrymore theatrical clan and an uncle to Ethel, Lionel, and John Barrymore, Sidney Drew had spent years on the stage as a popular light comedian. There he worked frequently with his first wife, Gladys Rankin, and after the pair originally entered films at Kalem in 1911, they joined the Vitagraph family in 1913. Mrs. Drew died soon after and Sidney was working on his own in films such as *Jerry's Mother-in-law* (1913) and *Goodness Gracious, or Movies as They Shouldn't Be* (1914).

A 1918 *New Jersey Telegram* item described the coming together of the twenty-four year-old Ms. McVey and the forty-nine year-old Drew:

> When the sudden rise of motion pictures ended the palmy days of lyceum entertaining Miss McVey made up her mind to become a screen actress, and the first picture in which she was cast was a Sidney Drew comedy. From that day she was invariably Mr. Drew's leading woman, and it was not long before a romance developed that culminated in their marriage.

The ceremony took place in July 1914, and together they found fame with a series chronicling the misadventures of an average married couple that soon became known as Henry and Polly. Mr. Drew directed the films, and told *Photoplay* in 1917:

> In our two years of producing one reel comedies we have never been able to buy a scenario complete as we produce it. We take them for the ideas they possess. The scripts are practically reconstructed by Mrs. Drew. I say practically because occasionally I – ah – offer a suggestion or two.

Mr. & Mrs. Sidney Drew in a publicity shot for their Metro Comedies. Author's collection.

Many of their light and witty shorts survive. *The Professional Scapegoat* (1914) has a recently discharged Sidney getting a job at a department store where he's discharged over and over – being the professional scapegoat for the store to take the blame for trivial complaints brought by customers. Summoned by the superintendent he's fired and gives an elaborate act of despair which satisfies the complaining customers. Mrs. Drew plays a salesgirl who at first has sympathy for the fired Sidney, but is soon in on the joke. Getting tired of the constant firing, he finds that he's an heir to a large fortune so he's able to quit the job and marry his salesgirl. Five years later their son breaks a saucer and when reprimanded by Sidney he goes through the same patented routine of despair that Sidney did at the store, much to his parent's amusement.

In *Boobley's Baby* (1915) Sidney has to stand on the crowded trolley every day to and from work. He notices that anyone carrying a baby always gets a seat, so he buys a doll, wraps it in a blanket, and on the next trolley ride everyone from men to old ladies make room for he and the "baby" to sit. At work he keeps the doll in a small bag. Problems begin when he begins a romance with Mrs. Drew at his office – she happens to see him on the train with the "baby" and assumes he's married and will have nothing to do with him. Angry at the situation he's gotten himself into, Sidney gets off the trolley and vents his frustrations on the doll. Mrs. Drew also gets off and sees Sidney throttle and tear the arms and legs off the doll. Thinking he's murdering the child she summons the cops, but of course the misunderstanding is cleared up for the happy ending.

The Drew's are an engaged couple in *Miss Sticky-Moufie-Kiss* (1915). Sidney has to go away to war but they pledge their love. Sidney returns three years later to find that his sweetheart now talks nothing but baby talk and says things like "Did my dwate big mankins realize he wud doin' to div up leading a nasty wasty bachelor man's life and stay home with his itty ongy blossomy wifie?" Stunned, he honors his pledge but on their honeymoon he can no longer stand it. Excusing himself, he goes down to the beach, wades out into the ocean, dress suit and all, until he disappears. Other shorts such as *The Fox Trot Finesse, A Case of Eugenics, By Might of his Right* (all 1915), and *His Wife Knew About It* (1916) made the pair immensely popular and in 1916 they left Vitagraph for the Metro Company.

Mrs. Sidney Drew. Author's collection.

With fame, the media wanted to know the secrets of their success, so the Drews had ample opportunity to discuss their thoughts on comedy material and filmmaking. Sidney told a 1919 *Detroit Journal*:

> I was practically born in the theatre and the theatre has been my world, but Mrs. Drew was born in the middle west and she knew the world of millions of American men and women to whom the little domestic incidents – such as getting cigar ashes on the carpet – are important.

> I really consider it a great compliment to my ability as an actor that I have been able to make people like my Henry, as I certainly am as far from him in real life as possible. But Mrs. Drew assured me there were such men and when she wrote some comedies about them and they went over big she proved it to me.

Mrs. Drew gave some of her theories to *Photoplay* in 1917:

> We believe the success of our comedies is largely due to the direct and human

subtitles, "continued the comedian's wife. "They get the story started with a swing and put the continuity over quickly and speedily. Moreover, they make the story mental rather than physical. They make it possible for the audience to think just what's in your mind. Plenty of subtitles, few people, and quick interest are the vital things.

It may sound egotistical but I sincerely think the subtitles give our comedies a distinct style of their own. I think you might term it a whimsical style. It is essentially our own, since we cannot even obtain scenarios to fit it. It has developed from a study of our own work and a belief that the intelligence should not be insulted and that the story must be real and not a thing of the imagination.

We have never accepted a script from a so-called "real" author as they build their stories and plays from their imagination. These may be adroit, of vigorous action and even powerful but they are *theatrical*.

We believe in giving credit to the intelligence of an audience. And, in attending the theatres to watch the reception of our comedies, we have found that some of our biggest laughs come by inference.

We see no indication of exhausting the field," said Mrs. Drew. "Others are concerned with the lover, the sweetheart, and the villain. Surely that is but half – or less – of life. Married life presents a thousand themes. Only a proportion lend themselves to humorous treatment, of course. But that proportion should keep us occupied for a long time to come.

With the ad line of "They Keep You Smiling" the Drews winning streak continued unabated at Metro. By this time they were equally sharing directorial duties, and at the end of 1918 they set up their own company with Amedee Van Buren's VBK Film Corporation, which distributed their one-reelers through Paramount. They also embarked on a successful cross-country tour of the play *Keep Her Smiling*, but in May 1918 Sidney's son from his first marriage, S. Rankin Drew, was a World War I casualty - killed in France while flying with the Lafayette Escadrille. The death affected the elder Drew deeply, causing a breakdown in his health that led to his death less than a year later on April 9, 1919.

While they were touring with their show the Drews had been renting studio space in the cities they were playing, such as Essanay in Chicago, etc., and shooting their shorts. When Sidney died they had completed five of their contracted seven films. With very little delay Mrs. Drew fulfilled the contract with *Bunkered* (July 13, 1919) and *A Sisterly Scheme* (August 24, 1919). Both films use the device of having Mrs. Drew, in her usual character of Polly, be the sister of the male lead who humorously advises her brother and helps him work out his relationship problems. Donald McBride, who had appeared as

Mrs. Drew's brother in many of their Vitagraph shorts, reprises his role in *Bunkered*, playing a golf champion who marries a young woman who can't play golf but thinks she must to support him. Of course she's ruining his game until Mrs. Drew steps in and gives her a clue that Jimmie will be fine alone on the links.

In *A Sisterly Scheme* John Cumberland plays the role of the brother, in love with a woman who ignores him. He hatches a scheme with her younger sister to pursue her to make the elder sibling jealous. Again things do not go as planned until Mrs. Drew straightens out all the confusion and points out that her brother and the younger sister are really in love. John Cumberland was a popular light comedian from the stage, who had great success with the Broadway comedy *Fair and Warmer* opposite Madge Kennedy and the farce *Up in Mabel's Room*. In background and style he was very similar to the late Mr. Drew, and would become very important in Mrs. Drew's ensuing work.

Mrs. Drew in her first solo outing *Bunkered* (1919). Author's collection.

In fact her next assignment would be a starring feature for Mr. Cumberland. *A Gay Old Dog* (1919) was adapted by Mrs. Drew from a story by Edna Ferber, and gives more of a seriocomic role for the star as he plays a young man whose parent's die leaving him responsible for a number of younger sisters. Devoting himself to their well-being, as the years go by he neglects himself, but tries to project the image of a "gay old dog," He is ultimately unhappy and alone. Directed by Hobart Henley, the film got good notices and was singled out for clever and insightful character touches.

Apparently happy behind the camera she next adapted an Albert Payson Terhune short story from the *Saturday Evening Post* for comedian Ernest Truex. Another light stage comic being tapped for movies, Truex was heading his own series of two-reelers for VBK, the first of which, *The Night of the Dub* (1920), benefitted from Mrs. Drews expertise. She next set up a deal with Pathé to direct, as well as write, a new series of comedies.

> Mrs. Sidney Drew has just completed "The Charming Mrs. Chase," first of her series of "After Thirty" comedies, adapted from the stories of Julian Street, in

which John Cumberland is starred. Production of the initial two-reel Drew comedy was started more than a month ago.

In its report on "The Charming Mrs. Chase," the Pathé Exchange devotes considerable space to the past accomplishments of Mr. Street, the author of the story. "Julian Street," says the Pathé report, "author of stories which Mrs. Drew is working, is one of America's most famous short-story writers. Two of his "After Thirty" series appeared in McClure's magazine and the three ensuing subjects ran in the Saturday Evening Post. (*Motion Picture News*, January 17, 1920)

When asked about her reasons for choosing the *After Thirty* stories she replied:

The story is the sort of thing Mr. Drew and I did before his death, the characters being very similar to Polly and Henry. (*Motion Picture News*, December 13, 1919)

John Cumberland in the Mrs. Sidney Drew-written and directed
The Stimulating Mrs. Barton (1920). Author's collection.

Four shorts were ultimately made – *The Charming Mrs. Chase, The Stimulating Mrs. Barton, The Emotional Miss Vaughan,* and *The Unconventional Maida Greenwood* (all 1920). Except for a minute of footage from *The Stimulating Mrs. Barton* at Library of Congress the films aren't known to exist, but contemporary reviews and commentary describe them as comedies of character and manners in the regular Drew tradition:

It was a fine stroke on Mrs. Sidney Drew's part when she selected John

Cumberland to succeed her late lamented husband in the comedies based upon Julian Street's "After Thirty" stories. With all due to Sidney Drew's ability, Mr. Cumberland is the best light comedian that has ever appeared under the Cooper-Hewitts. Possessing a fine sense of characterization, a fund of humor, and a fine personality, he is drawing attention to these comedies. Though they are filled with keen satire, and slice of life and food for thought, it is the manner in which they are interpreted which makes them so delightful. A great deal of credit is due Mrs. Drew for her admirable adaptations and direction. Just what "business" is hers and what is Mr. Cumberland's is hard to determine.

Satirizing the desire among a husband and wife to experiment after they have reached the age of thirty, the stories are truly unique. They are not meant for juvenile audiences, however – being too subtle and not filled with any broad comedy strokes to please the children. But there is no question of their appeal to adults. There is the same sparkle and tone to these pieces that were present in the Sidney Drew comedies. Which is, of course, a compliment to Mrs. Drew. Whether she is responsible for the titling is not known, but it is so in harmony with the idea expressed that we are going to credit her with it. It is no aspersion upon the actress who appears as the wife in the case to say that Mrs. Drew would fit admirably into her part. She probably feels like a baseball manager who prefers to guide the players from the bench rather than in the field. It gives her a better perspective to watch mistakes and eradicate flaws. (*Motion Picture News*, April 7, 1920)

Mrs. Drew did finally take a role in the third short *The Emotional Miss Vaughan*, saying that it was her intention to periodically return to the screen. Sadly she never did again, as following the *After Thirty* shorts she had only one more project. In 1921 she returned to Vitagraph to direct the screen adaptation of the play *Cousin Kate*. On stage Ethel Barrymore had a hit in the title role, and the film starred Alice Joyce as a small town novelist and her romantic entanglements with her cousin Amy's beau. Not wanting to hurt Amy, Kate tells the man that she doesn't really love him, but when Amy hooks up with another man Kate is free to have her beau.

As with most of Mrs. Drew's work, this feature appears to have been gentle and character driven, with focus given to the small details. The January 29, 1921 *Moving Picture World* reported:

> Simplicity and naturalness characterize this latest release of the Vitagraph Company, in which the entire cast co-stars with Alice Joyce to produce a really beautiful picture.

and added:

The artistic touches of Mrs. Sidney Drew's direction can be detected throughout. The titles are clever and well-placed, the photography and other technical arrangements are excellent.

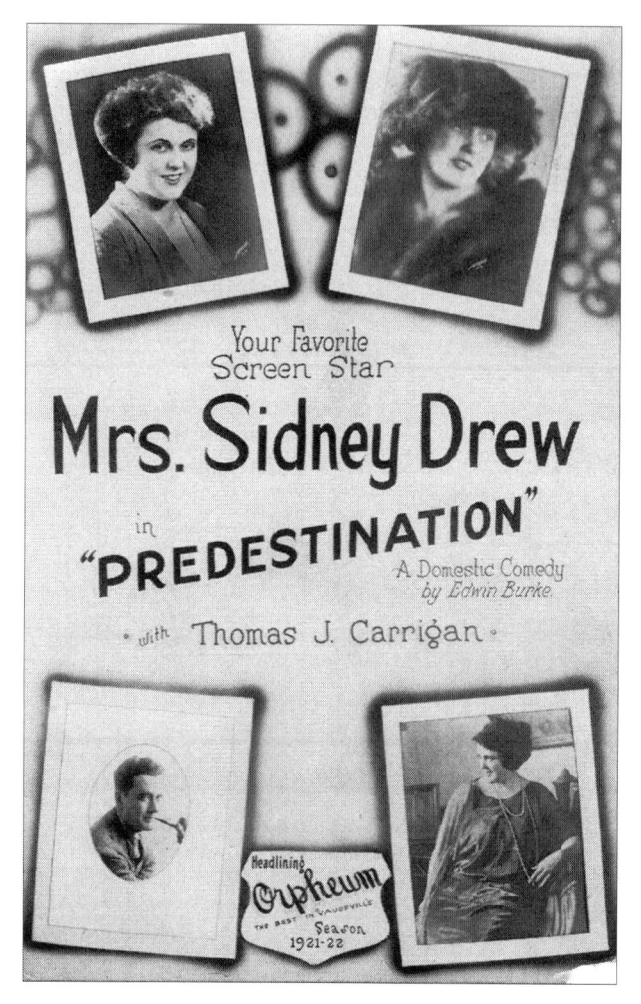

Theatre bill for Mrs. Drew's 1922 stage tour of *Predestination*.
Author's collection.

After *Cousin Kate* Mrs. Drew did do a 1922 stage tour on the Orpheum Circuit of the domestic comedy *Presdestination,* but no other films. Virtually nothing of her solo work is known to exist today, besides the already mentioned snippet of *The Stimulating Mrs. Barton*. When she died in 1926 at the premature age of thirty-five after a battle with cancer, the memory of her talents was already in eclipse:

The funeral of Mrs. Sidney Drew was attended by only twenty persons. And yet Mrs. Drew was one of the cleverest and kindest women ever in motion pictures. But apparently, after the death of her husband and her retirement from the screen, the movie colony forgot all about her. As a rule, Hollywood tries to be kind. In this case there's a black mark against it. (*Motion Picture Magazine*, 1926)

Since then Mrs. Drew's work and legacy have been treated in very much the same manner, and it's hoped that examples of her later films will be recovered to bring attention to her contribution to screen comedy.

The last of our directors to discuss is Ruth Stonehouse, a popular actress who briefly had the opportunity to write and direct a handful of her own starring comedies. Born in Denver, Colorado in 1894, she was interested in the performing arts from an early age, particularly dancing. With her father in the mining business, Ms. Stonehouse grew up in mining camps and had lived on a ranch in Arizona, before going to Monticello and Chicago where she became friendly with Gertrude Spoor, the daughter of Essanay Films founder George K. Spoor. The connection with the Spoor family led to her film career:

Ruth Stonehouse in a dramatic mood. Author's collection.

> Later I was sent to Monticello to school. There I used to dance for the girls and take part in all the concerts we had. Well, it just seemed like dancing was to be my career. I had never taken any lessons, but had learnt all from observation. I used to take my various positions from pictures I saw in magazines, and dreamed of the time when I would be a great dancer. When we came to Chicago, I played at many of the clubs here, dancing at all the exclusive receptions given by society folk. And at most of these I was somewhat under the care of Mrs. Spoor. You see, her daughter, Gertrude Spoor, and I had been great friends at school (Mr. Spoor is one of the owners of Essanay, and incidentally the S. of S&A), and it made it so nice for me. I attended all the teas and lawn parties. I did my classic dances, very similar to those popular dances of today, al fresco, and seemed to make a tremendous hit.

Well, I at last decided on a vaudeville career; had my act all intact and my time booked. I wrote to Gertrude Spoor, who had gone east to the "Castle" to school, and told her of my plans. She wrote back, "Don't do that. Why don't you go into pictures? Run out to the studio and see dad." I did. I went over on Sunday to talk to Mr. Spoor. I guess because I had been thrown with pictures so much thru my acquaintance with the Spoors it had never occurred to me to take them seriously; but upon the receipt of Gertrude's letter I went to see her father. He gave me a position, but wouldn't help me a bit. "Ruthie, if it's in you to make good, do it on your own ability." (*Motion Picture Magazine*, December 1914)

She joined the Essanay ensemble in 1910 as an ingénue and learned about films and acting by doing. Some current online biographies of Ms. Stonehouse oddly state that she co-founded and co-owned Essanay with Spoor and G.M. "Broncho Billy" Anderson, but I've found no evidence of this in any primary source material or in studies on the Essanay Company, such as David Kiehn's excellent *Broncho Billy and the Essanay Film Company* (Farwell Books, 2003). Besides that when the company was formed in 1907 Stonehouse would have been only thirteen years old. The truth is she was busy learning to be an actress and was constantly working in all types of films, including comedies such as *Mr. Wise, Investigator* (1911), *An Adamless Eden*, *Billy McGrath's Art Career*, and *Mr. Hubby's Wife* (all 1912) where she supported popular clowns like Victor Potel, Billy Mason, John Steppling, and Augustus Carney.

Wallace Beery and Ruth Stonehouse in an unidentified *Sweedie* Comedy. Courtesy of Robert Arkus.

For the most part these comedies were of the character-driven and situational type such as *His Birthday Jacket* (1912) in which she played a young daughter who wants to surprise her father with a new smoking jacket for his birthday. She bribes the butler to take his measurements at odd times so dad won't get suspicious, but after all is said and done the coat is about three sizes too small. Everyone has a good laugh and the daughter decides to skip surprises in the future.

Long I waited for an opportunity to show them what I could do, until I was desperate, when one day, at last, my chance came. I remember the play was called "Chains." Well, I did make good, but of course it has been one continual go forward and step back, then work up again – but I love the pictures. They give one such a wonderful advantage of seeing all the good and bad there is in them.

Chains was a 1912 release, and by 1913 she was mostly appearing in the studio's dramas, often opposite Francis X. Bushman. It wasn't until 1915 that she returned regularly to comedies, appearing with Bryant Washburn and in entries of the *George Ade's Fables* shorts such as *The Fable of the Divine Spark that had a Short Circuit*, *The Fable of the High Roller and the Buzzing Blonde*, and *The Fable of the Two Sensational Failures* (all 1915). This culminated in her starring role in Essanay's feature adaptation of George Ade's hit book *The Slim Princess* (1915). Set in Morovenia, Turkey, where fat is synonymous with beauty, Stonehouse plays the Princess Kalora, the slim daughter of the Governor General of Morovenia. The Governor can't marry off his pudgy younger daughter until Kalora is married, but so far has had no luck at that as she's too thin. He goes to great lengths to try to fatten her up, and orders her to stuff her clothing to trick someone into proposing.

At a party she meets an American, Alexander Pike, who falls for her, and shows her pictures in a magazine to prove that in his country slimmer persons are considered most beautiful. Having crashed the party Pike is discovered by the Governor's slaves and ejected. In the magazine left behind by Pike the Governor finds an ad that promises to make thin persons fat, so Kalora is bundled off to the U.S. where she rekindles her romance with Pike. When the Princess has to return to Morovenia, Pike visits the Governor posing as a Knight Templar and King of the Hoo Hoos who wants to marry Kalora. The Governor sees through the ruse, but is glad to give his consent, and the married pair is soon happily off to America.

After this feature she returned to shorts, again mostly dramas with occasional light spots such as *The Fable of Hazel's Two Husbands and What Became of Them* (1915), and two serio-comic titles, *Miss Freckles* and *Angels Unaware* (both 1915) where she played a tough little street waif named Freckles. In 1916 she left Essanay, which had been her home since 1910, and moved to Universal. Her initial work for the "Big U" was as a replacement for Grace Cunard in the Francis Ford-directed serial *The Adventures of Peg O' the Ring* (1916), but when Miss Cunard became available Stonehouse's scenes weren't used. Going on to the company's Bluebird brand features she had success in serious outings like *Love Never Dies* and *Kinkaid, Gambler* (both 1916) as well as lighter fare such as *Fighting for Love* and *Love Aflame* (both 1917).

In 1917 she was given the opportunity to write, direct, and star in a series of shorts. Out of the nine made seven were comedies. Starting out with *Dorothy Dares*, a story about a young girl in love with a haberdashery store clerk who is sent away to a girl's school to forget him by her disapproving parents, Stonehouse soon hit upon a recurring character. Mary Ann Kelly was the poor, but spunky daughter of an Irish washerwoman, and five shorts chronicled her misadventures in love, in brushing with society, and in wanting to be a gunfighter.

The first of a series of Mary Ann stories, "The Heart of Mary Ann" written and produced by Ruth Stonehouse and in which she plays the principal role, will appear on Thursday, February 22. This is a one act comedy drama with wide human appeal, and is an exceptional program release. If this first one can be judged a criterion the forthcoming Mary Ann photoplays will be in great demand. (*Moving Picture World*, February 24, 1917)

In *The Heart of Mary Ann*, the girl sees a poor woman turned away from a milk station as it is out of milk. She decides to set up her own station, and the next morning follows the milkman on his route pilfering every bottle he delivers for her own supply. Of course her neighbors soon miss their milk, and when they hear about her new milk station they rush there in a crowd to buy milk. Eventually the source of her supply is discovered, the local cop is called, and the film ends as he escorts Mary Ann on her rounds replacing all the "borrowed" bottles.

Daredevil Dan has Mary Ann obsessed with dime novels and aspiring to be a gunman. While out trying to hold up a soda shop and various folks she overhears three crooks planning a real job, so she turns detective and helps the police round up the gang. The last of the series, *A Walloping Time*, details the festivities that occur in the tenement section when Mary Ann's sailor father returns from a long sea voyage. The celebration turns into a battle royal between the Irish and Italian clans with Mary Ann in a ringside seat cheering the combatants on.

These and the other entries – *Mary Ann in Society* and *Puppy Love* – were written by Miss Stonehouse, along with Fred Myton and Charles Wilson Jr., with the regular role of her mother played by Lydia Yeamans Titus. Another comedy directed by Stonehouse, while not part of the *Mary Ann* group was decidedly in the same mold. *Tacky Sue's Romance* (1917) follows a poor girl's courtship with the son of a wealthy store owner. Called "Tacky Sue" because of her shabby clothes, the reason she spends no money on her attire is she's the sole support of a group of toddler orphans. Thinking that her beau is only nice to her out of pity, she stops seeing him, but eventually he wins her over and allows him and his father to help her take care of the children. Two dramas directed by the actress at this time were *The Stolen Actress* and *A Limb of Satan*, with the latter film again having similarities with her *Mary Ann* comedies. In *A Limb of Satan* she plays a mischievous and difficult orphan who has been adopted three times and always quickly returned. Much to relief of the manager of the asylum she runs away, and later steals money to aid a blind sculptor but her troubles end happily.

Ruth Stonehouse in a comic pose. Courtesy of The Museum of Modern Art.

With the completion of this string of directorial projects, Stonehouse left Universal, and starred in *A Phantom Husband* (1917), a comedy drama feature for Triangle. At the very end of the year it was announced:

> **Ruth Stonehouse to Have Own Company**. Ruth Stonehouse, Universal Bluebird star, and more recently with Triangle has signed a long-term contract to be featured in big productions. H. Berg, owner of the Overland Film Company, while in Los Angeles, made Miss Stonehouse an offer which, on November 21, was signed by her. The contract provides for the producing of six feature dramas during the year. (*Moving Picture World*, December 15, 1917)

It appears that nothing came from this deal. The contract kept her off screen for a year, during which time *Variety* and *Picture Play* reported that she was appearing in vaudeville. She returned to pictures in the beginning of 1919, but had only one more directorial credit, *Rosalind of Redgate*, a western short for Universal. From here on she was very busy as an actress, appearing in dramas, westerns, serials, and comedy features that includes *The Four-Flusher* (1919), *Parlor, Bedroom and Bath*, *Cinderella's Twin* (both 1920), and *Lights Out* (1923). In the mid-1920s she wrote one more film, the western

Rough Going (1925), but her career was slowing down, with most of her work done for smaller independent companies. In 1927 she married Felix Hughes, brother of screen writer Rupert Hughes, and when she made her last picture *The Devil's Cage* (1928) it was noted in a *Motion Picture Classic* article about retired former leading ladies:

> There are those that revel in domesticity. They are glad to relinquish fame. Ruth Stonehouse, now Mrs. Felix Hughes, sister-in-law of Rupert Hughes the novelist. For years she was an Essanay actress. Chadwick called her for a picture last month. She was thrilled. Back to greasepaint. It is incense divine. Back to Kleigs and direction. In three days she wanted to know when she would be through. It wasn't like the old days. The camaraderie was gone. Petty authorities irritated. Ruth Stonehouse has returned to her short-story writing course, her asparagus soufflés, her half-finished chaise-longue cover.

She remained retired and lived in Hollywood until her death in 1941 from a cerebral hemorrhage at age forty-eight.

Mary Pickford is bored of education in *The Hoodlum* (1919). Courtesy of Cole Johnson.

Women producers of comedy films were just as scarce as directors. Without a doubt the greatest female producer of the American cinema was Mary Pickford, and while not a comedienne per say, Pickford was funny, and comedy played an important part in her pictures and screen image. Much detailed information has been written on her elsewhere, but the basic facts are Gladys Mary Smith was born in Toronto, Canada on

April 8, 1893, and had already been on the stage for ten years as the main support for her mother and younger siblings when she began her film career at the Biograph Studio in 1909. Working under the tutelage of D.W. Griffith she did many of his signature dramas, but also did numerous comedies – even a series where she was co-starred with comic Billy Quirk. Titles such as *They Would Elope, Oh, Uncle, Getting Even* (all 1909), *The Smoker*, and *Mugsy's First Sweetheart* (both 1910) followed the romantic difficulties of young couples or newlyweds, and it was Pickford's feistiness and humor that set her apart from the other Griffith heroines like Lillian Gish or Mae Marsh.

A year-long stint at Imp in 1911 produced some comedies like *When the Cat's Away, Artful Kate, The Fair Dentist*, and *A Gasoline Engagement* (all 1911), and after a return to Biograph she soon embarked on her first features which were mostly melodramas until she hooked up with two of her most important collaborators – writer Frances Marion (more this chapter) and actor/ soon to be director Marshall Neilan. The above combination of talents resulted in the first signature Pickford films such as *Poor Little Rich Girl, Rebecca of Sunnybrook Farm, A Little Princess* (all 1917), *Amarilly of Clothes-Line Alley* (1918), and *Daddy-Long-Legs* (1919), where a dramatic story is leavened by large dollops of humor and Mary's clowning. Much of this seems to have originated with Mary herself, who gained more control of her films as her popularity soared. She's said to have insisted on the inclusion of the mud fight in *Poor Little Rich Girl*, while a very dramatic feature such as *Through the Back Door* (1921) stops for a knockabout sequence of Mary scrubbing the floor by strapping brushes on her feet and skating around through the water. Even the bleak Grimm's Fairy Tale of *Sparrows* (1926) has some lighter moments.

By the 1920s Pickford was in charge of her films and is credited as being one of Hollywood's most astute business women – but her main concern was her work. In 1957 she told a Columbia University Oral History interviewer:

> I suppose……it was that my pictures were my whole life, outside of my family. I never went any place. I never went to cafes, restaurants, never went dancing. I had no social life whatsoever. My whole life was wrapped up in the creative. As a mother lion or tigress, I had to assume the business role, in order to protect the thing I loved, my work……It was a protective measure……I run my own business; so I have to tend to these dry, dreadful meetings….I never enjoyed it, to tell you the truth….It's just a foreign atmosphere that I dislike. There's something about a typewriter that upsets me. It looks as if it's going to bite me – I don't know – I really detest it.

The most out and out comedies of her 1920s films include *Suds* (1920) where Mary is a London laundry slavey who dreams of romance, and besides slapstick routines in the laundry most of the comedy comes from her acquisition of a horse which she takes home to her second floor flat – where she puts its tail into Mary Pickford curls and rides it around the room, causing large chunks of plaster to fall on the people downstairs. *Rosita*

(1923) was a collaboration with director Ernst Lubitsch where Mary does a very creditable job taking on the Pola Negri-ish role of a Spanish street singer in a typical Lubitsch plot full of sly innuendo and playfulness. Today this is one of the harder of her films to see, as Pickford later had nothing good to say about the film and refused to preserve it.

Photographer Charles Rosher (center), director Sam Taylor (right), and Mary Pickford clown during the shooting of *My Best Girl* (1927). Courtesy of Cole Johnson.

    She was back to a little girl character in *Little Annie Rooney* (1925), a tough Irish street kid who spends most of her time fighting with the other neighborhood kids. Although there are serious moments such as the killing of her policeman father, the focus is on the slapstick antics in which she has great support from talented comedy kids like Spec O'Donnell and Eugene "Pineapple" Jackson. *My Best Girl* (1927) is a romantic comedy in the Colleen Moore mode with Mary playing a hard-working shop girl in a busy department store who has to contend with a difficult family and a budding romance with the son of the store owner. Director Sam Taylor and writer John Grey were veterans from Harold Lloyd's films, and as always Mary handled slapstick in the department store and romantic complications with equal aplomb. With sound Pickford seemed uncertain where to go – she had outgrown her popular little girl image and never found a talking one to take its place. After four sound features she retired in 1933, but remained active on the Hollywood scene for many years.

    Another actress who briefly became a producer was Clara Kimball Young. In 1917 at the beginning of the peak of her fame it was reported:

MISS YOUNG OWNS TWO COMPANIES – Clara Kimball Young, who is now being managed by Harry I. Garson, holds the unique distinction of being the only woman star to own and control two picture producing companies.

She not only heads, owns and controls her own producing company, known as Clara Kimball Young, which releases eight big pictures a year to the C.K.Y. Film Corporation, but she also owns the controlling interest in the Fun-Art Films, Inc., a New York corporation that will release two-reel comedies each month. The latter organization will feature Gordon Dooley and his sister Ray, beginning about September 15th. It has not been decided just how these comedies will be released, the announcement of which will be made soon, however. (*Motography*, September 22, 1917)

Fun-Art Films set up shop at the Thanhouser Studio in New Rochelle, New York on the two-reeler *A Rag, a Bone and a Hank of Hair* (1917). Gordon and Ray Dooley (see appendix) were popular stage comics from a busy New York stage family, with the rest of the cast consisting of Tula Belle, Helen Badgley, and Edward Kimball (Clara's father). The directorial duties were shared by Vincent Bryan and Johnny Hines, and although work was reported to have been started on more:

> The second picture, already under way at the Thanhouser Studio, will be a burlesque on "Cleopatra," called "Leo Patrick," it is announced, and this will be followed by "The Open Car Conductor." (*Motion Picture News*, November 17, 1917)

It appears that neither were finished or released, so the Dooley's went back to the stage and Fun-Art disappeared.

Clara Kimball Young is a name that pops up often in literature about the American cinema, but her films are

Producer and star Clara Kimball Young. Author's collection.

rarely shown, and if she's remembered at all today it's as a dramatic diva. What's forgotten is that she became a star at the Vitagraph Studio mostly appearing in charming comedies written and directed by her husband James Young in which she seems to have been the successor to Florence Turner in her skill and appeal. Born in the proverbial trunk she began performing at age two, and was the daughter of touring actors Edward H. and Pauline Kimball. As a young actress she met and married the successful leading man James Young, who had worked with the likes of Sir Henry Irving, Austen Daly, and Minnie Maddern Fiske, and the pair joined Vitagraph in 1909.

At first Clara appeared in smaller parts as daughters or other ingénue characters but when Young began directing in 1912 her roles expanded and she was soon a leading player. *The Picture Idol* (1912) presents Clara as a movie struck girl who's madly in love with a picture star played by Maurice Costello. Her worried father confers with the star and they hatch a plot where he comes to their home for dinner and acts like an uncouth boor, which quickly cures Clara of her movie-mania. *Delayed Proposals* (1913) also pairs her with Costello, and this time they are onboard a ship with Maurice wanting to pop the big question, but every time he tries to propose he's interrupted by a grouchy owner of a deck chair, Clara's mother, and even his own seasickness. Spending the remainder of the voyage terribly ill, he rushes to the deck in his pajamas just as the ship docks, and manages to finally propose in full view of everyone on the deck.

She also did a number of shorts teamed with Sidney Drew such as *Jerry's Mother-in-law*, *A Lesson in Jealousy*, and *Beauty Unadorned* (all 1913), but her moment of true brilliance came in their 1914 pairing *Goodness Gracious, or, Movies as they Shouldn't Be*. This little gem skewers and spoofs movie, theatrical, and literary clichés to a complete frazzle. Clara plays the hyper-animated heroine (whose eyelashes bat at more than twenty-four frames a second) Gwendoline who seeks work in the big city in a dry goods firm. The forty-plus year-old college boy son (Drew) of the millionaire owner falls in love with her, but villainous villain Ned Finley has his own designs on her, and to make things worse Sidney's wealthy father disapproves of their union. The absurdities come quick and fast with gags that make fun of phony painted backdrops, villains disguised as vegetation, sped up chases, and prerequisite "komic cops." All the performances are over the top but in a carefully considered way, and James Young's direction is tip top.

Young and Clara moved to features for "Big V" in 1914, but soon jumped across the river to Fort Lee, New Jersey to work for the World Film Co. Clara appears to have wanted to be a big dramatic star so her comedy was jettisoned as she focused on melodramatic features. She also acted the diva in real life as she became estranged from Young and became involved with her producer Lewis Selznick and later producer-director Harry Garson. When Young sued Selznick for alienating his wife's affections their problems hit the newspapers, even more so when Young attacked Garson with a knife in 1917. There were also legal lawsuits with Selznick, with he and Clara suing and counter-suing each other. Clara eventually married Garson, and her last big success was *Eyes of*

Youth (1919). After this Garson insisted on directing her films, and bad pictures as well as unwise management derailed her career.

Clara Kimball Young and Sidney Drew lead the movement in *When Women Go on the Warpath* (1913). Billy Rose Theatre Division, the New York Library for the Performing Arts.

Her last starring role was in 1925, after which she hit the end of vaudeville in an act that traded on her former movie fame. She returned to Hollywood in 1931 for small parts in low-budget and independent features, in addition to shorts such as the Three Stooges' *Ants in the Pantry* (1936) where she's a society matron that hires the trio to take care of the ants in her mansion. She retired in 1941, but when silent films began to be shown on television in the 1950s her name became known again and she made various personal appearances, but in poor health she moved to the Motion Picture Country Home and died in 1960.

Another producer that is remembered today for her involvement in the early work of animation giants such as Max Fleischer, Pat Sullivan, and Walt Disney is Margaret J. Winkler, but thanks to the success of Hal Roach's *Our Gang* shorts she also briefly jumped on the live-action comedy bandwagon with her own series of kid two-reelers. Ms. Winkler started her career at age eighteen as the secretary to Harry Warner. In 1921 both Max Fleischer and Pat Sullivan approached Warner Brothers for distribution of their shorts, but as Warner's was only interested in features they passed. Harry, impressed with Margaret, encouraged her to start her own distribution company, and helped her acquire *Out of the Inkwell* and *Felix the Cat*. She soon gave Walt Disney his first big opportunity with *Alice in Cartoonland*, and was very important to his future success as she had definite ideas on how he needed to improve his films.

> Announcing the Completion of the First Three
> **REG'LAR KIDS**
> FAST MOVING FUNMAKERS
> A GREAT SERIES OF SIX TWO REEL COMEDIES
> THE PICK OF AMERICA'S SCREEN CHILDREN
> DIRECTED BY BRYAN FOY
> READY FOR IMMEDIATE RELEASE
> **M. J. WINKLER**
> 220 West 42nd Street   New York

In 1925 she launched *Reg'lar Kids* and made a few shorts like *Ham and Eggs*, *The Masked Marvel*, *Afternoon "Tee," One Glorious Fourth*, and *Good Scouts*. Survivors like *The Masked Marvel* and *One Glorious Fourth* show that the series, despite talented kids like Spec O'Donnell and Carter De Haven Jr., not to mention the participation of pros like Brian Foy and Monty Brice behind the camera, was at best a lackluster clone of the Roach original. Winkler never attempted any other live-action series. She married distributor Charles E. Mintz in 1924, and gradually let him take over the business as they had a family. In 1927 they developed *Oswald the Lucky Rabbit* with Disney, but later severed their connection with Walt. They kept the ownership of Oswald, however (leading Walt to create a new character of a mouse). Winkler completely retired in 1930 and passed away at age ninety-five in 1990.

Chapter Three profiled the starring female clowns and the next three ladies were part of that crowd but are included here as their immense popularity led them to set up their own production companies (more details on this trio in my 2013 book *Lame Brains and Lunatics: The Good, The Bad, and the Forgotten of Silent Comedy*). One of the best-remembered women in this book is Marie Dressler, noted as the star of the "first silent comedy feature" *Tillie's Punctured Romance* (1914) – which was actually the first *slapstick* comedy feature. Dressler has been described with adjectives such as "mammoth," "buxom," "ample," and "roly-poly," but her talent was immense and she equally big-hearted, devoting much time to public causes that involved personal sacrifice and professional setbacks. She was born Leila Marie Koerber on November 9, 1869 in Coburg, Canada:

> The sad truth is I was born without looks or anything else in my favor. My mother said I was the worst looking thing she ever saw. I grew into girlhood with the graceful abandon of a colt, and for years my hands and feet were always in my way.

Her father, a dictatorial veteran of the Crimean War, ruled the family with an iron hand, so having gotten the acting bug Marie left home at fourteen. Spending the next ten years learning her trade and working up the hard way – through touring stock and light opera troupes – she hit New York in 1892 and soon became the comedy toast of Broadway. Working with stars like Eddie Foy and Joe Weber in shows like *Hotel Topsy-Turvy*, *King Highball*, and *Higgledy-Piggledy* led to starring vehicles like *The Lady Slavey* and the peak of her stage career, 1910's *Tillie's Nightmare*. In this she played Tillie Blobbs, a boarding house drudge who is promised an evening off to attend a traveling show. At the last minute Tillie has to stay home and work, but falls asleep and dreams up her own musical comedy extravaganza. The show was a mega-hit, and toured for many years, providing Marie with her signature song *Heaven Will Protect the Working Girl*.

Marie Dressler doing her best to look svelte in an early stage photo. Courtesy of Cole Johnson.

It also proved to be her entrée into movies. In 1914, Mack Sennett spotted her on the West Coast between jobs and hired her for a series of comedies with *Tillie's Nightmare* as the starting point. Concocting a spoof of the innocent country girl and the big city slicker around the Tillie character, Marie literally bursts upon the screen in *Tillie's Punctured Romance*. As coy as a baby rhino, she gallumps through the picture and towers over Charlie Chaplin, looking like she's going to permanently flatten him during their physical business together, which includes love play on the order of kicking and beaning each other with bricks. With her dark-circled eyes and bulldog face, Marie is grotesque in farm girl pigtails and hideous circus big top tent dresses, but despite all the absurdities her warmth still comes through. A huge success, it turned out to be her only Sennett film. *Tillie* started shooting under the title of *Dressler No. 1*, but an injury while shooting caused her to cancel her contract which probably led Sennett to get his money's worth by making the film a special feature. In spite of her problems with Sennett Marie was sold on the movies:

Lubin Signs Dressler: Comedienne Will Be Starred In Series Of Specially Written Comedies. Marie Dressler has signed a contract with the Lubin

Company and is to be starred in a number of featured comedies written especially for her.

Miss Dressler will be seen in five-reel comedies and she will make three of these each year. Elaborate preparations are being made for the first of these big reelers. (*Dramatic Mirror,* April 4, 1915)

Marie reported to the Lubin studio in Philadelphia for work, but again the "number of featured comedies" turned into only one – *Tillie's Tomato Surprise* (1915). Around thirteen minutes of surviving footage is known to exist today at Library of Congress, and elicits mostly head-scratching as it's very odd, with Marie doing a lot of heavy mugging in a strange plot about her nutty inventor friend "The Flying Scotsman" who flies around on a pair of homemade wings. After this feature Marie severed ties with Lubin, and according to the August 6, 1916 *Motion Picture News*:

William A. Brady, acting for the World Film Corporation has signed to appear exclusively in features supervised by himself, the famous "Tillie" of filmdom.

Tillie Wakes Up came out in January 1917, and this five-reel World release is probably the best of Marie's surviving early work. In it she played a neglected wife whose callous husband has only married her for convenience and treats her brusquely. A newspaper column gives her the idea to make him jealous so he'll appreciate her, and she hooks up with a neighbor's henpecked husband for a spree at Coney Island. Although she gives a more subdued performance than usual, much of the film is just an excuse to turn Marie loose on the Ferris Wheel, Steeplechase, and all the slides and revolving platforms in Luna Park. She even gets nauseous on the same Witching Waves ride that Buster Keaton and Al St John battle on in Roscoe Arbuckle's *Coney Island* (1918). In addition to the Coney locations, the film was shot at World's studio in Fort Lee, New Jersey.

Courtesy of The Museum of Modern Art.

This third and final *Tillie* title had the participation of a number of silent comedy veterans – her co-star was Johnny Hines, it was directed by Harry Davenport, Mark Swan wrote the story, and most importantly Frances Marion fleshed out the scenario. Starting her writing career as a reporter, Marion had originally met Dressler in 1911 during the San Francisco run of *Tillie's Nightmare*, and the two became very close (more on her later in this chapter). Over the years Marion would become a big Dressler supporter and write many scripts for her. *Tillie Wakes Up* is the first film to take advantage of the dramatic talents behind Marie's clowning, and it seems very likely this came from Frances Marion as it's a hallmark of the later scripts like *Min and Bill* (1930) that she would write for Marie.

Flushed with success, Marie formed the Marie Dressler Motion Picture Company to produce her own two-reelers and features. Her partner in this venture, and her life, was James H. Dalton, her business manager since 1907. They lived together as man and wife, and presented themselves as such to the press, although Dalton already had a wife in Chicago who wouldn't give him a divorce. Marie had a weak grip on the business aspects of her profession, a situation that was exacerbated when she hooked up with Dalton as he turned out to be a poor business manager and over the years a drain on her finances as he involved her in many lawsuits and even phony stock schemes.

Marie and Dalton set up a two million dollar corporation, but with their usual business acumen they spent the next couple of years bouncing the films around from distributor to distributor. Mutual was announced first but never materialized, as did a slew of titles – *Tillie's Day Off*, *Tillie's Divorce Case*, and *Elopement*, but only four shorts finally came out – *The Scrub Lady* (1917) for Goldwyn Pictures, and *Fired* (1917), *The Agonies of Agnes* (1918), and *The Cross*

Marie doing a publicity shoot for her World shorts. Author's collection.

Red Nurse (1918) through a combo of Goldwyn and World. It's hard to judge the series, as only the second reel of *The Scrub Lady* is known to exist today and is a fast and furious melee of Marie modeling various funny costumes and then engaging in wartime intrigue. Em Gee Film Library used to offer it under the title *The Love Riot* and described it as "a wild one." At any rate *The Scrub Lady* was shot in Fort Lee with veteran comedy writer Vincent Bryan her main collaborator as writer and director, not to mention support from Florence Hamilton, Fred Hallen, Harriet Ross, and European movie clown Raymonde Cacho. After this it appears that Marie moved to California for *Fired* and the final two films and directed them herself from scenarios by Marie and Frances Marion. Surviving photos show silent comedy regulars like William McCall, John Rand, and James T. Kelly supporting the star.

Some of the erraticness in the production and release of these shorts can be attributed to Marie's devotion to America's war effort during World War I. Beginning in 1917, she entertained troops and the next year threw herself into the selling of government bonds, touring the country along with Charlie Chaplin, Mary Pickford, and Douglas Fairbanks, as part of the Liberty Loan Drive. Another crusade began in 1919 with the formation of the chorus Equity Association. Having worked herself up the hard way from the chorus, Marie became president and figurehead for the Chorus Girl's Union.

Arthur Geary, Marie, and John T. Murray doing a *Passing Show of 1921* spoof on the Barrymores. Billy Rose Theatre Division, the New York Library for the Performing Arts.

The time spent on behalf of the war effort and the chorus members took energy and focus away from her career, and as the 1920s rolled in she found that she had begun to be regarded as a relic from a different era, and was mostly offered revivals of her previous hits or parts in "old timer's shows." Left devastated when Jim Dalton died at the end of 1921, this period was the low point of Marie's career and life. Things got so bad that in 1924 she was given a deal on a small servant's room at New York's Ritz-Carlton Hotel in exchange for hostessing at the hotel's restaurant. After almost ten years off the screen she had her first film work in the summer of 1926, when she shot footage for a series of *Travelaffs* shorts in Europe. These were to be produced by Harry Reichenbach and seem to have been designed to be humorous travelogues similar to the group Will Rogers made for Clancy-Pathé, which had him appearing in the world's capitals and making pithy wisecracks via title cards. Things did not go well for Marie's version, and the series never materialized.

But Marie's screen career did begin again thanks to Allen Dwan and Frances Marion. The story goes that Dwan was getting ready to shoot *The Joy Girl* (1927), a feature he was directing for Fox, when he spotted Marie in the Ritz-Carleton and offered her a supporting part. Around the same time friend Frances Marion found out about her lean times, and now a prolific screenwriter for MGM, came up with the script *The Callahans and the Murphys* and pitched the project and Marie to production head Irving Thalberg (see Chapter Nine). Jump starting her career, as well as Polly Moran's, Marie moved on to other character parts for MGM such as Marion Davies' over-bearing mother in *The Patsy* (1928), and branched out to other studios like First National and RKO.

Sound was now revolutionizing the industry, but after spending almost forty years on the speaking stage Marie had no problem adapting her style to talking films, and like W.C. Fields and Will Rogers the new technology made her film persona complete. She was more successful than ever. She became one of MGM's biggest stars with films like *Anna Christie*, and *Min and Bill* (both 1930), and continued on with *Caught Short* (1930), *Reducing* (1931), *Emma* (1932), *Prosperity* (1932), and *Tugboat Annie* (1933). Although this triumphant comeback must have given her great satisfaction, she wasn't able to enjoy it for very long. Almost as soon as she won the Academy Award for *Min and Bill* her health began to dramatically deteriorate. She was battling cancer, and by late 1932 there was really nothing more that could be done.

She stoically kept on working as long as she could, shooting just a few hours a day. Her last few pictures were made this way, and in *Tugboat Annie* in particular the strain shows in her face. Strangely she seems rejuvenated in *Dinner at Eight* (1933) turning in a wonderful performance. Perhaps her best loved and remembered moment comes at the very end of the film when Jean Harlow tells her that she was reading a book the other day. Marie's gargantuan take, physically reeling as if a truck has just smacked into the side of the building or the earth has suddenly shifted in its orbit, has to be seen to be believed. It is a fitting finale and farewell to her long career in comedy. By early 1933 she could no longer work. Audiences responded to her illness as if she was a beloved member of their own family, and during her last weeks the newspapers printed daily bulletins on the status of her health. The end came on July 28, 1934.

A stage contemporary of Dressler's, who had supported Marie as part of the chorus in 1906's *Twiddle Twaddle*, and made her own way in movies was Fay Tincher. Born in Topeka, Kansas on April 17, 1884 to an affluent family Fay was the eldest of four daughters and began elocution lessons and appearing in amateur theatricals at an early age. Set on a stage career, after high school she attended Chicago's Ziegfeld Musical College, and soon entered show business as a chorus girl in vaudeville and musical comedies in New York on Broadway and on tour.

Polly Moran and Marie feel the effect of the grape in *Caught Short* (1930). Courtesy of Sam Gill.

In 1905, she appeared as a "Sing Song Girl" in *The Sho-Gun* and joined Joe Weber's company where she stayed a number of years working in shows such as *Dream City, Hip! Hip! Hooray!* and the afore mentioned *Twiddle Twaddle*. During the next few years she appeared with huge stars like Lew Fields, William Collier, Lillian Russell, and Fay Templeton in the shows *Weber & Fields Jubilee, Hokey-Pokey*, and *Bunty Pulls the Strings*.

Her film debut occurred on the East Coast and the accepted version is that she was "discovered" by D.W. Griffith for his feature *The Battle of the Sexes* (1914), but she had already appeared in a few 1913 American Éclair shorts that were shot in New Jersey and distributed by Universal. The Griffith story sounded better so Fay stuck with that. As Cleo, a vamp who lures a middle-aged man away from his family, *The Battle of the Sexes* brought Fay much attention and a place in the di-

Studio portrait of Fay Tincher. Courtesy of Jim Kerkhoff.

rector's Reliance Studio ensemble. She did bits in the master's next two features *Home Sweet Home* and *The Escape* (both 1914), and appeared in one-reel dramas like *Too Proud to Beg* (1914). In January 1914, the company moved to California and soon:

> It was after I came west with the company that I started the black and white color scheme. I was the telephone girl in the Ethel and Bill series. Mr. Griffith said I looked like Mabel Normand and could do the broad comedy.

Fay became part of a Griffith-supervised unit making one-reel shorts under the brand name Komic Comedies, which were distributed by Mutual. The series was directed by Edward Dillon, who was also part of the regular acting ensemble along with Fay, Tod Browning, Max Davidson, Tammany Young, Elmer Booth, Joseph "Baldy" Belmont, and former Universal Ike Jr. Bobby Feuhrer (later Bobby Ray). Many of the Komic scripts were by Anita Loos (more this chapter) and the company maintained a hectic output of one release a week. A few months after the series was running the unit acquired the rights to the *Bill the Office Boy* stories of Paul West. An instant success, the *Bill* comedies appeared every other week and Tammany Young, later W.C. Fields flunky in *The Old Fashioned Way* and *It's a Gift* (both 1934) played Bill, the street-wise office boy with a knack for fouling up his co-workers plans. Fay co-starred as Ethel the office stenographer and became wildly popular.

The character was a gum-chewing, no nonsense working girl that was always scheming how to get more money from her boss or find a rich millionaire to marry. What immediately grabbed the audience's attention was the character's eccentric style of dress. Fay took Griffith's statement "She's just a plain black and white type, always photographs as you see her" and ran with it as she outfitted Ethel completely in black and white with garish striped outfits that made her look like a human zebra. The addition of large spit curls and continual gum-chewing gave Fay the effect she desired. Today just a handful of the shorts are known to exist. The funny *Ethel's Roof Party* (1915) has Ethel inviting her rich fiancée and his swanky friends to an open-air lunch on the office building's roof. Having been told that he's not invited under any circumstances, Bill gets his revenge by locking the only door and trapping Ethel and her guests on the roof. After much panic and a rescue by the fire department, Ethel's put-on airs are deflated and she finds out that her rich beau ("Baldy" Belmont) is not only a coward, but wears a toupee to boot!

The Bill and the Komic shorts came to an end in late 1915, when Griffith's unit became known as the Fine Arts Company and merged with Mack Sennett's Keystone and the companies of Thomas Ince to become one third of the Triangle Corporation. There Fay became the comic foil for stage star DeWolf Hopper in three of his features for the company – *Don Quixote*, *Sunshine Dad*, and *Mr. Goode, the Samaritan* (all 1916). The features gathered quite a bit of publicity, favorable reviews, and good notices for Fay, especially as Dulcinea in *Don Quixote*, but Hopper himself didn't really click with movie audiences and after a couple of other pictures returned to the stage.

Ethel the stenographer is confronted by cigarette butts in *Bill Gives a Smoker* (1915). Courtesy of Robert S. Birchard.

After her association with Hopper, Fay was then put into her own series of shorts. The May 20, 1916 *Motion Picture News* announced that Triangle was going to start producing two-reel comedies and:

The second two-reel subject is that which will star Fay Tincher. She will be remembered as having characterized the stenographer in the one-reel Komic brand made at this studio, and will have the support of Max Davidson, Jack Cosgrove, and Edward Dillon, who will also direct the production. Miss Tincher plays the part of an unusually fresh sales girl.

Eddie Dillon was put in charge of Fay's Triangle Comedy series and while many of her former compatriots were no longer available – Tod Browning and Chester Withey were directing, Elmer Booth had been killed in an auto accident – Max Davidson was still on hand and Anita Loos prepared most of the scripts. Eight shorts were made – *The Two O'Clock Train, Love's Getaway, Bedelia's Bluff, Laundry Liz, Skirts, The French Milliner, A Calico Vampire,* and *The Lady Drummer* (all 1916) – but only a chunk of the first one, *The Two O'Clock Train,* is known to exist. In the surviving fragment Fay portrays a brash shop girl. Trade magazine descriptions suggest that the overall series provided a wide range of characters for her – a lady drummer, a country maid with ambitions to be a big city vampire, and a headstrong socialite. The unifying link in these roles was Fay's no-nonsense demeanor and feistiness, which were in comic contrast to her tiny stature.

The surviving footage, clippings and photos show that while Fay got rid of Ethel's spit curls and gum-chewing, she kept the black and white costume motif as her trademark. She toned it down a bit, using less garish stripes and more solids, but even disguised as a man in the crook comedy *Skirts*, she kept it up by using a black and white checkered cap, etc. The series came to an end by December 1916, when it was announced that Anita Loos would be writing titles for the upcoming Douglas Fairbanks features. Years later, in her 1977 book *Casts of Thousands*, Loos reminisced about Fay with a little statement that not only cast aspersions on her acting talent, but also outed her (Fay was still alive at ninety-five):

> The heroines of many of my half-reel farces were played by Fay Tincher, who has long been forgotten. Ideal for these rowdy scripts, Fay required no acting ability. Let's say she had the pert allure of a "patsy" and could be a provocative target for slapstick. Fay was anything but a sex symbol, and – in those days before lesbians came out of the closet – her fans never dreamed that their rambunctious little idol harbored a preference for g-i-r-l-s!

Loos did make many statements late in life that took potshots at colleagues who were no longer around to defend themselves, but there is a hint of corroborating evidence in the 1920 U.S. Census, where Fay's living with screenwriter Maie B. Havey (more this chapter), who's listed as her "partner." Havey was involved in Fay's company for World Pictures, where's she credited for the scenario of *Oh, Susie, Behave* (1918), so the use of the term most likely refers to a business partner and not "significant other." The U.S. City Directories for Los Angeles show that the pair lived together for at least four years (1918

– 1921) and little is known about Fay's private life except that she was single. None of this proves whether Loos statement was really true or not, and I'm sure Fay would agree that it's none of our business anyway.

Edward Dillion and Fay Tincher are plotting his escape in the Triangle/Fine Arts feature *Mr. Goode, the Samaritan* (1916). Billy Rose Theatre Division, the New York Public Library for the Performing Arts.

Triangle had been rife with problems almost since its creation and the three producers decided to withdraw. Griffith bailed first on March 11, 1917, immediately signing a contract with Adolph Zukor at Artcraft Pictures and Fine Arts was dissolved. This marked the end of Fay's association with the director, who had shown less and less interest in her as it became clear that her true talents lay in comedy. Griffith never cared about comedy, and although he had also helped bring Mack Sennett, Mabel Normand, Max Davidson, and Douglas Fairbanks to the screen he was happy to let them develop their comedy films elsewhere. It also appears that Fay herself was frustrated about doing comedy shorts - she told *Theatre Magazine*:

> I started out in life – screen life, of course, as a vampire. I played a heavy role in "Battle of the Sexes," and then, after that, I started playing comedy roles. In "Don Quixote" I was featured with DeWolf Hopper, and later in other Fine Arts productions, "Sunshine Dad" and "Mr. Good." I hoped to play "heavies" or even genre leads, but my reputation as a comedienne always caught up with me and forced me to play in two-reel funnycisms.

Nevertheless she went out on her own and resurfaced in 1918 with the announcement of:

> **Fascinating Fay Tincher Comedies**. Fay Tincher, comedienne, and for a year and a half the head of her own company, is the latest addition to the World Film Corporation staff, according to the official announcement from the World Film Offices.

Fay had had the starring series for Fine Arts, but it hadn't been her own company. Now it was with distribution through World, who also released the films of Lewis Selznick's Equitable Pictures, William Brady's Shubert Pictures, and Jules Brulator's Peerless Pictures. Fay set to work in early 1918 making shorts under the direction of Al Santell, a former scenario writer at Keystone and American, who had directed Kolb & Dill at American and Ham & Bud for Kalem. After working with Fay he did shorts for Capital Comedies, Universal, and the Hallroom Boys, before graduating to features. He made dramas as well as comedies and continued working into the mid-1940s. In an unpublished 1970s interview Santell had this to say about the creation of Fay's company:

> I also tried to start a series with a girl named Fay Tincher who was a former D.W. Griffith comedienne and a man, a very wealthy man, M.D. Smith, who at the time owned practically all the tug boats around Virginia, Norfolk, and so forth, and he fell for Fay Tincher in a romantic way and financed a picture.

Fay's first two World comedies, *Main 1-2-3* and *Some Job* (both 1918), were shot on the east coast and then the unit moved to California. World leased the Willis and Inglis Studio on Fleming Street, which previously been Kalem's Hollywood studio, and at least one more was made where Santell had directed Lloyd Hamilton and Bud Duncan in Ham and Bud comedies just a couple of years before. Today the site is the KCET television studio. Fay maintained her two-tone color scheme and while it's uncertain exactly how many comedies the unit made, as none are known to exist and I've only found titles for three, surviving reviews give a hint of their style and reception:

> Main 1-2-3 signalizes the return of Fay Tincher to the silver-sheet after a too-long absence. We have to thank World for giving back to us a really original comedienne. True, in her absence from our midst Fay of the stripes has somewhat gained weight; in fact, the more we see of pictures the more we realize that, if food is scarce in some places, it most assuredly is not where the heroines of the silent drama abide. However, Fay has also gained weight in our opinion, for her production of "Main 1-2-3." It is the first time in our knowledge that the comedy of the crossed wires has been screened, and it is admirably done. The main idea, also, that of the little waif who has no home and gets a job in a furniture store so that she may live in the completely furnished flat in the window, is de-

liciously original. It is all good stuff, and we wish to extend to Fay a right royal welcome of approval. (*Motion Picture News*, July 6, 1918)

Some Job in which Fay Tincher appears in the leading role, far surpasses her first comedy released by World Film. She plays the part of a waitress in a small-town hotel who discovers a very nice captain in a nearby camp on which to shower her affections. Incidentally she succeeds in rounding up some German spies. The humor introduced is both the polite variety which introduces funny situations and of the gag variety in which Miss Tincher exercises her fine art of being tough. The better part of the picture is clever in both respects. A particularly funny touch is scored when the captain after fleeing mess because of more beans, gets a dish of them planted in front of him when he sits down at the hotel table. There are touches that equal this, throughout the two reels. Another when the captain gives the order "column right" and then, forgetting the men for the girl, finds them marching out in the ocean. The spy stuff is done seriously and Miss Tincher also does a dramatic scene when she bids the captain goodbye. (*Motion Picture News*, June 29, 1918)

But despite these and other warm welcomes back in the press – "Fay Tincher is a capable young miss who does all things on the screen with neatness and dispatch, from catching a burglar to darning her stockings. Fay was among the early movie comedians and after a protracted absence she returns in comedies that are being well received." – the run of her unit was brief. Al Santell remembered:

> Well, I knew this thing was not going to work out. As a matter of fact the deal had been set up by my agents and I told them in all honesty that I did not think that Fay Tincher at her age and her sort of ancient style which she used would go in modern comedies. So I advised him not to make the picture and he said well, I'll take your advice only I want to make the

Courtesy of Jim Kerkhoff.

picture. I promised Fay that I would make it, so if you don't make it somebody else will, so you might as well make the money. Well, I said, all right Mr. Smith, you want me to make it I'll make it but remember I'm telling you I think it's a lost cause. Well, it turned out to be a lost cause – he never did get a release for the series of pictures, no one went for the first picture.

Santell was not entirely accurate, for at least three shorts were made and distributed by World. It may be that exhibitors were looking for more "modern" comedies than Fay was offering,

In addition, surviving articles and comments by Fay suggest that she may have agreed to appear in shorts with the understanding that they would lead to starring features, and it appears that when this didn't happen, Fay moved on. Comedy shorts, while loved by audiences, were treated as poor stepchildren by the industry and if a performer wanted to be taken seriously they had to aspire to features, Another possible factor in the curtailing of the series may have been the deadly influenza epidemic that was sweeping the country in the fall of 1918, which temporarily shut down many studios and cinemas and took the life of Wayland Trask, Mack Sennett comedian.

World had publicized Fay as "the pocket-sized comedienne" and stated that she was in charge:

> Miss Tincher writes her own stories (in self-defense, as she puts it), chooses her own cast and directs her own pictures.

While some of this may be studio hype, she did receive script credit on *Main 1-2-3* and had definite ideas on the type of comedy that she wanted to perform. These are expressed, along with her attitude regarding shorts, in an interview with Grace Lee Mack for the *Photo-Play Journal*, where she recoiled after being asked if her World comedies would be of the "custard pie variety":

> I shall strive to them – the laughs I mean, legitimately or not at all. Of course comedy drama is my aim, that is about what my first two pictures are – two-reel comedies with a little drama, a laugh followed by a tear perhaps, and capped with a laugh. If I can make the people at home and the boys from over there a little happier because of my comedies, I shall be satisfied. Later, I expect to do five reel comedy dramas, that is if we can find the right kind of stories, but believe me, it is some job.

After the end of her company she next turned up in March 1919 in the Rupert Julian-directed *The Fire Flingers*, a seven-reel dramatic feature for Universal. Fay played a stenographer set to run off with her cheating boss, and basically seems to have reprised her role from *The Battle of the Sexes*. Not long after this feature hit the theatres, the press announced:

Fay Tincher, she of the black and white stripes and spit curls of the once famous Griffith comedies, is with us again but minus the stripes and curls. She is Al Christie's new star and the veteran comedy producer is directing her personally. Miss Tincher's vehicles will be two reels much similar to those that made her famous in the old days.

When Fay signed with Christie in 1919, the arrangement was beneficial for both of them. Having been making independent one-reelers since 1916, Christie was able to use Fay's proven popularity to mount a move to "two reel specials." She got his personal attention and a big build up from one of the biggest comedy producers of the silent era. After the first short, *Sally's Blighted Career* (1919), a new persona was devised for Fay and, perhaps due to the success of Polly Moran as Sheriff Nell, it was that of a wild and western cowgirl in shorts like *Dangerous Nan McGrew, Wild and Western,* and *Go West Young Woman* (all 1919).

Rowdy Ann (1919) is today the most accessible of Fay's films and is a little gem about a quick-drawing western tomboy who's sent east to a finishing school by her rancher father "for to larn to be a lady." Of course this rough and ready cowgirl gives everyone at her girl's school a run for their money, but after Ann prevents one of her roommates from eloping with a crook, she's a hero. Playing this character to the hilt, Fay strides around completely cock-sure, sizing everyone up as stands with her legs apart and hands on her hips. Her small size is in comic contrast to the character's bravado and tenacity, and outfitted in checkered flannel shirt, cowboy hat, boots, chaps, and oversized gun belt, she looks much like a little kid playing cowboy. Christie was fond of using cross-dressing as a comic device, producing two feature versions of *Charley's Aunt*. Ann puts on the flowing gown that she's required to wear for her classical dancing class, and adds her cowboy hat, boots, and gun belt to it. The juxtapositions challenge conventional notions of femininity.

Fay got quite a physical workout in the role, galloping on horses, throwing lassos and many punches. She even takes a few knocks in a boxing match with ranch hand Al Haynes early in the film. Christie had the reputation for producing more sophisticated and polite comedies than the usual run of slapstick shorts, but at the time Fay joined him he was adding more physical comedy while trying to retain the better developed story elements. Fay's sojourn with Christie turned out to be another brief stay, and a 1919 *Photoplay* article, titled *Is Polite Comedy Polite? Asks Fay Tincher*, gives us a good explanation why. The beginning of the piece presents Fay's initial excitement of working for Christie:

> I'm tickled to death! I'm going back into comedy – society comedies, too, if you please. You know Christie Comedies, don't you? They're nice refined little human dramas. They don't throw pies, they don't get you all mussed up, you know, real high-class stuff. There are going to be my special two-reel comedies.

But the rest of the article chronicles how these expectations are flattened as she amasses bumps and bruises doing the stunts for these "polite comedies." While the story presents all of these events with a "humorous" tone, it appears that Fay didn't find the experience funny and became disenchanted with the series.

In 1920 she had stopped making the western comedies and only appeared in three more shorts for Christie – *A Seaside Siren, Striking Models,* and *Dining Room, Kitchen and Sink*. Despite this, she still shows up prominently in Christie publicity ads into mid-1921, and went on a personal appearance tour with one of the earlier shorts, where she "delivered a monologue in which she told of her studio experiences and the manner in which Christie comedies are made." This gives the impression that a deal was worked out where Fay finished out her contract by drumming up publicity for the Christie product.

After this Fay was away from the screen for two years, and although the November 24, 1922 *Toledo Blade* reported –

Fay lays waste to Joe Murphy and Mark Hamilton with help from Jackie Morgan in the Gump Comedy *Oh, What a Day!* (1923). Courtesy of Robert S. Birchard.

Fay Tincher, "the striped girl" who has been in retirement for the last few years, has been engaged to support Lewis Sargent in some of his Messenger Boy stories, under the direction of Scott Darling.

-she's not known to have actually appeared in any of the Sargent comedies. She must have been negotiating with Universal, as the *Moving Picture World* announced on May 12, 1923:

Fay Tincher and Joe Murphy in Gump Comedies. Andy Gump, the famous cartoon character of comic strips in newspapers throughout the whole country, and known to millions, is to be a movie hero. He is not going to be an "animated cartoon," but a real, honest-to-goodness comedy character. Carl Laemmle found Andy's double in the person of Joe Murphy. Min, played by Fay Tincher, Chester, Uncle Bim, Widow Zander, and all the cast of the laughing group have also been found in real life and will be seen in these comedies.

Based on the enormously popular strip by Sidney Smith, which had premiered in 1917, the series was produced by Samuel Van Ronkel, who had a five-year contract with cartoonist Smith, and was distributed by Universal. The *Gumps* followed the misadventures of a middle-class family with the head of the house Andy a pompous bungler whose cry of "Oh Min!" when in trouble became a 1920s catchphrase. Fay's part of Min was described by Sidney Smith as "really the brains of the family. Gentle, loving and enduring, with a strong mother's instinct but a terror when aroused." Rounding out the cast was their little son Chester, a freckle-faced imp whose main pleasure in life seemed to be helping his father get into hot water.

Most of the characters in the strip had been drawn in a fairly realistic style and could be easily cast, but star Andy was pure cartoon. Incredibly tall and skinny with a big bald dome, jug-handled ears and beady eyes, Andy's most outstanding feature was his total absence of a chin. A giant push broom moustache led directly to his long, skinny pencil neck. The producers accomplished the nearly impossible task of finding a living person who looked like Andy Gump when they cast Joe Murphy, an ex-vaudevillian who had been playing supporting bits in shorts for L-KO, Keystone, Fox, Triangle, Reelcraft, and Educational. The series was a big success, and settled down to a regular production schedule.

Fay also turned up in other Universal product in 1924, making three appearances in the fourth series of their *The Leather Pushers* boxing shorts – *That Kid from Madrid*, *A Tough Tenderfoot*, and *Swing Bad the Sailor*. In addition she had a small role in *Excitement*, a feature comedy starring Laura La Plante as a thrill-seeking wife whose husband teaches her a lesson. The film was full of comedy regulars such as Bert Roach, Margaret Cullington, Rolfe Sedan, Lon Poff, and Fay was last billed as "Mammy."

After these 1924 appearances, Fay's career was swallowed up and swamped by the *Gumps*. The series lasted a total of five years and while some top-notched veteran comedy directors like Norman Taurog, Erle C. Kenton, Robert Kerr, and Vin Moore directed some of the shorts, the bulk were directed by Francis Corby, a cameraman who became an uninspired director and later returned to being a cameraman. The handful of *Gump* comedies that circulate today show that, although co-starred in billing and publicity, Fay actually took a back seat to Joe Murphy in the series, with the lion's share of footage going to Andy's slapstick trials and tribulations. Min's character was supportive, long suffering, and unfortunately very bland. Quite a step down from *Rowdy Ann* and leaves no doubt that Fay's exit from Christie was a big error.

When the *Gumps* came to an end in 1928, Fay's career did too. The arrival of sound and her typecasting as Min Gump are often suggested as possible reasons for her disappearance. But given her stage background and musical comedy experience, talking films shouldn't have been a hurdle. Another possibility is offered by historian Sam Gill, who reports that there are rumors that because of her sexual preference, Fay may have been on a fabled Will Hays blacklist that was created in the wake of the Arbuckle and William Desmond Taylor scandals.

In his book *The Day the Laughter Stopped*, author David Yallop gives a description of the list:

> In the summer of 1922 the Hays Office prepared a list of nearly two hundred people who were to be eased out of the business because they represented risks to filmdom's image – not because of their politics, because of habits like drug use, which contributed to the image of Hollywood as sin city.

Yallop claims that he saw an actual copy of said list, but Sam Gill offers that while there may have been an informal list, he's never seen or heard of a real document turning up in all the years he's spent researching silent comedy and working at the Academy's Margaret Herrick Library. Although it's true that Fay left Christie's employ a bit mysteriously and afterward never worked anywhere but Universal, without an actual copy of the list as a "smoking gun," this is all conjecture. It may have simply been that Fay had finally had enough of "two-reel funnycisms" and called it quits.

After the demise of the *Gumps*, Fay left the Hollywood area. She returned briefly when her sister died in 1932 and as the informant on the death certificate, is listed as living in Chicago. Between this point and her death virtually nothing is known. Researcher Billy H. Doyle searched for many years for information about Fay or her whereabouts and finally in 1991 found, through social security records, that she died in Brooklyn, New York on October 11, 1983. She was an amazing ninety-nine years old, had never married, and her final resting place is an unmarked grave at Silver Mount Cemetery on Staten Island in New York City.

The third of our starring clowns who managed their own company was the tall and extremely skinny Gale Henry. A dead ringer, and possibly the prototype, for Popeye's girlfriend Olive Oyl, she starred in her own popular series of comedies as well as provided sterling support for other comics. She was the daughter of Charles and Mai Henry, born in June of 1893 (some sources give her birth name as Trowbridge). The 1900 US Census states that she was born in Texas and living in Los Angeles where Charles was a saloon-keeper. Gale told a slightly different version of her early days to *Picture-Play* Magazine: "We lived on a ranch – mother, dad, and I, until I was fourteen, then we came to Los Angeles." In the 1910 Census she's seventeen and already an actress. She began her career onstage as a member of the Temple Opera Company, tersely described by Gale as "comic – not grand." Her looks defined her type of roles from the very beginning and again she reported to *Picture-Play*:

Heinie Conklin delivers Gale Henry and Billy Franey in an unidentified *Joker Comedy*. Courtesy of Robert S. Birchard.

> I saw an advertisement in the Los Angeles Times which called for seventy chorus girls. I answered the ad, in a little white dress which came not far below my knees, and a funny little straw hat; my mother had trimmed it with a wreath of tiny pink cotton roses, and the outfit was not unlike the comedy costumes I later used in my pictures. Think of the figure I must have cut among those more or less sophisticated girls – for I could neither sing nor dance. I went home that night – my hopes blasted! Not a word had been said about my coming back. But the next morning the postman brought me a card which requested that I "report for rehearsal" the next day. And that day was the very happiest of my life. To think that I, Gale Henry, was a full-fledged actress – for so I considered myself. The days that followed were happy ones, too, and what do you think – that cast included Fatty Arbuckle, Louise Fazenda, and Blossom Seely.

In 1914 she entered films at the Universal Film Company:

> I knew a girl who worked at Universal; she took me out with her one morning, and I got a job. That's all there is to it, except that I remained there for five years and was featured in two hundred comedies.

Joker Comedies had been formed by Universal in 1913 to compete with Mack Sennett's Keystones and the shorts were one-reel knockabouts that were cranked out at the rate of one or two a week. Gale joined the unit that was under the direction of Allen Curtis with Max Asher as the designated star, with an ensemble made up of Harry McCoy, Billy Franey, Louise Fazenda, and Bobby Vernon. McCoy left early to work for Sennett, as would Fazenda, Vernon, and scenarist Clarence Badger. Gale joined the group in early 1914, which soon included Milburn Moranti, Lillian Peacock, and Charles "Heinie" Conklin.

Gale is captured by Bobby Vernon, Heinie Conklin, and Billy Franey in *Lady Baffles and Detective Duck in When the Wets Went Dry* (1915). Courtesy of Robert Arkus.

Out of the huge number of Jokers that Gale appeared in only a handful are known to survive. *She Wrote a Play and Played It* (1916) stars Gale as Miss Scribbles, an amateur writer with a large bank account, who is pursued by a ham actor who agrees to put on her play. Everything that could go wrong with the performance does go wrong, and when she finds that the actor has eloped with her cash she gives up writing and marries her long-suffering suitor – the combination village undertaker, sheriff, judge, and dog catcher. In *A Burglar's Bride* (1917) she's the mooning scullery maid who's reading the novel *The Burglar's Bride* as she cooks, causing her to dump everything like canned goods, whole pepper shakers, and the book itself into the pot in her distraction.

The lady of the house and her mousey husband are going out, and leave Gale to look after things. Gale takes the opportunity to doll up in her employer's fancy gown. A real burglar, Soapy Jake, breaks in and thinks Gale is a rich lady. She's thrilled to see him and proposes on the spot – "Marry me or got to jail" – and since the cops who have trailed him are outside he agrees. Gale and Soapy are having their wedding breakfast when the employers come home early, and Soapy finds out that Gale is only the maid, which leads him to take flight out the window with Gale in hot pursuit. A handy manhole turns out to be his means of escape.

Universal also turned out other brands of comedies, and Gale showed up in some of the other releases. In 1915 Pat Powers produced the *Lady Baffles and Detective Duck* series, a spoof of cliffhanger serials in eleven one-reel chapters with titles like *The Dread Society of the Sacred Sausage*, and *The Signal of the Three Socks*. Max Asher played inventor and master of disguise Detective Duck who was always hot on the heels of his nemesis the mysterious crook Lady Baffles (Gale). At the end of 1917 Gale stopped working for Joker and was headlined in Universal's Nestor and L-Ko Comedies. Then in early 1918 she left the studio and the trade papers announced:

> **Gale Henry Forms Company.** Gale Henry, who has just returned from a three month vacation, has organized her own producing company and will make a series of comedies such has gained fame and prestige for her during her long engagement with Universal. Miss Henry has rented a space at Diando Studios in Glendale, and under the direction of Bruno J. Becker will begin immediately on her first production. Milburn Moranti, who supported the comedienne in both her Universal and L-Ko productions has been engaged to play the principal male role in the new comedies.

Billy Franey, Eddie Baker, Phyllis Allen, Hap Ward, and Richard Currier rounded out the regular supporting ensemble with the afore-mentioned Milburn Moranti, and Bruno J. Becker was Gale's husband. Becker had been Allen Curtis' assistant director at Joker and the couple married in 1916. As supervisor of her shorts and general manager of the new company it appears to have been very much a joint venture. Her organization was named the Model Comedy Co. and had a distribution deal with the Bulls Eye Film Corporation. Billy West was Bulls Eye's other big name, and their other releases included *Bulls Eye Master Comedies*, the Napoleon and Sally *Monkey Shines*, and a comic newsreel *The Weakly Indigestion*.

During her tenure at Universal Gale wrote many of the stories for her comedies and developed her screen persona. Like Louise Fazenda and Alice Howell she often played put-upon slaveys, but her angular and unconventional looks also made her perfect as lovelorn spinsters, over-bearing wives, and burlesque country girls. Her thinness gave her the appearance of a living stick figure – all gangly arms and legs, with incredibly expressive shoulders that would rise up to her ears with joy at the arrival of a new beau, or plunge and almost disappear due to some embarrassment or disappointment. Her nose was a sharp beak surrounded by large eyes that seriously threatened to cross in her signature big take of surprise. She had a mouth and eyebrows that seemed to be made of elastic, and a chin that dropped off suddenly into a long ostrich neck. Her hair was dark with bangs in the front and a bun in the back. On top was a wide brimmed hat, which looked like a satellite dish on her skinny body, usually garnished with a skimpy floral display. A tight, old-fashioned button-up blouse, with short sleeves to accentuate her long arms, a long plaid skirt, and clunky shoes finished her ensemble. Her over-all appearance had a feel of L. Frank Baum's Scarecrow of Oz – as if she was put together from odd, mismatching parts.

Gale gets a scolding from Hap Ward as Dick Currier hangs out the window in *Poor Fish* (1919). Courtesy of Jim Kerkhoff.

Known as "the Elongated Comedienne," her performing style could be very broad, but she also had a gift for small insightful gestures that could bring a moment of pathos and feeling into the knockabout. She was equally adept at being demure or projecting a world-weary cynicism. Keenly aware of the image she had created, Gale offered a few rules of thumb in 1919 to Giebler at *The Moving Picture World*:

"Do you find your work exacting?" I asked her.

"Oh, my, yes, "she said. "We artists have to strive so for effect. Look at this make-up. You have no idea how long it took me to figure out this gown."

"Is it a period gown?" I inquired.

"Hardly a period, "she answered, "I would call it more like an exclamation point. It was made to make people bust out laughing, you know.

"Gowns mean so much," continued Miss Henry. "They really are the distinction between drama and comedy. Take that instance you mentioned where I hit Max Asher with an axe. That was comedy because I wore a comedy make-up. Had I been garbed in a long trailing robe, a feather fan and wrist watch, I would have been either a vengeful vampire or a wronged wife, and it would have been drahmah."

Gale and company turned out the Models at a hectic pace – at least nineteen were released in 1919. Of the few survivors *The Detectress* (1919) presents Gale as a detective wannabe who's investigating a Chinatown ganglord's plot to steal the plans for an invention that will enable diners to see what's in the chop suey they are eating. A non-stop chase through the Chinatown maze of trapdoors and secret panels makes up the bulk of this short, but at the end everything turns out to be Gale's opium-induced dream and she's taken away in the "Nutwagon."

The Slavey (1919) chronicles Gale's misadventures in work and love as the girl-of-all-trades at a cheap boarding house. All that survives of *Poor Fish* (1919) is the climax, which has Gale and her beau Milburn Moranti on the run to elope with her parents in pursuit. Chased into an amusement park the race continues up and down the slides, and on the spinning floors of the sideshow funhouse. *Her First Flame* (1919) is set in the future of 1950, where women have taken over and men wear dresses and take care of the children. Gale is running for the office of fire chief and after she wins, loser Phyllis Allen kidnaps Gale's boyfriend, a frilly Milburn Moranti. When Milburn spurns her advances, Phyllis leaves him in a burning house, and Gale saves the day in a frantic last-minute rescue.

Although the Models were well-received it appears that the relationship between Bulls Eye and Gale's company was not smooth. Perhaps due to the grinding production pace or monotony from the sameness of the material, items began to appear about Gale's desire to make a feature "to be put on simply as a test picture; to show what Miss Henry can accomplish in five-reelers." Then in February 1920 the *Moving Picture World* announced:

> **Comedienne Gale Henry Is No Longer With Bulls Eye**. The Model Comedy Company announces that Gale Henry, comedienne and head of the company, severed connections with the Bulls Eye Film Corporation which has been dis-

tributing her releases, and has signed a contract with a prominent distribution company. She will produce only six two-reelers a year, instead of twenty-four a year as heretofore.

The period from 1920 to 1922 was an important transition in Gale's career. It appears that she and Bruno J. Becker divorced and that she took some time to examine how she wanted to continue in films. Although many statements were released about her future plans – starring in features or even a new series of twelve shorts for the Special Pictures Corporation – she appears to have decided to work at a more relaxed pace and became an ace supporting player.

Her popularity with viewers and dead-on comic timing were valuable assets, which put her in demand for features all through the 1920s. The first was *The Hunch* (1921) and she appeared in a total of eighteen. Most memorable were *Open All Night* (1924) where she was teamed with Raymond Griffith, and *Stranded* (1927). In *Stranded* she gives an excellent performance as a cynical, well-seasoned Hollywood bit player who takes a young Shirley Mason under her wing and teaches her the ropes of working at the studios. In all of Gale's work in features she has the air of a no-nonsense veteran who's taking advantage of every second of her screen time to give the audience maximum entertainment.

At the same time she made frequent guest appearances in other people's shorts. The costumes and hair styles may have been fancier, but it was the same old "two-reel Gale" willing to do anything for a laugh. Among others she worked at Christie with Neal Burns and Jack Duffy, and was a human exclamation mark in contrast to the balloon shapes of "Fatty" Alexander, "Fatt" Karr, and "Kewpie" Ross in the Joe Rock-produced *A Ton of Fun* comedies, but her moments of glory came with Charley Chase.

Chase began his starring career for Hal Roach in 1924, but earlier as Charles Parrott, he had been a director at Bulls Eye and knew that Gale was a perfect foil for him. Out of Gale's many appearances with Chase two particularly stand out. In *His Wooden Wedding* (1925) Charley has called off his wedding because his best man has convinced him that the bride has a wooden leg. The best man is after the diamond ring that Charley has given her, and later on a boat cruise Charley learns the truth and drops the ring down fellow passenger Gale's back to hide it. But Charley has trouble getting it back as Gale is a flirty spinster who thinks that his attempts to retrieve the ring are amorous advances. Finally Charley takes her to the ship's ballroom where he goads her into wilder and wilder dances which causes her make-up, watch, garter belt, and finally the ring to fall out on the dance floor.

A One Mama Man (1927) has Charley as a European count arriving in America, who through a series of complications that only happen in comedy shorts ends up being hired to impersonate himself at a society party. Gale, who had been a passenger with Charley on his voyage to America and knows that he really is the count, shows up at the party where he has to keep her from revealing the truth. Luckily Gale has an affliction, as a character explains in a title card – "Miss Glutz was in a streetcar accident – And the sound of a bell always shocks her into a trance!" Of course Gale's version of a trance has her suddenly freezing on a tilt like the Leaning Tower of Pisa with her eyes crossed. In a wonderful scene on the dance floor during the party Charley must repeatedly find new bells to ring to keep Gale in a trance so she can't reveal his true identity. Eventually everyone is happy when they find out who he really is, which leaves Gale to comment – "I've been trying to tell you. But there's too many damn bells around this place." Comedy fans are usually familiar with Gale from these appearances as the Chase films are popular and frequently screened today.

Charley Chase spots Gale about to expose his real identity to Burr McIntosh in *A One Mama Man* (1927). Author's collection.

When sound took over the film industry, Gale seemed to dive right in, appearing in two features, *The Love Doctor* and *Darkened Rooms* (both 1929), plus Charley Chase's first talkie *The Big Squawk* (1929). Her voice was fine and well-suited to her established character, but outside of an occasional role with Chase, she retired from the screen, most likely because she began a new screen profession. After divorcing Bruno J. Becker Gale had married Henry East, a Hollywood prop man, in 1925. In those days, part of a prop man's duties was to supply dogs if they were needed for a scene. Gale and Henry had adopted a little part bulldog/part terrier named Buddy, who proved to be a film natural. Soon, he was appearing in tons of features and shorts, including many on the Roach lot with pal Charley Chase, such as *What Price Goofy?* (1925), *Mighty Like a Moose* (1926), and *Dog Shy* (1926).

Buddy got the couple started in the dog training business, but another dog, Skippy, really put them on the map when he became famous as "Asta" in the *Thin Man* series, not to mention other pictures such as *The Awful Truth* (1937) and *Bringing up Baby* (1938). Eventually the Easts set up the East Kennels on two acres outside Hollywood and supplied dogs for movies and TV for many years. Gale's last known appearance is in Charley Chase's 1933 *Luncheon at Twelve* and from there she literally seems to have "gone to the dogs." Hardly the lovelorn spinster that she often played in films, she had a third marriage to Frederick Ernie Near, a dog trainer nineteen years her junior, and continued to run the dog kennel with ex-husband East. When she died of pneumonia on June 6, 1972, her acting career was sadly over-looked. Mostly remembered today for her shorts with Chase, it's hoped that more of her Joker and Model Comedies are recovered so that she'll have the opportunity to move from the forgotten category and take her rightful place among the great screen clowns.

More than directing or producing there were many opportunities for women as screenwriters. In addition to Mrs. Drew there were a number of ladies who specialized in writing comedy. Two of the most famous, who had the longest careers, were Anita Loos and Frances Marion. Loos was born in California in April 1889 and was a child actor on San Francisco stages:

> While I was acting in Pop's stock company, fate gave me a really proper steer into a brand-new line of endeavor. Pop used to run short movies between the acts of our plays; all movies were short in those days. I adored those old silent films, knew the particular style of each company – Selig, Vitagraph, Kalem, and, best of all, Biograph, which produced more literate stories played by a more sensitive group of actors. (*A Girl Like I*, 1966)

She began selling stories to Biograph where they were directed by D.W. Griffith. *The New York Hat* (1912) is a seriocomic tale about a legacy left by a dying mother for her daughter. According to the wishes of the mother the young village minister administers the funds for the girl, and when she wants a fancy New York hat he buys it for her, which causes local gossip that brings the church board in

A young Anita Loos. Courtesy of Cole Johnson.

judgment on him. The success of the film established Loos and led to her becoming a staff writer for the studio. By 1913 she was supplying a steady stream of stories to house comedy director Del Henderson along the lines of *The Hicksville Epicure, Highbrow Love, The Widow's Kids, Pa Says, A Cure for Suffragettes,* and *Bink's Vacation* (all 1913). Unfortunately practically all of these are unavailable, but the one viewable today, *Oh, Sammy!* (1913), is a definite oddity.

The story involves a Jewish sweatshop where the owner Einstein wants to palm his old maid daughter off on his worker Sammy. Einstein throws a party to announce the "engagement," and to give Sammy a diamond ring as a bribe, but Sammy has ideas of his own and ends up with the girl of his choice. What makes this film so strange is the choice to have all the Jewish characters (practically the entire cast) wearing huge and grotesque false noses – besides the outlandish racial profiling it makes the film look like it's populated by a flock of toucans.

When D.W. Griffith left Biograph to join Harry Aitken's Reliance/Majestic organization Loos went along, and among other things like items for Dorothy Gish such as *A Lesson in Mechanics* and *The Saving of Grace*, not to mention one of Max Davidson's *Izzy* Comedies *Izzy and his Rival* (1914), she wrote numerous scripts for the Komic Comedy one-reelers with Fay Tincher, Tod Browning, and Davidson. Eddie Dillon was director and part of the cast, and titles include *Nearly a Burglar's Bride, Nell's Eugenic Wedding* (both 1914), *A Flurry in Art,* and *The Deacon's Whiskers* (both 1915). When the company became Fine Arts and part of Triangle, Anita met a Broadway actor who had just arrived in California as part of the theatre stars acquired by Harry Aitken.

John Emerson had worked for the Shuberts and Charles Frohman and had been hired to act in and direct dramas. The pair first collaborated on Douglas Fairbank's *His Picture in the Papers* (1916) and its breezy and satiric tone was perfect for Fairbank's tongue-in-cheek personality. After working separately for a while – Loos writing the titles for *Intolerance* (1916), and stories for Fay Tincher's two-reelers like *Laundry Liz* and *A Calico Vampire* (both 1916), while Emerson directed dramas like *Macbeth* (1916) with Sir Herbert Beerbohm Tree – they were finally cemented as a team for Fairbanks with *The Matrimaniac* (1916):

> **Fairbanks Picks Anita Loos To Write Sub-Titles**. Anita Loos of the Triangle Fine Arts scenario department will henceforth write the sub-titles for all screen plays in which Douglas Fairbanks is starred.
>
> This arrangement has been made at the special request of Fairbanks himself, who is convinced that the drawing power of the pictures in which he appears can be greatly affected by the sub-titles.
>
> "Time and again," says Fairbanks, "I have sat through plays with Miss Loos and have heard the audience applaud her sub-titles as heartily as the liveliest scenes.

This has convinced me of the great value of the kind of work she does." (*Exhibitors Herald*, December 2, 1916)

In 1917 the pair moved with Doug over to Paramount/Artcraft for four more features – *In Again, Out Again, Wild and Wooly, Down to Earth*, and *Reaching for the Moon* – which were light-hearted romps that made jabs at pop culture subjects like eugenics, psychology, getting back to nature, etc. – all built around Fairbank's charming persona and included plenty of action and stunts. Anita later said:

> I had dramatized Doug's screen characters from what he was in real life. Stunts and jokes came first with Doug, while sex had to be barely indicated. If I ever ventured into sentiment, Doug would send for me and say, "Dammit, I'm no actor. I can't play a love scene." So I'd cancel the sex activities and have Doug jump off an airplane. (*The Talmadge Girls*, 1978)

Constance Talmadge, the heroine of twelve Anita Loo scenarios. Author's collection.

Emerson was credited as sole director, but it seems that Anita had a great deal of input there as well. During their work with Fairbanks the pair truly became a solid unit and in 1918 they split with Doug. Paramount gave them their own production unit and ballyhooed:

> **John Emerson and Anita Loos Productions**. John Emerson and Anita Loos are more than directors and scenario writers. They are artists who have developed a new sort of motion picture comedy-drama – the motion picture that doesn't take itself too darn seriously, the motion picture that speaks your language, that gives you a glow of good humor, that genially slaps you on the back, says "Look here! This is a bully story!," and proceeds to tell it to you.
>
> John Emerson and Anita Loos are responsible for Douglas Fairbanks' rollicking tales, "Down to Earth," "Reaching for the Moon," "The Man from Painted

Post," "Wild and Wooly," and "In Again, Out Again." They adapted "Hit the Trail Holiday" for George M. Cohan, and "Let's get a Divorce" for Billie Burke.

Their new productions will be made for several different stars. They will produce the first Shirley Mason pictures and have just completed the first Fred Stone story.

The names "John Emerson and Anita Loos" mean a great deal to exhibitor and to motion picture patron. Their new productions will be eagerly sought, for rare indeed is the exhibitor who hasn't been asked "When will you show another of those John Emerson-Anita Loos pictures – the ones with the funny stunts and gingery sub-titles?" (*Motion Picture News*, June 29, 1918)

In addition to Billie Burke, George M. Cohan, Fred Stone, and Shirley Mason, the pair did films with Marion Davies and Ernest Truex, and made their union legal in June 1919 when they married at Norma Talmadge's home in New York. When Joseph Schenck took over his sister-in-law Constance Talmadge's films in 1919 the first thing he did was hire Emerson and Loos to make them (see Chapter Five). Starting with *A Temperamental Wife* (1919) and ending with *Learning to Love* (1925) they wrote eleven comedies for the star, making her one of the screen's most popular in items such as *A Virtuous Vamp* (1919), *The Perfect Woman* (1920), and *Mama's Affair* (1921). Most of these films have been lost, leaving Talmadge's career overlooked and Emerson and Loos silent film reputation resting on their Douglas Fairbanks productions. In a February 1920 issue of *Photoplay* Anita gave her tips on "doping out the subtitles:"

Ruth Taylor and Mack Swain in the 1928 adaptation of Anita Loo's *Gentlemen Prefer Blondes*. Courtesy of Bruce Calvert.

Writing good subtitles and planning illustrated subtitle cards to be held before the camera is one of the hardest, yet pleasantest, sides of photography writing. It is the scenarioist's one chance to spread himself in clever, forceful verbiage. Use lots of subtitles – it's one of the secrets of good screen dramatization – but make them terse. The faster the action, the shorter the subtitle. Never forget that for every word you add to your subtitle card, another second or so must be added to the time it is held on the screen in order that the slowest-reading spectator may fully grasp it.

After 1925 their film work became more sporadic, occasional screenplays such as *Stranded* (1927) and *The Fall of Eve* (1929), plus they adapted Anita's book *Gentlemen Prefer Blondes* to be directed by Mal St Clair in 1928. In the sound era they worked at MGM on films such as *San Francisco* (1936), *Saratoga* (1937), *The Women* (1939), and *I Married an Angel* (1942). Emerson died in 1956, and Loos kept writing, producing a number of memoirs about her time in Hollywood right up to her death in 1981.

Frances Marion is primarily remembered today as a dramatic writer, but she did pen many comedies – lighter fare for the likes of Mary Pickford, Marie Dressler, Olive Thomas, and Constance Talmadge. Like Anita Loos her early life was spent in San Francisco:

Writer Frances Marion. Courtesy of The Museum of Modern Art.

Frances Marion was born in San Francisco and has spent most of her life there. She studied art, and for a number of years before she began screen writing was a designer of theatrical posters and an illustrator for magazines. She next "dabbled," as she puts it, in newspaper work, and finally began writing scenarios as a free lance.

In order to gain a thorough knowledge of the technique of picture making, she next got work as a humble extra in the Bosworth Studios. One of her earliest scenarios after that was "The Foundling" for Mary Pickford, and it is for that famous star that she has written the most of her photoplays since. Indeed, the two are closely associated in personal life as well as business. (*Photo-Play Journal*, May 1919)

This chapter has already touched upon Mary Pickford's contributions as a producer and comedienne, and of course many of her early signature films were written by Ms. Marion – *The Poor Little Rich Girl*, *Rebecca of Sunnybrook Farm*, *The Little Princess* (all 1917), *Amarilly of Clothes Line Alley* (1918), and *Pollyanna* (1920). Also mentioned was her work with Marie Dressler on films such as *Tillie Wakes Up* (1917), her independent shorts, and comeback films in the late 1920s and early 1930s (see Chapter Nine).

Besides major serious vehicles such as *Humoresque* (1920), *The Toll of the Sea* (1922), *Stella Dallas* (1925), *The Son of the Sheik* (1926), and *The Wind* (1928), other examples of her work in silent comedy includes Doug Fairbank's *He Comes Up Smiling* (1918), *The Flapper* (1920) with Olive Thomas, *The Primitive Lover* and *East is East* (both 1922) with Connie Talmadge, the Marion Davies films *Zander the Great*, *Graustrak* (both 1925), and *The Red Mill* (1927), in addition to *Potash and Perlmutter* (1923), *In Hollywood with Potash and Perlmutter* (1924), *The First Year*, *Partners Again* (both 1925), and *Excess Baggage* (1928). By the early days of sound she was one of Hollywood's top screenwriters, and between prestige pictures on the order of *The Champ* (1931) and *Dinner at Eight* (1933) she still found time to write Marion Davies comedies such as *Blondie of the Follies* (1932). Marion mostly left films after the death of MGM producer Irving Thalberg, doing some occasional uncredited re-writes, to work on plays, novels and paintings until her death in 1973.

Many writers began their careers as actresses and started supplying ideas for their own films before moving behind the camera full time. Bess Meredyth had been born in Buffalo, New York and started a career there as a newspaper writer. Also interested in music, she toured vaudeville with what she later referred to as a "pianologue act," and while on a break from the road in California in 1912 she began appearing as an extra with the Biograph Company. Working her way up to ingénue parts she soon moved to Universal where she became a comedy lead in their Joker and Nestor brands, initially appearing with William Wolbert in his *Willy Walrus* shorts like *Willy Walrus and the Baby*, and *Willy Walrus, Detective* (both 1914).

When Bess Got in Wrong (1914) survives at the Library of Congress and presents Bess as a terrible flirt, much to the annoyance of her boyfriend Lee. Although she promises to stop the next time they go to a party she flirts with three boys, all of whom promise to escort her home. Turns out they are friends of Lee, and he hatches a scheme where none of them take her home, so she has to go by herself.

Bess is nervous, but all is well until a young dude begins bothering her. Luckily an older working man comes by, gets rid of the dude, and sees that she gets home safely. Lee, feeling badly about the scheme, checks on her. When he gets there they argue, and the working man, who had been standing guard nearby, thinks Lee's another dude and decks him. Everything gets straightened out, and Bess and Lee patch things up.

Portrait of Bess Meredyth from her acting days. Author's collection.

Meredyth was a character comedienne, frequently playing difficult girls as in this and others like *The Wooing of Bessie Bumpkin* (1914). Not exactly pretty, she resembled Harry Langdon with curly blonde hair. She even had a short run as a comedic lady detectress in *Bess the Detectress, Bessie Pinkerton Holmes, Tick, Tick, Tick,* and *The Dog Watch* (all 1914). Interested in becoming a screenwriter she began writing many of her own comedy stories, like *When Bess Got in Wrong*, and dramas like *The Crack O'Doom* (1914), *The Mother Instinct*, and *The Human Menace* (both 1915), some for director Wilfred Lucas, who was her husband. In 1915 she stopped acting and began writing full time. Most of her comedy writing was done in the teens – in 1916 she wrote the scenarios for Carter De Haven's twelve episode *Timothy Dobbs, That's Me* series that chronicled a young soda jerk's attempts to become a movie star. Wallace Beery directed the films that included *The Sody Clerk, Hired and Fired, He Almost Lands an Angel,* and *Fame at Last* (all 1916). She would write others items for De Haven such as *The Topsy Turvy Twins* and *A Five Foot Ruler* (both 1917).

Meredyth also wrote a large number of the one-reelers of Eddie Lyons and Lee Moran – the most popular team in silent comedy before the arrival of Laurel & Hardy. Over about six years they made a staggering number of films together, and Bess wrote a large chunk of their 1917 output such as *Pass the Prunes* (1916), *Practice What You Preach*,

Treat 'Em Rough, Why, Uncle!, and *A Macaroni Sleuth* (all 1917). Later in 1917 Meredyth made the jump to features pictures, and outside of an occasional comedy focused on dramatic fare like *The Red Lily* (1924), *Ben-Hur* (1925), *The Sea Beast,* and *Don Juan* (both 1926). The changeover to sound saw her remain busy on big films on the order of *Strange Interlude* (1932), *The Affairs of Cellini* (1934), *Charlie Chan at the Opera* (1936), and *The Mark of Zorro* (1940). Married to director Michael Curtiz, she retired in the 1940s, and died in 1969.

Elsie Janis was a much beloved stage comedienne at the beginning of the Twentieth Century. Although mostly forgotten now, in her day she was the toast of two continents and one of the biggest names in vaudeville. Films were really a small part of her career, but she wrote as well as starred in five of her six silent features. She was born Elsie Bierbower on March 16, 1889 in Columbus, Ohio and made her stage debut there at the age of eight. She worked non-stop from that point, as in addition to her immense talent she had the stage mother of all stage mothers. They were inseparable for most of their lives, and in the November 1911 *American Magazine* Janis described some of that devotion:

> The usual hardships were not mine, because I have the most wonderful mother in the world; a mother who has guarded and shielded me from the rough corners of the world and made the path easy for my feet, a mother who has been father, sister, and brother to me, a mother who has fostered with remitting care and attention whatever talent I may have been born with, giving me every possible advantage and opportunity in developing my talent, a mother who has always been unselfishly interested in my career and whose devotion has made most of my fondest dreams come true.

From her earliest days Janis was known for her impersonations, and over the years they included Sarah Bernhardt, Weber & Fields, Lillian Russell, Eddie Foy, Ethel Barrymore, Harry Lauder, Bert Williams, Fanny Brice, and George M. Cohan. Famous in vaudeville, and popular singing and dancing in revues in America, London, and Paris, her

Elsie Janis. Author's collection.

first Broadway success was in 1906's *The Vanderbilt Cup* and over the years it was followed by *The Fair-Co-Ed* (1908), *The Slim Princess* (1910), *The Lady of the Slipper* (1912), *The Passing Show* (1914), *Miss Information* (1915), *The Century Girl* (1917), and *Oh, Kay!* (1927). Films came calling in 1915:

> Elsie Janis, long considered one of our best mimics, comediennes and musical comedy artists, has turned author and just completed her appearance, under the direction of Lois Weber, for Bosworth, Inc., in an original work by herself, "The Caprices of Kitty" a five-part feature which will be released on the Paramount program early in February. (*Moving Picture World*, January 16, 1915)

Bosworth, Inc. was formed in 1913 by actor Hobart Bosworth, with H.T. Rudisill and California capitalist and sportsman Frank A. Garbutt. Although the original object of the company was to make films based on Jack London stories, they soon branched out and in 1914 Phillips Smalley and Lois Weber joined as actor and directors. Married in real life, the pair had worked together at Universal and on his own Smalley had directed the Crystal Comedies with Pearl White, Chester Barnett, and Joseph "Baldy" Belmont. In 1914 Paramount Pictures was formed and distributed the Bosworth product. Janis did a total of four features for Bosworth in 1915 – *The Caprices of Kitty, Betty in Search of a Thrill, Nearly a Lady,* and *Twas Ever Thus* – and wrote all of them. The first two had her working with Weber and Smalley as directors – although Smalley alone was credited on *The Caprices of Kitty* it appears it was really a joint effort.

Sadly the films are unavailable today so details and impressions have to be gathered from contemporary reports. *Caprices* has Janis playing Kit, a spirited young girl enrolled at a very regimented girl's school who does her best to sneak out without her teachers knowing it whenever she gets a chance, giving her the opportunity for plenty of physical gags that involve climbing in and out of windows, scaling trees, and clamoring over fences. On one outing with a chaperone she manages to ditch the teacher and meet a young artist who becomes her fiancée. The rest of the plot concerns the restrictions in her father's will that she not see her lover for six months or lose her fortune, and somehow a sequence of racing a car at breakneck speed is worked in. The fledgling movie star was welcomed with open arms by critics:

> Elsie Janis, as a screen actress, appears in a dual capacity of playwright and star in "the Caprices of Kitty," which is the attraction at the Stanley for the first three days of the week. It is an irresistible comedy, with a tomboy role of the kind in which Miss Janis appears at her best. Here without the aid of songs or dialogue, her versatility is attested by the cleverness with which she conveys the idea of girlish mischief and merriment to the audience by pantomime and facile expression. She dances and skips about, climbs trees and performs other tomboy

tricks with the inimitable grace and all the time maintains the buoyancy and nerve of the capricious Kitty (*Philadelphia Telegraph*, March 6, 1915)

Her next picture, *Betty in Search of a Thrill*, seems to have been developed along very similar lines with the star as a sheltered convent girl, with another large fortune, who's consumed with a desire for thrills and to go out into the great big, beautiful world and see what it contains. The May 19, 1915 *Chicago Tribune* advised:

> Miss Janis frolics through her role with perfect naturalness and abandon. She is herself and does just what she pleases, which is mostly mimicking and tomboying, with an ease that makes her a pleasant thing to watch whether or not you happen to be much in sympathy with what she pleases.

Most stars who came to movies from the stage found that they had to pull back and take a more subdued approach, but Janis acknowledged the opposite:

> But I do not think the pictures can make actors. Take the line, the good old common line, "I love you." If I say it on the stage, I say it naturally. If I say it in a picture show I must work my lips, and thrust it in the camera, else the picture audience would not grasp it. If I say it for the picture the way I should on the stage, it would be lost. If I say it picture fashion on the stage the audience would laugh. For a picture you must exaggerate all you say and do. For the legitimate stage you must repress yourself, that's why I think the two schools are so radically different that the picture field will not breed actors. Acting must be learned on the stage. (*Boston Evening Transcript*, October 1, 1915)

Next on the production schedule was *Nearly a Lady*, for which there's no official director's credit – some sources cite Lois Weber and others name studio founder Hobart Bosworth. The plot, again by Janis, concerns Freddie, a young lady whose father has a large Montana ranch and who's in love with Jack, a cowboy on the ranch. After Jack accepts a job in New York, Freddie's annoyed that he hasn't written her, so when she meets the elegant, refined, and of course monocled Lord Cecil Grosvenor she accepts his marriage proposal to get back at Jack. She accompanies her lord to New York where she becomes the belle of society and meets Jack again when he rescues her from drowning during a swimming party. She realizes that she still loves him, and when everyone goes to the French Ball Freddie dresses as a man to observe them. When she returns home in drag the lord's sister thinks that a man has gone into her room, which gives Freddie the excuse to break off her engagement with the lord and marry Jack. Not only did this plot give the star the chance to do a male impersonation but also:

Elsie Janis and Owen Moore out west in *Nearly a Lady* (1915). Author's collection.

In addition to giving the star particular opportunity to show her real worth as an actress, "Nearly a Lady" shows her in several new feats, including expert swimming, lariat manipulation and horse-back riding. A lariat dance by Miss Janis, which is embodied in the story, surprised even the cowboys who appear in the picture, as did several exhibitions with the rifle. (*Moving Picture World*, August 7, 1915)

The fourth and final of her Bosworth films, *Twas Ever Thus*, gave Janis the opportunity to be a triple-threat – starring, writing, and directing. The plot structure is practically a dry run for Buster Keaton's *The Three Ages* (1923) with action set in the Stone Age, 1865, and then finally the present (1915 that is).

> Elsie Janis, in addition to being a perfect motion picture actress, knows how to write scenarios. Her work in "Twas Ever Thus" proves it. This picture has life to it, and action from the very moment it begins. We are first introduced to the Stone Age, Miss Janis as a bare-limbed girl, dressed in a panther skin, looks picturesque. She is wooed in the fashion of those days by being carried off by her ardent lover in spite of all attempts of her father to save her. Immediately the film moves on to the period of 1865, when crinolines and poke bonnets held sway. As Prudence Alden we see how a northern girl is wooed by a Southern doctor, their various vicissitudes including a case of mistaken identity, and finally a reunion of the lovers as it occurred in those days. Then we are brought up to 1915, where an ambitious authoress has her work rejected, and after being advised to go and get experience obtains plenty of it. In fact, so much so that she draws into the meshes the very publisher who turned her out, and his son, who marries her while she was masquerading as a kitchen maid. We see Miss Janis as a waitress in Child's, a private secretary, and a nurse. And in all of these parts she carries the interest to a successful termination. A very good story, very well acted. Hobart Bosworth played three parts; so did Owen Moore; so did Myrtle Steadman. This trio of fine players are about the best among the film actors.
>
> "Twas Ever Thus" will always hold a place among the interesting pictures of the period. (*Dramatic Mirror*, October 2, 1915)

After making these films in rapid succession she returned to the stage and when World War I broke out she was tireless, spending time in European war zones entertaining the troops, which won her the title of "Sweetheart of the A.E.F." (American Expeditionary Forces). When the war was over she brought her revue *Elsie Janis and her Gang* to Broadway at the end of 1919 with a cast that included many of the soldiers, plus several of the women who had worked with her during the war. She also returned to the screen:

> **Elsie Janis Becomes a Selznick Star**. Musical comedy and vaudeville star who entertained doughboys on the firing line signs contract with Myron Selznick for pictures to be marketed by Select. (*Moving Picture World*, June 28, 1919)

Work began on the East Coast with James Young, formerly of Vitagraph and Clara Kimball Young Productions, in the director's chair. Although the script was credited to Edmund Goulding and Frances Marion the press reported:

> **Elsie Janis Writes**. Elsie Janis, who is to appear in "Everybody's Sweetheart" in motion pictures, is helping Frances Marion and Edmund Goulding with

the manuscript. Miss Janis is no novice in the art of writing, as she has already written a scenario for herself and produced some years ago. She also has written much verse and several magazine and newspaper articles. (*New York Star*, August 13, 1919)

Another way that she put her imprint on the film was described in the August 9, 1919 *Motion Picture News*:

The extemporaneous lines that Elsie Janis uses while working on scenes, are often so original and to the point that Director James Young has formed the habit of having someone always ready with paper and pencil to take them down to be used for captions when the picture is cut.

Originally titled *Everybody's Sweetheart*, by the time it was released in November 1919 it had become *A Regular Girl*:

Elsie mugging in one of her comedies. Courtesy of The Museum of Modern Art.

One of the best things about the film is that it shows Elsie Janis as she was "over there." There are a number of scenes of her among the boys at the front and they make people realize what a boost to the army's spirit she must have been. The "gang" shown on the screen with her apparently registered the response they and their buddies must have shown in France.

The story of "A Regular Girl" was devised to illustrate Elsie Janis at the war and on stage. It begins with a society girl full of life but living to little or no purpose. Then she goes to France to do war work, and when she comes back the old things do not satisfy her. Pretending to be a maid she rejoins her "gang" and when they discover she is Elizabeth Van Somethingorother Schuyler, and not just their "Lizzie," she becomes their fairy godmother and sets to work finding jobs for all of them and others. She gives a circus first to raise money and then opens an employment agency. Her fiancée is drawn into her activities and she finally gives him the job of husband – so there is a "love interest" in the picture, but it doesn't interfere with the real "action," which is carried on by Lizzie, Mac, Shorty, Slim, and Red.

Matt Moore, as the fiancée, fits into the temper of the picture nicely, and the "boys" are played realistically by Tammany Young, Ernie Adams, Jerry Delaney, and Frank Murdock. Mrs. Jeffery Lewis makes the role of a boarding house keeper lovable. Robert Lyton appears as Elizabeth's father, and Robert Ayerton as a butler. The picture was directed by James Young. (*New York Times*, November 11, 1919)

A number of extras were needed to play wounded soldiers in the picture, so Miss Janis rounded up volunteers from a military hospital near the Selznick Studio. To their surprise they were given nice pay envelopes and a special supper, where they were entertained by the songs and imitations that the star had done in France.

Her next picture, *The Imp* (1920), was written by Elsie and Edmund Goulding and moved away from the star's war experiences. From the synopsis it sounds something of a crime spoof that gets set off after the star is hit in the head by a golf ball:

Jane Morgan, deeply interested in criminology, regains consciousness following a blow upon the head and imagines herself "The Imp," a notorious woman criminal who lived twenty years before. Under this delusion she dons boy's clothing and goes out into the night. Dr. Ferguson, a young specialist, disguises himself as "The Leopard, "a crook, and meets her in a dark street. They form an alliance and he takes her to Chinatown, where her sex is discovered. But the alliance is continued and a big robbery is staged in which he kills a butler. When she faints, as the police take him away to prison, she is carried to bed. Recovering, it is found that the delusion has been overcome and the happy ending is a matter of course. (*Exhibitors Herald*, April –June 1920)

After this she went back to the stage but made a return to film, and her sound debut, in the 1926 Vitaphone short *Behind the Lines*. A recreation of her entertaining the troops in France, she performs various songs like *When Yankee Doodle learns to Parley Vous* for the soldiers from the back of a flatbed truck. The next year illness caused her to lose her voice and forced her to withdraw from the Los Angeles run of her hit show *Oh, Kay!*, but when the film producer John McCormick bought the show for his wife Colleen Moore he had Janis adapt it for the screen with co-writer Carey Wilson and title writer George Marion Jr. After this hit for Colleen Moore, Janis hooked up with Paramount Pictures where she worked on the script for the Buddy Rogers/Nancy Carroll musical *Close Harmony* (1929), which led to her biggest film success *Paramount on Parade* (1930). Elsie came up with the idea for the revue, supervised the production, and contributed song lyrics.

Elsie acting mysteriously in *The Imp* (1920). Courtesy of The Museum of Modern Art.

She also wrote dialogue for Cecil B. DeMille's *Madame Satan* (1930) and *The Squaw Man* (1931), as well as worked on Douglas Fairbank's *Reaching for the Moon* (1930) and provided lyrics for Gloria Swanson's hit *Love Your Magic Spell is Everywhere* for *The Trespasser* (1929). Following her mother's death in 1930 Janis slowed down the pace of her work. She supervised and staged the revue *New Faces of 1934* and her last Broadway appearance came five years later in *Frank Fay's Vaudeville*. Her last film was *Women in War* (1940) a drama about war nurses. Settling from the East Coast to Beverly Hills, in her later years, before ill health prevented it, she would often go to the Sawtelle Veterans Hospital to sing and read for the service men. Elsie Janis died at age sixty-six in 1956.

Virginia Kirtley was a blonde beauty that was born in Missouri in 1888, and began career on stage in Los Angeles in 1910:

> She made her debut at the Burbank Theatre when Miss Florence Stone was playing a star engagement there, and attracted favorable comment by her talent and charm of personality.
>
> When Miss Anna Held was playing at the Mason, Miss Kirtley was offered an important position with that company, but not desiring to separate herself from her family she declined the offer and immediately was engaged by the Angelus Company. (*Los Angeles Examiner*, February 19, 1912)

From the small Angelus Motion Picture company she soon moved to Carl Laemmle's Imp and by the next year was working at Keystone, where she appeared in numerous 1913 and 1914 shorts such as *Love and Rubbish, Mabel's Dramatic Career* (both 1913), *A Flirt's Mistake*, and *In the Clutches of a Gang* (both 1914). Not having much of a chance to do more than look pretty and react to the wild gyrations of Ford Sterling, Roscoe "Fatty" Arbuckle, and Sennett himself, she did have the honor of being Charlie Chaplin's original screen leading lady in his first film *Making a Living* (1914).

From Sennett she moved to the American Film Manufacturing Company's *Beauty* brand of shorts where she appeared in numerous comedies like *Brass Buttons* (1914), *A Girl and Two Boys, Mrs. Cook's Cooking*, and *When the Firebell Rang* (all 1915), working mostly with director Frank Cooley and supported by Webster Campbell, Joe Harris, Fred Gamble, and Irving Cummings. She soon went over to Selig and Horsley, where she did mostly dramas, but in 1916 like Bess Meredyth she began writing stories for Eddie Lyons and Lee Moran's one-reelers. Virginia put Eddie and Lee through their comical paces in *With the Spirit's Help, The Barfly, Two Small Town Romeos* (all 1916), *A Million in Sight, To Be or Not to be Married*, and *The Night Cap* (all

Beautiful Virginia Kirtley. Author's collection.

1917). She also married Eddie Lyons in 1916 and began winding down both sides of her career. Her last acting work was with Selig, and according to a 1917 newspaper item:

Virginia Kirtley Has Come Back to Selig.

First Scene in her New Work Proves to be exciting

Well Known Star Will Play in Latest of Selig Feature Films

Virginia Kirtley, talented young actress, who has in the past been identified with many Selig features, but who of late has been devoting her entire time to the writing of scenarios, has returned to the Selig forces and will play a part in the feature now in course of production under the direction of Colin Campbell, "Who Shall Take My Life." Her return proved to be, for her at least, quite exciting, for in the first scene for which she was called, she was obliged to trip over two small boys on roller skates, then tumble down a long flight of stairs. Not only that, but pick herself up immediately and register comic indignation. "If this is a fair sample of what's to follow," remarked Miss Kirtley, "I think I'll prefer to stick to writing such scenes for other actors to enjoy; it's not nearly so painful.

Who Shall Take My Life? (1917) did prove to be her last film for a while as she retired and had a daughter with Mr. Lyons. Sadly he died in 1926, and she did make one more feature appearance – 1928's *The Midnight Adventure*. After marrying screen comic Eddie Fetherston she re-retired and died in 1956.

Beatrice Van was another pretty blonde. Born in Nebraska, she had no stage experience, and entered films as an ingénue at Keystone in 1913 where she appeared with fellow newbie Roscoe Arbuckle in titles such as *Passions, He Had Three, Help! Help! Hydrophobia, Peeping Pete*, and *A Bandit* (all 1913). She later remembered working on her first picture:

"I believe the first motion picture that I ever acted in would have cured most any girl; but I had made up my mind to stick and make good," said Beatrice Van, the Universal leading woman, to me.

"It was a slap-stick comedy and I had to jump off a rock into a lake with all my clothes on. Poor me! I couldn't swim a stroke! But I decided to keep still, especially as I heard the director say that it wasn't deep. So I shut my eyes, opened my mouth and jumped. I never did hit bottom; I never knew there was so much water in the world, and most of it seemed to go down my throat.

The first I knew they were "saving' me. I was scared to death, because I knew the picture was spoiled."

"I don't want to picture a real drowning," said the director, laughing (it's against all director's rules to be pleasant to a new recruit). "Just wade out again and splash around!"

"The real tragedy of my first day in the 'movies' came a few moments later when the men killed a big snake which had been snoozing a few feet from the scene of action." (*New Orleans State*, October 30, 1914)

After her baptism of water Beatrice moved from Sennett to Universal and appeared in many comedies like *One of the Finest*, *Such a Villain*, *A Quiet Day at Murphy's*, and *Lost By a Hair* (all 1914) for their Powers, Nestor, and Victor brands, as well as dramas for Rex and Bison. Following about a year's stay at Universal:

> Beatrice Van, engaged by President S.S. Hutchinson, of the American Film Company, as the feminine lead of the newly organized "Beauty" company No 2, now releasing twice a week on the Mutual's new $8,000,000 program, makes her initial bow to Mutual audiences in "When His Dough was Cake," released Sept. 11.
>
> Miss Van is not only talented, vivacious, beautiful, but she possesses an unlimited assortment of humor, and the ability to adapt herself to any role, regardless of how ludicrous it may seem. In the following releases screened by the second Beauty Company, Miss Van will continue to share honors with John Sheehan and John Steppling, who appear in her support in: "When His Dough was Cake" one of the most laughable comedies ever screened. Steppling will direct the staging of the second beauty releases as well as play in them. As a director, Steppling, judging by his work in "When His Dough was Cake, "will make just as much of a success as he has as a screen player. (*Moving Picture World*, October 2, 1915)

Beauty Comedies was an arm of the American Film Manufacturing Company, which was initiated in 1914 and turned out one-reelers with an ensemble that included Neva Gerber, Carol Holloway, Frank Borzage, John Sheehan, and later Oral Humphrey and Lucille Ward. Most of Van's *Beauty's* co-starred and were directed by John Steppling. Forgotten today, Steppling was a big film comedy name of the teens that came from an extensive stage career where he had worked for producer Daniel Frohman and toured in shows like *The Prisoner of Zenda* before joining Essanay in 1911. At Essanay he became popular with a series of *Billy McGrath* comedies, moved to Nestor, and settled in at American for these *Beauty* shorts and a series of *Billy Van Dusen* comedies. In 1917 he was part of the cast in Kalem's last round of Ham and Bud shorts, and from there he appeared steadily as a character actor in features such as *Joanna Enlists* (1918), *Bell Boy 13* (1923), and Raymond Griffith's *Wedding Bills* (1927) before he passed away in 1932.

> ## BEATRICE VAN
> *Original stories and continuities*
> *for*
> ## UNIVERSAL
> Starring Laura La Plante
>
> "BEWARE OF WIDOWS"
> "SILK STOCKINGS"
> "THANKS FOR THE BUGGY RIDE"
> "FINDERS KEEPERS"
> (Make 'Em Happy)
> *Starring*
> **NORMAN KERRY and LOIS WILSON**
> "THE IRRESISTIBLE LOVER"
> *Starring*
> **REGINALD DENNY**
> "CALIFORNIA STRAIGHT AHEAD"
> "THE FAST WORKER"
> "BE YOURSELF"

Exhibitor ad for Beatrice Van.

Van's *Beauty* titles included *Uncle Heck, By Heck, A Bully Affair* (both 1915), *What's in a Name?* and *The First Quarrel* (both 1916). 1917 to 1919 saw her transitioning from an actress to a writer. She was acting all over – comedy shorts at Universal paired with the likes of Max Asher, also features at the "Big U" plus others for Balboa, Fine Arts, and American. In features she supported Baby Marie Osborne, Wilfred Lucas, Francis Ford, Carmel Myers, and Margarita Fischer:

> **Beatrice Van in Society Role**. Beatrice Van has commenced work at the American Studios in support of Margarita Fischer in "The Tiger Lily," Joseph Franklin Poland's absorbing Italian-American romance, under the direction of George L. Cox. Miss Van is playing the role of "Doris Van Renssalaer," a spoiled society flapper, who is "The Tiger Lily's" rival for the love of a young millionaire. (*Moving Picture World*, May 17, 1919)

It was Margarita Fischer (see appendix) that Ms. Van began seriously writing for. She penned four light features for the star – *Miss Jackie of the Army* (1917), *Molly Go Get 'Em, Jilted Janet*, and *Ann's Finnish* (all 1918).

Beatrice Van Author of "Jilted Janet." "Jilted Janet," the clever comedy-drama in which Margarita Fischer has made a signal success, was written by Beatrice Van, who is the author of several of the Fischer pictures, among them "Molly Go Get Em." Elizabeth Maloney wrote the continuity for both of these comedy dramas. (*Moving Picture World*, March 16, 1918)

Her last acting role was in Fischer's 1920 feature *The Dangerous Talent*, and she spent the next fourteen years busily writing comedy for some of the era's most popular players. She started the twenties writing features for Bessie Love and Doris May (see appendix for both). May had become popular teamed with light comedian Douglas MacLean and Van wrote three early solo pictures for the comedienne – *Eden and Return* (1921), *Boy Crazy*, and *The Understudy* (both 1922). The trio was directed by William Seiter, one of the great comedy directors of the 1920s, whom Van would periodically work with through the decade.

She next joined the Carter De Haven unit that was making two-reelers for the R-C Pictures Corp. with distribution through FBO. Carter De Haven and wife Flora Parker De Haven (see appendix) specialized in witty and sophisticated shorts that continued the traditions established by Mr. and Mrs. Sidney Drew. Shorts such as *Their First Vacation, Twin Husbands, Entertaining the Boss* (all 1922), and *Christmas* (1923) were all built around situations in which Carter found himself entangled in small details that would accumulate and eventually snowball into an avalanche of troubles. *Christmas* portrays De Haven's attempts to buy a Christmas tree, get it home, decorate it, and eventually get rid of it. Again one of the nimblest comedy directors of the era, Mal St Clair, helmed all four shorts.

Her next assignment was another with St Clair, an adaptation of popular writer H.C. Witwer's *Fighting Blood* stories. Each episode of the boxing story was referred to as a "round," and the producers went out of their way to assure viewers that although the adaptation was done by a woman.....

> and right here is a good place to say that there are in the treatment or titling nothing that indicates other than a "sure masculine touch." For the latter quality is in evidence in chunks. (*Exhibitors Trade Review*, 1923)

Although the leads were played by George O'Hara and Clara Horton, much of the attention was given to, and almost all the comedy came from, the team of Al Cooke and Kit Guard. The pair was combined from 1923 to 1927 as comic relief in series like this, and *The Telephone Girl, Wisecrackers, The Beauty Parlor*, and more, not to mention features on the order of *Her Father Said No*, and *Legionnaires in Paris* (both 1927). Twelve "rounds" of *Fighting Blood* were made and included *The Knight in Gale, The Wages in Cinema*, and *The Switching Hour* (all 1923).

Comedy features with Reginald Denny such as *The Fast Worker* (1924), and

California Straight Ahead (1925) followed, as did more serious fare with Alice Terry and cowboy Harry Carey. Shorts kept her busy for the next year and a half. For the Fox Studio she adapted stories such as *Shoes* and *Transients in Arcadia* (both 1925) for their *O. Henry Stories* series, and then she ended up for a spell on the Hal Roach lot where she's credited on shorts such as *Along Came Auntie*, and Mabel Normand's *Raggedy Rose* (both 1926), plus the seriocomic western feature *No Man's Law* (1927). Another round of Witwer two-reelers with Al Cooke and Kit Guard ended her spate of shorts. This edition was based on Witwer's novel *Bill Grimm's Progress*, and besides Cooke and Guard the other cast members included Jack Luden, Margaret Morris, Grant Withers, "Lefty" Flynn, and Gertrude Short (see appendix) in episodes like *Bruisers and Losers*, and *A Knight Before Christmas* (both 1926) about a boxing taxi driver.

From left to right: Thelma Hill, Danny O'Shea, Lorraine Eason, Al Cooke, and Kit Guard in the Beatrice Van scripted *Beauty Parlor* series (1927). Courtesy of Karel Caslavsky.

Next she settled in at Universal to tailor vehicles for star Laura La Plante (see Chapter Five). The run included *Beware of Widows*, *Silk Stockings* (both 1927), *Thanks for the Buggy Ride,* and *Finders Keepers* (both 1928). Working with directors Wesley Ruggles and William Seiter, these pictures brought Ms. La Plante to the peak of her popularity. This stint at Universal saw Van also write *The Irresistible Lover* (1927) for Norman Kerry and Lois Wilson, and short-subject star Charley Chase's only starring feature *Modern Love* (1929), done on a loan-out from the Hal Roach Studio. Chase plays a fellow who has to keep his marriage to an up-and-coming dress designer secret in order to protect her job. The picture details Charley's problems with the arrangement. Although basically a silent the film did include a couple of sound sequences.

The transition to sound films saw Van writing the dialogue for the 1930 film version of the musical *No, No, Nanette*, and stories for most of RKO –Pathé's *Gay Girls* two-reelers such as *Take Em and Shake Em* (1931) and *Gigolettes* (1932), these two directed by William Goodrich (a.k.a. Roscoe "Fatty" Arbuckle). Finally her career wound down – after the Bela Lugosi thriller feature *Night of Terror* (1933) and the Andy Clyde short *The Super Snooper* (1934) she retired from screen work after twenty years.

Elinor Lynn and Lige Conley in *Step This Way* (1922). Courtesy of Sam Gill.

Marion Mack is best-remembered today as the spunky heroine of Buster Keaton's *The General* (1926), but besides appearing as a comedy ingénue she wrote and produced some of her own comedy projects. Born Joey Marion McCreery in 1902, she won a Hollywood beauty contest:

> **New Leading Woman in Mermaid Comedies.** Elinor Lynn has just been announced as the latest leading woman in Mermaid Comedies to be released through Educational Exchanges. Reports from Los Angeles promise that she will be a sensation.
>
> Just seven months ago Joey McCreery was at her home in Salt Lake City, happy – except with the desire to become a motion picture star. Then she picked up a copy of a Los Angeles paper and noted that Thomas H. Ince was conducting a

screen competition in co-operation with that paper. In Los Angeles she found herself one of the winners, and after appearing at the Ince lot for a while, she went to the Sennett studios. It was there that Jack White, supervising director of the Mermaid Comedies, found her (*Motion Picture News*, December 18, 1920)

As Elinor Lynn she appears as leading lady to Jimmie Adams and Lige Conley in Mermaid Comedies such as *Holy Smoke, Free and Easy* (both 1921), *Step This Way, Look Out Below*, and *Blazes* (all 1922). By 1923 she had taken the name of Marion Mack and appeared in some *Hall Room Boys* comedies like *Only a Husband* (1923). That same year she co-wrote and starred in the feature *Mary of the Movies* (1923) a seriocomic tale, based, she said, on her own experiences:

> Mary living in a small town in Arizona, is "movie struck" and goes to Hollywood seeking fame and fortune when her family meets with adversity. She meets an extra girl who helps her, and a fine young chap, who is also seeking to make his way. Through them she visits the studios looking for work, sees prominent players, and finally has to take the job as a waitress, where she is recognized by a boy from home who goes back and reports her failure. Her strong resemblance to a star, who is taken ill, gives her a chance and she makes good. During the filming of a desert scene a storm causes her to seek refuge at her home nearby and she arrives to save the home which is being sold at auction. The boy who has since inherited wealth, declares his love and all ends happily with the prospect of her soon being a real star. (*Moving Picture World*, June 21, 1923)

Mary of the Movies was the first feature film from Columbia Pictures, and Marion's co-writer was Lewis Lewyn, whom she first met when he took publicity photos of her as a Sennett girl and married in 1924. Creighton Hale played her love interest, and there were star cameos by Anita Stewart, Douglas MacLean, Zasu Pitts, Rosemary Theby, Louise Fazenda, Barbara La Marr, Johnny Walker, David Butler, and Herbert Rawlinson. After work in other features such as *One of the Bravest* (1925), *The Carnival Girl*, and *The General* (both 1926), she starred in (wearing a blonde wig), wrote, and produced the short *Alice in Movieland* (1928). Basically a condensed version of *Mary of the Movies*, it was distributed by Paramount, and had cameos by Blanche Payson, Eugene O'Brien, Creighton Hale, Ben Turpin, and Hank Mann as an effeminate director named Percy.

From here she retired from performing and worked with her husband on the shorts series he produced such as *The Voice of Hollywood, Hollywood on Parade, Hollywood Hobbies*, etc., into the 1940s. Before she died in 1989 she appeared in the Kevin Brownlow and David Gill documentary series *Hollywood* (1980) and *Buster Keaton: A Hard Act to Follow* (1989), and made appearances with screenings of *The General*, where she spoke about making the film.

The trio of Beta Breuil, Doris Schroeder, and Maie B. Havey didn't start their careers onscreen as comediennes but as honest to goodness story writers. Beta Breuil was born well-to-do in New York City in 1876, and educated in posh schools there and in Europe. After being widowed in two wealthy marriages she found herself "thrown on her own resources at an age past thirty," and tried the stage before becoming a writer at the Vitagraph Studio in 1910. Working under R.S. Sturgeon, head of the "Big V" scenario department, when he headed west in 1912 she took over the position. In addition to editing the Vitagraph scripts, she produced her own which included a large number of comedies. As early as 1910 she supplied scripts for star John Bunny such as *In Neighboring Kingdoms* (1910), *Seeing Double*, and *Bunny as Reporter* (both 1913), and other comedies like *Cutey and the Chorus Girls* and *Up and Down the Ladder* (both 1913 and described in the Florence Lawrence and Flora Finch sections of Chapter One).

Lobby card for Marion Mack's *Mary of the Movies* (1923).

She was said to have been a champion of the young Norma Talmadge, and started the *Belinda* series for her, which had Norma playing the young orphan Belinda who's hired as a maid of all work at Miss Ophelia's boarding house. Belinda and Miss Ophelia are more friends than employer and servant, and the series details their ups and downs, particularly concerning Miss Ophelia and men. In the surviving *The Lady and her Maid* (1913) Miss Ophelia comes into a fortune, but being tall, skinny, and unattractive still has no luck with men. Belinda is hard to look at also with freckles, missing teeth, and pigtails that stick out horizontally on either side of her head. They go to a beauty specialist and get a make-over, with Miss Ophelia now an elegant and statuesque beauty and Belinda a dead ringer for a cute French maid. Now all the men that rejected Miss O before are falling all over themselves for her, but she and Belinda turn up their noses, pack up the car, and drive off to greener pastures.

As head of the Vitagraph scenario department Ms. Breuil was quoted frequently in the motion picture trade journals giving advice to hopeful story writers. Here are a few of her tid-bits from a 1912 *Motion Picture News*:

> Do not send us plays instead of photoplays. Do not write long letters of complaint to the editor. The editor is quick to find and encourage those playwrights whose ideas seem to suggest a future in this line. No matter how wonderful the writer of the photoplay may think his play is, it may not even be mediocre.

> We do not want costume plays, fairy tales or nursery rhymes. We want strong, virile plots, with original or unusual business, short and long light society or farce comedies and strong modern dramas, Western scripts are often accepted.

In 1914 she left the Vitagraph organization and trade journal items have her freelancing for the North American Films Corporation, and an outfit named Mirror Films Inc. She worked on some films for the Rhode Island-based Eastern Film Company. Titles include *Daisies, Wisteria* (both 1915), *Violets* (1916), and *My Lady of the Lilacs* (1916 – 1919). Being the only person in the credits for these surviving films suggest that she may have produced and directed, as well as wrote, them. Her last credits are in 1918 – *Life or Honor?*, a mystery starring Leah Baird, and two films for Fox, Theda Bara's *When a Woman Sins*, and *A Daughter of France* with Virginia Pearson – after that the information ends.

Doris Schroeder was born in New York on Long Island and raised in Brooklyn, where she began writing on a local paper. In 1910 she became secretary to R.S. Sturgeon, head of Vitagraph's scenario department, and by 1913 was working under Beta Breuil. There she supplied stories for the studio's comic stars John Bunny, Sidney Drew and Hughie Mack

Trade magazine photo of Beta Breuil.

with titles such as *Bunny's Mistake, No Sweets,* and *The Late Mr. Jones.* She gave a 1914 issue of *Motion Picture Magazine* an idea of what it was like learning to write for the screen:

> After Mr. Sturgeon's departure from the east and Mrs. Breuil's succession to the editorship, I worked under that lady for two years, learning to appreciate just what was wanted, and learning to observe the small things in life that will make a good story. I have written and dramatized, and I have reconstructed, till I cannot remember the number of stories that have passed through my hands.

She soon transferred to Vitagraph's West Coast branch, and outside of an occasional comedy like *Kidding the Boss* (1914) her output for the next few years was almost entirely dramatic. After a brief stay at the American Film Manufacturing Company she settled in at Universal:

> Miss Doris Schroeder, well-known and popular among scenario scribes, has assumed charge of the reading staff at Universal studios. Miss Schroeder is well qualified to pass final judgement on the photoplay material submitted. For six years she was associated with the Vitagraph scenario department, the last three of which she was editor of the Pacific Coast studios. Prior to joining Universal Miss Schroeder has been engaged for almost a year as feature play writer for the American. (*Moving Picture World*, August 11, 1917)

1920 saw her stick a toe back into comedies for "Big U" with the short *My Lady's Ankle*, and the Eva Novak feature *The Smart Sex* (1921). That year Universal launched a series of comedies features starring naughty Marie Prevost (see Chapter Five), with Schroeder preparing the scripts. *Nobody's Fool, A Parisian Scandal* (both 1921), *Don't Get Personal, The Dangerous Little Demon, Kissed, Her Night of Nights,* and *The Married Flapper* (all 1922) all made Prevost a feature star. Schroeder also found the time to pen some similar pictures for Gladys Walton such as *Playing with Fire* (1921) and *The Lavender Bath Lady* (1922). In the latter twenties outside of an occasional lighter feature like *My Lady of Whims* (1925) with Clara Bow, and Viola Dana's *Naughty Nanette* (1927) Schroeder went back to dramas and even some Paramount westerns for Richard Dix.

These turned out to be good practice for her work in sound pictures, which was almost entirely westerns – Republic oaters with the likes of Don "Red" Barry, Bob Steele, and Sunset Carson, RKO horse operas with George O'Brien and Tim Holt, and finally finishing her film career with Hopalong Cassidy. After some early television work for "Hoppy" and the Lone Ranger she retired from screenwriting in 1951 after forty years in the business – but continued to write. In the 1950s and 1960s she turned out numerous television and film tie-in young adult novels for the Western Publishing Company. Subjects included shows such as *Rin Tin Tin, Lassie, Gunsmoke,* and *The Beverly Hillbillies*, as wells as personalities like Annette Funicello, The Lennon Sisters, and Patty Duke.

There's scant information on our next screenwriter, Maie B. Havey. Her work was mostly serious but she still managed to provide lighter material for some important comics. She started out in 1910 writing films at the Biograph Company for D.W. Griffith. *His Sister-in-law* (1910), *The Smile of a Child, In the Days of '49* (both 1911), and *Blind Love* (1912) starred Griffith performers such as Mary Pickford, Claire McDowell, and Blanche Sweet, and from Biograph she moved on to working for Edison, Reliance, Vitagraph, and Selig before settling in at Lubin at the end of 1913:

> Miss Maie B. Havey, who recently joined the Lubin scenario department, is having her initial Lubin photoplay produced. The story deals with the Northwest Mounted Police and is entitled "A Pack of Cards." It is being done in two reels, with special costumes and every advantage to give the picturesque realism of Northwest Canada. With doubtless a good story this picture should bring Miss Havey into prominence (*Moving Picture World*, December 13, 1913)

A Pack of Cards starred Edgar Jones, as did many of Miss Havey's Lubin films, and she also wrote scripts there for Harry Myers and Rosemary Theby (see appendix) before they began their series of comedies.

Havey's next stop was Universal, where for three years she turned out stories for the house brands Imp, Rex, and Victor. During this time she penned more comedies, the style of which were situational and more sophisticated. Carter De Haven, Edith Roberts, Eileen Sedgwick, and Jane Gail & Matt Moore all benefitted from her expertise in items like *The Little Lady across the Way* (1915), *The Wrong Mary Wright, His Little Room Mate, The High Cost of Starving*, and *A Five Foot Ruler* (all 1917). Leaving the "Big U" Havey spent 1918 in partnership with Fay Tincher (see earlier this chapter) as part of her Fay Tincher Film Company. The pair shared a home and Havey is credited for the script of *O, Susie Behave* (1918), one of the three know titles from the short-lived outfit.

After the dissolution of the Tincher Company Havey became head of the scenario department for Bessie Barriscale Pictures and wrote features for the star such as *Hearts Asleep, Tangled Threads, Her Purchase Price*, and *Kitty Kelly MD* (all 1919). Despite turning out numerous scripts for Barriscale she still found time to work with Fay Tincher and provide scenarios for some of the comedienne's Christie two-reelers:

> After casting about for over a month trying to find a proper type of story in which the comedienne can appear to best advantage, a story titled "Belinda's Bluff" has been secured from Maie B. Havey, a scenarist of prominence, which will furnish the basis for the next Christie two-reel offering. (*Motion Picture News*, April 17, 1920)

Havey's last known credit is the Bessie Barriscale feature *The Notorious Mrs. Sands* (1920) and from there the information on her ends.

Male writers such as Ralph Spence, Hiram "Beanie" Walker, and Al Boasberg, who wrote comedy inter-titles, were well known at the time and still have devotees today.

On the flip side Betty Browne, title specialist for the Mack Sennett Studio, is completely forgotten. She began her career in Hollywood writing for the fan magazines, and in 1918 and 1919 put out pieces on Jackie Saunders, Priscilla Dean, and Ann Little for publications like *Picture-Play Magazine*. Like fellow magazine scribe A. H. Giebler she made the jump to title writing and was extremely busy at the end of the 1920s working for the "King of Comedy" on shorts like *The Girl from Everywhere* (1927), *Love at First Flight*, *Taxi for Two, Motorboat Mamas* (all 1928), *Baby's Birthday,* and *Taxi Spooks* (both 1929). She even wrote the titles for the Marie Prevost feature *A Blonde for the Night* (1928) before the arrival of sound put her out of business and engulfed her in obscurity.

Ad for title writer Betty Browne.

The last woman to be profiled in this chapter, Dot Farley, could have been discussed in the beginning of this book with Florence Turner, Florence Lawrence, and Flora Finch as with them she was one of America's first important screen comediennes. At the same time she wrote an astounding number of scenarios, so she's been included here. Born in Illinois in 1890, like Turner and Lawrence she was raised on the stage, with her mother Alma Farley, an actress and opera singer. Some sources state that her real name was Dorothea while others say that she was named Alma after her mother, but she began her career at age three doing a song and dance in the show *Wedding Bells*. Known as "Chicago's Little Dot," she played Little Lord Fauntleroy and Little Eva, toured the Middle West in repertoire and musical comedy, and even had her own show, *Lost in Egypt,* before her voice failed in 1910 and she entered pictures.

> After a long siege of stock Miss Farley became well known in musical comedy as she possessed a fine baritone voice, but she developed throat trouble and an operation only served to make matters worse so she looked about for something in which she would not have to use her voice. A friend suggested she go and see the Essanay film people. Tom Ricketts saw her and after a short talk engaged her. (*Motography*, 1914)

From the get-go Farley was a character clown who played a succession of burlesque country girls, homely old maids, and flirtatious vamps. This was the throughline for the rest of her career – never developing one iconic and identifiable film persona, or even settling in at one studio. The list of production units that she worked for is truly head-spinning and even difficult to chart. Often billed as "the ugliest woman in motion pictures," this was of course an exaggeration, as Farley, like Louise Fazenda, was basically an attractive woman who went to some lengths to make herself a clown. The answer department of *Motion Picture Magazine* queried in 1914:

> You ask me how Dot Farley manages to get her face back in shape after making all those faces. I give it up, unless she uses a smoothing iron.

Working at Essanay in Chicago, Farley played with J. Warren Kerrigan and Augustus Carney in shorts like *Take Me Out to the Ball Game* (1910), but after a few months left with Thomas Ricketts when he joined the American Film Manufacturing

Dot Farley behind the scenes with her mother Alma. Courtesy of Robert S. Birchard.

Company. She mostly did one and split-reel comedies like *Hypnotising the Hypnotist*, and *The Harem Skirt* (both 1911), and was later sent to American's western unit in Southern California where she worked in western comedies and dramas with Adrienne Kroel and again J. Warren Kerrigan. After a year and a half she joined the St Louis Motion Picture Company and was the leading lady of their Shamrock Films appearing in a variety of comedies, westerns, and dramas – many of them from her own hand:

Dot Farley dozes as Augustus Carney (left) and J. Warren Kerrigan (behind Dot) enjoy the game in Essanay's *Take Me Out to the Ball Game* (1910).

She got her start in writing photoplays thus:

Once upon a time when she was with the St Louis Motion Picture Company, they were up against it and Miss Farley came to the rescue with "On the Verge."

It was a photoplay with a cast of only three people which was then almost unheard of in a picture play and in many other ways it was so entirely different from anything that they had ever had, that they were all enthusiastic over it. Since then Miss Farley has written a great number of the plays which have been produced by her company and in which she herself has acted. She says that she does not enjoy writing comedies as well as dramas and western stories, but that she writes a lot of comedies just the same. With characteristic modesty and generosity Miss Farley gives most of the credit for the success of her comedies to her director, Mr. G.P. Hamilton, the president of the Albuquerque Company, "who has a perfect genius for adding those little touches of humor which make or unmake comedy or slapstick farce, and in Mr. Hamilton's case it is always "make" and never "unmake," she said enthusiastically. (*Photoplay*, November 1914)

The "Mr. G. P. Hamilton" referred to is Gilbert P. Hamilton, a pioneering director and producer, who started his career around 1908, and at Essanay was an actor, cameraman, and eventually production supervisor. He and Farley met during her stint at Essanay and became a team, working together through the early part of the teens – directing her at American, Vogue, and the St Louis Motion Picture Company, in addition to organizing the Albuquerque and Century companies to produce her films. After a break with Farley in 1915, he finished his career directing features such as *The Golden Fleece* (1918) and *The Woman of Lies* (1919) for Triangle and World. For Shamrock Films Dot was writing and starring in comedies such as *How He Won Her* and *A Petticoat Ranch Boss* (both 1912), as well as dramas like *A Gypsy's Love* (1912). From here she moved on to the best-known period of her early career – a few months at the prestigious Keystone Studio.

Dot joined the Sennett mayhem with *A Deaf Burglar* (March 3, 1913), just six months after the formation of the company, and was immediately at home onscreen with Sennett, Mabel Normand, Ford Sterling, Fred Mace, Edgar Kennedy, Charles Avery, Rube Miller, Nick Cogley, Laura Oakley, and Arthur Tavares. Becoming the chief character woman, besides appearing as part of the general ensemble in outings like *A Strong Revenge*, *Hide and Seek*, and *A Fishy Affair* (all 1913), she often played Mrs. Sterling or Mrs. Mace as in *The Man Next Door*, or *A Dollar Did It*, in addition to major supporting roles.

Probably her best available Keystone today is *On His Wedding Day* (1913) where she steals the picture as Ford Sterling's coy and cross-eyed bride. The film opens with Dot flirting with the minister as the wedding party awaits the arrival of the bridegroom Oswell (Sterling). As he's hurrying on his way to the ceremony two rubes lace his flowers with pepper, which causes everyone else assembled into sneezing fits. When the minister runs out for air Oswell follows him into the nearby park to bring him back. In the park he sees Mabel Normand and after Dot he's struck by her beauty (or as he says by title "She's a goddess – uhm, what a difference"), so he makes a play for her and trounces her little boyfriend Charles Avery. Charlie hires a couple of thugs to beat up Oswell, and they also take his clothes so he's running around the park in his underthings avoiding cops and making women faint. Meanwhile back at the house Dot is still sneezing, and eyeing the minister. While Oswell is being chased he takes to the rooftops, and the chimney that he just happens to go down leads to Dot and the wedding group waiting below. The cops follow close behind him but Dot takes care of them and Oswell gets his cockeyed love.

Dot Farley recruits Eugenie Forde (extreme right) for the vote with the help of Victoria Forde (between them) in *When Roaring Gulch Got Suffrage* (1913). Courtesy of Robert S. Birchard.

Farley had a fondness for crossing her eyes for comic effect, and as we'll see this put her in good stead with Ben Turpin a few years later. Other surviving Keystones have her playing it a bit straighter as Mabel's mother in *The Bangville Police*, also as Sterling's wife whose baby is hanging out the window by a cord in *A Life in the Balance*, and a neighbor in *A Fishy Affair* (all 1913). This sojourn at Sennett gave her the opportunity to work with the best comedy minds in the business, and she must have made a good impression on the boss as she would be a semi-regular on the lot through the 1920s.

Despite Keystone being a much higher profiled outfit she returned to the St Louis Motion Picture Company, who at this time were producing Frontier Films for Universal release. There she headlined in a spate of 1913 western comedies on the order of *A Hasty Jilting* and *Flirty Florence*, was teamed with Victoria Forde for *The Frontier Twins Start Something* and *The Frontier Twins' Heroism* (see Chapter Nine), and even co-starred with

Lloyd Hamilton in *Dorothea and Chief Razamataz*. But after a few months she did another drive-through on the Sennett lot and played Fatty Arbuckle's sweetheart in *Fatty Joins the Force*, as well as various townsfolk in *Cohen Saves the Flag*, *The Gusher*, and *Some Nerve* (all 1913). This studio round-robin ended when she finally settled for a spell with the newly formed Albuquerque Film Manufacturing Company. Founded in the fall of 1913 with Gilbert Hamilton as its president and chief producer/director, their product was released through United Film Service which was part of Warner's Features Inc. Dot headlined in their one-reel Luna Comedies ("Two Comedies Weekly") as well as three-reel "specials" that were sometimes comedies, westerns, dramas, or a combination of the above. She was also turning out all kinds of scenarios for the company, and was her busiest period as a screenwriter.

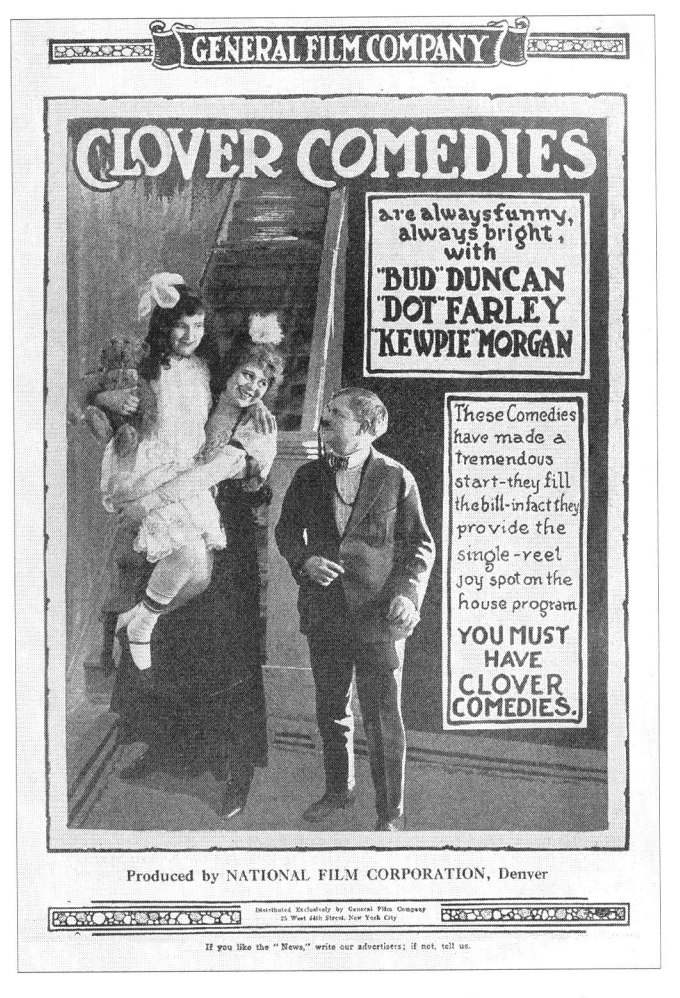

Dot and Bud Duncan in an ad for their *Clover Comedies*.

DOT FARLEY WRITES 'EM TOO. Dorothea Farley, who scored a decided hit in "Even Unto Death," a three-part drama recently released by Warners Features, Inc., is one of the most versatile stars in filmdom, with a big "V" in versatile. The word is used not because it sounds good, but because there is no other word.

Not only does she write her own plays, but she takes her own medicine cheerfully – that is, acts in them. As a scenario writer she has in her credit numerous photo plays that have been produced and, what is much more, produced with great success.

Early in life Miss Farley learned that "w-o-r-k," with capitals, was the only way to spell success, and she has yet to unlearn that lesson. Out at the Albuquerque Studios Dot is so busy writing, originating ideas and acting that Los Angeles has given her the soubriquet, the dynamoess. (*New Jersey Telegraph*, November 1, 1914)

Sadly practically none of the Albuquerque films are known to exist today, so we have to rely on trade magazine descriptions to get an idea of what they were like. As far as the Luna Comedy *An Accidental Parson* (June 24, 1915):

This week G.P. Hamilton is directing the production of "An Accidental Parson," in which a female inmate of an insane asylum escapes and plays the part of a minister with a mania for marrying people.

Before the real identity of the imposter is learned, she tied four knots for Cupid, and was busy with the preliminaries for the fifth couple. Miss Dot Farley appears as the accidental parson. (*Motion Picture News*, 1915)

For the three-reel drama *Even Unto Death* (November 1, 1914):

Jack Livingston saves the life of Dorothea Gordon, when she falls into a whirlpool, and they fall in love. Jack antagonizes Walter, her overbearing brother, and he opposes the match. One day the gossips see Jack climbing down from the porch, which opens off Dorothea's room. Walter, glad for the chance to avenge himself on Jack, attacks him, but is killed in the fight that follows. Jack escapes to an uninhabited island after burying Walter's body in the sea. The body is found, and a search is instituted for the murderer. Dorothea becomes ill, and Jack's brother tells him. He returns in time to take her in his arms, as she passes away. Jack then walks out into the sea carrying Dorothea's body and is drowned (*Motography*, November 14, 1914)

According to *Variety* a key member of the company was really almost drowned during the shooting:

Dot Farley, leading woman of the Albuquerque Film Co., had a narrow escape from drowning, Tuesday, of last week, while the company was shooting a picture off Catalina Island. Miss Farley was washed off a large rock by a big swell. The motor boat captain refused to drive his craft among the seal's rocks.

Director Gilbert P. Hamilton jumped in and pulled Miss Farley out unconscious.

It had been planned that a good swimmer double in the part, but Miss Farley objected.

Near the end of 1915 the pair left the Albuquerque outfit, and eventually the November 6, 1915 *Motion Picture News* announced:

The filming of the first Kuku Comedy was taken up by M.E. Spero Company during the past week at the old Masterpiece Studio, which has been leased. The first subject to be made is entitled "Sammy Vs. Cupid," in which Sammy Burns is featured with Dot Farley playing the feminine lead. G.P. Hamilton, late member of comedies for the United Program is in charge of the direction.

Sammy Burns was a British comic, who had spent many years in American vaudeville as part of the team of Burns and Fulton. He made his play for movies when producers were looking for performers with similar backgrounds to Charlie Chaplin in the hopes of finding gold and getting a seat on the Chaplin gravy train. Burns never really caught on, and after these shorts he moved on to a few for L-Ko and Nestor before headlining in a series of King Cole Comedies made on the east coast in 1919. His 1920s appearances were very sporadic – the Reelcraft short *Oh, Buoy* (1921), and a low-rent independent feature titled *Fun on the Farm* (1926). Three shorts made under the Kuku brand – *Sammy Vs Cupid*, *Sammy's Scandalous Scheme*, and *An Innocent Crook* (without Dot) – were eventually released under Mutual's Vogue Comedies banner, an outfit that turned out two-reelers from 1915 to 1917 starring Paddy McGuire, Rube Miller, and Ben Turpin.

Sammy's Scandalous Scheme (1915) still exists and stars Dot as Sammy's fickle and Charlie Chaplin-crazed girl friend. When he says something derogatory about her idol she decides she's through with him, but he dresses as Charlie and comes to her house, acting so badly that she's cured of her Chaplinitis. Burns does a passable Charlie, and made just as the Chaplin craze was taking off, the short goes out of its way to cram in as many images and references to the little tramp as possible. After these Burns comedies Farley and Hamilton went on to their last project together. They formed the Century Film Corporation (pre-dating Julius and Abe Stern's Century Co.), and made the dramatic feature *Inherited Passions*, a film about a woman who struggles with a tragic background which has created in her a type of "Jekyll and Hyde" personality. Initially released on the states rights market as *Inherited Passions* in 1916, it was shopped around for a couple of years with its title eventually modified to *Are Passions Inherited?*

Dot and Billy Bevan duck and cover in their 1919 Century Comedy *Frisky Lions and Wicked Husbands*. Courtesy of Robert S. Birchard.

Not only was this the last of the Farley and Hamilton collaborations, it's also Dot's last scenario. A definite turning point in her career, she stops writing and trying to make a mark as a dramatic performer and transitions into a crack comedienne for hire. Her first assignment was with her old Keystone director Henry "Pathé" Lehrman, who had just set up a new unit under the auspices of the Fox Studio. Dot was part of the ensemble of the first picture *The House of Terrible Scandal* (1917), and can be briefly glimpsed as a hotel resident in the surviving first reel, and went on to star in Sunshine Comedies like *A Milk-Fed Vampire* (1917), *Shadows of her Pest*, and *A Self-Made Lady* (both 1918). But as usual she couldn't stay in one place for very long:

General Film to Release New Comedies. General Film Company will begin releasing shortly a series of one-reel comedies featuring "Bud" Duncan, formerly of the Ham and Bud comedies, and Dot Farley, one of the favorite comediennes of the screen, it is announced. These subjects will be released once a week as Clover Comedies. They are being produced by the National Film Corporation, Denver Colo. O.D. Woodward is President. The first subject to be released will be "From Caterpillar to Butterfly," a story of domestic life. Other subjects in the series will be announced later. (*Motion Picture News*, March 23, 1918)

Made in Denver, the *Clover Comedies* were directed by Allen Curtis, who for many years had been the guiding light for Universal's Joker Comedies. Large Horace "Kewpie" Morgan was added to the mix and ads promised:

"Bud Duncan of Ham and Bud" fame – You Know Him!

"Dot" Farley, the "Scream Vampire" – You Know Her!

"Kewpie" Morgan, gigantic and jolly – Completing the Trio!

Ten one-reelers were made – *The Wooing of Coffee Cake Kate, The Poor Rich Cleaners, The Paperhanger's Revenge, Rip Roaring Rivals, Oh, the Women!, Love's Lucky Day, He Couldn't Fool His Wife, From Caterpillar to Butterfly, By Heck, I'll Save Her,* and *A Widow's Camouflage* (all 1918). *Rip Roaring Rivals* and *The Wooing of Coffee Cake Kate* were western spoofs with the boys as gunfighters and Dot respectively as "Nifty Nell, the vampiest vamp that ever vamped," and owner of the saloon in Gimpy Gulch.

The surviving *The Paperhanger's Revenge* has Bud and Kewpie as Ham and Bud type of wandering bums, who are hired to take the place of the local paperhangers when they go on strike. Dot is the cook at the wealthy Murphy mansion, who performs a lot of kitchen gags – flirting with the butler and hugging him while she's baking so she leaves handprints on his dark jacket, dealing with eggs that hatch into chicks, and showing the boys in when they come to do the wallpaper. The usual knockabout with paste, paper, broken furniture, and striking workers looking for revenge ensues before the end title arrives. The films suffer from their low-budget and lack of supporting talent, since they were filled with Denver-based actors, and seem to have been a plan to re-do the Ham and Bud comedies with the addition of Dot doing her thing. The series came and went without making much of an impression.

Luckily Dot was soon back in Hollywood for her next gig:

Dot Farley is Engaged by Universal. Universal announces that it has secured one of the screen's most fascinating comediennes in the person of Dot Farley, who will be seen in a number of L-Ko Comedies.

Miss Farley is now at work on her first two-reel comedy at Universal City. Prior to joining the L-Ko company she was featured in Sunshine Comedies by Pathé Lehrman. (*Motion Picture News*, 1919)

Mildred June (left) and Dot Farley (right) supervise Billy Bevan's wallpapering in *Ma and Pa* (1922). Courtesy of Robert S. Birchard.

No mention at all of the *Clover Comedies* is a good indication of how far they were off the industry radar. Besides the mentioned L-Kos she turned up in Century Comedies as well, but unfortunately these titles, which included *Frisky Lions and Wicked Husbands*, *Nellie's Naughty Boarder*, and *Brownie's Doggone Tricks* (all 1919), aren't known to exist today, so we can only imagine the results of Dot working with pros like Billy Bevan, Vin Moore, Phil Dunham, Frank Griffin, Brownie the wonder dog, Joe Martin, and the Century Lions.

Dot began the 1920s with a return to the Sennett studio, and actually consistently worked there for four years straight. At this point she had transitioned to a middle-aged character lady and was perfect to play caustic wives, nagging mother-in-laws, flirty widows, and Ben Turpin's cross-eyed mother. In the feature *A Small Town Idol* (1921) and shorts like *Where's My Wandering Boy This Evening*, *Pitfalls of the Big City* (both 1923), and *Romeo and Juliet* (1924) she demonstrates just where Ben got his ocular peculiarities. Sennett also kept her busy in the features *Home Talent* (1921) and *The Crossroads of New York* (1922), as well as plenty of shorts on the order of *Bungalow Troubles* (1920), *Astray from Steerage*, *By Heck* (both 1921), and *Ma and Pa* (1922). In addition to her activities for the King of Comedy she also found time to appear in some Elephant Comedies, *An*

Arabian Nightmare and *An Elephant on his Hands* (both 1920), opposite Hughie Mack for the Romayne Supercomedy Company, and play Lady Marian Fizzwater in Bull Montana's Robin Hood spoof *Rob 'Em Good* (1923).

In *The Acquittal* (1923) Dot essayed the type of character turn that she would continue to do until 1950. Courtesy of Robert S. Birchard.

Also in 1923 she began turning up in character roles in a myriad of feature films, with particularly nice parts in *So Big* (1924), *A Woman of the World* (1925), *The Grand Duchess and the Waiter* (1926), and *McFadden's Flats* (1927). Even when she would only have a tiny bit, such as her telephone switchboard operator in *Breakfast at Sunrise* (1927), she would make every second count and always enliven the proceedings. This was the boilerplate for the rest of her busy career – larger roles in shorts and character moments in features. She made the transition to sound without missing a beat, spending a lot of her time in the 1930s and 1940s playing Edgar Kennedy's mother-in-law in his *Average Man* comedies for RKO, but still turned up in features like *The Women* (1939), *Cat People* (1942), *Hail the Conquering Hero* (1944), *The Sin of Harold Diddlebock* (1947), and *Fighting Father Dunne* (1948). She retired after 1950's *The File on Thelma Jordan*, and died in 1971 at age ninety.

Chapter Seven
SUPPORTING CHARACTERS

The unsung ladies profiled in this chapter are a collection of mean landladies, vamps, spinsters, flirty fat girls, mother-in-laws, society snobs, dingbats, and busybodies who did yeoman service making up the universe of silent comedy. Whether fierce, maternal, or straight laced, they were well-seasoned veterans who were past-masters of timing, and at providing much needed comic tension. Some, due to their physicality, specialized in one specific type, while others were more chameleon-like and played all kinds of roles. The backbone of the genre - many of these woman were ubiquitous, turning up in film after film from practically all of the various comedy units, and had extremely long careers – starting on stage and going on in films into the sound era.

One of the joys of watching 1911 – 1914 Edison comedies is their crackerjack ensemble of comedy players – Arthur Housman, William Wadsworth, Jessie Stevens, Edward O'Connor, Dan Mason, and particularly Alice Washburn. While today her reputation has gone off the radar, she was the rock of the company and played maiden aunts, love-sick farm women, and suspicious servants, all with the common tendency to not suffer fools gladly and to take umbrage at the slightest provocation. Born in Oshkosh, Wisconsin, for many years she was involved in local amateur theatricals as an elocutionist, reciting pieces like Browning's *Soliloquy of a Spanish Cloister* and *Mrs. Jarley's Wax Works*. Eventually she went professional and toured with companies such as the Friend Players of Milwaukee and Proctor's Fifth Avenue Stock Company in shows on the order of *The Two Orphans, Our New Minister*, and *Trelawney of the Wells*.

Her film debut came with the Powers Company on the East Coast, and she also

The Edison Company's favorite biddy – Alice Washburn.

made a stop at Kalem before joining Edison in 1911. Right from the start she was their comic "biddy" – on tap for a succession of dowagers, servants, and maiden aunts. Many of the Edison comedies survive, but are difficult to see. Probably her most accessible film today is 1912's *A Serenade by Proxy*. Washburn plays Molly the cook who's wrapped up in the romantic stories she reads while she's peeling potatoes. Zeb the farmhand is crazy about her but she won't have anything to do with him as she thinks he's drab and unromantic. The young lady of the house suggests to Zeb that he come and serenade Molly that evening. The only problem is that Zeb can't sing, so he brings his Victrola and hides it behind a tree while he mimes to the tune. Molly is won over and agrees to elope with him the next evening. Although a slight and simple story, it's executed in a sweet and charming way by the cast and director C.J. Williams.

Other survivors include *How a Horseshoe Upset a Happy Family* (1912) where she plays the matriarch of the rowdy Murphy family who finds a horseshoe while out marketing. Believing it to be good luck she decides to keep it, but Mr. Murphy feels horseshoes have always been bad luck for him and wants no part of it. Sure enough, a telegram arrives from her mother stating that she's coming for a long visit so Murphy knows he's in for it. More bad luck ensues when a mirror gets broken, and when irate Murphy tosses the cursed horseshoe out the window it strikes a bystander on the head, who comes in and pummels our thrower. The final straw comes when mother-in-law arrives and presents Murphy with a "good luck" horseshoe all tinseled and trimmed with ribbons.

Aunt Elsa's Visit (1913) has a family receive a letter that their old maid aunt is coming for a stay. Everyone expects a crabby and finicky type so they stick the twelve year-old son with the task of meeting and keeping her away from the house while a party is taking place. Bobby is happy to find that the Aunt Elsa who shows up is a lively and fun person. Bobby hatches a scheme that involves Auntie showing up at the house as a cook hired for the party where she burns the food, breaks dishes, and generally makes a shambles of the festivities. As the mother and two daughters are in mourning for their party, father arrives with the real cook and a happy ending ensues. The Aunt Elsa character was even revived two months later for *Aunty and the Girls* (1913) where this time Bobby and Auntie make the two daughters think that they've been kidnapped by western desperadoes.

Running the gamut from a flirty maid in *A Proposal Under Difficulties* (1912) to a stern aunt who does her best to keep lovers Elsie MacLeod and Raymond McKee apart but is undone by Shep the dog in *With the Assistance of "Shep"* (1913), Washburn gave her all for her art and told a 1916 issue of *Film Flashes* that:

> One thing I like about me," says Miss Washburn, "is that I'm not averse to making myself ridiculous for the benefit of the film. I don't mind telling you that I never took any prizes at a beauty show, and that I'm no spring chicken; but so long as I seem to possess that intangible something that makes 'em laugh, why shouldn't I cash in on it?

After three years and about seventy-nine films she left Edison in 1914 and returned to Oshkosh:

> Alice Washburn, for a long time a comedienne in the Edison Company, is now lecturing in Wisconsin, giving funny accounts of her experience in motion pictures. Miss Washburn has given picture talks at the Orpheum and Colonial theatres and to the employees of the Diamond Match Company. (*New York Telegram*, June 20, 1915)

Her old Edison director C. J. Williams brought her out of retirement for the series of Frank Daniels comedies that he was helming for the Vitagraph Company. Starting with *Mr. Jack Goes into Business* (1916) she became Daniel's foil, and when they switched from *Mr. Jack* to the *Kernel Nutt* series she essayed the role of Kernel Nutt's crabapple wife. Following entries such as *Kernel Nutt in Mexico*, *Kernel Nutt Flirts with Wifie*, and *Kernel Nutt and High Shoes* (all 1916), her last role was as Witch Hex in Marguerite Snow's feature version of *Snow White* (1916) for Famous Players. After this she seems to have retired back to Oshkosh, and passed away there in 1929.

Eva Thatcher spying on Slim Summerville and Alice Maison in *The Kitchen Lady* (1918). Courtesy of Robert Arkus.

Where Alice Washburn was bird-like – little and skinny – Eva Thatcher was big and thick, with a rumpled face that looked like someone had slept in it. As Evelyn Thatcher she began her career at fourteen and was a long-time vaudevillian who was billed as "The Irish

Lady," and specialized in character songs. She toured with the show *Staley's Nightmare*, a one-act with music, and also had a "tall and small" act with a short comedienne named Martha Weis. Her first films were for the St. Louis Motion Picture Company whose *Frontier* shorts were distributed by Universal, and consisted of westerns and comedies, or often a combo of the two. Lloyd Hamilton and Dot Farley were also in the company, and Thatcher appeared with them in titles like *When Spirits Walk*, *The Circuit Rider of the Hills*, *His Better Self*, and *When Roaring Gulch Got Suffrage* (all 1913).

From here she went to Universal proper as a regular in Augustus Carney's *Universal Ike* comedies. Having become popular at Essanay as "Alkali Ike" Carney defected to the "Big U" in 1914 for a series that included *Universal Ike Has One Foot in the Grave*, and *Universal Ike Almost a Hero* (both 1914) with Eva filling in sometimes as his wife, and other times his mother-in-law. Carney soon left, but the series went on with Universal Ike Junior (Bobby Fuerher, later Bobby Ray), and Eva continued as mother figures in entries like *Universal Ike Junior and his Mother-in-Law*, and *Universal Ike Junior on his Honeymoon* (both 1914). Moving on to shorts for Vogue, and a selection of early Lonesome Luke comedies like *Luke, Crystal Gazer* (1916), one of her Vogue comedies, the aforementioned *Sammy's Scandalous Scheme* (1915), had her playing with Dot Farley and Charlie Chaplin imitator Sammy Burns.

Not long after, Eva worked with the man himself in *The Count* (1916), playing a cook who Charlie has a rendezvous with in her kitchen. A unique extra to her working with Chaplin is the survival of the rushes for his Mutual comedies, the basis for Kevin Brownlow and David Gill's 1983 series *Unknown Chaplin*, and the DVD of which included a special feature by Dr. Frank Scheide on the making of *The Count* which used a good selection of footage of Eva as herself working out physical bits and routines with Chaplin.

Her appearance with the most famous comedian in the world gave her relatively new film career a boost and she soon became a regular at the top comedy outfit of the day – the Mack Sennett Studio. Starting with *His Busted Trust* in 1916 and lasting through 1920's *Love, Honor and Behave* she was kept extremely busy playing a succession of boarding house landladies, suspicious wives, and combative mother-in-laws that made screen life difficult for Mabel Normand, Louise Fazenda, Chester Conklin, Mack Swain, and the other Sennett riff-raff. When her hubby Charlie Murray is trying to have fun with Phyllis Haver and the other bathing girls at a seaside hotel in *A Bedroom Blunder* (1917) Eva is the anchor that makes sure the fun doesn't occur. *Hearts and Flowers* (1919) has roué Ford Sterling out to marry dippy Louise Fazenda, who he mistakenly thinks is an heiress. When it's time for the wedding warhorse mama Eva shows up with Louise's three large ex-con brothers (Edgar Kennedy, Bert Roach, and Kalla Pasha) who terrorize Sterling until they are tamed by little Jack Ackroyd.

Thatcher appeared in some Sennett features as well such as *Down on the Farm*, *Married Life*, and *Love, Honor and Behave* (all 1920), but had her biggest role in *Yankee*

Doodle in Berlin (1919) where she plays the battleaxe Kaiserin, wife of Ford Sterling's Kaiser Bill, who does her best to keep husband and son Crown Prince in line. As the 1920s rolled along Thatcher moved on, but continued to work with the cream of the comedy crop. Next she ended up in star comic Larry Semon's ensemble where she had to endure dodging flying pastries, getting slammed with bags of flour, and having mice run down her back in Semon slapstick opuses like *The Bakery*, *The Rent Collector* (both 1921), *Golf*, and *The Counter Jumper* (both 1922). She was used to good advantage as Lupino Lane's mother-in-law in his five-reel Fox comedy *A Friendly Husband* (1923), and dramatic features took advantage of her talents as well. She turned up in the Lois Weber-directed *A Chapter in her Life* (1923), played a frontier woman in a number of Leo Maloney, Fred Hume, and Jack Perrin westerns like *Payable on Demand* (1924), *Ranchers and Rascals* (1925), *The Blind Trail* (1926), and *Blazing Days* (1927), but her best-known feature today is Buster Keaton's *College* (1927) where she plays the dean of the women's college and former flame of little Snitz Edwards. Not only do we get to see her partially undressed in one scene, but she's oddly unbilled in the role.

Eva Thatcher is Lige Conley's classic backseat mother-in-law in *Pleasure Bound* (1925). Courtesy of Karel Caslavsky.

Starting with the two-reeler *Pleasure Bound* in 1925 the bulk of her screen work was for Jack White Comedies doing what she did at Sennett, but this time for the likes of Lige Conley, Johnny Arthur, Dorothy Devore, Jerry Drew, George Davis, and Cliff Bowes. Highlights include Eva bearing the brunt of Lloyd Hamilton's ineptitudes when he's hired as the manservant for her rich family in *Breezing Along* (1927), and as Malcolm Sebastian's long in the tooth widowed Irish mother in *Shamrock Alley* (1927). She ends up matched to the kindly Jewish pawnbroker thanks to junior's efforts as cupid. In a change of pace she's an elderly gypsy who has the hots for skinny Monty Collins in *Wedding Slips* (1928), and amorously chases him all over her tent during a palm reading that goes awry. As the wife of college dean Al Thompson in *Hot or Cold* (1928) she's on the receiving end of snowballs, flying food, and other indignities thanks to the clumsiness of goofy freshman Al St John.

The early 1930s saw her film work dwindle but she was active in the theatrical club *The Troupers* and with them continued performing on stage. In 1933 the *Hollywood Filmograph* reviewed their "Irish night" benefit performance, a musical titled *Wash Day in Shanty Town*, which was written as well as performed by Thatcher, along with other movie character players like May Wells, and Edward Kimball (father of Clara Kimball Young). After retiring in 1936, she suffered difficulties after breaking a hip in 1938, and passed away in 1942.

Margaret Joslin wins the affections of Harry Todd (left) and Victor Potel (right) in *Snakeville's New Waitress* (1914). Courtesy of Sam Gill.

Another sturdily built individual was Margaret Joslin, who came to prominence at the Essanay Company playing Sophie Clutts, the most desirable woman (and basically the only one) in the mythical western town of Snakeville. Resembling the character of Mama from *The Katzenjammer Kids* comic strip, Ms. Joslin was born in Cleveland, Ohio in 1883, and her entry into show business seems to have been due to her marriage to actor Harry Todd – she spent a little time on the stage with him and when he entered films at Essanay in 1910 she did too. Their first appearances for the company were in Colorado and then G.M. Anderson moved the outfit to California. 1911's *Alkali Ike's Auto* detailed the rivalry of Augustus Carney and Harry Todd over the favors of Ms. Joslin, and was a huge hit that started a long series of western comedies with the three set in Snakeville.

Follow ups such as *Alkali Ike's Love Affair, Alkali Ike's Boarding House, Alkali Ike Plays the Devil,* and the surviving *Alkali Ike's Pants* (all 1912), where Ike beats out everyone for the privilege of taking Sophie to the big dance only to have his rivals steal his single pair of pants, made the trio very popular, and when Augustus Carney left the series in 1913 Victor Potel was added as Slippery Slim and the series continued without missing a beat. In spite of becoming known as possibly the "best comedy woman in movies," Ms. Joslin was more concerned with her daughter and home, telling *Motion Picture Magazine* in 1914:

> Whatever I am in this work," said she, "Mr. Anderson made me. The credit belongs to him. The public doesn't know that, perhaps, but it's a fact.

The one-reel *Snakevilles* continued until 1916 with entries such as *Sophie Picks a Dead One* (1914) where after being rejected by Sophie, combined with the cowboys not appreciating his work as their cook, Slippery Slim pretends to hang himself for attention. *Snakeville's Beauty Parlor* (1915) has Slim becoming assistant to the traveling beauty doctor, and their techniques put them both in jail. The rivalry for Sophie continues in *Versus Sledge Hammers* (1915) where an amorous count and Mustang Pete (Harry Todd) battle each other with mallets for Sophie's favors, and the late entry *Snakeville's Champion* (1915) has Ben Turpin winning his champion wrestling title against all comers, but not reckoning on his mistreated wife Joslin who mops up the floor with him at the final fade-out.

When Essanay closed its Niles, California studio in early 1916, Joslin and Todd spent a brief stint at Universal supporting Ernie Shields in shorts such as *It Can't Be True,* and *Twice at Once* (both 1916), in addition to Margaret having the title role in *His Temper-mental Mother-in-Law* (1916) with Billie Ritchie. Their next step was the fledgling Hal Roach Company where they dove into the ensemble for Harold Lloyd's Lonesome Luke comedies. In *Luke Joins the Navy* (1916) she's so overbearing as Snub Pollard's wife that he's happy to join Luke in enlisting to get away from her and their annoying brat. *Lonesome Luke, Messenger* (1917) has Harold pretending to be a telephone repairman to get into a seminary full of pretty girls and Joslin is the matron whose job it is to keep him out.

When Roach initiated the *Skinny* series of one-reelers starring fat boy Dee Lampton she was on hand as Skinny's mother, and she was kept busy as a foil for stage clown Toto and his replacement Stan Laurel. Both *Do You Love Your Wife?* and *Hustling for Health* (both 1919) has Joslin as the spouse of Bud Jamison. In the first Stan is a goofy janitor who causes problems in their apartment building, and *Hustling for Health* has Stan as a goofy friend brought home by neighbor Frank Terry who among other things romances their daughter and steals the food for their dinner.

Ben Turpin being done in by Harry Todd as Victor Potel and Margaret Joslin look on in *The Undertaker's Uncle* (1915). Courtesy of Sam Gill.

Joslin and Todd returned to working for Harold Lloyd, who had firmly established his young man with glasses character, and continued providing excellent support in shorts like *Just Neighbors, Going, Going, Gone, On the Fire*, and *Next Aisle Over* (all 1919). After leaving Roach, Harry Todd continued working, but Joslin only occasionally. She appeared in the features *Girl's Don't Gamble* (1920), *The Danger Point* (1922), and the John Ford-directed Tom Mix western *Three Jumps Ahead* (1923), along with her husband, before retiring to take care of their daughter. Long out of the business, she passed away in Glendale, California in 1956.

A third ample lady had a definitely Gaelic bent. As a film comedy stalwart for more than twenty years, Kate Price personified the tough Irish woman – often a cook, but also landladies, maids, laundry women, housekeepers, and mothers – all with last names like O'Brien, Sullivan, Mulligan, or Maloney. Born in Cork, Ireland in 1872 as Katherine Duffy, her family emigrated to Pawtucket, Rhode Island when she was two, and her younger brother Jack Duffy, himself a popular silent screen performer, was born there in 1882. Participation in a local dramatic club fired her interest in show business and introduced her to her husband, Joseph Price Ludwig:

> It's the comical roles that I've always liked to play," went on Kate, putting a smile into the telling. Then the smile disappeared and Kate Price said: "It was during

one of those amateur plays that I met me husband – that was twenty-two years ago. We were married eighteen years and two months, and were never separated in our work until he was taken ill and wasn't able to do anything.

Well,' she resumed with a sigh, "It was he who put me on the stage. He took me into vaudeville with him and our team name was "Price and Steele." Several times we left vaudeville for stock or a melodrama engagement. I remember we opened in Chicago at the Old Hopkins Theatre in "Her First False Step." I created the part of the Irish wash-woman." (*Motography*, August 15, 1914)

Kate Price supports Sidney Drew in *When Women Go on the Warpath* (1913) with Josie Sadler, Flora Finch, Clara Kimball Young, and Ethel Lloyd on the sidelines. Billy Rose Theatre Division, the New York Public Library for the Performing Arts.

The pair had an act similar to Johnny and Emma Ray's, and also appeared in music halls such as Tony Pastor's, Koster & Bials, the older Proctor Houses, and in Keith's first regular vaudeville theatre in Boston, appearing in various sketches, the most successful being *The Unexpected Visitor*, which they used continuously for seven years. But their stage careers came to an end when her husband's health failed:

We played together, my husband and I, always. Then four years ago he became ill and I stayed and took care of him until our funds were nearly gone. I didn't know what we would do when they were gone and I was pretending to my husband, right along, that we weren't badly off at all.

One day someone said to me "Kate, why don't you go to the Vitagraph studio and see if they can't use you? So I went and three days after I applied they called me on a picture. It was "Jack Fat and Slim Jim at Coney Island." (*Motography*, August 15, 1914)

That was 1910, and Kate quickly became a regular part of the Vitagraph family. In her early days at the studio she played all sorts of stock characters – widows who were the love interest for the old sea dog Captain Barnacle in *Captain Barnacle's Baby* (1911) and *Captain Barnacle's Messmates* (1912), wives sorely tried by their husbands – such as George Ober bringing home a baby elephant in *An Elephant on their Hands* (1912) or John Bunny hiring a cute secretary in *Stenographers Wanted* (1912), and even in blackface as a negro nurse in *A Juvenile Love Affair* (1912).

Kate Price as Buster Keaton's spouse in *My Wife's Relations* (1922).
Courtesy of Robert Arkus.

It appears that Kate's husband passed away in 1913. At the same time her roles got bigger and more important in the Vitagraph films. She's the bossy title character of *Jerry's Mother-in-law* (1913) where she comes for a visit and makes life miserable for Sidney Drew and Clara Kimball Young until Sidney manages to scare her off. In *Mrs. Malone's Fortune* (1914) she plays a washerwoman who inherits a fortune, but is eventually happy to return to her old life when she finds that the money really belongs to an orphan. She also wrote a couple of stories for her pictures, such as *Wanted, A Strong Hand* (1913) and *The Old Fire Horse and the New Fire Chief* (1914), where as the new lady fire chief she ousts former chief John Bunny from his longtime post. The studio even initiated a "Kate" series, where the actress would end up in occupations where she would be a fish out of water. The first was *Fisherman Kate* (1914), and was followed by *Officer Kate*, *Cabman Kate* (both 1914), *Getting Rid of Aunt Kate* (1915), and *Conductor Kate* (1916).

Her last two years at Vitagraph saw her becoming part of what the studio billed as its "Big Comedy Four," which was Ms. Price, Flora Finch, Hughey Mack, and William Shea as a re-occurring ensemble in outings such as *A Pair of Queens*, *Some Duel*, *Heavy Villains*, *Pat Hogan Deceased* (all 1915), and *Dooligan Ran for Mayor* (1916). Leaving the studio after six years, she made at least one last east coast picture:

> Her most recent appearance was with Fatty Arbuckle, the Triangle comedian, in "The Waiter's Ball," in which she shared the heavyweight honors with Arbuckle himself.
>
> Immediately after her work in this picture was concluded, she was signed to a long contract with Vim productions by Mark Dintenfass and Louis Burstein, to star with "Babe" Hardy, the famous Vim comedian and Raymond McKee in Vim comedies released on the General Film Service. (*Moving Picture World*, October 14, 1916)

Along with Hardy, McKee, Billy Ruge, Florence McLoughlin, and Joe Cohen, Kate was part of the last months of Vim, cranking out one-reelers like *The Precious Parcel*, *A Maid to Order*, *Fat and Fickle* (all 1916), and the surviving *A Warm Reception* (1916). When Vim succumbed in early 1917, part of it mutated into Amber Star Films, and then finally the Jaxon Film Corporation. Kate embarked on a series of *Sparkle Comedies* that teamed her with pint-sized Billy Ruge, who'd been half of the *Plump and Runt* comedies with Oliver Hardy. After about a year of odd couple combinations such as *Ambition*, *Weak End Shopping*, *In High Speed*, and *Monkey-Maid-Man* (all 1917), her next step was Hollywood.

This proved to be a huge turning point in her career as right away she ended up with nice roles like Mary Pickford's scrappy mother in *Amarilly of Clothes-Line Alley* (1918), and other big features such as *Ghost of Rosy Taylor* (1918), and *Dinty* (1920), plus occasional shorts on the order of *Goodnight, Nurse* (1918) with Arbuckle and Buster Keaton. Possibly her best remembered role today is as Keaton's married-by-accident Irish wife in his 1922 two-reeler *My Wife's Relations*. Kate is basically Buster's co-star, and a good deal of the short concerns the comedian trying to hold his own with Kate's tough father and brothers. Keaton seemed to be very fond of her talents and three years later she turned up in a cameo battling over Buster with other prospective brides in his *Seven Chances* (1925).

From 1920 on she's almost exclusively appearing in features, and was kept very busy in high profile films with stars like Mary Pickford and Colleen Moore. She had an excellent part in Pickford's *Little Lord Fauntleroy* (1921), and supported Colleen Moore in *Come on Over* (1922), *Irene* (1926), and *Orchids and Ermine* (1927). Other titles include *The Goose Woman*, *His People* (both 1925), and Larry Semon's *The Perfect Clown* (1925) as his tough landlady, but Kate's biggest and best role in features was as Mrs. Kelly, the matriarch of an Irish family, in *The Cohens and the Kellys* (1926), a thinly veiled movie version of Anne Nichol's hit play *Abie's Irish Rose*. Detailing the comic antics of Irish and Jewish families whose oldest son and daughter fall in love and marry, her spouse in the original film was Mack Sennett veteran Charlie Murray, and Kate continued in the role when it became a series with *The Cohens and Kellys in Paris* (1928) and *The Cohens and Kellys in Atlantic City* (1929).

Kate Price and Charlie Murray check out a new arrival in *The Cohens and the Kellys* (1926). Courtesy of Cole Johnson.

Late silents like *Quality Street*, *Casey Jones* (both 1927), and *Anybody Here Seen Kelly?* (1928) gave way to talkies such as *The Rogue Song* and *Shadow Ranch* (both 1930), although her largest sound roles were in the continuations of the Cohens and Kellys like *The Cohens and Kellys in Scotland* and *The Cohens and Kellys in Africa* (both 1930). Injuries received in an auto accident kept her off screen for a couple of years, but when she came back it was in uncredited bit parts in *Behold My Wife* (1934), *West Point of the Air* (1935), and *Easy Living* (1937). After finally retiring she died in Los Angeles at age seventy in 1943.

Billed as "the homeliest woman on the screen" Louise Carver was indeed that, not to mention large and fierce to boot. Although remembered for her 1920s Mack Sennett appearances, like the majority of the women in this book she came from a stage background, but in her case her theatre career was more extensive and successful than most. Born Louise Steiger in Davenport, Iowa, she set out to be a serious singer, but her looks forced her to detour into comedy. In 1920 she told an interviewer:

> All through my early life my "looks" seemed to pall upon me until one day while sitting in a railway station, a little girl who had been studying me intently for some minutes suddenly exclaimed: "O, Mama, look who's here! I believe it's Mrs. Santa Claus." If my face was as funny as Santa's, why not my face and figure make me a living? So I doped out a line of patter, got together a cheap wardrobe and still cheaper engagement in vaudeville, and now here I am, just like this picture, making faces and dollars at the same time.

Louise Carver is on pins and needles as Tom Murray, Nilde Baracchi, Rex Adams, and Billy Slade react in *Torpedoed by Cupid* (1916). Courtesy of James Snaden and family.

Touring for many years in vaudeville and revues with female partners, and later her husband Tom Murray, she worked her way up to a scene-stealing part in the George M. Cohan show *Fifty Miles from Boston* (1908) and starred opposite Lew Fields (of Weber & Fields) in *The Henpecks* (1911). She and husband Murray made their film debuts in 1916 for the Eagle Film Company in Jacksonville, Florida as part of the ensemble supporting transplanted European clown Marcel Perez. In the surviving *Lend Me Your Wife* (1916) Louise plays Perez's dragon-faced landlady who's willing to forgive the back rent he owes her if he marries her (which he regards as a fate worse than death). A recent rediscovery is *A Bathtub Elopement* (1916) where Carver and Murray play the annoying parents of Nilde Barrachi who insist that she marry goofy farmhand Andy, although Nilde prefers goofy farmhand Perez.

While working in Jacksonville Carver also found time to play opposite Victor Moore as his wife with operatic aspirations but no talent in the Klever Komedy *Ballads and Bologna* (1917). In the early 1920s the husband and wife team migrated to California where both settled in as regulars in comedy shorts and features. Louise worked for every comedy unit – Roach, Arrow, CBC, Christie – but most frequently and memorably at the Mack Sennett Studio. There she was unforgettable as the cigar-chomping cook giving Harry Langdon the stink-eye in *The First 100 Years* (1924), and had the priceless moment in *Masked Mamas* (1925) when Billy Bevan sees her at a masquerade party and tries to pull off her face, thinking it's an ugly party mask.

Louise Carver's about to plug Barney Hellum as Eddie Quillan and Alice Day sensibly head for the door in *Should Husbands Marry?* (1926). Courtesy of Jim Kerkhoff.

At the other comedy units she kept busy playing abusive mother-in-laws for the likes of Poodles Hanneford and Snub Pollard, or a militant lady subway rider who takes umbrage in *Crushed* (1924) when Lloyd Hamilton offers her a seat. She can be seeing terrorizing Billy West in *So Long Bill* (1925), the McDougal Alley Kids in *Luke Warm Daze* (1926), and Neal Burns in *Mister Wife* (1926). In *The Sting of Stings* (1927) she's actually an innocent bystander who just happens to walk through the back of a shooting gallery while Charley Chase is taking aim, and the big duck on her hat ends up being the perfect target. She also turns up as her nasty self in occasional features such as *Scaramouche*, *The Extra Girl* (both 1923), *Flying Luck*, *The Missing Link* (both 1927), *Barnum Was Right* (1929), and Buster Keaton's *Seven Chances* (1925) where she's the leader of the angry horde of women chasing Buster.

Despite her long stage background, the changeover to sound films saw her having less to do. After a few bigger roles such as El Brendel's mother-in-law in *The Big Trail* (1930), and *Hallelujah I'm a Bum* (1933), plus some Mack Sennett sound shorts and many for Columbia such as *Disorder in the Court*, *Lodge Night* (both 1937), *Love at First Fright*, and *Some More of Samoa* (both 1941), she was mostly seen in uncredited walk-ons until 1941. Tom Murray passed away in 1935, but Louise lived to age eighty-seven in 1958.

The next two ladies made their film debuts for Mack Sennett. Minta Durfee was the wife of star comic Roscoe "Fatty" Arbuckle and spent the bulk of her career in the shadow of her more famous husband. Although a pretty redhead she wasn't an ingénue, but a talented character comedienne who always brought interesting choices and details to her characterizations. She was born Araminta Durfee in Los Angeles in 1889, and began her career on stage with the Morosco Stock company as a singer in *The Milk White Flag* and dancing as a chorus member in *Zaza*. She also worked as an "end girl" (a dancer on the extreme left or right in the line) in the shows of Clarence Kolb and Max Dill, the west coast version of Weber & Fields, and in 1908 began an engagement at the Byde-A-Wyle Theatre in Long Beach, California where she met Arbuckle and married him a few months later.

For the next few years they toured around the world with stock companies run by Walter C. Reed and Ferris Hartman, and in 1913 Roscoe was hired by Mack Sennett. Minta became a part of the Keystone ensemble immediately after, and frequently worked with Roscoe in shorts such as *A Quiet Little Wedding*, *Fatty in San Diego* (both 1913), *A Flirt's Mistake*, and *The Under-Sheriff* (both 1914). Her red hair photographed dark in black and white, and although slim and slender she was a no-nonsense love interest that swung a deadly left. In *The Knockout* (1914) she holds her own against Al St John, so much so that when she's "rescued" by Roscoe, it's Al who needs the rescuing. Making the rounds with everyone else at the studio she played Mabel Normand's mother in spite of the fact that she was only three years older in *A Muddy Romance* (1913), and became a regular foil for Charlie Chaplin as he found his way in the new film medium.

Cruel, Cruel Love (1914) has Minta as Charlie's fiancée whose rejection of him drives him to take what he thinks is poison. In *The Star Boarder* (1914) she's Charlie's fawning landlady, who flirts with him and gives him preferential treatment in her boarding house even though she has a put upon husband and son (Edgar Kennedy and Gordon Griffith) that she bosses around. Edgar is itching to murder Charlie and finally gets his chance when the son photographs Minta and Charlie in a couple of embarrassing poses and shows them publicly in his magic lantern show for the boarding house denizens.

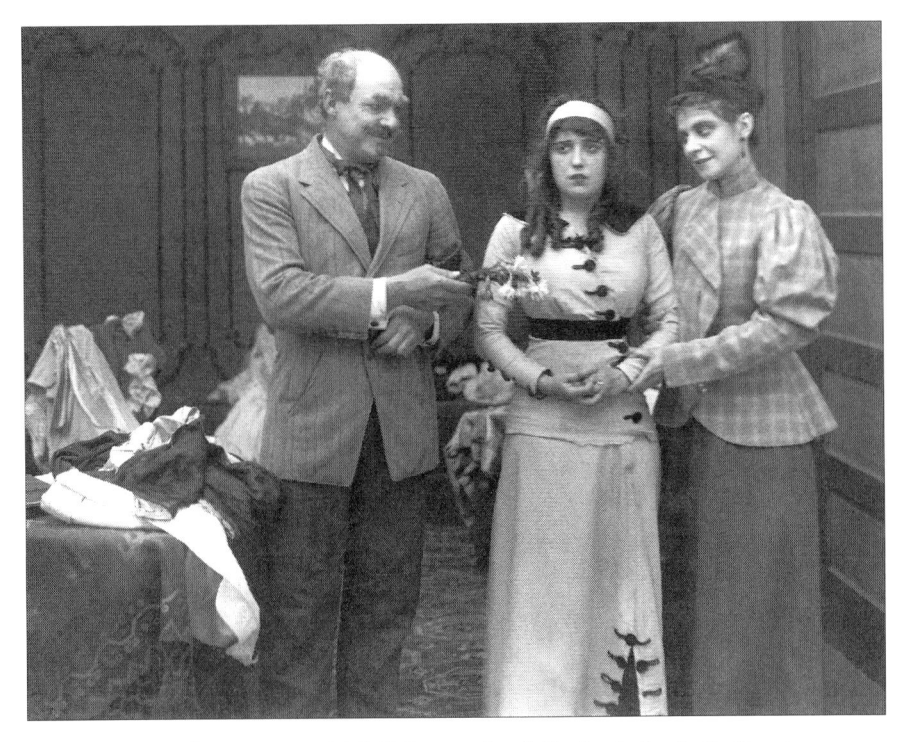

Minta Durfee supervises Mabel Normand and Charles Inslee in the Keystone *A Muddy Romance* (1913). Courtesy of The Museum of Modern Art.

Chester Conklin is her sneaky spouse Mr. Walrus in 1915's *A Bird's a Bird*. Ordered to get a turkey for a dinner with Minta's visiting parents, Minta has to first keep him from using their parrot and cat to fill the menu before he ultimately steals a neighbor's turkey. Everything hits the fan when the neighbors get invited to the feast with the parents and recognize their pilfered bird. *Ambrose's First Falsehood* (1915) casts her as Mack Swain's adoring and doting wife. In a plot similar to Laurel & Hardy's *Sons of the Desert* (1933) Mack goes out with a pal and a couple of good-time girls, telling Minta that he's called away on business. Of course the train that he's supposed to have been on has crashed, and he's presumed dead. Mack walks in while Minta is mourning, looking the worse for wear after a fight at a cabaret, so he tells her a whopper about how he was a hero, saving everyone left and right after the crash. Eventually he's found out – the crash was misreported in the paper and one of the good-time girls turns up at the house – so the short ends with Minta giving him her version of a train wreck.

At the very end of 1915 Minta, husband Roscoe, Mabel Normand, and Al St John headed to the East Coast to shoot films in Fort Lee, New Jersey. Minta appeared in *His*

Wife's Mistake and *The Other Man* (both 1916), but at this time she and Arbuckle separated and a slowing down of her film work began. Returning to California she did her last work for Sennett – a nice supporting role in Mabel's first starring feature *Mickey* (1918), as Mabel's snotty society girl cousin. She also appeared in the East Coast- shot World Pictures melodrama *The Cabaret* (1918) with June Elvidge and Carlyle Blackwell. She had been inactive for some time when she received an offer to headline in an independently made series of comedy shorts.

The *Minta Durfee (Mrs. Roscoe Arbuckle)* series was made by Truart Pictures, with distribution through the recently formed Plymouth Pictures, Inc. Five two-reelers – *The Wive's Union*, *He, She and It*, *When You are Dry*, *Whose Wife*, and *That Quiet Night* (all 1920) – were shot in Providence, Rhode Island. According to the September 18, 1920 *Moving Picture World*:

> The Pictures are new, recently produced, and deal intelligently and in a humorous vein with timely topics.
>
> Minta Durfee (Mrs. Roscoe Arbuckle) by her acting in these pictures, has placed herself in the very forefront of the short reel comediennes. She is ably assisted by a strong cast, headed by Billy Quirk, the well-known former Keystone actor. Tommy Grey wrote several of the stories and the titling and editing were attended to by the very able Tom Bret. Charles H. France, the well-known director, was responsible for the direction of the pictures.

Billy Quirk had never worked for Keystone, but had been a popular light comedian for Biograph, Solax, and Vitagraph, while Charles H. France had been a very solid director at Lubin, Selig, and Edison, responsible for numerous comedies like *A Pair of Boots* (1912) and *Getting to the Ball Game* (1914), in addition to Edison's *Buster Brown* and *Andy* series. Despite their track records most of these people hadn't worked in a while, and as none of the shorts are known to exist today it's hard to know how they turned out. Sadly the enterprise didn't raise a blip on the film industry E.K.G. screen.

Although they'd been long separated Minta stood by Roscoe during his trials for manslaughter – appearing in the courtroom and posing with him in photos. During the 1920s she did some stage work in shows such as the Will Morrissey revue *The Newcomers*, plus spent time in France where she finally divorced Arbuckle in 1925. They're said to have remained amicable, although she did occasionally go after him for back alimony. In the early 1930s she opened a shop on Hollywood Boulevard for "Fountain of Youth Toiletries" and ran ads asking her old film friends to "drop in and say hello." Eventually she returned to the screen as an extra, keeping busy from 1935 to 1971, and sporadically appeared on the radio with other stars from the silent days, sometimes performing old time melodramas such as *East Lynn*, *Ten Nights in a Barroom*, and *Nellie the Beautiful Cloak Model*.

Minta Durfee caught between Harry Bernard (left) and Ford Sterling (right) in *Dirty Work in a Laundry* (1915). Courtesy of The Museum of Modern Art.

Having never re-married Minta remained Mrs. Roscoe Arbuckle in the public's mind and got a certain amount of attention from reporters and journalists who would occasionally interview her, plus she'd also sometimes appear with other veterans on television programs such as the *Merv Griffin Show*, and others that would do tributes to the silent film era. Her last days were spent at the Motion Picture Country Home, and she passed away in 1975.

The other Mack Sennett "debutante" was the statuesque Blanche Payson. As mentioned before Louise Carver was large, but no one, including most of the male comics, was as large as Ms. Payson. At 6'4" she was the living embodiment of the phrase "large and in charge," but she was said to have been a sweetheart in real life, and worked with practically everyone at every studio, becoming one of the most ubiquitous faces of silent comedy. Unlike the majority of the women in this book Blanche did not have a show business background – instead she was a police officer. Born in Santa Barbara, California in 1881, she married traveling salesman Eugene A. Payson around 1908 and moved to San Francisco. In 1915 the Panama-Pacific International Exposition opened in San Francisco, and Blanche, the niece of Santa Barbara Chief of Police Daniel Walter Martin, was appointed to protect women from mashers and be a guard at the expo's Toyland exhibit.

Getting a good deal of exposure and publicity from the Exposition in newspapers and magazines like *Colliers*, she was "discovered" for movies by Sennett, who initially hired her to look out for his bathing girls at the studio, but soon put her in the films. Her debut came with *Wife and Auto Trouble* (1916) as William Collier's bad-tempered Amazon wife, and she proved herself a natural – projected just the right amount of menace to give an anchor for the comedy. From here the die was cast – for the next thirty years she would slow-burningly henpeck husbands, screw up her face into a knot of hostility, and pop people who deserved it in the eye or nose. Her Sennett appearances continued with *Bath Tub Perils*, *Dollars and Sense* (both 1916), *Her Circus Knight*, and *The Sultan's Wife* (both 1917), and she soon branched out into the wider world of silent comedy – taking Billy West to task in outings like *The Scholar, Bright and Early*, and *He's In Again* (all 1918), plus was on call at Vitagraph for Larry Semon and Montgomery & Rock comedies such as *Bears and Bad Men*, *Humbugs and Husbands* (both 1918), and *Zip and Zest* (1919).

Portrait of Blanche Payson in full police uniform. Author's collection.

When the 1920s rolled around she was busier than ever being the standard issued foil for Fox Sunshine Comedies, Jack White Comedies, Century Comedies, and Christie Comedies. Some of her memorable appearances include trying to rape a prissy Stan Laurel in *Half a Man* (1925), chasing an in-disguise Baby Peggy who's hot on a case in *The Kid Reporter* (1923), playing George Davis' hulking wife who goes out an ill-fated joyride with Al St John and family in *His First Car* (1924), and as the new bride of Lloyd Hamilton who surprises him with a brood of large children and sleeping quarters on the couch in *Crushed* (1924). Her best-remembered moment today is in Buster Keaton's *The Three Ages* (1923) as the burly and obstreperous cavewoman that Buster attempts to try out his love-making skills on, but she was constantly in demand as domineering wives for Bobby Dunn, Lee Moran, Eddie Gordon, and Jack Duffy, stern stepmothers to Baby Peggy and Lupino Lane, and being just plain mean to Harold Lloyd, Billy Dooley, Bobby Vernon, Dorothy Devore, Ben Turpin, and Clyde Cook. She was also active in features that include *Girl Shy* (1924), Colleen Moore's *We Moderns* (1925), *Charley's Aunt* (1925), *The Bachelor's Baby* (1927), *Bringing Up Father* (1928), and had a rare serious role as the brutal factory supervisor that works Lillian Gish to death in *La Boheme* (1926).

Sound films revealed a sharp and brusque voice perfectly in keeping with her well-established persona, and she went on menacing everyone on the Roach and Sennett lots, particularly as Wheezer's evil stepmother in *Dog Is Dogs* (1931) and Oliver Hardy's wife who he's desperately trying to clean up the house for in *Helpmates* (1932). Although she's only seen in a photo and has one brief scene on the phone that's enough to make it believable when we see Hardy return alone from picking her up with a black eye and a bent ceremonial sword. In the mid-1930s her reign of terror continued at the Columbia Pictures short subject unit, where she worked with The Three Stooges, Andy Clyde, El Brendel, and Harry Langdon in two-reelers like *Hoi Polloi* (1935), *A Doggone Mix-up* (1938), and *Swing You Swingers* (1939), plus brought her presence to features like *All Over Town* (1937), *You Can't Take It With You* (1938), and *Mr. Smith Goes to Washington* (1939).

Blanche remained busy at the beginning of the 1940s in shorts such as *Cuckoo Cavaliers* (1940), and *An Ache in Every Stake* (1941), plus features like *Li'l Abner* (1940) and *Ghosts on the Loose* (1943), but by the middle of the decade her work dwindled, and the June 25, 1944 *Brooklyn Eagle* reported:

> Blanche Payson – once a comedienne often cast as a domineering wife – manages an apartment house in Hollywood, and occasionally gets a bit part in pictures.

Her last screen appearance appears to be in the 1946 Paramount musical short *A Tale of Two Cafes*. From there she turned up occasionally at Mack Sennett veteran reunions, and passed away in 1964.

Another teen's comedienne got her start in pictures thanks to her riding and roping skills. Jane Bernoudy was born in New Castle, Colorado in 1893, and was a member of Wild West shows where she won awards for fancy riding, roping, and all-around horsemanship.

A certain part of Blanche Payson's anatomy is in the line of fire in *Follow the Leader* (1928). Billy Rose Theatre Division, the Library for the Performing Arts.

David Crutchfield and Jane Bernoudy made their ropes take every conceivable gyration, from the wedding ring or simple circle to the ring spinning vertically through which they skipped. Standing, jumping, sitting and even lying down made no difference, as they spun circles with eyes open or blindfolded. Then Jane Bernoudy placed her jacket on the ground and donned and removed it to the ceaseless spinning of her magic cord. (*The World's Work*, 1914)

Her western expertise was her ticket for entering films in 1913 to make westerns for Vitagraph, Kay-Bee, Broncho, and Bison. In 1914 she settled in at Universal and films like *Lasca* and *The Sheep Herder* (both 1914) were built around her skills, but she almost immediately gravitated to their comedies – starring in Joker one-reelers like *For the Hand of Jane*, and *Jane's Lover* (both 1914), in addition to working with Gale Henry and Billy Franey in entries such as *A Case of Beans* (1915). In 1915 she was teamed with lanky comic Victor Potel for a series of domestic comedies – some of which she would play his wife Mrs. Slim, such as *When Beauty Butts In* (1915), *When Slim Was Home Cured*, and *When Slim Picked a Peach* (both 1916), but for the most part she played the family maid Sally Sloppus.

Sally made her debut in *Bill's Plumber and Plumber's Bill* (1915) and was greeted with enough popularity to keep the series going through the next year and entries like *Slim, Fat or Medium* (1915), *Hired, Tired and Fired, Some Heroes, When a Wife Worries,* and *Love Laughs at Dyspepsia* (all 1916). With her pail and mop, lopsided maid's cap, checkered blouses, and voluminous aprons, Bernoudy toiled in the Alice Howell and Louise Fazenda territory of slightly addled young slavies, and told *Film Flashes Magazine* in 1916:

> I remember an awkward maid we used to have, "she said, "and I determined to make some use of her funny tricks and a most unique method she had of doing her hair. She used to be a scream as I remember her, and we kept her because she furnished us so much unconscious amusement. So I capitalized my looks and her ways, and I see no reason to regret my decision – as yet.

Western portrait of Jane Bernoudy. Courtesy of Robert S. Birchard.

After her run as Sally, Bernoudy continued in comedies for the "Big U" – working with Lyons & Moran in *Mixed Matrimony* (1917), and Carter De Haven with *The Topsy Turvy Twins* (1917). She also returned to a few western shorts like *Brute Force, Burning Silence,* and *The Mysterious Outlaw* (all 1917), and appeared in the features *Girl in the Checkered Coat,* and *Mr. Opp* (both 1917). Her last films were more comedies such as *Don't Flirt* (1918), and *The Hole in the Wall* (1919), the latter being one of her few survivors in which she plays the wife of artist Bobby Vernon where both of them are being driven crazy by their loud musical neighbors next door. They drill a hole in their adjoining wall so they can spray water to dampen the overeager musicians, but it all turn into a battle royal before the cops are summoned to settle the matter. Her last comedy was *The Movie Queen* (1919) after which she retired from the screen and was sadly forgotten.

Self-billed as the "thinnest woman on the screen," Caroline Rankin had the market cornered on shrewish wives and scrawny spinsters for a wide range of comedy producers that included Pathé, Crystal, Edison, Flamingo, Mittenthal, Sennett, Triangle, Vitagraph, King Bee, Hal Roach, Jack White, and Bray. Born in 1880 in Pittsburgh, Pennsylvania as the daughter of A.C. Rankin a temperance evangelist and influential republican, she may have become the black sheep of the family by going on the stage and having an extensive career that involved touring in *Mrs. Wiggs of the Cabbage Patch* and stock company work in Chicago, Cleveland, Cincinnati, and New York. She started her film work on the East Coast for Pathé in shorts like *Two Up a Tree* (1913), and *September Morn* (1914), and became a regular in Crystal Comedies.

Jane Bernoudy as Sally Sloppus with soon to be director Edward Sedgwick in *Lizzie's Waterloo* (1919). Courtesy of Robert Arkus.

The outrageous *A Change in Complexion* (1914) has skinny Rankin as the wife of stout Henry Bergman who fall asleep at their dinner table and are "blacked up" by their disgruntled cook Vivian Prescott. When they wake up they don't recognize each other in their dusky make-up and each assume that a "negro" has gotten in to their house, leading to much confusion, running from room to room, gun firing, and a final summoning of the police. Continuing to work in New York she became part of the ensemble in Edison Comedies, worked in some of the *Heinie and Louie* shorts with Jimmy Aubrey and Walter Kendig, and appeared in features such as *Lena Rivers, Without Hope* (both 1914), and *What Happened to Jones?* (1915) with Fred Mace and Josie Sadler.

Heading to Hollywood she landed at the Mack Sennett lot for shorts like *His Lying Heart* (1916), and *The Pawnbroker's Heart* (1917), and became known as "Spike" Rankin, probably due to her living stick-figure appearance at five feet and seven and a half inches at only eighty-five pounds. Steady work continued with plenty of work for Triangle, Billy West's King Bee Comedies, and more features like Douglas Fairbank's *He Comes Up Smiling* (1918) and *Heart's Haven* (1922). Her highest profile appearances came in two of Max Linder's American feature comedies. In *Be My Wife* (1921) she's the controlling Aunt Agatha of Linder's sweetheart Alta Allen, who, of course, doesn't like Max and forbids him from coming to their home. Trying various ploys to get by her, he ultimately wins the old lady over by staging a stunt where he's both a burglar and their rescuer, and in gratitude Agatha gives her permission to Max and Alta marrying.

Caroline Rankin chewing out an off-screen Eddie Boland in his one-reeler *Alias Aladdin* (1920). Courtesy of EYE Filmmuseum, Netherlands.

The Three Must-Get-Theres (1922), a feature-length parody of Douglas Fairbank's recent film adaptation of *The Three Musketeers* (1921), is a broad and wild burlesque, filled with anachronisms and surreal juxtapositions of different eras and styles. Linder plays Knockout Dart–in–Again, a young cavalier from the country who becomes an ally of the Three Must-Get-Theirs (Walrus, Octopus, and Porpoise) and falls in love with Connie, the Queen's handmaiden. Rankin is the spindly Queen Anne whose lover is the British fop Lord Duke Poussy Bunkumin, and the main action of the film has Dart-in-Again traveling to England to retrieve the brooch that the Queen had given to Bunkumin. Rankin and the rest of the cast of veteran slapstick performers that includes Bull Montana, Al Cooke, Harry Mann, and Bynunsky Hymen, add a great deal to the fun, but while the film is well-regarded today at the time the reviews were mixed and it did little business, causing Linder to give up on Hollywood and return to France.

The rest of the 1920s saw Rankin continuing her busy work schedule of numerous shorts, as well as more features such as John Ford's *The Village Blacksmith* (1922), and *Tea: with a Kick* (1923). She makes a hilarious appearance in Lloyd Hamilton's 1925 short *Hooked* as his wall-eyed stepmother sitting on their front porch trying to thread a needle. Ham comes out of the house and watches her for a bit as she tries to thread as one eye looks toward Canada and the other South America, and gingerly walks over and covers one of her eyes, giving her immediate success with the needle. Rankin was still working during the transition to sound pictures, and her last good-sized role was in the Jack Benny starring feature *The Medicine Man* (1930). From there she did uncredited bits until her retirement in 1939.

The opposites of the spindly Rankin were two round and fully-packed ladies – Merta Sterling and Sunshine Hart – who did yeoman service taking a lot of punishment in the name of comedy. Merta Sterling (sometimes listed as Myrta or Myrtle Sterling in credits and trade journals) was born in a log cabin in Wisconsin according to the March 10, 1917 *Motion Picture Weekly*, and as to her stage career:

> Eight years ago, she was a stenographer in the office of Klaw and Erlanger. They decided to revive "The Prince of Pilsen," and she had a hunch that she was just cut out to play the character woman. She succeeded in convincing her employers that she was right, and they told her she might learn the part and attend rehearsals. When they saw her work, they gave her the chance, inexperienced as she was, and she made good. She had a lot of vaudeville experience after that, and two years ago deserted to the movies.

She made her film debut in 1914 for Universal, appearing in some of their Joker Comedies such as *The Fascinating Eye* and *Willy Walrus, Detective* (both 1914) with William Wolbert in the title role. She became a regular in Kalem comedies and spent a couple of years in shorts such as *The Actress and the Cheese Hound*, and *The Bandits of Macaroni Mountain* (both 1915) as support of the studio's headliners like Ham & Bud, Ethel Teare, and again William Wolbert. Short, and as big around as she was tall, she was built like a cannonball, was bug-eyed and boisterous, and specialized in authority figures such as fussy mothers, suspicious wives, excitable spiritualists, and, as in *Raskey's Road Show* (1915), even lion tamers.

Of course dealing with the scuzzy Ham & Bud would make anyone excitable, and they tried her patience whether she was playing nurses, cooks, or especially their various landladies, although she got a bit of revenge when she turned up as Bud's wife during his nightmare in *From Altar to Halter* (1916). In 1917 she re-located to the L-Ko and Century companies, and although still playing shrewish wives and landladies, usually paired with Phil Dunham, they were featured roles with occasional leads in titles such as *The Little Fat Rascal, A Prairie Chicken* (both 1917), and *Rough on Husbands* (1918). Known as "the rotund and reckless comedienne," practically all of her starring films have vanished, leaving descriptions such as:

The overlooked Merta Sterling. Author's collection.

"The Little Fat Rascal" in which Merta Sterling does some of the most gosh awful stunts you ever saw a "plump lady" do on the comedy screen. Merta is "fattish." No gettin' away from that and for a lady of her proportions she has anything topped in the comedy field 49 ways from Sunday. (*Moving Picture Weekly*, July 21, 1917)

Myrta Sterling does not deny that she is fat, and the audience will agree that this L-KO sets a furious pace. It's two reels and the title "Fat and Furious," isn't nearly as funny as the comical stunts of the merry jokers in the L-KO company. Book this and give yourself a happy time at the box-office. (*Moving Picture World*, October 1917)

Although the bulk of her leading work is gone she can still be seen as support in *King of the Kitchen* (1918), in blackface as a cook in *The Freckled Fish* (1919), or playing second fiddle to the Century Lions in *A Lion's Alliance*, and *Lion Jaws and Kitten Paws* (both 1920).

Her stint with the Universal companies was the peak of her career. It culminated with her making *The Sage-Brush League* (1919), a five-reel starring feature for the short-lived Romayne Super Film Co. Billed as "The Female Charlie Chaplin," the film has disappeared and the little that's known about it comes from a May 1919 *Moving Picture World*:

Phil Dunham hiding Jessie Fox from Merta Sterling in *Brownie the Peacemaker* (1920). Courtesy of Sam Gill.

ROMAYNE SUPERFILMS READY WITH COMEDY – The Romayne Superfilm Company announces their second contribution to the trade in the shape of a five-reel comedy entitled "The Sage Brush League." The play was directed by Harry Gant, and Myrta Sterling, comedienne, is the featured player.

The story, which is very lively in character, revolves around the adventures of Bob Owen, a young chap from the East who inherits a ranch out West. Near the Owen's place is situated the Sunny Rest Ranch, which is maintained for the benefit of Eastern tourists who want to experience the wild, free life of the prairies and plains.

From this point on she free-lanced all over – turning up with Hank Mann in a number of his Arrow comedies like *The Janitor,* as an on the hoof Mata Hari, and *The Messenger* (both 1919), at the Hal Roach Studio in items such as *Years to Come* (1922), and *Scorching Sands* (1923), not to mention other shorts with the likes of Monty Banks and Lloyd Hamilton. Unfortunately she would usually contribute a comic bit or two and then exit from the rest of the picture. One of her better roles at this time was as the hefty and difficult sweetheart who Bobby Dunn has trouble marrying in his Arrow comedy *All is Lost* (1923).

By the mid-1920s her appearances became more sporadic, but she was still very effective as the wife that drives Charles Puffy to commit murder in his short *Not Guilty!*

(1926), in addition to supporting the Fox Monkeys in their starring feature *Darwin Was Right* (1924), and working in other pictures such as *The Star Dust Trail* (1924), and *Paid to Love* (1927) until the late 1920s.

Like Merta Sterling, Sunshine (Lucia) Hart weighed in at over two hundred and forty-five pounds and was defined by her pulchritude, giving her motto to a December 1925 *Exhibitor's Trade Review* as "Laugh and Grow Fat." She was born in Indiana in 1886, and spent nine years on the stage in stock, vaudeville, and Shubert shows before settling in as a resident of Edendale, California. Becoming a regular in the comedies made there, Coy Watson Jr., who often played her son in shorts, remembered her more in his 2001 book *The Keystone Kid* as a neighbor and the mother of his classmate Leora Hart than as an actress.

Making her film debut in 1914, she became a familiar face (and shape) in early 1920s Jack White-produced comedy shorts, often turning up with comedian Lige Conley as a bossy maternal figure in two-reelers like *Free and Easy* (1921), *Casey Jones Jr.*, and *The High Life* (both 1923). Her best role during her days with the White unit was in *Family Life* (1924) a one-shot short about the misadventures of Sunshine, her hubby Mark Jones, and rotund son Tommie Hicks as they coped with housing problems and an attempt at a camping trip. Gaining recognition for her work she soon branched out, appearing on the Roach lot as Stan Laurel's mother-in-law in *Save the Ship* (1923), and soon settled into a regular berth at the Mack Sennett Studio.

Driving difficulties with Sunshine Hart, Mark Jones, and son Tommie Hicks in *Family Life* (1924). Courtesy of Sam Gill.

From 1923 to 1930 Sunshine was the butt of a lot of Sennett fat jokes. A good example of which occurs in 1926's *Love's Last Laugh* where as a passenger on an ocean liner Sunshine's daily workout in her cabin causes the boat to violently rock back and forth sending her fellow passengers flying all over the ship. Comic mothers were her stock-in-trade, and besides usually playing Ruth Hiatt's mom in *The Smith Family* comedies, she filled the same role at various times for Alice Day, Alma Bennett, Madeline Hurlock, and Thelma Parr in some of her better-known shorts such as *Honeymoon Hardships*, *The Iron Nag* (both 1925), *Smith's Baby*, *Spanking Breezes* (both 1926), *Crazy to Act* (1927), and *Motorboat Mamas* (1928).

Also appearing in a few features such as *Syncopating Sue* (1926) and *Five and Ten Cent Annie* (1928), her best all-time role was in Mary Pickford's romantic comedy *My Best Girl* (1927). As the excitable and over dramatic matriarch of Pickford's dysfunctional family Sunshine held her own amongst comedy pros like Lucien Littlefield, Vivien Oakland, and Mack Swain, and in her subsequent trade ads Sunshine proudly displayed this note from Ms. Pickford:

One of the happy memories of "My Best Girl" is the fact that you played my mother. I am grateful to you, Sunshine, for the brave, splendid way you have carried on.

Sadly her career didn't last much longer. While working on another Pickford film she broke an ankle which left her bedridden until her death in 1930 at age forty-three.

The little old lady of 1920s comedy was Florence Lee, or as a 1922 *Exhibitors Trade Review* referred to her: "Miss Lee is one of the finest portrayers of grandmothers on the screen." (See appendix for the young and blonde Florence Lee). Although she has very little to do in the film, she's best remembered today as Virginia Cherrill's grandmother in Charlie Chaplin's *City Lights* (1931), but she was a maternal figure for everyone from Snub Pollard to Sid Smith, and was equally adept at handling gags as she was at sentiment.

Never a big name player, detailed information on her life is sparse, but her *Variety* obituary states that she was seventy-four at her death in 1962, which places her birthdate around 1888, and that she appeared on stage for six years with D.W. Griffith. Her earliest known films are in 1911 for his Biograph Company, and she was married to Biograph actor and soon to be director Del Henderson. The date of their marriage is unknown but according to D.W. Griffith's first wife Linda Arvidson the pair was already wed by 1910. Lee was part of the performing ensemble at Biograph, playing young women or the occasional wife in titles like *Teaching Dad to Like Her*, *The Diving Girl* (both 1911), *A Close Call*, and *His Auto's Maiden Trip* (both 1912) for directors such as Griffith, Frank Powell, and Mack Sennett. In 1913, when her hubby Henderson began alternating directing duties with Edward Dillon, Lee predominantly worked for him and even began writing scenarios. Some of the one-reelers they did together include *A Rainy Day*, *Cinderella and the Boob*, *Faust and the Lily* (all 1913), and *A Natural Mistake* (1914).

Biograph went bankrupt and closed its doors in 1916. Henderson moved on directing features for various companies, but Lee was off the screen for six years. She returned in 1922 and quickly found her niche as every comic's momma. Like male comic Jack Duffy she developed an old age character and effectively played it for years. At that time she was only in her late thirties, but was playing in her sixties. *Screenland Magazine* noted in 1931: "She has to make up cleverly to look as old as that. She has been playing grandma to half the players in Hollywood." A brief role that shows her in transition is as a customer in a general store in the Jackie Coogan feature *Peck's Bad Boy* (1922) – she's made up older but stands erect and seems youngish, but by the next year her persona was fully developed.

By 1926 she'd been mother or grandmother to Monty Banks, Baby Peggy, giant Jack Earle, Harry Langdon, Malcolm "Big Boy" Sebastian, and others in shorts such as *Little Miss Hollywood*, *A Corn-Fed Sleuth* (both 1923), *The Golf Bug*, *Feet of Mud* (both 1924), and *Sea Scamps* (1926). She's the silver-haired Madonna that gives a tearful goodbye to son Lloyd Hamilton as he leaves their country home and in a few steps is in the big city in *The Movies* (1925), in addition to being Johnny Arthur's long-suffering mom in *My Stars* (1926) who has to put up with his impersonations of movie stars to win over fickle Virginia Vance. She also essayed older family members in features such as *Top O' the Morning* (1922), *Mary of the Movies* (1923), and *The Johnstown Flood* (1926).

Her hands down best part came in the Our Gang two-reeler *Ask Grandma* (1925). The plot concerns Mickey Daniel's difficulties with an overbearing mother who won't let him just be himself. She makes him take ballet lessons, dress like Little Lord Fauntleroy, and adhere to a long list of etiquette rules (all beginning with "Don't"). His grandma secretly helps him out, playing baseball and boxing with him, in addition to advising him to follow his natural instincts. When his crush on Mary leads him into a fight with bully Johnny, Mickey proves himself and his mother sees the error of her ways. Lee is wonderful as grandma, and brings a perfect combination of heart and moxie to the role. She handles the slapstick with aplomb as well – when grandma gets ready to play ball she limbers up with silent speed backflips and somersaults, during the big fight while cheering Mickey on she gives a couple of demonstration slugs to her stuffy daughter, and when bully Johnny's father Noah Young gets involved and starts going after Mickey,

A relatively young looking Florence Lee during her early teens stint at Biograph.

grandma and mom give him the what-for. The film gave Lee the opportunity to display her warmth and sincerity while at the same time use her well-developed slapstick chops.

Florence Lee as the perennial mother with Marion Mack in *Mary of the Movies* (123).

The rest of the 1920s saw her busily continuing on – more shorts with Big Boy and Our Gang like *Fair and Muddy* (1928), and *Ginger Snaps* (1929), plus a spate of westerns with the likes of Leo Maloney, and Buzz Barton such as *The High Hand* (1926), *The Little Buckaroo*, and *The Bronc Stomper* (both 1928). After her non-speaking appearance in *City Lights* (1931) she can be spotted in other bits in titles like Marie Dressler and Polly Moran's *Politics* (1931), but appears to have retired soon after. Her husband Del Henderson went on as a character player until 1950 and passed away in 1956. She survived him by six years before her own demise in 1962.

Another maternal figure in silent comedy was Dorothy Vernon, who just happened to be the real-life mother of Sennett and Christie star Bobby Vernon. Her background is very sketchy – born in Germany as Dorothea Ahrens in 1875, and it's not known when she entered show business or came to America, but as Bobby was born in Chicago in 1897 as Sylvion de Jardins, there must have been a Mr. de Jardins in the picture at some time. Since Bobby began working on stage as a child it's reasonable to assume that his mother was also, and there is a Dorothy Vernon listed in 1907 vaudeville and the 1909 show *Fashion Plates* on the western Burlesque Wheel. When Bobby began working at Universal in 1913 he was first billed as Sylvion de Jardins, but quickly became Bobby Vernon. Dorothy begins appearing in films in 1919, after Bobby is well established, and one of her earliest films is Billy West's *Ship Ahoy* (1919) as a denizen of Billy's tough boarding house. She was a regular in Hank Mann's Arrow comedies such as *Junk* and *Leap Year* (both 1920), usually as his battle-axe wife. In *A Gas Attack* (1920) Hank has a hard time avoiding her wrath and her rolling pin, and after a trip to dentist fills him up with so much gas that he floats away to a desert island she's there as well as a native version of her usual self.

From 1920 on Dorothy was working everywhere – supporting Bobby Dunn and Eddie Lyons at Arrow, in Century Comedies, Joe Rock Comedies, Billy West Comedies, Jack White Comedies with Big Boy and without, not to mention countless Christie shorts with Jack Duffy, Billy Dooley, Neal Burns, and of course son Bobby. Over the years she made multiple appearances in Hal Roach's Our Gang two-reelers playing various Gang members mothers in *Commencement Day, Cradle Robbers* (both 1924), *The Big Town, Dog Days* (both 1925), *Buried Treasure, Telling Whoppers* (both 1926), *The Glorious Fourth*, and *Heebie Jeebies* (both 1927). Also busy in features and she has been spotted in *Conductor 1492* (1924), *The Man on the Box* (1925), *The Missing Link* (1927), and *Show People* (1928).

Dorothy Vernon has it in for Hank Mann and an unknown actress in *A Gas Attack* (1920). Courtesy of Sam Gill.

During the silent era Dorothy was married to Harry Burns, an assistant director and actor. Burns had been William S. Campbell's assistant on the *Chester Comedies* that starred the chimp Snooky the Human-Zee, and later helmed a short-lived group of *Iris Comedies* with Little Napoleon, who like Snooky was an offspring of the movie monks Napoleon and Sally. Dorothy had prominent roles in *Little Napoleon* comedies such as *The Monkey Cop* and *A Small Town Hero* (both 1922). Later Burns became editor and publisher of the trade paper *The Hollywood Filmograph*.

Dorothy worked for many years after the change-over to sound in shorts and features (a 1930s Broadway Dorothy Vernon was a different actress) such as *The Fighting Parson* (1930), *Melody Cruise* (1933), *The Wrong Miss Wright* (1937), and *The Heckler* (1940). Her husband Harry Burns passed away in 1939, followed a few months later by her son Bobby, who was only forty years old. Dorothy continued working, doing bits parts until the late 1950s, making it to ninety-four when she died in 1970.

Babe London was a silent comedy fixture who was typecast as the funny fat girl because she was more than plump at two hundred and fifty plus pounds. But besides her weight she always brought extra zest to a comedy with her sunny smile and engaging personality. London had grown up "movie struck," and was determined to be part of the fun. In 1972 she told interviewer Anthony Slide in *The Silent Picture*:

> I was living in Oakland, and I don't know how this ever came to my eye, but they had an ad in the paper, advertising for talent for a movie, from this company that was at the old Essanay Studio. So I sent snapshots in, and I got a letter back asking me to come down for an interview. So I did, and they ended up selling me a course in make-up for thirty-five bucks. It was just a little one-horse company. So I learned to make-up, and they also did make a little one-reeler, and I played the lead in it. I was a good type. They announced that they were going to Los Angeles to make pictures. So I got father and mother and the whole family to move to Los Angeles so I could go into pictures.
>
> Well, nothing ever came of the picture – I don't think it was ever released. Anyhow, I had some professional 8 x 10 photographs made, I just went around. I didn't know anything about the business except enough to go to casting directors and register. And I gradually got in. About two weeks after I talked to them, I did a lead with Eddie Lyons and Lee Moran at Universal. They had a regular character woman, but she was sick, so it made space for me. And on and off through the years I did a picture with them.

She had been born Jean Ruth Glover in Des Moines, Iowa in 1901, and the family moved to California when she was young. Living in Oakland in 1915 she remembered skipping high school to watch Douglas Fairbanks shoot scenes for *The Americano* (1916) at their World's Fair. Just a few years later, in 1919, she made her debut at eighteen with

Lyons & Moran in one-reelers like *The Expert Eloper* (1919). Besides other work with them she got a career boost that same year with a good role in Charlie Chaplin's *A Day's Pleasure* (1919) as Tom Wilson's seasick girlfriend:

> Chaplin was awful nice. He was a son-of-a-gun. He said "Babe, if you stick with this, you're going to make it." And I had quite a good little part in that picture, because most people didn't have much, but I had a nice scene with him, close-ups and stuff.

Babe London smiles on co-stars Al St John and Ruth Hiatt in *Fares, Please!* (1925). Courtesy of Sam Gill.

Not long after this she became part of the stock ensemble at Vitagraph for Joe Rock and Earl Montgomery in shorts like *Sauce and Senoritas*, *The Laundry*, and *A Parcel Post Husband* (all 1920), in addition to free-lancing around working with John Bunny's son George in *Why Worry?* (1921), and making her first appearances with her good friend Stan Laurel in his solo two-reelers *The Weak-End Party* (1922), and *The Handy Man* (1923). She also worked in features such as *When the Clouds Roll By* (1919), *Merely Mary Ann* (1920), and *When Romance Rides* (1922). In 1923 she became an important part of Christie comedies:

> I was there for a long time as a featured comedienne. I worked in practically every picture Al Christie directed while I was there. He seemed to like me. He got a kick out of me as a bum Mary Pickford. He put a Mary Pickford wig on me, you know, with curls and all that.

> We always had a script at Christie's. They were considered the highest class comedy movies made at that time. We sort of looked down our nose at Mack Sennett comedies. They were rough. We thought them pretty corny, according to our way of thinking, because ours had scripts and stories, and they had nice sets, and quite a lot of production value, excellent photography. They were more situation comedies; there was very little hokum or slapstick in them. Dorothy Devore was one of their biggest stars, and they had Neal Burns and Bobby Vernon.

As she said she supported everyone on the Christie lot – was an annoying little girl who thought that Bobby Vernon in disguise as a child made a great playmate in *Second Childhood* (1923), had a yen for Jimmie Adams in *Done in Oil* (1923) as a lunch counter cook, and in *Kidding Katie* (1923) she's Dorothy Devore's fat older sister who has a beau she's never met before coming to visit, so Babe and mom make Dorothy pretend to be a little girl so she'll be no competition for Babe. Christie did headline her in one comedy, *A Hula Honeymoon* (1923), where she and country sweetheart Henry Murdock win a contest for a honeymoon in Hawaii. While over there Henry starts a flirtation with a Hawaiian girl, so Babe learns how to hula to win him back. A unique angle on the picture is that it was actually shot on location in Honolulu and on board ship going over.

> My contract ran out, and I went over to Educational. I did a lot of pictures with Norman Taurog over there. They were pretty good. I worked a lot with Lloyd Hamilton. I think he was a great comic, and you don't hear much about him now. Some of the greatest comics you don't hear of anymore.

One of her first appearances for Educational was as Lloyd Hamilton's country girlfriend in *Jonah Jones* (1924) who has to vie for Lloyd's attentions when he falls for society girl Dorothy Seastrom. In *Red Pepper* (1925) Al St John is riding his bike to work when he gets yoo-hooed from a flirty Babe on the sidewalk. Al stops and gives her a ride on his handlebars, but unfortunately her weight causes a quick crash. Other pairings with Hamilton and St John include *Half a Hero*, *Fares, Please* (both 1925), and *Live Cowards* (1926). She also supported Lige Conley in outings like *Spot Light*, and *Cheap Skates* (both 1925), and in some of the studio's Cameo Comedies had a chance for a leading role. *Scrambled Eggs* (1925) has her arriving to meet her mail order fiancée George Davis, who's a bit surprised when he sees her as the photo she sent him had her girth dramatically reduced. Within the limitations of slapstick comedy Babe played her characters honestly, and with her sweet smile and bubbly personality there's always a tinge of pathos for her usually rejected characters:

> I always wanted to play straight roles. Even in some of my comedies I used to cry real tears. I never mugged very much in comedy. I played it straight, because I was always the wallflower, losing my man to the pretty girl. I've always had

a feeling for the dramatic. I played with great sincerity even in my comedy days.

She continued turning up in features like Buster Keaton's *Go West* (1925) where she played the daughter of an in-drag Roscoe Arbuckle, *The Fortune Hunter*, *All Aboard* (both 1927), and *Tillie's Punctured Romance* (1928), but after the short *Top Speed* in 1929 her appearances became a lot more sporadic. In 1931 she returned for one of the best roles in her career in Laurel & Hardy's *Our Wife*. Playing Ollie's chubby fiancée Dulcy, whose irate father Jimmy Finlayson locks her in her room after he gets one look at Hardy's photograph, the pair decide to elope, which is easier said than done when Stan Laurel has come along to help. Of working with the team Babe remembered:

> Stan did most of the directing. He explained the scene to me, and we'd play it. Of course, you would play it in your own style, but there wasn't much improvisation as far as I was concerned. There was another director who got screen credit for Our Wife; he would take over when Stan would step in and work. But Stan did all the directing – mostly.

Babe London was such a ubiquitous comedy player in the 1920s that she got her own photo postcard. Author's collection.

Outside of turning up in *Penny Wise* (1935), one of Joe Cook's New York made Educational comedies, she was away from the screen until the early 1940s when she did all kinds of uncredited bits in features such as *Six Lessons from Madame La Zonga* (1941), *Jackass Mail* (1942), *The Paleface* (1948), and *The Good Humor Man* (1950). In 1951 she played Shemp Howard's dream girl Nora in *Scrambled Brains,* one of the most offbeat of the later Three Stooges comedies. Shemp has had a nervous breakdown, and Moe and Larry pick him up after a stay in a sanitarium. Although he's said to have been cured he's still having hallucinations – the main one being that he sees his ugly and toothless fiancée Nora as a beautiful blonde bombshell. A slimmed-down Babe appears as Nora, which created problems for her getting work:

> I used to weigh 255 pounds, and I was typed as a fat girl. And my doctor told me I had to take this weight off: my heart was tired. So he said if I wanted to go on living I had to take the weight off. So I did.

After that I got a bit of work occasionally. It was like starting anew. I'd be called down for an interview, and they'd say, "Who are you? You aren't Babe London!" And I'd say "Oh, yes I am." But I wouldn't fit the script. Once you get typed in pictures and established, and then change your type radically, it's very hard.

She continued doing bits for a number of years and later lived at the Motion Picture Country Home, even marrying musical director Phil Boutelje in 1975. She passed away in 1980, and during her later years her pastime was painting, focusing on portraits of stars and locations from the silent era:

> I'm painting this thing, which I call "The Vanishing Era." The way I came to it is rather interesting. You know, the only time we old-timers get together is at funerals. So I was at Mack Sennett's funeral, and it was a very large funeral. All the still-living Keystone Kops were honorary pall-bearers, and I saw everyone there, Louise Fazenda, Chester Conklin, all my friends from the old days. After the ceremony, in front of the church, you kinda stand around and greet each other – people you haven't seen in years. So I thought, well this is symbolic of the passing of the era. I had started to paint in the meantime, and it came to me, why don't I paint a series of the old silent comics, and some of the landscapes and memorabilia. A painted saga of the old silent days.

The female Lon Chaney, or "woman of a thousand faces," of the supporting comediennes was the unsung Vera White, who was really as unknown to audiences of her time as she is today. Small and dark-haired with features seemingly made of rubber, as she amply demonstrates thanks to some rampant fleas in Our Gang's *Thundering Fleas* (1926), she played any and all types of characters, and although anonymous to moviegoers the people making the films, particularly Stan Laurel and Hal Roach, were well aware of her skills and used her over and over. Born in Australia in 1894, she married Joseph T. Everett in 1913 and the two toured vaudeville for many years as Joe and Vera White. Reviews of their act mention Vera doing a well-received Charlie Chaplin routine and generally making a better impression than Joe, who they said was better at tumbling than comedy.

Variety reported that their film debut came in 1918 for the National Film Company, and they seem to have finally wound up at the Hal Roach Studio in 1921. Vera quickly became ubiquitous on the lot supporting Harold Lloyd, Snub Pollard, Paul Parrott, Eddie Boland, and even Gaylord Lloyd as a resuscitated Lonesome Luke. Joe appeared in some 1921 Roach titles like *The Pickaninny, Late Hours, Never Weaken, The Chink,* and *I Do* without making an impression, and appears to have left films when the couple divorced in 1922. Memorable among Vera's many, many Roach roles is the disinterested spinster who's set to marry an amnesiac Snub Pollard in *Where am I?* (1923), a stressed-out social director doing her best to deal with Our Gang's antics in *One Terrible Day* (1922), but her best remembered character was the spit-curled good-time girl who's teamed up with Kay Deslys to entertain Laurel and Hardy in *We Faw Down* (1928).

The Cock-Eyed Family (1929) consists of Ben Turpin, baby Billy Barty, Sherwood Bailey (back seat), and Vera White as Turpin's optically-challenged wife. Courtesy of Karel Caslavsky.

In addition to her work at Roach she made the rounds of all the various comedy units – supporting Brownie the wonder dog in *A Howling Success* (1923) for Century Comedies, working with Jimmie Adams and Jack Duffy on the Al Christie lot, playing the innocent towns lady who's startled by Stan Laurel popping a blown-up paper bag in *Dr. Pyckle and Mr. Pride* (1925), and practically out cross-eying Ben Turpin as his optically challenged wife in *The Cross-Eyed Family* (1929). She even pops up in features such as *Keep Smiling* (1925) with Monty Banks, and the drama *Is Your Daughter Safe?* (1927). With the transition to sound her appearances dropped off, and one of her few documented talking film roles was as a villager in Laurel and Hardy's *Swiss Miss* (1938). Although overlooked before and after she passed away in 1956, her films and performances are available on home video, shown theatrically, and still enjoyed today.

One of the cutest and funniest girls in movies was Martha Sleeper. Probably the most vivacious member of the Hal Roach stock company, she did yeoman work at the studio, especially in support of Charley Chase and Max Davidson. Born in 1910, she studied dance as a child in New York, and a trip to Hollywood in 1923 led to the movies. At age twelve her first film was the dramatic feature *The Mailman* (1923) and she soon became a regular in the Buddy Messenger two-reelers made by Century Comedies. Playing one of Buddy's "gang" along with Spec O'Donnell, Arthur Trimble, "Bubbles" Berry, and Pete the pup, sadly most of these titles like *The Racing Kid*, *Happy Days*, *Trailing Trouble*, *Please, Teacher,* and *Low Bridge* (all 1924), are lost today, and the one survivor, *Budding Youth* (1924), starts at the end of the first reel and only has about a minute of footage with Martha before it moves on to the boy's misadventures playing baseball.

Quickly hired by producer Hal Roach, it's said that the initial thought was to have her join Our Gang, but appearing with them in *Every Man for Himself* (1924) and *Better Movies* (1925) shows that she was far too mature looking, and so after spending the rest of 1924 doing smaller bits in shorts like *A Ten Minute Egg*, and *Should Landlords Live*, she graduated to being leading lady for Charley Chase in *The Rat's Knuckles*, and *Bad Boy* (both 1925). Seeming older than her fifteen years, Martha's a perfect match for the youthful Chase, and usually plays the down-to-earth girl who spurs him on to prove himself. *The Rat's Knuckles* (1925) introduces her as:

Martha Sleeper and Charley Chase from *Fluttering Hearts* (1927). Courtesy of Karel Caslavsky.

"Flirty" McFickle - -

Jimmy's sweetheart had one of those street car hearts - -

Always room for one more - -

and Martha does a lot of gum chewing working at a hash house counter. Convinced that Charley's going to make a fortune with his latest invention, a humane mousetrap, the pair spends much time imagining what it will be like when they're rich, but Martha dumps him the first time he doesn't sell the invention. *Bad Boy* (1925) has her as another lunch room girl, still coy and flirty, but much more steadfast than in *Rat's Knuckles* – that is until she sees Charley performing a fruity ballet for one of his mother's society benefits. Referring to him as a "leaping tuna," she won't have anything to do with him. Trying to prove himself tough enough for her he shows up at the local dance hall acting the part of a "hard boiled yegg" – giving him and Sleeper a chance to do some funny dance parodies – but eventually he's found out which leads to a big brawl where Charley proves himself by battling the pug-uglies and winning Martha.

Other films they did together include *Mum's the Word* (1926) where Charley's mother has a new husband, and because she doesn't want him to know that she's old enough to have an adult child, Charley has to pose as the replacement butler. Despite his new father taking an instant dislike to him Charley sticks it out as he's fallen in love with Martha the maid. The climax comes when he finds that the maid is in the father's room at night. Thinking that they're having an affair Charley confronts them to find that Martha is actually step-father's daughter whom he was concealing as well. *Crazy Like a Fox* (1926) has Martha as a society girl who's being forced to marry her father's best friend's son. While she's running away she winds up at the train station and meets Charley, who just happens to be the son in question. Of course neither of them knows that the other is their intended and they fall in love. Because of Martha Charley decides to go and act crazy at his prescribed bride's house so they'll be glad to get rid of him. When Charley shows up Martha conveniently doesn't want to see him (otherwise the film would be over then), and there's much footage of Charley acting nutty for the benefit of her parents. Finally Martha comes downstairs and they recognize each other, leaving Charley to prove to her that he's not crazy.

In addition to being in the studio's ensemble and working with the likes of Arthur Stone, Lucien Littlefield, Clyde Cook, and Glenn Tryon, Roach gave her one starring comedy, the delightful *Sure–Mike!* (1925). Martha joined the ranks of Alice Howell, and Fay Tincher as a gum-chewing and addle-pated little working-class girl who slaves away in a fancy department store. When we first see her she's late for work, and her idea of rushing is wearing roller skates and getting pulled along by a bulldog, which of course leads to her creating a pedestrian pile-up on the sidewalk and almost getting run-in by the cops. When she finally gets to the store the rest of the plot of this quick one-reeler concerns her infatuation with her fancy supervisor, but her dreams of nabbing him and moving up the social ladder are finally flattened when she discovers that he already has a fat wife and five rowdy kids. Making use of Sleeper's perky charm and signature wide-eyed takes of surprise, the short moves along at break-neck speed, and it's a shame that the idea wasn't developed further or that she never got another starring short.

Martha Sleeper, Chester Conklin, Ethel Wales, and a crying Delmar Watson in *Taxi 13* (1928). Author's collection.

Besides her work opposite Chase, Sleeper's best known films today are the ones she made as part of Max Davidson's screen family. In four shorts – *Jewish Prudence, Flaming Fathers, Fighting Fathers* (all 1927), and *Pass the Gravy* (1928) – she played the daughter that was the old man's pride and joy, but still caused him a lot of aggravation, particularly when she would take up with boys he didn't approve of. Max is driven to distraction in *Flaming Fathers* (1927) as he and mama are afraid that Martha is going to elope with beau Eddie Clayton, so he follows the pair to the beach and suffers one embarrassment after another. When he's finally pinched by the cops the lovers get their chance to run off.

Gaston Glass is a young lawyer who wants to marry Martha in *Jewish Prudence* (1927), but Max tells him they can only wed after he wins his first case. Turns out that his first case is against Max, so not only does the old man lose but has to keep his word and turn Martha over to Glass. *Pass the Gravy* (1928) is the peak of the series where Max has cooked and is about to eat his neighbor's prize-winning rooster. Martha is engaged to the neighbor's son and the pair goes to great lengths to try and put Max wise to the situation – mostly by enacting hilarious scenes that make the old man think they've lost their minds. Sleeper and Gene Morgan steal the picture with their pantomimic versions of chickens getting their heads cut off, laying eggs, etc., while trying to cover their tracks so the boy's father doesn't catch on.

Sleeper left the Roach organization in 1928, after *Should Tall Men Marry,* and moved on to a few comedy features such as *Skinner's Big Idea*, and *Taxi 13* (both 1928), but soon went on to supporting parts in dramas like Joan Crawford's *Our Blushing Brides*, *War Nurse* (both 1930), *Ten Cents a Dance* (1931), *Penthouse* (1933), and *Spitfire* (1934), but for the most part this later work was lackluster and made no use of her real skills – that of a comedienne. Frustrated by the Hollywood system she began appearing in plays on the West Coast and in 1935 finally moved to New York where she spent a decade on the Broadway stage in plays such as *Russell Mantle* (1936), *Save Me the Waltz* (1938), *The Cream in the Well* (1941), and *The Rugged Path* (1945-46) with Spencer Tracy.

She made one return to Hollywood to work for her old director Leo McCarey in his 1946 feature *The Bells of St. Mary's*, where she played the not-so-reputable mother of a young girl that comes under the care of Bing Crosby's Father O'Malley. At the same time she became known for designing clothing and whimsical jewelry, and devoted the latter part of her life to these pursuits – in fact Sleeper's clothes and jewelry pieces are still highly regarded and sought after today. Living for many years in Puerto Rico, she occasionally appeared in local theatre productions there and died in 1983.

Daphne Pollard leaning in on the far right as part of Pollard's Lilliputians. Billy Rose Theatre Division, the New York Public Library for the Performing Arts.

A relatively late arrival to films was Daphne Pollard, who didn't join the ranks of character comedy women until 1927. Born Daphne Trot in Australia in 1890, she spent much of her early career crisscrossing back and forth between stages in England and America. She made her stage debut at age eight as a member of the child opera company

Pollard's Lilliputians (whose alumni also included comics Snub Pollard, Billy Bevan, and director Alf Goulding). The troupe toured the world and after adopting Pollard for a last name Daphne ended up in the U.S. in the 1908-09 show *Mr. Hamlet of Broadway*. During this jaunt in America she also toured vaudeville and appeared in *A Knight for a Day*, *The Candy Shop*, and *The Passing Show of 1915*.

Not long after she switched to England, working with George Robey in the 1917 revue *Zig Zag*, and continuing in other London shows such as *Box O Tricks*, *Joy Bells*, *Jig Saw*, and *After Dinner*. By the early 1920s she was back in America, rumored to have made her film debut with a bit in the Mack Sennett feature *The Crossroads of New York* (1922), and enjoying a long run on the Orpheum Circuit. It's said that Mack Sennett had scouted and been interested in her as early as 1915, but she didn't sign a contract with him and settle into films until 1927.

Sennett featured her in a series of *Sennett Girl Comedies* where girls like Carole Lombard and Sally Eilers provided the sex appeal while Daphne supplied the laughs. Many of the shorts have sequences in "Sennett Color," which was a good excuse to show off the girls as well as a gimmick for extra attention. Sennett gave Daphne a big promotional build-up as "the internationally famous musical comedy and vaudeville star," and she would get special billing before the title on the first one, *The Girl from Everywhere* (December 11, 1927). Set in a movie studio where director Mack Swain is trying to film his super production in spite of problems that range from a temper mental German star to lions on the loose, movie goers got their first look at Pollard as Minnie Stitch, the studio's dippy wardrobe mistress. Tiny, (4'9"), with a prominent rear end that she would stick out or pad for comic effect, she was always the little but feisty eccentric determined to have her way despite whatever hurdles were thrown in her way.

In *Run, Girl, Run* (1928) Daphne is the coach of the college track team who is going to lose her job if her team doesn't win the upcoming meet. She has her hands full with the grumpy dean and Carole Lombard as her track star, who's more concerned with sneaking out at night to meet her boyfriend and powdering her nose during a race than running. When Daphne confiscates her powder puff during the big meet it ends up, through circumstances that only occur in silent comedies, being grilled as a funnel cake and returned to Daphne who spends a good chunk of screen time trying to eat it, and then spraying powder out of her mouth like a geyser.

The Campus Carmen (1928) has the girls of the Sunnydale School forbidden to perform a production of *Carmen* by their prissy dean. Set to play the male lead Daphne talks the girls into doing the show anyway, so they hire a hall. With liabilities that include slow-on-the-uptake Johnny Burke as the theatre janitor, Daphne's ripe singing and trouble with her hat and moustache, not to mention a cow that's playing the bull having a calf during the show, the ultimate performance goes exactly as you'd expect. The title card writers worked overtime on this one – with gag arias that include:

Daphne's choice of seat mate surprises H.L. Kyle (left) and Andy Clyde in *The Swim Princess* **(1928). Author's collection.**

Beneath yon tree you Spanish Onion –

Upon your head I'll raise a bunion!

Matchmaking Mama (1928) has Daphne dominating the entire short as the wealthy Mrs. McNitt. Her goofy second husband is played by Johnny Burke. Each have a daughter from a previous marriage – Daphne's is Carole Lombard, who she's trying to get hitched to the local rich boy, and Johnny's daughter is Sally Eilers, a nice girl who the rich boy really likes. Daphne's determined to send Sally back to school so Carole can snare the money. Everything is tied around rehearsals for a performance of a show (excuse for the Technicolor sequence). Eventually Sally gets her rich boy and Carole marries the fruity dance teacher, which causes Daphne to go after hubby Johnny. The last shot of the film has Johnny ensconced in the top of a tree with Daphne busily chopping the trunk with an axe.

After a bit in the feature *The Goodbye Kiss* (1918) Daphne made the transition to sound with Sennett in many shorts like *The Lion's Roar* (1928), *Sugar Plum Papa* (1930) and *Hawkins and Watkins* (1932), and soon branched out to other units such as RKO and Pathé. Besides some funny two-reelers with Shemp Howard for Vitaphone, her best-remembered work was with Laurel and Hardy at the Hal Roach Studio. In *Thicker than Water* (1935), and *Our Relations* (1936) the 4'9" Pollard played 6'2" Oliver Hardy's most vicious and domineering screen wife ever. Daphne began curtailing her appearances in the late 1930s, and after a brief flurry of bits in early 1940s features like *Tillie the Toiler* (1941), and *Kid Dynamite* (1943) she retired.

Children and animals are always sure-fire "scene stealers", and some of the best in silent comedy were Mary Ann Jackson, Hannah Washington, and Cameo the dog. Mary Ann Jackson was the female equivalent of freckle-faced boys such as Mickey Daniels and Spec O'Donnell. Her deft comic timing and extremely expressive face put her in a class by herself, and made her a comedy veteran by the age of three. Born on January 14, 1923, to a family of movie children, her older sister Peaches (see Appendix) had a sizeable career in features like D.W. Griffith's *The Greatest Thing in Life* (1918), and *Circus Days* (1923) with Jackie Coogan. Her brothers Bobby and Dick worked also, and Mary Ann being brought to the set at age two while one of the boys was working was well documented:

Mary Ann Jackson puts on the dogs in *Smith's Cousin* (1927). Courtesy of Cole Johnson.

He was called for extra work at Sennett's. His mother accompanied him and, having no one with whom to leave Mary Ann, took her along. It had never occurred to Mrs. Jackson to seek a picture career for her because she wasn't pretty like Peaches. But at the studio the company took a fancy to the funny baby and put her in the picture too. When the day's rushes were run, it was found that she had taken the scene completely away from a veteran comedian. (*Picture-Play Magazine*, 1929)

Two-year old Mary Ann Jackson is the child actress who has been engaged by Sennett. She is probably the youngest actress in Hollywood, at least the only baby to boast of a real contract. Mary Ann was discovered on the set one day when she came to the studio to watch her brother work. An added scene in the picture called for a baby to walk through some custard pies on a table. Mary Ann got her chance, and never were pies trod upon with such dignity and poise. So Mary Ann will be a Sennett starlet for some time to come. She is the sister of Peaches and Bobby Jackson, well-known screen children. (*Moving Picture World*, August 1, 1925)

Director Eddie Cline was credited with "discovering" Mary, and her first film was his *Dangerous Curves Behind* (1925). At first she was used as an all-purpose scene-stealer in shorts like *Goose-Land*, *Spanking Breezes*, and *A Blonde's Revenge* (all 1926) where she terrorizes Ben Turpin as he tries to give a speech, before being headlined with Raymond McKee and Ruth Hiatt in the studio's *Smith Family* series. These misadventures of a middle-class family were a more situational type of comedy for Sennett, although there were still ample helpings of sight-gags and slapstick.

The premiere episode, *Smith's Baby* (1926), concerns Mr. & Mrs. Smith trying to have an evening out at the movies while baby Bubbles (Mary Ann) is being watched by her grandmother. Of course nothing goes smoothly at the movies or at home, with the entire movie audience constantly disrupted by Mr. Smith's frequent calls home, and baby Bubbles managing to flood the house. The series became a solid hit – continuing on for four years and twenty-seven entries. Stories included the Smiths going on vacation, buying a new house, Bubbles starting kinder garden, Mr. Smith joining the army, and going shopping at a busy department store, not to mention being visited by various uncles and cousins. All of the above situations are always complicated thanks to something engineered by Mary Ann, and the studio, well aware of her position as the main laugh-getter, advertised:

Baby Mary Ann Jackson is a wonder. She's good for as many laughs as she has freckles, and that's plenty.

Smith's Candy Shop (1927) has Jimmy Smith opening his own store. In addition to being sabotaged by a rival who substitutes his sugar for concrete, Bubbles brings a couple of candy hungry elephants to the shop. *Baby's Birthday* (1929) is all about Mary's party, which doesn't proceed well when a neighborhood brat steals the ice cream and replaces it with lard. Mary Ann's contract with Mack Sennett expired in 1928, and she was immediately hired by Hal Roach to become a member of *Our Gang*, but because a large number of the Smith comedies had been shot in advance she actually appeared in both simultaneously, as the previously made Smith shorts continued to be released until March 1929.

Her first comedy for Roach, *Crazy House* (June 2, 1928), has her fitting right into the Gang, and soon they were building shorts around her like the sadly lost *The Holy Terror* (1929) and the surviving *The Spanking Age* (1928), where Mary Ann and Wheezer have to live with a mean stepmother and her bratty daughter Jean. Besides Mary's great takes and reactions, an interesting aspect of this film is that all the scenes are shot at the kid's level, so the adults are never seen above the waist. With her scrappy tomboy manner, black pageboy hairdo, and tons of freckles Mary was the perfect contrast to Jean Darling's blonde coquetry, and with her own sizeable comedy skills was able to more than hold her own with longtime Gangsters like Joe Cobb and Farina.

Although a no-nonsense tomboy, she was often pining away with unrequited love for Harry Spear or Joe Cobb as in *Wiggle Your Ears* (1929) which is a puppy-love triangle with Harry preferring Jean over Mary. It's filmed entirely in close-ups, making it a comic equivalent to Carl Dreyer's *The Passion of Joan of Arc* (1928). Mary was also frequently saddled with Wheezer as her younger brother, and in *Little Mother* (1929) she even has a second brother, Beezer, to take care of after their mama has gone to heaven. Mary handles the sentiment of the story with the same aplomb as the slapstick, and all ends happily with the kids thinking their mother has returned when her twin sister comes to take care of them.

When sound arrived Mary proved to be as good with dialogue as she was takes, and now had Jackie Cooper and Chubby Chaney to have crushes on. Our Gang became more popular than ever and she stayed until 1931's *Fly My Kite*. Like other Gang members such as Sunshine Sammy Morrison, Mary Kornman, and Mickey Daniels before her Mary Ann spent time in vaudeville after leaving the series:

10 Picture Players Barnstorming with Femme Baseballers

Combination femme baseball team and 10 picture players embark May 16 on a tour of the country. Team will play in the afternoon while the players make personal appearances in local establishments.

At night the big get-together will be a "movie stars ball." This will give the small towners a glimpse of some Hollywood "names" and also a chance to do a turn on the dance floor. It's figured to attract femmes as well, because of the style angle.

Vincent Ray organized the company and will transport them in buses. Players making the trip are Shannon Day, Virginia Pearson, Molly O'Day, Priscilla Dean, Pauline Garon, Carmen Granada, Mary Ann Jackson, Rose Rosirio, and Jackie Hooray. (*Variety*, May 13, 1931)

Mary Ann Jackson with Harry Spear in *Wiggle Your Ears* (1929). Courtesy of Robert Arkus.

One can find listings that suggest that she may have travelled with her own solo act as well, and was out on the road for more than a year before returning to Hollywood in October 1932. Years later Mary Ann told Leonard Maltin and Richard W. Bann for their book *The Little Rascals: The Life and Times of Our Gang*, that she finally gave her mother an ultimatum:

> This is not for me. I don't want the responsibility or the rejection. I'm not an actress, I'm not talented, leave me alone, let me get on with my life!

From there she did do a few bit parts in films, including some stand-in work for Edith Fellows, but then married young and concentrated on raising a family.

Today Mary Ann has a bit of a film comedy fan base, thanks to her sound *Our Gang* appearances, but another kid comedy regular, black comedienne Hannah Washington, is completely forgotten. Born at the end of 1923, Hannah was the niece of popular west coast singer and dancer Mildred Washington, who was billed as "the Dancing Demon from Washington," and in addition to being a fixture at nightspots like Sebastian's Cotton Club also turned up in films such as *Hearts of Dixie* (1929) and *Blonde Venus* (1932) before her death from appendicitis in 1933. Hannah began her film career at age three, doing bits in features such as *Sea Horses* (1926), and *The Notorious Lady* (1927), and then found her niche at the Bray Company.

Bray had been a pioneer in film animation, and made a move into live-action shorts in the late 1920s. Besides shorts with Jack Cooper and other comics they initiated a knock-off version of Our Gang dubbed *McDougal Alley Kids* comedies. Hannah became their "Farina," with the moniker of "Oatmeal." Bray even copied Roach's gender-bending – Farina was a boy who usually dressed as and was referred to as a girl, and Oatmeal, played by a girl, was referred to and dressed as a boy. Like Farina, Hannah was the tag-along younger sibling, who toddled around in big shoes and would always create problems for the gang, like in *The Big Pie Raid* (1927) where she finds and brings a skunk to the big pie fight. Her McDougal appearances also include *The Deuce*, *The Orphans*, *Magic Game*, *Cattales* (all 1927), *A Lot of Baloney*, *Fowl Play*, and *Bathing Beauty Babies* (all 1928).

After about a year and a half of the McDougal's Hannah moved on to appearances in other kid's series such as the *Mickey McGuire* comedies that starred Mickey Rooney, and Weiss Brothers' *Winnie Winkle* comedies. At the same time she gathered some attention playing opposite Billy Dooley in the Al Christie-produced two-reeler *A Gallant Gob* (1928), where goofy sailor Dooley gets stuck with taking care of little Hannah, who this time plays a girl. This seems to have brought her to the attention of Abe and Julius Stern who distributed their short comedies through Universal and began using her in their *Newlyweds and their Baby* and *Buster Brown* comedies,

Hannah became an important part of the *Buster Brown* shorts, as by the time she joined the series Pete the pup had jumped ship and gone to Hal Roach's *Our Gang* comedies. The Sterns had always relied heavily on Pete's antics and reactions for laughs, and his replacement Tige was downright creepy – some poor dog in white-

Hannah Washington does a little dog whispering on Billy Dooley in *A Gallant Gob* (1928). Courtesy of Cole Johnson.

face make-up with painted on eyebrows. Effeminate Arthur Trimble who played Buster wasn't at all funny either, so Hannah became their ace in the hole for the later Brown entries. A good example of this is *Knockout Buster* (1929) in which the opening half of the picture is a boxing match between Buster and his fat friend Albert Schaefer. Hannah plays the referee who gets all of the laughs, and most of the punches, as she tries to dodge the blows to no avail, even taking one on the chin that turns her into a human pinwheel spinning wildly on the ringside ropes.

The film then switches to Buster's camping trip in the country with his family, including stowaway Hannah, which leads her to explore a nearby farm. For almost seven minutes the picture becomes a solo Oatmeal comedy, with Hannah stalking a chicken, getting bitten in the seat by a goose, and ultimately discovering a watermelon patch (what else). She finally gets chased back into the plot by an irate farmer with Buster, Mary Jane, and Tige joining in the action to bring the film to a close. Other installments such as *Busting Buster* (1928) have Oatmeal helping out at Buster's soda fountain, *Teacher's Pet* (1928) has the kids sneaking into school late, and Oatmeal is the football team's secret weapon in *Half-Back Buster* (1928).

After the series ended in 1929 Washington's appearances became sporadic and difficult to chart. She's listed as a native child in *King Kong* (1933) and her last real role appears to be as the slave girl Sally Ann in Shirley Temple's *The Littlest Rebel* (1935). Looking over her silent films, Al Christie was the most upscale producer that she worked for. It's a shame that she didn't do more for him or work for Sennett, Jack White, or any of the other majors, instead of being stuck in the Bray and the Stern Brothers' low-budget leftovers. With good material (or at least some kind of material) her funny presence and timing could have been developed and resulted in some solid comedy films.

Just like kids, there were many canine comedians in silent film – Teddy, Brownie, Pal, Buddy, and Pete – but perhaps the best, plus the only comedienne of the litter, was Cameo. Owned by supporting comic Hap Ward, who was part of the ensemble in Gale Henry's Model Comedies, she was a black and white bull terrier, and her full name was Camisole:

> She was born in 1919, and being very sickly, was fed warm milk and lime-water every thirty minutes from a medicine dropper until she was old enough to take nourishment from a baby's bottle. To her owner's careful nursing she owes her life (*Los Angeles Times*, January 1, 1924)

In 1920 Hap Ward became main support in Chester Comedies' Snooky the Human-Zee two-reelers, and Cameo appears to have made her debut there in entries such as *Ladies Pets*, and *Ready to Serve* (both 1921). It wasn't long before she branched out as a sidekick to the likes of Baby Peggy and Lige Conley for *Peggy, Behave!* (1922), and *This Way Out* (1923), but she really showed the range of her talents at the Mack Sennett Studio.

Cameo all ready for her close-up. Author's collection.

In *Nip and Tuck* (1923) she plays an unbelievable poker game with Billy Bevan and Harry Gribbon. Cheating for her master Billy she nonchalantly takes a few peeks at Harry's cards, and whenever he catches her she looks away with split-second timing, leading to a hilarious back and forth routine. *Asleep at the Switch* (1923) has her getting drunk and smoking a big black cigar, while managing to trounce Ben Turpin at checkers, and in *Smile Please* (1924) she gives grief to Harry Langdon. According to Hap Ward she never had a repertoire of learned routines or tricks, but instead would understand what he told her to do, and then do it.

From the mid-1920s on she was all over the silent comedy map – more shorts such as *The Hollywood Kid* (1924), *Low Tide*, and *Baby Be Good* (both 1925), in addition to many "A" features like *Penrod and Sam* (1923), *A Self-Made Failure* (1924), Mary Pickford's *Little Annie Rooney* (1925), and *Frisco Sally Levy* (1927). She even recreated *Nip and Tuck*'s poker game with Heinie Conklin and Tom Wilson in the blackface World War I comedy *Ham and Eggs at the Front* (1927). Known as "the Buster Keaton of dogdom," Cameo went from studio to studio as the total film dog, and the Los Angeles Times also reported:

> Once Cameo had "Kleig eyes" from working under the powerful lights and now she wears always on the set her pair of tiny yellow goggles.

Although this sounds like pure fabrication, photos exist of her on the set wearing those little goggles. In 1928 Ward bought a car in Cameo's name with savings from her salary and:

> With her master Hap H. Ward, Cameo left Los Angeles last Sunday on a two year's tour of the United States, with personal appearances scheduled at theatres in hundreds of cities and towns.

> Mr. Ward's statement that Cameo understands what she is told to do, rather than going through a routine of tricks, was bourne out when it came time to take a photo. Told to "get in and drive the car," Cameo jumped upon the seat of the Oakland, a car from Reeve-Gautzman Oakland-Pontiac distributors, and put her paws on the wheel. (*Los Angeles Times*, June 10, 1928).

Cameo reports to Billy Bevan with the details on Harry Gribbon's cards in *Nip and Tuck* (1923). Courtesy of Karel Caslavsky.

Following this publicity tour Cameo's screen appearances, perhaps due to her advancing age, became less frequent. Later sightings include the Snub Pollard /Weiss Brother short *Here Comes a Sailor* (1929), and two 1931 features, *Misbehaving Lady* and *Penrod and Sam*, helmed by her five-time director William Beaudine. On February 21, 1935 the *Los Angeles Times* reported:

Famous Film Dog Dies of Grief at Van Nuys

A tragedy in the lives of two famous dogs ended today with the burial of Cameo, an 18 year-old Boston bull terrier, which died Monday from apparent grief over the recent kidnapping of her son Buster, also a film dog.

Buster was never returned, and yesterday grief-stricken Cameo, remembered for her acting in numerous moving pictures, died in the arms of her master, Hap Ward, former comedian.

Cameo was actually sixteen years old (one hundred and twelve in dog years), so despite the Hollywood hyperbole it's more likely that her passing came from her ripe old age.

Elinor Vanderveer (right) and Symona Boniface (left) wonder what Charley Rogers is up to in *Madame Q* (1929). Courtesy of Cole Johnson.

The last, but not the least, of our character ladies is the unsung Elinor Vanderveer. Basically a dress extra who rarely received billing, Ms. Vanderveer became a memorable comic screen presence due to her regal bearing and exquisite timing. Although portraying the ultimate society lady on screen, she came from a more modest background. Born in Brooklyn, New York she lived for many years in Seattle where her husband was a lawyer for the Industrial Workers of the World. After their early 1920s divorce she and their daughter headed to Hollywood, and Vanderveer began popping up on screen in 1924.

She can be spotted in numerous features such as *Paths to Paradise* (1925), *Skinner's Dress Suit*, *Flesh and the Devil* (both 1926), and *The Girl in the Pullman* (1927), but it was in the Hal Roach Studio's shorts that she was given the opportunity for a smidgen of attention. Almost always on hand in the crowd at theatre performances, dinners, or society parties where Laurel & Hardy, Charley Chase, and Our Gang ended up at, some of her best moments include unflinchingly and resignedly taking a pie in the face in *The Battle of the Century* (1927), and the sad and quizzical look she gives Marion Byron after she's sat on her ice cream cones in *A Pair of Tights* (1929).

The sound era saw her continuing on the Roach lot, even getting a large role as Waldo's snobby mother in Our Gang's *Washee Ironee* (1934), as well as appearing with the Three Stooges and in features like *Frankenstein* (1931), *Movie Crazy* (1932), *All This, and Heaven Too* (1940), and *Hellzapoppin* (1941). After a nice bit as a staring woman in the *Pete Smith* short *Pest Control* (1950) she worked until 1953, and passed away in 1976.

Chapter Eight

BATHING BEAUTIES AND LOVE INTERESTS

The ladies in this chapter were a highly decorative group. The bathing beauties of course spiced up the proceedings with large doses of sex appeal, while the leading ladies provided love interest for the male comics. Many of the bathing girls would graduate from the beach and cross over to the leading lady category, and along the way a number of these women would prove that they could be just as funny as their star comic sisters.

The Sennett Squad from left to right – Hazel Williams, Claire Cushman, Thelma Hill, Georgia Hale, Andree Bayley, and Elsie Tarron – circa 1924. Courtesy of Cole Johnson.

Mack Sennett really hit upon something when he first filmed Mabel in her one piece for *The Diving Girl* (1911) and *The Water Nymph* (1912). He basically came up with a more refined version of the "French Postcard," and moved to the logical conclusion that if one girl in swim wear on the screen caused a sensation – a bevy of them would become an industry standard. And they did – like his Keystone Cops, every unit had to have their own version. There were the L-Ko Girls, Fox Sunshine Beauties, Vanity Fair Girls, not to mention all the unnamed bathing squads from the smaller companies who would show up to frolic for moviegoers at the drop of a hat, regardless of any plot logic, simply because they were an expected ingredient.

One of the earliest bathing girls was much more than just decoration. Vera Steadman was a record holding diver and swimmer from the Los Angeles Athletic Club. She was born in Monterey, California in 1900 and had no previous experience on the stage or screen when she joined Keystone in 1915. It was her devotion to water sports and her good looks that brought her to Sennett's attention. Her first film was *Those College Girls* (1915) and she alternated showing off her swimming prowess in comedies like *The Surf Girl* (1916) with being eye candy in other such as *Her Native Dance* (1917). In 1918 she got one of the leads opposite Sennett himself in *The Country Girl*, but the film was never released, and she ultimately graduated to leading ingénue in *Her Blighted Love* and *The Summer Girls* (1918) which led to other offers:

> **Vera Steadman Returns**. Vera Steadman, formerly one of the leading comediennes at the Keystone Comedies, has joined the Universal forces and will be seen shortly in a one–reeler entitled "Happy Returns," being directed by Jack Dillon. She is also seen in the two-reel special animal comedy directed by William S. Campbell and entitled "And the Elephant Still Pursued Her."(*Motion Picture News*, 1919)

Vera Steadman, with support from Bobby Vernon, demonstrates her swimming skills in *Why Wild Men Go Wild* (1919). Courtesy of The Museum of Modern Art.

Vera spent 1919 making the rounds of the various comedy units. Only a handful of titles are known. She appeared at Universal in the Jack Dillon-directed one-reel comedies *Happy Returns* and *Temporary Alimony* (the above mentioned "And the Elephant Still Pursued Her" seems to have had a title change before its release). During a stay at Fox Sunshine Comedies she did some diving for Virginia Rappe in *His Musical Sneeze*, was an elegant leading lady for madcap Larry Semon in *Traps and Tangles* and *Scamps and Scandals*, and most importantly ended up on the Al Christie lot. Her first film for Christie was opposite Bobby Vernon in *A Rustic Romeo* (1919), and outside of her appearances in the features *Scrap Iron* (1921) and *Meet the Prince* (1924), the studio would be her screen home until 1931.

During her Christie tenure she made more than seventy comedies and supported every male comic on the lot – Bobby Vernon, Jimmie Adams, Neal Burns, and especially "goofy gob" Billy Dooley. A few of the shorts include *Back from the Front* (1920) *Exit Quietly* (1921), *Pardon My Glove* (1922) *Fool Proof* (1923), *Getting Gertie's Goat* (1924), *Sea Legs* (1925), *Run Tin Can* (1926), *A Mooney Mariner* (1927), *Gobs of Love* (1928), and *Sappy Service* (1929), not to mention the Christie features *813* (1920), *Stop Flirting* (1925), and *The Nervous Wreck* (1926). Playing multiple variations on the basic comic sweetheart, from time to time the opportunity arose to have her poolside or at the beach. Having continued her competitive swimming in the 1920s, and racking up more records, often no logical reason had her in the water, as in the surviving *Why Wild Men Go Wild* (1920) where out of the blue she gives Bobby Vernon a diving demonstration to end the picture.

The arrival of sound saw a drop off in her career. After a couple of 1931 talking shorts for Christie the rest of her work was uncredited bits in features such as *Morning Glory* (1933), *Frisco Kid* (1935) and *A Star is Born* (1937).

> **A Touch of Irony** There was an ironical ring in a scene in *Mind Your Own Business* at Paramount not long ago. Property men went out to get some scrap books to use in a sequence and they came back with a flock from the old Christie comedy studio, now being vacated. The books were loaded with write ups and pictures of Vera Steadman, who was once a top comedy star, but who was playing a bit in the particular scene in which the scrap books were being used. (*Hollywood*, 1937)

The extra work continued in films like *Zaza* (1938), *The Doctor Takes a Wife* (1940), and *Meet John Doe* (1941), but came to an abrupt end in 1941:

> Hollywood scenarists have written many stories of bravery but here is a real life story that tops them all. A year ago Vera Steadman, the famous silent day star, was struck by an automobile. Her back and both her legs were broken. Before operating, doctors said she had only a slight chance to live. And if she survived the operation, they said she'd probably be a cripple for life. The operation saved her life but Vera Steadman could not leave her hospital bed for six months. Four months ago she was released from the hospital in a wheelchair – a brace

on her hip and braces on both legs. Doctors said she'd never walk again. But Vera Steadman didn't believe them. The other day, at a Los Angeles school for paralytics, I watched Vera Steadman walk again. It was a painful process but the pain will lessen each day. Vera Steadman will not be a cripple – thanks to bravery and determination far surpassing any movie plot. (*Hollywood*, 1942)

Within two years she did indeed walk again, and although she left the movie business she was on hand for many of the Sennett company reunions before her death in 1966.

Most silent comedy fans know Bartine Burkett from her appearance with Buster Keaton in *The High Sign* (1921) but as most of her films are lost, her work is largely unknown. She was a prolific leading lady who worked at a number of different studios for a variety of well-known comics. Born in Shreveport, Louisiana, her family moved to Hollywood in 1914 when she was sixteen. After performing with a little stock company in her home town, she became smitten with movies, and determined to give them a try. She began making the rounds of the studio casting offices around 1917.

Christie Comedies portrait of Vera Steadman. Courtesy of The Museum of Modern Art.

Bartine landed a stock position at the Lasky Studios at five dollars a day with a three day a week guarantee. After a few months she moved to Universal and was soon active in their Joker, Star, and L-Ko Comedies.

She turned up in Stan Laurel's early films *Phony Photos* and *Hickory Hiram* (both 1918). Sadly both of these are considered lost, but *Adventurous Ambrose* (1918) does survive and concerns Mack Swain's farmer Ambrose inheriting a seaside inn. Complications and mistaken identities of course ensue and at the end of the picture Ambrose is more than happy to return to his farm. Bartine is on hand as one of the girls at the seaside who are ready to frolic on the beach with Ambrose when his wife is otherwise occupied. Keeping busy working with the likes of Eddie Lyons and Lee Moran, Chai Hong, Eddie Barry, Harry Mann, and even supporting Bobby Vernon at Christie in *Mum's the Word* (1918), Bartine's career got a boost when she landed the female lead in the Century "special" *The Geezer of Berlin* (1918).

Universal had recently had a success with the dramatic feature *The Kaiser, the Beast of Berlin* (1918), and *Geezer* was their own parody version. Bartine plays the daughter of large baker Hughie Mack in a small village of Belgium. The Kaiser comes to take over the country, but thanks to the efforts of Bartine and her baking assistant boyfriend, played by Monty Banks, he ends up getting cooked in their bakery oven. Taking broad potshots at the German command with names such as Von Turpentine and Chancellor Von Bethman – Bowlegs, the studio claimed to have spared no expense on the parody; rebuilding all the sets that had been destroyed in the dramatic feature. The film gathered a good deal of attention and much of it went in Bartine's direction:

Bartine Burkett as a Fox Sunshine Girl. Author's collection.

Bartine Burkett, one of the most engaging and interesting of screen ingénues has been cast in an interesting role in "The Geezer of Berlin."

This Jewel Production is a travesty on "The Kaiser, the Beast of Berlin." Miss Burkett plays the role made famous in the former production by Ruth Clifford, only in "The Geezer of Berlin" the blacksmith of Louvain becomes a baker, and his daughter a doughgirl. (*Moving Picture Weekly*, July 30, 1918)

Continuing at L-Ko with titles such as *Hello Trouble* (1918), *It's a Bird*, and *Hearts in Hock* (both 1919), she then moved over to Fox Sunshine Comedies and became one of their Sunshine Comedy girls in *Virtuous Husbands, Wild Waves and Women*, and *Back to Nature Girls* (all 1919), but her stay at Fox wasn't without incident as illustrated by this May 1919 *Variety* item.

Bear Injures Bartine Burkett Los Angeles May 7. Bartine Burkett was attacked by a bear at the Fox Studio and seriously injured.

1920 saw her work with Keaton in the often-seen *The High Sign*. Buster plays a drifter who gets a job at Ingham "Seven-Foot" Pickett's shooting gallery. Pickett is head of the Blinking Buzzards, a group of bandits who are demanding $10,000 dollars from

Bartine's father August Nickelnurser. After seeing Buster in the shooting gallery Bartine decides he's the person to be dad's bodyguard, but the Blinking Buzzards order Keaton to rub Nickelnurser out – or as a title explains "Guarding a man from danger and killing him at the same time is SOME job." Buster is ultimately won over by Bartine's charms and takes care of the gang in a great action climax. Not given much to do Bartine is still sweet and charming, making a very attractive first leading lady for Buster's initial starring short.

Although the short was his first and shot in January and February 1920, Keaton was not entirely happy with his maiden effort so it wasn't released until April at 1921 after his series of comedies had already well established itself. From working with Buster, Burkett appeared in the First National feature *The Turning Point* (1920) and returned to Universal. In the middle of 1920 she was teamed with leading man Austin Howard for a series of eleven one-reel star comedies which were billed in the exhibitor trade journals as:

New Fun!   New Fashions!   New Faces!

The New Star Comedies   One Reel

Featuring the Comedienne de Luxe   Bartine Burkette

(*Moving Picture Weekly*, August 7, 1920)

All were directed by Horace Davey and were short and sweet domestic comedies. The first of the series *Kid-ing the Landlord* (1920), has the couple blessed with a new baby but then chronicles the misfortunes the pair have trying to hide the infant from their landlord. In *The Nuisance* (1920), hubby is a fight fan and when Bartine goes out with a friend and leaves him to take care of their baby he's so desperate to see the big prize fight that he bundles the kid up and takes it along. Although refused admittance, he finally gets the little one in by disguising it in a hat, whiskers, and moustache etc. Hubby has a great time at the fight but forgets about the baby. He has to go back and get it before Bartine finds out. The only known survivor of the series, *Cards and Cupid* (1920), has Bartine coming to town to marry her fiancé Jack, but as he's just lost all his money in a card game his best buddy "borrows" his wife's wedding ring and lends it to Jack for Bartine. The wife in the meantime has reported the ring being stolen and the cop who just happens to end up as a witness for Jack and Bartine's wedding recognizes the ring from its description and arrests them. Eventually all the confusion gets sorted out at the jailhouse.

After headlining in the Star series, Bartine remained busy for Universal working with Harry Sweet and Charles Dorety in Century Comedies such as *High Life, Playing Possum, His Fearful Finish*, and *The Nervy Dentist* (all 1921), in addition to the feature *High Heels* (1921), and even moonlighted in some of CBC's *Hallroom Boys* two-reelers, like *High and Dry* and *False Roomers* (both 1921). 1922 saw her appear in two Metro features *I Can Explain* and *Don't Write Letters* opposite Garth Hughes and continue at Century:

Bartine Burkett and Buster Keaton in her best-known film *The High Sign* (1921).

Miss Burkett Supports Moran. Bartine Burkett, leading woman in many recent Century Comedies, is again seen in support of Lee Moran in Lee's latest, which the director Fred Hibbard has just finished. Miss Burkett, one of the prettiest girls of the screen, has found time to play in the supporting casts of Mary Pickford, Katherine MacDonald, Buster Keaton and William Desmond besides doing her latest work on the Century lot.

Her latest work in support of Lee Moran was in *Ten Seconds*, in which she took the part of a society bud who elopes with her chauffeur and is quietly married to him in The Little Church around the Corner. Fred Hibbard directed this story of the prize ring and did not spare Moran in the ring scene. (*Exhibitors Trade Review*, March 18, 1922)

Besides *Ten Seconds*, her other pictures with Moran included *The Straphanger* and *Red Hot Rivals* (both 1922) but at this time she took a break from movies which is explained by an item on her return:

Bartine Burkett, who deserted the screen some two years ago to join the ranks of married women, is to return via "The Movie Queen" a new Century Comedy, which is now ready to be placed in production. (*Exhibitors Herald*, March 8, 1924)

Bartine Burkett reacting to one of the many things that Al St John does in *The Live Agent* (1925). Courtesy of EYE Filmmuseum, Netherlands.

After her marriage to Ralph Zane, Bartine now worked at a more leisurely pace. She made two reelers for Century like *Pretty Plungers*, *A Lofty Marriage*, (both 1924), *Itching for Revenge*, and *Dry Up* (both 1925) with Harry McCoy, Al Alt, Hilliard Karr and Eddie Gordon, and the features *Cornered* (1924), *He Who Gets Slapped* (1924), which she was unfortunately cut out of, and Cecil B. DeMille's *The Golden Bed* (1925).

The best known of her later films is the recently restored and revived *Curses!* (1925), which paired Bartine with Al St. John and was anonymously directed by Roscoe "Fatty" Arbuckle. After being banned from the screen following his infamous manslaughter trials, Arbuckle produced, wrote and directed two years' worth of two-reelers for Reelcomedies, Inc. which were distributed by Educational Pictures. *Curses!* was the last of the series and is a rip-roaring spoof of western serials with Bartine as the poor heroine, Little Nell, who is bedeviled by the blood thirsty villain, Buttonshoe Bill. Movie conventions and implausibility are roasted to a crisp in one of the wittiest comedies of the 1920s.

1926 was Bartine's last year in silent films. She followed *Curses!* with another appearance opposite Al St. John in the Biff Comedy release *The Live Agent* (1926). Al and Bartine want to get married, but her father, who happens to be Al's boss, is against it. He agrees, providing Al can sell a record amount of life insurance policies for his company by the end of the day. The rest of the short details Al's attempts at sales and his eventual hitting of the jackpot. *The Live Agent* consists of the same cast and crew, including nominal director Grover Jones, as *Curses!*, so there's a possibility that this was shot for Reel Comedies, Inc. by Arbuckle but was sold to the Biff Company, who distributed shorts by the Van Pelt Brothers and Trem Carr (who later was a co-founder of Monogram Pictures and produced tons of low-budget westerns and programmers). Bartine returned to Universal for her last known silent comedies, *Her Ambition*, and *Why George* (both 1926).

After a nearly fifty year retirement Bartine returned to work in the early 1970s and was again busy in movies and television. In addition to films such as *Galaxina* (1980) and *The Devil and Max Devlin* (1981) she was all over television – on programs like *The*

Mary Tyler Moore Show, The Rockford Files, and *Adam 12,* plus appeared in tons of commercials, best remembered as a hip motorcycle riding granny in a series of spots for Boone's Farm Strawberry Hill Wine. She was also critical on the way the elderly were presented in the media.

> Bartine Zane is an elderly actress who is dismayed at the way elderly women are portrayed in the movies. "Because of a general misconception," she complained, "a great many elderly women who work in films are obliged to dress and look like old frumps of the 1890 -1920 vintage. For instance, though hats are almost one hundred percent taboo for the entire female population at present (one does not see them, even in church, anymore), we are required to wear them as well as odd, unattractive dresses which end somewhere between midcalf and ankle." Bartine Zane recalled a television commercial in which she was required to wear a hat with faded roses, a small fur neck piece, and a huge feather boa. "I looked ghastly!" Why," she asked, "do elderly women have to look like pre historic specimens? (*American Film*, September 1977)

She also talked about working with Keaton in Kevin Brownlow and David Gills' 1987 documentary *Buster Keaton: A Hard Act to Follow* and had made it to the ripe old age of ninety-six when she passed away in Burbank on May 20, 1994.

One of the more athletic of the Sennett girls was Mary Thurman. Although only 5'3" and one hundred and twenty three pounds, she was an all-around track and field athlete as well as expert in all aquatic sports. She, of course, was also a great beauty with red hair and gray eyes. Born in Richfield, Utah in 1893 as Mary Mavoureen Christiansen, after high school she attended the University of Utah and became involved in their drama group which toured all the small towns with two shows, one of which was Shaw's *Arms and the Man*. More interested in dramatics she never graduated as during the play's tour she married fellow student Victor Thurman in 1912. The couple settled in Mary's home town of Richfield and found teaching jobs – Mary teaching elementary school and Victor at the middle school. Both were interested in Hollywood – Mary as an actress and Victor as a writer. They took a trip there in 1915 and never returned to Richfield.

It's thought that Mary entered the film business in a Sennett bathing contest wearing a swim suit that she made herself. She began working for Triangle and appeared in the DeWolf Hopper Feature *Sunshine Dad* (1916). For the next three years Mary played

Mary Thurman as a rollerskating goddess in *Love Loops the Loop* (1918). Author's collection.

ingénue for Chester Conklin, Ford Sterling, Louise Fazenda, Al St. John, and particularly the always ready to flirt Charlie Murray. Wayland Trusk would usually come along with Murray, playing Mary's jealous husband or admirer in shorts such as *Friend Husband* and *Watch Your Neighbor* (both 1918). *A Bedroom Blunder* (1917) is set at a beach resort where Murray is trying his best to be alone with Mary, but gets much interference from her hubby Trask and his own battle-axe wife played by Eva Thatcher. Intrigue in a cabaret is the plot of *Love Loops the Loop* (1918). Mary is the star of the roller-skating floor show, and this time Murray, Wayland Trask and old Harry Booker are all crazy about her which leads to shootings, faked deaths, and a good part of the cast ending up on roller skates for the action climax. The end of 1919 saw some more changes in Mary's life. She divorced Victor in December and moved to a more important studio:

> **Mary Thurman Enters Drama.** It has just been announced from the western studios of the Famous Players Lasky Corporation that Mary Thurman, the famous Sennett beauty, has been secured to play the principal lead in the Paramount production of "Poor Boob" in support of Bryant Washburn.
>
> This announcement came as a surprise, as it was not generally known that Miss Thurman had left the Sennett Studios. It was learned that at Miss Thurman's request Mr. Sennett returned to her two years' contract with that organization when the player explained to him that she had a desire to enter another line of endeavor. A great future is predicted for her in her new line of work (*Moving Picture World*, January 11, 1919).

Her first four features – *The Poor Boob*, *Spotlight Sadie*, *This Hero Stuff*, and *The Prince and Betty* (all 1919) continued her working in comedy, and besides Bryan Washburn, paired her with Mae Marsh, William Russell, and William Desmond for "A" producers like Goldwyn, Paramount, and American. She soon moved into drama working frequently with well-known director Allan Dwan.

> **Mary Thurman to Star in Dwan Productions** Mary Thurman, schoolteacher, bathing beauty and leading lady, will blaze forth as a star in the Allan Dwan production "In the Heart of a Fool" to be presented by Mayflower Photoplay Corporation, through First National Exhibitions Circuit on September 6.
>
> She also is featured in two more Dwan productions, "The Scoffer" scheduled for publication November 15, and The Sin of Martha Queed" which will probably be shown in January (*Exhibitors Herald*, September 4, 1920)

Besides the aforementioned *In the Heart of a Fool*, *The Scoffer* (both 1920) and *The Sin of Martha Queed* (1921) Dwan also directed her in *A Broken Doll* (1921) and most famously *ZaZa* (1923) where as Floriane, the rival of star and fellow Sennett alumnus Gloria Swanson, she has a knock down, no holds barred cat fight with La Belle Swanson.

One of her rare comedy features was *Leap Year* (1924) with Roscoe "Fatty" Arbuckle. Roscoe plays a rich hypochondriac who is beset by various women who want to marry him for the fortune he's going to inherit. Mary is his steadfast nurse who loves him, and although he loves her as well the farcical plot complications keep them apart until the end of the picture. This was Arbuckle's last feature for Paramount and was unreleased before his scandal broke in 1921. Although it never came out in America it was finally released in Europe.

Eva Thatcher (left) and Wayland Trask (right) force Mary Thurman and Charlie Murray into a compromising situation in *Friend Husband* (1918). Courtesy of Robert S. Birchard.

In *Leap Year* Mary sports a page boy hair-do and she was one of the first stars to make it popular, predating Colleen Moore and Louise Brooks. For the next few years Thurman was kept busy in all types of dramatic features with co-stars such as Edmund Lowe, Helene Chadwick, and Hope Hampton. On location in Florida for *Down Upon the Swanee River* (1925) she caught malaria. It seemed that she had fought it off so she continued working, but she developed pneumonia. During her last few days her mother and old friend Juanita Hansen were at her side but she died in New York on December 22, 1925. She was only thirty years old, and her final film *The Wives of the Prophet* was released posthumously in January 1926.

Elinor Field was a beautiful blonde born in 1902 in Plymouth, Pennsylvania. Her family later moved to California, and as a teenager at Los Angeles Poly High School, she was spotted for film work in an amateur theatrical. She began as an extra at Triangle Komedies in 1917 and worked her way up to larger parts. Eventually she became a leading lady in one-reelers such as *His Speedy Finish, His Cool Nerve,* and *Half and Half* (all 1917) where she was directed by pros such as Harry McCoy, Charles Avery and Reggie Morris and appeared with McCoy, Morris, Hugh Fay and Harry Depp (her future co-star at Strand). She was also paired with a young Raymond Griffith for titles such as *His Thankless Job, His Fatal Move* and *His Foothill Folly* (all 1917).

She soon became one of the girls in Sennett-Paramount releases such as *A Dog Catcher's Love, A Bedroom Blunder* (both 1917), *The Kitchen Lady,* and *Those Athletic Girls* (both 1918), and her next step was Christie Comedies. She worked most frequently with Bobby Vernon, supporting him in *In and Out, Love and a Gold Brick, Petticoats,* and *Some Romeo* (all 1918), but soon Christie moved her into being the female lead in his separate brand of Strand Comedies which were released by Mutual. Elinor spent much of 1918 and all of 1919 working with Cullen Landis, Harry Depp, and director Scott Sidney on one reelers such as *Cupid on Quarantine* (1918), *Easy Payments,* and *The Wig-Wag System* (all 1919). According to James M. Sheldon President of the Mutual Film Corporation:

Elinor Field poses with Keystone Teddy. Author's collection.

> Now Mr. Sheldon announces that Miss Field will be starred in Mutual Strand comedies, the one-reel farces which have been so distinctly successful during the last year.
>
> "She's just the girl we've been looking for," said Mr. Sheldon after his attention had been called to Miss Field's work and he had viewed some of the things she had done "She does comedy just the way that we want comedy done for the Strands."

Miss Field will work under the direction of Scott Sidney, who has been responsible to a large degree for the quality and character of the Mutual Strands. (*Moving Picture World*, July 27, 1918)

In *Winnie's Wild Wedding* (1918) Elinor is a flirtatious girl who wants to marry her boyfriend, but her father mandates that she must have three additional proposals before he'll consent to the first. She arranges two more very quickly, but nearly slips up on the third. *Beans for Two* (1918) makes fun of the fad for trading stamps when Elinor and her hubby Harry Depp find that they get double quantities of stamps for canned beans. Carried away by the items they want to get with the stamps, they buy a mountain of cans of beans and are soon driven crazy and practically have their marriage destroyed by eating nothing but beans.

Peggy's Burglar (1919) has Elinor and her hubby suspecting that each other has turned burglar. Elinor thinks that he's stealing her furs, and hubby finds her working with some burglar-like tools. When a cop shows up at their house each tries to save and alibi for the other. When 1920 rolled around she took a break from shorts and made a leap to features. She did a number of dramas such as *Once to Every Woman*, *The Kentucky Colonel*, and *The Blue Moon* (all 1920), and of course comedies like *Girls Don't Gamble* (1920) and *Hearts and Masks* (1921)

"Hearts and Masks" has been one of the most widely read of the McGrath books. The film version was done by Mildred Considine, and was directed by William Seiter. Miss Field appears in the role of Alice Gaynor, the willful and adventure hungry young girl who passes herself off as a maid in her uncle's mansion, succeeds in capturing Galloping Dick, a notorious crook, and in snaring the heart of a famous author. Brilliant costumes, and a lavish setting for the fashionable masked ball at the climax of the exciting action is reached, are features of the production. (*Exhibitor's Herald*, May 21, 1921)

She even played the title role in Colonel William Selig's serial *The Jungle Goddess* (1922) described in the ads as "15 Episodes packed with thrills, wild animals and jungle romance." The bulk of the rest of her career was spent at Universal, where her first assignment was as

Portrait of Elinor Field. Author's collection.

leading lady in the third series of *Leather Pushers* shorts starring Reginald Denny as a gentleman boxer. After entries like *He Raised Kane* (1922), *The Chickasha Bone Crusher*, and *When Kane met Abel* (Both 1923) she move to western features and shorts with Hoot Gibson, Jack Hoxie and Jack Mower. Titles included *Don Quickshot of the Rio Grande*, *Western Skies* (both 1923), and *The Bull Tosser* (1924). Some were serious and others more comic, but after 1924 her career came to a fairly abrupt halt. Over the next few years she would turn up in uncredited bit parts in Sennett shorts such as *The Bargain Hunt* (1928) and *Pink Pajamas* (1929), but her film work seems to have come to a final end in 1934 when she was thirty-two, although she lived until 1998.

Another young girl that got her start in the Sennett "beauty chorus" and moved on to other studios was Marvel Rea. Blonde and vivacious, she was born in 1901 in Ainsworth, Nebraska and moved to California in 1910. Beginning with Sennett in 1917 when she was only sixteen, she was at first a standard issue bathing girl – one of the crowd in comedies such as *Whose Baby?*, *A Bedroom Blunder*, *That Night* (all 1917), *Friend Husband*, and *His Smothered Love* (both 1918) but by the end of 1918 she had worked herself up to featured roles in *Her Screen Idol* and *The Summer Girls*.

Although making headway with the "King of Comedy" she left the Sennett fold –

Marvel Rea, one of the Sennett bathing girls, is now a member of the Christie Comedy Company. (*Moving Picture World*, Fall 1918)

Her stay there was very brief as she was soon back at Sennett, turning up in shorts such as *Why Beaches are Popular*, *When Love is Blind*, plus the feature *Yankee Doodle in Berlin* (all 1919). Leaving again, this time she played female leads at Fox Sunshine Comedies, working with comics such as Jack Cooper, Glen Cavender, Edgar Kennedy and Bobby Dunn her titles include *Hungry Lions and Tender Hearts*, *A Lightweight Lover*, and the surviving *The Heart Snatcher* (all 1920). Marvel plays the daughter of rich Harry Booker, and at the start of the picture they're having a big party at their mansion. Jack Cooper is a tramp that crashes their shindig. He makes a play for Marvel but is rebuffed in all the confusion so he dumps chloroform in the orchestra's tuba, which causes it to spray and knock out everyone at the party. This gives Jack the opportunity to rob the safe and then he hightails it to the second reel. Now we have a change of setting to a blacksmith shop and Jack shows up as the assistant to the blacksmith, Kewpie Morgan, and has a romance with his Amazon daughter, Blanche Payson. After numerous blacksmith gags, Marvel, Harry Booker and Bobby Dunn show up from reel one when their car needs to be repaired by the smithy. Jack rebuffs Blanche for Marvel, and the ending is a wild chase with sledgehammers and gun powder. The action and comedy is fast and furious, not giving Marvel much to do but look pretty and watch the bodies and projectiles that fly by her.

Marvel primarily worked with director Roy Del Ruth at Fox, but another director in the company, the young Jack White, not long after *The Heart Snatcher* teamed up with comedian Lloyd Hamilton and set up their own production company with distribution through Educational Pictures. White picked Marvel to be leading lady for their new series of *Mermaid Comedies*, and their inaugural effort was *A Fresh Start*. (1920)

An unusually frizzy-haired Marvel Rae. Author's collection.

Jimmie Adams and Lige Conley have just gotten out of jail, but as they pilfered some funds from the warden the police force is after them again. After eluding the cops they get jobs in a cabaret where Marvel is the queen of the floor show – diving into a pool and showing off her figure in a one piece. Both boys fall hard for her and begin fighting over her, but she already has an extremely jealous husband. When he finds some mash notes from the boys that ask her to meet them in the park he goes ahead with his pistol ready. Jimmie gets there first, finds out who her husband is, and sets up Lige to get shot. They both end up being moving targets but eventually get away and return to their boarding house – just where Marvel and Hubby happen to live. After much running between rooms a couple of lions end up on the premises for the big action climax.

Chockfull of gags delivered at a fast and furious pace, *A Fresh Start* started Jack White Comedies out on the right foot, and a fetching Marvel in a variety of costumes didn't hurt either. Continuing with four more of the White comedies she was paired with Lloyd Hamilton in *Duck Inn* and *The Simp* (both 1920) and returned with Jimmie Adams, Sid Smith, and Lige Conley respectively in *Nonsense* (1920), and *For Land's Sake* (1921). At this point she abruptly left the series and disappears from films, although it's thought she did some uncredited work through 1932. Her personal life was troubled, a short lived 1918 marriage that was terrible, and in 1936 she was abducted by three men and "criminally assaulted." Sadly, she committed suicide the next year by ingesting ant poison. She was only thirty five.

Probably the bathing girl supreme – the most popular while at Sennett and the busiest after – was Phyllis Haver. Born Phyllis O'Haver in Douglas, Kansas in 1899, she and her mother moved to Los Angeles when she was four. She met Marie Prevost when she was nine and they became best friends and went to Manual Arts High School together. At fourteen she began playing piano in movie theatres accompanying films, and then:

"I was just actually pushed into pictures," She said, with her frank, frequent smile. "I hadn't any desire to go – hadn't any ambition to work."

"I had a boyfriend who worked out at Lasky's. I was going to Manual Arts High School in Los Angeles. He asked me to come out one Saturday if I wanted to and see the studio and how they made motion pictures. I was crazy to go, of course, and I did."

"One director working there that day saw me and he offered me a job on the spot. He said he had a part right that minute for me, and even wanted me to borrow make up and work."

"I simply giggled my head off at him. I told him I was in school – didn't want to work. That night he called me at my house. Three days later he called me again. I finally decided to do it. I only had a month more in school and my eyes had been troubling me. I played the part of a cigarette girl. Then I did extras a while and then one day I was sent for on the Sennett lot. Honestly, it was funny. I'm mighty lucky. That's all it ever is really - luck. They hardly let me get on the lot before they hired me. I can't understand it. I've been there ever since." (*Photoplay* Fall 1921)

Reportedly starting at Sennett doing extra work around 1915, by 1917 she began having featured roles in comedies such as *A Dog Catcher's Love* and *Whose Baby?*, where she was on contract for twelve dollars a week and learned comedy by doing and by the people she was working with. In 1921 comic Charlie Murray told a *Picture–Play Magazine* reporter:

Phyllis Haver (left) and her good friend Marie Prevost during their Sennett Bathing Girl days. Author's collection.

"I train 'em all," he said proudly. "Whenever they bring in a new chick to be a principal, they turn her over to Uncle Charlie. There was Mabel first, and then Mary Thurman, and after she graduated into five reels I took little Phyllis Haver under my wing. Now she's got her own company here, so I'm showing Harriet how to act."

Essentially starting as visual adornment, by the time of *His Wife's Friend* (1918) and *Never Too Old* (1919) she had worked her way up to secondary roles. In 1919 she became one of the leads with billing for titles such as *Among Those Present, Salome vs. Shenandoah,* and *His Last False Step* (all 1919). In *Hearts and Flowers* (1919) Phyllis has the third lead with Ford Sterling and Louise Fazenda and plays a prune grower's daughter who is smitten with schmaltzy orchestra leader Sterling. When Sterling is led to believe that goofy flower girl Louise Fazenda is heir to a $2,000,000,000 estate, he makes a play for her and leaves Phyllis flat. To get back at him Phyllis dresses as a man and flirts with Louise to thwart the relationship with Sterling. In the meantime Phyllis' former suitor, Billy Armstrong is baffled by the man (Phyllis in drag) going in and out of her room. When the day comes for Sterling to marry Louise her three ex-convict brothers (Edgar Kennedy, Bert Roach, and Kalla Pasha) show up to look him over, and just before the knot is tied Phyllis and Billy Armstrong drop by and report that Louise is not an heiress. Trying to get away Sterling is chased by the tough brothers, who eventually pick him up and throw him from room to room as they play baseball with him as the ball. Eventually they bring him back to marry Louise, but she's already married miniature suitor Jack Ackroyd. When the brothers make fun of him for his puny size he beats them up for the happy ending. *Hearts and Flowers* is a rare, but excellent example, of one of Sennett's comedies for Paramount release, and while still displaying her ample physical charms Phyllis has the opportunity to show off her acting and comedy talents.

Besides her work in shorts she also had roles in a number of Sennett features such as *Married Life* (1920) *Love, Honor and Behave* (1920) *A Small Town Idol,* and *Home Talent* (both 1921). 1921 saw her frequently playing alongside Ben Turpin as his love interest in titles such as *Love's Outcast, Love and Doughnuts, Bright Eyes* and *Step Forward*. It has been rumored that in real life she was Mack Sennett's love interest at this time and was being groomed to star in her own feature productions:

Phyllis Haver to Head Own Company as Star. Phyllis Haver, has been promoted by Mack Sennett and will henceforth be seen at the head of her own company as the star in a series of full length comedy drama productions to be published through First National. Her first starring vehicle, not as yet given a title, will be ready for production within a short time. (*Exhibitor's Herald*, September 30, 1922)

Phyllis' feature project was to be from a story by Sennett himself titled *Millie of the Movies*, and in early 1923 it was announced that Ralph Graves was hired to be her leading man in what was now titled *The Extra Girl*. The director attached to the project was William A Seiter, but by April 1923 it was reported that Phyllis had parted company with the Sennett organization altogether. At first Winifred Bryson was announced as the new lead but it was eventually done by Mabel Normand with direction from F. Richard Jones.

Whatever the reason for her split with Sennett, Phyllis' career was on the upswing. A big break for her was an important role in Maurice Tourneur's prestigious production *The Christian* (1923). Sadly the film is lost today but Phyllis gathered excellent notices:

Charlie Murray assists Phyllis Haver, with kibitzing by Heinie Conklin, in a Mack Sennett version of Salome in *Salome Vs Shenandoah* (1919) Courtesy of Robert Arkus.

> The outstanding bit, and a surprise for those who recognize the Sennett bathing girl, is the playing of Phyllis Haver. She does a genuinely fine piece of dramatic portrayal in the role of an unwed mother who kisses her baby goodbye and gives it into the care of the orphanage before she dies. Miss Haver registers a real "choke in the throat" in this scene. (*The Film Daily*, January 28, 1923).

The Christian was a turning point in her career that the trade magazines were still talking about a few years later:

> It came one day. Some girls might not have recognized it as "My Chance" Phyllis did. It was just what she had been waiting for. A real acting part. Not

a heroine, not even a lead. But a role you could get into. The wronged girl in the "The Christian" – Pathetic, shabby, pitiful. Great drama possibilities – yes. Hardly the part you'd pick for a famous beauty about to graduate. But Phyllis grabbed it. And played it - and wow! She went over. She bridged the gap from beauty to actress in one graceful leap. (*Motion Picture Classic*, Fall 1928)

She was now off and running in dramatic and comedic features. Between 1923 and 1929 she did a whopping forty six features with co-stars such as William S. Hart, Colleen Moore, John Gilbert, Norma Shearer, Milton Sills, Tom Mix, John Barrymore, George O'Brien, Harrison Forde, Emil Jannings, Lon Chaney, and her old pal Marie Prevost. Highlights include *The Perfect Flapper, The Snob, So Big* (all 1924), *Up in Mabel's Room, Don Juan, Fig Leaves, Three Bad Men,* and *What Price Glory?* (all 1926). Another dramatic feather in her hat was her performance of the thieving adventuress Mayme who lures Emil Jannings away from his happy family in *The Way of All Flesh* (1927). Her solid and steady work led to a starring contract:

> **Phyllis Haver Signs Three-Year Contract**. Phyllis Haver this week joined the group of individuals who have signed Metropolitan contracts the past fortnight or so when she affixed her signature to an agreement with Metropolitan whereby she will act before that studio's cameras for three years more. Since signing with Metropolitan a year ago, Miss Haver was cast in "The Nervous Wreck," "Up in Mabel's Room," "Don Juan, " "What Price Glory," No Control, " and " The Little Adventuress." She is now supporting Emil Jannings in "The Way of All Flesh" the other recent signers of Metropolitan contracts are Marie Prevost, Franklyn Pangborn, and E. Mason Hopper (*Motion Picture News*, Winter 1927)

The Metropolitan Company was Cecil B. DeMille's (DeMille – Metropolitan Pictures) which released their films through Producers Distributing Corporation (PDC) and later Pathé. Phyllis' early Metropolitan Pictures included *No Control, The Little Adventuress, The Rejuvenation of Aunt Mary,* and *The Fighting Eagles* (all 1927) which led up to her major starring feature *Chicago* (1927). In this first film version of the Broadway play, written by Maurine Dallas Watkins, Phyllis plays goldigger Roxie Hart who strings along her patsy husband, murders her lover, and ends up in a sensational three-ring trial organized by flamboyant lawyer Billy Flynn. As the scheming and conniving Roxie, Haver gives perhaps her best performance, and has great support from Eugene Pallette, Julia Faye, Victor Varconi, and Robert Edeson. Although credited to Frank Urson the picture was supervised and mostly directed by DeMille, and while for many years was considered lost, a print was found in his private collection and after restoration by UCLA became available in 2006.

After *Chicago* she continued her starring features for DeMille such as *Tenth Avenue* and *Sal of Singapore* (both 1928), plus had a loan-out to D. W. Griffith as the playgirl seductress in *The Battle of the Sexes* (1928). *The Shady Lady* (1928) and *The Office Scandal* (1929) were silent with talking sequences so she was making the transition to sound films, but *Thunder* (1929) with Lon Chaney was her last picture. In April 1929 she married millionaire William Seeman and retired from the screen. In November 1931 she told a New York newspaper:

> "I've never regretted my decision," she said today, entrancingly beautiful in a gown of black silk. "I'm so happy that I wouldn't consider going back. They cabled me all the way from Germany to play opposite Emil Jannings in "The Blue Angel." I refused. Marlene Dietrich later took the role and became famous. I've turned down stage offers, too, because the work would take me away from my husband."

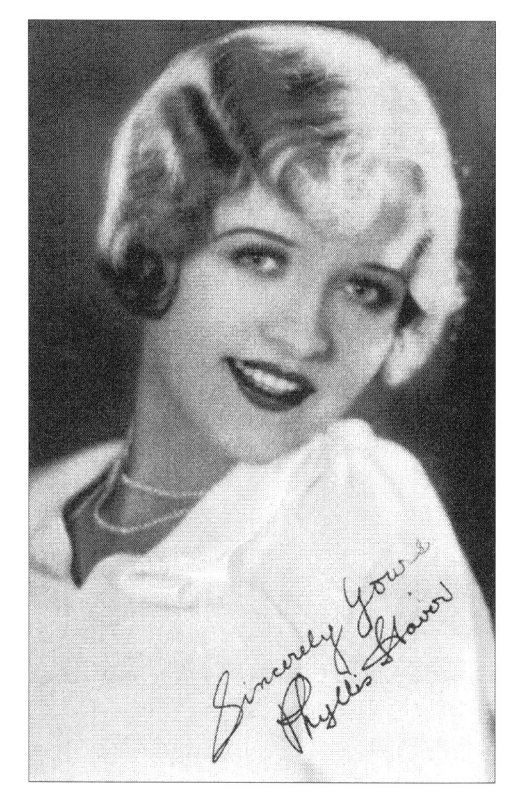

A 1920s movie star portrait of Phyllis Haver. Author's collection.

It seems like her career would have continued to develop in interesting ways if she hadn't walked away from it for marriage. Sadly after sixteen years she and Seeman divorced in 1945. Following the divorce she settled in Sharon, Connecticut and lived alone for the next fifteen years. She made a brief re-appearance in the public eye to honor Mack Sennett on *This Is Your Life* in 1954. Sennett's death on November 5, 1960 was said to have depressed her. Mrs. Samuel Graham, her housekeeper-companion, told *The New York Journal American*:

> "She never knew that Mr. Sennett was living in extreme poverty during the last year," Mrs. Graham said "She read about in the obituaries and was shocked."

Two weeks later she joined her old boss when she committed suicide by an overdose of barbiturates. Still beautiful and wealthy, she had outlived friends like Marie Prevost and many others she had worked with at the Sennett Studio when she ended her life at age sixty-one on November 19, 1960.

One bathing girl that particularly made good and became a talented but unjustly overlooked comedienne was Thelma Hill. Born Thelma Hillerman in Emporia, Kansas, her birthdate is given as 1906, the date on her death certificate, but it appears that she was born a couple of years earlier. A newspaper notice for her parents June 1905 divorce lists her as an infant, and the 1920 census gives her age as seventeen. Thelma grew up in Azusa, California, about twenty five miles from Los Angeles. According to the publicity story her mother had a small café in Azusa. Fatty Arbuckle and his crew, shooting location scenes, were eating there when the teenaged Thelma spilled soup on the large comic while serving the food. This attention led to her ending up with a screen test and becoming a Mack Sennett girl, one of the youngest. She got her first film experience in comedies such as *Up in Alf's Place* (1919) and *Great Scott* (1920). With her dark hair, big eyes, and spunky personality it was not long before she began getting noticed. In addition to her work for Sennett, she was part of the bathing crew and had little bits in some of the independent Chester Conklin Comedies made by Special Pictures such as *Home Rule, The Soft Boiled Yegg,* and *His Model Day* (all 1920).

The early 1920s saw Thelma carrying on as visual adornment in the Sennett shorts, plus doubling for Mabel Normand in her studio features like *Molly O'* (1921), *Suzanna,* and *The Extra Girl* (both 1923). Nicknamed "Pee Wee" (she was only five foot tall), she continued making an impression. After doing some publicity photos in a Mah Jongg themed bathing suit, and wearing it in *Super-Hooper-Dyne-Lizzies* (1925) she became known as "The Mah Jongg Bathing Girl". Swim suit appearances in shorts such as *Picking Peaches, The Half-Back of Notre Dame, The Hollywood Kid, Yukon Jake,* and *His New Mamma* (all 1924) ultimately led to a

The beautiful and funny Thelma Hill.
Courtesy of Cole Johnson.

move into more solid character bits. Occasional loan-outs such as playing Neely Edwards' leading lady in *So This is Paris?* (1926) and the surviving *The Cat's Whiskers* (1925) led her to be showcased by Sennett in specialty turns, such as a funny appearance in *Hooked at the Altar*, and a terrific spoof Apache dance in *A Yankee Doodle Duke* (both 1926).

After a major role as Vernon Dent's wife in *Hoboken to Hollywood* (1926) she played the first of her "Sennett nerdy girl" characters in *A Prodigal Bridegroom* (1926). With horn-rimmed glasses, heavy eyebrows, and frumpy clothes, Thelma was the girl that Ben Turpin would leave for Madeline Hurlock or Ruth Taylor, but he'd soon regret that decision as Thelma would get a make-over and emerge as her cute self. Also portraying this character in *Crazy to Act* and *The Pride of Pikeville* (both 1927), Thelma got the opportunity to prove that she was a true physical clown as she suffered slapstick indignities like getting dunked in mud holes and losing her skirts as she mooned over Turpin.

1927 to 1929 was the peak of her career as she branched out from the Sennett Studio to the larger world of silent comedy. She headlined with Lorraine Eason in the FBO series *The Wisecrackers* and *The Beauty Parlor*, where shorts such as *Turkish Howls, Cry and Get It, Artist's Brawls,* and *Survival of the Fattest* (all 1927) had them playing shop girl telephone operators with the team of Al Cooke and Kit Guard as their comic support. Fox comedies tapped her for *Hold Your Hat* and *Love is Blonde* (both 1928), plus she made two memorable appearances on the Hal Roach lot. In *Dumb Daddies* (1928) Max Davidson thinks she's a vamp who has her hooks into his son Spec O'Donnell, but it turns out the old man's just watching them rehearse a play. Her most frequently seen performance today is in Laurel and Hardy's *Two Tars* (1928). Thelma and Ruby Blaine play two good-time girls that sailors Stan and Ollie meet and take for an afternoon joy ride, which in usual Hal Roach fashion turns into a reciprocal violence nightmare. At the same time she won roles in features like *Hearts of Men, Crooks Can't Win, The Chorus Kid,* and *The Play Girl* (all 1928). The most easily seen today is *The Fair Co-ed* (1927), in which she is Marion Davies' sidekick.

The climax of the silent film phase of her career saw her starring in FBO's *Toots and Casper* series. Produced by Larry Darmour and starring little Bud Duncan, the shorts were based on the popular comic strip by Jimmy Murphy which chronicled the misadventures of wife Toots, henpecked hubby Casper, their baby buttercup, and family dog Spareribs. The strip was basically a forerunner of the *Blondie* variety of domestic comedy strips, with Casper always getting the worst of any situation. Thelma wore a blonde wig to look like her comic strip counterpart, and Bud Duncan was so tiny that the five-foot Thelma towers over him, making her look long and leggy. Starting in 1928 twelve shorts were made, with the early ones written and directed by St. Elmo Boyce, Thelma's fiancée. Sadly, Boyce committed suicide, and it was reported that Thelma began having problems with drinking and depression. Available Toots and Casper shorts include *Fooling Casper, What a Wife, Family Meal Ticket, Casper's Week End* (all 1928) *Smile, Buttercup, Smile* and *Spareribs Reforms* (both 1929).

The arrival of sound stalled Thelma's rising career. In contrast to her spritely and charming silent persona she's awkward and unfocused in the new medium. Her bathing girl background didn't prepare her for the acting demands of sound, although when signed to a two-year contract by Sennett for his talking output she took an optimistic stance for the press:

> "I am all enthused what the next two years may bring me," exclaimed the pretty brunette. "I was scared to death the first time I faced the microphone, but I have made three talkies now and feel just as much at home as I did when we had only cameras to face. I am taking dancing lessons now too and if I ever get sufficient courage I am going to take singing lessons as I think both will be necessary with sound films now in vogue.

Thelma Hill (right) as Marion Davies' sidekick in
The Fair Co-Ed (1927). Courtesy of Bruce Calvert.

Along with Harry Gribbon and Andy Clyde, Thelma was a mainstay in the Sennett studios' 1929 talkies like *The Old Barn, Broadway Blues, The Big Palooka,* and *The Lunkhead,* but before the end of the year she was replaced by the vivacious Marjorie Beebe. Her sound performances did improve with experience. She has some of her old spontaneity and pep back as the female lead in the Pathé short *Two Plus Fours* (1930), not to mention a nice cameo in Frank Capra's *Miracle Woman* (1931) and a very funny bit in the 1934 Hal Roach short *Mixed Nuts* as one of the chorus girls that the government allots money for retraining at a stuffy girls' school. When entomologist Dougie Wakefield's Arabian sand fleas get loose they naturally pick Thelma for their new home. Her reactions to the bugs gives her a specialty routine that's part dance and part seizure. Although brief, it's the funniest moments in the film and harks back to her Sennett days, reconfirming what an excellent physical clown she was.

After 1930 her film appearances had become very sporadic and finally ended in 1934. She married Johnny Sinclair, a comic, stuntman, and a gag man for W.C. Fields. Sinclair was known as a drinker and barroom brawler. He was involved in a fracas that resulted in the death of boxer Eddie Diggins, and got comic Lloyd Hamilton banned from the screen, not to mention putting a crimp in Sinclair's career. Thelma's last years were plagued by alcoholism. Off the screen for four years, she was in a sanitarium and died in 1938, only in her early thirties.

Perhaps the best-remembered Sennett girls today are Sybil Seely and Virginia Fox – the two that became leading ladies to Buster Keaton in his popular series of two-reelers. It seems likely that Buster's director, Eddie Cline, suggested both girls, as he had previously worked with them at Sennett. Sybil Seely's real name was Sibye Trevilla and she was born in 1902 in Los Angeles to a vaudeville family that had a swimming act known as The Three Trevilla Brothers, which consisted of her brothers, Jack, Guy and Ford, in addition to their mascot, Winks, billed as "the Seal with the Human Brain." Considering this family background it seems appropriate that she entered films as a bathing girl. Starting in the late teens Sybil was seen briefly in Sennett shorts such as *Hearts and Flowers, Salome vs. Shenandoah* (both 1919), *By Golly* (1920), in addition to the features *Down on the Farm, Married Life*, and *Love, Honor and Behave*." (all 1920)

Joining Buster Keaton's company in 1920 was a step up for the actress as she was now a leading lady with plenty of screen time. *One Week* (1920) was her first appearance with the comedian, and with her charming personality, pert approach to comedy, and striking natural beauty she's the perfect love interest for the deadpan Buster. Sadly, she only appeared in four more shorts with Keaton – *Convict 13, The Scarecrow* (both 1920) *The Boat* (1921), and *The Frozen North* (1922) – before moving on to Fox Comedies where she supported Charles Dorety in *Please Be Careful* (1922) and Clyde Cook in *The Eskimo* (1922). Retiring from the screen after marrying screenwriter Jules Furthman, she remained in Hollywood until her death at eighty-two in 1984.

Virginia Fox was Buster's most frequent vis-a-vis, appearing in nine of his nineteen shorts. Born in Charleston, West Virginia in 1903, Sennett reportedly discovered her when she visited the studio while on a break from boarding school. She began appearing in 1919 shorts such as *Why Beaches are Popular,* and *Hearts and Flowers,* and soon worked her way up to small roles in *Fresh from the City, Great Scott,* and *Fickle Fancy* (all 1920) Also appearing in the features *Down on the Farm, Married Life,* and *Love, Honor and Behave* (all 1920), she was an ingénue in the Fox comedies *Monkey Business* (1920) *The Golfer,* and *His Meal Ticket* (both 1921) where she supported Bobby Dunn, Big Joe Roberts, Ethel Teare, and Jimmy Savo.

A post-Keaton Sybil Seely in the Fox Comedy *Please Be Careful* (1922) with Charles Dorety (center) and James Finlayson (right). Courtesy of Sam Gill.

Virginia Fox Engaged for Keaton Comics. Virginia Fox, the dainty little comedy queen whose dimples have been indelibly impressed upon the minds of motion picture fans throughout the country, hereafter will be seen in Metro Keaton comedies.

For Buster Keaton the merry comedian who never smiles, has selected her from a long list of candidates for honors as his new leading woman. (*Motion Picture News*, September 1920)

Her first role with Keaton was as his Hogan's Alley Juliet in *Neighbors* (1920), and she played his mostly unobtainable object of affection in *The Haunted House, Hard Luck, The Goat, The Playhouse* (all 1921), *The Paleface, Cops, The Blacksmith, The Electric House* (all 1922), and *The Love Nest* (1923). After working with Buster she starred in the Robertson-Cole Pictures Corp. feature *Itching Palms* (1923), a haunted house comedy that had been originally titled *Now You See It,* but when she married the young writer Darryl F. Zanuck in 1924 she left the screen to raise a family. Her last known appearance was a cameo in the Warner's feature *The Caveman* (1924) written by her husband, and she spent the rest of her life as Hollywood royalty when Zanuck became the head of 20th Century Fox. Her son Richard became a prolific and well known producer, and Virginia Fox passed away at eighty in 1982.

Virginia Fox and Big Joe Roberts check out Bobby Dunn's form in *The Golfer* (1921). Courtesy of Beth Goffe.

One of the more unusual Sennett girls was Madeline Hurlock, who was "the dark lady of the Slapsticks" – a cool, femme fatale that was always ready to pull a scam or lead some unsuspecting comic astray. Stunning and statuesque, Ms. Hurlock was born in Federalsburg, Maryland, and after attending Neff College in Philadelphia she joined the stock company at the city's Little Theatre. At this point her chronology is vague, but according to the August 25, 1917 *Moving Picture World* she had been on the West Coast working for Universal:

> **Madeline Hurlock Heroine in Real Romance**. Baltimore MD. – Maryland is quite a place for romance and Baltimore is the big center, so probably that is the reason why Madeline Hurlock, the charming star of the Universal Company, probably was obliged to race all the way here from Los Angeles to marry. You see she met Sgt. Jack McGovern, who is now acting as quartermaster's sergeant

at Camp Meade, when he was in California last summer with the Thirteenth U. S. Cavalry. It was a great love match from the very beginning. So very recently valiant Sgt. McGovern got information that he is likely to be sent to France, so he wired for Miss Hurlock, and she arrived in Baltimore on Saturday night. She was met by Sgt. McGovern and some friends, and they immediately went to Ellicott City and were married.

Although the item refers to her as "charming star of the Universal Company" she may have been in the background stock company as there are no known Universal titles for her. After the marriage her next step appears to be a move to New York where she became a busy chorus girl. In 1919 and 1920 she appeared in the chorus of the Broadway musical *The Rose of China*, and at the same time in the after-theatre revue *Midnight Whirl* that was performed on the Century Theatre's roof. It's said that it was the Century roof appearances that led her back to Hollywood. She was working at Paramount doing extra work on features like *The Cheat* (1923), and not really getting anywhere when Gloria Swanson noticed her on the set and called attention to her beauty. This led to larger bits and when Sennett Studio had trouble finding a vamp for a Ben Turpin comedy they called the Lasky Casting office for suggestions and Madeline ended up signed with the "King of Comedy."

Where's My Wandering Boy this Evening? (1923), a Ben Turpin film, was her Sennett debut. As the big city vamp that tempts the cock-eyed comic Madeline held her own with comedy veterans like Dot Farley, James Finlayson, and Billy Armstrong. The film spawned the sequel *Pitfalls of the Big City* (1923), and Madeline was off and running using her charms on Turpin, Billy Bevan, and Harry Langdon in slapstick opuses like *The Dare Devil*, *Inbad the Sailor* (both 1923), *The Half Back of Notre Dame*, and *The Cat's Meow* (both 1924). Madeline's performing style in contrast to most of the Sennett performers was low-key and restrained-which caused Sennett concern on what to do with her:

> I tried her out and most of us were puzzled at first because we put her in one thing and another and she didn't seem to do anything. Just stood around as far as I could see. And we thought she was a total loss, or I did. But after a while we began to hear from exhibitors. They showed interest in her - liked her personality - asked who she was. Then I began to understand that there was something about the way she did stand around, perhaps, that was interesting to the public – her poise. So I began to surround her with the kind of material that would bring her out. And she herself, the more she becomes used to this work, is developing characteristics and stunts which are certain to make her into a sure-fire personality if she keeps on. (*Photoplay*, August 1928)

Over the next few years she brought her smolder and sex appeal to about four dozen shorts, and even kept her cool with the Sennett Lions in *Scarem Much* (1924), *The Lion's*

Whiskers (1925) and *Circus Today* (1926). Years later, talking about her career in a letter to film historian Steve Rydzewski, Madeline said:

The regal Madeline Hurlock and Numa in 1925's *The Lion's Whiskers*.
Courtesy of Cole Johnson.

My directors were mostly Del Lord and Eddie Cline. I liked both of them. Most of my films were made with Turpin. I didn't like him at first, thinking him what used to be called "fresh." As I got to know him, I found him friendly and amusing. He did not take himself seriously, nor did I take myself so. Harry Langdon was a worrier. Andy Clyde was a good actor, and a gentle, lovable man. By the way Frank Capra was at the studio part of the time I was there. He wasn't a director then, but what was known as a gagman.

Later the studio gave Madeline an occasional lead and began varying her character a bit, giving her working-girl roles in *Flirty Four-Flushers* (1926) and *Catalina, Here I Come* (1927). She also had a loan out to the Hal Roach Studio and played with Laurel and Hardy in *Duck Soup* (1927), and turned up in the features *Don Juan's Three Nights* (1926) and *The Best of Friends* (1928). When sound came in Madeline retired. She told Steve Rydzewski:

I was fed-up with films and Hollywood and could hardly wait to get back to New York. When I left the Sennett Studio my weekly salary was $750. Had I stayed on, it would have been $1000. In 1928, I went to London, Paris, Italy, and Switzerland – my first trip abroad.

In 1930 she married well-known playwright Marc Connelly, author of *Merton of the Movies* and *The Green Pastures*, but they divorced and she then married Pulitzer Prize winning author Robert E. Sherwood. Among other things Sherwood wrote the plays *The Petrified Forrest*, *Idiot's Delight* and *Abe Lincoln in Illinois*, in addition to the screenplay for *The Best Years of Our Lives* (1946) for which he won an Oscar. After Sherwood's death in 1955 Madeline lived in New York until she passed away at eighty-nine in 1989.

Actresses that played love interests generally weren't funny. They were charming and attractive, but their function was to be straight women for the male comics. They were the motivation for the plots of the films, particularly the feature-length comedies, where the need to impress the girl and obtain their favor was the catalyst that moved events along. The big three of the silent comedy love interests, who are best known today because they worked with the still popular Charlie Chaplin and Harold Lloyd, are Edna Purviance, Mildred Davis, and Jobyna Ralston.

For decades the most familiar of this trio has been Edna Purviance, particularly thanks to the amazing longevity of Chaplin's twelve Mutual two-reelers, which have been in almost constant theatrical showings, on television, and in the home video market, ever since their original release. Born in Paradise Valley, Nevada in 1896, as a youngster Edna moved to Lovelock, Nevada. After graduating from high school she went to San Francisco where her older sister Bessie lived, and worked in an office while she took business courses. The trajectory of her life was changed dramatically by a chance meeting:

As usual Edna Purviance is the cool counterpoint to Charlie Chaplin' bravura in *A Woman* (1915). Author's collection.

You see, I had taken stenography with my high school course in Nevada, and when we moved to California I finished a complete business course and seriously studied the piano. Vaguely, I imagined that someday I might be a big musician, and then one evening I accidently met Mr. Chaplin thru a mutual friend. Mr. Chaplin asked me if I would like to act in pictures with him. I laughed at the idea, but agreed to try it. I never thought I would ever go thru with another after that first picture. I want to tell you that I suffered untold agonies. Eyes seemed to be everywhere. I was simply frightened to death. But Mr. Chaplin had unlimited patience in directing me and teaching me. I learnt everything I know from him. (*Motion Picture Life*, 1918)

Although, later publicity pieces said she attended Vassar College in the east, and starred in amateur theatricals, Edna's career got its start because she was in the right place at the right time. Chaplin had just arrived in California from a brief stay in Chicago where he made his initial film, *His New Job* (1915), for the Essanay Company. Chaplin brought Ben Turpin and Leo White with him from Chicago, but he needed to assemble a company. Most important, he needed to find a leading lady. Edna's first appearance was in *A Night Out* (1915) portraying a woman that Charlie spots while he's out on a spree and follows home only to find she's the wife of the burly head waiter that he's had a run in with earlier in the evening. As she got more relaxed and comfortable before the camera Edna's screen time increased and her presence became an important catalyst for the development and refinement of Chaplin's tramp persona.

Having no previous acting experience Edna was a natural with a very modern, non-actorly style. Where the women at Keystone had been a harder edged and combative group - always ready to return a kick or trade slaps - Edna's screen persona was warm, supportive and had a natural refinement. She brought the element of romance to the films which deepened the tramp's character and gave the films broader appeal. She and Chaplin developed a real-life romantic relationship and their intimacy transferred to the screen. Chaplin was even able to begin exploring pathos in films such as *The Tramp* and *The Bank* (1915), something that would not have been possible without the emotional grounding from Edna's screen presence.

Quickly becoming a very important part of Chaplin's company (and life) she continued on with him as he moved up the Hollywood ladder:

When Mr. Chaplin signed his $670,000 contract with the Mutual Film Corporation, he took most of his company with him, and in March 1916 we began work here at the Mutual Studios in Los Angeles. Our first picture was "The Floorwalker," followed by "The Fireman." The one you saw us working on just now going to be released under the title of "The Vagabond." I consider it the best we have done so far for the Mutual. (Unidentified Clipping)

In the Mutual series Edna played the daughter of authority figures (*The Fireman, The Pawnshop,* 1916) wealthy or society girls (*The Count, The Rink,* 1916, *The Cure* and

The Adventurer, 1917), or put upon young girls (*The Vagabond, Behind the Screen*, 1916) needing Charlie's help. Her outstanding role in the series is her poor immigrant girl in *The Immigrant* (1917). In a touching and nuanced performance Edna is the heart of the film, and is the reason we really care about Charlie's run-ins with surly waiter Eric Campbell. By this time she was completely in sync with Chaplin's working methods and described them in 1919 to *Motion Picture Classics*.

Charlie Chaplin gives Edna Purviance an open-air shampoo in *The Vagabond* (1916).

He writes and directs his own pictures and I tell you, I have to be wide awake and on the alert to keep pace with him, for I never know at what instant he will think up some big scene and, when he is in the mood, he likes to work quickly and steadily. It is always interesting to watch him develop the action, for he insists that there must be a cause leading up to the fights, the runaways or whatever it is. He acts out our parts for us, and I assure you he can even play my role better than I can, for he is a natural imitator.

1918 saw Chaplin moving to another company, First National Pictures, and building his own studio. Edna remained important in his films – playing the awkward bar singer in *A Dog's Life* (1918), *Shoulder Arm*'s down trodden French girl (1918), and her most dramatically challenging role, the unwed mother of Jackie Coogan in *The Kid* (1921). As always she played her characters directly and simply, but after *The Kid* her roles were less important and more of a plot ingredient. By that time her relationship with Chaplin had cooled and he had married Mildred Harris.

She was getting older, or as Rollie Totheroh, Chaplin's cameraman, later explained it:

By this time Edna was getting pretty heavy but her little face still had charm in it. And she got to drinking pretty heavy. One day we were looking at rushes and Charlie could see it.

Having formed United Artists in 1919 along with Mary Pickford, Douglas Fairbanks and D.W. Griffith, Chaplin wasn't free to release through them until he finished his First National contract with *The Pilgrim* in 1922. Once free he decided his first film for U.A. would be a starring picture for Edna. *A Woman of Paris* (1923) was suggested to Chaplin by stories told to him by Peggy Hopkins Joyce the first official "gold digger."

Edna plays Marie St. Clair a young woman in a small French village who is in love with equally young painter Jean. Since their parents look down on their relationship the pair plan to elope to Paris, but while Marie is waiting for Jean at the train station he is delayed when his father is taken ill, so Marie goes to Paris on her own. The film jumps to Paris a year later when Marie is now the mistress of the wealthy Pierre Revel. Used to her life of luxury, but unhappy with the lack of emotional commitment from Revel, she meets Jean again when he has moved to Paris to pursue his painting. Jean wants them to start over again. He wants her to give up her Parisienne life and marry him. Marie is not sure what she truly wants, and in the meantime Jean's mother convinces him not to marry Marie. Hurt, Marie flaunts her life with Revel in Jean's face, and after a confrontation at a posh restaurant, he goes into the lobby and shoots himself. When Jean's body is brought home his mother takes the gun and sets out to kill Marie but when she finds her prostrate with grief over Jean's death she forgives her. The coda of the film has Marie and Jean's mother back in the country running a home for orphan children. The last scene has Marie and Pierre Revel pass on the country road without knowing it.

Very sophisticated and adult for 1923, *A Woman of Paris* was not a popular hit, but was a very influential film to directors such as Ernst Lubitsch, Mal St. Clair, and Monte Bell. Edna gives a very mature and skillful performance, but the film is stolen by Adolphe Menjou as Pierre Revel, whose career got the boost that Chaplin had hoped to give to Edna.

A Woman of Paris was released in October 1923 but a few months later, on New Year's Day 1924, Edna was involved in an incident that could have come from the film itself. She was a guest at the apartment of oil millionaire Courtland Dines, and later in the day they were joined by Mabel Normand. When Mabel's chauffeur arrived a few hours later to pick her up, an altercation between Dines and the chauffeur occurred leading to the driver shooting the playboy with a revolver that belonged to Mabel. Dines wasn't killed, but the press had a field day with the story, and although the events were never fully explained the result was terrible publicity for Edna, and the banning of *A Woman of Paris* by a number of theatres.

Chaplin moved on to other leading ladies like Lita Gray, Georgia Hale, and Myrna

Kennedy for his films *The Gold Rush* (1925) and *The Circus* (1928) but he again made an attempt to jump start a dramatic film career for Edna. Early on in the shooting of *The Circus* in 1926 Chaplin produced the feature *A Woman of the Sea* (working title *Sea Gulls*). Having been enthusiastic over Josef von Sternberg's independent feature *The Salvation Hunters* (1925), Chaplin hired Sternberg to write and direct this picture for Edna. Years later in his 1965 autobiography, *Fun in a Chinese Laundry*, Sternberg had this to say:

> The film was to revolve around Edna Purviance, a former star of his, with whom, among notable films, he had made the impressive Woman of Paris. She was still charming, though she had not appeared in pictures for a number of years and had become unbelievably timid and unable to act even the simplest scenes without great difficulty. Aware of this Mr. Chaplin credited me with sufficient skill to overcome such handicaps, and in the completed film she actually seemed at ease.
>
> The tentative title of the film was The Sea-Gull (no relation to the Anton Chekov tragedy) and it was based on a story of mine about some fisherman on the California coast. When the filming had ended I showed it exactly once at one theatre, then titled A Woman of the Sea and that was the end of that. The film was probably returned to Mr. Chaplin's vaults and no one has ever seen it again.

Candid pose of Edna Purviance at the Chaplin Studio. Courtesy of The Museum of Modern Art.

No one knows the reason that Chaplin never released the picture, and although photos from the production survive, the film itself was ultimately destroyed in 1933 as part of a tax settlement for the Chaplins.

Edna remained on contract to Chaplin and got a weekly salary whether she worked or not. In 1926 she was loaned to the French company Rapid Films and left for Paris in December to begin shooting her last silent film. *Education of a Prince* (*La Reine Liska Silistre*) was directed by Henri Diamant-Berger and was about a young crown prince in Paris who is being schooled in the ways of the world by an older bon vivant. This has been arranged by his widowed mother Queen Liska of Silistria (Edna) as she feels his upbringing has been too strict and severe. Sacha, the young Prince, falls in love with a dancer, but due to trouble back in his country he has to say goodbye to her and returns to accept the crown and his duty to his country. Complications like an uprising ensue, but thanks to his Parisienne dancer the rebels are overthrown and all ends happily for the royal family. Long unavailable, the film played in France and England but wasn't released in America.

With the arrival of sound Edna retired from films. In 1938 she married a pilot, John P. Squire, who transported cargo during World War II, and the couple was happy until Squire's death from a sudden heart attack in 1945. 1946 saw her return to Hollywood where she was re-united with Chaplin and her old friends at the studio when Chaplin tested her for a role in his upcoming *Monsieur Verdoux* (1947). Although he ultimately decided that she didn't have the necessary European sophistication for the role, Chaplin restored her weekly salary and she remained on his payroll even after he left the United States. Her last years involved a long battle with throat cancer before she passed away at age sixty-three in 1958.

Another pretty blonde, not funny in herself, who became a screen icon for her work opposite Harold Lloyd was Mildred Davis. The small, petite Davis was born in Philadelphia in 1900 and was said to have been a descendant of the famous Quaker William Penn. When she was six the family moved to Tacoma, Washington, and after an early interest in dance:

**Mildred Davis and Harold Lloyd in 1922's *Dr. Jack*.
Author's collection.**

"I began as a movie fan when I was twelve," she said, with her little-girl smile. "I had the walls of my room just plastered with pictures of movie actresses, and I liked the ones who wore curls and ruffly dresses-like Mary Pickford and Viola Dana." (*Motion Picture Classic*, 1920)

When she was fifteen she decided to give movies a serious try:

"Of course, I met with many obstacles" (Mildred smiled at the memory), "but once I make up my mind I never let discouragement creep in, so I journeyed to Los Angeles and tho I had no stage experience and had never seen a motion picture camera, I hunted up a booking agent and applied for work. I suppose I expected to become a star at once and receive a thousand a week, but I was happy when they selected me from among several girls for the Mutual Comedies at thirty five a week." (*Motion Picture Magazine*, 1921)

After Mutual she worked in some Universal Bluebird productions, and had a role in the Bryant Washburn feature *Marriage a la Carte* (1916). Davis' pre-Lloyd movie making experience was more extensive than is usually noted. She worked for Pathé, Universal, and Metro – in shorts such as *What'll We Do with Uncle?* (1917) and *Bud's Recruit* (1918 – both written by King Vidor), and the features *Fighting Mad* (1917), *A Weaver of Dreams* (1918), and *All Wrong* (1919) with stars like Bryant Washburn and Viola Dana. On her parent's insistence she put her career on hold and returned to school. Bebe Daniels, who had been Harold Lloyd's regular leading lady for four years' worth of short comedies, decided to take an offer to appear in features for Cecil B. DeMille in early 1919.

Lloyd and producer Hal Roach had to find a replacement for Daniels, and Roach had noticed Mildred in one of her Pathé features with Bryant Washburn. Pathé was Roach's distributor as well and they were also keen on her appearing with Lloyd. Eventually Mildred was tracked down back at school and a contract with Roach was signed. But no sooner had she started working with Lloyd, making the two-reelers *From Hand to Mouth* (1919) and *His Royal Slyness* (1920), than he had the accident during a photo shoot with a live bomb that maimed his right hand and left him temporarily blinded. With his main star sidelined Hal Roach moved quickly and put Lloyd's second banana Snub Pollard into his own starring one-reelers, with Mildred as his leading lady.

In shorts such as *All at Sea, Call for Mr. Caveman, Giving the Bride Away, How Dry I Am, Looking for Trouble, The Floor Below* (all 1919), and *Red Hot Hottentots* (1920) Mildred played the usual comedy roles of beach bathing girl, damsel in distress, and nagging wife. Harold recovered in four and a half months so he and Mildred resumed in January 1920 on *Haunted Spooks*. After his return, Lloyd's popularity went through the roof, and shorts like *Get Out and Get Under, Number Please* (both 1920), *Among Those Present* and *Never Weaken* (both 1921) got more sophisticated and moved up to three reels. He was poised to move into features. To our modern eyes the character played by

Mildred in his films is an odd combination of woman and child, but for Harold she was an ideal, a goal to be obtained, which helped propel the plots when he made the jump to features with 1921's *A Sailor-Made Man*.

Pal gives Mildred Davis some tips on scene-stealing during the making of *Too Many Crooks* (1927). Courtesy of Cole Johnson.

Mildred starred opposite Lloyd in three more features, which included the classics *Grandma's Boy* (1922) and *Safety Last!* (1923). Following shooting *Safety Last!* her contract with Hal Roach expired, but instead of resigning she married Lloyd on February 10, 1923. She retired after their marriage as she was soon pregnant with their daughter Gloria, but before she had appeared in two features that were released later in the year. Principal Picture's *Temporary Marriage* was a society picture that starred her opposite Kenneth Harlan, and *Condemned* was a Grand Asher-released Ben Wilson Production, a comedy whose cast also included Carl Miller, Kate Price, George Cooper and Virginia Warwick.

Mildred was said to have wanted to return to the screen, but Harold wasn't totally on board with the idea. Other projects were floated around and in 1925 there was much talk about her starring in a film version of *Alice in Wonderland*, but nothing came of it. She did make one last film, the comedy romance *Too Many Crooks* (1927), for Paramount. The plot was about a society girl who is writing a crime novel, and hires a bunch of crooks to give her atmosphere and details for her book. Directed by Lloyd's regular director Fred Newmeyer, with support from Lloyd Hughes, George Bancroft, and El Brendel, it's hard to assess today as it's lost, but at the time the plot was criticized and some reviewers even took potshots at Mildred about her weight. After this she settled in as the mistress of Greenacres, the palatial estate of the Lloyd family, and died on August 18, 1969.

Wallace Howe and Jobyna Ralston try to put the breaks on Eddie Baker (left) and Paul Parrot (right) in *The Golf Bug* (1922). Courtesy of Robert Arkus.

Jobyna Ralston was Harold Lloyd's third long term leading lady. She combined the winsomeness and charm of Mildred Davis with the feistiness and dark hair of Bebe Daniels. Born Jobyna Raulston in South Pittsburgh, Tennessee in 1900, her unusual first name was in tribute to the actress Jobyna Howland, a favorite of her parents. Early on, her mother, a professional photographer, encouraged a dramatic career for her daughter, and in 1919 Jobyna made her film debut in a series of *Cuckoo Comedies*. Produced by Mark Dintenfass, who had made the propaganda feature *My Four Years in Germany* (1918), the two reelers starred comic Bobby Burns and were shot in Jacksonville, Florida. Burns had recently been part of the team of Pokes and Jabs for the Wizard, Vim and Jaxon companies, and for this, his first starring solo series, surviving films and photos show that he often appeared in blackface. Titles included *Starting Out in Life, All Out of Luck, Ball Bearing but Hard Running,* and *The Shimmy Gym* (all 1919) and it seems that every opportunity was taken to show Jobyna in negligees or skimpy athletic wear. Raulston was shortened to Ralston, and some writer must have been confused by her first name as it sometimes turned up in publicity items and ads as Juliana.

Not lighting any fires, the *Cuckoos* were short-lived, and Jobyna moved to New York. There she studied dance with famous choreographer Ned Wayburn. 1921 was a busy year – she made her stage debut in the chorus of the George M Cohan show *Two Little Girls in Blue* and appeared on screen again in another Florida-made series, this time for Reelcraft Comedies and again with Bobby Burns. Sun–Lite Comedies had the addition of Billy Quirk as the male lead, and were produced by Morris and Julius Schiller with titles like *Mother's Lamb, Eastern Breeze, The Brown Derby* and the surviving *Don't Marry* (all 1921). It's not definite whether or not the shorts with Jobyna and Burns were left over *Cuckoo* material or all new productions, but again the series was brief as Reelcraft went bankrupt in the fall of 1921.

Also that year she appeared as leading lady for the Marx Brothers in their fabled silent comedy short *Humor Risk*. Jobyna has been identified in surviving photographs from the film, made independently in New York, which appears to never have been released and is considered lost today. Produced by the Marxes and written by Jo Swerling, the short was directed by Richard Smith, a busy Hollywood comedy director, writer, player, and husband of comedienne Alice Howell. According to Yvonne Stevens, Smith's stepdaughter, the director encouraged Jobyna to go to California, which she did quickly enough to end up as an extra in Harold Lloyd's *A Sailor-Made Man* which was shot from August 26 to October 21, 1921. After more extra work she landed a featured role in the drama *The Call of Home* (1922), and from there became Max Linder's leading lady in *The Three Must-Get-Theres* (1922). Jobyna is sweet and sincere, in addition to being the only touch of calm in this wild spoof of Douglas Fairbanks' *The Three Musketeers* (1921).

Jobyna Ralston gracing her first of six films with Harold Lloyd in *Why Worry?* (1923). Author's collection.

Her role as the female lead in this comedy feature was good for her career, and she soon found a regular place on the Hal Roach lot as the love interest for comic James Parrott. Billed as "The Doodlewit of Screen Comedy," Parrott had a three-year run of one reelers for producer Roach. Born in 1898 he had entered the film business thanks to his older brother Charles Parrott (better known as Charley Chase), who had cast his brother in his directorial efforts at Fox, Bulls Eye, and Reelcraft. James also worked on his own as a day player at Roach, and in 1922 took the screen name of Paul Parrott and set off on his own series of madcap, anything-for-a-laugh shorts. Ethel Broadhurst was Parrott's first leading lady, but about six months in, starting with *Friday the 13th* (1922), Jobyna became a fixture in the series. Over the next year and a half in forty-plus one-reelers such as *Take Next Car, The Golf Bug, Shine 'Em Up* (all 1922), *Paste and Paper, Mr. Hyppo,* and *Tight Shoes* (all 1923) Jobyna added a dollop of feminine charm to the slapstick gag-fests. 1923 also saw her named a WAMPAS Baby Star, and when the reigning star of the Roach Studio needed a new leading lady, she was in the right place at the right time.

La Salle Film Co. ad featuring a dark-haired Madge Kirby.

Harold Lloyd and Mildred Davis were about to marry, and Mildred was planning to retire. Jobyna stepped into *Why Worry?* (1923) as the nurse for wealthy hypochondriac Harold and damsel in distress caught up in a South American revolution. Right from the start there was a chemistry between Jobyna and Lloyd which led to more believable romantic relationships than he had with either Bebe Daniels or Mildred Davis. At this point Lloyd was leaving the Roach organization and setting out with his own production company, and took Jobyna with him for more features together – *Girl Shy*, *Hot Water* (both 1924), *The Freshman* (1925), *For Heaven's Sake* (1926), and *The Kid Brother* (1927). After four years of working with Lloyd, Jobyna set out on her own.

She continued to work in comedies, such as *Sweet Daddies* (1926) opposite the team of Charlie Murray and George Sidney, and *Special Delivery* (1927) where she played her well-rehearsed Harold Lloyd heroine with comedian Eddie Cantor. She also did dramas such as *Lightning*, *A Racing Romeo* (both 1927), *The Big Hop*, and *The Power of the Press* (both 1928), although her biggest film was the World War I aviation saga *Wings* (1927). When sound arrived she made three final films – *The College Coquette* (1929), *Rough Waters* (1930), with Rin Tin Tin, and *Sheer Luck* (1931). She married her *Wings* co-star Richard Arlen, and after the birth of their son, she retired in 1933. She died after a long illness at the Motion Picture Country Hospital in 1967.

The most unsung of the leading ladies are Madge Kirby, Molly Malone and Charlotte Merriam. Madge Kirby was born in England, according to some sources as Madge Vincent – others say Madge Whitehead – but she got the last name Kirby from a first marriage. She came to the United States at age nine, and at fourteen went on the stage appearing with Richard Carle and Lew Fields, in addition to performing in vaudeville with Fred Walton. 1912 saw her begin her film career with the Biograph Company. During her four years there the dark-haired ingénue began in small roles in D. W. Griffith dramas such as *The Musketeer of Pig Alley*, *The Painted Lady* (both 1912) and *The Telephone Girl and the Lady* (1913), but spent much more time in the one-reel comedies directed by Del Henderson. By 1914 she had graduated to leads in comedies such as *Getting the Sack*, *All on Account of the Cheese*, (both 1914) and *In the Boarding House* (1915).

In *Bertha, the Buttonhole-Maker* (1914) she plays the title role in a spoof of ripe melodramas where the dastardly boss of the sweatshop conspires to get the pretty Madge alone in the factory. When she spurns his advances he even locks her in a room filling up with water. Luckily her over-age sweetheart and a group of misfit comedy cops somehow manage to rescue her in the nick of time. In *The Boob and the Magician* (1915) she is one of the two pretty assistants to a magician doing his act in a small-town theatre. All goes well until the magician gets a rube to come up from the audience to assist with a trick, and the hick ends up wreaking the act, even locking the magician in a tank full of water while he sits down to have lunch with the two female assistants. When Kirby left Biograph in the beginning of 1916 she became one of the most prolific leading ladies of the teens.

Her first move was to the ensemble of Vogue Comedies where she appeared with Rube Miller and Arthur Tavares in short comedies like *Germatic Love*, *Rube's Hotel Tangle*, *Jealousy a la Carte*, and *Love, Music and Cannon Balls* (all 1916), and then passed through Imp, Victor, American, Fox, and LaSalle Comedies playing in support of Carter

DeHaven, Billy Mason, and Jay Belasco. She was also support in the crime drama feature *The Flash of Fate* (1918) before landing at Vitagraph with Larry Semon. On the way to hooking up with Larry she'd begun regularly appearing in a blonde wig, in which she was always the fair-haired damsel in distress in Semon one-reel slapstick opuses such as *Stripes and Stumbles* and *Dunces and Dangers* (both 1918).

Bathing Beauties and Big Boobs (1918 - perhaps the most provocative and misleading title in silent comedy history) involves Larry and friends frolicking at the beach, whereas *Romans and Rascals* (1918) has minstrel Larry as a dead ringer for Emperor Caesar (also Larry) who takes his place and has a romance with Madge as Cleopatra. At the end of 1918 Semon made the move to two-reelers with Madge continuing as his love interest in *Huns and Hyphens, Bears and Bad Men, Frauds and Frenzies, Pluck and Plotters,* (all 1918) and *Traps and Tangles* (1919). Never having the opportunity to be funny on her own, she embodied the part of the heroine in peril, and fulfilled the same function when she joined Hank Mann's ensemble in 1919. Mann had made his name starring at Keystone, L-Ko, and Fox, and his new independent series was produced by Morris Schlank and had Madge, Vernon Dent, and little Jess Weldon in support. Starting with surviving one reelers such as *The Messenger, Hopping Bells, The Nickel Snatcher* (all 1919) and moving on to two reel shorts like *Naughty Nurses, A Gum Riot, Mystic Mush,* and *The Bill Poster* (all 1920) she's often the girl that the bashful Hank flirts with from afar, or the lady needing rescue.

Madge Kirby tries to talk some sense to Vernon Dent (left) and Hank Mann (right) in one of their Arrow Comedies. Courtesy of Robert Arkus.

Always warm and plucky, Kirby seems like she should have moved on to greater use in the 1920s, but in 1922 she left movies when she married Fresno District rancher Edward Frank Loescher. She passed away in Fresno at age seventy-two in 1956.

Brown-haired Molly Malone was born in Denver, Colorado. Her father was involved in mining and his work took the family to diverse places like Australia, South Africa and Mexico, in addition to all over the United States. She began working as a model and at age nineteen made her film debut. With no previous dramatic experience she began in small parts with the West Coast Vitagraph Company, and at first was an ingénue in serious fare at Lasky, Lubin and Universal such as *A Mountain Nymph* (1916) *The Pullman Mystery*, and the John Ford Westerns *Strait Shooting, A Marked Man, Bucking Broadway, The Scarlet Drop, Thieves Gold*, and *The Phantom Riders* (all 1917), where she was teamed with Harry Carey.

While still with Universal Malone began cutting her comedy teeth in shorts such as *To Be or Not to Be Married* (1917) with Eddie Lyons and Lee Moran, and *Adventurous Ambrose* (1918) opposite Mack Swain, and then in mid-1918 she became leading lady for "Smiling Bill" Parsons, in his two-reelers for the National Film Corporation such as *Widow's Might, Birds of a Feather*, and *Matching Billy* (all 1918). Parsons was an older, heavy-set, and very bald comic who specialized in a put-upon everyman character. He was usually paired with younger ladies like Malone, Teddy Sampson, and Billie Rhodes (whom he married) playing his spouse or sometimes girls that the henpecked Parsons would have a platonic flirtation with. Graduating from Parsons, Molly did a couple of shorts for Christie Comedies like *Sally's Blighted Career* (1919) and then joined Roscoe "Fatty" Arbuckle at the very end of his series of Comique Comedies for Paramount release.

Today her shorts with Arbuckle are her most frequently seen films. Little is known about *The Bank Clerk* (1919), as it and *A Desert Hero* (1919) are considered lost, but *Back Stage, The Hayseed* (both 1919), and *The Garage* (1920) are in wide circulation. In all three Malone plays the girl that Fatty takes a shine to – she's the fire chief's daughter in *The Garage*, the general store owner's daughter in *The Hayseed*, and in *Back*

Molly Malone supporting Roscoe Arbuckle in the two-reeler *A Desert Hero* (1919) Courtesy of Cole Johnson.

Stage she's the over-worked assistant of the bullying Strong Man. She had something of a look of a rag doll, with her delicate features, button eyes, and unruly hair, and she was a spirited and peppy love interest – not above slapping Harry McCoy when he gets too fresh or pushing Fatty into a water tub. Malone appears to have been very close to the rotund Arbuckle - not only was she the mascot of the Vernon Tigers, his baseball team, but she continued to work with Roscoe after his fortunes drastically changed in the 1920's.

After *The Garage* Arbuckle moved into features for Paramount, and Malone starred in her own brief series of comedies that Al Christie produced for the Southern California Producing Co. under the brand name Supreme Comedies. They were distributed by the Robertson – Cole Exchanges and titles included *Molly's Millions, Molly's Mumps, Her Doctor's Dilemma*, and *Come into the Kitchen* (all 1920). Sadly none of these are available or known to circulate so it's hard to say what her starring shorts were like. As the twenties began Malone was in demand for features. She was the female lead in comedies such as *It's a Great Life* (1920), and leading lady to Will Rogers and Jack Pickford in the Goldwyn-produced *Just Out of College* (1920), *An Unwilling Hero*, and *A Poor Relation* (both 1921). She was also in numerous westerns with Hoot Gibson, Guinn "Big Boy" Williams and Lefty Flynn, plus supported Johnny Hines in *Little Johnny Jones*, (1923), and Wesley Barry in *Battling Bunyon* (1924).

She returned to shorts in 1923 with her old pal Roscoe Arbuckle. Early that year, after his three infamous trials for manslaughter, Arbuckle began work on a short comedy starring himself entitled *Handy Andy* to try and recover his career. Molly was his leading lady but in February censorship czar Will Hays banned Roscoe from the screen and *Handy Andy* was scuttled – but not completely. A company, Reelcomedies, Inc., was soon set up for Arbuckle to anonymously direct shorts, and it appears that footage from the aborted *Handy Andy* was used for a new release starring circus clown Poodles Hanneford. Molly appeared

Molly Malone. Author's collection.

with Hanneford in this new version of *Handy Andy* that was released and reviewed under that title in October 1923. Perhaps to cover its origin by the end of October its title was changed to *Front*. In surviving photos Hanneford is dressed in Arbuckle's signature plaid shirt, high water pants, and derby, in addition to looking somewhat padded. The question is whether there were any long shots with Arbuckle kept from the original and used in the new release version, but until the actual film turns up it is just a question.

Malone continued with the unit, working with Hanneford in *The New Sheriff* and *The Bonehead* (both 1924) – both re-workings of the earlier Arbuckle comedies *The Sheriff* (1918) and *Back Stage* (1919). From here she became a regular at Christie Comedies. Starting with *Court Plaster* (1924) she would support Neal Burns, Bobby Vernon, Jimmie Adams, and goofy gob Billy Dooley in outings such as *Love Goofy*, *Don't Pinch* (both 1925) *Whoa, Emma!*, and *A Dippy Tar* (both 1926). She finished the decade mostly in independent western features such as *Bad Men's Bluff* (1926) and *The Golden Stallion* (1927) and bounced around for single shorts for Bray, Jack White, Christie, and Universal. Her last known film is 1929's *The Newlywed's Pest*, after which she appears to have left the screen. An undated clipping from the mid-1930s talks about her working in the photo department of MGM and hoping to become a portrait photographer, but her 1952 Variety obituary lists her passing away at age sixty-three under the name Mrs. Edith Greaves.

Our third over looked leading lady is Charlotte Merriam. Born in Fort Sheridan, Illinois in 1903 she was an army brat, as her father was Col Henry Clay Merriam, later commanding officer at Fort Preble in Maine. Her early desire was to be a concert pianist, and while she did continue her musical studies over the years she ended up in films in 1919 at age sixteen in some Pete Morrison western two-reelers for Universal like *The Flip of a Coin* (1919):

> **Charlotte Merriam in Moran Comedies**. Charlotte Merriam, who played opposite Pete Morrison, one of Universal's Western stars, has been given parts in the Lyons-Moran comedies. Miss Merriam is well suited to heavy parts in comedies. She will divide the feminine honors in the comedies with Mildred Moore. (*Moving Picture World*, May 31, 1919)

Eddie Lyons and Lee Moran were one of silent comedies' most popular duos, and Charlotte received her comedy basic training during a year and a half working with the pair. None of the twenty one-reelers she made with them, such as *A Dog Gone Shame*, *Ten Nights in a Tea Room* (both 1919) *Sweet Patootie*, and *Oiling Uncle* (both 1920), are known to exist. In addition to her work with Lyons and Moran, she also had nice supporting roles in two dramatic features – Billie Rhode's *The Blue Bonnet* (1919) and *The Honey Bee* (1920) for the American Film Co. Although extremely young, she was quickly making a solid impression.

Charlotte Merriam in "The Honey Bee." Charlotte Merriam is an actress of seventeen who is seen in the vivacious role of "Blondie" in "The Honey Bee" with Mme. Marguerite Sylvia. During her two years' motion picture career she has made an enviable reputation for herself in comedy parts. However, Miss Merriam has a decided preference for dramatic work and is working toward that end. (*Motion Picture News*, May 1, 1920)

In the middle of 1920 she moved to Christie Comedies and worked with veteran comics like Fay Tincher, Bobby Vernon, Earle Rodney, Eddie Barry, and Neal Burns in outings such as *Two Pairs and a Peach, Kiss Me Caroline, A Seaside Siren* and *Shuffle the Queens* (all 1920). That same year she hooked up with producer/director Reggie Morris and became one of the stars of his Comiclassic Productions that were distributed by Special Pictures Corporation:

Charlotte Merriam, star of "Comiclassic" release, is already working on her second comedy for Special Pictures. Her first comedy is ready for release. "Up in Betty's Bedroom" is its title and it was directed by Reggie Morris, who made "Married Life" for Mack Sennett. "A Sunny Scandal" is the title of her second picture which Morris is also directing. (*Motion Picture News*, 1920)

Frank Griffin, an old Sennett veteran, was production manager for the Comiclassic series, and besides Morris the other main director was Harry Edwards. The unit first began production at the Balboa Studios, moved to the Balshofer Studio, and finally ended up in the large Jesse D. Hampton Studios on Santa Monica Boulevard. Charlotte was surrounded by talented people like Ford Sterling, Neely Edwards, Jay Belasco, Eddie Baker, and Margaret Cullington, and titles included *A Pajama Marriage* (1920), *A Ballroom Romeo, Watch Your Husband,* (both 1921) and *Are Husbands Happy?* (1922). Suddenly Reggie Morris and his company were no longer working for Special Pictures:

Formal portrait of Charlotte Merriam. Courtesy of Robert S. Birchard.

Reggie Morris will Produce Films for Arrow. The Reggie Morris Productions, Inc., located at 7100 Santa Monica Boulevard, Hollywood, Cal, Reggie Morris, president and Frank H Marshall, vice-president, are now making two-reel comedy productions under the name of Speed Comedies, released through the Arrow Film Corporation for the independent market and featuring the following people: Neely Edwards, Charlotte Merriam, Jack Duffy, Margaret Cullington, Eddie Baker, and Gertrude Robinson. (*Exhibitors Trade Review*, Fall 1921)

In the surviving *Papa's Night Out* (1921) Charlotte plays the daughter of Jack Duffy and Margaret Cullington. Duffy is a big fight fan, but he's so henpecked by Cullington that he has to keep his tickets to the big fight a secret. Charlotte's beau Neely Edwards comes to call, and Duffy decides he's yellow so Neely decides to fight in the evening's boxing match. Everyone decides to sneak out to the fight - Charlotte dresses as a boy, Duffy disguises himself in his wife's clothes, and when the wife sees her clothes sneaking out she puts on his suit and top hat. At the fight (where the referee is Jimmy Finlayson) Neely is ready to fight, but the fighter he's bought off doesn't show up so he instead has to fight real tough pug Eddie Baker. Although Charlotte's there rooting for him, Neely's taking a beating until he gets the idea to put chloroform on his boxing glove which practically knocks out the entire fight staff.

Other survivors include *No Vacancies* and *The Trouble Doctor* (1921) but like Comiclassics, *Speed Comedies* was short-lived. Although the production companies folded Charlotte remained connected to Reggie Morris, so much so that his wife May named her as co-respondent in her December 1923 divorce suit. With the end of *Speed Comedies* Charlotte returned to Christie comedies and would work with them on and off through 1926. During that time she mostly worked with Neal Burns and Jimmie Adams in shorts like *Ocean Swells* (1922), *Dog Sense, Done in Oil*, and *Call the Wagon* (all 1923). Her last Christie production was 1926's *Beauty a la Mud*. Charlotte is the daughter of Billy Engel who runs a high class beauty parlor under the name "Madame Louise." Her father wants her to marry a pompous, celebrated beauty expert, but Charlotte instead loves Jimmie Adams, who father detests. To be close to Charlotte, Jimmie disguises himself as the beauty expert and spends most of the short improvising beauty "treatments" for hapless customer. When he accidentally gets rid of the tremendous warts on the face of the rich Mrs. Gotrox (Blanche Payson) father quickly warns up to Jimmie as his future son-in-law.

This period was the real peak of her career. In addition to the Christie shorts she had good supporting roles in a number of class "A" features. Titles include the Maurice Tourneur fantasy comedy *The Brass Bottle* (1923), two Colleen Moore films - *Painted People* and *So Big* (both 1924), and the swashbuckler *Captain Blood* (1924) for Vitagraph. One of her oddest assignments was the surviving *When Winter Went* (1925), a five-reel feature cobbled together by her former director and paramour Reggie Morris from left over footage from *Speed Comedies*. A linking device was created with Raymond Griffith trying to read a story about the Old South. The Old South (and old *Speed*) footage has Charlotte, Jack Duffy, and Eddie Baker, but that story keeps getting interrupted as problems and events take Griffith away from his book. This independent production was released by the redundantly named Independent Pictures and came and went quickly without making an impression.

Charlotte Merriam getting the star treatment in a *Comiclassic* exhibitor ad.

In 1925 she married actor and future cowboy Rex Lease and for a time retired from the screen, but returned after their divorce:

> Although a two year absence from the screen may be suicidal to the career of most actresses it has left no mark on the activities of Charlotte Merriam. Two months ago she accepted the part of a maid in "Pleasure Crazed" and before the picture was finished the part had grown into a subtle portrayal of a wise cracking and blackmailing characterization. In direct contrast, she is now playing the part of a wealthy debutant and reveling in an elegant array of gowns. The picture is Dolores Costello's "Second Choice" and Charlotte is playing opposite Chester Morris. (*Hollywood Filmograph*, 1929)

While she was off the screen the industry had transitioned to sound, but she jumped right in with sizable supporting roles. This lasted for a couple of years, with her best sound role being the dipsomaniac mother who's under the thumb of her sinister chauffeur, Clark Gable, in *Night Nurse* (1932) starring Barbara Stanwyck. After this she was demoted to uncredited bits in big studio films and small parts in low budget outings like the infamous *Damaged Lives* (1933) and other product from Monogram, Tower Pyramid, and Franchon Royer Pictures. She retired in 1934, having married actor Don Douglas. Widowed in 1946, she remained in Los Angeles and passed away in 1972.

Another popular leading lady that's well–remembered today is Kathryn McGuire. Thanks to her appearances with Buster Keaton in *Sherlock Jr.* and *The Navigator* (both 1924) she's frequently seen by most silent film fans. Born in Peoria, Illinois in 1903, her family later moved to Aurora, Chicago and when she was fourteen, California. As a very young girl she began dancing, and was studying when she ended up at the Mack Sennett Studio by chance:

> One day a friend of hers had an engagement at the Sennett studio and Kathryn went along. Somebody of importance got a look at Kathryn, and wanted to make a test. And that's the way she got started. (*Motion Picture Classic*, 1928)

Signed in 1919 she spent a steady three years at Sennett playing small roles in *Trying to Get Along*, *Uncle Tom without a Cabin* (both 1919), *Gee Whiz*, and *By Golly!* (both 1920), plus the features *Down on the Farm* (1920) *Molly O'*, and *Home Talent* (both 1921). She eventually worked her way up to the feminine lead in titles like *Wedding Bells Out of Tune* and *Hard Knocks and Love Taps* (both 1921). In 1921 she moved on from Sennett and into features working with Maurice Flynn and Strongheart the Dog. Returning to the Sennett lot she turned up in the features *The Crossroads of New York* (1922) and *The Shriek of Araby* (1923), in which she was the lucky girl who played Ben Turpin's love interest.

After being named one of the original WAMPAS Baby stars in 1922 along with Colleen Moore, Lila Lee, and Lois Wilson she did a few dramas and the Pete Morrison western *Pioneer's Gold* (1924) before becoming Buster Keaton's leading lady for two films in a row. Kathryn doesn't have much of a chance to do more than look sweet and pretty in *Sherlock Jr.* (1924), but in *The Navigator* (1924) she and Buster are the only characters through much of the film. Both are spoiled rich kids who get set adrift on a deserted ocean liner, and must come up with ingenuity that they've never used before to learn how to survive and run the ship. Having rejected Buster's earlier proposal of marriage Kathryn comes to rely on him as he proves his worth to her. Like Marion Mack in *The General* (1926) McGuire has much more to do in the film than the regular Keaton heroine and gets quite a physical work-out taking part in his various stunts. Like Mack, Kathryn's "help" often causes more problems for Buster, but once she accepts him as her suitor and protector she assumes a comic air of acceptance for all of his idiosyncrasies. This is McGuire's largest role, and more than any other film gives her the opportunity to show off her own comic talents.

Katherine McGuire and Buster Keaton having trouble adjusting to their close proximity in *The Navigator* (1924). Courtesy of Cole Johnson.

From *The Navigator* she spent the next couple of years in various westerns and action dramas with Jack Hoxie, Roy Stewart, David Butler, and Frank Merrill but in 1926 she returned to comedy and shorts. Taking up residence in Jack White two-reelers she was busy supporting Lupino Lane, Johnny Arthur, Charley Bowers, and Dorothy Devore in shorts such as *Movieland* (1926), *Howdy Duke*, *Wedding Yells*, *The Draw-Back*, *Naughty Boy* (all 1927), *There It Is*, and *Cutie* (1928). She then supported Colleen Moore in *Lilac Time* and the recently rediscovered *Synthetic Sin* (both 1928) and went back to

Westerns with Tom Mix and Hoot Gibson. In 1927 she had married First National's publicity director George Landy, and began tapering off her film work. After a couple of talking appearances in the feature *The Lost Zeppelin* and the Jack White short *Love a la Mode* (both 1930) she retired. Landy died in 1955, and Kathryn returned in a few small bits in television series like *The Thin Man* (1958) and *Dragnet* (1959) and spent the rest of her life in Los Angeles before passing at seventy-four in 1978.

To finish up this chapter are five actresses who spent a substantial amount of their early screen training as ingénues in silent comedies before they went on to become well-known stars of 1930s and 1940s screwball comedy classics. Jean Arthur was born, and worked as a commercial model in New York. Young and brunette, she set out to California where she spent time on contract to Fox and turned up in two-reelers supporting the Fox Monkeys in *Monks a la Mode* (1923) and *Spring Fever* (1924) with Harry Sweet. She also appeared in Fox features like *Cameo Kirby* (1923) in addition to other shorts such as *My Little Brother* and *Case Dismissed* (both 1924) for Universal before spending three years in independent western programmers for outfits like Action Pictures, and Goodwill Productions supporting the cowboys Buddy Roosevelt, Tom Tyler, Bob Custer, and Bill Cody.

Why Monty Banks thinks Jean Arthur is an angel in *Horse Shoes* (1927). Courtesy of EYE Filmmuseum, Netherlands.

Luckily she got sprung from this cinematic corral with more comedy shorts like *Eight Cylinder Bull*, *The Mad Racer* (both 1927), and *Hello Lafayette* (1927), not to mention graduating to Monty Bank's leading lady in his features *Flying Luck* and *Horse Shoes* (both 1927). She was Karl Dane and George K. Arthur's love interest in *Brotherly*

Love (1928), and the arrival of sound gave audiences a chance to hear her unique voice in films like *The Canary Murder Case*, *The Saturday Night Kid* (both 1929) and *Street of Chance* (1930). A change of hair color and roles in *The Whole Town's Talking* (1935) and *Mr. Deeds Goes to Town* (1936) led to other classics such as *Easy Living* (1937), and *The More the Merrier* (1943) where she took her place alongside Irene Dunne and Claudette Colbert as one of the top screwball heroines of the genre.

Carole Lombard of course, belongs in the above pantheon of screwball deities, where the combination of her goddess looks and down to earth personality endeared her to movie audiences of her time as well as today. Born Jane Peters in Fort Wayne, Indiana in 1908, she and her mother moved to Los Angeles after her parent's 1916 divorce, where she happened to be discovered by director Allan Dwan.

> I saw a kid playing baseball on the street with some other kids. She was a cute-looking tomboy - about twelve- a hoyden, out there knocking hell out of the other kids, playing better baseball than they were. And I needed someone of her type for this picture. She'd never acted, so we talked to her parents and they let her do it and she was very good.

The film in question was 1921's *A Perfect Crime*, and although she returned to her normal childhood afterward her career was set. When she turned fifteen she joined a local stage troupe and did extra work. In 1925 she got a contract with Fox where she was dubbed Carol Lombard (the finale "e" on Carol would be added later). Besides appearing in two-reelers she had parts in *Marriage in Transit* (1925), the Buck Jones' westerns *Gold and the Girl* and *Durand of the Badlands* (both 1925), as well as bits in *The Plastic Age*, *Ben-Hur* (both 1925), and *The Johnstown Flood* (1926). Despite all this progress her rising career was almost permanently derailed when her face went through a windshield in a 1926 auto accident:

> I had an accident once and had nine stitches taken across the left cheek. But you can hardly see the scar now.
>
> My upper lip was so stiff from this accident that for several months I could hardly move it. There's nothing so expressionless as a woman with a stiff upper lip, so I'm really glad that it came back to normal. Massage did the trick. It is all right now. (*New York Daily Mirror*, May 20, 1934)

Fox dropped her contract after the accident, but thanks to successful plastic surgery she was able to return to the screen. In early 1927 she was signed by Mack Sennett and became one of the main features of his Sennett Girl Comedies. Two-reelers such as *The Girl from Everywhere* (1927) *Run, Girl, Run*, *The Swim Princess*, *His Unlucky Night*, *The Campus Carmen*, *The Campus Vamp* (all 1928), and *Matchmaking Mama* (1929) gave her the opportunity to work with and learn from comedy pros like Mack Swain, Daphne

Pollard, Billy Bevan, and Dot Farley, as well as develop her screen presence as Sennett kept her constantly in front of the camera. Features such as *My Best Girl* (1927), *Power*, *The Divine Sinner*, *Me, Gangster*, and *Ned McCobb's Daughter* (all 1928) also led to her first lead in 1929's *High Voltage*. In the early days of sound she appeared in all kinds of dramas, crime films, westerns, as well as comedies, but it wasn't until 1934's *We're Not Dressing* and *Twentieth Century* that the Carole Lombard that film fans know and love fully emerged. Her later major movies included *Hands Across the Table* (1935), *My Man Godfrey* (1936), *Nothing Sacred* (1937), and her last, *To Be or Not to Be* (1942), before her life was cut short at only thirty-three in a 1942 plane crash.

Carole Lombard had an early role in the Fox Studios feature comedy *Marriage in Transit* (1925).

Myrna Williams, who would become famous as Myrna Loy, was born in the small western town of Raidersburg, Montana on August 2, 1905. Having started dancing as a young girl, after her father died in the 1918 Spanish-influenza epidemic her mother moved the family to California and enrolled Myrna in the toney Westlake School for Girls. When she got flack about getting caught sneaking into Hollywood for dancing lessons she transferred to Venice High School where she was exposed to a wide variety of culture and arts:

During my time at Venice High, I taught dancing at the Ritter School of

Expression in Culver City. My pupils were tiny tots – babies practically – who didn't do much dancing, but we did manage to teach them something. My salary, forty dollars a month, went from Mrs. Ritter to my mother. I also filled in for a friend as a splicer at the Hal Roach Studio. The film had already been cut, and all I did was put the pieces into a machine and pull a lever to splice them. I don't remember the picture – there was a dog in it, I think. (*Myrna Loy: Being and Becoming*, 1987)

Leaving the school before graduating she was determined to dance and got a job with Fanchon and Marco, a successful dance team, doing stage prologues for big films at Grauman's Egyptian Theatre. Following prologues for *The Ten Commandments* (1923) and *Thief of Bagdad* (1924) she began getting nibbles from the movie studios. The *Thief of Bagdad* ensemble was hired for an orgy scene in Raoul Walsh's *The Wanderer* (1925), and after noted photographer Henry Waxman took some photos of her they were seen by Rudolph Valentino and his wife Natacha Rambova. Nothing came from the screen test that the couple gave Myrna for *Cobra* (1925), but when Rambova made her own film *What Price Beauty?* in 1925 (although the film wasn't released until 1928) Loy was given a part in a futuristic dream sequence. After changing her name to Loy from the "too ordinary for a performer, Williams," bits followed in films such as *Ben-Hur*, *Pretty Ladies* and *Satan in Sables* (all 1925) when she finally got noticed and signed by Warner Brothers.

My apprenticeship began in the imposing old Warner's building on Sunset (now a television studio). They put me into one part after another in rapid succession. It's a production before you even reach the set, you know, because you're up at five-thirty, at the studio by seven. Your hair has to be done, which meant spending hours under the dryer in those days. Your make-up has to be applied, not only to your face. If you had bare arms or legs, as I did in those early roles, they used body makeup. Those makeup people were always your friends - Ernie Westmore, who headed the department, and all the others. They got you first thing in the morning, scolding and chattering: "What were *you* doing last night? You look *awful*!" You took a lot of punishment from them, but it was all in fun, and they really saved you on bad days. When they had finished, you put on your costume, your jewels, and reported to the set by nine o'clock. I've done that all my working life.

She alternated more exotic and vamps roles with some solid comic turns as all-knowing maids in *The Caveman*, and Ernst Lubitsch's *So This is Paris* (both 1926). She also became a regular in the comedy features that starred Louise Fazenda and Clyde Cook such as *Simple Sis*, *A Sailor's Sweetheart*, (both 1927) and *Pay As You Enter* (1928), where she absorbed some of the comic technique of Fazenda, Cook and William Demarest.

Her other comedies included *Finger Prints* (1927) and her oddest assignment - the World War I blackface opus *Ham and Eggs at the Front* (1927). Myrna, Heinie Conklin, Tom Wilson and a large percentage of the cast were blacked up in this currently lost parody of the popular *What Price Glory?* (1926). She began getting female leads in pictures such as *State Street Sadie* (1928) and *Fancy Baggage* (1929) when sound hit the industry:

> The process was extremely awkward, even for those of us who could "talk." Cameras were still very noisy then. You could hear the constant *rrrr* of the reels turning, so they enclosed them in sound proof boxes with windows. This hampered the camera's mobility and ours, compounding the fact that we were terribly conscious of the microphones hidden all over the set – in the flowers, under the furniture, everywhere. Many people that I'd supported in my first years couldn't make the jump. Stars were falling like leaves in that studio. Marie Prevost, a beautiful little comedienne, Patsy Ruth Miller – so many of them just seemed to disappear. They didn't have voice coaches, who would have said "Can you get your voice down a bit? It's too high, too light." Having studied with a voice teacher in Los Angeles while I was still in school, I had something to go on when sound came crashing in, despite my low, soft sort of voice. The sound men had to open it up all the way. But I learned to use it effectively and it worked for me.

Myrna Loy in dusky make-up for the blackface comedy feature *Ham and Eggs at the Front* (1927). Author's collection.

What she did have to deal with in sound films was getting typecast as an exotic – mysterious Orientals, Indians, Mexicans, gypsies, etc. – in pictures like *Desert Song*, *The Black Watch* (both 1929), *Turn Back the Hours*, *Crimson City*, and *The Mask of Fu Manchu* (1932). Through perseverance better roles came her way in *A Connecticut Yankee*, *Arrowsmith* (both 1931), *Emma*, *Love Me Tonight*, and *The Animal Kingdom* (all 1932), plus she even proved her comedy skills in *Topaz* (1933) opposite John Barrymore. Her teaming with William Powell in *The Thin Man* (1934) changed her career. Her articulate, witty and sexy Nora Charles set the course for the rest of her screen life. Although, she would play serious roles in films such as *Test Pilot* (1938), and *The Best Years of Our*

Lives (1946) she's best remembered for comedies like *Libeled Lady* (1936), *Double Wedding* (1937), *I Love You Again* (1940), *Love Crazy* (1941) and the *Thin Man* films. In her later years she continued working in films and on television until 1982. During her retirement she received multiple honors from places like the Kennedy Center and the Academy Awards before she passed away in 1993 at age eighty–eight.

Lupe Velez became known for her comedic fractured English in sound films like *Palooka* (1934) and her starring *Mexican Spitfire* series, but she began her career as a somewhat more demure heroine in silents. Born in 1908 as Guadalupe Velez de Villabos in San Luis Potosi, Mexico, her father was a colonel in the Mexican army and her mother was an opera singer. It was sitting in the wings and watching her mother perform that made Lupe decide to be an actress. As a young teen she was sent to the Our Lady of the Lake Convent in San Antonio, Texas, where she learned English (which was much better than her screen portrayal), but returned to Mexico at age fifteen when she obtained a role in the musical comedy *Ra-Ta-Pan*. When the company disbanded Lupe returned to help support her family as her father had been killed in a revolution, but through two influential Americans, Mr. and Mrs. Frank A. Woodward, she came to the attention of stage star Richard Bennett, who hired her for his upcoming Los Angeles production of *The Dove*. On arrival in California Lupe was dropped from the production because of her extreme youth and inexperience. Luckily she appeared soon after in a benefit for Los Angeles traffic policemen, where she was seen by, and signed for, the Hal Roach Studio.

Today she can be seen as the female lead opposite Charley Chase in *What Women Did for Me* (1927) as well as a role in Laurel and Hardy's *Sailor's Beware* (1927). Her stay on the Roach lot was brief as she soon got a better break as a leading lady for Douglas Fairbanks. *The Gaucho* (1928) was directed by F. Richard Jones, who had recently been director-general at Roach, and he cast her as Doug's fiery, Latin love interest. This appearance set her career off full force, and she was soon working with Lon Chaney in *Where East is East*, opposite Gary Cooper in *The Wolf Song*, not to mention having the starring role in D.W. Griffith's *Lady of the Pavements* (all 1929). The transition to sound saw her score in dramas like *The Squaw Man* (1931) and *Kongo* (1932), but it wasn't long before she returned to comedy with *The Half Naked Truth*, (1932), *Strictly Dynamite* (1934) and others. In 1940 *Mexican Spitfire* launched her series of the same name, and she kept busy breaking English grammatical rules until her unfortunate suicide in 1944.

Another ingénue who got her first film experience at the Hal Roach Studio was Jean Harlow. She was born Harlean Carpentier in Kansas City, Missouri on March 3, 1911 and was the only child of parents who divorced when she was ten years old. Nicknamed "Baby" by her family, she grew up with her grandparents until she was sent to the Ferry Hall School for Girls in Lake Forest, Illinois. From there she eloped at age sixteen, marrying Charles Fremont McGraw, and the young couple moved to California. According to the publicity story, her introduction to pictures came when she accompanied a friend who had an appointment at the Fox Studio, and interested in what she saw on the visit began applying for extra work. Her earliest work came in features such as *Honor Bound* and *Moran of the Marines* (both 1928) and she was soon signed to a contract with the Roach organization.

Lupe Velez administers to Charley Chase in 1927's *What Women Did for Me*.
Courtesy of Robert Arkus.

Her most famous appearances at the Studio were in the 1929 Laurel and Hardy shorts *Liberty, Bacon Grabbers,* and especially *Double Whoopee* (where she shows off her form in skimpy lingerie), but she also worked with Charley Chase in *Chasing Husbands* (1928), supported Edgar Kennedy in *Why Is a Plumber?* and *Thundering Toupees* (both 1929), and vamped Bryant Washburn in *The Unkissed Man* (1929). Working with this caliber of comedy experts had to rub off on the young actress, and she enjoyed the rollicking atmosphere of the studio. Laurel and Hardy later included an affectionate in-joke in their 1931 short *Beau Hunks*, where the girl that causes Ollie (and as it turns out most of his fellow platoon members) to join the Foreign Legion is shown in a photo to be Harlow (referred to as "Jeenie-Weenie").

After her stay at Roach she continued turning up as an extra, and can be spotted in the recently revived *Why Be Good?* (1929) with Colleen Moore, and Charlie Chaplin's *City Lights* (1931). What changed everything was landing the female lead in Howard Hughes' aviation epic *Hell's Angels* (1930). Creating a sensation this was followed by important films such as *Public Enemy* and *Platinum Blonde* (both 1931), which led to her being signed by MGM and a steady string of hits such as *Red Dust* and *Red Headed Woman* (both 1932) ensured she was typecast as the tough blonde with a heart of gold. She exhibited her expert comedy chops in *Dinner at Eight, Bombshell* (both 1933), and *Libeled Lady* (1936) and in spite of the scandal surrounding the suicide of her second husband Paul Bern, she remained one of the studios biggest stars. Her last film was 1937's *Saratoga*, not quite finished when she died from uremic poisoning at the age of twenty-six.

Chapter 9

DISTAFF DUOS

On the subject of female comedy teams during the silent era the sad fact is that there were barely any. While there were tons of male teams like Lyons & Moran, Montgomery & Rock, Wallace Beery & Raymond Hatton, and, of course, Laurel & Hardy, not to mention male/female pairings such as the Drews, John Bunny & Flora Finch, and Harry Myers & Rosemary Theby, only four women duos stand out.

The first pairing came in 1913 for the St. Louis Film Company, who were producing *Frontier* brand westerns and comedies for Universal release. Dot Farley and Victoria Forde were part of the regular company and in June of that year they were paired as the "Frontier twins" in a handful of shorts. The first was *The Twins of the Double X Ranch*, which was followed rapidly by *The Frontier Twins Start Something* and *The Frontier Twins Heroism*. The twins were a pair of juggernauts who left a path of destruction in their wake seemingly just for the sheer enjoyment of it. Sadly none of the entries are known to exist, but this *Moving Picture News* synopsis of *The Frontier Twins Start Something* gives a good description of their bloodthirsty rampaging:

> The beginning of this story is the ending of the twin's punishment for the prank they played upon their luckless uncle, the professor, in their former appearance. They have been locked up in jail, behind the ranch that big bluff Joe, who loves Vic, has had mercy upon them and brought them some good things to eat. Naturally he gives Vic more than Dot and right then the trouble begins. Dot and Vic have a small tussle

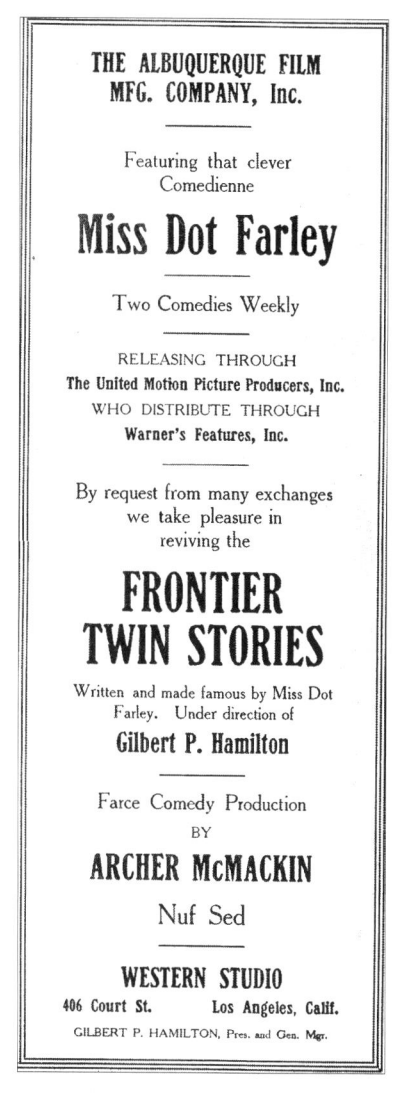

THE ALBUQUERQUE FILM
MFG. COMPANY, Inc.

Featuring that clever
Comedienne

Miss Dot Farley

Two Comedies Weekly

RELEASING THROUGH
The United Motion Picture Producers, Inc.
WHO DISTRIBUTE THROUGH
Warner's Features, Inc.

By request from many exchanges
we take pleasure in
reviving the

FRONTIER TWIN STORIES

Written and made famous by Miss Dot
Farley. Under direction of
Gilbert P. Hamilton

Farce Comedy Production
BY
ARCHER McMACKIN
Nuf Sed

WESTERN STUDIO
406 Court St.   Los Angeles, Calif.
GILBERT P. HAMILTON, Pres. and Gen. Mgr.

1914 exhibitor ad about Dot Farley and director Gilbert P. Hamilton planning to resuscitate the Frontier Twins.

405

as to which shall consume the eatables and Joe gets his face plastered with jelly as his share of the feast.

Father and mother come to visit their erring youngsters and are so impressed by their promises to be good that they release them. Mother thinks that young ladies should learn to cook and she has Dot and Vic peal apples and potatoes as a handy first lesson. When she has left them to the pursuit of their respective occupations the girls throw apples at their uncle until he is forced to forego his afternoon nap in the hammock. Wun Lung, the cook, takes his place and the girls unwittingly tie him in the hammock instead of their uncle.

They create so great a disturbance throwing apples and potatoes at Mammy and the cowboys and the burro that the entire ranch organization appeals to mother for protection, father and Joe having gone to town on business. This fond parent is helpless to control her offsprings, and the delegation decides to take vengeance in its own hands. Headed by Mammy with the butcher knife, the pursuit is begun.

Meanwhile the twins had taken their supposed uncle, hammock and all, down to the irrigation ditch and soused him in the mud and water. This treatment failing to have the desired results they tie the luckless Chinaman to a tree and heave apples at him until they grow weary. Then they leave him and hide out. The pursuit is continued, but soon this changes to a search, for the twins have effectually disposed of themselves in some place unknown.

Nobody misses the cook and the twins are asleep so things naturally return to their former place at the ranch while the youngsters dream of their next batch of mischief.

Farley and Forde appeared in other Frontier comedies together such as *When Roaring Gulch Got Suffrage* and *A Hasting Jilting* (both 1913), but this partnership came to an end when Farley left the St. Louis company and joined the ensemble of Keystone Comedies. However briefly produced the Frontier Twins comedies seem to have made an impression at the time as more than a year later when Dot Farley became part of the Albuquerque Film Mfg. Co. the outfit announced a revival of the Frontier Twins stories. According to publicity items Farley had prepared scenarios for the new series but director Gilbert P. Hamilton was having trouble finding the right person to play the other twin, and it doesn't appear that the revival ever happened.

The next female team while not twins, were actual sisters. Moppets Jane and Katherine Lee became a huge hit in the late teens for the Fox Film Corporation, and were known as the "Fox Kiddies" and "William Fox's Baby Grands" in their starring series of eight features that included *Trouble Makers* (1917) and *We Should Worry* (1918).

Born to a show business family, their background is well recounted in this June 6, 1920 blurb from the *Cleveland Plain Dealer*:

> Mrs. Lee was a "hoofer" in vaudeville a few years ago, which means that she was a professional dancer of the ball room variety. Her act was known as "Irene Lee and Her Kandy Kids," a dancing act in which she had two dancing partners. Her husband was a juggler who often appeared on the same bill with her. However, she divorced him some time ago, and, being given custody of her children she gave them her name. Strangely though, both Jane and Katherine were born on the sixth of April. Katherine was born in Glasgow while Mrs. Lee was touring the British music halls, and three years later Jane arrived in Hamberg, where her mother had concluded a continental tour.

Katherine was born in 1909, and started in films in 1913. Jane, born in 1912, followed her sister in films the next year. Both girls made their debuts for Universal in shorts for their Imp and Gem brands. Right away they were popular with audiences and reviewers and they soon moved over to Fox to support stars such as Theda Bara and Stuart Holmes in features on the order of *Romeo and Juliet* and *The Spider and the Fly* (both 1916). That same year they scored much attention with good roles in Fox's spectacular mega-hit *The Daughter of the Gods* with diving and swimming star Annette Kellerman. It didn't take long for the studio to announce:

The "Terrible Two" – Jane (left) and Katherine (right) Lee. Courtesy of Sam Gill.

> Jane and Katherine Lee, small of size but big in reputation, two of the best known and most loved of motion picture children, have been rewarded by William Fox with a five-reel production in which they will have the stellar roles. (*New York Telegraph*, June 17, 1917)

Two Little Imps (1917) was their first starring film, and these were not sweet or simpering Kewpie dolls but ornery and cheeky little hellions. Their formula was quickly solidified in their next picture:

> "Trouble Makers" is the "Peck's Bad Boy" of the screen and shows the clever little stars in a series of mischievous episodes each of which ought to be followed by a sound spanking, but none of which are. It was written especially to exploit the two youngsters and few bits of child mischief have been overlooked by the scenario writer.

> They tease the policeman, put tacks under chairs, spill sugar in the pantry, throw cream puffs at the baker's wife, upset a rack of clothes in a tailor's shop, pester the old gardener and harass the colored cook. They go in swimming when they ought to be in Sunday school and hide in the church choir loft when the policeman chases them.

A regular unit was set up to make their films. Kenean Buel, a veteran of the stage and the Fox Film Co., was selected as their director, and starting with *Trouble Makers* he also wrote *American Buds, We Should Worry,* and *Doing Their Bit* (all 1918) as well. America's entry into World War I saw the girl's films turn their focus to the war effort – involving them with spies and shaming their elders into doing their civic wartime duty. After five pictures Kenean Buel moved on and he was replaced by seasoned comedy expert and graduate of the Mack Sennett Studio Arvid E. Gillstrom. *Swat the Spy* (1918) was his first writing and directing effort for the Lees and is the only of their features known to survive today.

The girl's father is a chemist who is working on a new explosive for the U.S. government. The family's entire household is staffed by German spies – the butler, the housekeeper, the maid, the chauffeur, etc., etc. Since dad is distracted by his experiments and mom is about to have a new baby they don't notice that they're surrounded by Huns. That's left to Jane and Katherine, who retaliate by clipping the Kaiser-like moustache of the butler while he sleeps, splattering their beloved Kaiser's picture with pies, and generally bedeviling the Huns until they wind up in the hands of the United States Department of Justice. In addition to their onscreen wartime efforts the girls made personal appearances at recruiting stations and put on concerts to entertain troops.

1918 was the peak of the Lee's career and although they are forgotten today at that time they were immensely popular:

> These Lees are not a Chaplin, Pickford or Fairbanks to be copied or imitated – they are just freak babies – freaks, because they have extraordinary sagacity, unparalleled precociousness (for their age), unexampled intelligence for ones so young in the work they are performing, and a natural ability that could never be instilled in kidlets of their size and years if it weren't a gift.

They are a certain proposition. Fox, his directors, scenario writers, and the rest of the Fox staff, may either or all say they contribute so much to any feature the Lee kids are in, but they are all wrong. They do nothing. The Lees do everything, for the Lee children have everything all their elders could not possibly have when it comes down to performing in a picture.

Arvid E. Gillstrom

announces his engagement as Director with the

Fox Film Corporation

First Release

Jane and Katherine Lee

in

"Swat The Spy"

Written and Directed by
ARVID E. GILLSTROM

Sadly the January 1919 issue of *Variety* announced a decision that would start a down turn in the pairs' career:

Lee Kiddies Finishing. Jane and Katherine Lee, under contract to William Fox for several years, are to sever their connection with the firm in May.

The Lee Kiddies have been starring in children features, produced mainly in the east. Three months ago they went to the coast to work there for the winter.

Their Fox contract expires in May and it will not be reviewed by them.

Jane and Katherine Lee get the drop on Katherine Griffith in their feature *Smiles* (1919). Courtesy of Sam Gill.

The family decided to set up their own corporation, in partnership with producer Louis T. Rogers, for a series of shorts. A talented company was assembled and began production in March 1919. Director Tefft Johnson had helmed Bobby Connelly's popular "Sonny Jim" series for Vitagraph, and writer Philip Bartholomae was a Broadway contributor to *The Greenwich Village Follies* and author of the shows *Very Good Eddie* and *Girl of my Dreams*. A handful of shorts, such as *The Infant-ry*, and *Love Us, Love Our Dog* were made, but distribution was erratic when Louis Rogers Productions went bankrupt, and Mrs. Lee sued for breach of contract. In 1921 Masterpiece Film Distributing Corporation released the shorts *The Circus Imps*, *The Dixie Madcaps*, and *The Hicksville Terrors*, but Mrs. Lee was back in court charging that *The Hicksville Terrors* was "assembled from previous film taken and discarded" from the other two shorts. This must have given an idea to Fox as they came back into the picture with the shorts *The Wise Birds* and *A Pair of Aces* (1921), which according to the *Moving Picture World* were "re-edited versions of some of their former successes. The pictures have been edited by Ralph Spence and cut down to two reels. The first of the series is called *A Pair of Aces*, and is made up of situations and bits of business culled from several of the original features."

The girls themselves left films in 1920 and launched a vaudeville act that played the Palace Theatre in New York and toured the Keith Circuit. Outside of singing and dancing in two Vitaphone shorts – *Jane and Katherine Lee* (1927) and *Vitaphone Billboard* (1936) – they turned their backs on movies and worked on stage in America and London through the 1930s. Jane later returned to films in uncredited bit roles in features such as

Knock on Any Door (1949) and *Cheaper by the Dozen* (1950) but died young at forty-five in 1957. By the time that Katherine passed away at fifty-nine in 1968 their popularity had been forgotten and most of their film work lost. Today only a few such as *Swat the Spy* (1918), *Circus Imps* (1921), and *The Dixie Madcaps* (1921) are known to survive, making it difficult for a reappraisal and appreciation of their contribution to film comedy.

For our next team we go from child stars to long-experienced comedy warhorses. As discussed earlier Marie Dressler and Polly Moran had spent most of their lives on stage and in films entertaining audiences. After both hitting a peak of popularity in the teens, by the early 1920s they experienced a lull in their careers and were off the screen for a number of years. The vehicle that brought them back and paired them for the first time was *The Callahans and the Murphys* (1927). At the time, ethnic comedies were big box office in Hollywood. The trend had begun on Broadway with the huge hit *Abie's Irish Rose* and the film industry jumped on the bandwagon with their own versions such as *The Cohens and the Kellys* and *Kosher Kitty Kelly* (both 1926).

Marie Dressler (left) and Polly Moran (right) locking comedic horns in their second teaming *Bringing Up Father* (1928). Courtesy of Sam Gill.

The Callahans and the Murphys was the brain child of writer Frances Marion, who adapted the book of author Kathleen Norris and went to producer Irving Thalberg to urge that the old girls play the leads. Playing the heads of Irish-American families, Marie and Polly battled and boozed in a rough and tumble slapstick plot. The film played well to preview audiences and reviewers, and MGM exhibitor ads heralded "Here's Looking at You, Girls! May your Future as a Comedy Team be as Great as its Beginning in The Callahans and the Murphys!" But when put into general release Irish and Catholic groups protested, leading to certain scenes being re-edited and in some places the picture was withdrawn altogether. With only ten minutes extant at the Library of Congress it's hard to say how actually offensive the film was, but although not the hit the studio had hoped for, it did jump start their careers again and linked them as a team in audience's minds.

While both continued on with character parts in other MGM features preparations were made for their next pairing, an adaptation of George McManus' well-known comic strip *Bringing Up Father* (1928). Again the scenario was written by Frances Marion, and Polly played Maggie with J. Farrell MacDonald as her spouse Jiggs. Marie came in as Maggie's best friend Annie Moore and the plot left plenty of room for, as one reviewer put it, "their usual Irish battles." This time the film was well-reviewed and popular. At this time sound was taking over the industry and the girls cemented their teamwork in the new medium with the Al Christie short *Dangerous Females* (1929). This was followed by the MGM features *Caught Short* (1930), *Reducing* (1931), *Politics* (1931), and *Prosperity* (1932), a string of hits for the team that was ultimately curtailed by Dressler's failing health. After her death in 1934 Polly continued on as a popular screen zany into the 1940s.

In 1927 another sister act hit the screen. Rosetta and Vivien Duncan were longtime vaudevillians who had a major hit with their 1923 stage show *Topsy and Eva*. The musical used Harriet Beecher Stowe's *Uncle Tom's Cabin* characters and situations as an extremely loose thread to hang their regular vaudeville routines and songs. Pretty Vivien played Little Eva, with the comedienne Rosetta as Topsy. After touring the show to great success all over the world the sisters were tapped to transfer their hit to the silent screen. The resulting film, *Topsy and Eva* (1927), has languished in limbo, practically since its initial release, due to its bounty of racial stereotypes and politically incorrect material. Rosetta Duncan, its lead performer, spends the entire production "blacked-up" in burnt cork make-up, shuffling and popping her eyes as the black imp Topsy. While very difficult for modern audiences to accept, within the convention of blackface she's very funny and carries the film, managing to transcend the stereotype with great comic timing and by thumbing her nose at conventional film logic and structure. All in all the film is an entertaining and one-of-a-kind mixture of outrageous physical comedy, racial humor, and Victorian melodrama that deserves a fresh look.

The credited director Del Lord was without peer as a director of slapstick action and chases. Having worked his way up from being a Keystone cop, stuntman, general assistant, cameraman, and even a stunt driver of Sennett's paddy wagons and autos, by the early 1920s he was a full-fledged director of wild and crazy Billy Bevan comedies such as *From Rags to Britches* (1925) and *Ice Cold Cocos* (1926). The late 1920s saw him branching out into features, but full-length films didn't go as smoothly for him as *Topsy and Eva* was his second assignment and very troubled. Since this was a silent film the musical numbers (some of which had consisted of singing and dancing cotton pickers) had to be dropped, so elaborate sequences of Sennett-style slapstick was put in their place.

Rosetta (left) and Vivian Duncan (right) in a lobby card for their feature *Topsy and Eva* (1927). Courtesy of Cole Johnson.

From the onset the Duncans were rumored to have been difficult about adapting to filmmaking and surrendering their "baby" to other hands. Lois Weber, the original director of the project, left as she felt the material was too racist, after which Lord was brought in and shot the bulk of the footage. After United Artist's production head Joseph Schenck looked at the finished product he prevailed upon D.W. Griffith to overhaul the film. In a letter, Griffith's assistant Raymond Klune elaborated that Schenck:

> turned it over to Mr. G shortly after his arrival here and asked him to do something with it. He shot quite a few additional scenes and recut the greater part of it, and from the comments I have heard he improved it to a rare degree... He did not supervise *Topsy and Eva* – he remade it.

The supporting characters were well cast, with Gibson Gowland as Simon Legree and Noble Johnson's Uncle Tom making perhaps the strongest impressions, but the Duncans are really the whole show. Unfortunately audiences, possibly confused by scenes that veer from Griffith drama to broad Sennett slapstick, didn't respond to the film and it didn't do well on release. As for the Duncans their only other silent film was a cameo in the W.C. Fields/Chester Conklin picture *Two Flaming Youths* (1927), and they made their talkie debut in *It's a Great Life* (1929). Outside of the 1935 Vitaphone short *Surprise!*, the sisters worked intermittently in vaudeville and nightclubs.

Anita Garvin and Marion Byron were brought together by producer Hal Roach in the final days of silent films. They only made three starring shorts as a team but they laid the groundwork for Roach's later sound comedies that starred Thelma Todd with Zasu Pitts and Patsy Kelly. Anita Garvin was born on February 11, 1907 in New York City and at the tender age of twelve became a Mack Sennett Bathing Beauty, appearing in the Sennett stage show *Seeing Brooklyn* and at publicity and promotional events. From there she became a showgirl for the legendary Florenz Ziegfeld in his *Follies* and other shows, and when the tour of *Sally* hit Los Angeles in 1924 Anita quit for the movies.

Anita Garvin as a fiery Latin dancer in Lupino Lane's *Fandango* (1928). Courtesy of Wallace Lupino scrapbook.

The very first thing I did was a picture with Bobby Vernon. I was supposed to be a dancer on the floor, and Vernon flipped a piece of butter on the floor and I took a pratfall. (*Filmfax* #40, 1993)

This was in the Christie comedy *Bright Lights* (1924), which still exists, and in addition to Anita's exactly described big scene there's footage of her fixing a couple of her soon-to-be famous murderous glares on Bobby. Young and ambitious, Anita soon moved on to other comedy units:

After only a few months I expected to be getting lead roles, so I moved across the street to Century Studios. All these small studios were located around Sunset and Gower in Hollywood, and were called names like Poverty Row or Gower Gulch. At Century I got to work with Arthur Lake, who was a real nice guy with a great sense of humor. Later on, Charles Lamont, who'd been an assistant director at Christie, became a director at Educational Pictures. He offered me the lead in a picture he was making with Lupino Lane. And so I went to Educational and made pictures there.

She also spent time at Fox and, very importantly, the Standard Cinema Corporation where; "I first met Stan (Laurel) while working for Joe Rock, a producer who made his films by renting space at Universal. Stan also directed some comedies with Jimmy Aubrey that I worked on." Laurel was impressed by Anita's comedic skills, and she soon made her debut on the Hal Roach lot in the Laurel directed *Raggedy Rose* (1926). It was in the creative and family atmosphere at Roach that Anita's talents and screen persona bloomed, leading to the performances for which she's remembered today.

Leo White and James Finlayson (left) observe Anita Garvin making Hallam Cooley nervous in the Billy West-directed Fox short *Old Wives Who Knew* (1928). Courtesy of Robert Arkus.

From the start Garvin was a commanding physical presence – tall, dark hair and eyes, with incredible legs. Her character was also quick witted, knew what she wanted, and didn't suffer fools gladly – which became her stock-in-trade. Her days at Roach were spent in constant irritation and exasperation with the likes of Laurel & Hardy, Charley Chase, James Finlayson, and even Our Gang. Her succession of wives, girlfriends, and "good time" girls all had a sultry smolder covered with an icy exterior, and a contemptuous glare that could burn its way through solid lead. From her years as a showgirl she was a true pro, able to do her work with little fuss and ado, and get some great moments in one take:

> One day while I was working with Charley Chase, Stan asked me if I would do him a favor, and of course I said yes. He asked me to do a little bit that turned out to be the famous pie-falling scene in *Battle of the Century* (1927). All he told me to do was go to wardrobe and ask for a circular skirt that would make the fall even funnier. In the picture I come into the scene during this terrific pie fight. I slip and fall on the pie, and ever so carefully and daintily shake out bits of pie

from under the circular skirt. I added a little something more by shaking my leg. That was ad libbed.

In another interview she added "It took about ten minutes to shoot."

Despite being busy at Roach, Anita still found the time to take her smolder over to Jack White Comedies where she joined in with Lupino Lane's acrobatics in *Fandango* and *Roaming Romeo* (both 1928), and had a brief first marriage to star comic Jerry Drew (a.k.a. Clem Beauchamp). She also appeared in a few features like *Trent's Last Case* (1929) with Raymond Griffith.

Marion Byron was born La Mae Bilenkin on March 16, 1911. The youngest of five sisters born to Russian immigrants, one of Marion's older sisters became a vaudeville performer under the name Betty Byron and Marion adopted Byron as a last name too. Like Anita Garvin, Marion started her career on the stage as a chorus girl, and on the west coast had roles in shows like *Tip-Toes*, *The Cradle Snatchers*, and *The Music Box Revue*. She entered films in 1926 and gained a great deal of attention as Buster Keaton's leading lady in *Steamboat Bill Jr.* (1928). Later that year Hal Roach put her to work in comedies with Charley Chase and Max Davidson. Nicknamed "Peanut" because of her tiny and petite size (4'11," 88 lbs.), she was extremely cute and sexy but still had a little girl quality with her big eyes and flat chest.

Marion Byron and Anita Garvin being separated by Max Davidson in *Feed 'Em and Weep* (1928) as a stunned Charlie Hall looks on. Courtesy of Cole Johnson.

In 1928 the Roach Studio was enjoying a huge success with the teaming of Stan Laurel and Oliver Hardy. Hoping that lightning might strike twice Anita and Marion were put together as the female equivalent. Three shorts were shot between July and October of 1928, and where Stan and Ollie had the "fat and skinny" physical contrast going the girls had "tall and small." Anita, with her worldly-wise manner and already proven slow-burn was a shoo-in for the "Hardy" role, and sweet, innocent, and slightly ditzy Marion was given the "Laurel" part.

The first two films are very similar and strongly based on the Laurel & Hardy blueprint. *Feed 'Em and Weep* (December 8, 1928) presents the girls as waitresses hired for a big rush at Max Davidson's train depot diner. Echoes of *From Soup to Nuts* (1928) abound, including a note from their employment agency describing them as "the best we could do under the circumstances," frequent falls with trays full of food, and Marion serving in her long underwear. In *Going Gaga* (January 5, 1929) they are amateur sleuths on the trail of a kidnapped baby, and a long sequence of the girls climbing in a window and sneaking into a nursery at night is right out of *Habeas Corpus* (1928) or *Night Owls* (1930). In both films Anita is the leader and has many Oliver Hardy "let me do it" moments that backfire in her face. Marion is the slow-witted tag-along, outfitted in a clownish, old-fashioned costume reminiscent of Alice Howell and Louise Fazenda, and topped off with an odd little cloth hat that makes her resemble Harry Langdon. Max Davidson is their main foil as an exasperated authority figure that suffers greatly from their ineptitude.

Their last and best known film together, *A Pair of Tights* (February 2, 1929), takes the team in a different direction that moves away from Laurel & Hardy hand-me-downs, and develops a more female point of view. The simple plot has Marion's boyfriend Stu Erwin bringing his boss Edgar Kennedy over to meet her roommate Anita. They go out for a drive, and while Anita was hoping to get dinner out of the deal she settles for ice cream cones, a simple thing which in usual Hal Roach fashion escalates into all-out war. Working from the premise of the problems that single girls have on dates Anita still slow-

Anita Garvin and Marion Byron during the making of *A Pair of Tights* (1929).

burns and Marion gets into trouble, but the things that they have to put up with – lack of money, tightwad boyfriends, overbearing dates – feel more organic and grounded in reality. In particular Marion's comedy costume and slow-wittedness is gotten rid of, and she's back in up-to-date attire as a cute flapper who's a victim of circumstances.

Sadly they never got to develop the single girls theme any further as Marion Byron's stay at the Roach Studio was brief. She seems to have left by the end of 1928 bringing an end to her pairing with Garvin. Byron appeared in many early talkies features like *Broadway Babies* (1929), *So Long Letty* (1929), and *Golden Dawn* (1930), but by the mid-1930s her roles became increasingly small. Married to screenwriter Lou Breslow she left films in 1938. After many years of retirement she was contacted when Kevin Brownlow and David Gill were preparing their documentary *Buster Keaton: A Hard Act to Follow* (1987), but she died in 1985 before an on-camera interview could take place. Anita Garvin stayed with Roach and made many early sound appearances with Charley Chase, and Laurel & Hardy. In the mid-1930s her career took a backseat to raising her family, but she still turned up in shorts for RKO and Columbia, and worked with Laurel & Hardy in *Swiss Miss* (1938) and *A Chump at Oxford* (1940). Gradually retiring from films, years later she was rediscovered and feted by the Sons of the Desert, the international Laurel & Hardy fan club, and she passed away on July 7, 1994.

PART II: SELECTED BIOGRAPHIES

In addition to the ladies discussed in the previous chapters there are innumerable others who made up the very fabric of the silent comedy universe – players that went from film to film, and studio to studio, as snooping landladies, bratty children, girls next door, mean mothers-in-law, femme fatales, awkward spinsters, and henpecking wives. Unsung and taken for granted, without them a comedy star's screen life would be calm and peaceful – but not at all funny. The following is a "who was who" of silent comedy women:

Gypsy Abbott (1893 – 1952)
Abbott was a dark-haired comedienne with extensive stage experience. Born in England, she spent eight years on the stage – three years of stock in Chicago, playing ingénue parts with star Nat Goodwin, and appearing in dancing and singing sketches on the Orpheum and Pantages circuits. Her film debut was made for the Balboa Co., where she made shorts and features with lead players such as Jackie Saunders, Neva Gerber, Henry B. Walthall, and her husband, future director Henry King. She also turned up in independent features like *The Key to the City*, and *The Man Who Could Not Lose* (both 1914) with Carlyle Blackwell, plus the David Horsley-produced *Vengeance Is Mine* (1916) opposite Crane Wilbur. In 1916 she joined the ensemble at the newly established Vogue Comedies, where she spent the next year and a half abetting the antics of Ben Turpin, Paddy McQuire, and Rube Miller in two-reelers such as *Bungling Bill's Bow-Wow*, *Shot in the Fracas* (both 1916), and *When Ben Bolted* (1917). Her last film before retiring from the screen was the independent *Lorelei of the Sea* (1917) which starred Tyrone Power Sr.

Balboa trade ad photo of Gypsy Abbott.

Aber Twins (Charlene 1912 – 2013 & Arlene (a.k.a. Minniela) 1912 - ?)
Fort Worth, Texas-born twins who caused a lot of confusion for sailors Lupino Lane and Wallace Lupino during shore leave in *Hello Sailor* (1927). Besides a few film appearances, the girls worked as models and were musicians and singers who performed in the Broadway shows *Smiles* (1931) with Fred Astaire, and *Strike Me Pink* (1933). Charlene later married David Marx of the Marx Toy Company, and was a supporter of charity events, plus raised thoroughbred horses before passing away at one hundred and one in 2013.

Josephine Adair (1917 -?)
Child actress who had been in stage musicals such as *Lady Billy* (1920) and *Music Box Revue* (1921), and made the rounds in the early 1920s appearing in comedy shorts for Mack Sennett, Fox Sunshine Comedies, Century, and Lloyd Hamilton that include *Puppy Love, You and Me, The Educator* (all 1922), *Skylarking* (1923), and *Speed Boys* (1924). At the end of the decade she returned to the stage for the musicals *Say When* (1928) and *Whoopee!* (1928) with Eddie Cantor.

Claire Adams (Clara Adams, Peggy Adams) (1896 – 1978)
Canadian-born brunette who was leading lady in many of Victor Moore's one-reel Klever Komedies. She started her career as Clara Adams in the ensemble at Edison Films where she appeared in numerous comedies such as *Curing the Office Boy* (1912), *Aunt Elsa's Visit*, and *A Taste of His Own Medicine* (both 1913). At the outbreak of World War I she left films for the nursing corps, returning in 1917 as Peggy Adams for Victor Moore comedies, where she supported him in titles like *Nutty Knitters, Oh! U Boat* (both 1917), and *Adam and Some Eves* (1918). After some Paramount Flagg two-reelers like *Romance and Brass Tacks* (1918) she moved on to features, changed her name to Claire, and for the most part left comedy behind. Her major films include *The Penalty* (1920) with Lon Chaney, *Just Tony* (1922), *Helen's Babies* (1924), and *The Big Parade* (1925). Although her career ended with the silent era she made sporadic later appearances, such as the quickie sound feature *What a Mother-in-Law!* (1934), and the TV series *Empire* (1963).

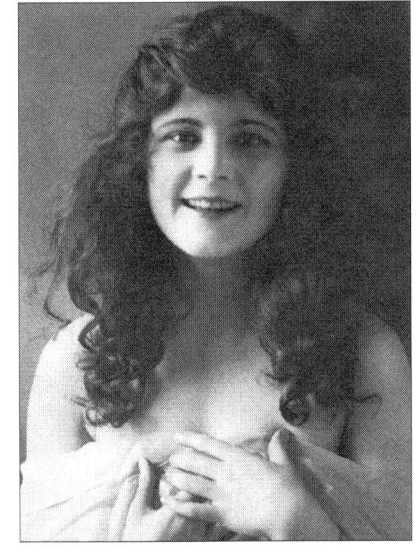

A young Claire Adams during her days at Edison. Author's collection.

Stella Adams (1883 – 1961)

Texas-born character actress who spent over fifteen years as support in comedy shorts, the majority of them produced by Al Christie. After twelve years on stage in stock companies such as the Cummings and Lee Comedy Co. where she played ingénue and leads, Adams started her film career in 1909 working with Hobart Bosworth in the Selig drama *In the Sultan's Power*. Following a stint at Éclair she settled in at the Al Christie unit of Nestor, and over the next four years supported Eddie Lyons, Lee Moran, Betty Compson, Billie Rhodes, and Harry Rattenberry in shorts such as *Her Friend the Butler* (1913), *When the Girls Joined the Force* (1914), and *All in the Same Boat* (1915). When Christie left Nestor and went out on his own Adams came along for comedies like *The Making Over of Mother* (1916) and *Those Wedding Bells* (1917), but left the screen for almost nine years. Returning in 1926 she again worked for Christie, and in 1927 became one of the stars of Stern Brother's *Keeping Up with the Joneses* series, based on the comic strip by Arthur "Pops" Momad. Twelve entries were made, after which she returned to Christie, and in the early days of sound played bits in features such as *Bachelor Mother* (1932), *The Vampire Bat* (1933), and *Theodora Goes Wild* (1936) before retiring in 1936.

Long-time Christie supporting player Stella Adams.

Lassie Lou Ahern (1920 -)

Child actress, who appeared in many Hal Roach shorts, not only with Our Gang but also Will Rogers and Charley Chase in titles such as *Derby Day* (1923), *Sweet Daddy* (1924), *The Family Entrance* (1925), and *Thundering Fleas* (1926). Her features include *Surrender*, with large roles in *Uncle Tom's Cabin* (playing a boy – Eliza's child Little Harry), and *Little Mickey Grogan* (all 1927). Leaving films, she and her sister Peggy toured supper clubs and hotels as the Ahern Sisters from 1932 to 1939, and Lassie returned as an uncredited performer and dancer in films such as *Mister Big* (1943) and *Gaslight* (1944), in addition to 1970s TV shows like *Love, American Style*, *The Magician*, and *The Odd Couple*.

Peggy Ahern (1917 – 2012)
Older sister of Lassie Lou Ahern, who spent a lot of time working at the Hal Roach Studio and regularly appeared with Our Gang in shorts such as *Cradle Robbers*, *The Sun Down Limited* (both 1924), *Dog Days*, *The Love Bug* (both 1925), *War Feathers* (1926), and *Olympic Games* (1927). Also turning up in features like *Excuse Me* and *Not So Long Ago* (both 1925), the sisters left films when sound arrived and toured supper clubs with their musical act. Peggy later appeared in the documentary *Our Gang: Inside the Clubhouse* (1984) talking about her time with the Gang.

Claire Alexander (1897 – 1927)
New York girl who began her career for Fine Arts and Famous Players to become the regular ingénue for two years of George Ovey's *Cub Comedies*. After one-reelers such as *Jerry and the Blackhanders* (1916), *Jerry's Picnic* (1917), and *Jerry in Yodel Land* (1917) she moved over to Universal to support Asian comic Chai Hong in *A Pair of Deuces* and *Charlie the Hero* (both 1919). She retired after appearing with Baby Marie Osborne in the feature *Child of M'sieu* (1919).

Alta Allen (Alta Crowin) (1904 - ?)
Pretty ingénue, who according to publicity pieces was born in Dundee, Scotland, but may have really been born in Oakland, California. While appearing as a dancer in San Francisco she was discovered for Fox Sunshine Comedies, and was the leading lady for their five-reel feature *Skirts* (1920). Hampton Del Ruth, Mack Sennett's former supervising director, was in charge of Fox comedies, and he and Ms. Allen married on Thanksgiving Day in 1920. After she appeared opposite Max Linder in his American features *Seven Years Bad Luck* and *Be My Wife* (both 1921), Del Ruth set up Hampton Del Ruth Productions and made the comedy *The Marriage Chance* (1922) with her as the lead. She was to star in others but the company was short-lived and soon filed for bankruptcy. Afterwards she supported Lloyd Hamilton in his missing feature *A Self-Made Failure* (1924), and westerns such as *Daring Chances* (1924) and *The Set-Up* (1926) with the cowboys Jack Hoxie and Art Accord. Her film career ended in 1926 after a small role in Mabel Normand's *Raggedy Rose*, but she may have made later appearances on stage as Rhea Del Ruth in plays written by her husband such as *The Latest Murder*.

Irene Allen (1892 – 1958)
Heavy African-American actress who worked for Hal Roach and Mack Sennett in the 1920s, most notably as the servant in Smith Family comedies such as *The Chicken* (1928) and *The New Aunt* (1929). She continued appearing in shorts and features until the late 1930s.

Phyllis Allen (1861 – 1938)
Memorable Mack Sennett performer, who at 5'8" and one hundred and eighty pounds specialized in battleaxes and domineering wives. Born on Staten Island in New York, this longtime stage veteran was a vaudeville headliner with an act titled *The Dazzler*, in addition to being a talented singer and pianist. After making her film debut for Selig in 1910, she was in residence on the Sennett lot from 1913 through 1916 appearing frequently with the Chaplins (Charlie and Sydney), Fatty Arbuckle, Mack Swain, and all the usual Keystone suspects. In 1916 she began working in Fox comedies, and made the rounds to practically all the Hollywood comedy units such as Universal, Gale Henry's Model Comedies, and Vitagraph in titles like *The Headwaiter, Her First Flame* (both 1919), and *Footprints* (1920) to name only a few. She even had a return engagement with Charlie Chaplin for *Pay Day* (1922) and *The Pilgrim* (1923). Also appearing in features such as *White Youth* (1920), she retired in 1928.

Metro Pictures star May Allison.
Courtesy of Cole Johnson.

May Allison (1890 – 1989)
Georgia-born leading lady, who came from the stage. Her first appearance was as "Beauty" in *Everywoman*, and she had the title role in *The Quaker Girl* opposite De Wolf Hopper. She also appeared in New York in *Apartment 12-K* before making her film debut in 1915's *A Fool There Was* with Theda Bara. After working with W.H. Crane in *David Harum* (1915) she began working in shorts and features for the American Film Manufacturing Company such as *Pardoned, The End of the Road* (both 1915), *The Gamble*, and *The Man in the Sombero* (both 1916) where she was teamed with Harold Lockwood. A popular screen pair, they made over twenty films together before his death from influenza in 1918. On her own she began working for Metro Pictures and in addition to dramas, she headlined in romantic comedies such as *The Winning of Beatrice, Her Inspiration, In for Thirty Days* (all 1918), and *Castles in the Air* (1919). In some like *A Successful Adventure* (1918) and *Peggy Does Her Darndest* (1919) she had support from the young Sunshine Sammy Morrison, and *Peggy* and *Castles in the Air* were directed by comedy pro George D. Baker. By the mid-1920s she was busy in support in features like *I Want My Man* (1925), *Men of Steel, The Greater Glory* (both 1926), *One Increasing Purpose* (1927), with her last film being *The Telephone Girl* (1927).

Bee Amann (Betty Amann) (1905 – 1990)
Actress born in Germany to American parents, but was raised in the United States, and after a role in the Fox feature *The Kick Off* (1926) became a Mack Sennett girl where she appeared in many shorts such as *The Beach Club*, *The Campus Carmen* (both 1928), and *The Rodeo* (1929). During this time she also turned up as Larry Semon's leading lady in his very last film *A Simple Sap* (1928), in addition to the FBO western feature *The Eagle's Talons* (1928). From here she went to Germany, and like Louise Brooks was starred in prestigious productions such as *Asphalt* (1929) and early sound items like *The White Devil* (1930) as Betty Amann. Because she was Jewish she left Germany in the early 1930s and worked in England, but briefly returned to Germany before coming back to America. Her later work included the short *Strictly Confidence* (1933) with Jimmy Finlayson, and features like *In Old Mexico* (1938), *Nancy Drew…Reporter* (1939), and Edgar G. Ulmer's *Isle of Forgotten Sins* (1943).

Claire Anderson (1895 – 1964)
Pretty, Detroit-born blonde, who began her career in 1914 as an ingénue at Reliance/Majestic as a replacement for the departed Blanche Sweet, and appeared in comedies as well as dramas such as *A Temperance Lesson* and *The Primitive Spirit* (both 1915). Switching to comedy she joined the Sennett/Triangle Company and was an all-purpose heroine in *Cinders of Love*, *The Lion and the Girl*, and *Bathtub Perils* (all 1916). When Sennett left Triangle she remained for two more years turning out titles like *The Ring and the Girl*, *His Baby Doll* (both 1917), and *His Double Life* (1918). Making a jump to features she appeared in many on the order of *The Mask* (1918), *The Spitfire of Seville* (1919), *When We Were 21* (1921), and *The Yellow Stain* (1923) before retiring in 1925.

Mary Anderson (1897 – 1986)
Anderson was a Brooklyn-born ingénue who began her career at age seventeen at the nearby Vitagraph Studio in support of John Bunny in shorts such as *Tangled Tangoists*, *Father's Flirtation*, and *The Old Maid's Baby* (all 1914). She also worked with Norma Talmadge, Clara Kimball Young, Sidney Drew, and Kate Price, and in 1915 moved to Vitagraph's West Coast company where she advanced to the female lead in items like *Pansy's Papa*, *Some Chicken*, *Miss Adventure*, and *Taking the Honey Out of Honeymoon* (all 1916). By 1917 she was appearing in the studio's features, and soon branched out to Universal, Metro, and Charles Ray Productions. In 1922 she was hired by producer C.C. Burr to headline his series of two-reel *All Star Comedies* alongside Charlie Murray and Raymond McKee. After shorts such as *Faint Hearts* (1922), *The Four Orphans*, and *The Fatal Photo* (both 1923), she made two 1923 features, *Shell Shocked Sammy* and *Enemies of Children*, before leaving the screen.

Cecile Arnold (right) and Vivian Edwards (left) make a fuss over Mal St Clair much to Harry McCoy's dismay in *Their Weak Moments* (1917). Author's collection.

Alice Ardell (1902 – 1996) **See Chapter Five**

Arby Arly (?)
Rather plain leading lady whose only known work was supporting comic George Ovey in his 1922 series of lower-budgeted Folly Comedies for the Pacific Film Company. Titles include *Holding His Own*, *Henessey of the Mounted*, *Hands Up*, and *Mummy's Nightmare* (all 1922).

Cecile Arnold (1893 – 1931)
Blonde ingénue who appeared in over thirty Keystone comedies on and off from 1914 to 1917. As a flirtatious other woman she supported Charlie Chaplin, Chester Conklin, Charlie Murray, and Syd Chaplin in shorts like *His Musical Career* (1914), *His Second Childhood* (1914), *Hushing the Scandal* (1915), and *Her Nature Dance* (1917). Her stint with Sennett was interrupted by appearances in the *Ziegfeld Follies* and the show *Robinson Crusoe*. After her return to Keystone she often used the last name Arly, worked mostly on one-reel Triangle comedies, and married Sennett assistant director Frank "Duke" Reynolds. When Reynolds joined the military in 1917 Cecile left the screen.

Jean Arthur (1900 – 1991) **See Chapter Eight**

In 1915's *Pretenses* Sylvia Ashton (back right) grimaces at hubby John Steppling while bride and groom Carol Holloway and John Sheehan are horrified. (The best man on the extreme right is a young William Frawley). Courtesy of Robert S. Birchard.

Sylvia Ashton (1880 – 1940)
Heavy-set, matronly actress, who after working on the stage began her film career in the Biograph comedies directed by Mack Sennett and Del Henderson. She also worked in the early days for Nestor, Komic Comedies, and Bison. In the late teens she made her way back to Sennett for shorts like *Her Fame and Shame* (1917), and moved into features such as Cecil B. DeMille's *Old Wives for New* (1918). Very busy in the 1920s playing mothers and aunts (she was known as "Mother Ashton" at the studios), one of her most memorable roles was as Mama Sieppe opposite Chester Conklin in Eric von Stroheim's *Greed* (1924). Following features such as *Ladies Night in a Turkish Bath* and *The Barker* (both 1928) she retired due to ill health and passed away in 1940.

Gertrude Astor (1887 – 1977)
Tall (5' 9") and shapely blonde Astor excelled at playing tough dames, such as actresses and gangster's molls, in numerous shorts and features. Born in Cleveland, Ohio, she entered vaudeville playing slide trombone in a women's band that toured all over the United States. After early film work in New York she trekked to Hollywood and began appearing regularly at Universal in all types of pictures, but frequently in comedies for their Victor and Nestor brands, in addition to Star comedies opposite Eddie Lyons and Lee Moran. By the 1920s she was a regular in features, with the latter part of the decade the peak of her career – with her most famous role coming as Lily of Broadway – a hard-bitten thief who's trying to retrieve a stolen jewel from an unsuspecting Harry Langdon

in *The Strong Man* (1926). Her other important films from this period include *Behind the Front*, *The Cheerful Fraud* (both 1926), *The Cat and the Canary* (1927), and *Rose-Marie* (1928). She also brought her comedy expertise to the Hal Roach Studio where she essayed "other women" in shorts such as *Laughing Ladies* (1925), *Dizzy Daddies*, *Wife Tamers*, *Tell 'Em Nothing* (all 1926), *The Family Group*, and *Chasing Husbands* (both 1928). The early days of sound saw her continue in some nice supporting roles, but by 1935 she was turning up in uncredited bits, which she did in films and television until 1966 – lasting in the business for fifty years. She died in 1977 at age ninety.

Marion Aye (1903 – 1951)
A Mack Sennett Bathing Beauty who went on to Fox Comedies, appeared in *The Sportsman* and *The Hick* (both 1921) with Larry Semon, worked in Metro comedies in 1922 with Stan Laurel (*The Weak-End Party*) and Bull Montana (*The Punctured Prince*), plus appeared in features until the mid-1920s.

Gertrude Astor tries to prevent Dick Gilbert from punching out Tyler Brooke's lights in *Laughing Ladies* (1925). Author's collection.

Agnes Ayres (Agnes Eyre) (1898 – 1940)
Actress best remembered as Rudolph Valentino's love interest in *The Sheik* (1921). Having grown up near Chicago, she began her career in 1915 as an extra at the Essanay Studio, even appearing in a bit in Charlie Chaplin's only Chicago-made short *His New Job* (1915). She moved on to Frank Powell produced and directed independent features such as *Motherhood* and *The Debt* (both 1917), before ending up at Vitagraph in 1917. The studio soon paired her with Edward Earle for a series of situational married life comedies that were inspired by the success of the Mr. and Mrs. Sidney Drew shorts. The Drews had recently left Vitagraph for Metro Pictures, so this series was designed to fill the void.

Three years' worth of comedies were made with titles such as *His Wife's Hero* (1917), *The Rubaiyat of a Scotch Highball* (1918), and *The Buried Treasure* (1919). C. Graham Baker and Kenneth S. Webb directed many of the shorts, with scenarios often adapted from O. Henry stories. From here Ms. Ayres kept busy in dramatic features which besides *The Sheik* included *The Affairs of Anatol* (1921), *Clarence* (1922), and *The Ten Commandments* (1923). The latter 1920s saw a dropping off in her career, and in 1927 she became one of the fading feature stars hired by Hal Roach to give class to his two-reelers when she appeared opposite Stan Laurel in *Eve's Love Letters* (1927). She continued working until 1929, and is said to have been financially wiped out in the stock market crash. Returning to films in the mid-1930s, she turned up in shorts and uncredited bits in features, but permanently left the screen in 1937.

Baby Peggy (1918 -) **See Chapter Five**

Leah Baird (1887 – 1971)
Leading lady, who appeared in shows such as *The Mummy and the Humming Bird* and *The Gentleman from Mississippi* before making her film debut in 1910 at Vitagraph. Working in all types of pictures she supported John Bunny in items like *Chumps, Stenographers Wanted, Working for Hubby* (all 1912), and *Bunny and the Bunny Hug* (1913). In 1913 she moved over to Universal's Imp Company to co-star with King Baggot in titles such as *Ivanhoe, Mr. and Mrs. Innocence Abroad* (both 1913), and *Absinthe* (1914), plus features such as *Neptune's Daughter* (1914) before returning to the "Big V." After appearing in features like *The Devil's Payday* (1917), *Wolves of Kultur* (1918) and *When Husbands Deceive* (1922), her films became more low-budget and at the end of the 1920s she returned to shorts – appearing with Taylor Holmes in a series of *Henry and Polly* marital two-reelers like *Their Second Honeymoon*, and *King Harold* (both 1927). She left the screen when sound arrived but returned in the 1940s and did uncredited bit roles until 1957.

Betty Balfour (1903 – 1977) **See Chapter Five**

Gertrude Bambrick (1893 – 1974)
Actress who spent most of her career at the Biograph Studio, starting with small parts in 1912 and eventually working her way up to female leads in comedies such as *Just Kids, A Saturday Holiday* (both 1913), *Who's Looney Now?, Liberty Belles* (both 1914), and *Divorcons* (1915) for the directors Del Henderson and Edward Dillon. Bambrick retired when she married actor and director Marshall Neilan in 1916. Although they divorced in 1921 she never returned to the screen.

Nilde Baracchi (1889 - ?) **See Chapter One**

Bonnie Barrett (?)
A champion child swimmer and diver, who started in the water at fifteen months old and began making film appearances at age two in Jack White Juvenile Comedies such as *Three Cheers* (1923). Often teamed with Malcolm "Big Boy" Sebastian in series entries like *Baby Be Good* (1925), *Sea Scamps* (1926), and *Funny Face* (1927), she left films at six in 1927.

Billie Beck (Helen Gould Beck, Sally Rand) (1904 – 1979)
One of the many dancers brought to films by producer Al Christie, Ms. Beck had started her career as a teenage dancer at a Kansas City nightclub and moved on to Gus Edward's vaudeville company, the *Ziegfeld Follies*, and the Palais Royale. An illness caused her to terminate a tour of the Orpheum Circuit and while recuperating in California she was discovered by Christie, and appeared in a few shorts like *Court Plaster* (1924) with Neal Burns. After working as an acrobat for Ringling Brothers and appearing in summer stock, she eventually returned to vaudeville, changed her name to Sally Rand, and developed her famous fan dance. A sensation at the 1933 Chicago World's Fair, she remained a popular performer until her death in 1979.

Marjorie Beebe (1908 – 1983)
Beebe was a talented comedienne who almost made the big time with Mack Sennett. She came to California with her mother as a teenager and by 1924 was working at Universal. After supporting comics like Bobby Ray and Oliver Hardy in *Hey Taxi* (1925) and Harry Sweet in *What! No Spinach?* (1926) she moved over to Fox where Imperial comedy two-reelers such as *A Low Necker, An Old Flame,* and *Why Blondes Leave Home* (all 1927) led to feature appearances. Proving herself in supporting roles in comedies like *Colleen* and *Ankles Preferred* (both 1927), she got her first starring role in *The Farmer's Daughter* (1928). The attention and good notices for this film caused her to be signed by Mack Sennett as one of his early sound stars. Her Sennett shorts include *A Hollywood Star*

An early Fox Studios study of Marjorie Beebe. Author's collection.

(1929), *He Trumped Her Ace* (1930), *The Bride's Mistake, Ex-Sweeties* (both 1931), and *Too Many Highballs* (1933), not to mention the feature *Hypnotized* (1933). After Sennett went bankrupt in 1933 her career lost its steam, and although she turned up in some westerns like *Orphans of the Pecos* and *The Fighting Deputy* (both 1937) and Fox's homage to Sennett, *Hollywood Cavalcade* (1939), she retired in 1940.

Alice Belcher (1880 – 1939)
Homely older actress, whose face would frequently be veiled or obscured and then finally revealed to give comics like Ben Turpin or Billy West the opportunity for a big reaction take. Ms. Belcher was convent schooled, and was an artist's model before breaking into pictures in 1916. Despite her mirror-breaking face she was always flirtatious, and in addition to numerous Mack Sennett shorts she also worked with Lloyd Hamilton, Max Davidson, Big Boy, Thelma Todd & Patsy Kelly, and the Three Stooges. Her feature appearances include *Second Hand Rose* (1922), *Blondes by Choice* (1927), *The Devil's Brother* (1933), and *Meet the Boyfriend* (1937). The year before she died she even appeared as herself in a 1938 Paramount *Unusual Occupations* short.

Alma Bennett (1904 – 1958)
Sultry brunette with a bit of a resemblance to Bebe Daniels, who vamped comics such as Larry Semon, Harry Langdon, and Eddie Quillan. Making her debut in 1919 she appeared in shorts for Al Christie and supported Lyons & Moran, at the same time having parts in features such as *The Right to Happiness* (1919), *Lilies of the Field* (1924), and *The Lost World* (1925). After vamping Larry Semon in *Her Boy Friend* (1924) she became a regular in Mack Sennett two-reelers that include *Don't Tell Dad* (1925), *The Jolly Jilter* (1927), and *The Best Man* (1928), although her most memorable role was as the object of Harry Langdon's obsession in his feature *Long Pants* (1927). After the changeover to sound she continued in features and shorts for Sennett and Jack White before retiring in 1931.

The always sultry Alma Bennett. Author's collection.

Belle Bennett (1891 – 1932)
1920s dramatic performer, best-remembered for her star turn in the lead in the original *Stella Dallas* (1925), who was a regular in comedy shorts in the early days of her career.

Coming from a circus background she began in films in 1913 as an ingénue for Lubin, Nestor, Bison, Majestic, and Balboa, but soon settled in at George Ovey's Cub Comedies for producer David Horsley such as a *A Shot Gun Romance* (1915), *Jerry in the Movies*, and *Jerry's Millions* (both 1916). She also did many shorts opposite Edward Sedgwick at Universal, and even worked with Wallace Beery in *Sweedie, the Janitor* (1916). By 1917 she was getting good parts in dramatic features for Universal and Triangle, and had a run on Broadway in the 1921 production of *The Wandering Jew*. Besides *Stella Dallas* some of her better known titles include *The Way of All Flesh* (1927), *Mother Machree*, *The Battle of the Sexes* (both 1928), and *The Iron Mask* (1929). Her career was cut short by her early death from cancer at age forty-one.

Billie Bennett (1874 – 1951)
Small, dark-haired character actress, who specialized in domineering spouses for the likes of Fatty Arbuckle in *Fatty's Chance Acquaintance* (1915) and Smiling Billy Parsons for *Bill's Opportunity* (1919). After fifteen years on the stage she entered films in 1912 at the United States Motion Picture Company, and appeared in Universal's Joker and Nestor Comedies before taking up residence at Keystone. Later doing yeoman service for Fox and Strand Comedies, she moved into supporting roles in features such as *Robin Hood* (1922), *Lady Windermere's Fan* (1925), and *One Romantic Night* (1930) before leaving films in 1930.

Billie Bennett's tough on Roscoe Arbuckle in *Fatty's Chance Acquaintance* (1915). Courtesy of Jim Kerkhoff.

Catherine Bennett (1901 – 1978)
Sister of Enid and Marjorie Bennett, who in the early 1920s was a leading lady for comics such as Stan Laurel and Monty Banks in two-reelers like *When Knights were Cold, Paging Love, Taxi Please*, and *Always Late* (all 1923). Her later work consisted of more shorts like *Control Yourself* with Sid Smith, plus the features *The Wild Bull's Lair* and *Soul Mates* (all 1925).

Marion Bent (1879 - 1940)
Wife and stage partner of Pat Rooney Jr., and together the pair were vaudeville headliners for many years, in addition to being one of show business's best loved couples. The daughter of cornet player Arthur Bent, she started her career as a child and first appeared with Rooney in the 1903 musical extravaganza *Mother Goose*. The couple married soon after and spent the next thirty years singing and dancing. Movies tried to tap into their success and they made a few pictures sporadically during the silent days – a couple for Lubin such as *The Busy Bell Boy* and *He's a Bear* (both 1915) and some for Universal like *I'll Get Her Yet* (1916). After a film break of more than a decade they returned with the early sound shorts *Sweethearts*, *The Love Tree*, *Love Birds*, and *The Three Diamonds* (all 1929). Bent retired in 1932 due to the onset of arthritis, and passed away in 1940.

Jane Bernoudy (1893 – 1972) **See Chapter Seven**

Lillian Biron (1898 – 1957)
Independence, Kansas-born blonde who became an all-purpose comedy shorts leading lady in the teens and early twenties. She began her film career after a year on stage in stock at Vogue Comedies, and soon moved on to Triangle one-reelers such as *A Berth Scandal*, *Skirts Strategy*, and *Wheels of Love* (all 1917). At the same time she appeared in some mainstream Mack Sennett shorts on the order of *A Dog Catcher's Love* (1917), *Those Athletic Girls*, and *Her Screen Idol* (both 1918). After some work for Vitagraph for the next two years was she the leading lady for diminutive comic George Ovey in his Gaiety Comedies, which were billed as "one reel a week of fast fun and farce." In 1920 she made a move to Century Comedies where she worked with Charles Dorety, Bud Jamison, Baby Peggy, and Brownie the Wonder Dog. She stayed with Century through 1922, although made a few side trips to work with Joe Rock, Jimmie Adams, the Hallroom Boys, and Little Napoleon. Her later shorts included *A Blue Ribbon Mutt* (1920), *Sunless Sunday* (1921), *The Whirlwind*, *A Monkey Cop*, and *The Kickin' Fool* (all 1922), not to mention the action feature *Below the Deadline* (1921), before she left films in 1922.

Lillian Biron (left) with Dorothy Vernon and Walter Wilkenson in the Iris Comedy *The Monkey Cop* (1922). Courtesy of Sam Gill.

Alice Guy Blache (1873 – 1968) **See Chapter Six**

Violet Blythe (1892 – 1983)
Blythe was the wife of comedian Lupino Lane with her own background in British musical comedy and music hall. After their 1917 marriage Ms. Blythe appeared with her husband in film shorts in England such as *Hullo! Who's your Lady Friend?* (1917), and occasionally turned up in his Hollywood comedies like *Maid in Morocco* (1925) and *Battling Sisters* (1929). The family returned to Britain in 1930, and she continued working with Lane on stage and screen, particularly in his monster stage hit *Me and My Girl* (1937).

Delia Bogard (1921 – 1995)
Blonde child actress who played Tomboy Taylor, the main sidekick of Mickey Rooney's Mickey McGuire in the series of the same name. Based on Fontaine Fox's popular comic strip *Toonerville Folks*, Mickey (Himself) McGuire was a tough Irish kid and the self-styled leader of Tomboy Taylor, Hambone Johnson, and Teeth McDuff in their adventures and battles with rich kid nemesis Stinky Davis. Producer Larry Darmour started the series rolling in 1927 and cast the then unknown Rooney and the other kids in the leads. Silent titles include *Mickey's Pals* (1927), *Mickey's Nine, Mickey the Detective* (both 1928), and *Mickey's Menagerie* (1929). The series made the transition to sound, and Bogard continued as Tomboy until 1933, when she was replaced by Shirley Jean Rickert from Our Gang. Afterward she did some uncredited bit roles into the late 1940s.

Symona Boniface (1894 – 1950)
Boniface is well-known for her work with the Three Stooges and came from the stage, to make her first film appearances in the 1920s. She has a large role in Charley Chase's 1925 short *The Caretaker's Daughter*, and has bits in other Roach shorts like *Baby Brother* (1927), *Movie Night*, and *Leaping Love* (both 1929). Turning up in numerous sound features such as *The Black Cat* (1934), *Ninotchka* (1939), and *Wilson* (1944), she had bigger roles in Columbia two-reelers with the Stooges, Andy Clyde, and El Brendel. Best remembered as the society ladies Mrs. Bixby in *Micro-Phonies* (1944) and Mrs. Smythe-Smythe in *Half-Wits Holiday* (1947), she worked right up to her

Casting directory ad for Symona Boniface.

death in 1950 and even after, as producer Jules White used her in stock footage in his 1956 Stooges short *Scheming Schemers*.

Priscilla Bonner (1899 – 1996)
Dramatic ingénue who played serious parts in many comedy features. One of her first roles was with Will Rogers in *Honest Hutch* (1920), and she also appeared in Dorothy Devore's *Hold Your Breath* (1924) and *Charley's Aunt* (1925) with Syd Chaplin. Best remembered for her work opposite Harry Langdon in *The Strong Man* (1926) and *Long Pants* (1927), she also supported Clara Bow in *It* (1927). Her other features include *The Red Kimona* (1925), *Three Bad Men* (1926), and *Golden Shackles* (1928). Retired when she married Dr. Bertrand Woolfan in 1928, she never made a talking film. Remaining in Hollywood, she and her husband were later friends and the landlord of director Preston Sturges.

Olive Borden (1906 – 1947)
Popular 1920s actress, who got her start at age fifteen as a Mack Sennett Bathing Girl. Soon moving on to Jack White Comedies, she became a leading lady for comic Lige Conley in shorts such as *Neck and Neck*, *Wide Open*, and *Air Pockets* (all 1924). Her next stop was the Hal Roach Studio where she supported the likes of Charley Chase, Arthur Stone, Hunky-Dorrey (Earl Mohan and Billy Engle), and Glenn Tryon in *Too Many Mamas*, *Should Landlords Live?* (both 1924), *Should Husbands be Watched?*, and *Tell It To a Policeman* (both 1925). Work at Gotham, Vitagraph, Paramount and back at Sennett led to her signing with Fox, where she became a star in comedies such as *Fig Leaves* (1926), *The Joy Girl*, *Pajamas* (both 1927), in addition to the dramas *Three Bad Men* (1926) and *The Monkey Talks* (1927). After a falling out with Fox she ended up freelancing, and her career ran out of steam in the early days of sound. Following a return to shorts her last film was 1934's *Chloe, Love is Calling You*, a shoe-string production shot in Florida. The rest of her life was a series of ups and downs, and she died in a Los Angeles skid row mission at age forty in 1947.

Before she became a star at Fox, Olive Borden appeared in many Hal Roach and Jack White shorts. Author's collection.

Clara Bow (1905 – 1965) **See Chapter Five**

Betty Boyd (1908 – 1971)
A former dancer in prologues and presentations at movie theatres, Boyd became a regular leading lady in Lloyd Hamilton and Jack White Comedies of the late 1920s. She also supported Monty Collins, Harold Goodwin, and played "Black Betty, the Pirate Queen" in Lupino Lane's *Pirates Beware* (1928). After being named a WAMPAS Baby Star in 1929 she seemed on the verge of stardom, but her career stalled in sound.

Lois Boyd (?)
Light-eyed brunette who started in films as a Mack Sennett beauty in 1919. After some work at Roach and Fox Sunshine Comedies she gathered attention as Monty Bank's leading lady in a few of his Grand Asher two-reelers such as *Paging Love*, *The Covered Schooner*, and *The Southbound Limited* (all 1923). From there she turned up in Century Comedies like *Sweet and Pretty* (1923) and *Taming of the East* (1925), but she's best remembered as the love interest for Frank "Fatty" Alexander, Hilliard "Fatt" Karr, and Bill "Kewpie" Ross in their Joe Rock produced Standard Comedies. The petite and very game Ms. Boyd took numerous falls and much physical knockabout in support of these three high calorie comics. She appeared in the first half of their series – from 1925 to 1927 in shorts such as *All Tied Up* (1925), *Wedding Daze* (1926), *The Vulgar Yachtsmen* (1926), and *Old Tin Sides* (1927). Her few features include *The Last Man on Earth* (1924), *A Woman's Heart* (1926), and *Thumb's Down* (1927).

Publicity photo of Jack White Comedies regular Betty Boyd. Author's collection.

Kitty Bradbury (1875 – 1945)
White-haired character actress, best known for playing Edna Purviance's mother in Chaplin's *The Immigrant* (1917) and *The Pilgrim* (1923). Ms. Bradbury also worked with Buster Keaton in his short *The Goat* (1921) and feature *Our Hospitality* (1923). Starting in films around 1916 she also appeared in dramatic features such as *Intolerance* (1916), *The Brand of Lopez* (1920), and *The Man Between* (1923) before she disappeared in the mid-1920s.

Estelle Bradley (1908 – 1990)

Bradley was a beauty contest winner who was Miss Atlanta in 1924 and a semi-finalist for Miss America. After a couple of bit roles in features she joined the ensemble at Jack White Comedies in 1925 and made her debut opposite Lige Conley. She also supported Al St John, Lloyd Hamilton, Phil Dunham, and Monty Collins in shorts such as *Cheap Skates* (1925), *One Sunday Morning* (1926), *High Sea Blues* (1927), and *Three Tough Onions* (1927) into the early 1930s. Married to comedy director Charles Lamont, she retired in 1932.

Estelle Bradley and Phil Dunham clinch in *Queens Wild* (1927). Courtesy of Robert S. Birchard.

Beta Breuil (1876 - ?) **See Chapter Six**

Mary Brian (1906 – 2002)

Brian was a dark-haired ingénue who played the love interest or daughter for a number of popular comedians. Her career began as a teenager when she placed second in a beauty contest and the prize was a screen test for director Herbert Brennon, who cast her as Wendy in his 1924 adaptation of *Peter Pan*. Soon she was in demand as support for comics like Raymond Griffith (*A Regular Fellow* 1925), the team of Wallace Beery and Raymond Hatton (*Behind the Front* 1926 and *Partners in Crime* 1928), and W.C. Fields (*Running Wild* and *Two Flaming Youths* both 1927). She made a smooth transition to sound, appearing in solid titles like *The Royal Family of Broadway* (1930), *The Front Page* (1931), *Blessed Event* (1932), and was re-united with W.C. Fields for *The Man on the Flying Trapeze* (1935). Her career slowed down after 1937, but she toured on stage and as part of the USO during World War II. She later worked in television and was a regular on the 1950s series *Meet Corliss Archer*.

Ethel Broadhurst (1897 – 1945)
Vaudeville dancer, who toured with the Dolly Sisters in *Oh, Look,* and spent a season working for Florenz Ziegfeld. In 1920 she became one of the Vanity Fair Girls at the Hal Roach Studio supporting Eddie Boland in shorts such as *Alias Aladdin* and *Greek Meets Greek*. Looking something like a Kewpie Doll with big eyes and bee-stung lips, she soon moved up to being Boland's main leading lady, and did the same for Paul Parrott in one-reelers like *Loose Change* and *Stand Pat* (both 1922). Her last films were made in 1922, but a few such as *Don't Butt In* and *Pay the Cashier* were held back and finally released in 1926.

Ethel Broadhurst (right) and Jean Hope (left) take care of Eddie Boland in one of their Vanity Girls Comedies. Courtesy of Robert Arkus.

Billie Brockwell (1875 – 1949)
Stage actress from stock and Broadway productions who began her film career at Lubin, and worked at Nestor before becoming a Keystone regular in 1914. Appearing in many of Charlie Murray's *Hogan* comedies, as well as *Love in Armor, Gussle's Wayward Path* (both 1915), and *The Village Vampire* (1916). When her daughter Gladys Brockwell became a popular film actress, Billie retired to manage her business affairs. After Gladys Brockwell died in an auto accident in 1929, Billie acted again in a couple of features before permanently retiring.

Ann Brody (Ann Brody Goldstein) (1884 – 1944)
Small, round actress who excelled at playing Jewish mothers, and began her stage career at age nine in east side New York children's theatre before touring the country in traveling stock companies. She made her film debut in 1912 for Vitagraph and became a regular member of the company, working with Norma and Constance Talmadge, Wally Van, Hughie Mack, Flora Finch, and Mr. & Mrs. Sidney Drew in titles such as *Hughey of the Circus, Levy's Seven Daughters* (both 1915), and *The Princess of Park Row* (1917). During the 1920s she spent several years in Hollywood where she appeared in features like *Clancy's Kosher Wedding* and *Jake the Plumber* (both 1927), in addition to playing "Mama" to Max Davidson's "Papa" in *Why Girls Say No* (1927), *Hurdy Gurdy*, and *So This Is College* (both 1929). In the mid-1930s she returned to New York and the stage, appearing in the Broadway productions of *Having Wonderful Time* (1937/1938) and *The Time of Your Life* (1940) before passing away in 1944.

Betty Bronson (1906 – 1971)
Seventeen year-old who went from being a bit player to a movie star when she was personally picked by author James M. Barrie to play the title role in *Peter Pan* (1924). Bronson beat out seasoned veterans such as Mary Pickford and Gloria Swanson for the part, and her youth and freshness were perfect for the character. After her star-making turn, she continued working for Paramount in excellent pictures such as Are *Parents People?*, *A Kiss for Cinderella*, and even played Christ's mother in MGM's *Ben Hur* (all 1925). Following more silents like *The Cat's Pajamas* (1926), *Ritzy* (1927), and *Companionate Marriage* (1928), her sound appearances were not as successful, so she basically retired after marrying in 1932. She did return to performing in the 1950s, acting in films like Sam Fuller's *The Naked Kiss* (1964) and *Blackbeard's Ghost* (1968), not to mention television shows such as *My Three Sons* and *Run for Your Life* until her death in 1971.

Louise Brooks (1906 – 1985)
Brooks is a screen icon, famous for playing Lulu in G.W. Pabst legendary 1929 film *Pandora's Box*, who appeared in many comedies in the early part of her career. Born in Cherryvale, Kansas, she started dancing as a young girl and at age fifteen left school to become a member of the Denishawn Dancers. In 1924 she moved on to the Broadway shows of George White and Florenz Ziegfeld, and the next year made her first film, *The Street of Forgotten Men* (1925), at Paramount's Astoria Long Island Studio. She made a number of 1926 comedies there such as *It's the Old Army Game* with W.C. Fields, *Love 'Em and Leave 'Em*, *A Social Celebrity*, and *The Show-Off*, before going to Hollywood and continuing with *Now We're in the Air*, *Evening Clothes* (both 1927), and *A Girl in Every Port* (1928). Famously, she turned her back on Hollywood and went to Germany, where she made *Pandora's Box* and *Diary of a Lost Girl* (both 1929). When she returned to the United States in 1930 the studios didn't care and only offered her small bits. Her last film was the 1938 Republic oater *Overland Stage Raiders* opposite a young John Wayne. Spending her last years in Rochester, New York, she was basically taken care of by the George Eastman House, and wrote a couple of books of memoirs before her death in 1985.

Iva Brown (?)
London-born beauty who had a brief run as a comedy shorts leading lady in 1920 when she supported Lloyd Hamilton in *Dynamite*, and Al St John in two of his Warner Brothers produced two-reelers *Ship Ahoy* and *Cleaning Up*. Her career ended after the 1922 independent western feature *Diamond Carlisle*.

Kate Bruce (1860 – 1946)
Actress from the stage who started in films in 1908 as part of D.W. Griffith's original Biograph company, becoming the matriarch of the group as she always played the mother or grandmother of Mary Pickford, Blanche Sweet, Mae Marsh, and the Gish

sisters. Best remembered in dramas, she also appeared in many of the Mack Sennett-directed Biograph comedies such as *The Manicure Lady* (1911), *With a Kodak*, and *The Furs* (both 1912). She left Biograph with Griffith and continued working with him in features like *True Heart Susie, A Romance of Happy Valley* (both 1919), and *Way Down East* (1920). By the mid-1920s her appearances had slowed down, although she did have a nice role in the Charley Chase comedy *Are Brunettes Safe?* (1927). Her last role was in Griffith's final film *The Struggle* (1931) and she passed away in 1946.

Leota Bryan (1891 - ?)
Bryan was the wife of writer and director Vincent Bryan and had a stage background in musical comedy with the La Salle Theatre Stock Company of Chicago. When her husband was working as a writer on Charlie Chaplin's comedies for the Mutual Company, Leota played ingénue roles in entries such as *The Floorwalker, The Count*, and *The Rink* (all 1916). This seems to be the extent of her film career, and in 1923 the Bryans were arrested for possession of narcotics and eventually underwent a cure treatment.

Billie Burke (1884 – 1970)
Stage star best remembered today for her sound film appearances as dizzy matrons, confused mothers-in-law, or good witches of the west. Born in Washington, D.C. to a circus family, she toured the world with her circus clown father, and began her stage career at eighteen in London. Broadway beckoned, and she appeared in the hits *Mrs. Dot, Suzanne, The Runaway*, and *The Land of Promise*, in addition to marrying impresario Florenz Ziegfeld in 1914. She made her film debut for Thomas Ince in *Peggy* (1916), which she followed up with the fifteen part action serial *Gloria's Romance* (1916). After a few dramas she settled into a string of popular light comedy romances for Paramount Pictures which included *The Make-Believe Wife* (1918), *Sadie Love, Wanted: A Husband* (both 1919), *Away Goes Prudence, The Frisky Mrs. Johnson* (both 1920), and *The Education of Elizabeth* (1921).

She returned to the stage for the remainder of the twenties but returned to film when sound arrived and made her signature films *Dinner at Eight* (1933), *Topper* (1937), *The Wizard of Oz* (1939), *The Man Who Came to Dinner* (1942), and *Father of the Bride* (1950). She kept busy working in movies and television until 1960 with one of her last appearances as comic relief in the John Ford drama *Sergeant Rutlidge* (1960).

Bartine Burkett (1898 – 1994) **See Chapter Eight**

Heavyweight Rose Burkhardt (right) made solid support
for Ethlyn Gibson and Billy West in *Mustered Out* (1920).
Author's collection.

Rose Burkhardt (?)
Heavyweight, Chicago-based character actress who specialized in domineering wives and society dowagers, who has been spotted in Selig Polyscope films as early as 1910's *A Sleepwalking Cure*. By 1917 she was working for Sunshine Film Corp. of Chicago in some of their "Sunny Films" shorts like *Some Baby* and *A Forceful Romance* opposite the three hundred and sixty pounds Floyd Williams. Ms. Burkhardt was reported as weighing in at three hundred and forty-one herself, and in addition to working at Essanay she was a mainstay in the ensemble at the Emerald Motion Picture Company. Supporting Emerald president Frederick J. Ireland in the door-slamming farce *When the Cat's Away* (1920), and Billy West in *Mustered Out* (1920), her best-known film today is Alice Howell's *Cinderella Cinders* (1920) where Burkhardt is Howell's large employer, the rich Mrs. Doughbills. Emerald became part of the Reelcraft Pictures Corporation, but the outfit folded in 1922 which seems to have marked the end of Ms. Burkhardt's career as well.

Bertha Burnham (?)
Pretty brunette, who supported Ernest Shields and Eddie Boland in early 1915 Joker Comedies made by the Archer MacMackin unit. Her titles include *Dixie's Day Off* and *Love, Fireworks, and the Janitor* (both 1915), but she was soon replaced by Queenie Rosson and Jane Bernoudy.

Evelyn Burns (1877 – 1958)
Matronly actress who specialized in society ladies in the 1920s, turning up frequently in Hal Roach shorts such as *High Society* (1924), *Is Marriage the Bunk* (1925), and *Bad Boy* (1925), in addition to bits in features like Harold Lloyd's *Hot Water* (1924). She seems to have disappeared from films with the changeover to sound.

Ethel Burton (1898 - 1985)
Tall brunette who's pre-cinema career was as a model for well-known illustrators such as J.C. Leyendecker and C. Coles Phillips, in addition to writing and managing charitable entertainments in and around New York City. Her screen debut was for Vitagraph, and she soon hooked up with comedians Bobby Burns and Walter Stull at the Wizard Company for comedies like *Mashers and Splashers* (1915). Moving with Burns and Stulls to the Vim Company in Florida she was the regular leading lady in their Pokes and Jabbs comedies like *Strangled Harmony* (1915), *Frenzied Finance*, and *A Pair of Skins* (both 1916). In support in many of the Burns and Stull shorts was a young Oliver Hardy, and Ms. Burton also appeared with him in one-reelers such as *He Winked and Won*, *The Other Girl*, and *The Love Bugs* (all 1917). When Vim closed many of the people behind the scenes and in front of the camera reorganized, and with the addition of Charlie Chaplin imitator Billy West formed the King Bee Film Corporation. Playing Edna Purviance to West's ersatz Chaplin in shorts like *Backstage, Dough-Nuts, Cupid's Rival (all 1917), The Straight and Narrow*, and *The Handy Man* (both 1918), she married director Arvid E. Gillstrom and basically left the screen after *Playmates* (1918), although she occasionally turned up in items directed by her husband such as the Lee Moran two-reeler *His High Horse* (1925).

Mae Busch (1891 – 1946)
Perhaps best-remembered for her sound film appearances as a shrewish Mrs. Oliver Hardy in *Sons of the Desert* (1933) or as Charlie Hall's a bit too-friendly wife in *Them Thar Hills* (1934), and *Tit for Tat* (1935), Mae Busch spent much time in silent comedy shorts as

Mae Busch during her early days with Triangle. Authors collection.

well as dramatic features. Born in Australia, she was on the stage for many years appearing with star Eddie Foy and touring with the revue *The Lasky Beauties*. She's said to have made her film debut doing a stunt for Mabel Normand in *The Water Nymph* (1912), but it wasn't until 1915 that she really joined the Mack Sennett ensemble for shorts like *Ye Olden Grafter, Love in Armor, The Best of Enemies* (all 1915), *Wife and Auto Trouble*, and *Because He Loved Her* (both 1916). She moved over to Fox to appear in some of their Foxfilm comedies and features such as *The Fair Barbarian* (1917). The films *The Devil's Passkey* (1920) and *Foolish Wives* (1922) for director Erich von Stroheim gave her career a boost and she became a star – working in prestigious productions like *The Christian* (1923) and *The Unholy Three* (1925). Rumors of being difficult and a nervous breakdown derailed the upward trajectory of her career, but she became a busy character actress. Her first appearance at the Hal Roach Studio came in the All Star Comedy *Love 'Em and Weep* (1927), and she became a regular there in the early 1930s. Besides her work there she also did shorts for RKO, and had bits in features. By the late 1930s most of her roles were uncredited, but she worked until her death at fifty-four in 1946.

Marion Byron (1911 – 1985) **See Chapter Nine**

Marie Cahill (1874 – 1933)
Musical comedy star billed as "the Goddess of Laughter" who was famous for productions such as *The Tin Soldier, The Wild Rose, Nancy Brown,* and *The New Yorkers*, not to mention her reoccurring signature routine which involved her telephone conversations with a friend named Ethel. In 1915 Ms. Cahill first transferred her antics to the screen with an adaptation of her stage success *Judy Forgot* for Universal. Two years later she embarked on some two-reelers that were distributed by Mutual – *Gladys' Day Dream, When Betty Bets,* and *Patsy's Partner* (all 1917). After this brief jaunt in films she returned to the stage and worked continually until the 1931 show *Merry-Go-Round*.

Stage star Marie Cahill during her short-lived movie career. Author's collection.

Betty Caldwell (Elizabeth Caldwell) (1908 – 1998)
Actress who went to Hollywood High with Fay Wray and Betty Boyd, and was a comedy leading lady in Educational two-reelers with Charley Bowers and Lupino Lane like *You'll Be Sorry* (1928) and *Fire Proof* (1929). Besides working with the team of Al Cooke and Kit Guard in their shorts and the feature *Her Father Said No* (1927), she also appeared in many westerns such as *Greased Lightning*, and *Girl-Shy Cowboy* (both 1928) with the likes of Kermit Maynard, Ted Wells, and Rex Bell before she left the screen in 1929.

Cameo (1919 – 1935) **See Chapter Seven**

Sadie Campbell (1912 - ?)
Blonde and curly child actress who was a leading lady for Buddy Messinger in his series of starring shorts for Century Comedies. Starting at age ten in 1923 Ms. Campbell supported Buddy in shorts such as *Smarty* (1923), *Quit Kidding*, and *A Young Tenderfoot* (both 1924). She also appeared uncredited as a fairy in Herbert Brenon's feature version of *Peter Pan* (1924).

Lucille Carlisle (Lucille Zintheo) (1895 – 1958)
Beautiful brunette who was the regular leading lady (on screen and off) in the early 1920s for Larry Semon. Before appearing with Semon she entered show business when she won a 1916 "Brains and Beauty" contest for *Photoplay Magazine*, and the next year she was on stage in the G.M. "Broncho Billy" Anderson produced Broadway musical *His Little Widows*. Her first film with Semon was *Boodles and Bandits* (1918), and she was soon very busy playing vamps, innocent country girls, aristocrats, or using her musical background when played the star of the shows in *The Stage Hand* (1920) and *The Show* (1922). Originally billed as Lucille Zintheo, she switched over to Carlisle with *The Star Boarder* (1919), and worked with Semon until 1923's *No Wedding Bells*, a very appropriate title as it appears she left the comedies due to the ending of their off screen relationship. Although it's said that she was up for the role of Esmeralda in the Lon Chaney *The Hunchback of Notre Dame* (1923), she left the movies and married successful businessman Leland H. Milikin. Outside of doing some radio work before and during the Second World War, she retired into private life.

Detective Larry Semon takes Lucille Carlisle into his confidence in *Dull Care* (1919). Courtesy of Jim Kerkhoff.

Ora Carew (1891 – 1955)
Coming from "sister acts, single acts and in sketches" in vaudeville and various stock companies, she made her film debut for Reliance / Majestic and then joined Keystone. Teamed there with long-time character comedian Joseph "Baldy" Belmont for a series of light romantic comedies which were more situational and less dependent on physical comedy, their series included *Dollars and Sense* (1916) and *Her Circus Knight* (1917) and were mostly directed by Walter Wright. After this group of films her career seems to have stalled. After a move into dramatic features such as *Getting Her Man* (1924) and *Cold Fury* (1925), her appearances sputtered out by the late 1920s. Returning to the stage, she later ran a cosmetics shop.

Helen "Ollie" Carlyle (1892 – 1933)
Brunette, born Helen Hellman to a prominent Los Angeles banking family, who became a busy Keystone comedy ingénue in 1914 and 1915. Usually playing small roles like maids or party guests in shorts such as *Hogan's Mussy Job, Love in Armor, That Little Band of Gold, Gussle's Wayward Path,* and *My Valet* (all 1915), her one female lead was in the Roscoe Arbuckle one-reeler *When Love Took Wings* (1915) where she's the object of rivalry between Roscoe and Joe Bordeaux who's revealed to be bald at the end of the picture! Marrying Sennett scenario editor and production manager Hampton Del Ruth during this time she retired from the screen, but after their 1920 divorce she returned to acting on the stage and made two final films, *Models and Wives* (1931) and *Forgotten Commandments* (1932) before she died at age forty in 1933.

Jewell Carmen (Evelyn Quick) (1894 – 1984)
An attractive blonde, who as Evelyn Quick appeared in many 1912 – 1913 Keystones such as *The Professor's Daughter, A Strong Revenge,* and *The Gangsters* (all 1913). Not long after the release of the last film Ms. Quick was involved in a case as one of a number of underage girls who were entertaining men at the Vernon and Venice Country Clubs.

Jewel Carmen during her stint as a frequent co-star for Douglas Fairbanks. Author's collection.

For some reason this sent Sennett and the bulk of the Keystone male comics to location shooting in Mexico until the whole thing blew over. After appearing in some L-Ko comedies like *The Jailbirds Last Flight* and *Ignatz's Icy Injury* (both 1916), she changed her name to Jewell Carmen and became a popular foil for Douglas Fairbanks in his features *Flirting with Fate, Manhattan Madness, The Half-Breed,* and *American Aristocracy* (all 1916). She made many more features, married director Roland West in 1918, appeared in his *Nobody* (1921), and her last film was *The Bat* (1926). Later a business partner with West (by then her ex-husband) and his current girlfriend Thelma Todd in the restaurant Thelma Todd's Sidewalk Café, she retired from the public eye after the investigation into Todd's death and died in her eighties in 1984.

Betty Carpenter (1899 – 1982)
Pretty blonde ingénue who made an impression in the Universal drama *The Kaiser, the Beast of Berlin* (1918), and became a leading lady for the likes of Billie Ritchie, Hugh Fay, and Slim Summerville in Fox Sunshine Comedies such as *The Fatal Marriage* (1918) and *A Lady Bell Hop's Secret* (1919). Perhaps due to the risks involved in making comedies, a 1918 incident left Carpenter, Sylvia Day, and Mary Rooleston badly bruised when a wagon they were riding in was struck by a train, she moved into features which included *Such a Little Queen* (1921), *Cardigan* (1922), and the popular Johnny Hines comedy *Burn Em Up Barnes* (1921). She retired after marrying Herman Axelrod in 1921, and became the mother of writer, director, and producer George Axelrod, famous for *The Seven Year Itch* (1955), *The Manchurian Candidate* (1962), and *Lord Love a Duck* (1966).

Mary Carr (1874 – 1973)
Long-time stage actress, who started out as a school teacher but became an actress in Philadelphia where she toured with the Gerard Stock Company and married actor William Carr. Specializing in mother roles in silent and sound features and shorts, she was famous for her star performance in *Over the Hill to the Poorhouse* (1920), and played supporting maternal figures in comedies such as *A Self-Made Failure* (1924), *The Wizard of Oz, Hogan's Alley* (both 1925), *Stop, Look and Listen,* and *Atta Boy* (both 1926). Her sound films include *Lights of New York* (1928), *Stout Hearts and Willing Hands,* and *One Good Turn* (both 1931) with Laurel & Hardy. She continued working until 1951, and lived to age ninety-nine.

Perennial screen mother Mary Carr played dramatic support in numerous comedies. Author's collection.

Helen Carruthers (1892 - 1925)
Ingénue who appeared in numerous 1914 Keystone comedies such as *The Property Man, Mabel's Blunder, His Musical Career,* and *Tillie's Punctured Romance.* The next year she had a vaudeville act that failed, and unable to get work attempted suicide. In 1918 she married Baron Franciscus Gerard Zur Muhlen, a Dutch sugar merchant from Java, and fell to her death from a New York hotel window in 1925.

Peggy Cartwright (1912 – 2001) Canadian-born child actress who worked for D.W. Griffith and Harold Lloyd in addition to being Our Gang's very first leading lady. After appearing as a toddler in *The Birth of a Nation* (1915) and *Intolerance* (1916) she became a regular in shorts such as Universal's *Billy the Bandit* (1916) with Smiling Billy Mason. Her best known work was with Harold Lloyd in *From Hand to Mouth* (1919) where she proved herself a real seven-year-old pro in some very intricate business and elaborate chases with Lloyd.

Peggy Cartwright and Sunshine Sammy in trouble from thugs, among them William Gillespie and Charles Stevenson, in *Young Sherlocks* (1922). Courtesy of Sam Gill.

After some features such as *The Third Generation* (1920), *Penrod*, and *Afraid to Fight* (both 1922), she was the female lead in the first five Our Gang comedies – *One Terrible Day, Fire Fighters, Young Sherlocks, Our Gang,* and *A Quiet Street* (all 1922). From here she moved on to independent productions like *Robin Hood Jr.* (1923) and a number of Jack White's Our Gang inspired *Juvenile Comedies* like *Three Cheers* (1923), *The Junior Partner,* and *Over the Fence* (both 1924). Ending her Hollywood career after playing Madge Bellamy as a child in John Ford's *The Iron Horse* (1924) she moved to England and appeared on stage in shows such as *Americana* and movies like *Hindle Wakes* and *Magic Night* (both 1932). After marrying comedian Phil Baker she mostly retired from performing outside of appearing with him on the radio. In 1989 she made a charming appearance in Kevin Brownlow and David Gill's *Harold Lloyd: The Third Genius* recounting her experiences working with Lloyd.

Louise Carver (1869 – 1958) **See Chapter Seven**

Lottie Case (?)
Character actress, active in the teens, who worked for the Liberty and Alhambra Film Manufacturing Companies (both distributed by Kriterion) and Universal in titles such as *School Boy's Memories or, Kids at School*, and *The Bold, Bad Burglar* (both 1915). In 1916 she joined the stock company at the fledgling Hal Roach organization and supported Harold Lloyd in numerous *Lonesome Luke* and early glasses character shorts that included *Lonesome Luke, Lawyer*, *Lonesome Luke, Mechanic*, *The Flirt* (all 1917), and *Here Comes the Girls* (1918).

Dolores Cassinelli (1888 – 1984)
Cassinelli was a Chicago-born actress who started her career there for the Essanay Company. Small roles in 1911 soon led to leads in shorts such as *Cupid's Leap Year Pranks*, *Detective Dorothy* (both 1912), *Mr. Dippy Dipped*, and *Love Incognito* (both 1913). After moving on to Selig in 1916 she became a star for the Emerald Motion Picture Company, appearing in dramas and as a regular in their *Tom and Jerry* comedy two-reelers, playing Mrs. Jerry in outings like *Tom and Jerry in a Fog*, and *Tom and Jerry in the Chorus* (both 1916). She later became something of an exotic clothes-horse in features for Leonce Perret and Albert Capellani, and in the 1920s turned up in independent films such as *Anne of Little Smoky* (1921), *Christopher Columbus* (1923), and *The Midnight Girl* (1925), before ending her film career in 1925. She later sang opera on the radio.

Nema Catto (1888 – 1986)
Stage dancer in vaudeville and burlesque who was the wife of performer Frederick J. Ireland, who was the George M. Cohan of Chicago theatre. In the mid-teens Ireland founded the Emerald Motion Picture Company in the Windy City, with Nema appearing in many of the Emerald offerings, such as some of Chaplin impersonator Billy West's films for the outfit like *Mustered Out* (1919), and the two-reel farce *When the Cat's Away* (1920) which starred her hubby Ireland in the lead. In 1920 Emerald merged with the Bulls Eye Film Company, the Bee Hive Film Exchange, and the Interstate Film Co. of New York to form the Reelcraft Pictures Corporation. Unfortunately the concern went bankrupt the next year and ended Catto and Ireland's film careers. Her younger sister Rhea Catto McLaughlin also appeared on stage and in the Emerald product.

Nita Cavalier (Juanita Cavalier) (1901 -1969)
Blonde ingénue whose walk-on parts in features like *A Thief in Paradise* (1925) led to becoming the female lead in western quickies such as *The Twin Triggers*, *The Dead Line* (both 1926), and *Tearin' into Trouble* (1927) with the likes of Buddy Roosevelt, Bob Custer, and Wally Wales. In 1927 she became the leading lady for Bray's live-action *Skylark Comedies*, where he was teamed with goofy Perry Murdock in two-reelers such as *Beauty and the Bump* (1927), *The Duke's Dirty Doings*, *The Bare Co-Ed*, *Lost in the Lurch*,

and *Hick in Hollywood* (all 1928). After supporting Edward Everett Horton in his short *Horse Shy* (1928) and the transition to sound, she toured a comedy sketch on the Keith Circuit with Mae Busch in 1929, and returned to pictures and Perry Murdock with some talking *Broadway Comedies* such as *The Wages of Gin* (1931), in addition to some mid 1930s action melodramas for William Pizor Productions.

Nora Cecil (1878 – 1951)

Irish-born actress, who specialized in gossips, mean landladies, and girl's school principals well into the sound era. She spent twelve years on stage in vaudeville and musical comedy in England and America before entering films in 1915 in Fort Lee, New Jersey. Already playing spinsters and orphanage matrons, she began her long career as a comic antagonist in features such as *The Social Secretary* (1916), *Tillie Wakes Up*, and *The Poor Little Rich Girl* (both 1917). Eventually heading out to Hollywood she continued being generally disapproving in *Darwin Was Right* (1924), *Lightin'*, *His Majesty Bunker Bean* (both 1925), and *The Fortune Hunter* (1927) with Syd Chaplin. The transition to sound saw her not missing a beat, as she kept working in many Hal Roach shorts with Charley Chase and Thelma Todd, in addition to countless features such as *The Old-Fashioned Way* (1934), *Nothing Sacred* (1937), *Stagecoach* (1939), *I Married a Witch* (1942), and *The Miracle of Morgan's Creek* (1944) where she was a perfect comic foil for everyone from W.C. Fields to Monty Wooley. She worked non-stop to 1947.

Nora Cecil and Charley Chase have a tangle in *Girl Grief* (1932). Courtesy of Robert Arkus.

Dixie Chene (1894 – 1972)

Chene was an ingénue who had been a dancer in vaudeville, touring in the act *Mary Jane and Buster Brown* with her older sister Hazel. She entered films in 1912 at Universal, and after a stint at Kay Bee settled in for two years at Keystone in shorts such as *The Noise of Bombs* (1914), *Gussle the Golfer* (1914), *Giddy, Gay and Ticklish* (1915), and *A Lucky Leap* (1915). Leaving Sennett for L-Ko, she returned to the stage in the late teens.

Virginia Cherrill (1908 – 1996)

Cherrill was a blonde society girl who's famous for her one silent screen role as the blind flower girl in Charlie Chaplin's *City Lights* (1931). Having no previous acting experience she met Chaplin socially, and it's thought that he may have hired her as he felt she resembled Edna Purviance. Although ultimately fine in the role, the working relationship between Ms. Cherrill and Chaplin was strained, due to her inexperience and Chaplin's frustration with his own creative blocks, with the comedian even firing her at one point. After the film's release she was signed by Fox and appeared in titles like *Girls Demand Excitement*, *The Brat*, and *Delicious* (all 1931), but she never caught on, and after two British productions, *Late Extra* (1935) and *Troubled Waters* (1936), she left the screen. Keeping herself busy with marriages and charity work, she made a memorable appearance in Kevin Brownlow and David Gill's documentary *Unknown Chaplin* (1983) where she gave her inside info on Chaplin and *City Lights*.

Ann Christy (Gladys Cronin, Gladys Harvey) (1905 – 1987)

Small, dark-haired ingénue, originally named Gladys Cronin, who began her career in 1926 with extra work in Century Comedies. As Gladys Harvey she was Snub Pollard's love interest in his Weiss Brothers' two-reeler *Fire* (1927) and quickly moved over to Christie Comedies where her name was changed to Ann Christy for her leading roles in shorts like *Dumb Belles*, *Queer Ducks*, *No Sparking* (all 1927), and *Say Uncle* (1928). Small parts in features like Harry Langdon's *Long Pants* (1927) led to her playing the title role in Columbia's *The Kid Sister* (1927). In 1928 she was chosen to succeed Jobyna Ralston as Harold Lloyd's love interest in his last silent film *Speedy* (1928), and followed that up with *The Water Hole* (1928), *Just Off Broadway*, and Hoot Gibson's *The Lariat Kid* (both 1929). When sound arrived she returned to shorts for Universal, Mack Sennett, and Hal Roach such as *The Take-Off* (1929), *Good-Bye Legs, Hello Television* (both 1930), *Big Ears* (1931), and *Dream House* (1932), plus appeared in the feature *The Fourth Alarm* (1930) and *Behind Stone Walls* (1932) before she married a Texas businessman and retired in 1932.

Ann Christy with Jimmie Adams (middle) and William Irving (right) in *No Sparking* (1927). Courtesy of Robert Arkus.

Ethlyne Clair (1904 – 1996)
Atlanta-born beauty who put aside her art studies when she began appearing in small roles in features such as *Sandra* (1921), *The Golden Bed*, and *Chickie* (both 1925). In 1926 she was put under contract by Universal's Century Comedies and played Mrs. Newlywed in the studio's *The Newlyweds and Their Baby* series. In two-reelers like *Snookum's Tooth*, *The Newlywed's Quarantine* (both 1926), and *Snookum's Playmate* (1927) she appeared with Sunny McKeen, Jed Dooley, and Sid Saylor, besides turning up in other Centurys with Charles King and Charles Dorety. While continuing with *The Newlyweds* until 1928 she also worked in westerns such as *Painted Ponies* (1927), *Riding for Fame* (1928), and *Gun Law* (1929). Unfortunately she didn't transfer well to sound films, and after a few small roles retired in 1932.

Bessie Clark (?)
Actress from the stage, who began her career there at the age of eight in stock and road shows, who was part of the ensemble in L-Ko Comedies and moved on to being leading lady for George Ovey in Cub Comedies such as *Jerry's Big Game* (1916).

Trilby Clark (1903 – 1983)
Australian-born beauty who appeared in musical comedy and a few films in her native country before coming to New York and working in *The Greenwich Village Follies*. After the feature *Big Dan* (1923) with Buck Jones she appeared in comedies for Fox, and in 1924 was hired by Century Comedies to play in shorts opposite the likes of Hilliard Karr and Billy Engle. Features with Harry Carey and Pete Morrison followed, and in 1927 she re-located to England where she starred in late 1920s and early 1930s features such as *Maria Marten* (1928) and *The Night Porter* (1930).

Virginia Clark (?)
Comedy ingénue who started out as a child performer in Edison and Majestic production such as *The Orphan, Bill's Sweetheart* (both 1913), *His First Love*, and *The Tie that Binds* (both 1914). Besides turning up in *Gloria's Romance* (1916) with Billie Burke, she also worked for Perry Comedies, Billy Quirk, Pokes & Jabbs at Vim, and in Billy West King Bee comedies like *The Hobo* (1917). She was teamed with Claude Cooper and Kenneth Clarendon for Commonwealth Comedy Company shorts such as *The Hod Carrier's Million* (1917), and her last work appears to have been as Jimmy Aubrey's leading lady for his series of 1918 Tom Bret-produced comedies that included *His Vinegar Bath, Twins Bedrooms,* and *Why Not Marry.*

Emma Clifton (Emma Bell Clifton) (1893 - ?)
Actress, who resembled a plump Mabel Normand, and was a Keystone leading lady in *Double Crossed* and *Between Showers* (both 1914) but soon defected to Sterling Comedies.

The daughter of screenwriters Wallace C. Clifton and Emma Bell, she started her own film career after visiting her uncle at the Lubin Studio in 1912. Coming west with the company she joined Keystone in 1913, and then Sterling in 1914. For Sterling she supported star Ford Sterling in outings such as *Love and Vengeance*, *The Fatal Wedding*, and *A Shooting Match* (all 1914) before soon leaving the screen.

Ivy Close (1890 – 1968)
International beauty born in England who briefly had her own starring series of comedies in America. In 1908 she became famous when she entered and won the Daily Mirror's "Most Beautiful Woman in the World" contest. This led to her appearing on stage, and in 1910 she married Elwin Neame. After making her film debut with Hepworth

Ivy Close had a short-lived comedy series for Kalem before returning to England. Author's collection.

in 1912, she and Neame set up the Ivy Close Film Company. They made dramas like *Dream Paintings*, *The Lady of Shalott* (both 1912), and *The Legend of King Cophetua* (1913), as well as the comedies *The Terrible Twins*, *Ghosts*, *Two Elderly Cupids* (all 1914), and *The Haunting of Silas P. Gould* (1915). May 1916 saw the Kalem Company sign Ms. Close for a series of comedy one-reelers. Production began at the studio's Jacksonville, Florida plant, with direction by Robert Ellis and a supporting cast made up of Henry Murdock, Arthur Albertson, William McKay, Mary Taylor-Ross, and Frances NeMoyer.

After a dozen titles, that included *The Girl and the Tenor*, *Tangled by Telephone*, *That Pesky Parrott*, and *The Battered Bridegroom* (all 1916), the series was discontinued when Close decided to return to England when her husband Neame was called up for World War I service and a brother, Raymond Close, was killed in the trenches of France. Unfortunately at the moment none of the series is known to exist. Her later work included the British features *The Ware Case* (1917), *The Irresistible Flapper* (1919), and *The Worldlings* (1920), but her most famous role was as the female lead in Abel Gance's epic *La Roue* (*The Wheel*, 1923). She left films after the German-made features *Die Halle der Jungfrauen* (*The Hall of the Maidens*, 1928) and *Der Fidele Bauer* (*The Jolly Peasant*, 1929). Although her first husband Neame died in a motorcycle accident in 1923, their family became a British film dynasty which included well-known director and cinematographer son Ronald, another son Derek was a scriptwriter, and grandson Christopher and great-grandson Gareth were both producers.

Margaret Cloud (?)
Beautiful brunette who made the rounds as a comedy ingénue for Century, Christie, and Bull Montana in shorts such as *Horse Sense* (1922), *Take Your Choice*, and *The Two Twins* (both 1923). After taking up residence as a bathing girl at the Mack Sennett lot in 1923 she was in two-reelers on the order of *Down to the Sea in Shoes* (1923), *The Hollywood Kid*, *His New Mamma* (both 1924), *The Plumber* (1925), and the feature *His First Flame* (1927). After roles in two independent features, *He Who Laughs Last* (1925) and *Broadway Madness* (1927), she retired from the screen.

Dorothy Coburn (1905 – 1978)
Beautiful brunette whose daily swim in the Culver City Community Pool led her to being sent to the Hal Roach Studios to double Helene Chadwick in swimming and diving for the two-reeler *Wise Guys Prefer Brunettes* in May 1926. She doubled for others for a few months but soon moved up to roles in *Putting Pants on Phillip* (1927), *The Finishing Touch* (1928), *Do Gentlemen Snore?* (1928), and other Roach comedies. In 1928 as part of an odd economy move the Roach company let Coburn, Edna Marion, and Viola Richard go, and afterward Coburn turned up at Universal where she appeared in a number of Syd Saylor's *Let George Do It* Comedies like *Rubber Necks* (1928) and *Sailor Suits* (1929), in addition to Charley Chase's 1929 feature *Modern Love*.

Dorothy Coburn shares a laugh with Stan Laurel and Oliver Hardy during the making of *The Finishing Touch* (1928). Courtesy of Cole Johnson.

Goldie Colwell (1893 – 1982)
Scottish-born character actress, who began her career on stage in 1911 in a Kansas City rep. company and moved to films for Selig the following year. There she appeared in many dramatic shorts and eventually Tom Mix's light-hearted western comedies such as *Why the Sheriff is a Bachelor*, *The Ranger's Romance* (both 1914), and *Cactus Jim's Shop Girl* (1915). In 1915 she went over to David Horsley's comedies, first for MinA and then Cub, where she supported George Ovey in titles like *A Mix-Up in Males*, *Waking Up Father*, *Jerry's Busy Day*, and *The Oriental Spasm* (all 1915). After a brief spell in 1916 doing more dramatic fare for brands like Bison, Centaur, and Victor, she returned to Cub for items such as *Jerry's Big Mystery* and *Jerry and the Vampire* (both 1917) before her career ended in 1919.

Mathilde Comont (Mathilde Caumont and Mattie Comont) (1886 – 1938) **See Chapter One**

Betty Compson (1897 – 1974) **See Chapter Four**

Grayce Connell (?)
Showgirl who appeared in numerous revues and cabarets shows, including at G.M. Anderson's Gaiety Theatre in San Francisco, and had a brief stint at Keystone in shorts like *His Last Laugh* and *Bath Tub Perils* (both 1916) before returning to the stage.

Della Connor (?)
Pretty blonde who began her career on stage as a child with Gus Edwards, and around 1900 became a popular show girl in musicals like *Sally in Our Alley*, *The Office Boy*, and *Sergeant Brue*. Her first film work was as a comedy ingénue for Pathé, and she joined the George Kleine organization in 1914 for features such as *Officer 666* (1914) and *The Woman Next Door* (1914). She soon became the regular leading lady in Kleine's *The Mishaps of Musty Suffer* series (1916 – 1917), where she supported star Harry Watson Jr. with her good looks, and provided the only sympathetic character in Musty's trials and tribulations. Also appearing with Leon Errol in the Kleine produced *Nearly Spliced* (shot in 1916 but released in 1921), her career wound down and her last title is the 1926 western short *Rustler by Proxy*.

Norma Contero (?)
Dark-haired ingénue who was a leading for Al St John in many of his Fox Studio two-reelers such as *Small Town Stuff* (1921) and *All Wet* (1922).

Virginia Lee Corbin (1910 – 1942)
Pretty blonde who began her career as a child actress and made a smooth transition to adult leading lady. After modeling for artists she made her film debut at six in 1916, and first worked at D.W. Griffith's Fine Arts Studio in *Let Katie Do It* and *Intolerance* (both 1916). From there she moved to Universal and appeared in a number of their Rex and Victor shorts such as *By Conscience's Eye* (1916), *The Old Toymaker*, and *Somebody Lied* (both 1917). Previously at Fine Arts she had worked with brothers Sidney and Chester Franklin, and in 1917 they embarked on a series of tongue-in-cheek kid-starring adventure films for Fox that included *Jack and the Beanstalk*, *Aladdin and the Wonderful Lamp* (both 1917), *Treasure Island*, and *Fan Fan* (both 1918). Virginia, co-starred with master Francis Carpenter, was their pint-sized leading lady, and with the children playing their roles seriously the films were charming spoofs of adult super productions. Hitting the awkward age of ten in 1920 she left films for a few years and appeared on the Keith-Orpheum vaudeville circuit. Her act consisted of "songs, dances, impersonations, but

the outstanding incident of her act is her portrayal of a newsboy, ragged and unkempt, who enters the home of a rich man, is delighted with the toys scattered about the room, and heartbroken when gruffily ordered to get out."

After a few years of getting good notices for her act she returned to pictures as a young lady and became a dependable and popular comedy leading lady in features like *Hands Up!*, *Ladies at Play* (both 1926), *The Perfect Sap*, *Play Safe* (both 1927), *Bare Knees*, and *The Little Snob* (both 1928). Although she made the transition to sound she wound down her career after marrying in 1929, and left the screen to have a family. Sadly the remainder of her life was not happy – her first husband divorced her for habitual drunkenness in 1936 and won custody of their two children. In 1940 she tried to make a comeback in movies, but she died in a sanitarium in 1942. The official cause of death was tuberculosis, but it's said to have been the result of her drinking. She was only thirty-two years old.

Virginia Lee Corbin in the late 1920s. Author's collection.

Anne Cornwall (1897 – 1980) **See Chapter Five**

Blanche Cornwall (1868 - ?)
Part of the ensemble at Alice Guy's Solax Film Company, who appeared in all types of films including numerous comedies with Billy Quirk, Fraunie Fraunholz, and Lee Beggs such as *Lend Me Your Wife*, *Canned Harmony* (both 1912), *Burstup Holmes*, *Cooking for Trouble*, and *The Coat that Came Back* (all 1913). Her career appears to have ended in 1913.

Minerva Courtney (?)
Courtney was an odd little blip in the line of film comediennes. By 1915 Charlie Chaplin had become the national rage with audiences unable to get enough of the little tramp. To fill this demand outright imitators such as Billie Ritchie and Ray Hughes were recruited by eager film producers, and in 1915 Minerva Courtney offered her version of Charlie in three shorts made by the Metropolis Film Manufacturing Company – *Minerva Courtney in her Impersonation of Charles Chaplin*, *Minerva Courtney as Chaplin; Putting It Over*, and *Minerva Courtney as Chaplin in Her Job in the Laundry*. Although Ms. Courtney is said to have been "well known in vaudeville circles as an impersonator of men," the first film of the three still exists and shows that her imitation was, frankly, unexceptional. The slender plot has Minerva as an out of work actress asking for a job at a film studio. After be-

ing turned down she pleads "Please give me a chance. I can do as good as Chaplin and can even impersonate him!" So the studio lets her re-enact scenes from *The Champion* (1915) as Charlie. Although she's the right size and has Chaplin's slight build, Courtney looks more like Mickey Rooney as Mickey McGuire, even with the Chaplin moustache. She also has no sense of timing and isn't funny at all. Overall the film is a curiosity, and confirms the *Moving Picture World*'s opinion that the shorts were "hastily prepared and technically a bit crude." After this Courtney vanished from films.

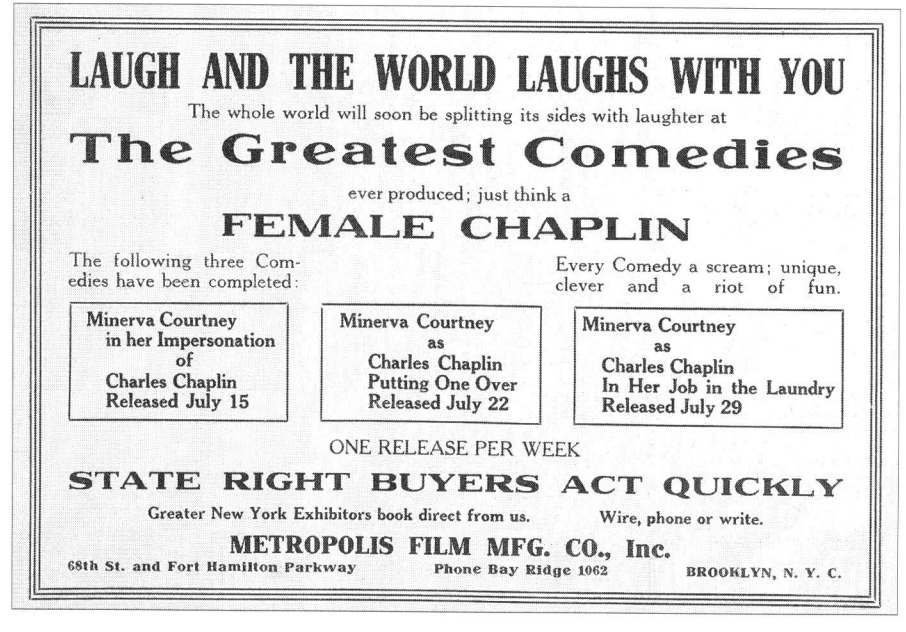

> # LAUGH AND THE WORLD LAUGHS WITH YOU
> The whole world will soon be splitting its sides with laughter at
> ## The Greatest Comedies
> ever produced; just think a
> ## FEMALE CHAPLIN
>
> The following three Comedies have been completed:
>
> Every Comedy a scream; unique, clever and a riot of fun.
>
> | Minerva Courtney in her Impersonation of Charles Chaplin Released July 15 | Minerva Courtney as Charles Chaplin Putting One Over Released July 22 | Minerva Courtney as Charles Chaplin In Her Job in the Laundry Released July 29 |
>
> ONE RELEASE PER WEEK
>
> ## STATE RIGHT BUYERS ACT QUICKLY
> Greater New York Exhibitors book direct from us.   Wire, phone or write.
> **METROPOLIS FILM MFG. CO., Inc.**
> 68th St. and Fort Hamilton Parkway   Phone Bay Ridge 1062   BROOKLYN, N. Y. C.

Trade magazine ad for Minerva Courtney's Charlie Chaplin imitations.

Ivy Crosthwaite (1897 – 1962)
A champion woman swimmer of the Pacific Coast who had spent time on stage, and because of her aquatic skills became a Keystone bathing girl. Starting with the short *Their Husbands* (1913), she became a leading lady in Triangle Sennett films such as *Fickle Fatty's Fall, A Game Old Knight* (both 1915), and *By Stork Delivery* (1916). Married to Keystone cop and assistant director Adolph Linkof, Crosthwaite retired from films and later managed a coffee shop at Los Angeles' Santa Fe Railroad offices.

Josephine Crowell (Josephine Bonaparte Crowell) (1859 – 1932)
Long-time stage actress born in Canada, who worked for many years with producers and stars such as Frank Keenan and Klaw & Erlanger before entering pictures at Biograph. Although she made her screen name in dramatic parts in D.W. Griffith epics like *The Birth of a Nation* (1915), *Hearts of the World* (1918) and others, this busy character actress

was equally at home in comedy. Perfect as a snobby matron or overbearing mother-in-law, some of her most memorable comedic moments are with Harold Lloyd in *Hot Water* (1924), in Charley Chase's *Dog Shy* (1926), opposite Edward Everett Horton in *Dad's Choice* (1928), and her last film, *Wrong Again* (1929), with Laurel & Hardy.

Margaret Cullington (Margaret Cullington Fitzroy) (1885 – 1925)
Overlooked character player who had the market cornered on battle-axes and old maids. She made her debut in 1916 doing shorts for Universal and supporting George Ovey in Cub Comedies, sometimes with her first husband Louis Fitzroy, such as *A Merry Mix-Up*, and *Jerry's Stratagem* (both 1916). She soon appeared in features like *Betty Takes a Hand* (1918), *Wolves of the Border* (1923), and *Excitement* (1924), but most of her work was done in short comedies. She was an on and off regular in Christie Comedies and Reggie Morris' *Speed Comedies* for Arrow, plus had her only major starring role as Maggie in the three *Bringing Up Father* two-reelers Al Christie produced in 1920. Also supporting Eddie Lyons, Jimmie Adams, and Monty Banks, she sadly died young in 1925. According to her Variety obituary the death of her second husband, Lieutenant William Fowler who was killed in a plane crash three years before, was directly responsible for her passing and leaving a fourteen year-old son.

Margaret Cullington and an unknown actor in Special Pictures' 1920 *A Ballroom Romeo*. Courtesy of EYE Filmmuseum, Netherlands.

Florence Curtis (1896 – 1972)
Dark-haired dancer who had appeared in stage acts such as *The Cohan Revue* and *Jack Hunt's Merry Makers* before she joined Vitagraph to become Larry Semon's leading lady in 1917 one-reelers that include *Tough Luck and Tin Lizzies*, *Rooftops and Ruffians*, and *Plagues and Puppy Love*. She also supported the forgotten "Big V" comedian Walter Hall in 1918 before leaving the screen.

Yola D'Avril (1907 – 1984)
Actress, born in Lille, France, who was a dancer before making films in Europe, where she worked with Gloria Swanson in the feature *Madame Sans Gene* (1924). Ms. Swanson advised her to go to Hollywood, and there Ms. D'Avril began appearing in Christie

Comedies such as *Yes, Yes, Babette* (1925), *Fresh Faces*, and *Have Courage* (both 1926). Features like *Orchids and Ermine* (1927), *Lady Be Good*, and *Vamping Venus* (both 1928) soon followed. When sound arrived she continued playing humorous French girls in features and Mack Sennett shorts such as *A Hollywood Theme Song* (1930) and *The College Vamp* (1931) until the early 1950s.

Irene Dalton (1900 – 1934)
Attractive damsel in distress in the early 1920s, she appeared in many Christie Comedies and a few shorts like *The Author* (1923) with Al St John, supported Lloyd Hamilton in six two-reelers that included *The Vagrant* (1921) and *Rolling Stones* (1922), plus did a couple of features such as *Children of Jazz* and *Bluebeard's Eighth Wife* (both 1923). In addition to working with Hamilton she later became his second wife for just a few months in 1927 – 1928. Her last film appearance was in 1923, and she died young at age thirty-three, passing away in 1934 just a year before Hamilton.

Irene Dalton and Lloyd Hamilton (right) try to pretend that Bobby DeVilbiss isn't hanging around in *Rolling Stones* (1922).
Courtesy of Robert S. Birchard.

Marcella Daly (Dorothy Drew) (1901 – 1966)
Pretty brunette who began her career in small roles in 1918, doing uncredited work in big budget productions such as *Rosita* (1923) and *Dorothy Vernon of Haddon Hall* (1924), and eventually moving up to featured supporting roles. In 1925, under the name Dorothy Drew, she starred in four independent dramas that were directed by Del Henderson –

Defend Yourself, Pursued, Accused (all 1925), and *The Pay-Off* (1926) which didn't lead to any other starring work. Going back to Marcella Daly she became a regular ingénue in Jack White and Fox two-reelers like *The Movies* (1925), *Careful Please, Midnight Follies, The Tennis Wizard* (all 1926), and *Roses and Romance* (1927), plus was busy as support in the features *The Prince of Pep* (1925), *Black Paradise* (1926), *Married Alive, Silk Stockings* (both 1927), and *Two Lovers* (1928) before her career ended.

Viola Dana (Virginia Flugrath) (1897 – 1987)
The middle of three Brooklyn-born Flugrath sisters (along with Edna Flugrath and Shirley Mason), who became a major star of the teens and twenties. Like her siblings she was on stage as a child, appearing with Joseph Jefferson in *Rip Van Winkle*, in addition to other shows such as *The Squaw Man* and *The Littlest Rebel*, even scoring a hit as the title character in *The Poor Little Rich Girl*. Joining the rest of the family with the Edison Company's acting ensemble in 1912 she appeared in many comedies like *The Butler and the Maid* (1912), *My Friend from India, The Adventure of the Hasty Elopement*, and *Seth's Sweetheart* (all 1914). She began breaking out as a star in 1915 under the direction of John Collins. The couple married and their films together included *Gladiola* (1915), *The Cossack Whip* (1916), *Aladdin's Other Lamp, The Girl Without a Soul*, and *Blue Jeans* (all 1917) before Collins died of influenza in 1918.

**Viola Dana in the 1920s.
Author's collection.**

She continued on as a popular star for Metro and others all through the 1920s in pictures like *Cinderella's Twin* (1920), *The Off Shore Pirate* (1921), *Roughed Lips* (1923), *Merton of the Movies, Open All Night* (both 1924), *Kosher Kitty Kelly* (1926), and *That Certain Thing* (1928). Her career wound down in the early 1930s but she returned on television in the 1950s and 1960s. She appeared as herself and offered humorous and moving commentaries in the Kevin Brownlow and David Gill documentaries *Hollywood* (1980) and *Buster Keaton: A Hard Act to Follow* (1987).

Viora Daniel (1902 – 1980)
California-born brunette who began her career with Paramount in 1920. While there she supported Roscoe Arbuckle in *The Life of the Party* (1920), in addition to other comic features like *The Sins of St. Anthony* and *The Fourteenth Man* (both 1920). After appearing with Max Linder in *Be My Wife* (1921) she became a regular in Christie Comedies, working with Neal Burns, Bobby Vernon, Jay Belasco, and Earl Rodney. Her two-reelers for the comedy producer include *Let Me Explain, In for Life, A Pair of Sexes* (all 1921), *A Barnyard Cavalier, Cold Feet*, and *That Son of a Sheik* (all 1922). After this she turned up sporadically in features such as *Old Shoes* (1925), *Quarantined Rivals*, and *Bulldog Pluck* (both 1927), but left films in 1927.

Bebe Daniels (1901 – 1971) **See Chapter Five**

Phyllis Daniels (1886 – 1959)
Character actress, and mother of Bebe Daniels, who after extensive stage experience entered movies in 1912. She appeared in many Kalem comedies with Ruth Roland and John E Brennan such as *Ranch Girls on a Rampage* (1912), *The Laundress and the Lady* (1913), and *The Confiscated Count* (1914). She later became the Keystone wardrobe mistress and did bits in Sennett and Triangle shorts like *Skirt Strategy, His Hidden Talent, Their Husbands* (all 1917), and *Hide and Seek, Detectives* (1918).

Thelma Daniels (?)
Daniels was a dark-haired beauty who began her vaudeville career at the age of six, and danced for many years on the Orpheum and Harris Circuits. She was recruited by Al Christie for Christie Comedies and appeared opposite Bobby Vernon in *Dummy Love* (1926), but soon moved over to Stern Brother's Comedies where she played often with Syd Saylor in *Let George Do It* comedies like *George the Winner* (1926) and *George Meets George* (1928), plus took over their *It Happened to Jane* series when Wanda Wiley left for entries such as *Jane's Honeymoon* and *Jane's Hubby* (both 1927). In addition to other Stern product like their *Mike and Ike* shorts, she moonlighted at Weiss Brothers in the ersatz Laurel & Hardy comedies of Snub Pollard and Marvin Loback. Thelma supported the imitating pair in *Mitt the Prince, Once Over* (both 1928), and *The Big Shot* (1929). Her features included *The Laffin Fool* (1927) and *The Amazing Vagabond* (1929), and after a couple of sound shorts she left the screen.

Constance Darling and Charles King in the *Century* Comedy *What'll You Have?* (1927). Courtesy of Jim Kerkhoff.

Constance Darling (?)
Darling was an ingénue who was groomed by Century Comedies to be a comedy leading lady. Between 1925 and 1927 she worked with the likes of Al Alt, Edna Marion, and Blanche Payson, although most of her time was spent playing opposite Charles King in the studio's *Excuse Makers* series. Her titles include *Raisin' Cain*, *A Rough Party* (both 1925), *Honeymooning with Ma*, *Please Excuse Me* (both 1926), *Snookum's Playmate*, *What's Your Hurry?*, and *Keeping His Word* (all 1927).

Helen Darling (1895 – 1972)
Born Helen Mitchell MacCorquodale in Portland, Oregon, this former café dancer was brought to films by producer Al Christie in 1919 and quickly became a leading lady in Christie Comedies such as *Save Me, Sadie* (1920), *Falling for Fanny*, and *No Parking* (both 1921). She also appeared in shorts like *Single and Double* and *Twin Husbands* (both 1921) for Universal as well as some Morris Schlank produced Arrow Broadway Comedies with Harry Gribbon and Eddie Barry before leaving the screen in 1922. Her last known credit is for the story of the Universal western short *Hearts of the West* (1926). Her younger sister Margaret MacCorquodale was actress Lassie Young.

Jean Darling (1922 - 2015)
Cute little blonde who replaced Mary Kornman as Our Gang's leading lady. Joining the Gang in 1927 for adventures such as *Ten Years Old* (1927), *School Begins* (1928), and *Wiggle Your Ears* (1929), she was often the femme fatale who would cause jealousy and battles between the boys. Leaving the series in 1929, just after the transition to sound,

she continued her career in films, vaudeville, radio, television, and on Broadway as the original Carrie in *Carousel*. For many years she appeared regularly at film festivals with her *Our Gang* shorts.

Beth Darlington (?)
Cute brunette, who started her career in 1921 as a bathing girl in Jack White Comedies and worked her way up to being a comedy lead. After a bit in the feature *The Lamplighter* (1921) she became leading lady for Eddie Lyons in some of his Arrow Comedies such as *Just in Time* (1921) and *Keep Moving* (1922), many written by Robert MacGowan, and soon settled into a stint at the Hal Roach Studio where she supported Charley Chase in many of his early "Jimmie Jump" one-reelers like *The Fraidy Cat*, *Outdoor Pajamas*, and *Sitting Pretty* (all 1924), played Will Rogers' daughter in his Alfalfa Doolittle shorts *Our Congressman* and *A Truthful Liar* (1924), plus worked with Our Gang, Paul Parrott, and Snub Pollard. The last leg of her career was at Century Comedies, headlining in shorts like *Too Much Mother-in-Law* and *Married Neighbors* (both 1925) with the likes of Buddy Messinger, Charles King, Al Alt, Hilliard Karr, Billy Engle, and Eddie Gordon.

Beth Darlington and Charley Chase in a Hal Roach publicity photo. Courtesy of Cole Johnson.

Grace Darmond (1898 – 1963)
Cool blonde, born in Canada, who was discovered by the Selig Company in a school play and joined their acting ensemble in 1914 at age sixteen. Initially spending her time in comedy shorts such as *A Pair of Stockings*, *When the Clock Went Wrong*, *The Lure of the Ladies*, and *An Egyptian Princess* (all 1914), she graduated to dramatic features for Selig in 1915, not to mention comedies like *A Black Sheep* (1915) before moving over to Vitagraph for serious fare like *In the Balance* (1917) and *The Other Man* (1918). The rest of her career saw her mostly in dramas, but she would occasionally return to comedy for two Al Christie features, *So Long Letty* (1920) and *See My Lawyer* (1921), plus *White and Unmarried* (1921), *I Can Explain* (1922), and *Honesty - The Best Policy* (1926). The latter

part of the 1920s saw her appearing in the lower-budgeted independents, and she left the business in 1927, but did return to do uncredited walk-on in the early 1940s.

Carrie Daumery (1863 – 1938)
Daumery was a thin, older character actress who appeared in many comedy features and specialized in European countesses or other kinds of society matrons. Although not funny in herself, her severe presence was often used for comic effect. Born in Brussels, she went on the stage at age seventeen, eventually playing with Sarah Bernhardt, and appeared in some early French films. World War 1 put an end to her European career, and after the war an impoverished Ms. Daumery and her son, a recovering battle veteran, relocated to London and then California. She was soon making the rounds of the studios as an extra when she caught the eye of director Rex Ingram, who cast her as Alice Terry's mother in *The Conquering Power* (1921). More roles followed and her comedy features included *Forbidden Paradise* (1924), *Lady Windermere's Fan* (1925), *Young April* (1926), *Upstream* (1927), *The Cardboard Lover* (1928), and *The Last Warning* (1929). After some featured roles in the early days of sound she became an uncredited bit player until 1937.

Alice Davenport disciplines Al St John in *The Hayseed* (1921).
Courtesy of Sam Gill.

Alice Davenport (1864 – 1936) (Alice Shepard)
One of the earliest Keystone players, this perennial mother figure had started her stage career at the age of five and spent twenty-five years in stock companies and vaudeville.

A 1893 – 1896 marriage to actor Harry Davenport (later Dr. Meade in 1939's *Gone with the Wind*) left her with the last name and two daughters – Ann and Dorothy (later Mrs. Wallace Reid). After brief stints at Nestor and Horsley she joined Keystone when the company hit the West Coast in 1912, around the time of *Stolen Glory* (October 14), and remained an important player through 1919. Almost always turning up as the no-nonsense mother or mother-in-law of Mabel Normand or Roscoe Arbuckle, she could also be flirty wives or stage-struck matrons. Sennett actress Dixie Chene told historian Sam Gill that there were a lot of underage girls at Keystone, and not only was Davenport called "Mother Davenport" by the girls, but that she and Phyllis Allen watched out for the teens as far as the men on the lot. Having moonlighted a bit in 1916 for Kalem and Rolin, Ms. Davenport left Sennett for good in 1919 to become a regular in Fox Sunshine Comedies supporting the likes of Slim Summerville, Ethel Teare, and Al St John. Less active in the 1920s, her feature appearances include *Skirts* (1921), *Unmarried Wives* (1924), *Legend of Hollywood* (1924), and *The Dude Wrangler* (1930).

Marion Davies (1897 – 1961) **See Chapter Five**

Mildred Davis (1901 – 1969) **See Chapter Eight**

Virginia Davis (1918 – 2009)
Before Mickey Mouse or Annette Funicello, Virginia Davis was the original Walt Disney star. At the age of five she became the first Alice in his breakthrough *Alice in Cartoonland* series. Born in Kansas City, Missouri, Virginia began dancing and taking acting lessons at a young age, and appeared in ads shown in local movie theatres. Disney saw her in an ad for Wareneker's Bread at the time he was planning a jump from from his animated *Laugh-O-Grams* to a combination of live-action and cartoon. Approaching Davis' parents, Disney now had a heroine and made a pilot, *Alice's Wonderland* (1923) in Kansas. When it was picked up by producer M.J. Winkler, Virginia and her family moved with the Disney unit to California. The early Alice shorts were more live-action than animation (which was expensive) and Virginia, who with her long blonde curls was a miniature Mary Pickford, acted with regular Hollywood kids like Spec O'Donnell and Tommy Hicks in situations and gags that were very inspired by Our Gang. After ten shorts that included *Alice's Fishy Story, Alice Gets in Dutch* (both 1924), and *Alice Cans the Cannibals* (1925) she left the series. Working in small bits as a dance extra in films like *Three on a Match* (1932), *College Holiday* (1936), *My Gal Sal* (1942), and *The Harvey Girls* (1946), Virginia stayed in touch with Disney and later worked at the studio inking and painting, as well as doing voice work on *Snow White and the Seven Dwarfs* (1937) and *Pinocchio* (1940). In her eighties she was rediscovered and appeared at film festivals with surviving Alice shorts.

Charlotte Dawn (?)
Dainty brunette singer from the stage, who became the ingénue in *The Kick in High Life* and *Wet and Warmer* (both 1920), two of Henry Lehrman's independent comedy shorts for First National Pictures. Continuing her singing career in California and New York in venues such as *Marquard's Café* in San Francisco and *The Bluebird Café* in Los Angeles, Ms. Dawn may have returned to films in the late 1920s in Stern Brothers comedies such as *Watch George* (1928) with Sid Saylor, but at the moment this is unconfirmed.

Consuelo Dawn (Connie Dawn) (1907 – 1976)
Striking dark-haired leading lady who first started showing up in Fox two-reelers such as *A Cloudy Romance* (1925) and *A Flaming Affair* (1926), and passed through Mack Sennett shorts on the order of *Soldier Man, Masked Mamas*, and *The Divorce Dodger* (all 1926) before becoming Neely Edward's regular partner in Universal Bluebird Comedies. Paired in a year of one-reel domestic outings such as *In for Life, The Little Pest*, and *Surprised Honey* (all 1927), Dawn's career tapered off after with her last film being the western feature *Two-Gun Caballero* (1931).

Doris Dawson (1909 – 1986)
A pretty brunette, born in Towaco, New Jersey, who broke into films as a hand double. Eventually all of her was seen on screen when she became a "Christie Girl" in the late 1920s, appearing in shorts like *Swiss Movements* (1927) with Jimmie Adams and *Just the Type* (1928). She moved into features such as *The Little Shepard of Kingdom Come* (1928) and played Harry Langdon's sweetheart in his last independent (and missing) feature *Heart Trouble* (1928). Her talkie roles were small and her career ended in 1934.

Alice Day (1906 – 1995) **See Chapter Five**

Marceline Day (1908 – 2000)
Younger sister of Mack Sennett star Alice Day, who also started her career at the studio supporting the likes of Harry Langdon in *The Luck of the Foolish* and *The Hansom Cabman* (both 1924). She soon moved on to Universal shorts such as *Discord in 'A' Flat* and *The Party* (both 1925) as leading lady to Arthur Lake, and then made the jump to low-budget features like *Looking for Trouble* and *College Days* (both 1926). 1926 saw her named a WAMPAS Baby Star, and better films like *The Beloved Rogue* (1927) led to a contract with MGM for pictures such as *Rookies, London After Midnight, Captain Salvation* (all 1927), and her best-known role in *The Cameraman* (1928) with Buster Keaton. Her later films ended up being B westerns and cheapie features, including the infamous *Damaged Lives* (1933) before her career ended in 1933.

Marceline Day encourages Buster Keaton in *The Cameraman* (1928) as Harold Goodwin (left) and Sidney Bracey (right) plan to throw him out. Courtesy of Robert Arkus.

Priscilla Dean (1896 – 1987)
Actress who became a popular leading lady in crime melodramas such as *The Wicked Darling* (1919) and *Outside the Law* (1920), but began her career in comedy shorts. Born in New York to stage actor parents, she began appearing with them as an infant, and worked in the companies of well-known performers such as Joseph Jefferson and Jones A. Herne. Her initial films were for the Biograph Company, and from there she moved through Imp, Edison, and William Brady productions before she joined the ensemble of Vogue Comedies in the fall of 1915. She supported the likes of Paddy McGuire, Russ Powell, and Arthur Moon in opuses such as *Oh, For the Life of a Fireman, Heaven will Protect a Working Goil, Bungling Bill's Peeping Ways,* and *Knocking Out Knockout Kelly* (all 1916). After a brief stint at Kalem she moved to Universal where she worked with the team of Eddie Lyons and Lee Moran. Titles like *The Battle of Chili Con Carne, A Silly Sultan, Love and a Liar* (all 1916), *Treat Em' Rough,* and *Why Uncle!* (both 1917) led to other Universal shorts and features. By 1918 the studio was headlining her in her own features, and a teaming with director Tod Browning saw popular films that included *The Virgin of Stamboul* (1920), *Under Two Flags* (1922), and *White Tiger* (1923). By the later 1920s her career began to run out of steam and she returned to comedy shorts in Hal Roach All Star productions like *Slipping Wives, The Honorable Mr. Buggs* (both 1927) and *All for Nothing* (1928). Her sound films were sporadic for small, low-budget outfits and her career ended in 1932.

Doris Deane (1900 – 1974)
Former dancer who began her film career at Universal, and in 1923 moved on to two-reel shorts directed anonymously by Roscoe "Fatty" Arbuckle. In addition to acting in titles such as *Easter Bonnets* (1923), *The New Sheriff*, *His First Car*, *Stupid But Brave*, and *Lovemania* (all 1924), she married Arbuckle in 1925. Although a charming and humorous leading lady her career didn't continue and after cameo appearances in the Buster Keaton features *Sherlock Jr.* (1924) and *Seven Chances* (1925) she left the screen, only coming back for the Arbuckle-directed short *Marriage Rows* (1931) and some brief television work in the 1950s.

Doris Deane comforts Al St John in *Lovemania* (1924). Courtesy of Sam Gill.

Hazel Deane (Hazel Schilling) (1901 – 1986)
Deane was a statuesque beauty born in British Columbia, Canada. After her family moved to California she became a lifeguard at Malibu Beach and from there a bathing beauty in Fox Sunshine Comedies such as *A Tight Squeeze* (1918) and *Money Talks* (1919). She soon moved on to the National Film Corporation and Special Pictures for shorts like *Matrimaniacs* (1920) opposite Neal Burns, and the Chester Conklin starrers *The Soft Boiled Yegg* and *Who Am I?* (both 1920). Besides occasional feature appearances like *The Devil Within* (1921) and *West of the Pecos* (1922), she became a Mack Sennett girl, and in 1923 was hired by, but spent a brief time in, Christie Comedies. After playing one of the women who refuse Buster Keaton's marriage request in *Seven Chances* (1925) she spent the rest of her career in action pictures such as *The Grey Vulture*, *The Devil's Gulch*, *Trouper 77* (all 1926), and *Speedy Smith* (1927). During World War II she entertained troops working for the USO.

Annette De Foe (Annette DuCroix) (1890 – 1960)
Brunette beauty of French parentage, who started her film career in 1916 for the E & R Jungle Film Company appearing in Napoleon and Sally Comedies like *Rival Detectives* (1916). The next year, alongside Raymond Griffith, Charles Arling, Amy Jerome, Bill Hauber, and Frank Alexander, she became part of the ensemble of Foxfilm Comedies, and was leading lady in shorts such as *An Aerial Joyride* and *Social Pirates* (both 1917). She also appeared in features for Fox, Triangle, and Lester Cuneo Productions such as *Indiscreet Corinne* (1917), *Fame and Fortune* (1918), and *Lone Hand Wilson* (1920), before ending her career in 1922.

Patsy De Forest (1894 – 1966)
After two years on stage, this dark-haired comedy ingénue began her film career at Lubin as the leading lady for Clarence Elmer in his *Patsy Bolivar* series, as well as opposite Davy Don in his *Otto* shorts. In mid-1916 she transferred to Vitagraph and played Hughie Mack's love interest under Larry Semon's direction in shorts like *Sand, Scamps and Strategy* and *Hash and Havoc* (both 1916) until she was bumped up to Vitagraph features in 1917. Breaking out to independent features like *Bullin' the Bullsheviki* (1919), her last two pictures were the Fox Buck Jones westerns *Square Shooter* and *Sunset Sprague* (both 1920).

A relatively serious portrait of Patsy De Forest. Author's collection.

Flora Parker De Haven (Mrs. Carter De Haven) (1883 – 1950)
Perth Amoy, New Jersey-born comedienne, who, along with her husband Carter De Haven, made one of the silent screen's most popular husband and wife teams. She began her career in New Orleans in stock, and later became the leading woman for comic Nat Goodwin. She played the lead in *The Queen of the Moulin Rouge* and toured vaudeville with her husband De Haven. Carter made his film debut for Universal and Flora soon followed, appearing with him in *The College Orphan* (1915), *Where are My Trousers*, and *A Five-Foot Ruler* (both 1917), in addition to working on her own in *The Madcap*, *The Seekers*, *The Whirlpool of Destiny*, and *Behind Life's Stage* (all 1916).

Flora De Haven and William Desmond in *Twin Beds* (1920). Courtesy of Bruce Calvert.

In 1919 the pair left Universal for "Smiling Bill" Parson's National Film Corporation, and since Sidney Drew had recently passed away they helped themselves to the "Mr. and Mrs." billing. The rest of her career was spent with De Haven in shorts such as *Honeymooning* (1919), *Kids is Kids* (1920), *Twin Husbands* (1922), and *Christmas* (1923), in addition to a few features like *Twin Beds* (1920), *The Girl in the Taxi*, and *Marry the Poor Girl* (both 1921). Her last appearance was in 1923, and after she and De Haven divorced she remained in Hollywood, where her children Gloria De Haven and Carter De Haven Jr. were busy in the film industry, before she passed away in 1950.

Amy Dennis (1899 - ?)
Dennis was an ingénue who made her stage debut at a tender age in New York stock companies and on Broadway. Her first film was the dramatic feature *York State Folks* (1915) for the Dra-Ko Film Company, but two years later she was part of the ensemble for Selig's Hoyt Farce Comedies, a two-reel series based on the stories of comedy playwright Charles Hoyt. The sixteen year-old Ms. Dennis was the leading lady in *A Brass Monkey, A Contented Woman, A Runaway Colt, A Dog in the Manger, A Hole in the Ground* (all 1917), and more. Also for Selig she supported Lew Fields in the dramatic circus picture *The Barker* (1917). She later made sporadic appearances in features such as *The Woman the Germans Shot* (1918) and *Sooner or Later* (1920), but mostly returned to the stage.

Carmen De Rue (Baby De Rue) (1908 – 1986)
Child actress, daughter of director Eugene De Rue, who made her debut in serious fare such as *The Squaw Man*, and the serial *Lucille Love: The Girl of Mystery* (both 1914) before settling into comedy work in the kid's pictures made at the Sterling Film Company. Along with Paul Jacobs, Gordon Griffith, Violet Radcliffe, and Violet Johnson she headlined in one-reelers such as *A Race for a Life, The Close Call, A Bear Escape* (all 1914), and *Billie was a Right Smart Boy* (1915) which were directed by Robert Thornby and Robert Z. Leonard for Universal release. From here she became part of Majestic's juvenile company under the supervision of the brothers Chester and Sidney Franklin (who in turn were supervised by D.W. Griffith) for comedy shorts like *Pirates Bold, The Kid Magicians, The Straw Man* (with former Alkali Ike Augustus Carney), and *Billie's Goat* (all 1915), as well as the dramas *The Little Life Guard*, and *The Doll-House Mystery* (both 1915).

The outfit soon morphed into the Fine Arts Company with release through Triangle, and she continued appearing in features such as *Going Straight, Gretchen the Greenhorn, A Sister of Six* (all 1916), and *Cheerful Givers* (1917). The Franklin Brothers moved to the Fox Film Corporation and embarked on a series of tongue-in-cheek adventure films that starred their half-pint ensemble in the leading roles. Carmen joined Virginia Lee Corbin, Francis Carpenter, Violet Radcliffe, and Gertrude & Buddy Messenger in elaborate feature-length spoofs that included *Jack and the Beanstalk, Aladdin and the Wonderful Lamp*, and *Babes in the Woods* (all 1917). Corbin and Carpenter were the heroic leads, and Carmen played roles such as the King of Cornwall, a slave dancing girl, and the Good Fairy. Her last films were *The Girl with the Champagne Eyes* (1918) and the Franklin *Mikado* spoof *Fan Fan* (1918), before retiring into private life.

Kay Deslys (Kathleen M. Herbert) (1899 – 1974)
Plump, London-born comedienne, who began her stage career at age five and worked for Sir Robert Arthur, Gus Edwards, the Keith and Pantages circuits, and the Shuberts. Moving into pictures in 1923, she was truly an unsung member of the Hal Roach stock company, and is best remembered for playing floozies in Charley Chase's *Innocent Husbands* (1925) and Laurel & Hardy's *Their Purple Moment* (1928). Occasionally, as in *Should Married Men Go Home?* (1928), she would turn up as a long-suffering wife. Her feature film appearances include *The Gold Rush* (1925), as one of Georgia Hale's dance hall girlfriends, and *The Case of Lena Smith* (1929). She continued in sound films for many years, with funny turns in Roach comedies like *Below Zero* (1930), and as a lady bus driver in the Pete Smith short *Bus Pests* (1945). Her last known film was *Pat and Mike* (1952).

Dorothy Devore (1899 – 1976) **See Chapter Five**

Ray Dooley (1896 – 1984)
Legendary stage performer and mainstay of the *Ziegfeld Follies*, who specialized in playing bratty children, usually opposite W.C. Fields. Born into a theatrical family of eccentric comedians, her brother Johnny became a headliner in the *Follies* and on his own, while her other brothers Gordon and William were busy as well. Her one silent film appearance came with her brother Gordon in the short *A Rag, a Bone, and a Hank of Hair* (1917), which was to be the first of a series of Fun-Art Film Comedies, a company set up by star Clara Kimball Young, but turned out to be the only entry made (see Chapter Six). Outside of one sound film, *Honeymoon Lane* (1931), Dooley limited her appearances to the stage. Married to comedian and producer Eddie Dowling, she spent most of her later career working with him.

Adrienne Dore (? – 1992)
Showgirl who appeared in the *Midnight Revue* at the Cocoanut Grove singing *I'd like to See a Little Bit More of You*, and was also a runner-up in the Miss America Beauty Pageant of 1925 as Miss Los Angeles. She entered films in 1926 when she was signed by Universal, and spent time in the *Excuse Makers* series for Century Comedies where she supported star Charles King in entries like *Love's Hurdle* (1926). Near the end of the silent era she took up residence at Jack White Comedies as a young flapper in shorts like *Wife Trouble* (1928), *Pep Up*, and *Delicious and Refreshing* (both 1929). She also appeared in talkie shorts for Vitaphone, Christie, and Lloyd Hamilton such as *Peaceful Alley*, *Adam's Eve* (both 1929), and *Johnny's Week End* (1930), plus had some good roles in sound features on the order of *The Wild Party* (1929) with Clara Bow, and *Union Depot* (1932), before leaving pictures in the mid-1930s.

Jean Doree (?)
Blonde ingénue and professional dancer, who got her start in pictures by doubling for well-known stars in dance specialties. In 1925 she began playing small bits in Mack Sennett comedies with Harry Langdon and Ralph Graves, and from there made her way to Stern Brothers Comedies where she supported Sid Saylor in his *Let George Do It* shorts like *On Furlough* (1927), *On Deck*, and *The Disordered Orderly* (both 1928), in addition to other Stern opuses such as *Taking the Count* (1928) and *Take Your Pick* (1929).

Nancy Dover (Judith Barrett) (1909 – 2000)
Texas-born dancer seen by producer Al Christie in the show *The Connecticut Yankee*, and hired to work with Bobby Vernon and Billy Dooley in shorts such as *The Sock Exchange* (1928) and *Happy Heels* (1929). She also appeared in Jack White Talking Comedies like *Romance De Luxe* (1929) and the Hal Roach produced Harry Langdon shorts *Skirt Shy* (1929), *The Head Guy*, *The Fighting Parson*, and *The Big Kick* (all 1930). Other shorts as well as features such as *Dynamite* (1929) and *Cimarron* (1931) followed before she changed her name to Judith Barrett and continued working in pictures like *The Gracie Allan Murder Case* (1939) and *Road to Singapore* (1940) until 1940.

Alice Dovey (1884 – 1969)
Stage comedienne who appeared in Broadway hits such as *Very Good Eddie* and *The Pink Lady*. She began her brief film career in 1915 with the dramatic feature *The Commanding Officer*, but soon moved on to headline for the Gaumont Company in Casino Star Comedies such as *The Reformer* (1915) and *Every Lassie Has a Lover* (1916). She retired after marrying actor and playwright Jack E. Hazzard in 1917.

Marie Dressler (1869 – 1934) **See Chapter Six**

Mrs. Sidney Drew (1890 – 1926) **See Chapter Six**

Sarah Duhamel. See Chapter One

Rosetta Duncan (1894 – 1959) **See Chapter Nine**

Vivian Duncan (1897 – 1986) **See Chapter Nine**

Gonda Durand (1896 – 1960)
Mack Sennett bathing beauty who had appeared on stage with the Morosco Stock Company before joining the Sennett organization in 1915. Mostly appearing with the other girls, she did occasionally have a featured role such as the café vamp in *Taming Target Center* (1917). She retired from films in 1919, and later married comedy and western character heavy Robert Kortman.

Minta Durfee (1889 – 1975) **See Chapter Seven**

Dorothy Dwan (1906 – 1981)

Big-eyed ingénue, who became leading lady and real-life wife to comedian Larry Semon. After some early films such as *The Silent Vow* (1922), *The Breed of the Border*, and *Sinners in Silk* (both 1924), her career took a leap up when she was cast opposite Semon in his feature *The Perfect Clown* (1925). She also supported Larry in *The Wizard of Oz* (1925), *Stop, Look, and Listen* (1926), and *Spuds* (1927). Outside her work with her hubby most of her other features were westerns on the order of *The Great K & A Robbery* (1926), *The Land of the Law* (1927), and *Tumbling River* (1927). After Semon's death in 1928, Ms. Dwan worked for a while in silent and sound features that include *California Mail*, *The Peacock Fan* (both 1929), and *The Fighting Legion* (1930). After re-marrying in 1930 she retired from films and eventually became a registered nurse.

Publicity portrait of Dorothy Dwan. Author's collection.

Mabel Dwight (?)

Stage actress who during her long career appeared as Mrs. Ogden in 1905 during the New York run of *The Virginian*, in addition to numerous spectacular productions at the New York Hippodrome such as *A Trip to Japan* and *Marching Through Georgia*, opposite comic "Spook" Hanson. In 1914 she took up residence with the Edison Company and became part of their comedy ensemble, playing gossips, maids, aunts, suffragists, and landladies in shorts such as *Father's Beard* (1914), *A Sport of Circumstances*, *Food for King's and Riley* (with Oliver Hardy), *The Sufferin' Baby* (all 1915), *The Real Dr. Kay*, and *A Mix-Up in Black* (both 1916). She also appeared in the 1917 Edison features *The Last Sentence* and *Builders of Castles* before ending her career.

Ruth Dwyer (1898 – 1978)

A leading lady, in action films, westerns, and comedies such as *The Evil Eye* (1920), *His Mystery Girl* (1923), and *Stranger of the North* (1924). Best remembered as Buster Keaton's love interest in *Seven Chances* (1925), she spent the rest of the 1920s mostly as the second female lead in features such as *A Hero for a Night* (1927) and *Alex the Great* (1928), in addition to the Johnny Hines' comedies *The Brown Derby*, *Stepping Along* (both 1926), and *White Pants Willie* (1927). In sound films she did uncredited walk-ons until the early 1940s. She later became an agent, casting small parts and extras for Hollywood films shot in San Francisco.

Peggy Eames (1918 – 1987)
Child vaudeville performer, who moved into films, to become a supporting kid in numerous Our Gang Comedies such as *Uncle Tom's Uncle* (1926), *Bring Home the Turkey*, *Seeing the World*, and *Tired Business Men* (all 1927). In addition to appearing in the feature *The Wedding March* (1928), she did a post Our Gang vaudeville tour teamed with former Gang headliner Mickey Daniels.

Dorothy Earle (Esther Lucille Elmendorf) (? - 1958)
Twenty-two year-old from Ithaca, New York who became the leading lady and real-life wife of the transplanted European comedian Marcel Perez. Earle joined Perez in 1919 when he was making a series of Jester Comedies for producer William Steiner, and supported him in entries such as *Can You Beat It?*, *Chicken in Turkey*, and *You're Next* (all 1919). The pretty blonde worked with her husband through the rest of his career, which included shorts for Reelcraft and Sanford Productions, plus features like *Pioneers of the West* (1925), which Dorothy co-wrote, and *Out All Night* (1927). After Perez's premature death from cancer in early 1929, Dorothy left the screen, and with her son Marcel Jr. returned to the East Coast where she eventually remarried.

Marcel Perez comes to Dorothy Earle's rescue in
Here He Is (1921). Courtesy of Sam Gill.

Lorraine Eason (1904 – 1986)
Entered pictures in 1923 through a contest for *Photoplay Magazine*, spent some time at Sennett, and played Echo in the fantasy *The Temple of Venus* (1923). After some work in *The Leather Pushers* series opposite Billy Sullivan, and westerns such as *Circus Lure* (1924), *Slow Dynamite* (1925), and *The Grey Devil* (1926), she became a comedy leading

lady – working with Charley Chase, supporting Wallace Beery and Raymond Hatton in their hit feature *We're in the Navy Now* (1926), and appearing with Al Cooke and Kit Guard in their FBO series of *Wisecrackers Comedies* based on the stories of H. C. Witwer. She continued with Cooke and Guard for their next series of *Beauty Parlor Comedies*, and returned to action features with Buzz Barton and Ranger the dog before ending her career in 1928 as the second lead in the comedy feature *Must We Marry?*

Doris Eaton (Doris Eaton Tavis) (1904 – 2010)
Stage legend, who along with her brother Charles and sister Mary, became a Ziegfeld dancer at age fourteen in 1918, appearing in various editions of the *Ziegfeld Follies* and *Ziegfeld Midnight Frolic*. She made her film debut with a small part in *At the Stage Door* (1921), and after starring in three 1922 features in England she returned to the U.S. for some two-reel Century comedies such as *High Kickers* and *Fashion Follies* (both 1923) as head of the "Gorham Follies Girls." Her other films include *Taking the Count* (1928), *The Very Idea* (1929) and seventy years later *The Man in the Moon* (1999) the Andy Kaufman bio-pic with Jim Carrey. During the 1930s her stage career dried up so she became a dance instructor at the Arthur Murray Dance School, and continued dancing, making regular appearances at Broadway's annual AIDs benefit. Her last appearance was a month before her death at age one hundred and six.

Lorraine Eddy (1904 – 1972)
Eddy was a saucy blonde who came from a background in stock companies and touring with shows like *Strawberry Blonde* and *Topsy and Eva* with the Duncan Sisters. In 1927 she was appearing in a musical comedy in Hollywood when she was seen by producer Al Christie and hired to play in his comedies for Paramount. For the next few years she supported Jimmie Adams, Neal Burns, and Billy Dooley in shorts like *Oh, Mummy* (1927), *Holy Mackerel* (1928), and *Oriental Hugs* (1928). Also while working for Christie she appeared in the early part-talkie feature *The Carnation Kid* (1929) opposite Douglas MacLean, and they married in 1931. The marriage lasted until 1936, and afterwards Eddy returned to the film industry as a costume designer and in the make-up department for independent features such as *Song of My Heart* (1948) and *The Babe Ruth Story*

Christie Comedies star Lorraine Eddy. Author's collection.

(1948), in addition to Monogram Pictures product like *Gentleman Joe Palooka* (1946) and *Jiggs and Maggie in Society* (1947). Retiring in 1949, she passed away in 1972.

Mattie Edwards (Martha Mattie Settle) (1866 – 1944)
Pioneer black film comedienne who came from the stage. Having appeared in vaudeville as early as 1887 with groups like P.G. Lowry's Minstrels, she worked with Bert Williams and George Walker in their show *In Dahomey* (1903) and was in the Klaw & Erlanger 1912 extravaganza *The Round-Up*. In 1913 she joined the Lubin Company when they set up a unit to make one-reelers with black casts in Jacksonville, Florida. Ms. Edwards was teamed with John (Junk) Edwards for three years' worth of shorts such as *Zeb, Zack and the Zulus* (1913), *Mandy's Chicken Dinner*, *Swami Sam* (both 1914), *Black Art*, *The Rakoon Hose Company* (both 1915), and *Under a Barrel* (1916). Unfortunately surviving examples show that the films were built around denigrating black stereotypes and were made by the studios' regular white directors Arthur D. Hotaling, Will Louis, and Jerold T. Hevener. Between stage work her other film appearances included more black-cast comedy shorts for Chicago's Ebony Film Co. like *Good Luck in Old Clothes* (1918), and the early Oscar Micheaux features *Within Our Gates* and *The Brute* (both 1920). Later she settled in Los Angeles where she did bits in Hollywood pictures like *Give Us the Night* (1936) and *Champagne Waltz* (1937) before passing away at seventy-eight.

Vivian Edwards (1896 – 1983)
Tall brunette who began appearing at Keystone in 1914, working with Chaplin in *The Property Man*, *The Face on the Barroom Floor*, *Those Love Pangs*, and others, in addition to supporting Charlie Murray in "Hogan" entries such as *Hogan's Mussy Job*, *Hogan, the Porter*, and *Hogan's Aristocratic Dream* (all 1915). Mostly turning up in small featured roles, she also appeared in a number of the one-reel Triangle Komedies that were shot on the Sennett lot and supervised by Hampton Del Ruth like *Her Donkey Love* and *A Tuner of Note* (both 1917).

Vivian Edwards tries to stop Fritz Schade from dousing Bill Hauber with water in *Only a Farmer's Daughter* (1915). Courtesy of Sam Gill.

Sally Eilers (1908 – 1978)
A sultry brunette who began her career as a teenager doing extra work in films such as *The Red Mill*, *The Cradle Snatchers*, and *Sunrise* (all 1927). Said to have been discovered by Mack Sennett when she visited her friend Carole Lombard at his studio, the producer made her the female lead in his 1928 comedy-romance feature *The Goodbye Kiss*, as well as two-reelers like *The Campus Vamp* (1928) and *Matchmaking Mamma* (1929). She made a smooth transition to sound films where she was leading lady in some westerns with her husband Hoot Gibson, and some of Buster Keaton's MGM films like *Doughboys* (1930) and *Parlor, Bedroom and Bath* (1931). Making a big splash in the dramatic success *Bad Girl* (1931), her other noteworthy films include *Over the Hill* (1931), *State Fair*, *Sailor's Luck* (both 1933), and *Strike Me Pink* (1936). She continued working in less important pictures, such as *I was a Prisoner on Devil's Island* (1941) and *Strange Illusion* (1945) until 1950.

Lillian Elliott (1874 – 1959)
Longtime stage performer, who was known as "the leading exponent of German dialect on the American stage," and appeared in musicals such as *Hanky Panky* as well as dramas like *Help Wanted*. The 1915 film version of *Help Wanted* was her movie debut, but it wasn't until the 1920s that she became a regular film player. Features such as *Too Much Married* (1921) and *One Glorious Night* (1924) led to her being teamed with Max Davidson in *Old Clothes* (1925), and she was soon playing "Mama" to his "Papa" in classic Hal Roach two-reelers like *Don't Tell Everything*, *The Call of the Cuckoos*, and *Should Second Husbands Come First?* (all 1927). Small and plump, with Davidson she was often a flirty rich widow who can't stand Max's bratty son, and possessed a withering glare which she makes good use of when Spec O'Donnell turns up in drag as the "maid" in *Don't Tell Everything* (1927). During the sound era, she made a few more appearances on the Hal Roach lot – *Hasty Marriage* (1931) with Charley Chase and Our Gang's *Free Eats* (1932) – but was mostly seen in features such as *Polly of the Circus* (1932) or *Mrs. Wiggs of the Cabbage Patch* (1934) as landladies, mothers, or society matrons. Married for many years to actor James Corrigan, she was the mother of popular 1940s and 50s character actor Lloyd Corrigan, and retired in 1943.

Babe Emerson (Kathleen Emerson) (?)
Blonde ingénue, who appeared in 1917 and 1918 L-Ko Comedies such as *Fat and Furious*, *Deep Seas and Desperate Deeds* (both 1917) and *Cannibals and Carnivals* (1918). Little is known about her, but her screen time was regularly spent with Myrta Sterling, Al Forbes, and Russ Powell.

Fern Emmett (1896 – 1946)
Character actress, who specialized in irritable landladies, town gossips, and put upon wives. Coming from the stage, she was married to supporting player Henry Roquemore, and they both began appearing in films in 1927. Emmett's first films were two-reelers for Al Christie such as *Hot Papa* (1927), *Mad Scrambles* (1927), and *Fighting Fanny* (1928) where she supported the likes of Jack Duffy and Neal Burns. With the changeover to sound she became even busier appearing in many comedy shorts directed by Roscoe Arbuckle such as *Idle Roomers* (1931), *Bridge Wives*, and *Mother's Holiday* (both 1932), not to mention horror films like *The Vampire Bat* (1933), *The Mummy's Tomb* (1942), and *Dead Men Walk* (1943), plus countless other features and westerns right up to her death in 1946.

May Emory (1880 – 1948)
Real-life wife of comedian Harry Gribbon, who spent sixteen years on stage as an actress and singer in *The Ziegfeld Follies* and other shows, in addition to appearing on major vaudeville circuits with and without her husband. The pair made their film debut at Keystone in 1915, and the statuesque and a bit zaftig Ms. Emory was often ogled by the likes of Ford Sterling in shorts such as *That Little Band of Gold* (1915) or played the alluring "other woman" as she does in *Teddy at the Throttle* (1917). She joined her husband at L-Ko, but returned to Sennett and soon retired to run a beauty parlor. She passed away in New York thirteen years before Harry in 1948.

Cecile Evans (Ceci Evans) (1902 – 1960)
Schoolgirl from the San Joaquin Valley, who entered show business at age fifteen when she won a bathing beauty contest that led to a contract with Mack Sennett. Spending ten years with the producer in shorts like *Down to the Sea in Shoes* (1923), *The Hollywood Kid* (1924), *Hot Cakes for Two* (1926), and *Motorboat Mamas* (1928), her big moment of attention came when Sennett insured her legs for $100,000 leading to her being ballyhooed as "The Girl with the $100,000 Legs." Besides her Sennett shorts she also appeared in the features *Worldly Goods* (1924), *The Goose Hangs High* (1925) and *The Prince of Headwaiters* (1927) before leaving films in 1928.

Muriel Evans (1910 – 2000)
Actress who grew up on film sets as her mother was a maid at First National Studios, and began doing bit roles in 1926. At the same landing parts in stock theatre productions in 1927 she became an ingénue in Jack White comedies, supporting comics such as Lupino Lane and Jerry Drew in *Sure Cure* (1927), *Wife Trouble* (1928), *Good Night Nurse*, and *Joyland* (both 1929). A brief marriage saw her leave films, but she returned as a blonde in 1932 at the Hal Roach Studio where she was a frequent leading lady for Charley Chase. Her Roach shorts include *Young Ironsides* (1932), *Fast Workers*, and *His Silent Racket* (both 1933). She moved on to features doing small bits in "A" pictures like

Hollywood Party (1934) and *Mr. Deeds Goes to Town* (1936), while becoming a leading lady in numerous low-budget westerns such as *The New Frontier* (1935), *Smoke Tree Range* (1937), and *Westbound Stage (1938).* Having remarried in 1936 she eventually retired with her last film being the Pete Smith short *Studio Visit* (1946). She later dabbled in radio and television, and eventually due to ill health became a resident at the Motion Picture Country House. The year before her death she appeared in the documentary *I Used to be in Pictures* (2000) and talked about her film days.

Bessie Eyton (1890 – 1965)
Santa Barbara-born actress, who started her film career with Selig in 1911, and played in a vast number of their dramatic productions until 1917. From there she moved to serious features such as *The Still Alarm* (1918) and *The Usurper* (1919). She did something of an about face in 1920 when she was signed by the Plymouth Producing and Distributing Service to star in their series of *Top Notch* Comedy shorts for the states' rights market. Titles included *Movie Mad, A Dishonest Crook, Higher Education,* and *An Indiscreet Flirt* (all 1921). After this group of two-reelers she made two more dramatic features before retiring in 1925.

Elinor Fair (Eleanor Crave) (1903 – 1957)
Fair was a Virginia-born ingénue who began her film career in 1916 under the name Eleanor Crave. Making her debut at Fox at age thirteen in two William Farnum dramas, she soon became Elinor Fair and after more experience supported Clara Kimball Young, Belle Bennett, and J. Warren Kerrigan. In 1919 Fox teamed her with comic Albert Ray in the light comedy feature *Married in Haste.* A popular success, the studio paired them in six more comedies in rapid succession, all concerning the tribulations of a young couple on their road to matrimony. The series included *Words and Music By -, Be a Little Sport, Vagabond Luck,* and *Tin Pan Alley* (all 1919). After her teaming with Ray she continued working in all kinds of features, often with lower budgets, but in the later 1920s, after appearing in *The Volga Boatman* (1926), she came under the aegis of Cecil B. DeMille and appeared in many films for his independent company, such as comedies like *Bachelor Brides* (1926) *My Friend from India* (1927) and *Let 'Er Go Gallagher* (1928) as well as pictures like *The Yankee Clipper* (1927). She made the transition to sound in westerns, but was soon playing uncredited bit parts until 1934's *Bolero, The Scarlet Empress,* and *Broadway Bill.*

Fanny (?)
Mule which co-starred with Slim Summerville in a group of Universal Bluebird one-reelers that included *Red Suspenders* and *Oh! What a Kick!* (both 1927).

Dot Farley (1890 – 1971) **See Chapter Six**

Elfie Fay (1879 – 1927)
Little and scrawny character actress, who had been a big-time stage comedienne in the early 1900s, and was the sister of film comic and director Hugh Fay. The daughter of Hugh Fay Sr. who was half of the popular Irish stage team of Barry and Fay, Elfie became a headliner herself at age sixteen in shows such as *Mamselle Awkins*, *The Belle of New York*, and *The Belle of Avenue A*. Also having performed in London, she came to films in 1924 and specialized in playing old biddies in shorts for Fox, Roach and Jack White such as *A Movie Mad Maid* (1924), *Never Too Old* (1926), and *Hot Cookies* (1927), some directed by her brother Hugh, plus supported comic Billy West in his Rayart feature *Trouble Chaser* (1926). At the time of her death she had become a regular in the Weiss Brother's *Izzy and Lizzie* series as the matriarch of the Irish clan in shorts like *Ham and Herring* and *Nize People* (both 1927). Her death at age forty-eight is said to have been brought on by grief over the death of her brother nine months before.

Julia Faye (1893 – 1966)
Dark-haired ingénue, born in Richmond, Virginia, who spent the bulk of her career working for Cecil B DeMille. After college she became a fashion model, where it's said she was discovered by DeMille, although her first films were tiny parts in Fine Arts Productions supervised by D. W. Griffith such as *The Lamb* and *Don Quixote* (both 1915). She also spent 1916 appearing in Mack Sennett and Triangle comedies like *His Auto-Ruination*, *Bucking Society*, *The Surf Girl*, and *A Lover's Might*. Her first DeMille production was 1917's *The Woman God Forgot*, which led to more like *Old Wives for New* (1918), *Don't Change Your Husband* (1919), *Something to Think About* (1920) and *Saturday Night* (1922). She also was co-starred with light comic Bryant Washburn for Paramount's *Venus in the East*, *A Very Good Young Man*, *It Pays to Advertise*, and *The Six Best Cellars* (all 1919). Through the 1920s while appearing in DeMille dramas like *The Ten Commandments* (1923), *Triumph* (1924), *The Road to Yesterday* (1925) and *The Volga Boatman* (1926), she still found time for many comedies like *Changing Husbands* (1924), *Bachelor Brides*, *Meet the Prince* (both 1929) *Turkish Delight*, and *Chicago* (both 1927). In the sound era she continued to work for DeMille but was mostly seen in uncredited bit parts in features and on television until 1963.

Versatile actress Julia Faye. Author's collection.

Louise Fazenda (1889 – 1962) **See Chapter Three**

Elinor Field (1902 – 1998) **See Chapter Eight**

Madalynne Field (1907 – 1974)
Field was a two hundred and fifty pound blonde who entered movies as a teenager in 1925. Her size made her a comedy natural and she appeared in shorts for Fox, Universal, Bray (*A Sorority Mix-Up* (1927) as "Beefy"), and William Pizor, plus features such as Colleen Moore's *Ella Cinders* (1926). Often in tiny bits as the big girl who the boys aren't interested in, she made an impression in Mack Sennett's 1927-1928 *Sennett Girl Comedies* such as *The Campus Carmen* and *Run, Girl, Run* (both 1928) where she became best friends with the series star Carole Lombard. After sound arrived Field mostly retired from the screen, becoming unofficial business manager for Lombard and marrying director Walter Lang.

Flora Finch (1867 – 1940) **See Chapter One**

Margarita Fischer (1886 – 1975)
Big-eyed and dark-haired actress, who became a popular leading lady of the teens. Born in Missouri Valley, Iowa, she was so popular as a child performer that when she was twelve her minstrel father formed a company and starred her as "Babe Fischer." She went on to work in stock companies and vaudeville, along the way appearing with names such as Walter Sanford, T. Daniel Frawley, and Joseph Medill Patterson. Entering pictures in 1910 for Selig she turned up in a wide variety of films that included comedies such as *Romeo and Juliet Out of Town, Her First Long Dress,* and *Settled Out of Court* (all 1910), before a brief stay at the American Film Manufacturing Company where she met, worked with, and married the actor Harry "Bud" Pollard. By the end of that year she transferred to the Imp Company, where she was joined by Pollard, although by 1913 he had split and Fischer was mostly appearing with Robert Z. Leonard in Rex films such as *Sally Scraggs: Housemaid, His Old-Fashioned Dad,* and *The Boob's Dream Girl* (all 1913).

American Film Manufacturing Company star Margarita Fischer. Author's collection.

The next year saw she and Pollard as a regular team at American, where he co-starred with her and directed *Beauty* brand shorts like *A Flurry in Hats, A Modern Othello,* and *Cupid in a Dress Coat* (all 1914). 1916 saw her launch into features – first with Pollard behind the camera for items like *Miss Jackie of the Navy* (1916), and many comedies for American such as *Molly Go Get 'Em*, *Jailed Janet* (both 1918), *Put Up Your Hands*, *Charge It to Me* (both 1919), and *The Week-End* (1920). This was the peak of her career, and after 1921 she made only three more pictures, her last being Pollard's version of *Uncle Tom's Cabin* (1927) for Universal, which headlined Fischer as Eliza. After making some low-budget talkie features Harry Pollard died in 1934, and Fischer remained in California until her death at eighty-nine in 1975.

Cissy Fitzgerald (1873 – 1941) **See Chapter One**

Bess Flowers (1898 – 1984)
Texas-born actress, who after small roles in the 1920s became "The Queen of Hollywood Dress Extras," and worked as such until the mid-1960s. Starting in 1922, probably her best and largest role was in the missing James Cruze-directed feature *Hollywood* (1923), but her other features included *Irene*, *Laddie* (both 1926), and *Blondes By Choice* (1927), as well as playing Mrs. Laurel in the Laurel and Hardy two-reeler *We Faw Down* (1928). By the time sound arrived she had settled in the extra ranks, although she occasionally had a bit more to do in Three Stooges shorts like *Termites of 1938* and *Tassels in the Air* (both 1938).

Edna Flugrath (1892 – 1966)
Oldest of the Brooklyn-born Flugrath sisters, the others, Virginia and Leonie, became Viola Dana and Shirley Mason. All the girls had extensive stage experience – Edna appeared in stock and vaudeville, was in *Peggy* with Peter F. Dalley, and *Newport News* with Thomas Jefferson, in addition to being the premiere danseuse at the Metropolitan Opera House. She entered films with the Edison Company and became part of their ensemble in numerous comedies such as *Uncle Mun and the Minister*, *A Proposal Under Difficulties* (both 1912), *Mother's Lazy Boy*, and *The Girl, the Clown, and the Donkey* (both 1913). Moving to England in 1914, she worked with and married the director Harold M. Shaw. Most of her later films were done in the U.K., although her last film, *The Social Code* (1923), was done with sister Viola Dana for Metro.

Artye Folz (1920 – 1969)
Tall, chubby girl with glasses and freckles who was always the annoying know-it-all in kid's comedies such as the McDougal Alley Kid's *The Big Pie Raid* (1927) and the "Smitty" Comedy *Tomato Omelette* (1929). She went on in sound to make appearances in features like *Sunnyside Up* (1929) and the Our Gang shorts *Teacher's Pet* (1930) and *The Pooch* (1932).

Eugenie Forde (1879 – 1940)
Busy character actress, and mother of comedy leading lady Victoria Forde, who had appeared on stage with Chauncey Olcott, William Faversham, and Blanche Walsh. Making her film debut in Nestor's *Desperate Desmond* comedy entries like *Desperate Desmond Almost Succeeds* (1911) and *Desperate Desmond Fails* (1912), she continued with many other of the company's westerns and comedies. More work was done for Bison, Balboa, and the St Louis Motion Picture Company's Frontier Films that included *Where Wits Win*, and *When Roaring Gulch Got Suffrage* (both 1913). After joining Selig in 1915 she worked frequently with Tom Mix (who later become her son-in-law) and alternated films with Selig and the American Film Manufacturing Company. She later appeared in occasional shorts for Christie Comedies, and was support in numerous features on the order of Mabel Normand's *Sis Hopkins* (1919), *Cameo Kirby* (1923), and *Captain Salvation* (1927).

Victoria Forde (1996 – 1964) **See Chapter Four**

Helen Foster (1906 – 1982)
Kansas-born actress from a theatrical family, her father was a member of the well-known Woodward Stock Company, who began her film career in independent westerns such as *Reckless Courage* and *The Bandit's Baby* (both 1925), and soon moved over to Jack White and Educational two-reelers in support of Lloyd Hamilton, Lupino Lane, and Johnny Arthur in shorts like *The Tourist, Maid in Morocco* (both 1925), and *Move Along* (1926). In the late 1920s she was on contract to Universal, appearing in westerns and serials, and in 1929 was a WAMPAS Baby Star. She continued in minor roles until 1956.

Jack White ingénue Helen Foster.
Author's collection.

May Foster (1873 – 1951)
Character actress, who specialized in western and rural types, and was busy in features as well as comedy shorts. Born in Illinois, she made her first film appearances in westerns for Rex and Bison in the teens, but really settled in films in 1920 with a good part in the Charles Ray feature *45 Minutes from Broadway* (1920). Her comedy work included the shorts *The Road to Ruin* (1920), *The Hound of the Tankervilles* (1922), *Snowed Under* (1923), and *Gee Whiz, Genevieve* (1924) where she supported Neely Edwards, Ned Flanagan, Victor Potel, Bull Montana, and Will Rogers. After features such as *The*

Midnight Alarm (1923), and Pola Negri's *A Woman of the World* (1925) her appearances became smaller and more sporadic, but she still turned up in pictures like *The Docks of New York* (1928) and *The Scarlet Empress* (1934) until 1935.

Virginia Fox (1902 – 1982) **See Chapter Eight**

Christine Francis (1903 – 1952)
Francis was a cute, little brunette from Tacoma, Washington who had most of her roles in mid-1920s films directed by Fatty Arbuckle or Buster Keaton. Coming to Los Angeles as an aspiring actress, she appeared in a 1922 touring production of *Abie's Irish Rose* before entering pictures. Francis was the leading lady in shorts such as *The Broncho Express* (1924) and *Dynamite Doggie* (1925) opposite Al St John. She also turned up in *Stupid But Brave* (1924), *Be Careful, Dearie* (1926) and Buster Keaton's feature *Sherlock Jr.* (1924) as the candy shop girl. A friend of

One of the most used photos from silent comedy shows Buster Keaton and Christine Francis in a posed shot from *Sherlock Jr.* (1924). In the film itself Christine plays the girl in the candy shop.

Roscoe Arbuckle's second wife Doris Deane, she later worked as the script/continuity girl on Keaton's famous *The General* (1926) and in 1938 married well-known aviator and Hollywood stunt flier Dick Grace. She's sometimes mistaken for Ruth Holly, a similar looking but different actress.

Betty Francisco (1900 – 1950)
Blonde, who moved from the *Ziegfeld Follies* to films in 1920. At first appearing in dramas and westerns with the likes of William Desmond and Buck Jones, she had a very brief stay at Sennett, and in the late 1920s cornered the market on tough blondes in comedy features such as *Uneasy Payments, Too Many Crooks, The Gay Retreat* (all 1927), and especially Harry Langdon's *Long Pants* (1927). When sound came in she continued as support in films like *Broadway,* and *Smiling Irish Eyes* (both 1929), but her roles got smaller as the 1930s started. She retired after marrying New York stock broker Fred Spradling.

Evelyn Francisco (1904 – 1963)
Sister of Betty Francisco, who like her older sister Betty, joined the movies from the *Ziegfeld Follies*. Starting as one of the Mack Sennett bathing girls in many two-reelers such as *Flip Flops* (1923), *Picking Peaches* (1924), and *He Who Gets Smacked* (1925), she moved over to the Christie lot and appeared in several of his Educational releases with Bobby Vernon, Neal Burns, and Jack Duffy like *Bright Lights* (1924) and *Off His Beat* (1925). Christie also used her in his Julian Eltinge-starring feature *Madame Behave* (1925), and the rest of her career was spent in shorts such as *Nize Monkey* (1926) with Buddy Messinger, and doing smallish parts in features such as *The King of Kings, The King of the Herd* (both 1927), and *The Godless Girl* (1929).

Valentina Frascaroli (1890 – 1955) **See Chapter One**

Nitra Frazer (Anitra Frazer MacTavish) (1892 - 1979)
Dark-haired, Brooklyn-born actress, who began her career on the stage around 1908 when she was selected to appear in De Wolf Hopper's *The Pied Piper of Hamlin* (1908). From there she graduated to *The Jolly Bachelors* (1910) with Nora Bayes and Jack Norworth and eventually was given an important part in the operetta *The Spring Maid* (1911). Theatrical shows always took a break in the summer, and in the summer of 1913 Ms. Frazer decided to give movies a try. The Vitagraph Studio was close to her home, and after her screen debut there met with success she became a stock member of their ensemble, finding a place in their comedies. She was soon picked to be leading lady to star comic Wally Van, and besides working with him in titles such as *Cutey and the Twins* (1913), *Cutey Becomes a Landlord, Love, Snow and Ice*, and *Cutey's Awakening* (all 1915) they soon married. In addition to the Van shorts she turned up in other comedies like *Hughey of the Circus* (1915) and *When Hooligan and Dooligan Ran for Mayor* (1916). The pair left Vitagraph in 1917, and following their first independent production *Love, Pep and Petrol* (1917) Ms. Frazer retired from the screen.

Dale Fuller (Marie Dale Phillipps) (1885 – 1948)
A versatile and unsung comedienne, as well as a dramatic actress, who toured on stage with May Vokes, and appeared in stock, vaudeville, and musical comedy. Making her film debut in 1915 in Mack Sennett's Triangle comedies, she was regularly seen as unattractive wives or overbear-

Eccentric comedienne and Erich von Stroheim actress Dale Fuller.

ing mothers in two-reelers like *Crooked to the End* (1915), *Bath Tub Perils*, *The Surf Girl*, and *A Scoundrel's Toll* (all 1916). When Sennett exited Triangle she remained through 1918 in shorts such as *The Camera Cure* (1917) and *His Punctured Reputation* (1918). In the 1920s, after some Chester Comedies she moved into character roles in features like *Manslaughter* (1922), *Souls for Sale* (1923), *Tea, with a Kick* (1923), and *Ben Hur* (1925), plus was a favorite of director Eric von Stroheim and had interesting roles in his *Foolish Wives* (1922), *Greed* (1924), *The Merry Widow* (1925), and *The Wedding March* (1928). In the early days of sound she was seen to advantage in *Emma* (1932) and *Twentieth Century* (1934), but after *A Tale of Two Cities* (1935) she disappeared from the screen.

Jane Gail (Ethel S. Magee) (1881 – 1963)
All-purpose actress who was at home in comedy and drama. This stock company veteran became a popular player at Imp, and had her own "Jane" series of comedy-dramas that included *Jane of Moth-Eaten Farm*, and *The Jealousy of Jane* (both 1913). Working frequently under the director George Loane Tucker, she starred in his *Traffic in Souls* (1913) and accompanied him to England and the Cosmofotofilm Co. for the films *She Stoops to Conquer*, and *England Expects* (both 1914). Back in the United States she returned to Universal and appeared in a number of Victor comedies with Matt Moore such as *Ashamed of the Old Folks* (1916), *The Fireman's Bride*, and *Pots and Poems* (both 1917). Her feature appearances include *20,000 Leagues Under the Sea* (1916), and after *Bitter Fruit* (1920) she left the screen.

Wallace Lupino (left) Toy Gallagher, and George Davis (right)
behind the scenes on the Educational Pictures lot.
Wallace Lupino Scrapbook.

Toy Gallagher (Louise Gallagher) (?)
Irish-born, dark-haired actress, who came to Hollywood to write a series of articles for a New York newspaper on "Breaking into the Movies." The story goes that while inter-

viewing Mack Sennett he offered her work in his pictures instead, which led to appearances under her real name of Louise in his 1924 shorts *Three Foolish Weeks* and *The Sea Squawk*. Following a bit in Harold Lloyd's *The Freshman* (1925), plus western features such as *Action Galore* (1925) with Buddy Roosevelt and Al Hoxie's *The Texas Terror* (1926), she settled in at Jack White Comedies, was re-named Toy, and was frequently paired with Phil Dunham in Cameo Comedies like *The Radio Bug, Plumb Goofy*, and *His Off Day* (all 1926). Later moving up to two-reelers with Lloyd Hamilton such as *Peaceful Oscar* and *New Wrinkles* (both 1927), plus Lupino Lane in *A Half-Pint Hero* (1927), she ended her career with the arrival of sound in 1928.

Anita Garvin (1907 – 1994) **See Chapter Nine**

Carmelita Geraghty (1901 – 1966)
Geraghty was the beautiful daughter of screenwriter Tom Geraghty who was a regular "other woman" in Mack Sennett comedies of the late 1920s. Following her father into the film business she started as a continuity clerk for directors such as Marshall Neilan and Chester Franklin before starting her acting career in the feature *Bag and Baggage* (1923). Becoming a WAMPAS Baby Star in 1924 she supported Larry Semon in his two-reeler *Trouble Brewing* and appeared in a couple of shorts with boxer Jack Dempsey. Her features at this time included *High Speed* (1924), *My Lady of Whims* (1925), and *My Best Girl* (1927). After appearing in the 1928 full-length Sennett feature *The Goodbye Kiss* she became a fixture in his shorts, supporting Billy Bevan, Carole Lombard, and Johnny Burke in titles like *Hubby's Weekend Trip, The Campus Carmen* (both 1928), and *Clunked on the Corner* (1929). Her sound features included *Fifty Million Frenchmen* (1931) and *Malay Nights* (1933), before she married screenwriter Carey Wilson and retired from the screen to start a second career as a painter.

Neva Gerber (1894 – 1974)
Action actress best-remembered as a western heroine and serial star opposite Ben Wilson in opuses like *Officer 44*, and *The Power God* (both 1926) who spent a substantial part of her early career in comedy shorts. Born in Chicago, by 1912 she was working for Kalem and in 1914 became a regular with the Balboa Company. The next year she joined the American Film Company and under their *Beauty* brand co-starred in numerous one-reelers like *Cupid Takes a Taxi, Mumps and Bumps, Almost a Widow* (all 1915), *Ella Wanted to Elope*, and *Getting Wrong* (both 1916) with Webster Campbell and Frank Borzage as leading men. On joining Universal in 1916 she teamed up with actor, director, and producer Ben Wilson and spent most of the rest of her career working for him. In a career that lasted until 1930 she appeared in westerns such as John Ford's *Hell Bent*, and *Three Mounted Men* (both 1918), in addition to serials like *Trail of the Octopus* (1919), *The Screaming Shadow, The Branded Four* (both 1920), *The Mystery Box* (1925), and two

of their most popular – 1926's *Officer 44* and *The Power God*. When Ben Wilson died in 1930 she left the screen, and had a number of marriages before her death in 1974.

Emily Gerdes monopolizes Billy West as Ethel Broadhurst stands by in *Hello Bill* (1923). Courtesy of Sam Gill.

Emily Gerdes (1890 – 1974)
Plain and skinny character actress, who seems to have been the prototype for Miss Prissy in Warner Brothers' later Foghorn Leghorn cartoons. Got her start in Mary Pickford features such as *Rebecca of Sunnybrook Farm* (1917) and *How Could You, Jean?* (1918), and spent the 1920s in numerous shorts and features. She worked with Lyons & Moran in *Heart Trouble* (1919) and *Oiling Uncle* (1920), Billy West in *Hello Bill* (1923) and *Fiddlin' Around* (1925), in addition to other shorts with Buster Brown, Charley Bowers, and Cliff Bowes. Her feature appearances include *Bell Boy 13* (1923), *Dynamite Dan* (1924), *Heir-Looms* (1925), and her most often seen film today *Ella Cinders* (1926), where she annoys Colleen Moore as Prissy Pill. She continued in sound films until 1940, mostly in walk-ons in features like *Banjo on My Knee* (1936) and *The Grapes of Wrath* (1940).

Ethelyn Gibson (Ethel Gibson) (1897 – 1972)
Blonde who was the longtime support of Charlie Chaplin imitator Billy West, in addition to being his real-life wife. Born in Akron, Ohio, in 1914 she was in the Ziegfeld Follies and toured vaudeville, as an incident at the Columbia in Atlanta, Georgia made the pages of the April 1914 *Variety*: "Ethel Gibson and George Milton leads at Columbia, were arrested for an indecent tango. Milton was fined $50 and Miss Gibson fled town, leaving a contempt writ hanging onto her." By 1915 she was appearing with West in his vaudeville act *Is He Charlie Chaplin?* Their first films such as *His Married Life* and *Bombs and*

Boarders (both 1916) were made for Unicorn Film Service, and they soon moved over to the King Bee Co. and shot the films in Florida, New Jersey, and finally Hollywood. Ms. Gibson was part of the ensemble in the King Bees as West's leading ladies were Ethel Burton, Leatrice Joy, and Myrtle Lind, but with a move to Bulls Eye in 1919 she became her husband's main support for the next few years in titles such as *A Rolling Stone* (1919), *The Beauty Shop* (1920), *He's In Again* (1921), *Love* (1924), and *Rivals* (1925). In 1926 West teamed with his brother George in West Brothers Productions and distributed a number of series through the independent Weiss Brothers Artclass Pictures. Ethelyn was starred in their *Winnie Winkle* comedies, which were based on the popular comic strip about a working girl and her family. The series ended in 1928 as did Gibson and West's marriage. That same year she set up Ethelyn Gibson Productions, Inc. to make talking serials, the first of which was to be *The Five Cards*. After this there's no information about the remainder of her career, and she passed away in Ohio in 1972.

Oliver Hardy makes time with Ethelyn Gibson, much to Billy West's surprise in *Rivals* (1925). Courtesy of Robert Arkus.

Margaret Gibson (Patricia Palmer) (1894 – 1964)
Statuesque blonde, whose tumultuous life had a detrimental effect on her screen career. Her parents were actors, so she made her stage debut at twelve, appearing in vaudeville and stock companies. In 1912 she entered films with Vitagraph's West Coast company where she appeared in all types of films including comedies such as *Any Port in a Storm* (1913), and *All on Account of Towser* (1915). Eventually she moved on to Centaur where she was their leading lady in dramas and exotic stories like *Marta of the Jungles*, *The Star of India*, and *Tangled Hearts* (all 1916). 1917 saw her become a headliner at Christie Comedies, working with Neal Burns and Eddie Barry in one-reelers on the order of *With the Mummies' Help*, *Skirts*, *Her Merry Mix-Up*, and *Almost Divorced* (all 1917). That

year she was arrested for vagrancy (at the time a code word for prostitution) and drug dealing, and although eventually acquitted she changed her name to Patricia Palmer. Returning to Vitagraph for dramas and western shorts, she also went back to Christie for a spate of 1919 comedies, a few where she supported star Fay Tincher like *Sally's Blighted Career, Mary Moves In*, and the surviving *Rowdy Ann*.

The 1920s saw her occasionally popping up at Christie, and starring opposite Guinn "Big Boy" Williams in western such as *Across the Border* and *The Cowboy King* (both 1922). She was arrested again in 1923, this time on blackmail and extortion charges, and although she again wasn't convicted it battered her career even more. She did a few more features, comedies on the order of *Hold Your Breath* (1924), *Who's Your Friend* (1925), and *Naughty Nanette* (1927), but by 1929 she was out of the business. She later married, spent much time overseas, but finally settled back in Hollywood, got religion, and at her death even confessed to having killed director William Desmond Taylor.

Eugenia Gilbert (Eugenie Gilbert) (1902 – 1978)
Pretty brunette, born in East Orange, New Jersey, who first was a professional toe dancer. She entered pictures at age fifteen as an extra, and started getting roles in a 1920 series of low-budget comedy shorts from the American Lifeograph Company that revolved around a young man named Paul, with titles such as *Paul's Peril* and *Paul's First Kiss*. Moving to supporting work in features like *A Certain Rich Man* (1921) and *The Half-Breed* (1922), in addition to being action star Richard Talmadge's leading lady in *Wildcat Jordan* (1923), she became a Mack Sennett girl. Soon she was paired with the likes of Harry Langdon and Ralph Graves for *The Sea Squawk* and *The Plumber* (both 1925) and was a foil for Alice Day in *A Soapsuds Lady, Hotsy Totsy* (both 1925), and *Gooseland* (1926). From Sennett she moved to Fox Imperial Comedies like *Officer of the Day* (1926) and then worked for Hal Roach in the *All Star* short *Get 'Em Young* (1926) with Stan Laurel and Harry Myers. Besides roles in features she returned to Roach and appeared with Charley Chase in *There Ain't No Santa Claus* (1926), *Many Scrappy Returns, One Mama Man* (both 1927), and *Movie Night* (1929). The latter part of the 1920s saw her in the Weiss Brother's serial *Perils of the Jungle* (1927), and she ended her career in action and western pictures such as *The Mysterious Airman* (1928) and *Courtin' Wildcats* (1929). Following her film career she was a model in Los Angeles fashion shows in the early 1930s.

Florence Gilbert (1904 – 1991)
The Chicago-born Gilbert was a leading lady who entered pictures in the late teens. Besides doubling for Mary Pickford, she worked for Christie Comedies and supported Monty Banks in numerous shorts like *A Fliver Wedding* (1920), *Where's My Wife*, and *Fresh Air* (both 1921). She moved on to Bull Montana comedies such as *One Wild Day, Snowed Under* (both 1923), and *Breaking Into Society* (1924) before she was put under

contract by Fox, where she played second leads in the prestigious features *The Johnstown Flood* and *The Return of Peter Grimm* (both 1926) as well as kept busy in shorts such as the *Van Bibber* series with Earle Foxe and one-shots like Lige Conley's *King of the Kitchen* (1926). After marrying in 1926 she left the screen, and later married famous Tarzan author Edgar Rice Burroughs.

Monty Banks has his eye on Florence Gilbert in *Love Taps* (1922).
Courtesy of Robert S. Birchard.

Helen Gilmore (1862 – 1936)
Tall (5'10 1/2") and overpowering actress who specialized in harridans and made frequent appearances as mean landladies or bossy mothers-in-law. She began acting at age eight in 1870, and after thirty years on the stage started her film career in 1903 working for Universal, World Film, and Kalem. 1915 saw her supporting Pokes and Jabbs at Vim, and she was a regular in George Ovey's 1917 Cub Comedies. Also signed by Roach that year, she stayed there until her retirement in 1931. During that time she terrorized Harold Lloyd, Paul Parrott, Stan Laurel, Charley Chase, and even Our Gang, in addition to playing the Widow Douglas in *Tom Sawyer* (1917) and *Tom and Huck* (1918), plus turning up in other features such as *Dangerous Paths* (1921) and *Too Much Business* (1922) with Edward Everett Horton. She passed away in 1936 at age seventy-four.

Helen Gilmore gets the drop on Snub Pollard and Harold Lloyd in *Two Scrambled* (1918).
Courtesy of Karel Caslavsky.

Dorothy Gish (1898 – 1968) **See Chapter Five**

Lea Giunchi (1884 -) **See Chapter One**

Louise Glaum (1888 – 1970)
Brunette who began her film work in comedy but eventually became popular as a dramatic diva. Having appeared on stage in stock in Chicago, she later supported star Nat Goodwin on the West Coast, and also toured on the road. She made her film debut for Pathé, and was soon doing comedies for Al Christie at Nestor as well as dramas for Kalem and Thomas Ince's Broncho. In 1914 she became the leading lady for Augustus Carney in his *Universal Ike* series of shorts, and even stayed on when Carney was replaced by Bobby Fuehrer (a.k.a. Bobby Ray) as Universal Ike Junior in tiles like *Universal Ike Has One Foot in the Grave*, *Universal Ike in Pursuit of Eats*, and *Universal Ike Junior in Me, Him and I* (all 1914). After this series the rest of her career was spent in drama, supporting William S. Hart in *Hell's Hinges* and *The Return of Draw Egan* (both 1916), before eventually becoming a Theda Bara-type in pictures such as *Sex*, and *The Leopard Woman* (both 1920). Her career ended with *Fifty-Fifty* in 1925.

Paulette Godard (1910 – 1990)
Popular actress of the 1940s, who first gained attention playing the Gamin in Charlie Chaplin's *Modern Times* (1936). Having started working in small parts in 1929, she was also a Goldwyn Girl in musicals such as *Whoopee* (1930), *Palmy Days* (1931), and *Kid Millions* (1934) before being discovered by Chaplin and cast as his co-star in his last silent film. Following *Modern Times* she appeared with Chaplin again in *The Great Dictator* (1940), and became very busy in light comedies and dramas like *The Women* (1939), *The Ghost Breakers* (1940), *So Proudly We Hail* (1943), and *The Diary of a Chambermaid* (1946) into the 1950s.

Ray Godfrey (Rae Godfrey) (1896 - ?)
Beautiful actress, who did acrobatic work in road shows before entering pictures with Vim where she was the regular leading lady for Babe Hardy and Billy Ruge in their series of *Plump and Runt* comedies. Spending 1916 in shorts such as *Hungry Hearts*, *Spaghetti*, *An Aerial Joyride*, and *Love and Duty*, Ms. Godfrey then moved over to L-Ko to support Mack Swain in *Ambrose* two-

Ray Godfrey as the title role in L-Ko's *Ambrose's Icy Love* (1918). Courtesy of EYE Filmmuseum, Netherlands.

reelers like *Ambrose's Icy Love*, and *Ambrose, the Lion Hearted* (both 1918), in addition to comedies for Nestor, Bulls Eye, and Reelcraft. After features that included *Marked Cards* and *The Mask* (both 1918), her career ended with *Smashed Back* (1926).

Marta Golden (1868 – 1943)
Golden was a Pennsylvania-born stage warhorse who toured around the country with numerous sketches and songs for many years. Hitting big-time vaudeville in 1908, she worked with Ferris Hartman's Company and at San Francisco's Alcazar Theatre. Also on the West Coast she substituted for Marie Dressler at the Gaiety Theatre in 1914, and was a member of the Bishop Players at the Liberty Stock Co. Selling a script to Essanay in 1915 led to her appearing in a number of their comedies such as the Hal Roach-directed *All Stuck Up*, and Charlie Chaplin's *A Woman* and *Work* (all 1915). Following her work with Chaplin she moved over to Keystone for *Crooked to the End*, and the title role in *A Janitor's Wife's Temptation* (both 1915) opposite Fred Mace. The topper for this foray into films was her role in Chaplin's last Mutual comedy *The Adventurer* (1917) where Golden memorably gets a scoop of ice cream down her back. After a bit in Chaplin's *A Dog's Life* (1918) she returned to the stage, touring with a sketch titled *The Pickpocket* which she wrote as well as produced. Her last film role was as support for Dolores Del Rio in the Edwin Carewe feature *Revenge* (1928).

Rosa Gore (1866 – 1941)
Tall and thin actress, who was adept at playing snoopy landladies or gossips. With her husband Dan Crimmins she was half of the popular vaudeville team of Crimmins and Gore (real names Alexander and Minnie Lyons) who toured the globe with their act *What are the Wild Winds Saying?*, as well as appearing in the stage version of *The Wizard of Oz*. Making their film debuts for Pathé in 1913, Ms. Gore appeared in comedies with Charles Arling and Henry Bergman such as *An Itinerant Wedding* and *The Cook's Revenge* (both 1913), before moving on to Vitagraph. In 1915 they began working for producer George Kleine in features like *The Commuters* (1915) as well as entries of his comedy series *The Mishaps of Musty Suffer*, and other shorts with George Bickel and Leon Errol. Spending the rest of the silent era appearing all over the map of silent comedy – L-Ko, Jimmy Aubrey, Larry Semon, Fox – not to mention features on the order of *La La Lucille* (1920), *Seven Chances* (1925), and *Play Safe* (1927) – Ms. Gore continued after the change-over to sound until 1935. Passing away in 1941, she was followed by husband Crimmins in 1945.

Rosa Gore shows some overage delivery boys to Chester Conklin in a Fox Sunshine Comedy. Courtesy of Robert S. Birchard.

Baby Early (Gorman) (1906 – 1982)

Blonde-haired little actress who began working for producer Pat Powers at the age of five, and was soon teamed with Matty Roubert for a series of comedies like *Injuns*, *The Skeleton*, and *Getting Their Picture Took* (all 1912). Known as "The Powers Kids" the pair spent most of their screen time as pint-sized troublemakers. The niece of actress Elsie Albert, who appeared in many films alongside her, Baby Early continued in comedies and dramas, mostly for Universal, until she was eleven in 1917.

Bobbie Gould (Dot Gould) (?)

Dark-haired comedienne who was very busy for a couple of years in Sterling comedies. Her early work was for Imp and the Oz Film Manufacturing Co. in features such as *The Patchwork Girl of Oz* (1914). Joining the Sterling ensemble she supported star Ford Sterling in shorts like *Snookee's Day Off* (1914) and co-starred with Max Asher and John Brennan in items like *An Ill Wind*, *The Fatal Hansom*, *Love and Water* (all 1914), *The Runaway Closet*, and *The Battle of Running Bull* (both 1915). Becoming popular as the character Dot, and headlining in *Dot's Chaperone* and *Dot's Elephant* (both 1914), she became known as Dot Gould. Her last known film was an *Independent Woman* (1915) for the Reliance Company.

Betty Jane Graham (1923 – 1998)

Graham was a curly-headed blonde moppet who played the female lead in the Van Buren Company's late 1920s *Smitty Comedies*. Based on the comic strip by Walter Berndt, Graham shared the series with freckle-faced Donald Haines and little Jackie Coombs in titles such as *Camping Out*, *No Picnic* (both 1928), *Circus Time*, and *Tomato Omelette* (both 1929). After the series she worked for many years in small child's parts and some of her films included *King of Jazz* (1930), *Huckleberry Finn* (1931), *20,000 Years in Sing Sing* (1932), *Ah Wilderness* (1935), *All This and Heaven Too* (1940), and *Heart of the Rio Grande* (1942). Said to have been the best friend of Judy Garland, she left films in the mid-1940s, but returned later for bits in productions like *El Dorado* (1966).

Charley Chase, Lassie Lou Ahern (center) and Katherine Grant (right) in 1924's *The Family Entrance*.

Katherine Grant (1904 – 1937)
Very good at playing shrewish or suspicious wives, Katherine Grant was a beauty contest winner who had worked on stage with Gus Edwards and began her screen career as an extra at the Hal Roach Studio in 1921. After working in shorts for Fox and Universal she returned to Roach as support for Stan Laurel. Although she quickly became Charley Chase's regular leading lady in classics like *Innocent Husbands*, *His Wooden Wedding*, and *The Uneasy Three* (all 1925), she suddenly disappeared from films in early 1926. Sadly, this is reported to have been due to personal problems that had her spending time in and out of sanitariums, where she eventually died at age thirty-two in 1937.

Betty Gray (1895 – 1919)
Petite brunette, who like Mabel Normand started out as a model for well-known illustrators such as Charles Dana Gibson, Clarence Underwood, and Harrison Fischer. Based in New York, she got her start in films for Pathé and Biograph in 1912, and appeared in comedies like *Gee! My Pants* (1912), *$1000 Reward* (1913), and *The Tango Flat* (1914), in addition to dramas. In 1914 she moved over to the Vitagraph Company and appeared *Too Many Husbands* (1914) with Mr. & Mrs. Sidney Drew, *The Timid Mr. Tootles*, and *The Smoking Out of Bella Butts* (both 1915) with Flora Finch. When Roscoe Arbuckle

made some Keystone shorts on the East Coast in 1916 Betty supported him in *His Wife's Mistake* and *The Other Man*. Her last film was the propaganda feature *Why America Will Win* (1918), as she sadly died in the influenza epidemic at age twenty-five in 1919.

Charlotte Greenwood (1890 – 1977)
Memorable long-legged stage comedienne, who sadly only made two silent film appearances. After achieving stardom in shows like *The Passing Show of 1912*, *The Tik-Tok Man of Oz*, and *Pretty Mr. Smith*, she was brought to the screen by her regular stage producer Oliver Morosco and Paramount Pictures to headline in the feature comedy *Jane* (1915). Having been teamed on stage with comedian Sydney Grant, producer Morosco teamed again for the film. The next year saw her major stage hit *So Long Letty* and due to the sequels *Linger Longer Letty*, *Letty Pepper*, and other stage work, she didn't return to films until more than ten years later when she supported the team of George K. Arthur and Karl Dane in *Baby Mine* (1928). Although it's unavailable, the arrival of sound saw her become much more of a movie regular – starring in a version of *So Long Letty* (1929), and shorts like *Love Your Neighbor*, and *Girls Will be Boys* (both 1931), and more importantly being major support in high profile features like *Palmy Days*, *Flying High*, and *Parlor, Bedroom, and Bath* (all 1931) to Eddie Cantor, Bert Lahr, and Buster Keaton. She continued making funny appearances in films that include *Springtime in the Rockies* (1942), *The Gang's All Here* (1943), and *Oklahoma!* (1955).

Ena Gregory (1906 – 1993)
Blonde actress who was a WAMPAS Baby Star and brought her good looks to comedy shorts with Monty Banks, Bobby Dunn, Century, and the Hal Roach Studios before moving on to numerous western features in the mid-1920s (her first husband was director Albert S. Rogell). At the end of the silent era she began working under the name of Marion Douglas, but her career didn't go past the early days of sound.

Ena Gregory and Arthur Stone in the Hal Roach Comedy *Should Landlords Live?* (1924). Courtesy of Brussels Cinematek.

Lita Grey (Lillita MacMurray) (1908 – 1995)
Young actress who played the flirty angel in Charlie Chaplin's *The Kid* (1921) and was starring as his leading lady in *The Gold Rush* (1925) when she suddenly became Mrs. Chaplin at fifteen due to pregnancy. Georgia Hale took over the role, and Lita had two children with Chaplin before a sensational divorce in 1927. She later toured as a singer in vaudeville and cabaret, appeared in a few minor films, and late in life gave a charming interview about working with Chaplin in Kevin Brownlow and David Gill's *Unknown Chaplin* (1983).

Julia Griffith (1880 – 1961)
Tall and middle-aged blonde, who often played dowagers in numerous uncredited bits in late 1920s and early 1930s Mack Sennett comedies. Turning up as wedding guests, party guests, train passengers, or audience members, she came in handy for crowd scenes and can be seen in titles like *Don't Tell Dad* (1925), *A Blonde's Revenge* (1926), *Smith's Cousin* (19127), and *Love at First Flight* (1928). She can also be spotted in Hal Roach shorts such as *Should Men Walk Home?* (1927) and *Honkey Donkey* (1934), plus had more substantial roles in Weiss Brothers Artclass comedies such as *Better Behave* (1927) with Poodles Hanneford and Ben Turpin's *The Cockeyed Family* (1928). Besides shorts, she also appeared in features like *A One Man Game* (1927), *Vagabond Lady* (1935), and *Hellzapoppin* (1941) through 1943.

Dan Russell enjoys his repast with Katherine Griffith (left) and William Irving (right) in an L-Ko Comedy.

Katherine Griffith (1876 – 1921)
Character comedienne, who spent many years on stage in musical comedy and vaudeville before coming to pictures. She was a regular in Powers Comedies, often playing mother to the "Powers Kids" Matty Roubert and Baby Early, as they caused trouble in outings such as *Injuns* and *Getting Their Picture Took* (both 1912). She also did comedies as well as dramas for Kalem, Rex, Tiffany, Oz, Sterling, and Morosco Companies, and was the matriarch of an early Hollywood family that included her husband Harry and sons Gordon and Graham who were popular child players. In 1916 she became part of the ensemble at L-Ko Comedies, usually teamed up with Dan Russell in shorts like *The Right Car but the Wrong Berth*, *Murder By Mistake* (both 1916), and *Heart Sick at Sea* (1917). Also appearing in meaty roles in prestigious features such as Mary Pickford's *Pollyanna* (1920) and *Huckleberry Finn* (1921), Mrs. Griffith's busy career was cut short by her sudden death from a stroke in late 1921 on the set of the Marshall Neilan film *Penrod* (1922).

Clara Guiol (1909 - 1995)
Sister of director/writer Fred Guiol. She began appearing in small roles in Hal Roach comedies in the early 1920s when her brother was a crew member and camera assistant. The dark-haired Clara worked at the studio for years supporting Charley Chase, Our Gang, Laurel & Hardy, and everyone else on the lot, and some of the titles she turns up in include *A Quiet Street* (1922), *Cradle Robbers* (1924), *Should Men Walk Home?* (1927), *The Lighter That Failed* (1927), and *Two Tars* (1928). She continued at the studio until the mid-1930s.

Dorothy Gulliver (1908 – 1997)
Brunette beauty who came to Hollywood after winning a Salt Lake City beauty contest that was sponsored by Universal Studios. Starting in bit parts in "Big U" comedy and western shorts, as well as serials, she landed the female lead in their *Collegians* series – forty-four two-reel shorts that followed the ups and downs of a college athlete and his friends. Lasting from 1926 through 1929 titles included *The Last Lap* (1926), *Flashing Oars* (1927), *The Bookworm Hero* (1928), and *Sporting Courage* (1929), plus there was even an early sound feature-length entry entitled *College Love* (1929). After *The Collegians* ended Dorothy appeared in sound features such as *Painted Faces* (1929), *Outlaw Justice* (1932), and *Fighting Caballero*

Portrait of Dorothy Gulliver, female lead in Universal's *Collegians* series. Author's collection

(1935) for various producers, but by the late 1930s her roles became smaller and the production companies more low-budget. She worked sporadically in films and on television in the 1940s and 1950s, and later had a nice role in John Cassavetes' 1968 drama *Faces*.

Lillian Hackett (1896 – 1973)
Brunette, who began her film career in 1919 in Hallroom Boys Comedies such as *The Chicken Hunters* (1919) and *A Close Shave* (1920). Also appeared in Fox Sunshine Comedies and at the Roach Studio before settling in at Jack White Comedies for a string of Lige Conley comedies that included *Hold Tight, Kick Out* (both 1923), *Midnight Blues*, and *There He Goes* (both 1924). A selection of her feature appearances are *Once a Plumber* (1920) with Lyons & Moran, *Danger* (1923), *In Hollywood with Potash and Perlmutter* (1924), and *Ladies at Ease* (1927).

Dorothy "Dot" Hagar (1896 - ?)
Beauty who specialized in playing vamps and "other women" in Triangle Keystone comedies such as *Crooked to the End* (1915) and *A Tugboat Romeo* (1916). When Mack Sennett left Triangle she stayed on and continued working in shorts like *Honest Thieves* (1917) and *His Double Life* (1918), and also features such as *Old Hartwell's Club* and *His Enemy, the Law* (both 1918). Besides the serial *King of the Circus* (1920) with Eddie Polo, and features like *The Smart Sex* (1921), she spent time as one of the Vanity Fair Girls who supported Eddie Boland in Hal Roach shorts such as *Queens Up* (1920) and *Man Haters* (1922). Her last film was the Baby Peggy feature *The Darling of New York* (1923).

Georgia Hale (1906 – 1985)
Sultry brunette who grew up in Chicago, where she appeared in musical comedy and stock, in addition to being "Miss Chicago" in 1922's *Pageant of Progress*. After entering pictures in 1923 she worked for a time as a bathing girl and extra in Mack Sennett comedies, and can be spotted in photos and as a member of the wedding party in Harry Langdon's *His Marriage Wow* (1925). That same year she landed the female lead in Josef von Sternberg's independently made *The Salvation Hunters* where she was seen by Charlie Chaplin, who hired her to replace the pregnant Lita Grey as his leading lady in *The Gold Rush* (1925). Remembered today for that film and for her relationship

Late 1920s beauty shot of Georgia Hale. Author's collection.

with Chaplin, her other movies included *The Great Gatsby* (1926), *The Wheel of Destiny* (1927), and *The Last Moment* (1928), but her career ended after one sound picture in 1931. She later worked as a dance instructor and memorably told her story of working with Chaplin in Kevin Brownlow and David Gill's *Unknown Chaplin* (1983).

Lillian Hamilton (1893 – 1997)
Former toe dancer and actress with the Burbank Theatre stock company in Los Angeles who entered films as an extra with D. W. Griffith and the Biograph Company in films such as *The School Teacher and the Waif* (1912). She also passed through Universal, Selig, and the Premier Company of the St. Louis Motion Picture Producing Company in a mixture of comedies and westerns, and settled at Imp in Roy Clements-directed comedies like *Safety First and Last*, and *Slim, Fat or Medium* (both 1915). After a brief stint working with chimps Napoleon and Sally in E & R Jungle Films like *The Home Breaker* (1916) she became a regular in the slapstick ensemble at Vogue Comedies, where she was leading lady to Sammy Burns, Rube Miller, Paddy McGuire, and Ben Turpin. Her Vogue two-reelers included *Sammy's Dough-Filled Romance, Doctoring a Leak, Picture Pirates* (all 1916), *Sticky Fingers, Lured and Cured*, and *When Ben Bolted* (all 1917). After Vogue closed shop she moved over to the Al Christie-produced Strand Comedies such as *For Art's Sake* and *Her Rustic Romeo* (both 1918) before leaving pictures in 1918.

Harriet Hammond (1899 – 1991)
Michigan-born beauty, who gave up thoughts about being a concert pianist to become a Mack Sennett bathing girl. Starting in 1918 she adorned four years of two-reel comedies on the order of *She Loved Him Plenty, The Village Chestnut* (both 1918), *Hearts and Flowers, A Lady's Tailor* (both 1919), *Great Scott* (1920), *Officer Cupid*, and *Astray from Steerage* (both 1921) as well as the Sennett features *Yankee Doodle in Berlin* (1919), *Married Life* (1920), and *Home Talent* (1921). With her great beauty and warm camera presence she moved into features – some dramas like *Bits of Life* (1921) and *The Golden Gift* (1922), others comedies such as Roscoe Arbuckle's *Leap Year* (shot in 1921) and *Confidence* (1922). While shooting a 1922 Buck Jones western a premature explosion resulted in injuries and burns to her face. She returned to films in 1925, having a good role in the comedy *Man and Maid* (1925) opposite Lew Cody, and supported Harry Carey in the westerns *The Man from Red Gulch* (1925), *Driftin' Thru*, and *The Seventh Bandit* (both 1926). After the 1928 silent *Queen of the Chorus*, she made one talking appearance in the comedy short *The Chumps* (1930) and left films.

Part II: Selected Biographies

Raye Hampton (1875 – 1944)
Hampton was a large, battle-axe type of character actress, born in Texas, who toured the U.S. and Canada in vaudeville and burlesque before entering films around 1920 to play domineering wives for Milburn Moranti in his Reelcraft two-reelers such as *Kick* and *A Bungalow Bungle* (both 1920). She later settled into westerns supporting stars like Buddy Roosevelt, Wally Wales, and Buffalo Bill Jr. in features on the order of *Western Grit* (1924), *Action Galore* (1925), and *The Obligin' Buckaroo* (1927).

Portrait of overlooked character actress Raye Hampton. Courtesy of Jim Kerkhoff.

Juanita Hansen (1895 – 1961)
A blonde beauty who became popular as a Mack Sennett bathing girl, and moved on to other starring films but eventually found herself unemployable in Hollywood. Born in Iowa, she entered films with small parts at the Oz Film Company in titles like *The Magic Cloak* and *The Patchwork Girl of Oz* (both 1914). After more work at Paramount, American, and Fine Arts, she became a regular on the Sennett lot in 1916, where she lent her good looks to *His Pride and Shame*, *Black Eyes and Blue* (both 1916), *Her Nature Dance*, and *A Clever Dummy* (both 1917). She also appeared in Triangle shorts and was the leading lady for the comedy team of Clarence Kolb and Max Dill in their feature production *Glory* (1917). She later moved into serials for Universal and Selig and was quite popular, but high living and drug addiction caused many problems for her with the studios, and after major issues on Pathé's *The Yellow Arm* (1921) her career hit the skids. After 1923 she was off the screen and despite a Broadway play in 1928 she still had more problems. After a final film appearance in Monogram's *Sensation Hunters* (1933) she spent many years at carnivals and traveling shows lecturing on the evils of drugs, eventually becoming a clerk at a railroad company before her death in 1961.

Mack Sennett and serial star Juanita Hansen. Author's collection.

Lois Hardwick (1917 – 1968)
Child actress, and the fourth and final Alice in the Walt Disney cartoon/live-action *Alice in Cartoonland* shorts such as *Alice's Circus Daze*, *Alice's Three Bad Eggs*, *Alice the Whaler*, and *Alice in the Big League* (all 1927). In addition to parts in features like *Seventh Heaven* (1927), *The Crowd*, and *Lilac Time* (both 1928), she was hired by the Stern Brothers to re-

place Doreen Turner for the last year and a half of their *Buster Brown* Comedies. Lois co-starred as Mary Jane opposite Arthur Trimble in entries such as *Buster Minds the Baby*, *Teacher's Pest* (both 1928), *Knockout Buster*, and *Stop Barking* (both 1929).

Marion Harlan (1904 – 1971)
Daughter of character actor Otis Harlan, who was on stage with her family from the age of three. Her father made his film debut in 1915 and Marion followed him in the early 1920s as a comedy ingénue in shorts for Bull Montana and Bobby Vernon such as *The Two Twins*, *Rob 'Em Good*, *Easter Bonnets* (all 1923), *High Gear* (1924), and *Great Guns* (1925). Roles also opened up in lighthearted features like *Hit and Run* (1924) and *Thank You* (1925), in addition to westerns and dramas such as *Rough Going* and *Wings of Youth* (both 1925). In 1925 she signed a contract with Fox, and appeared in two-reelers like *Shoes*, *The Flying Fool*, and *The Peacemakers* (all 1925), not to mention the Tom Mix and Buck Jones westerns *Tony Runs Wild* (1925), *A Man Four-Square*, and *The Gentle Cyclone* (both 1926), before she married Walter Kennedy in 1926 and retired from pictures.

Jean Harlow (1911 – 1937) **See Chapter Eight**

Marcia Harris (1868 – 1947)
Harris was a tall and thin actress from the stage who entered films in the teens after years in plays such as *Mrs. Wiggs of the Cabbage Patch* and *What Happened to Jones*. Specializing in maiden aunts and officious teachers, one of Ms. Harris' first films was the Gaumont two-reeler *The Reformer* (1915), but she spent most of her time as support in New York-made features such as *The Poor Little Rich Girl* (1917),

Marcia Harris is surprised at the attentions of Alice Joyce in *So's Your Old Man* (1926). From the Alice Joyce Collection – courtesy of Bruce Lawton.

Prunella (1918), and *The Flapper* (1920). In the 1920s she worked in D.W. Griffith dramas like *Orphans of the Storm* (1921), *Isn't Life Wonderful?* (1924), and *The Sorrows of Satan* (1926), but at the same time had good comic roles in *The King on Main Street* (1925), *Love Em and Leave Em* (1926), and especially as W.C. Fields' long-suffering wife in *So's Your Old Man* (1926). By the late 1920s she'd moved to California, and after supporting Karl Dane and George K. Arthur in *Brotherly Love* (1928) and Corrine Griffith in *Saturday's Children* (1929) her screen roles tapered off and ended in 1932.

Sunshine Hart (1886 – 1930) **See Chapter Seven**

Olive Hasbrouck (1907 – 1976)
Ingénue who began her career in westerns at Universal, and soon moved over to their comedies starring Arthur Lake. She supported Lake from 1924 to 1926 in shorts such as *The Girl Hater, Alone at Last* (both 1924), and *Dog Biscuits* (1925), in addition to playing Nannie Cohen in the hit feature *The Cohens and Kellys* (1926). In the later 1920s she appeared in shorts for Christie, plus features like *The Shamrock and the Rose* (1927), and numerous westerns on the order of *The Cowboy Cavalier* (1928) and *The Royal Rider* (1929).

Phyllis Haver (1899 – 1960) **See Chapter Eight**

Maie B. Havey (?) **See Chapter Six**

Wanda Hawley (Wanda Petit) (1895-1963)
Hawley is an overlooked blonde comedienne who at her peak starred in numerous situational comedy features for Realart. Having started her career on the stage, where she toured in productions of the popular *Peg O' My Heart*, she entered film in 1917 at Fox under the name of Wanda Petit, and appeared in a variety of dramas, westerns, and comedies. From Fox she supported Doug Fairbanks in *Mr. Fix-It* (1918) and came under the wing of Cecil B. DeMille for *Old Wives for New* and *We Can't Have Everything* (both 1918). Through DeMille she was signed by Paramount and spent the next four years being leading lady to light comics Bryant Washburn and Wallace Reid, as well as starring in her own features for Paramount's subsidiary Realart. Her titles include *The Poor Boob, Peg O' My Heart* (both 1919) *The Best Six Cellars, Miss Hobbs* (both 1920), *Her Sturdy Oak, A Kiss in Time* (both 1921), *Too Much Wife, Bobbed Hair* (1922) and *Nobody's Money* (1923). In 1923 she had a contract dispute with Paramount and went out on her own, but despite a few good offerings such as the Christie feature comedies *Reckless Romance* (1924) and *Stop Flirting* (1925), she bounced from studio to studio, soon ending up in low budget offerings from independent outfits like Embassy, Banner, Trem Carr, and Sun Motion Pictures. In the late 1920s she returned to the stage on the Keith-Albee circuit in the playlet *The Wedding Ring*, and when sound hit Hollywood she made one short for Al Christie, *Her Husband's Women* (1929), and two western features with cowboy Jay Wilsey before leaving films in 1931.

Helen Hayward (?)
Actress who specialized in battle-axes, who is remembered for playing Harry Langdon's virago mother-in-law in his self-directed feature *The Chaser* (1928). After many years on the stage in stock and Shakespearian roles she began appearing in films as early as 1916 in titles like *The Wrong Door* (1916) with Mr. & Mrs. Carter De Haven, the dramatic feature *Remembrance* (1922), and Chaplin's *The Gold Rush* (1925). She first worked with Langdon as a neighbor in *Three's a Crowd* (1927) and then had her major role the next

year in *The Chaser*. In her later years she was a member of the stage club The Troupers, along with Louise Carver and Eva Thatcher, privately taught stage and screen acting, and appeared in small bits in films like *Show Boat* (1936).

Connie Henley (?)
Dark-haired ingénue who after a couple of shorts for the United States Moving Picture Corp. had a brief career at Century Comedies where she supported Charles Dorety and Harry Sweet in two-reelers like *Home Brew, A He-Male Vamp,* and *A One Cylinder Riot* (all 1920). Her last known film was the Hoot Gibson short *The Cactus Kid* (1921).

Gale Henry (1893 – 1972) **See Chapter Six**

Anna Hernandez (Anna Dodge) (1867 – 1945)
Small and chubby supporting actress who spent many years in stock and rep companies until she and her second husband George Hernandez joined the ensemble at Selig in 1911. Specializing in maternal types in dramas as well as comedies such as *Where There's a Will There's a Way, Out Generated* (both 1911), *A Night Out* (1912), and *Hiram Buys an Auto* (1913), she also turned up in episodes of Selig's *Chronicles of Bloom Center* one-reelers, and moved into features like *Hoodoo Ann* (1916), *Nancy Comes Home* (1918), and *The Jack-Knife Man* (1920). In the 1920s she took up residence on the Mack Sennett lot and in addition to playing Mabel Normand's mother in *Molly 'O* (1921) and *The Extra Girl* (1923) she made numerous silent and sound shorts like *Black Oxfords* (1924), *A Yankee Doodle Duke* (1926), *The Bride's Mistake* (1931), *Speed in the Gay Nineties,* and *The Singing Plumber* (both 1932), before retiring in 1933.

Aggie Herring (1876 – 1939)
Herring was an Irish character actress who began her stage career at age seventeen in stock and vaudeville, before entering films in 1912 with the New York Motion Picture Company. Over the years she was comic relief for stars such as Olive Thomas, Harold Lloyd, Mary Pickford, and Jackie Coogan in pictures like *Madcap Marge* (1917), *The Hoodlum* (1919), *Among Those Present* (1921), *Oliver Twist* (1922), and *McFadden's Flats* (1927). Continuing in sound features, she also appeared in many early Mack Sennett sound shorts such as *Courting Trouble* (1932) and *Too Many Highballs* (1933), and worked right up to her death in 1939.

Aggie Herring advises Marguerite Clark in *A Girl Named Mary* (1919). Courtesy of Bruce Calvert.

Wilna Hervey (Wilna Wilde) (1894 – 1979)
This 6'3", three hundred pound actress was really a painter, but because of her unusual size ended up in movies, starting out doing bits in Sidney Drew and Reelcraft shorts. In the early 1920s she became a regular in the *Toonerville Trolley* Comedies as Katrinka, the large and powerful housekeeper of the Skipper of the trolley. When the *Toonerville* films ended Hervey moved over with star Dan Mason to an imitation series called *Plum Center* Comedies playing the character of Tillie Olson. Only making films to support her art pursuits, her film career ended when the *Plum Center* series finished in 1923. In addition to appearing in the two series with Dan Mason, she became the life partner of his daughter Nan, and the two were together until Hervey's death in 1979.

Ruth Hiatt (1906 – 1994)
Blonde best remembered today for the *Smith Family* series – Mack Sennett's stab at situational and domestic comedy. From 1926 to 1929 Hiatt played the young wife opposite Raymond McKee as her hubby and little Mary Ann Jackson as their scene-stealing baby. Earlier she had been leading lady for Lloyd Hamilton in the early 1920s, and had been a female-lead-in-residence for Jack White Comedies where she was also paired with Lige Conley, Cliff Bowes, and Lee Moran until she went to Sennett in 1925. Following features like *The Missing Link* (1927), sound arrived, and Hiatt returned to work with Lloyd Hamilton in a number of his talkie comedies, and then moved around in small bits in shorts and features until the mid-1930s.

Ruth Hiatt shares a furry friend with Syd Chaplin in *The Missing Link* (1927). Courtesy of Sam Gill.

Mamie Hicks (?)
Plus-sized bit player who turned up in shorts such as *Speed Boys* (1924) and *Smith's Modiste Shop* (1927), and was the mother of Tommy Hicks, a freckle-faced fat boy who regularly appeared in numerous kid comedies and other items for Universal and Educational like *Family Life* and *Crushed* (both 1924).

Josephine Hill (1898 – 1989)
Actress who was leading lady in some late teen Universal comedies such as *Two Tired, Babies is Babies* (both 1919), and *Pills for Papa* (1920) with Neal Burns, and a number

of Al Christie two-reelers like *Pure and Simple* (1921) and *Hokus Pokus* (1922) opposite Bobby Vernon, but spent the bulk of her career in westerns with the likes of Hoot Gibson, Art Accord, Leo D. Maloney, and her first husband Jack Perrin. After many oater features, her career ended in 1933.

Thelma Hill (1906 – 1938) **See Chapter Eight**

Fay Holderness (1888 – 1963)
Holderness was a silent comedy regular who turned up in an uncountable number of shorts, and was usually seen as a combative spouse or a no-nonsense nurse. Entering films in 1914, in a few years she began to be noticed for roles in Chaplin's *A Dog's Life* (1917) and D.W. Griffith's *Hearts of the World* (1918), and was soon appearing at all the comedy units in Hollywood supporting the likes of Oliver Hardy, Billy West, Alice Howell, Mack Swain, and Phil Dunham. By the mid-1920s she was a member of the Hal Roach Stock Company, and also turned up in features like *The Last Man on Earth* (1924) and *Lonesome* (1928). In sound she continued to be on hand for tons of Roach and Sennett shorts, and continued working until the early 1950s.

Max Davidson (left), unknown, and Fay Holderness in an unused scene from *The Boy Friend* (1928). Courtesy of Bruce Calvert.

Carol Holloway (1892 – 1979)
Pretty blonde who started her career on the stage as a member of the Carleton Stock Company, appeared as Youth in productions of *Every Woman*, and appeared on Broadway. She entered films in 1913 for Lubin where she worked in *Patsy's First Love*, *Patsy Among the Fairies* (both 1915), and other entries of Clarence Elmer's *Patsy* comedies, and when she moved over to the American Film Manufacturing Company she frequently supported John Steppling in his *Billy Van Dusen* series. She also starred in

During her career Carol Holloway worked for Lubin, American, La Salle, and Vitagraph. Author's collection.

many of their Beauty Comedies such as *Pretenses, Too Much Married*, and *A Gay Blade's Last Scrape* (all 1915). After working for the LaSalle Comedy Co. she did some serials for Vitagraph, and then supporting roles in features, including many westerns, such as *The Saphead* (1920), *The Ramblin' Kid* (1923), *Beau Brummel* (1924), and *Jake the Plumber* (1927), but her roles got smaller and smaller before she retired in the early 1940s.

Ruth Holly (?)
Holly was a small brunette, born in New Orleans, who was a supporting player, and an occasional female lead, in Monty Banks two-reelers such as *Be Careful, The Artist* (both 1922), *Hangin' Around, Oil's Well* (as a saucy senorita), and *Spooks and Spirits* (all 1923), as well as his 1925 feature *Keep Smiling*. She also appeared in Buster Keaton's *Sherlock Jr.* although is often mis-credited as the candy shop girl (actually Christine Francis). Holly turns up briefly as the leading lady of the picture that projectionist Buster is showing, *Hearts and Pearls*, who turns around and changes into Katherine McGuire. Married to a Hollywood doctor, she continued working on and off in uncredited bits in features such as *A Single Man* (1928), *Free and Easy* (1930), and *Friendly Enemies* (1942).

Jean Hope (?)
Local, Los Angeles-born blonde who began her career on stage as a child toe dancer. In 1920 she became part of the Vanity Fair Girls, the female ensemble that supported comic Eddie Boland in Hal Roach one-reelers such as *Alias Aladdin, June Madness*, and *Greek Meets Greek* (all 1920). In 1921 she married Eddie Boland and continued in his shorts, as well as appearing in Century Comedies. After the 1923 feature comedy *Gimmie*, her career slowed down, with her last known appearance being the Snub Pollard Weiss Brothers short *Fire!* (1926).

Edith Hoskins (?)
Pretty blonde from vaudeville and musical comedy who worked at Lubin before moving over to Fox Comedies where she was Hank Mann's leading lady in shorts such as *A Bon-Bon Riot* and *His Love Fight* (both 1917).

Jannie Hoskins (Jane Florence Hoskins) (1923 – 1996)
Younger sister of Our Gang stalwart Allen "Farina" Hoskins; she joined the series in 1923. Originally dubbed "Aroma," she was usually called "Mango," and often played Farina's sister until the early 1930s.

Mae Hotely (Mrs. Arthur D. Hotaling) (1872 – 1954)
Hotely was a versatile character clown who starred in numerous split and one-reel comedies for the Lubin Company. In interviews and publicity pieces Ms. Hotely gave her birthplace as Paris, France, but it appears that she was actually born May Shearor in

Maryland. After working on stage in stock companies she joined the early movies, although her 1913 claim of "having been a picture actress for 15 years" seems to be as exaggerated as her birth in Paris. It's known that she began at Lubin in 1907 working with her husband director Arthur D. Hotaling, whom she'd married in 1902. The pair were the "king and queen" of Lubin's comedy production and made their shorts in Philadelphia and later, during the winter months, in Jacksonville, Florida, where Ms. Hotely had support from a young Oliver Hardy in outings such as *Casey's Birthday* (1914) and the surviving *A Lucky Strike* (1915). In 1915 Mae was co-starred in a series with stage comedian Billie Reeves but soon left the screen. Arthur Hotaling continued directing into the 1920s, and Mae made one final appearance in the 1929 feature *Girls Who Dare*.

Mae Hotely was Lubin's female comedy headliner for eight years until 1915. Author's collection.

Alice Howell (1886 – 1961) **See Chapter Three**

Hazell Howell (1898 – 1965)
A Los Angeles native, Howell made her film debut in the 1920 adaptation of George M. Cohan's *45 Minutes from Broadway*. After large roles in other features like *A Full House* (1920) and *Desperate Youth* (1921) she took a break to get married. When she returned to pictures in 1925 it was in Fox features, in addition to two-reelers such as *Neptune's Stepdaughter, A Parisian Knight* (both 1925), and *The Swimming Instructor* (1926). Besides the Charley Chase short *The Way of All Pants* (1927), she also turned up in *Spuds* (1927) playing "Bertha from Berlin" opposite Larry Semon and Monty Banks' *A Perfect Gentleman* (1928). When sound arrived she was demoted to uncredited bit parts, and one of her last roles was as the wife who mistakenly buys her husband a piano in Laurel & Hardy's *The Music Box* (1931).

Helen Howell (1895 – 1957)
Dark haired vaudeville actress who made her film debut in the late teens supporting "Smiling Billy" Parsons and appeared in some of the *Hallroom Boys* shorts, first with Ned Flannigan and Neely Edwards, and then Edwards with Hugh Fay. In 1921 she was teamed with comic Al Alt for a short-lived series of romantic comedy two-reelers

produced by the Union Film Company, and distributed on the states' rights market by Reelcraft Pictures Corporation and the even more independent Allied Distribution Corporation. Despite behind the scenes and in front of the camera help from veterans such as Al Martin and former *Pokes and Jabbs* star Bobby Burns, survivors like *Bungalow Love* and *The Lost Engagement Ring* (both 1921) are particularly uninspired. Howell went on to become the ingénue in *Plum Center Comedies*, where she met a young gagman named Frank Capra and became his first wife.

Yvonne Howell (Julia Rose Shevlin) (1905 – 2010)
Howell was the daughter of comedienne Alice Howell, and made her debut as a Century Follies Girl in the 1924 Century Comedy *Harem Follies*. Little and cute, she was originally featured as a bathing girl, but worked her way up to roles in shorts for Hal Roach, FBO, Standard, and Educational such as *Flaming Flappers* (1925), *A Fraternity Mix-Up* (1926), and *Hop Off* (1928) opposite Charley Bowers. Also appearing in a few features like *Somewhere in Sonora* (1927) and *Take Me Home* (1928), she retired after marrying cameraman and director George Stevens. Mother of American Film Institute founder George Stevens Jr., she lived to be one hundred and four before passing in 2010.

Gladys Hulette (1896 – 1991)
Dainty brunette who had been a child actor on the stage, playing with Nazimova and Bertha Kalich in *Kreutzer Sonata*, in addition to *The Blue Bird*. Her last stage appearance was in 1911's *Little Women*, but by that time she had already begun doing occasional film work for Edison, Vitagraph, and Imp such as *Princess Nicotine* (1909). Finally settling in as part of the acting company at Edison, she at first played children but eventually became a young leading lady in numerous comedies. Titles include *Bobbie's Long Trousers*, *Why Girls Leave Home* (both 1913), *Courting Betty's Beau*, *An Absent Minded Cupid* (both 1914), *Joey and his Trombone*, and *Count Macaroni* (both 1915).

In 1916 she moved to the Thanhouser Company, and after more shorts for them graduated to romantic comedy features like *Prudence, the Pirate* (1916) and *Pots-and-Pans Peggy* (1917). Re-locating to the West Coast she made many features such as *Mrs. Slacker* and *Annexing Bill* (both 1918) for the Astra Company. 1921 saw her with an excellent role in the major release *Tol'able David* opposite Richard Barthelmess, and her other big features include *The Iron Horse* and *The Family Secret* (both 1924). After the mid-1920s the steam seems to have run out of her career, and besides making one Hal Roach short, *Be Your Age* (1926) opposite Charley Chase, she finished the decade in low-budget outings like *A Bowery Cinderella* (1927) and *Life's Crossroads* (1928). She disappeared from films during the change-over to sound, but came back for a few walk-ons in films such as *Torch Singer* (1934) until 1934.

Jewell Hunt (1895 - 1975)

Hunt was a dark-haired ingénue for the Vitagraph Company who was born in Georgia but raised in Brooklyn. Her talent as a dancer led to her screen career, and besides performing, she also had the Dolly Varden Studios on 5th Avenue where she taught many of New York's elite "400." Spotted by Vitagraph head J. Stuart Blackton dancing at a function at the Waldorf-Astoria Hotel, she became part of their film family in 1915. Frequently working with comedy directors C.J. Williams and Larry Semon, she often supported comics like Kate Price, Hughie Mack, and Semon himself in outings like *Getting Rid of Aunt Kate* (1915), *Losing Weight* (1916), and *Chumps and Chance* (1917), in addition to starring in titles such as *The Little Trespasser* and *Myrtle the Manicurist* (both 1916). Only appearing for Vitagraph, her film career lasted from 1915 to 1917.

Jewell Hunt had a two-year career with Vitagraph from 1915 to 1917. Author's collection.

Madeline Hurlock (1899 – 1989) **See Chapter Eight**

Lucille Hutton looking coy in the L-Ko Comedy *The Million Dollar Smash* (1916). Courtesy of Robert Arkus.

Lucille Hutton (Juanita Lucille Hutton) (1898 – 1970) Ingénue who made her film debut in 1916 at age eighteen in L-Ko Comedies. Before that, she had appeared on stage with the Morosco Stock Co., and after two years at L-Ko supporting the likes of Billie Ritchie, Phil Dunham, and Merta Sterling in shorts such as *A Bold, Bad Breeze* (1916), *A Limburger Cyclone* (1917), and *The Little Fat Rascal* (1917), she moved on to Christie and Universal comedies. In the mid-1920s she appeared in features like *East Side – West Side* (1923) and *Dick Turpin* (1925) before landing at Jack White Comedies. Working in their Mermaid and Cameo brands with Al St John, Monty Collins, Johnny Arthur, and Lloyd Hamilton, some of her titles include *Open House* (1926), *Hot Lightning* (1927), and *Wedding Slips* (1928). The early days of sound saw her continuing in shorts for White and Universal, but she retired in 1931.

May Irwin (1862 – 1938) **See Chapter One**

Ann Ivers (?)
Ingénue who appeared in some of the 1915 Hal Roach-directed Essanay comedies such as *Street Fakers* and *Off for a Boat Ride* alongside comedy regulars like Bud Jamison, James T. Kelly, and Jack Pollard. In addition to the Bosworth Pictures feature *Martin Eden* (1914), she also worked in Charles Parrott-directed Foxfilm Comedies like *His Bomb Policy* (1917). It appears that she left pictures for World War I Red Cross service as she told *Film Fun* magazine that "she doesn't mind being slapped in the face with an open-faced pie, but since her latest picture, in which she was stuck with a fork and burned with a hot iron and had to fall over a railing on the side of a house, Red Cross work under shrapnel fire has no terrors for her."

Mary Ann Jackson (1923 – 2003) **See Chapter Seven**

Peaches Jackson (Charlotte Jackson) (1913 – 2002)
Older sister of *Smith Family* and *Our Gang* star Mary Ann Jackson who began her screen career in 1917. Some of the many features she appeared in include D.W. Griffith's *The Greatest Thing in Life* (1918), and she supported Mabel Normand, Mary Pickford, and Jackie Coogan in *Jinx* (1919), *Through the Backdoor* (1921), and *Circus Days* (1923). After 1925 features such as John Ford's *Kentucky Pride*, her career wound down, and she made unbilled appearances as a dancer in the sound films *She Wanted a Millionaire* (1932) and *Dancing Lady* (1933). She later married Hawaiian-born Tony Guerrero, and the pair moved to Honolulu and opened up The Tropics, a long-time well-known restaurant in Waikiki Beach.

Elsie Janis (1889 – 1956) **See Chapter Six**

Amy Jerome (1895 - ?)
Stage actress born in Kansas City, Missouri, that spent several years in stock companies, which included touring the Hawaiian Islands, and joined the ensemble at Foxfilm Comedies in 1917. Alongside Charles Arling, Annette DeFoe, Martin Kinney, Bill Hauber, and Frank Alexander she appeared in shorts like *A Footlight Flame* and *Social Pirates* (both 1917). Also for Fox she appeared in the comedy western feature *Durand of the Bad Lands* (1917) and ended her film career playing Sarah in the independent biblical epic *Restitution* (1918).

Josephine (?)
Little capuchin monkey, which was best known for stealing laughs from Buster Keaton in *The Cameraman* (1928). Owned and trained by ex-organ grinder and animal wrangler Tony Campanaro, she seems to have made her earliest appearances in 1921-1922 *Campbell Comedies* like *Schoolday Love* and *Monkey Shines* (both 1922), before moving

to the Hal Roach lot for his all-animal *Dippy-Doo-Dad* shorts, and then turning up all over in two-reelers and features such as *Hold 'Em Yale* (1928) and *The Four Feathers* (1929). Since there were similar monkeys active in films (Chicago and Jocko, for two) it's hard to determine many of her performances, but she did seem to have routines and gestures that were her own. There was also a Josephine who according to the trades celebrated her forty-first birthday on the set of *Words and Music* (1948), but it's not known if it's the same monk. Coy Watson Jr., her sometime co-star in the *Campbell Comedies* remembered:

Josephine's scene in *Two Tars* (1928) with Stan Laurel & Oliver Hardy sadly ended up on the cutting room floor.

> I worked in three pictures with a ring-tailed monkey named Josephine and a boxer dog named Pal. Their owner and trainer was Tony Campanero, the owner of several animals he kept in Culver City. In his great Italian accent he would tell me "Coy, you be ah careful wit ah Josephine today, she no feel-a-berry good."
>
> Tony got into films because Josephine had been Tony's organ grinder monkey on the street. In our Campbell Comedies the monkey and dog were great. The monkey rode on the dog' back as Tony shouted directions at them from off-camera.
>
> Remember in those days of silent pictures, owners could direct their animals by voice: "Lie down now, Pal. Josephine, tip your hat." Tony would also wave his arm as he called to Josephine saying, "Josephine, jump on Coy's shoulder, jump over!" Then he'd open his mouth wide and tell her to "Say Aah!" She'd open her mouth and say "Aah' back at him to look like she was talking. Sometimes a subtitle would pop onto the screen to tell what the monkey was saying.
>
> I remember how Tony had such patience with the animals (*The Keystone Kid*, 2001)

Margaret Joslin (1883 – 1956) **See Chapter Seven**

Gloria Joy leads the "Butterfly Girls" chorus in *Moonlight Nights* (1925). Courtesy of Cole Johnson.

Gloria Joy (1910 – 1970)
Black-haired, curly-headed moppet who started her film career at age eight and worked steadily into her teens in the late 1920s. At three years old she began appearing on stage with the Majestic and Morosco Stock Companies, in addition to touring vaudeville. In 1917 the Balboa Company was looking for someone to replace baby Marie Osborne, who had moved on to greener pastures, and little Gloria was hired. Her starring features for the company included *No Children Wanted*, *Miss Mischief Maker*, and *Little Miss Grown-Up* (all 1918). After these features she went on to shorts for Pathé and R-C Pictures such as *The Fortunes of Corinne* (1918), *Corinne Come Here* (1919), and *Sweet Thirteen* (1922). By 1925 she was a teenager and hooked up with the Rayart Pictures Corporation as a young leading lady, first in a series of *Butterfly Comedies* and then followed in *Joybelle* shorts like *Artist Blues*, *Moonlight Nights*, *Hay Fever Time* (all 1925), and *Wet Paint* (1926). Although cute and charming, she comes off as a bit of a neutral presence in these later shorts, with most of the heavy comedy lifting done by Max Asher, Joe Moore, Conrad Hipp, and Eddie Fetherston. After the Rayart serial *Phantom Police* (1926) with Herbert Rawlinson she was away from pictures for a few years before coming back in the early 1930s for a few low-budget items on the order of *Lariats and Six-Shooters* (1931) and *Girl Trouble* (1933). She ultimately left pictures in 1934.

Leatrice Joy (1893 – 1985)
Dark-haired actress who became a popular star of the 1920s, who had begun her career in the teens in slapstick shorts. Starting out as an extra in 1915, after a supporting role in Mary Pickford's *The Pride of the Clan* (1917) she became the leading woman

for Black Diamond Comedies, a small company that shot their films in Wilkes Barre, Pennsylvania. Although sometimes billed as Beatrice Joy, she was their plucky heroine, who became known as Susie, in numerous 1917 one –reelers such as *Her Fractured Voice, Getting the Evidence, Susie Slips One Over,* and *Susie's Scheme*. Getting attention in this series Hollywood beckoned and she headed out west to become the love interest for Charlie Chaplin imitator Billy West. Following West two-reelers on the order of *His Day Out, The Orderly, The Messenger,* and *The Handy Man* (all 1918) she made her way into features and worked up to leading roles. While doing many dramas she also acted in comedies like *Bunty Pulls the Strings* (1921) and *Bachelor Daddy* (1922). Soon she was "discovered" by Cecil B. DeMille for epics such as *Manslaughter* (1922) and *The Ten Commandments* (1923), but was also starred in many romantic comedies like *Changing Husbands* (1924), *The Clinging Vine, Eve's Leaves* (both 1926), *Nobody's Woman* (1927), and *Man-Made Widow* (1928). She began free-lancing at the end of the silent era before retiring after a couple of talking films. Later she would return in occasional roles in films and on television, and made a memorable appearance in Kevin Brownlow and David Gill's 1980 documentary series *Hollywood*.

Natalie Joyce (1902 – 1992)
This graduate of Broadway musical shows made her stage debut in *The Passing Show of 1918*, and appeared in the *Ziegfeld Follies* from 1919 to 1921. Re-locating to Los Angeles she was dancing in a café when discovered by producer Al Christie and she joined his organization in 1922 supporting Neal Burns, Jimmie Adams, and Billy Dooley in shorts such as *Be Yourself* (1923), *Savage Love* (1924), and *A Briny Boob* (1926). Besides shorts she also worked in features like Tom Mix's *The Circus Ace* (1927) and *A Girl in Every Port* (1928). Moving into sound, she did a few more shorts and some bits in features until 1932.

Mildred June (1902 – 1940)
Pretty brunette, who made a charming foil for Billy Bevan in Mack Sennett comedies such as *Be Reasonable* (1921) and *Gymnasium Jim* (1922). Mildred and her family had moved to Los Angeles around 1917, and after attending Hollywood High she started in films as a Sennett Bathing Beauty in 1919. Besides her work at Sennett she also made some Fox Imperial Comedies like James Parrott's *A Deep Sea Panic* (1924), plus *Matrimony Blues* and *Fighting Kangaroo* (both 1926) with Lige Conley, a number of shorts for Samuel Bischoff, Universal one-reelers opposite Charles Puffy

Odd Sennett publicity photo of Mildred June among the ducks. Author's collection.

and Arthur Lake, and visited the Hal Roach lot for *Starvation Blues* (1925), *Dizzy Daddies*, and *Dog Shy* (both 1926). Her feature appearances included *Rich Men's Wives* (1922), *Fashionable Fakers* (1923), and *The Snarl of Hate* (1927) before her career ended in the late 1920s.

Dorothy Kelly (1894 – 1966)
A versatile actress for the Vitagraph Company, who appeared in many of the studio's dramas as well as comedies. Born in Philadelphia, she was raised in New York and after studying at the National Academy of Design she worked as an artist and illustrator before abandoning it when she joined Vitagraph in 1911. Over the years her comedy films included *The Troublesome Stepdaughters*, *The Lovesick Maidens of Cuddleton*, *Bettina's Substitute, or There's No Fool Like an Old Fool* (all 1912), *Bunny's Honeymoon*, *Disciplining Daisy* (both 1913), *Sonny Jim in Search of a Mother*, *Miss Raffles*, *A Double Error* (all 1914), *A Madcap Adventure*, and *Easy Money* (both 1915). As time went on she graduated to more of the studio's dramatic fare, and after supporting comic Ernest Truex in his comedy feature *Artie the Millionaire Kid* (1916) she finished her days at Vitagraph in serious features like *The Money Mill* and *The Maelstrom* (both 1917). Having married business man Harvey Havenor in 1916, her final film was World Picture's *The Awakening* (1917) before retiring from the movies.

Edith Kelly (?)
Ingénue who appeared in many late teens Century comedies like *Choo Choo Honeymoon* and *Hey Doctor!* (both 1918) where she supported star comics like Alice Howell, Hughie Mack, Billy Armstrong, and Neal Burns.

Fanny Kelly (1875 or 1877 – 1925)
Hefty actress of Scottish descent, who came from vaudeville with her husband Pat Kelly, and spent of most of her film career at the Mack Sennett Studio playing Irish cooks or domineering wives. Some of her Sennett appearances include shorts such as *Sheriff Nell's Tussle* (1918), *Hard Knocks and Love Taps* (1921), and *Romeo and Juliet* (1924), plus the features *Yankee Doodle in Berlin* (1919), *Love, Honor, and Behave* (1920), and *The Extra Girl* (1923). She can also be spotted in Fatty Arbuckle's *Love* (1919), as Mickey Daniel's mother in *Giants vs. Yanks* (1923), and in *The Telephone Girl* comedy *Sherlock's Home* (1924) before her early death in 1925.

Madge Kennedy (1891 – 1987) **See Chapter Four**

Judy King (Priscilla King, Priscilla Whelan) (1901 – 1987)
Canadian–born, dark-haired actress billed as "the pint-sized comedienne," and originally worked as Priscilla King with her first husband Tim Whelan in the vaudeville sketch *Suite*

Sixteen. When Whelan became a gag writer for Harold Lloyd, King played the flapper in *Girl Shy* (1924), and turned up from 1924 through 1927 in shorts such as *Red Pepper*, *The Heart Breaker*, and *Strong for Love* (all 1925), plus Fox features like *The Best Bad Man* (1925), *Upstream*, and *The Gay Retreat* (both 1927). King later remarried, and was also the sister of Mona Ray, who played Topsy in the 1927 version of *Uncle Tom's Cabin*.

Natalie Kingston (Natalie C. Ringstrom) (1905 – 1991)
Statuesque brunette, who had been a dancer with Fanchon and Marco, and joined the Mack Sennett Bathing Beauties in 1923. She soon became a regular leading lady for Harry Langdon in shorts such as *All Night Long* (1924), *His Marriage Wow*, and *Lucky Stars* (both 1925), in addition to also supporting the likes of Billy Bevan, Ralph Graves, and Ben Turpin. Leaving Sennett at the end of her contract in 1925 she appeared in comedy features like *Wet Paint*, *Kid Boots* (both 1926), and *Lost at the Front* (1927), even venturing into dramas such as *Street Angel* (1928) and the serials *Tarzan the Mighty* (1928) and *Tarzan the Tiger* (1929). After a few roles in talkie shorts and features she married banker George J. Andersch and retired from the screen.

Natalie Kingston after her days at Sennett supporting Harry Langdon. Author's collection.

Madge Kirby (1884 – 1956) **See Chapter Eight**

Virginia Kirtley (1888 – 1956) **See Chapter Six**

Lillian Knight (?)
Brunette beauty who was "Miss Los Angeles of 1924," and adorned many 1925 Mack Sennett comedies such as *From Rags to Britches*, *Sinners in Silk*, *He Who Gets Smacked*, and *Bashful Jim*. Besides playing Billy Bevan's leading lady in *Super-Hooper-Dyne-Lizzies* (1925) she was a French maid in the feature *Stage Madness* (1927). There was a different Lillian Knight who appeared in dramas in the 1910s.

Mary Kornman (center) giving Joe Cobb (left) grief with the rest of the Gang in *The Fourth Alarm* (1926). Author's collection.

Mary Kornman (1917 – 1973)
The heroine of the early *Our Gang* comedies was the daughter of Roach Studio staff photographer Gene Kornman, and joined the Gang in their third short *Young Sherlocks* (1922), when she was five years old. Cute, with a little pug nose, Mary became the love interest for Mickey Daniels, and besides sometimes being a real flirt, she was often the voice of reason who made the boys stop and almost think over the consequences of the latest scheme they were hatching. She appeared in forty-one entries of the series, and being slender and very long-legged she was taller than many of the guys in the Gang by the time she left in 1926. She toured in vaudeville for a while, sometimes teamed with Mickey, and by the time sound hit Hollywood she was trying to re-establish herself as an adult performer. Unfortunately not having much success outside of Roach's early 1930s *Boy Friends* Comedies and occasional feature appearances such as *College Humor* (1933), *Flying Down to Rio* (1933), and *Queen of the Jungle* (1935), she retired to private life.

Mildred Kornman (1925 -)
Younger sister of Our Gang leading lady Mary Kornman who began appearing in the Gang and other Hal Roach comedies in 1926. As a toddler in films such as *The Nickel Hopper* (1926) and *Ten Years Old* (1927) Mildred was cute, but never caught on like her older sister. She left films in the late 1930s and as an adult became a successful fashion model under the name Ricki Van Dusen.

Alice Lake (1897 – 1967)
Lake was a Brooklyn, New York-born actress who went from amateur dancing and pantomime theatricals to Brooklyn's Vitagraph Studio. Her debut was 1912's *The Picture Idol* and she appeared in other Vitagraph titles like *Who's Who in Hogg Hollow* (1914), *Insuring*

Cutey, and *Levy's Seven Daughters* (both 1915). Following a brief stint with Thanhouser, she worked in some of the East Coast-made Keystones of Roscoe "Fatty" Arbuckle such as *The Moonshiners*, *The Waiter's Ball* (both 1916), and *A Reckless Romeo* (shot in 1916 but released in 1917). Heading out west with Arbuckle she did a couple of shorts like *Grab Bag Bride* and *A Finished Product* (both 1917) for Triangle, and then re-joined Arbuckle to be a regular in his Comique Comedies *Out West*, *The Bell Boy*, *Moonshine*, *Good Night, Nurse!*, and *The Cook* (all 1918). After her stint with Arbuckle she did a few for Mack Sennett such as *Whose Little Wife Are You?* (1918), *Cupid's Day Off*, *Rip & Stitch: Tailors*, and *East Lynne with Variations* (all 1919), before moving into features. She became very popular as a dramatic star in early 1920s features like *Shore Acres* (1920), *Hole in the Wall* (1921), *Broken Hearts of Broadway*, and *The Unknown Purple* (both 1923), but her career waned by the end of the decade, and by the time sound arrived she was doing background work. In an interview Olivia De Havilland spoke about her first days in Hollywood and mentioned being surprised to see Alice Lake as an extra, as she had been a great favorite of hers.

Dixie Lamont (?)

Leading lady in Century Comedies for Universal and also Jimmy Aubrey's starring shorts for Vitagraph. *Squeaks and Squawks*, *Pals and Pugs*, and *Springtime* (all 1920) saw her supporting Aubrey with the likes of Oliver Hardy and Leo White, while at Century she worked with Harry Sweet, Cliff Bowes, Zip Monberg, and the Century Lions. Later she worked with Gloria Joy and appeared in western shorts with Leo Maloney and Jack Perrin, as well as supported Fearless the Dog in the two-reeler *A String of Diamonds* (1926). Her features include *The Western Musketeer* (1922) and *Wolf's Trail* (1927).

Ramona Langley (1893 – 1983)

Performer from the stage who had appeared in the musical revue *A Modern Eve*, who made her film debut in 1913 as a member of Phillips Smalley's Rex Company in shorts like *The Pretender* (1913). It wasn't long before she switched to Al Christie's Nestor Comedy unit as the female lead for Eddie Lyons, Lee Moran, and John Steppling, where they turned out one-reel comedies at a rapid pace. During that year she appeared in around twenty-six comedies, such as *Curses! Said the Villain*, *His Wife's Burglar*, *An Elephant on his Hands*, *Teaching Dad a Lesson*, and *Her Friend the Butler* (all 1913). At the very beginning of 1914, during the shooting of *She Was Only a Working Girl* (1914), Langley, Lee Moran, and John Steppling were playing a spoof abduction scene when the actors fell on the slippery concrete floor with the two men landing on top of Langley. Suffering from internal injuries, Victoria Forde took over the role in the picture, and Ms. Langley never returned to the company or to the movies. Her final films were released in the beginning of 1914.

Beatrice La Plante (1891 – 1973) **See Chapter Five**

Laura La Plante (1904 – 1996) **See Chapter Five**

Villie Latimer (a.k.a. Billie Latimer) (?)
Extremely tall and thin, hatchet-faced actress who specialized in busybodies and spinsters in shorts such as *Chasing the Chaser* (1925) and *Love Em and Weep* (1927). Her largest roles seem to have been for the Hal Roach Studio, but she also appeared in shorts like *Twins* (1925), and Mack Sennett's *Smith's Modiste Shop* and *The Girl from Nowhere* (both 1927), plus features on the order of *The Girl I Loved* (1923) and *The Spieler* (1928).

Villie Latimer (second left) and Hilliard Karr (far right) among others take dentist cards from Wanda Wiley in *Painless Pain* (**1926**).

Rhea Catto Laughlin (? - 1978)
Younger sister of dancer Nema Catto, Rhea had her own stage career, and appeared in the films produced by her brother-in-law Frederick J. Ireland for the Emerald Motion Picture Company. In 1916, Emerald embarked on a series of *Tom and Jerry* two-reel comedies. About ten shorts were made and Rhea played Mrs. Tom in the films. The June 24, 1916 issue of *Motography* reported: "Rhea Catto Laughlin gained her experience on the vaudeville stage, and is seen in a "clinging, weepy role in these comedies." She continued on in the Emerald product supporting Chaplin imitator Billy West in his shorts for the company like *Mustered Out* (1919) and the two-reel farce that starred her brother-in-law *When the Cat's Away* (1920). Emerald had become part of the Reelcraft Corporation and when the company went bankrupt in 1921 it ended the film careers of the family.

Mae Laurel (Mae Charlotte Dahlberg) (1888 – 1969)
Australian-born vaudevillian, who toured the country as half of the Hayden Sisters before teaming up with Stan Jefferson (a.k.a. Laurel) in 1918. Their act had titles such as *Raffles the Dentist* and *No Mother to Guide Her*, and although a husband in Australia kept them from marrying they were every bit a team off-stage as on. Although not much of an actress, Mae appeared in many of Stan's early films such as *Mud and Sand* (1922) and *Frozen Hearts* (1923), usually as some kind of bold and boisterous other woman, but despite giving Stan his new surname of Laurel her temper and professional jealousies frightened off many producers and held back his progress in movies. Eventually producer Joe Rock and director Percy Pembroke conspired to send Mae back to Australia in 1926. She did return a decade later in 1936 to sue Stan as a former common-law wife, and create some bad press for him, before the case was settled out of court.

Jane La Verne (Mary Jane Kutzman) (1922 -)
Child actress who co-starred with Reginald Denny in Universal feature *That's My Daddy* (1927). Other comics she supported include George Jessel in *George Washington Cohen* and Charley Chase in his short *Imagine My Embarrassment* (both 1928). Her last films were 1929's *Melody Lane* and *Show Boat*, where she played the roles of Magnolia as a child and her daughter Kim.

Laura La Varnie (Laura Anderson) (1853 – 1939)
Older character actress who had spent thirty-five years on the stage in stock, vaudeville, and working for the Shuberts, before entering films in 1909. At first she was a member of the ensemble in Biograph films, and turns up in many comedies like *A Disappointed Mama* (1912), *Bertha the Button Hole Maker* (1914), and *The Boob and the Magician* (1915). From there she moved over to Sennett where she specialized in domineering wives and social-climbing dowagers in features like *Mickey* (1918) or shorts on

Laura La Varnie takes a minute to smell the roses before the inevitable butting occurs in *The Yellow Dog Catcher* (1919). Courtesy of Dr. Robert Kiss.

the order of *The Pullman Bride,* and *Are Waitresses Safe?* (both 1917). She jumped ship for Fox Sunshine Comedies in 1919 racking up appearances in items such as *The Yellow Dog Catcher,* and *Her First Kiss* (both 1919). In the 1920s she worked in shorts supporting Buster Keaton, Mabel Normand, Glenn Tryon, and Mickey McGuire, in addition to features such as *Skirts* (1921), *Vanity Fair* (1923), and *Devil's Holiday* (1930).

Florence Lawrence (1890 – 1938) **See Chapter One**

Margaret Leahy (1902 – 1967)
British shop girl who won a 1922 *Daily Sketch* newspaper movie competition to play the second lead in the Norma Talmadge film *Within the Law* (1923). When Ms. Leahy was picked the winner she was sent to America with much fanfare to begin working with director Frank Lloyd, but the story goes that it was soon discovered that while attractive she couldn't act. To save face while not jeopardizing the Talmadge film, producer Joseph Schenck announced that Ms. Leahy would instead star opposite Buster Keaton in his first feature production *The Three Ages* (1923). When Buster objected Schenck reportedly told him that "comic leading ladies don't have to act," and she's pleasant but wooden in the finished film. Although she was also named a 1923 WAMPAS Baby Star, she married, settled in California, and never made another film.

Publicity photo of Daily Sketch contest winner Margaret Leahy whose only film role was as Buster Keaton's love interest in *The Three Ages* (1923). Author's collection.

Florence Lee with Charles Dorety (doing his Buster Keaton imitation) in the Century Comedy *Third Class Male* (1921). Courtesy of Robert Arkus.

Florence Lee (- 1962) **See Chapter Seven**

Florence Lee (?)
Pretty blonde ingénue, who had the same name as the character actress who specialized in mother and grandmother roles (see Chapter Seven). This Florence started her comedy career in 1921 supporting Sid Smith in *Hallroom Boys* Comedies, and soon moved over to Century Comedies where she worked with Baby Peggy in shorts such as *The Kid's Pal* and *Playmates* (both 1921). Married to famous

boxer Jack Dempsey's trainer Teddy Hayes, she appeared in some of Dempsey's *Fight and Win* shorts for Universal, plus a few western features like Bob Custer's *Man Rustlin'* (1926).

Frances Lee (1906 – 2000) **See Chapter Five**

Gwen Lee (Gwendolyn La Pinski) (1904 – 1961)
Lee was a supporting actress of the 1920s, born in Nebraska, who began her career as a department store model and then became a dancer. Spotted by director Monta Bell she landed a contract at MGM in 1925. Originally a brunette, as she appears as the femme fatale in the Lupino Lane two-reeler *Time Flies* (1926), she quickly became a blonde and specialized in support for stars such as Colleen Moore and Norma Shearer in films on the order of *The Boy Friend* (1926), *Orchids and Ermine*, *Her Wild Oat* (both 1927), *Sharp Shooters*, *The Actress*, *Show Girl*, and *A Lady of Chance* (all 1928). Despite solid early talkies like *Chasing Rainbows*, *Free and Easy*, and *Caught Short* (all 1930) her career hit a snag in sound and she was soon demoted to bit parts. Also plagued by personal problems her movie work ended in 1938.

Jane Lee (1912 – 1957) **See Chapter Nine**

Katherine Lee (1909 – 1968) **See Chapter Nine**

Lila Lee (1901-1973)
Child-like ingénue, born in New Jersey and nicknamed "Cuddles," who began acting on stage at a very early age. Discovered while playing on the street by performer/song writer Gus Edwards, she toured vaudeville with *His School Days* Company for ten years. Although she may have made a few sporadic early appearances her film career began in 1918 when Jesse Lasky brought her to Paramount. After making a very big impression in Cecil B. DeMille's *Male and Female* (1919), she became the light-comedy leading lady for Wallace Reid and Roscoe "Fatty" Arbuckle in popular comedy features such as *Hawthorne of the USA* (1919), *The Dollar-a-Year-Man*, *Gasoline Gus*, *Crazy to Marry* (all 1921), *One Glorious Day*, and *The Ghost Breaker* (both 1922). With memorable dramatic performances such as Rudolph Valentino's sweet

Lila Lee, popular leading lady for Roscoe Arbuckle and Wallace Reid in the 1920s. Author's collection.

and long suffering wife in *Blood and Sand* (1922), the early 1920s were the peak of her career. Although she continued to work for decades her tempestuous life affected her career. Most of her later work was very routine, but highlights include *The Unholy Three* (1930) and Olsen and Johnson's *Country Gentlemen* (1936). After a break of more than a decade she returned to acting on television in the 1950s, and *The Emperor's New Clothes* (1966) and *Cottonpickin' Chickenpickers* (1967) were her last films. In the 1920s she was married to actor James Kirkwood, and their son James became a writer who, besides two novels about Hollywood (*There Must Be a Pony* and *Some Kind of Hero*, which included characters based on his mother), also wrote the play *P.S. Your Cat is Dead* and the book for the mega hit musical *A Chorus Line*.

Lillian Leighton (Lillian Brown Leighton) (1874 – 1956)
Heavy-set character actress who was a newspaper woman before embarking on a stage career. She toured the country with her self-written vaudeville sketch, in addition to appearing in stock and even managing her own company. Her movie career began in 1911 with the Selig Company in Chicago, and right away she was playing mothers, cooks, and hotel keepers in shorts like *His First Long Trousers*, *Getting Married* (both 1911), *Mistaken Identity*, and *Murray the Masher* (both 1912). She also played Mrs. Katzenjammer in the studios film version of *The Katzenjammer Kids* comic strip which included titles like *They Go Tobogganing* and *Unwilling Scholars* (both 1912). Eventually she moved to Selig's West Coast studio where she was a regular as Mrs. Plum in their 1915 comedy series *The Chronicles of Bloom Center*. When the series ended she had a brief stint at Vogue Comedies and then joined the E & R Jungle Film Company as the human co-star to the simian team of Napoleon and Sally, supporting them in entries such as *Some Detective!* and *Uncle's Little Ones* (both 1916).

Lillian Leighton shares the screen with Sally the chimp in E&R Jungle Films' *Uncle's Little Ones* (1916). Courtesy of EYE Filmmuseum, Netherlands.

Eventually she made the leap to features and was in demand for "A" pictures such as *Joan the Woman* (1916), *Male and Female* (1919), *Peck's Bad Boy* (1921), *Ruggles of Red Gap* (1923), and *Tumbleweeds* (1925). In the late 1920s she began making semi-regular appearances at the Hal Roach Studio and lent her comic expertise to *Your Husband's Past*, *Be Your Age* (both 1926), *Flaming Fathers* (1927), *Blow By Blow*, and *Fair and Muddy* (both 1928), working with Charley Chase, Max Davidson, and Our Gang. Still busy in the early days of sound, she continued to turn up as aunts, teachers, and pioneer women in *Feet First* (1930), *The Bitter Tea of General Yen* (1933), *Millions in the Air* (1935), and *Trapped by Television* (1936) until 1937.

Irene Lentz (1901 – 1962)
Lentz was a brunette second-lead heroine in Mack Sennett comedies, and as "Irene" later became one of the best-known costume designers in Hollywood history. She came to California from South Dakota to study piano at USC and attend the Wolfe School of Design. Although she opened a gown shop after graduation, she entered movies where she appeared in features such as *A Tailor-Made Man* (1922) and became a regular on the Sennett lot in *The Duck Hunter* (1922), *The Dare-Devil* (1923), *Ten Dollars or Ten Days*, and *Picking Peaches* (both 1924). Going back into fashion she married director F. Richard Jones in 1929, who funded her gown shop on the Sunset Strip. After Jones' death a year later from tuberculosis she became known under the single name "Irene" as one of the studio's best designers for films such as *Shall We Dance*, *Topper* (both 1937), *The Palm Beach Story* (1942), *Meet Me in St Louis* (1944), *Anchors' Away* (1945), *The Yearling* (1946), and *The Pirate* (1948) and many more, racking up two Oscar nominations. Despite her success Lentz had alcohol-related problems and killed herself by jumping from the eleventh floor of the Hollywood Knickerbocker Hotel at age sixty.

Julie Leonard (Julie Leonard Polito) (1902 – 1987)
Dark-haired ingénue who got her start as one of the Vanity Fair Girls in Hal Roach's Eddie Boland Comedies like *Running Wild* and *Prince Pistachio* (both 1921). Making the rounds as leading lady she appeared at Century Comedies in *A Lot of Bull* (1922) opposite bullfighter turned comedian Charles Molina, and supported Stan Laurel in his 1922 Metro Comedy *Mud and Sand*. Two years later Leonard became Laurel's regular foil in his 1924 – 1925 series for producer Joe Rock that included *West of Hot Dog*, *Somewhere in Wrong* (both 1924), and *Dr. Pyckle and Mr. Pride* (1925). Leonard retired from the screen and became the first wife of director Norman Taurog, and in addition to being the sister of writer Jack Leonard, she was the aunt of child star Jackie Cooper.

Julie Leonard and gob Stan Laurel in the Joe Rock-produced *Navy Blue Days* (1925).

Lila Leslie (Lillie Leslie) (1890 – 1940)
Australian stage actress who started her film career in 1913 in dramas as part of the Lubin stock company. After moving into features in the late teens she joined character actor Paul Weigel for a series of *Cruelly Wed* comedies. The two-reelers were produced, written, and directed by Sig Herzig, with distribution by Arrow, and were domestic comedies about a longtime married couple. The only circulating example today, *The Slyest Bidder* (1921), chronicles hubby Henry's adventures as an auction nut who can't keep himself from bidding and filling up their home with unwanted junk. Of course, wifie turns the tables

Lila Leslie playing Big Boy's mother in an unidentified short.

to teach him a lesson. After this series Leslie supported Roy Atwell in some Universal shorts, appeared in Christie two-reelers like *Dandy Lions* and *Grandpa's Girl* (both 1924), in addition to many features such as *Skinner's Dress Suit* (1926) and *Getting Gertie's Garter* (1927). At the end of the decade she became a regular in Jack White comedies playing Malcolm "Big Boy" Sabastian's mother in *No Fare* (1928), *Helter Skelter* (1929), and other shorts. Her last appearance is as Shirley Temple's mother in the two-reel *What's To Do?* (1933).

Katherine Lewis (1906 – 1949)
Lewis was a Newark-born ingénue who began her career at Vitagraph, making regular appearances starting in 1915. Appearing in many dramas she also supported transplanted Broadway comic Frank Daniels in entries of his *Mr. Jack* and *Captain Jinks* comedy series. In 1919 she began working on and off at for producer Al Christie, which included shorts like *Sally's Blighted Career, Rowdy Ann, Mary Moves In* (all 1919), *Hearts and Diamonds* (1920), *Saving Sister Susie* (1921), and *Chop Suey* (1922). She was also in demand for comic features - supporting Lyons & Moran in their full-length *Everything but the Truth* (1920), *Twins Beds* (1920) with Mr. & Mrs. Carter De Haven, and Douglas MacLean's *A Man of Action* (1923). Before ending her career in 1927 she also appeared in *The Nutcracker* (1926) with Edward Everett Horton, and Phyllis Haver's *Your Wife and Mine* (1927).

Beatrice Lillie (1894 – 1989) **See Chapter Three**

Caryl Lincoln (1903 – 1983)
Pretty brunette contract player for the Fox Studio who cut her teeth in two-reel comedies such as *Slippery Silks* and *Roses and Romance* (both 1927) before moving on to be leading lady for Tom Mix, Rex Bell, and Thunder the dog in *Wolf Fangs* (1927), *Hello Cheyenne*, and *Wild West Romance* (both 1928). She continued in sound westerns with Bob Steele, Buzz Barton, and Bob Custer, but by 1933 she was seen only in walk-ons, which she did on and off for a number of years in films such as *Cheaper by the Dozen* (1950), *Please Don't Eat the Daises* (1960), and *The Nutty Professor* (1964).

Myrtle Lind makes herself comfortable on the running board. Author's collection.

Myrtle Lind (1898 – 1993)
Keystone leading lady who joined the King of Comedy in 1916, and appeared in shorts such as *His Hereafter, Pills of Peril* (both 1916), *Pinched in the Finish*, and *A Maiden's Trust*

(both 1917). She also worked in Triangle one-reelers on the order of *A Counterfeit Scent* (1917) and *Wronged by Mistake* (1918). After some Chaplin imitator Billy West films like *The Straight and Narrow* and *Playmates* (both 1918) she returned to the Sennett lot for many of his 1918-1919 Paramount Comedies – *The Village Chestnut* (1918), *The Little Widow*, and *No Mother to Guide Him* (both 1919) – plus the full-length *Yankee Doodle in Berlin* (1919). After the features *Winners of the West* (1921) and *Forget Me Not* (1922) she retired from the screen.

Emma Littlefield (1883 – 1934)
Wife of comedian Victor Moore, who was his long-time stage partner in their sketch *Change your Act, or Back to the Woods*, and in shows such as *Forty-Five Minutes from Broadway* (1906), *The Talk of the Town* (1907), and *The Happiest Night of his Life* (1911). In 1917 Moore began making one-reelers for Klever Komedies, and Littlefield supported him in many of them like *He Got There After All*, *Commuting*, and *Rough and Ready Reggie* (all 1917). Her only films are in this series with her husband, and she passed away in 1934.

Ethel Lloyd (1886 – 1923)
Lloyd was a Brooklyn-born character actress with an extensive stage background. Besides appearing with Maude Adams in *Chanticleer* and Henry Miller in *The Rainbow*, she also had the lead in the musical comedy *Just Out of College*, in addition to playing in vaudeville and stock. Tired of touring, in 1913 she applied for films at Vitagraph in her native Brooklyn and became a resident member of their stock company. Often turning up as put upon daughters or humorous maids, some of her titles include the feature *A Florida Enchantment* (1914), and shorts such as *Beauty Unadorned* (1913), *Jerry's Uncle's Namesake* (1914), and *Mr. Jarr Brings Home a Turkey* (1915). Her last film work were the features *The Little Miss Brown*, *Victor's at Seven* (both 1915), and *The Ransom* (1916), after which she left the screen and died young in 1923. (Some sources have erroneously cited Ms. Lloyd as being the first wife of comedian Lloyd Hamilton, But Hamilton's first wife, whom he married in 1913, was eighteen year-old Ethel Anderson who outlived Hamilton when he died in 1935).

Gayle Lloyd (?)
Pretty light-haired ingénue who was an Al Christie girl supporting comics such as Neal Burns, Jack Duffy, and Bobby Vernon in Christie Educational and Paramount shorts like *French Fried*, *Hot Papa* (both 1927), *Say Uncle*, and *Slick Slickers* (both 1928).

Christie Comedies publicity photo of Gayle Lloyd. Author's collection.

Carole Lombard (1908 – 1942) **See Chapter Eight**

Babe London (1901 – 1980) **See Chapter Seven**

Anita Loos (1889 – 1981) **See Chapter Six**

Aileen Lopez (?)
Dark-haired dancer in vaudeville and the popular musical *Little Jessie James*, who was brought to films by Al Christie for a flurry of activity in 1926. In addition to being leading lady in Jack White and Lloyd Hamilton comedies such as *Mister Chump*, *Flaming Romance*, and *Teacher, Teacher* (all 1926), she also supported Fearless the Dog in the short *Detective K-9* (1926).

Del Lorice (?)
A dark-haired ingénue who was part of the Vanity Fair Girls, the beauty ensemble that supported comic Eddie Boland in a series of 1920 and 1921 Hal Roach one-reelers. During this time she was married to comedy director Percy Pembroke, and later played a vamp in Lloyd Hamilton shorts such as *The Optimist* (1923) and the Marie Prevost feature *Don't Get Personal* (1922).

Louise Lorraine (1901 – 1981)
Dark-haired beauty who started her career as an extra and soon ended up making shorts for Century Comedies with Harry Sweet, Charles Dorety, and Baby Peggy such as *The Dog Doctor*, *A Bunch of Kisses* (both 1921), and *Sweetie* (1923). She also appeared in many westerns shorts and features, some opposite her first husband Art Accord, and later appeared in the comedy features *Exit Smiling* (1926), *Rookies* (1927), *Legionnaires in Paris* (1927), in addition to *Chinatown Charlie* and *The Wright Idea* (both 1928) where she was leading lady for Johnny Hines. Her sound films were mostly westerns before she retired in 1932.

Late 1920s publicity photo of Louise Lorraine. Author's collection.

Bessie Love (1989 – 1986)
Texas-born leading lady, whose cowboy father moved the family to California. As a teenager she came to the attention of D.W. Griffith, who put her under contract to his Fine Arts Company which released through Triangle. Starting in small parts in items like *The Flying Torpedo* (1916) she quickly jumped to leading lady status and supported Douglas Fairbanks in *The Good Bad Man*, *The Mystery*

of the Leaping Fish, and *Reggie Mixes In* (all 1916). By the end of that year she was starring in her own comedy/drama vehicles such as *The Heiress at Coffee Dan's* (1916), *Cheerful Givers*, *The Sawdust Ring*, *Wee Lady Betty*, and *Polly Ann* (all 1917).

With the dissolving of Triangle she moved to Pathé and Vitagraph for more dramatic features, but after 1925's adventure film *The Lost World* she returned to comedy with a number of breezy pictures like *New Brooms*, *The King on Main Street* (both 1925), *Meet the Prince*, *Young April*, *Going Crooked* (all 1926), *Rubber Tires* (1927), and *Has Anybody Here Seen Kelly?* (1928). She made an excellent transition to sound in popular musicals like *The Broadway Melody* (1929), *Chasing Rainbows*, and *Good News* (both 1930), but after leaving MGM she moved to England in 1935. There she worked on stage, and in films and television for many years, and some of her later film appearances are *The Roman Spring of Mrs. Stone* (1961), *Children of the Damned* (1964), *Isadora* (1968), *Sunday, Bloody, Sunday* (1971), *Ragtime* (1981), and her last, *The Hunger* (1983). She also talked about working in silent films in Kevin Brownlow and David Gill's 1980 documentary series *Hollywood*.

Bessie Love as leading lady for Douglas Fairbanks in *Reggie Mixes In* (1916). Billy Rose Theatre Division, the New York Public Library for the Performing Arts.

Beatrice Lovejoy (?)
Slapstick ingénue of the late teens, who started her career with D.W. Griffith and moved on to comedies for Triangle-Keystone, Bulls Eye, and Universal. Some of her titles include *One Night Only* (1919) with Billy West imitator Harry Mann, and *Monkey Stuff* (1919), where she supported star orangutan Joe Martin.

Myrna Loy (1905 – 1993) **See Chapter Eight**

Barbara Luddy (1907 – 1979)
Seventeen year-old beauty who co-starred with the British Georgie Harris in a series of mid-1920s *East Side – West Side Comedies* for the Fox Studio. The five two-reelers were variations on Anne Nichols' stage hit *Abie's Irish Rose* and included *Pawnshop Politics* (1926) and *The Bathing Suitor* (1927). After the series ended in 1927 Luddy appeared in a few features, and became popular on the radio. In 1955 she was the voice of Lady in the Walt Disney classic *Lady and the Tramp*, which led to her becoming a Disney voice regu-

lar for *Sleeping Beauty* (1959), *101 Dalmatians* (1961), *Winnie the Pooh and the Honey Tree* (1966), and many more. She also continued with small parts in movies and TV shows until 1977.

Anna Luther (1897 – 1960)
Dark-haired actress, who started in Reliance dramas in 1913 and then moved on to Lubin and Selig before joining Keystone in 1915. Her comedies for Sennett include *Crooked to the End* (1915) and *Bath Tub Perils* (1916). She soon went over to Fox where she appeared in their Foxfilm Comedies *Her Father's Station* and *Love and Logs* (both 1917), plus features like *The Beast* (1916) and *Melting Millions* (1917). After doing features in the early 1920s she left films in 1924, but sporadically returned in uncredited roles until 1957.

Barbara Luddy was the female half of the five *East Side – West Side* Comedies made by the Fox Company. Author's collection.

Sharon Lynn (1901 – 1963)
Nightclub singer and songwriter, who was a comedy ingénue in late 1920s features such as *Clancy's Kosher Wedding* and *Jake the Plumber* (both 1927), in addition to shorts like *Dad's Choice* (1928) with Edward Everett Horton. With her stage background she was in demand for early musicals such as *Sunnyside Up* and *Fox Movietone Follies of 1929* (both 1929). But her career never really took off, and her last major role was as James Finlayson's paramour Lola Marcel in Laurel & Hardy's *Way Out West* (1937).

Mary "Betty" Mabery (1907 – 1972)
Mack Sennett bathing beauty born in New York City, she attended Glendale High School and UCLA, and was recruited for the Sennett organization in 1926. Having specialized in athletics in preparation for a career as an athletic instructor, much of her screen time was at the beach or in collegiate settings. Her two-reelers include *Smith's Picnic* (1926), *The College Kiddo, Catalina, Here I Come, The Golf Nut* (all 1927), *The Beach Club*, and *The Best Man* (both 1928). After leaving Sennett she became an action and western leading lady, supporting the likes of Bob Steele, Bob Custer, and Ranger the dog in *Lightning Speed, Dog Law, Manhattan Cowboy, The Law of the Mounted* (all 1928), and *Headin' Westward* (1929). In 1928 she married, and after a bit in the Sennett feature *Midnight Daddies* (1930) she retired to join her husband in their mining business in Ely, Nevada.

Marion Mack (Joey McCreey, Elinor Lynn) (1902 – 1989) **See Chapter Six**

Dorothy Mackaill (1903 – 1990)
Mackaill was a blonde beauty who became a popular leading lady in late 1920's feature comedies. Born in England she ran away from home to become a dancer in London, eventually becoming a chorus girl in Paris before joining the *Ziegfeld Follies* in New York. There she became a good friend of Marion Davies, and followed her into the movies in 1920. By 1925 she had made a name for herself with successful films such as *Shore Leave* (1925) and *The Dancer of Paris* (1926), and she was soon launched in a number of romantic comedies, often teamed with Jack Mulhall, such as *The Lunatic at Large*, *Man Crazy* (both 1927), *Ladies Night in a Turkish Bath*, and *Lady Be Good* (both 1928). After one of her best-regarded performances in the part-talking drama *The Barker* (1928), she had a very busy period in a wide variety of early sound films such as *Man Trouble* (1930), *Once a Sinner*, *Safe in Hell* (both 1931), and was even the female lead opposite Ed Wynn in his starring *The Chief* (1933)., but she retired in 1937. Later she did occasional roles on television and her last appearance was on *Hawaii Five-O* in 1980.

Gladys McConnell (1905 – 1979)
Oklahoma native who got her start in Universal shorts with Neely Edwards and Bert Roach before moving over to Fox shorts with the likes of Earl Foxe, Gene Cameron, Hallam Cooley, and Lige Conley such as *The Feud*, *A Polar Baron*, *A Lickpenny Lover*, and *The Steeplechaser* (all 1926). After a couple of small parts in Fox features like *The Midnight Kiss* (1926) and *Marriage* (1927), plus becoming a 1927 WAMPAS Baby Star, her main claim to fame was as Harry Langdon's leading lady in the first of his self-directed features *Three's a Crowd* (1927) and *The Chaser* (1928). Her best role was in *The Chaser* where the court orders her to change roles with hubby Harry, leading her to become a mannish bully that nearly drives him to suicide. Both Langdon films were box office failures, but she appeared in more features and serials, in addition to Lloyd Hamilton's first sound short *His Big Minute* (1929), before retiring in 1930.

After getting her start in Fox two-reelers Gladys McConnell became Harry Langdon's co-star in his directed and starring comedies *Three's a Crowd* (1927) and *The Chaser* (1928). Author's collection.

Gertrude McCoy (Gertrude Lyon) (1896 – 1967)
Statuesque leading lady, born in Rome, Georgia, who spent time on stage in musical comedy and stock, appearing in shows such as *The Two Orphans*. Her first film work was at Biograph under D.W. Griffith, and she passed through Pathé before settling in the

company at Edison Films. For a number of years she was a regular part of their comedy ensemble appearing shorts such as *The Summer Girl, Mike's Hero* (both 1911), *Curing the Office Boy, Kitty's Holdup* (both 1912), *A Serenade by Proxy,* and *The Long and Short of It* (both 1913). She even played the recurring role of "Winsome Winnie" in *That Winsome Winnie Smile* (1911), *Winnie's Dance* (1912), and *Winsome Winnie's Day* (1913), plus penned a few scenarios such as the comedy *Circumstances Make Heroes* (1913).

By 1914 she moved over to their dramatic fare, and made her feature debut with Edison in pictures like *June Friday* and *The Ploughshare* (both 1915). After leaving Edison she worked in numerous East Coast-made features such as *The Blue Bird* (1918), and then in 1919 she married British-born actor/director Duncan McRae. The pair moved to England and McCoy spent the rest of her career in English dramas such as *Chappy: That's All* (1924) and *Nelson* (1926).

Gertrude McCoy was the star of many Edison comedies of the teens. Author's collection.

Ruby McCoy
Dark-haired beauty who had been the cigarette girl at the Montmartre Café in Hollywood, and a beauty contest winner before she began making the rounds of the short subject units in the late 1920s. Her appearances in comedies for Jack White, Sennett, Century, and Hal Roach include *Green-Eyed Love, When George Hops, The Campus Vamp,* and *Chasing Husbands* (all 1928). The changeover to sound seems to have stalled her career, and her last known role is a bit in the Universal feature *Broadway* (1929).

Madame Sul-Te-Wan (Nellie Conley) (1873 – 1959)
Pioneering black film actress, who came from a theatrical background of dancing and musical companies, to settle in California in the early teens and break into movies. Starting in 1915, she appeared in all kinds of films, generally without billing, and turns up in numerous comedies such as *Who's Your Father?* (1918), *His Musical Sneeze* (1919), *The Show* (1922), and *College* (1927). Although usually playing maids, cooks, or on occasion voodoo witch women, she worked non-stop until passing away at the Motion Picture Country Home in 1959, with some of her memorable later films being *Kentucky* (1938), *King of the Zombies* (1941), and *Carmen Jones* (1954).

Marion McDonald (Marion Elizabeth McDonald) (1904 – 1956)

Dark-haired beauty, who became a Mack Sennett Bathing girl in the early 1920s when her family moved from Massachusetts to Los Angeles. Her first known film is 1924's *East of the Water Plug*, and through 1927 she supported Alice Day and the Smith Family, not to mention vamped and flirted with the likes of Billy Bevan, Eddie Quillan, and Ralph Graves in shorts such as *From Rags to Britches* (1925), *Circus Today* (1926), *Pass the Dumplings* and *Smith's New Home* (both 1927). After a bit in the feature *The Prince of Head Waiters* (1927), Marion married businessman Stephen A Quinerly, and retired from movies.

Inez McDonnell (?)
Dark-haired ingénue, born in Mexico to American parents developing oil lands, who began doing extra work in Universal films after her family moved back to Southern California. Her earliest known role was in the Eddie Polo adventure serial *Do or Die* (1921), which was followed by supporting roles in Century Comedies such as Baby Peggy's *Carmen Jr.* and *Tips* (both 1923), plus *A Spooky Romance* (1923) with Jack Cooper.

Roxana McGowan (1897 – 1976)
Brown-haired beauty, born in Chicago, who became a Mack Sennett bathing girl in 1917 and adorned shorts such as *Villa of the Movies*, *Teddy at the Throttle*, *His Widow's Might*, *A Bedroom Blunder* (all 1917), *The Kitchen Lady*, *Love Loops the Loop*, and *Two Tough Tenderfeet* (all 1918). She appeared in Sennett shorts through the Keystone, Triangle, and Paramount periods, in addition to the feature *Yankee Doodle in Berlin* (1919) and the live road show that toured with it. After a brief early marriage to comedy director and writer Albert Ray, she married director John M. Stahl in 1931, which lasted until his death in 1950.

Kathryn McGuire (1903 – 1978) **See Chapter Eight**

Alice Maison (1900 - 1976)
Maison was a dancer and model who studied with Meiklejohn and was the poster girl for the 1916 Panama – California Exposition. She became a Sennett bathing girl in 1917 with roles in *The Pawnbroker's Heart* (1917), *The Kitchen Lady*, *It Pays to Exercise*, and *Those Athletic Girls* (all 1918). Moving over to Fox, she soon ended up in Christie comedies where she worked with Neal Burns and Bobby Vernon in shorts like *A Rambling Romeo*, *Hokus Pocus*, and *Tis the Bull* (all 1922). After her last film, the 1923 feature *Lawful Larceny*, she continued dancing on stage, studying and working for famous dance instructor Ernest Belcher in Chicago, and appearing in revues in New York with Leon Errol and at the Palais Royal.

Mary McIvor (1904 – 1941)
Pretty blonde who started her career as a teenaged extra, and began getting small parts in features in 1917, mostly with William Desmond, whom she would marry in 1919. In late 1918 and early 1919 she was a regular leading lady for "Smiling Bill" Parsons in his Capitol Comedies for Goldwyn release like *Chasing Rain-Beaux* (1919). Her career slowed down after her marriage to Desmond and her last film was opposite him in *The Burning Trail* (1925). The couple had been married for twenty years when McIvor died of heart attack at age thirty-six in 1941.

Ella McKenzie (1911 – 1987)
Niece of Robert and Eva Heazlett McKenzie and raised as their daughter, she began her acting career in 1915 at Essanay with the rest of the family. In the 1920s she was overweight as a teenager and often turns up playing annoying fat girls or overbearing children in all kind of comedy shorts such as *Short Socks* with Bobby Vernon and Lupino Lane's *Naughty Boy* (both 1927). She continued in the 1930s and later slimmed down and married well-known comic Billy Gilbert.

Ella (far right) and Fay McKenzie (in front of Ella) are part of the school kids with Tommie Hicks (left) in the Mermaid Comedy *Oh, Teacher!* (1924). Courtesy of Karel Caslavsky.

Eva Heazlett McKenzie (1889 – 1967)
Wife of character player Robert McKenzie and mother of Ida Mae and Fay, she had been a stock company actress and entered films in 1915 with her husband at Essanay. Usually appearing as a maternal figure, she was support in tons of comedy shorts for comics like Billy West, Lloyd Hamilton, Alice Howell, Bobby Dunn, and Monty Banks. In the late 1920s she was a regular in West Brothers' *Winnie Winkle* series as Winnie's mother, and continued her film appearances into the 1940s.

Fay McKenzie (Eunice Fay McKenzie) (1918 -   )
Youngest member of the McKenzie acting clan, who began appearing as an infant, and turned up in all kinds of shorts and features all through the 1920s. Very busy in sound films, she was a western heroine in oaters such as *Ghost Town Riders* (1938), *Death Rides the Range* (1939), and *The Singing Sheriff* (1944), as well as bits in *The Party* (1968) and *S.O.B.* (1981). She also turned up in many television shows like *Mr. Lucky* (1960) and *Bonanza* (1961).

Ida Mae McKenzie (1911 – 1986)
Daughter of Robert and Eva McKenzie who began acting at Essanay in 1915 along with her cousin Ella. In 1920 she was the leading lady to Snookie the Human-Zee in a number of Chester Comedies like *A Trayful of Trouble* (1920) and *Beat It* (1921) released by Educational Pictures. She continued to appear in shorts and features into the 1940s, was later a regular on Red Skelton's TV show, and eventually became a contestant coordinator for 1970s and 1980s game shows such as *Hollywood Squares*, *The New High Rollers*, and *Las Vegas Gambit*.

Ida Mae McKenzie with little Arthur Nowell, Cameo, and Snooky in *Snooky's Wild Oat* (1921). Courtesy of Karle Caslavsky.

Florence McLaughlin (1898 – 1972)
Actress born in Jacksonville, Florida, who did most of her work in the local Jacksonville comedy studios. She began her career around 1914 for Lubin, and was soon busy at the Vim Company appearing as leading lady in their *Plump and Runt Comedies* with Oliver Hardy and Billy Ruge. Titles include *The Serenade, The Candy Trail,* and *A Precious Parcel* (all 1916). Along with Hardy she moved over to Billy West's starring King Bee Comedies, and was support in outings like *The Hero* and *Dough Nuts* (both 1917), and when the company moved to the East Coast she went along for *The Millionaire* and *The Goat* (both 1917). While in the East she appeared in a few of the Commonwealth Comedy Company's *Three C Comedies* with Pearl Shepard, Lou Marks, and Oom Paul, but soon returned to Jacksonville to finish her career in Josh Binny *Funny Fatty Filbert Comedies* like *Fred's Fictitious Foundling and Freda's Fighting Father* (both 1918).

Elsie MacLeod (1890 - ?)
MacLeod was a fair-haired ingénue who began appearing with the Edison Company in 1911, first in child roles and then becoming their youngest leading lady. During her four years with the company she was a busy member of their ensemble and acted alongside the likes of Arthur Housman, Dan Mason, Alice Washburn, Andy Clark, and others in one-reelers like *No Cooking Allowed* (1911), *Dress Suits in Pawn* (1912), *Her Face was her Fortune* (1913), *The Sultan and the Roller Skates, Lo! The Poor Indian,* and *A Tango Spree* (all 1914). Branching out she acted at Kalem in the serial *The Hazards of Helen* (1914), went to Universal for films like *Father Buys a Bale, Fickle Elsie* (both 1914), and *The Law of Life* (1915), plus at Joker appeared with transplanted European clown Marcel Perez in *A Day at Midland Beach* (1915).

After a good role as Michaela in Theda Bara's *Carmen* (1915), she joined Marcel Perez at the Vim Company in Jacksonville, Florida in four *Bungles* one-reelers. Perez soon left, but MacLeod stayed at Vim supporting Oliver Hardy and Billy Ruge in their *Plump and Runt* misadventures. Shorts such as *The Battle Royal, What's Sauce for the Goose, The Water Cure,* and *The Schemers* (all 1916) kept her busy through 1916. For the next few years she was in demand for features support-

Elsie MacLeod went from Edison, to Vim, to feature films before ending her career in 1921. Courtesy of Karel Caslavsky.

ing Viola Dana in comedies like *Aladdin's Other Lamp* (1917), *Opportunity* (1918), and *The Gold Cure* (1919), in addition to dramas on the order of *The Beautiful Lie* (1917), *Madame Jealousy* (1918), and *The Right Way* (1921) before ending her career in 1921.

Molly Malone (1888 – 1952) **See Chapter Eight**

Marie Manley (1893 – 1953)
West Virginia-born actress who entered films for the Centaur Film Company's series of action shorts based on the adventures of explorer Henry M. Stanley (of Stanley and Livingston). Titles included *Stanley's Search for the Hidden City*, *The White King of the Zaras*, and *Stanley Among the Voodoo Worshipers* (all 1915). From here she moved to much lighter fare when she joined the Keystone Studio for outings such as *Perils of the Park* and *The Snow Cure* (both 1916). She remained busy for the next few years in Triangle Komedies, where she worked with Harry McCoy, John F. Dillon, and Harry Depp in titles that include *A Dishonest Burglar*, *Twin Troubles*, *An Innocent Villain*, *A Love Case*, and *A Dark Room Secret* (all 1917).

Alice Mann (1899 - 1986)
Comedy ingénue who began her career at Lubin supporting comics like Davey Don and Billie Reeves in shorts such as *Limberger's Victory* (1915), *Otto the Soldier*, and *Millionaire Billie* (both 1916). After a stint at the Mittenthal Studio for some *Heinie & Louie* shorts, she joined the comedy unit at Vitagraph films and worked with Hughie Mack and Jimmy Aubrey in outings like *Hash and Havoc* (1916) and *Rips and Rushes* (1917) under Larry Semon's direction. In 1917 she did her best-known work in Roscoe Arbuckle's Comique Comedies like *His Wedding Night*, *Oh Doctor*, and *Coney Island*. Following this she sporadically appeared in mostly independent features on the order of *Scrambled Wives* and *The Family Closet* (both 1921) until 1925.

Mildred Manning (1890 – 1963)
Dark-haired beauty, who came from the musical comedy stage, where she had appeared in shows such as *Little Nemo*, *Over the River*, *Oh, Oh, Delphine*, and *Dancing Around* at New York theatres like The New Amsterdam and the Winter Garden. She made her screen debut with the Biograph Company under D.W. Griffith and worked in shorts such as *A Chance Deception* (1913), *Concentration*, and *The Charity Ball* (both 1914). After passes through Universal and Thanhouser, she settled in at Vitagraph for items like the surviving *Captain Jinks, the Cobbler* (1916) with transplanted Broadway comic Frank Daniels, and became the female lead in their *O. Henry* comedy series that included *Past One at Rooney's*, *Vanity and Some Sables*, *The Love Philtre of Ikey Schoenstein* (all 1917), and *The Thing's the Play* (1918). Vitagraph also put her in features such as *Mary Jane's Pa* and *The Princess of Park Row* (both 1917), and she spent the rest of her career in dramatic pictures until 1923.

Martha Mansfield (Martha Early) (1899 – 1923)
Eighteen year-old model and Broadway actress chosen by Max Linder to be the leading lady in his 1917 American-made shorts for the Essanay Company. Born Martha Erlich, she appeared in the Linder films *Max Comes Across, Max Wants a Divorce,* and *Max in a Taxi* as Martha Early, and after working with Max she became a Ziegfeld Follies girl and changed her name to Martha Mansfield. Her big break came in the John Barrymore version of *Dr. Jekyll and Mr. Hyde* (1920) and she continued on with other popular pictures such as *The Little Red Schoolhouse* and *Potash and Perlmutter* (both 1923). Sadly, while shooting *The Warrens of Virginia* in 1923, her 1860's period dress caught fire and she died of severe burns the next day.

Jack Egan (left), Addie McPhail, and baby Sunny McKeen slide to Stella Adams feet in *The Newlyweds' Servant* (1927). Courtesy of Sam Gill.

Addie McPhail (Addie Dukes) (1905 – 2003)
Vivacious ingénue who did some stage work in Chicago before breaking into films in 1925 doing bits in Stern Brothers comedies. After appearing in some *Newlyweds and their Baby* shorts, she became a regular in the Sterns' overlooked 1927 – 1928 *Keeping Up with the Joneses* comedies. Directed by Gus Meins the series co-starred Harry Long, Stella Adams, and Gene "Fatty" Layman, with *Keeping in Trim, Passing the Joneses* (both 1927), *A Big Bluff,* and *Reel Life* (both 1928) as a few of the titles. She also appeared in shorts for Fox and Weiss Brothers such as Ben Turpin's *She said No* (1928) and *Jack and Jilted* (1928) directed by Billy West, in addition to the early William Wyler directed feature *Anybody Here Seen Kelly?* (1928). Very busy in the early days of sound in many Jack White and Mack Sennett shorts for Educational Pictures with Al St John, Lloyd Hamilton, and Andy Clyde, during this time she worked with Roscoe Arbuckle and they married in 1932. Widowed in 1933 she continued her film work, but having re-married she retired in 1941.

Marjorie Marcel (?)
Marcel was a small and petite British-born beauty who had appeared in English films, and made an impression in America in the New York and Chicago stage productions of *Scandal*. In 1922 she was signed to a long-term contract by Julius and Abe Stern to be a leading lady in their Century Comedies, where she worked Jack Cooper, Buddy Messenger, Billy Engle, and Pal the dog. She later briefly replaced Wanda Wiley in the Stern's *What Happened to Jane* series.

Edna Marion (1906 – 1957) **See Chapter Five**

Frances Marion (1888 – 1973) **See Chapter Six**

Helen Marlowe (?)
A Jack White discovery who began appearing in his Cameo Comedies in 1925, playing opposite Cliff Bowes and Phil Dunham in one-reelers such as *Slow Down*, *Sweet and Pretty*, and *Scrambled Eggs* (all 1925). Later moving on to small parts in features like *The Albany Night Boat* and *The Flying Buckaroo* (both 1928), by the mid-1930s she was working as a stand-in at the Fox Studio.

June Marlowe (Gisela Valaria Goetten) (1903 – 1984)
Brunette-beauty who achieved lasting film immortality in a blonde wig as the school teacher Miss Crabtree in Our Gang's early sound films. Born in St. Cloud, Minnesota, her family moved to Los Angeles in 1920 and while attending Hollywood High she was discovered in a school play by director Mal St Clair. Her first film appearance was in his comedy series *Fighting Blood* (1923), and she appeared in other two-reelers such as *Killing Time* (1924) with Lloyd Hamilton and Harry Langdon's pre-Mack Sennett short *Horace Greeley Jr.* (1925) before moving on to second leads in features like *When a Man's a Man* and *The Tenth Woman* (both 1924). In 1924 she settled in at Warner Brothers and frequently supported their stars Irene Rich and Rin Tin Tin. She set a record working with Rinty, appearing with him in five outings that included *Find Your Man* (1924), *Tracked in the Snow Country*, *Clash of the Wolves* (both 1925), and *The Night Cry* (1926).

In addition to being a 1925 WAMPAS Baby Star the rest of the 1920s saw her working at Universal, supporting Charlie Murray and George Sidney in *The Life of Riley* (1927), not to mention Rin Tin Tin imitator Silverstreak in *Fangs of Justice* (1926). After two final silent films made in Europe she began sound with Rinty in his Mascot serial *The Lone Defender* (1930), before memorably playing Miss Crabtree in a mere six of the Our Gang comedies. Her last film was in 1935.

Gene Marsh (1893 - 1957)
Marsh is a forgotten comedienne who spent two and a half years at the Reliance-Majestic Company in shorts such as the Komic Comedy *Dizzy Joe's Career* (1914) and *Down the Hill to Creditville* (1914) with Dorothy Gish. Briefly going to Keystone, this

tall brunette's best known appearance is as the King's favorite wife who flirts with Charlie Chaplin in *His Prehistoric Past* (1914). Soon switching over to the fledgling Hal Roach Company she was "Mazie Nut" in the ensemble supporting Harold Lloyd in early Lonesome Luke Comedies like *A Mix-Up for Mazie* (1915), *A Foozle at the Tee Party* (1915), and *Luke Foils the Villain* (1916). After early 1916 she disappeared from the screen. In 1919 she married vaudevillian Dale Bale, who performed under the stage name Bill Bailey, and traveled with him around the country. During the depression they moved overseas and eventually opened a nightclub, The Coconut Grove, in Singapore, where they both passed away.

Gene Marsh is stuck on Snub Pollard in *Luke, the Candy Cut-Up* **(1916). Courtesy of Richard Simonton.**

Mrs. Joe Martin (Miss Topsy Tree) (?)
Lady chimpanzee who headlined in numerous 1919 to 1920 Century comedies such as *A Jungle Gentleman*, *The Good Ship Rock n' Rye* (both 1919), *A Baby Doll Bandit*, and *Over the Transom* (both 1920). Her main human co-star was Jimmie Adams, and the December 27, 1919 *Universal Weekly* description of her wedding to Universal's animal star Joe Martin speaks for itself:

> Social leaders in the animal world are discussing with rare relish the recent wedding of Mr. Joe Martin, the educated orang-outang of Universal City and Miss Topsy Tree, considered the season's most beautiful debutante among monkeys. She is a female impersonator and was known on the vaudeville stage as "Milton." She has been working in Century and Rainbow comedies.
>
> Joe Martin, who is a Universal star in his own right, proposed to Miss Tree in some moment of mental anguish and was surprised and pained to discover that she accepted him. In a beautiful alcove built for the purpose on one of the stages at Universal City the impressive ceremony was performed. Bobby Mack, the widely known character player, was commissioned as Justice of the Peace for the event and read the marriage service with his finest baboonical accent.

The bride was beautifully gowned in white satin and wore a flowing veil, trimmed with orange blossoms, which she ate immediately after the service. The groom was dressed in evening clothes, which is feared he filched from some undersized waiter. He carried his collapsible hat in the manner in vogue among pall-bearers and stood throughout the service with legs akimbo.

At the conclusion of the ceremony, Mr. Mack tried to avail himself of the judicial privilege of kissing the bride. Mrs. Joe Martin did not appear averse to the salutation, extending her lips fully eight inches. As Justice Mack nerved himself for the ordeal, the infuriated bridegroom rushed at him shouting dire threats against the venerable gentleman who was about to kiss the bride.

Mr. and Mrs. Joe Martin left immediately after the ceremony on their honeymoon. They will visit the Japanese, Canadian and New York streets at Universal City. After December 30, they will be at home to their friends in a beautifully furnished little bungalow at the Universal City arena.

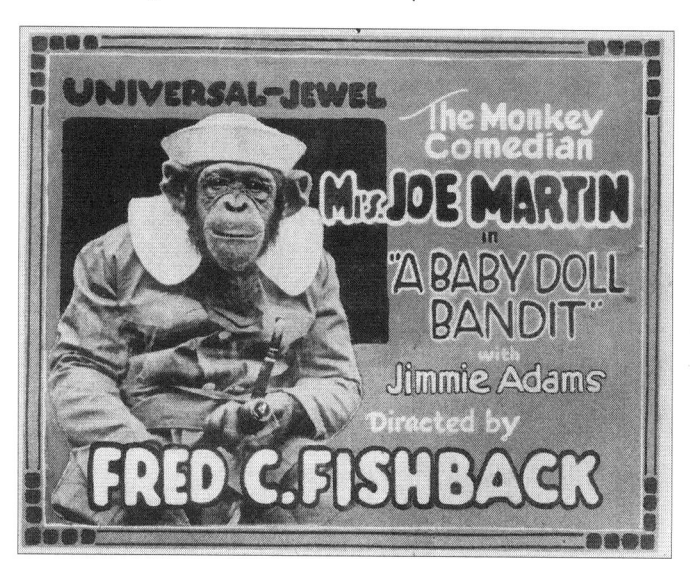

Mrs. Joe Martin in her starring short *The Baby Doll Bandit* (1920).

Grace Marvin (1883 – 1949)
Chubby character actress who made her debut at Bison in 1915, and soon settled in at Universal where she worked under Lois Weber and appeared in numerous comedies for Victor such as *A Walloping Time, Your Boy and Mine,* and *The Soubrette* (all 1917). In 1918 she became a regular in Eddie Lyons and Lee Moran's one-reel Star Comedies, usually playing the missus of the more character Moran. The surviving *Give Her Gas* (1918) has

Lee, Grace, and their two kiddies setting out for a spin in their brand new Model T. Along the way they pick up Eddie Lyons and his wife, and of course go from one disaster to another. Marvin continued with the team through 1920 and other shorts include *Damaged Goods*, *House Cleaning Horrors* (both 1918), *Fun in "A" Flat*, *All in the Swim* (both 1919), *The Latest in Pants*, and *Concrete Bisquits* (both 1920). Having appeared in occasional features such as *The Love Girl* (1916) and *The Mask* (1918), the 1920s saw her playing dramatic maternal roles in *The Long Chance* (1921), *The Gray Dawn* (1922), and twice playing Mama to Max Davidson's Papa in *No Woman Knows* (1921) and *Second Hand Rose* (1922). Her appearances became less frequent as the 1920s progressed with her last known picture being the Tom Mix western *A Horseman of the Plains* (1925).

Shirley Mason (Leonie Flugrath) (1900 – 1979)
Youngest of the Brooklyn-born Flugrath sisters (the others included Edna Flugrath and Viola Dana), who created the part of Little Hal on stage in *The Squaw Man* with William Faversham at age four, plus also appeared as Little Moonie in *Rip Van Winkle* and Peter in *Passers-By*. Joined Edison with the rest of the family and became part of the acting ensemble in various comedies like *Betty's Buttons* (1911), *Mary had a Little Lamb* (1912), *A Youthful Knight* (1913), and *Andy Learns to Swim* (1914). In 1915 she started using the name Shirley Mason and by 1917 was busy in dramatic features on the order of *The Light in Darkness* (1917), and *The Unwritten Code* (1919), but also appeared in comedies like *Come on In* (1918) and *Good-Bye Bill* (1919) that were written and directed for her by John Emerson and Anita Loos. She was busy as a medium-sized star all through the 1920s, and some of her comedies include *Ever Since Eve* (1921), *Sweet Rosie O'Grady* (1926), *Let It Rain* (1927), *So This Is Love*, and *The Wife's Relations* (both 1928). After a few early talkies she left the screen in 1929, but later made a few television appearances in the 1950s.

Rose Mass (?)
Leading lady to the supremely unfunny Al Joy in his series of independent shorts for Ricordo Films, Inc. Shot at the Pyramid Studios in Astoria, Long Island, it appears that titles such as *Spooky Money*, *The Orphan*, and *Over There* were completed in 1925 and 1926 but weren't released by distributors Cranfield and Clarke until 1927. In addition to Ms. Mass, Joy's supporting ensemble included Pierre le Collosse, Paul Panzer, Lou Marks, Thomas Burillo, George Du Count, and Lucio Lomay, with Joseph Richmond and Joe Basil taking turns behind the megaphone.

Maude (?)
Mule which was part of the menagerie in early 1920s Century comedies, and co-starred frequently with comic Harry Sweet in two-reelers such as *The Kickin' Fool*, *Me and My Mule* (both 1922), and *Hee!Haw!* (1923).

Mary Maurice (1844 – 1918)
Maurice was a long-time stage actress whose career encompassed Shakespeare, shows like *The Arkansas Traveler* and *Rip Van Winkle*, not to mention taking time off to have a family, all before she joined the Vitagraph Company at age sixty-five in 1909. Playing everyone on the lots mother or grandmother, she became known as "Mother Maurice" or just plain "Mother" among the company as well as the public. Whether it was in comedies such as *The Picture Idol* (1912), *The Locket* (1913) with John Bunny, Sidney Drew's *Is Christmas a Bore?* (1915), or dramas like *The Battle Cry of Peace* (1915), Ms. Maurice worked non-stop for Vitagraph right to her death in 1918.

The aristocratic Mary Maurice, who played everyone's mother, in comedies as well as dramas, at the Vitagraph Studio. Author's collection.

Louella Maxam (Lola Maxam) (1896 – 1970)
Blonde ingénue, born in St Augustine, Florida, who after early appearances in 1913 for Universal and Selig, including the serial *The Adventures of Kathlyn* (1913) and westerns with Tom Mix, became a Mack Sennett heroine in his Triangle releases such as *An Oily Scoundrel, Bucking Society,* and *His Lying Heart* (all 1916). During her time with the "King of Comedy" she was frequently paired with Mack Swain, and supported his Ambrose character in outings like *His Bitter Pill, A Movie Star, Vampire Ambrose,* and *Ambrose's Rapid Rise* (all 1916). She moved from Sennett to do a few dramas but mostly did more westerns back at Selig with Mix, and also Canyon Pictures shorts and features with Franklyn Farnum, Buck Jones, and Bud Osborne (sometimes as Lola Maxam) until 1920. Having married a Los Angeles deputy sheriff she moved from the movies to become a juvenile delinquent investigator for Los Angeles County and the Burbank Police Department until she retired in 1961.

Betty May (1904 – 1949)
Colorado-born actress who began her film career with Century Comedies in 1922 supporting Lee Moran and even Queenie the horse in two-reelers such as *Upper and Lower, Ten Seconds, True Blue* (all 1922), and *The Home Plate* (1923). She moved on to a few features like the Bill Cody western *Love on the Rio Grande* (1925) and *Flaming Fury* (1926) with Ranger the dog. Leaving films in the 1920s she returned in the early days of sound for uncredited walk-ons in titles such as *Broadway Bill* (1934) but left again in 1936.

Doris May (1902 – 1984)
Pretty actress, born in Seattle, Washington, who excelled at elocution, music, and dance

as a young girl, and began her film career as an extra where she was "discovered" by producer Thomas Ince. Starting in 1917 she became a leading lady for popular star Charles Ray in Ince-produced comedy-romances such as *His Mother's Boy* (1917), *Playing the Game* (1918), and *Hay Foot, Straw Foot* (1919). In 1919 the producer paired her with light comic Douglas MacLean and had a huge hit with *23 ½ Hours Leave* (1919), so he immediately made them a regular team for five more features – *What's Your Husband Doing?*, *Mary's Ankle*, *Let's Be Fashionable*, *The Jailbird*, and *The Rookie's Return* (all 1920). Leaving Ince and MacLean she supported Jackie Coogan in *Peck's Bad Boy* (1921), and then moved on to a string of starring features directed by William A. Seiter that included *Eden and Return* (1921), *Boy Crazy*, *Gay and Devilish*, and *Up and at 'Em* (all 1922). Her career lost steam by the mid-1920s, and after supporting comic Johnny Hines in *Conductor 1492* (1924) she appeared in three more features before leaving films in 1927.

Blanche Mehaffey (1906 – 1968)
Red-haired showgirl, who appeared in the *Ziegfeld Follies* as well as *Ziegfeld's Midnight Frolics* on the New Amsterdam roof with Will Rogers. Discovered in the *Follies* by producer Hal Roach, she began working at his studio in 1923 and at first was an all-purpose leading lady for the likes of Snub Pollard and Charley Chase until she was teamed up with Glenn Tryon for a series of shorts that included *The Goofy Age*, *Meet the Missus* (both 1924), and *Whose Baby are You?* (1925), plus the features *The Battling Orioles* and *The White Sheep* (both 1924). In 1925 she moved to Universal where she mostly appeared in westerns opposite Hoot Gibson, and the rest of her career was spent in independent features for outfits like Tiffany, Superlative, Mayfair, and Trem Carr Productions until *The Wages of Sin* in 1938.

Former Ziegfeld girl Blanche Mehaffey spent most of her onscreen career working with Glenn Tryon at the Hal Roach Studio. Author's collection.

Rose Melville (1867 – 1946) **See Chapter Three**

Bess Meredyth (1890 – 1969) **See Chapter Six**

Charlotte Merriam (1903 – 1972) **See Chapter Eight**

Violet Mersereau (1892 – 1975)

Mersereau was a New York City born actress who started a stage career at age nine in roles such as *Rebecca of Sunnybrook Farm*, in addition to appearing with star Maxine Elliott and in *The Clansman*. She joined D.W. Griffith's company at Biograph in 1908, where she was in the ensemble for dramas such as *The Cricket on the Hearth* and *His Duty* (both 1909), as well as comedies like *Her First Biscuits* (1909) and *The Passing of a Grouch* (1911). In 1911 she moved over to Nestor Films and had leads in items such as *His Vacation*, *Only an Iceman* (both 1911), and *The New Clerk* (1912). After a brief sojourn making westerns at Bison, she took up residence at Imp, and in 1915 was teamed with William Garwood for many comedies on the order of *The Unnecessary Sex*, *Getting His Goat* (both 1915), *His Picture*, and *The Gentle Art of Burglary* (both 1916). 1917 saw her graduate to Universal features, and for the most part the rest of her career settled in drama. The 1920s saw her as the star of Art-O-Graph Film Company's features *Finders Keepers* and *Out of the Depths* (both 1921), and she was support in *Lend Me Your Husband* (1924) and *The Wives of the Prophet* (1926). After appearing as Johnny Hine's leading lady in *Luck* (1923), her last comedy work appears to have been a series of independently made Molly May shorts such as *Her First Night with the Bootleggers* (1926) produced by Arthur J. Lamb. She left the screen in 1926. Her younger sister Claire also appeared in films.

Arthur Lake buys up Gertrude Messinger's box lunches in *Whose Baby?* (1929). Author's collection.

Gertrude Messinger (1911 – 1995)

Busy child actress who began her career at age four in 1915. Her father was a carpenter at Universal so Gertie and her siblings Buddy and Marie all got started early in front of the camera. In 1917 she became part of the ensemble in Sidney and Chester Franklin's tongue-in-cheek kid's adventure pictures at Fox such as *Aladdin and the Wonderful Lamp* (1917) and *Treasure Island* (1918). Besides roles in features like *The Luck of the Irish* (1920) and *Penrod and Sam* (1923), she supported Johnny Jones in his Pathé two-reelers such as *Makin' Movies, Broadcasting* (both 1922), and *Stung* (1923). By the late 1920s she was a teenage ingénue for comics like Arthur Lake, and in the early days of sound was part of the Hal Roach *Boyfriends* series along with Mickey Daniels, Mary Kornman, Grady Sutton, and her first husband Dave Sharpe. She spent the next twenty years in mostly uncredited bits in features such as *Zenobia* (1939), *Syncopation* (1942), and *Samson and Delilah* (1949) until 1952.

Marie Messinger (1905 – 1987)
Older sister of Buddy and Gertrude Messinger who appeared with them in the kiddie adventure features produced by Chester and Sidney Franklin which included *Aladdin and the Wonderful Lamp* (1917) and *Ali Baba and the Forty Thieves* (1918). Busy in the 1920s in features such as *When Seconds Count* (1927) and *South of Panama* (1928), as well as comedy shorts on the order of *All for a Girl* (1925), *Restless Bachelors*, and *Silk Sock Hal* (both 1928). She left the screen in 1929 but later did work behind the scenes.

Bliss Milford (?)
Dark-haired actress, born in North Dakota and raised in Chicago, who spent five years on the stage in shows for illustrious producer Charles Dillingham such as *The County Chairman*, *The Candy Shop*, and *Sentimental Sally*. Living near the Edison Studio she thought to fill in the summer, when the theatres were closed, by doing extra work. This was in 1911 and she quickly became one of their comedy ingénues, spending four years with the company in shorts like *Freezing Auntie*, *The Grouch* (both 1912), *Interrupted Wedding Bells*, *Mother's Lazy Boy* (both 1913), *Mr. Sniffkin's Widow*, and *The Tango in Tuckerville* (both 1915). In 1915 she left Edison for Thanhouser, and made features with Edwin August's Kinetophote Company such as *The Beloved Vagabond* (1915). Married to director Harry Beaumont, after a few more features she retired in 1918.

Patsy Ruth Miller (1904 – 1995)
1920s leading lady, best known for playing the gypsy girl Esmeralda opposite Lon Chaney in 1923's *The Hunchback of Notre Dame*. Born in St. Louis, Missouri, she was discovered by the Russian actress Nazimova during a 1920 trip to Hollywood to visit relatives. Cast as Nichette in Nazimova's *Camille* (1921), she played opposite Rudolph Valentino and moved on to other features such as *Where's My Wandering Boy Tonight?*, *Fortune's Mask* (both 1922), and *Hunchback*. After being named one of the original WAMPAS Baby Stars she was off on a busy career, and eventually gravitated to comedy features on the order of *A Self-Made Failure* (1924), *Hogan's Alley* (1925), *Oh, What a Nurse!*, *So This is Paris* (both 1926), *Wolf's Clothing*, *Hot Heels* (both 1927), *Beautiful*

But Dumb (1928), *Twin Beds*, and *The Hottentot* (both 1929). Although she made the transition to sound, she stepped back from working after marrying director Tay Garnett in 1929. She made a few later appearances, including talking about her memories of *Hunchback* in Kevin Brownlow's documentary *Lon Chaney: A Thousand Faces* (2000).

Andy Clyde and Marvin Loback (back) let Harry Langdon and Charlotte Mineau know that they are not alone in *Flickering Youth* (1924). Courtesy of Robert Arkus.

Charlotte Mineau (1886 or 1891 – 1979)
Elegant and tall brunette, who may have been French and born near Paris, or born in Michigan. She joined the Essanay Company in Chicago in 1914, having come from Selig, appeared in *George Ade Fables, Sweedie Comedies,* and had a featured role in Charlie Chaplin's first Essanay comedy *His New Job* (1915). Soon moving to the West Coast she joined Chaplin's Mutual company and is seen in *The Floorwalker, The Vagabond* (both 1916), and *Easy Street* (1917) among others. From there she became a regular in Mack Sennett shorts until 1925, also working in the Sennett features *Love, Honor and Behave* (1920), *Married Life* (1920), and *The Extra Girl* (1923). She appeared in a very different character role in Mary Pickford's *Sparrows* (1926), and became a member of the Hal Roach stock company in many shorts such as *Baby Clothes, Should Husbands Pay?, Wise Guys Prefer Brunettes* (all 1926) and *Sugar Daddies* (1927). She later married character player Christian Frank, and her career wound down in the early 1930s.

Anna Mingus (?)
Wife of comedian and director Robin Williamson, and part of the acting ensemble at Vim Comedies. She appeared in Pokes & Jabbs and Plump & Runt comedies such as *A Day at School* and *The Serenade* (both 1916).

Minnie Ha Ha (Minnie Prevost Devereaux) (1858 - ?)
Native American actress who was a great favorite of Mabel Normand, and had important roles in her features *Mickey* (1918) and *Suzanna* (1923). Said to have been part of the tribe that was living on the grounds of Inceville, Minnie made her film debut in Thomas Ince-produced Broncho shorts such as *Old Mammy's Secret Code* (1913), sometimes playing black characters. Co-starring with Roscoe Arbuckle in the comedy *Fatty and Minnie Hee-Haw* (1914) she's very funny, and after that turned up in numerous two-reelers like Billy West's *The Slave* (1917), and *The Son of a Gun* (1918) with Billie Ritchie, in addition to *Up in Mary's Attic* (1920) and other comedy features. Minnie also racked up many westerns and dramas such as *The Coward* (1915) and *The Four Horsemen of the Apocalypse* (1921) before leaving films in 1923.

Minnie HaHa thinks that Leon Barry is coming on too strong to Mabel Normand in *Suzanna* (1923). Courtesy of Cole Johnson.

Belle Mitchell (1889 – 1979)
Brunette ingénue who racked up an incredible sixty-plus years in movies, stage, and television work. Born in Michigan, she entered vaudeville and toured extensively in sketches and revues before starting in films at Essanay's Niles, California studio in 1915. Appearing in Broncho Billy Anderson westerns, she was also busy in the tail end of the outfit's *Snakeville Comedies* where she supported Ben Turpin, Victor Potel, Margaret

Joslin, and Harry Todd in opuses such as *How Slippery Slim Saw the Show, Snakeville's Eugenic Marriage* (both 1915), *A Safe Proposition*, and *A Waiting Game* (both 1916). When the Niles studio closed she relocated to the fledgling Hal Roach Studio where she was in numerous early Harold Lloyd one and two-reelers like *By the Sad Sea Waves, Step Lively* (both 1917), *A Gasoline Wedding, Take a Chance* (both 1918), *Just Dropped In* (1919), and *An Eastern Westerner* (1920), in addition to finding time to work with Stan Laurel in *Just Rambling Along* (1918), *Do You Love Your Wife?* (1919) and others. The 1920s saw her return to vaudeville in Los Angeles. Outside of an appearance in the Charlie Murray – George Sidney feature *Flying Romeos* (1928) she returned to films with a vengeance in 1932 and worked in small bits non-stop until 1978. Some of her later movies and television shows include *San Francisco* (1936), *Meet Me in St. Louis* (1944), *Ghost Chasers* (1951), *My Little Margie* (1953), *Lust for Life* (1956), *77 Sunset Strip* (1962), *Mister Ed* (1964), *Funny Girl* (1968), *Airport* (1970), and *Soylent Green* (1973).

Janethel Monahan (1907 - ?)
Female star of the Juvenile Film Corporation's 1916 kids comedies produced by James A. Fitzpatrick (of later color *Traveltalks* fame) for his Cosmofoto Film Company. The films were released on the state's rights market and featured Janethel and her brother Joseph. Fitzpatrick said that he discovered the children while conducting a dramatic school in Brooklyn and built the series around them. Titles included *Chip's Backyard Barnstormers, A Chip Off the Old Block*, and the surviving *Chip's Rivals* (all 1916). The gimmick for the entire series of shorts was having Joseph imitate Charlie Chaplin at some time in each entry. Janethel was his leading lady and got to spoof Edna Purviance in outings like *Chip's Burlesque on Carmen* (1916). Only lasting for a handful of shorts Fitzgerald moved on to other projects.

Bee Monson (Beatrice Monson) (?)
Minneapolis-born ingénue who, according to Educational Pictures press books, was known as "the honey girl" because of her work during World War I entertaining soldiers at Fort Douglas, near Salt Lake City. The bee-hive is the emblem of Utah and her nickname was derived from that. After the war she moved to Los Angeles and began doing small parts in Marion Kohn productions. Moving on to Monty Banks comedies, she was seen by producer Jack White and comic Lloyd Hamilton, who hired her to be Ham's leading lady in his shorts *April Fool* (1920) and *Moonshine* (1921). Her career seems to have ended after appearances in the Jack Hoxie western *The Sheriff of Hope Eternal* (1922), and some Fox Sunshine Comedies such as *False Alarm* (1922).

Mavis Montel (?)
Montel was an ingénue who appeared in some *Universal Star Comedies* such as *A Hero 'n Everything* (1920) with Monty Banks.

Peggy Montgomery (1904 – 1989)
Illinois-born beauty who spent most of her career in westerns like *Hoof Marks* (1927), *The Brand of Courage*, *Arizona Days* (both 1928), *Bad Men's Money*, and *Wyoming Tornado* (both 1929), but made a few appearances in shorts at the Mack Sennett Studio. In *There He Goes* (1925) and *Saturday Afternoon* (1926) she supported the up and coming Harry Langdon, and *Love's Languid Lure* (1927) saw her as the lucky sweetheart of cross-eyed Ben Turpin. Her career ended with the change-over to sound in 1929.

Muriel Montrose (left) keeps her eye on Arthur Lake and Marceline Day in the Century Comedy *Heart Trouble* (1925). Courtesy of Sam Gill.

Muriel Montrose (1906 - 2001)
Little, dark-haired ingénue, who was born in Denver, Colorado. Her family moved to Hollywood in the early 1920s, and while a senior at Hollywood High she began appearing in Universal's Century Comedies such as *Heart Trouble* (1925) with Arthur Lake. She also doubled Clara Bow and did stunts, and was a late 1920s Sennett girl for titles like *The Jolly Jilter*, *Hubby's Quiet Little Game* (both 1927), and *Soldier Man* (1928). After playing the leading lady in the obscure independent feature *Ready, Set, Go* (1928), a college comedy that starred Spec O'Donnell, she married John Stephens Dow and retired from the screen. In the 1950s her son Tony Dow became popular as Wally Cleaver on the television show *Leave It to Beaver*. Muriel died at age ninety-four in Canoga Park, California.

Colleen Moore (1902 – 1988) **See Chapter Five**

Eunice Murdock Moore (? – 1934)
Character actress from the stage that specialized in dowager roles. The wife of comedy

director Vin Moore, she began her film career at L-Ko Comedies in 1917 shorts like *Rough Stuff*, *Where is My Che-ild*, and *Surf Scandal*. Quickly graduating to feature films she kept busy in pictures such as *Carolyn of the Corners* (1919), *Huckleberry Finn* (1920), *The Beauty Prize* (1924), and *The Man from the West* (1926) until 1934.

Marcia Moore (1898 – 1920)
Moore is a forgotten ingénue who appeared as leading lady for numerous Universal brands like Nestor, Victor, Powers, and Joker. Born in Chicago, she worked in that city's Bush Temple stock company, plus toured the country in vaudeville and the show *Salomy Jane*. Beginning her film career in 1909 as a child actress at Essanay in titles such as *The Old Curiosity Shop*, she went over to Selig where she played Dorothy in their versions of *The Wonderful Wizard of Oz*, *Dorothy and the Scarecrow of Oz*, and *The Land of Oz* (all 1910). Moving around to Rex, Bison, Broncho, Vitagraph and Lubin for dramas and westerns like *The Prairie Trail* (1913), *An Arrowhead Romance* (1914), and *The Lorelei Madonna* (1915), she settled in at Universal in 1916 working with Lyons & Moran, Ernest Shields, Carter De Haven, Jane Bernoudy, and Pat Rooney in one and two-reelers such as *Beer Must Go Down*, *Borrowed Plumes*, *Pat's Pasting Ways* (all 1916), *Who Said Chicken?*, *Kicked Out* (both 1917), *Don't Flirt* (1918), and *Lizzie's Waterloo* (1919). She died very young two days after her second marriage in 1920.

Marjorie Moore (?)
Red-headed ingénue who came from vaudeville, night clubs, and presentations acts at motion picture theatres. During her brief film career she played the love interest for comics Lloyd Hamilton and Lupino Lane in shorts such as *Between Jobs* (1927) and *Fandango* (1928).

Mildred Moore (1899 – 1941)
Brunette beauty who had appeared in Flo Ziegfeld's *Midnight Frolics*, and danced at the Cocoanut Grove after coming to Los Angeles. Movie companies came calling and she was soon appearing in comedies for Fox and Christie. In 1919 she became the leading lady in the popular comedies of Eddie Lyons and Lee Moran, spending two years supporting them in entries like *His Body for Rent*, *Who's Her Husband* (both 1919), and *Some Shimmiers* (1920). She also turned up in some of Universal's light-hearted westerns shorts like *Held Up for the Makins* and *His Nose in the Book* (both 1920) with Hoot Gibson, and ended her career with the Art Accord serial *The Moon Riders* (1920).

Polly Moran (Pauline Moran) (1884 – 1952) **See Chapter Three**

Gigetta Morano (1887 – 1986) **See Chapter One**

Marie Mosquini (1899 – 1983)

Snub Pollard's long-time leading lady was born in Los Angeles and at age fourteen became the "gal Friday" for the fledgling Hal Roach Studio. Besides her duties of answering phones, ordering props, checking out costumes, and even patching films, she began playing various bits in the comedies. These appearances gradually increased and she eventually became a full-time actress, appearing notably in the Harold Lloyd comedies, with meaty roles in such shorts as *Young Mr. Jazz* (1919) and *His Royal Slyness* (1920). Teamed with Pollard in 1920, she appeared in umpteen shorts with him, and also found time to support Stan Laurel, Paul Parrott, and Will Rogers. After leaving Roach in 1924 she worked in Universal shorts with Charles Puffy and a few features, the most famous being Fox's *Seventh Heaven* (1927). She retired from the movies in 1930 when she married Dr. Lee DeForest of audion tube and Phono-Films fame.

A glamorous pose for Snub Pollard's regular screen partner Marie Mosquini. Author's collection.

Edna Murphy (1899 – 1974)

Pretty brunette who found her way to films from being a top New York photographer's model. She made her movie debut in 1918 for Vitagraph, and for the most part appeared in dramas until 1925 when she started turning up in comedy features like *Clothes Make the Pirate* (1925), *The Little Giant*, *Oh What a Night* (both 1926), *McFadden's Flats*, and *All Aboard* (both 1927). She made some appearances on the Hal Roach lot, some dramatic like the serial *Her Dangerous Path* (1923) and the feature *The King of the Wild Horses* (1924), in addition to the comedy shorts *45 Minutes from Hollywood* (1926) and *The Unkissed Man* (1929). With the arrival of sound she was paired with Edward Everett Horton in *The Sap* (1926) and *Wide Open* (1930), but her career ended in 1933.

Kathleen Myers (1899 – 1959)

A regular comedy leading lady of the 1920s who worked with Jimmy Aubrey, Larry Semon, Jimmie Adams, and Billy West, although her best known film today is *Go*

Kathleen Myers, best-known for playing Brown Eyes the cow's human rival for Buster Keaton's affections in *Go West* (1925). Author's collection.

West (1925) where she supported Buster Keaton (although the object of his affections was Brown Eyes the cow). She also appeared in serials and all kinds of westerns and dramatic features until 1928.

Alice and Edna Nash (Edna ?-1985, Alice ?-?)
Identical teenage twins who appeared in Vitagraph comedies such as *Bunny and the Twins* (1912), *Two of a Kind* (1913), and *Which?* (1913). The title of the surviving *Mixed Identities* (1913) could have been used for all their outings as they were always built around people mistaking one twin for the other. Publicity items maintained that their co-players and behind the scenes crews at the studio had trouble telling them apart as well. After *The Athletic Family* (1914) the girls left Vitagraph but returned for the 1918 feature *Love Watches*. In addition to their films the pair appeared on stage in Charles Dillingham produced musical extravaganzas at the New York Hippodrome such as *Everything* (1918 – 1919), *Happy Days* (1919 – 1920), and *Good Times* (1920 – 1921) where they sang, danced, and shared the stage with DeWolf Hopper, Harry Houdini, The Hannefords, Cissie Hayden, and Joe Jackson.

Frances Ne Moyer (?)
Pretty brunette who spent much time in the Jacksonville, Florida-made comedies of Lubin and Kalem. She started at Lubin in 1910, and worked with Mae Hotely, Oliver Hardy, Raymond McKee, George Reehm, Bobby Burns, and Walter Stull in shorts like *An Interrupted Courtship* (1910), *His Vacation* (1912), *Training a Tightwad* (1913), *Outwitting Dad* (1914), and *A Lucky Strike* (1915). After an appearance in the Theda Bara drama *Gold and the Woman* (1916), she joined Kalem and made appearances in their *Sis Hopkins* and *Ivy Close* Comedies such as *The Wishing Ring*, *A Double Elopement*, and *Peaches and Ponies* (all 1916).

Agnes Neilson (Mrs. Agnes Tibbetts) (? - 1936)
Small and plain character actress usually cast as domineering wives or mothers-in-law, who had been part of the singing and dancing vaudeville act The Neilson Sisters that toured from 1894 to 1920. Based on the East Coast she was a regular in the Sennett and Comique shorts like *A Reckless Romeo*, *The Butcher Boy*, *The Rough House*, and *Coney Island* (all 1917) that Roscoe Arbuckle made in the New York area. She also appeared in Billy West's New Jersey shot *The Goat* (1917) and some of Victor Moore's east coast Klever Komedies such as *Adam and Some Eves* (1918). She also turned up in the features *The Girl Who Didn't Think* (1917), Marion Davies' *April Folly* (1920) and *Insinuation* (1923). Her later stage work included small parts in Mae West's *Diamond Lil* (1928) and *The Jayhawker* (1934) with Fred Stone. At the time of her death she was in rehearsals for the WPA Theatre Project's "Living Newspaper" production *Crime* (1936).

Agnes Neilson, best-known for hen-pecking Roscoe Arbuckle in his Comique Comedies, does the same thing in *Adam and Some Eves* (1918) to Victor Moore (right) and Davey Don (back).

Lois Neilson (1895 – 1990)

California-born actress who became a 1919 and 1920 Universal starlet, appearing in numerous L-Ko, Rainbow, and Century shorts such as *A Roof Garden Rough House, Brown Eyes and Bank Notes, Dainty Damsels and Bogus Counts* (all 1919), and *Loose Lions and Fast Lovers* (1920). Her co-stars included Zip Monberg, Bud Jamison, Harry Sweet, Merta Sterling, Billy Engle, Jimmie Adams, Brownie, and the Century Lions. Even doing a few dramatic two-reelers like Leo Maloney's *The Honor of the Range* (1920), by the early twenties she was doing smaller roles such as one of the shipwrecked women in Stan Laurel's *Half a Man* (1925). She left the screen after marrying Laurel, and besides being his first wife she was the mother of his daughter Lois.

Eva Nelson (1893 - ?)

Texas-born brunette, who was a dancer in musical comedies and vaudeville before joining Keystone in 1914. During her brief time there she worked frequently with Charlie Chaplin and Roscoe Arbuckle in shorts like *A Rural Demon, Cruel, Cruel Love, A Bath House Beauty,* and *Mabel's Married Life*. As part of the group that left Sennett to be part of Henry Lehrman's new L-Ko company, she usually worked in support of Billie Ritchie. Sadly the bulk of the L-Kos are lost and unavailable, but Nelson is very good in the surviving *Live Wire and Love Sparks* (1916) as Ritchie's put-upon wife who hatches a scheme and gets her revenge. Her other L-Ko comedies include *Almost a Scandal* (1915), *Stolen Hearts and Nickels* (1915), and *Billie's Waterloo* (1916). When Lehrman moved over to Fox Sunshine Comedies, Nelson went along for her last known appearances.

Evelyn Nelson (1899 – 1923)
Chloride, Arizona-born slapstick ingénue, whose career began in 1919. During her short time in movies she worked in Bulls Eye and Special Pictures' two-reelers such as *Don't Park Here* and *A Pajama Marriage* (both 1920), as well as supported Jimmy Aubrey and Oliver Hardy in the Vitagraph comedies *The Decorator, The Trouble Hunter, The Backyard,* and *His Jonah Day* (all 1920). She moved on to do many western features with stars like Jack Hoxie, George Chesebro, and William Fairbanks into 1923, but committed suicide that year. A note was found with her body implying that she had killed herself to join her friend Wallace Reid. She was twenty-three years old.

Marguerite Nichols (Mrs. Hal Roach) (1895 – 1941)
Los Angeles-born actress, who started her career in 1915 as an extra with the Balboa Company and quickly worked her way up to leading roles. Also appearing for the American Film Manufacturing Co., she co-starred with Henry King and Mary Miles Minter, and played Baby Marie Osborne's mother in the features *Little Mary Sunshine* (1916) and *When Baby Forgot* (1917). The older sister of ingénue Norma Nichols, she joined the young Rolin Film Co in the fall of 1916 to support comedian Dee Lampton in his series of *Skinny* comedies like *Skinny Gets a Goat* and *Skinny's Shipwrecked Sand-Witch* (both 1917). She married producer Hal Roach and retired from the screen.

Norma Nichols (? - 1989)
Sister of Marguerite Nichols who became a Keystone leading lady in shorts like *The Property Man, Dough and Dynamite, Fatty's Jonah Day* (all 1914), and *Fatty's Tintype Tangle (1915)* where she supported male stars such as Charlie Chaplin, Chester Conklin, Roscoe Arbuckle, and Charles Murray. Leaving Sennett she had a brief stint at Selig and soon ended up at Kalem as the love interest for the scuzzy bums Ham and Bud in opuses that included *Ham Agrees with Sherman, Ham and the Masked Marvel,* and *The Tank Town Troupe* (all 1916). After a few features on the order of *The Tides of Barnegat* (1917) and *The Legion of Death* (1918), in addition to supporting Ruth Roland in the Pathé serial *Broadway Bob* (1920), she became part of the Vanity Fair Girls that supported comic Eddie

Norma Nichols as Roscoe Arbuckle's sweetheart in *Fatty's Jonah Day* (1914). Author's collection.

Boland in numerous Hal Roach comedies. Her sister Marguerite had married producer Roach in 1918, and besides appearing in shorts like *Mamma's Boy*, *The Sleepyhead* (both 1920), *Oh, Promise Me* (1921), and *The Man Haters* (1922), she's said to have worked in the studio's scenario department in the early 1920s. After a brief spell supporting comic Larry Semon in 1921 shorts like *The Bakery*, *The Rent Collector*, *The Fall Guy*, and *The Bell Hop*, plus the feature *The Call of Home* (1922), she retired from the screen.

Asta Nielsen (1881 – 1972) **See Chapter Four**

Marian Nixon (1904 – 1938)
Pretty brunette who became a regular comedy leading lady in the mid-1920s. Born in Wisconsin, she began her career at age nineteen in 1923 doing bit roles in features such as *The Shriek of Araby* and Mary Pickford's *Rosita*. Contracts at Fox and Universal led to her appearing in numerous westerns opposite Buck Jones and Hoot Gibson. In 1925 she began working with light comedian Reginald Denny with *I'll Show You the Town*, and in the next few years racked up five outings with Denny that included *What Happened to Jones?* (1926) and *Out All Night* (1927). Today her most highly regarded and often shown silent film is *Hands Up!* (1926) where she plays one of the two love interests of suave comic Raymond Griffith, but she also worked with Edward Everett Horton and Glen Tryon in *Taxi! Taxi!* (1927) and *How to Handle Women* (1928). Making a very successful transition to sound, some of her remembered talking films are *Pilgrimage* (1933), *We're Rich Again* (1934) and the Will Rogers' features *Too Busy to Work* (1932) and *Doctor Bull* (1933). Having married director William Seiter in 1934 she retired two years later for family life.

Marian Nixon kept busy in the 1920s working with Reginald Denny, Raymond Griffith, and Edward Everett Horton. Author's collection.

Amber Norman (1901 – 1972)
Norman was a sultry blonde who specialized in vamps in shorts such as *A Briny Boob* (1926) with Billy Dooley, *Many Scrappy Returns* (1927) with Charley Chase, and Jack White comedies like *Wife Trouble* and *Playful Papa* (both 1928). Her silent features include *Hill's Four Hundred* (1926), *Uneasy Payments* (1927), and *The Port of Missing Girls* (1928), and her sound work was mostly uncredited bits in features, often as streetwalkers or showgirls, like *Love and the Devil* (1929), *Werewolf of London* (1935), and *Woman of the Year* (1942).

Mabel Normand (1895 – 1930) **See Chapter Two**

Eva Novak (1898 – 1988)
Sister of actress Jane Novak, who became a comedy ingénue at L-Ko Comedies and worked there in shorts like *The King of the Kitchen* (1918) and *The Freckled Fish* (1919) until she broke into features in 1919. Her full-length comedies included *Up in Mary's Attic* (1920) with Harry Gribbon, and Leo McCarey's first unsuccessful directorial effort *Society Secrets* (1921). She soon became in demand opposite male stars such as William S. Hart, Jack Holt, and most frequently, Tom Mix. She retired in 1930, and only worked occasionally until 1948, when she began doing numerous unbilled roles in movies and TV shows until 1966.

Jane Novak (1896 – 1990)
Older sister of Eva Novak, Jane preceded her sibling into films after appearing in stock and vaudeville. The girls' aunt was Vitagraph actress Anna Schafer, and Jane began working alongside her aunt in 1913. In 1915 she became one of the first leading ladies hired by Hal Roach's fledgling Rolin Film Co. and appeared opposite Harold Lloyd in titles like *Willie Runs the Park*, *From Italy's Shores*, and the surviving *Just Nuts* (all 1915). The remainder of her career was spent in drama and included productions for Universal, Fox, Ince, William S. Hart, Maurice Tourneur, and Paramount such as *Wagon Tracks* (1919), *Three Word Brand* (1921), *Lazybones* (1925), and *Redskin* (1929). Said to have made a fortune in the 1920s in real estate that she lost in the stock market crash, after the arrival of sound she made sporadic uncredited appearances in features like *The File on Thelma Jordan*, *The Furies* (both 1950), and *About Mrs. Leslie* (1954). The year before her death she recounted her first meeting with Harold Lloyd and Hal Roach in Kevin Brownlow and David Gill's *Harold Lloyd: The Third Genius* (1989).

Joint portrait of the busy sisters Jane (left) and Eva Novak (right). Author's collection.

Vivien Oakland (1895 – 1958)
Vivacious blonde who came from a popular vaudeville act with her husband John T. Murray to be the "other woman" in scores of 1920s Hal Roach Comedies with Glenn

Tryon and Charley Chase, such as *Mighty Like a Moose* (1926), *Along Came Auntie* (1926), *Two Time Mama* (1927), and perhaps her most memorable appearance *Scram* (1932), in which she plays an innocently drunken judge's wife opposite Laurel & Hardy. Later getting a bit matronly, she kept busy playing wifely comedy foils at RKO for Edgar Kennedy and Leon Errol until her retirement in 1951.

Laura Oakley (1879 – 1957)
Character actress in the early days of Keystone who began her theatrical career at age twelve singing and dancing at the Tivoli Opera House, and touring with The Bostonians and Kolb & Dill. Entering films for Imp and working with Fred Mace, she joined Keystone in 1912, and played roles such as Ford Sterling's wife in *A Fishy Affair*, and the Queen in *Those Good Old Days* (both 1913). Returning to Universal in 1913, she was the honorary chief of police for Universal City, and appeared in films for their brands like Nestor, Rex, and Powers such as *Aunt Betty's Revenge, Sally Scraggs; Housemaid* (both 1913), and *Hawkeye and the Cheese Mystery* (1914). Also spending time at Kalem in items like *Don't Monkey with the Buzz Saw* and *The Winking Zulu* (both 1914), she settled into dramas such as *The Dumb Girl of Portici* (1916) and *The Vanishing Dagger* (1920) before retiring in 1920.

Besides acting at Keystone and Universal, the neglected Laura Oakley was the honorary chief of police for Universal City. Author's collection.

Patsy O'Byrne (1884 – 1968)
Kansas-born character actress who specialized in cooks, gossips, maids, and mean landladies. Said to have come from the stage where she worked at the New York Hippodrome, she entered films around 1919, as she's been spotted in Larry Semon's *Between the Acts*. She became a cinema staple around 1924 working at the Hal Roach Studio in shorts such as *The Cake Eater* with Will Rogers, as well as *Wide Open Spaces, Short Kilts*, and *The Goofy Age* (all 1924). She then had a two-year apprenticeship at the Mack Sennett lot, where she inflicted her presence on Ralph Graves, Billy Bevan, and Alice Day. From there she branched out to features on the order of *My Old Dutch* (1926), and shorts for Christie, Weiss Brothers, and back again at Roach. Some her two-reelers include *Fire* (1926), *The Pride of Pikeville, Meet the Folks* (both 1927), *Their Purple Moment*, and *Taxi Beauties* (both 1928). Sound films saw her as busy as usual making small character appearances in numerous features such as *Doctor Bull* (19333), *It's a Gift* (1934), *Ruggles of Red Gap* (1935), *The Pride of the Yankees* (1942), and *Sorrowful Jones* (1949) until 1952.

Little known is that besides her comedy skills she had a pair of beautiful legs and in the 1930s would double the legs of stars when close-ups of those limbs were needed.

Kathleen O'Connor (1894 – 1957)
Former beauty contest winner and telephone girl from Dayton, Ohio who worked her way up from extra work at the Sennett studio to comedy leading lady for Hal Roach in shorts with Toto the clown such as *Fare, Please* and *The Junk Man* (both 1918). She soon moved over to Universal where she was teamed with comic Harry Mann for Nestor and L-Ko two-reelers like *Vamping the Vamp* and *Home, James* (both 1918), even supporting Stan Laurel in his early short *Who's Zoo?* (also 1918). She made the jump to features working with Tom Mix in *Ace High* (1918) and *Hell-Roarin' Reform* (1919), and continued supporting stars such as Harry Carey, Marie Prevost, and William S. Hart in pictures such as *A Gun Fightin' Gentleman* (1919), *The Married Flapper* (1922), and *Wild Bill Hickok* (1923) until 1924.

Georgia O'Dell (1892 – 1950)
Tall, hatchet-faced character actress who specialized in snobby rich matrons and domineering wives for comedy shorts producers such as Jack White, Al Christie, and the Weiss Brothers, for whom she made life difficult for the likes of Big Boy, Bobby Vernon, Jerry Drew, Jack Duffy, and Ben Turpin in items like *Wedding Wows* (1927), *Just Dandy*, *Seeing Things* (both 1928), and *Only Her Husband* (1929). She continued turning up in character bits until 1938.

Georgia O'Dell playing the grand dame in the *Big Boy* Comedy *The Gloom Chaser* (1928). Courtesy of EYE Filmmuseum, Netherlands.

Dolly Ohnet (?)
Supporting player, who was very busy in comedies of the teens. She started out in 1913 as part of Del Henderson's comedy company at Biograph where she appeared in shorts such as *A Compromising Situation* (1913), and provided stories for items like *The Rise and Fall of McDoo* (1913). By 1914 she was working for Universal in their Joker, Nestor, Powers, and Victor comedy brands. The comics she supported there include Gale Henry, Billy Franey, Ernie Shields, Eddie Lyons, Lee Moran, and Eileen Sedgwick in titles such as *The Way He Won the Widow*, *Lady Baffles and Detective Duck in The Signal of the Three Socks*, *Little Egypt Malone* (all 1915), *Love Me, Love My Biscuits*, *The High Cost of Starving* (both 1917), and *The Fickle Blacksmith* (1918). Her film career seems to have ended before 1920.

Edna May Oliver (Edna May Nutter) (1883 – 1942)
Grand dragon lady of the 1930s American cinema, memorable in films such as *Little*

Women (1933), *David Copperfield* (1935), and *Drums Along the Mohawk* (1939), who began her film career as comedy support in the 1920s. Pursuing the theatre at age fourteen she toured around the country, even working as a pianist with an all-girl band, before she made it to Broadway in 1917. There she appeared in musicals and plays such as *Oh Boy* (1917-1918), *The Half Moon* (1920), and *Cradle Snatchers* (1925-1926), not to mention a run as Parthy Ann in the original production of *Show Boat* (1927-1929). Her work on Broadway led her to films made in the New York area such as at C.C. Burr Productions and Paramount's Astoria Studio. Among her features she was comic relief in *Lovers in Quarantine* (1925) with Bebe Daniels, and the Richard Dix starring *Manhattan* (1924), *The Lucky Devil* (1925), and *Let's Get Married* (1926). Off screen for a couple of years she returned with the transition to sound in 1929 where she remained an audience favorite until her death in 1942.

Violet Oliver (?)
Stage performer from the West Coast who had appeared in the title role in the Bert Lennon production of *Little Bo Peep*, and became a leading lady for Lige Conley in Jack White Comedies such as *High Power* (1922) and *Casey Jones Jr.* (1923). During her stay with White Comedies there was much publicity in the trade magazines about Ms. Oliver being the Sun Maid girl and that "a likeness of Miss Oliver is on every package of Sun Maid Raisins." This doesn't appear to have been the case as the official Sun Maid information gives Lorraine Collett Petersen as the girl on the box, but it's possible that Miss Oliver was used on calendars and other publicity. After her short stint in films she returned to the stage and toured with Sophie Tucker on the Orpheum Circuit.

Gertrude Olmstead (1897 – 1975)
Chicago-born ingénue, who made her film debut in 1920 at Universal in light hearted Hoot Gibson westerns such as *Tipped Off* (1920), *The Driftin' Kid*, and *Out o' Luck* (both 1921). Until 1929 she functioned as all-purpose leading lady, comfortable in every genre. Her numerous comedies included the serial *The Adventures of Robinson Crusoe* (1922) with Harry Myers, the shorts' series *Fighting Blood* (1923), and features such as *The Monster*, *California Straight Ahead* (both 1925), *The Cheerful Fraud* (1926), *The Callahans and the Murphys* (1927), *Bringing Up Father*, and *Sporting Goods* (both 1929). Married to director Robert Z. Leonard since 1926, she made a solid transition to sound in films such as Al Jolson's *Sonny Boy*, and *The Show of Shows* (both 1929) but retired at age thirty-one.

Peg O'Neal (1894 – 1960)
Funny character clown who supported Lige Conley in many of his 1923 and 1924 comedies such as *Casey Jones Jr.* (1923), *Neck and Neck*, and *Air Pockets* (both 1924). Born in Iowa, she had a very diversified theatrical background appearing on the Redpath-Vawter

Chautauqua Circuit and with the Avon Players, where she played Shakespeare in addition to modern ultra-realistic dramas. Starting her film career at Lubin in 1913, she appeared in other Jack White Comedies such as *Low Tide* (1925) and Lloyd Hamilton Comedies like *Framed* (1925). Also turning up in features like *Mixed Faces* and *Top O' the Morning* (both 1922), after 1925 she mostly returned to the stage and only made sporadic film appearances.

An overeager Peg O'Neal has Lige Conley in a headlock in *Casey Jones Jr.* (1923). Courtesy of Sam Gill.

Zelma O'Neal disapproves of Al St John's toilette in *Who Hit Me?* (1926). Courtesy of Sam Gill.

Zelma O'Neal (Zelma Schrader) (1903 – 1989)
Pert and eccentric comedienne who was well-known on the stage and appeared in mid-1920s Jack White Comedies as leading lady for Al St John and Cliff Bowes. After these shorts she returned to Broadway for two of her biggest shows – *Good News* (1927) where she introduced *The Varsity Drag*, and *Follow Thru* (1929), in which she sang *Button Up Your Overcoat*. She made a few sporadic sound film appearances, such as the film version of *Follow Thru* (1930) and *Peach-O-Reno* (1931) with Wheeler & Woolsey, before retiring in the late 1930s.

Sally O'Neil (1908 -1968)
O'Neil was a Bayonne, New Jersey actress, born as Virginia Louise Noonan, who began her career in vaudeville under the name Chotsie Noonan. She started in films in 1925 and quickly became popular teamed with Joan Crawford and Constance Bennett in *Sally, Irene and Mary* (1925). Besides supporting Buster Keaton in *Battling Butler* (1926), O'Neil had leads in pictures like *Mike* (1926) and *Frisco Sally Levy* (1927), in addition to featured roles in *The Callahans and the Murphys* (1927), *The Battle of the Sexes* (1928), and *On with the Show!* (1929). Moving into sound she performed with her sister Molly O'Day in *The Show of Shows* (1929), and continued in features like *The Brat* (1931), *Ladies Must Love* (1933), and *Convention Girl* (1935) until 1938.

Sally O'Neil (right) with Belle Bennett in D.W. Griffith's *The Battle of the Sexes* (1928). Courtesy of Cole Johnson.

Sue "Bugs" O'Neil (Molly O'Day) (1911 – 1998)
Younger sister of Sally O'Neil, who was also born in Bayonne, New Jersey under the family name of Noonan, and began her film career at age fifteen at the Hal Roach Studios in shorts like *Yes, Yes, Nanette*, *Flaming Flapper* (both 1925), *Long Pants*, *Wandering Papas*, and *45 Minutes from Hollywood* (all 1926) playing bored or wise-ass teenagers. After a year-long break she returned to the screen with a new name, Molly O'Day, as a young leading lady in the popular Richard Barthelmess film *The Patent Leather Kid* (1927). From there she moved on to more pictures like *The Little Shepard of Kingdom Come* (1928), and continued on in talkies such as *Sob Sister* (1931), *Gigolettes of Paris* (1933), and *The Life of Vergie Winters* (1934) before ending her career in 1935.

Louise Orth (1891 -?)
Orth was a Denver-born actress who had appeared on stage with Blanche Ring and female impersonator Julian Eltinge. After nine months with the Biograph Company in comedies such as *A Barber Cure* and *Riley's Decoys* (both 1913), she settled in at L-Ko where she and Gertrude Selby shared the position of leading lady to the company's reigning psychopath Billie Ritchie in shorts like *Cupid in a Hospital*, *Almost a Scandal*, and *Silk Hose and High Pressure* (all 1915). Orth stayed with L-Ko until 1916, and afterward made only one feature, *Three Black Eyes* (1919), before retiring from the screen.

Baby Marie Osborne (1911 – 2010) **See Chapter Four**

Kathryn Osterman (1883 – 1926)
Popular stage comedienne, born in Toledo, Ohio, who spent many seasons in vaudeville and in touring shows such as 1908's *The Girl Who Looks Like Me* (written by comedy expert Mark Swan) and *True to Nature* (1914). She also appeared on Broadway in *Modest Suzanne* (1912) and was partnered with comic Louis Simon for revues such as *The Jump Ups* (1913-1914). Her first brush with the movies came in the very early days at the Biograph Company where she appeared in a number of 1903 comedies for the unit that included *Lucky Kitten*, *In My Lady's Boudoir*, and *He Loves Me, He Loves Me Not*. Concentrating on her stage work she came back to films in 1915 for the feature *The Bludgeon* for the Equitable Motion Pictures Corporation. At the same time she was signed by the World Comedy Stars Film Corporation to star in a number of one-reelers. At least two were made, *Housekeeping Under Cover* and *Sauce for the Gander* (both 1915) but the unit was very short lived, disbanding in August 1915, and Osterman left films to return to the stage.

Muriel Ostriche (1896 - 1989)
Pretty blonde who started her career as an extra at Biograph in 1911 after being approached in the street by assistant director W. Christy Cabanne. She later moved on to doing background for Powers and Pathé, and then got her first leads for the Éclair Film Company. She appeared in all types of their films, including comedies such as *Oh, You Ragtime* (1912) and *An Accidental Servant* (1913), before going on to a brief stay at Reliance. She settled in at Thanhouser in 1913 and made a name for herself there, so much so that the company set up the Princess Film brand for her starring films. Often teamed with Boyd Marshall, her *Princess* shorts included *Lobster, Salad and Milk* (1913), *A Rural Free Delivery* (1914), and *Pleasing Uncle* (1915). When Charles Hite, Thanhouser's president, died in 1914, she grew dissatisfied with the company and moved on.

After brief stays with Imp and Vitagraph, and being voted the "Moxie Girl" in a national contest sponsored by the soft drink, she signed a three-year contract with the World Film Company where she was support in feature dramas on the order of *The Road to France* (1918) and *The Bluffer* (1919). In 1920 Muriel Ostriche Productions was set up for a series of comedy shorts to be distributed by the Arrow Film Corp. The titles, which included *Betty the Vamp, Meet Betty's Husband, Betty Sets the Pace,* and *Betty's Green-Eyed Monster* (all 1920), were all directed by comedy expert Arvid E. Gillstrom. The next year she embarked on a series of dramatic features for Salient Film, appearing in *The Shadow* (1921), but soon retired for marriage and children.

Ossi Oswalda (1897 – 1947) **See Chapter Four**

Mabel Paige (1880 – 1954)
Comedienne, who appeared in numerous comedies for Lubin, and later was a busy character player in the 1940s and 1950s. Born in the proverbial trunk to stock actors, she began her own career at four, and ten years later at age fourteen was the main attraction of her own Mabel Paige Company. Billed as "the youngest singing and dancing soubrette on the American Stage," they toured the southern states to keep away from the child-protecting Gerry Society, and eventually set up the Paige Theater in Jacksonville, Florida. Her first films were made in 1912 for the Comet Film Company in comedies like *A Realistic Rehearsal*, but she soon switched over to Lubin's Jacksonville studio. She spent the next few years working with Oliver Hardy, Bobby Burns, and Raymond McKee in shorts like *No Trespassing* (1912), *You Can't Beat Them* (1914), *Mixed Flats* (1915), and *It Happened in Pikesville* (1916). After miscellaneous films for Wizard and the Eight Bell's film Co., she took a long break from movies. Married to actor Charles Ritchie, she went back to vaudeville and appeared on Broadway before going to Hollywood in 1942. Cornering the market on lively old ladies she appeared in numerous pictures on the order of *Murder, He Says* (1945), *If You Knew Susie, Johnny Belinda* (both 1948) and *The Sniper* (1952), in addition to plenty of television, until her death.

Muriel Ostriche in a 1913 Maurer, Schultz & Co. postcard. Author's collection.

Shirley Palmer (1908 – 2000)
Brunette actress who got her start in two-reelers for the Fox and Hal Roach Studios such as *A Bankrupt Honeymoon, Scared Stiff* (both 1926), and *Forgotten Sweeties* (1927). Most of her work was as a second female lead in many dramas and adventure pictures, including a few comedies like *Yours to Command* (1927), *Beautiful but Dumb* (1928), *Campus Knights* (1929), and *Ladies Must Play* (1930). Sound saw her roles dwindle before her retirement in 1934.

Corinne Parquet (?)
Attractive brunette who after a tiny role in Roscoe Arbuckle's *His Wife's Mistake* (1916), became his leading lady in *The Waiter's Ball* (1916) and *A Reckless Romeo* (1917), part of a series of shorts the comedian made in Fort Lee, New Jersey. Although made at the same time as *The Waiter's Ball* in 1916, *A Reckless Romeo* was released a year later and is the last known credit for Ms. Parquet.

Thelma Parr (1906 – 2000)
Oregon-born brunette, who studied to be an artist, but instead became a Mack Sennett girl starting with *His Marriage Wow* (1925). She quickly became Ralph Graves' regular leading lady in his starring two-reelers such as *Hurry Doctor!*, *The Window Dummy* (both 1925), *Wide Open Faces*, and *Funnymooners* (both 1926). She also had the lead in *The Gosh Darn Mortgage* (1926), and continued working with the likes of Billy Bevan, Alice Day, the Smith Family, and Ben Turpin in *Smith's Landlord*, *A Blonde's Revenge* (both 1926), *Should Sleepwalker's Marry?*, and *Peaches and Plumbers* (both 1927). Having appeared in the Rayart features *The Scorcher* (1927) and *The Devil's Tower* (1929) her career came to a sudden end with a 1928 car accident that left her with some facial scars. After a comeback attempt in the Lee Moran Educational Pictures short *My Harem* (1930) she retired from the screen.

Mack Sennett leading lady Thelma Parr and butterfly. Courtesy of Cole Johnson.

Blanche Payson (1881 – 1964) **See Chapter Seven**

Lillian Peacock (Lillian M. Webb) (1894 – 1918)
Peacock was a pretty ingénue who began working in Universal's Imp and Joker comedies in 1914. In addition to the Power' *Lady Baffles and Detective Duck* series, she was a member of the Joker ensemble of Max Asher, Gale Henry, Billy Franey, and Milburn Moranti in shorts like *When Hiram Went to the City* (1915), *His Highness the Janitor* (1916), *Canning the Cannibal King* (1917), and *The Pie Eyed Piper* (1918). After sustaining internal injuries when she fell from a moving car while filming, she was to continue working on and off but died a year later due to her injuries.

Peggy Pearce (1894 – 1975)
One of the most beautiful of the early silent comedy leading ladies, Peggy wasn't funny on her own but added a lot of appeal to the comedies with her warm personality and striking looks. Very busy in the teens, she began her career at Biograph in 1913, and soon ended up at Keystone where she worked with Ford Sterling and Charlie Chaplin. Like

Hank Mann and others, Peggy moved to the Sterling Film Co. and L-Ko for items such as *Love and Sour Notes* and *Poor But Dishonest* (both 1915), but then returned to Sennett in 1916. She later did shorts and features for Triangle, and in one of her last films was support to Louise Glaum in *Sex* (1920).

Lillian Peacock held captive by Max Asher in *Lady Baffles and Detective Duck in The Great Ore Mystery* (1915). Courtesy of Sam Gill.

Peggy Pearce alarmed by Dan Russell's antics in L-Ko's *Father's First Murder* (1915).

Pepper (? -1924)
Dark Maltese cat, which became a popular part of the Mack Sennett menagerie alongside Teddy the Great Dane and Cubby the bear. Said to have been a stray kitten which just showed up one day at the studio and was adopted by Sennett, she had definite screen presence – eventually becoming known as "the Sarah Bernhardt of alley cats." Her earliest appearance may be the 1913 split-reeler *A Little Hero*, where she tries to brunch on Mabel Normand's new canary until Mabel's little lapdog rounds up a canine posse to stop her. She frequently worked with Louise Fazenda, and her titles include *A Bedroom Blunder* (1917), *The Kitchen Lady* (1918), *Reilly's Wash Day* (1919), *Down on the Farm* (1920), *On a Summer's Day* (1921), and *Bow Wow* (1922).

Thelma Percy (1903 – 1970)
Sister of star Eileen Percy, who like her sister was born in Belfast and began her career as a child on the stage. Entering films at seventeen in 1920, much of her short screen life was spent in comedy – features such as *The Beggar Prince* (1920) and Max Linder's *Seven Years Bad Luck* (1921), as well as many shorts like *The Stage Hand*, *April Fool* (both 1920), and *An Idle Roomer* (1922) where she was a foil for Larry Semon, Lloyd Hamilton, and Harry Sweet. She left pictures in 1922.

Derelys Perdue (1902 – 1989)
Missouri-born brunette who began dancing at the age of six, and after coming to Los Angeles danced with the Marion Morgan Dancers and broke into films in the dance sequences of films such as *Man – Woman – Marriage*, *The Conquering Power*, and Mack Sennett's *A Small Town Idol* (all 1921) where she danced with Ramon Navarro. She quickly graduated to being a leading lady in dramas and a few comedies like *Blow Your Own Horn* (1923) and *The Last Man on Earth* (1924). Named a WAMPAS Baby Star in 1923, in 1925 she ended up at Universal and became Mrs. Newlywed in the studio's long-running series of *The Newlyweds and their Baby* two-reelers, where she played the mother of devil child Sunny McKeen. Numerous entries such as *The Newlywed's Neighbors* (1926), *The Newlywed's Success*, *The Newlywed's Hard Luck* (both 1928), *The Newlywed's Headache*, and *The Newlywed's Pest* (both 1929) followed, and she even found time to appear in a couple of Sid Saylor's *Let George Do It* one-reelers – *Television George* and *Hot Puppies* (both 1929). Except for an occasional appearance in a western like *Quick Triggers* (1928) and *The Smiling Terror* (1929), the latter part of career was taken over by the comedy shorts before she retired in 1929.

Kathryn Perry (1897 – 1983)
New York City-born brunette who began on stage as a musical performer in numerous revues and musical shows starting in 1911. During the decade of the teens she appeared in various editions of the *Ziegfeld Follies*, *Ziegfeld's Midnight Frolic*, *The Passing Show*, and

book shows such as *Robinson Crusoe Jr.*, *The Century Girl*, and *Miss 1917*. Her film career began in support of Owen Moore in his comedy features for the Selznick Company. Starting with *Sooner or Later* (1920) she soon became his leading lady as well as marrying him in 1921. Besides appearing in comedies on the order of *Why Girls Leave Home* (1921) and *Reported Missing* (1922) with Moore, she also turned up in dramas like *Main Street* (1923) and *Wings of Youth* (1925). In 1925 she signed with Fox and was starred in their two-reel

Kathryn Perry and Hallam Cooley in the Fox two-reeler *Moving Day* (1926). Courtesy of Karel Caslavsky.

Married Life series, where she was teamed with Hallam Cooley in the misadventures of the average married couple Helen and Warren. Sixteen entries such as *All Aboard*, *The Peacemakers* (both 1925), *Moving Day* (1926), *An Old Flame*, and *Rumors for Rent* (1927) were made between 1925 and 1927. Also continuing in comedy features like *The First Year*, *Early to Wed* (both 1926), and *Is Zat So?* (1927), after leaving Fox she was back with Owen Moore in the silent *Husbands for Rent* (1927) and the sound crime drama *Side Street* (1929). The rest of her talking film career consisted of walk-ons in features such as *Air Mail* (1932) and *My Man Godfrey* (1936). She left films in 1936 and remained married to Owen Moore until his death in 1939.

Delia Peterson (Della Peterson) (?)
Peterson was a blonde beauty who became a Mack Sennett girl, and adorned shorts such as *Meet My Girl*, *Ice Cold Cocos*, and *Masked Mamas* (all 1926). She soon moved over to Fox Imperial Comedies where she supported the likes of Lige Conley and Alice Howell in *King of the Kitchen* and *Madame Dynamite* (both 1926). Her other appearances include *The Latest from Paris* and *The Big City* (both 1928), in addition to playing Billy Dale's love interest in his Cameo Comedy *The Lucky Duck* (1928). Her last known film is the Bob Curwood western feature *The Secret Outlaw* (1928).

Carmen Phillips (1895 - 1936)
Dark, exotic-looking actress born in San Francisco whose early stage career began there with the Princess Opera Company. She also toured in Ferris Hartman's company with

Roscoe Arbuckle, and worked at Keystone before he did, appearing as part of the ensemble in 1913 shorts such as *A Deaf Burglar*, *The New Conductor*, and *Barney Oldfield's Race for a Life*. Moving over to Universal brands like Powers, Victor, Rex, and Nestor in 1914 and 1915, she had occasional leads in comedies like *A Family Affair* and dramas like *Shackles* (both 1916). After a stint at Vitagraph she then became Hank Mann's foil in his starring Fox shorts that include *The Cloud Puncher* and *Chased into Love* (both 1917). Her dark looks made her perfect for vamp roles, and she did a Theda Bara spoof with Hank in the Charles Parrott-directed *There's Many a Fool* (1917). From here she played supporting roles in features and numerous westerns until 1926's *A Six Shootin' Romance*.

Sally Phipps (Nellie Bogdon, Bernice Sawyer) (1911 - 1978)
Saucy, red-haired ingénue who was busy in many late 1920s Fox comedy shorts and features. Born in Oakland, California as Nellie Bernice Bogdon, after her parents split up when she was four Nellie was sent to live with foster parents who worked at the Essanay Studio in Niles, California, and there she made her film debut under the name Bernice Sawyer in Broncho Billy Anderson films such as *Broncho Billy and the Baby* and *The Outlaw's Awakening* (both 1915). Returning to Oakland she was re-discovered for films by the Fox Studio in 1926 at age fifteen when she became a jazz baby in Imperial Comedy two-reelers like *Light Wines and Bearded Ladies* (1926), *A Kangaroo Detective*, *Gentlemen Prefer Scotch* (both 1927), and *Hold Your Hat* (1928), many which teamed her with Nick Stuart. Named a 1927 WAMPAS Baby Star, Fox moved her into features that included *Love Makes 'Em Wild*, *High School Hero* (both 1927), and *Why Sailors Go Wrong* (1928). When she hit eighteen she had a falling out with Fox, and after making her talkie debut in the Clark & McCullough short *Detectives Wanted* (1929) she bailed on the last two years of her contract and fled to New York. There she appeared in the Kaufman and Hart Broadway hit *Once in a Lifetime* (1930-1931), but after the Joe Penner Vitaphone short *Where Men are Men* (1931) her career ended.

Fox starlet and WAMPAS Baby Star Sally Phipps. Author's collection.

Mary Pickford (1892 – 1979) **See Chapter Six**

Barbara Pierce (1905 - 1972)
California-born and a former debutant from a wealthy family, she had local stage work

with the Community Players of Santa Barbara and the Pasadena Community Players, as well as experience in Boston and New York. She became a leading lady on the Mack Sennett lot for Billy Bevan and Sid Smith in shorts like *Lizzies of the Field*, *Wall Street Blues*, and *Wandering Waistlines* (all 1924). Moving on to be one of Buster Keaton's militant brides in *Seven Chances* (1925), she appeared with Adolphe Menjou in *The Grand Duchess and the Waiter* (1926), plus supported Laurel & Hardy in *Sailor, Beware* (1927), but eventually returned to the Sennett lot and became something of a background bathing girl in shorts like *The Girl from Everywhere* (1927), *Run, Girl, Run*, *The Campus Carmen*, *Smith's Rowboat Race*, and *The Campus Vamp* (all 1928).

Zasu Pitts (1894 – 1963)
Good example of a performer who marched to a different drummer – even her first name, a combination of two aunts, set her apart. With reactions and a sense of timing uniquely her own, she was so distinctive a comedienne that it overshadowed her very real talents as a dramatic actress. Kansas-born but raised in California, Zasu began her career in 1917 with roles in features like Mary Pickford's *The Little Princess*, and as part of the ensemble in La Salle Comedies and Joker Comedies. Soon working steadily, in supporting roles as comic maids or country girls, in 1923 director Erich von Stroheim cast her as the lead in his film *Greed* (1924). Although she gave an incredible performance in one of the most famous films of the silent era, it didn't really transform her career. Outside of another tragic role in von Stroheim's *The Wedding March* (1928) she continued her idiosyncratic comic roles in films like *What Happened to Jones?* (1926) and *Casey at the Bat* (1927). The changeover to sound made her more popular than ever, with a hesitant voice and delivery that matched her fluttery gestures. Besides the well-known series of Hal Roach two-reelers that teamed her with Thelma Todd, Ms. Pitts starred in "B" productions such as *Love Birds* and *Their Big Moment* (both 1934), was support in "A" films like *Mr. Skitch* (1933) and *Ruggles of Red Gap* (1935), plus worked on television right up to her death in 1963.

A mid-1920s serious pose of comedienne Zasu Pitts. Author's collection.

Daphne Pollard (1890 – 1978) **See Chapter Seven**

Part II: Selected Biographies

Vivian Prescott (?)

A forgotten leading lady in comedies of the early teens, who had been a child actress on stage and starred in hit shows like *A Child of the Regiment* (1907) and *Sal the Circus Gal* (1909). Prescott entered films in 1909 for the Biograph Company and while there worked for D.W. Griffith and Frank Powell, but her best roles came with Mack Sennett in shorts such as *The Manicure Lady* (1911) and *With a Kodak* (1912). After a couple of years she went to Lubin and Imp, then went on to star in Crystal Comedies, often teamed with Charlie DeForrest and Joseph "Baldy" Belmont in items like *Baldy is a Wise Old Bird* (1913) and *His Lucky Day* (1914). Crystal publicized her as "the Refined and Cyclonic Comedienne" (which seems to cover all the bases), but after marriage she left the screen and disappeared from the public eye in 1917.

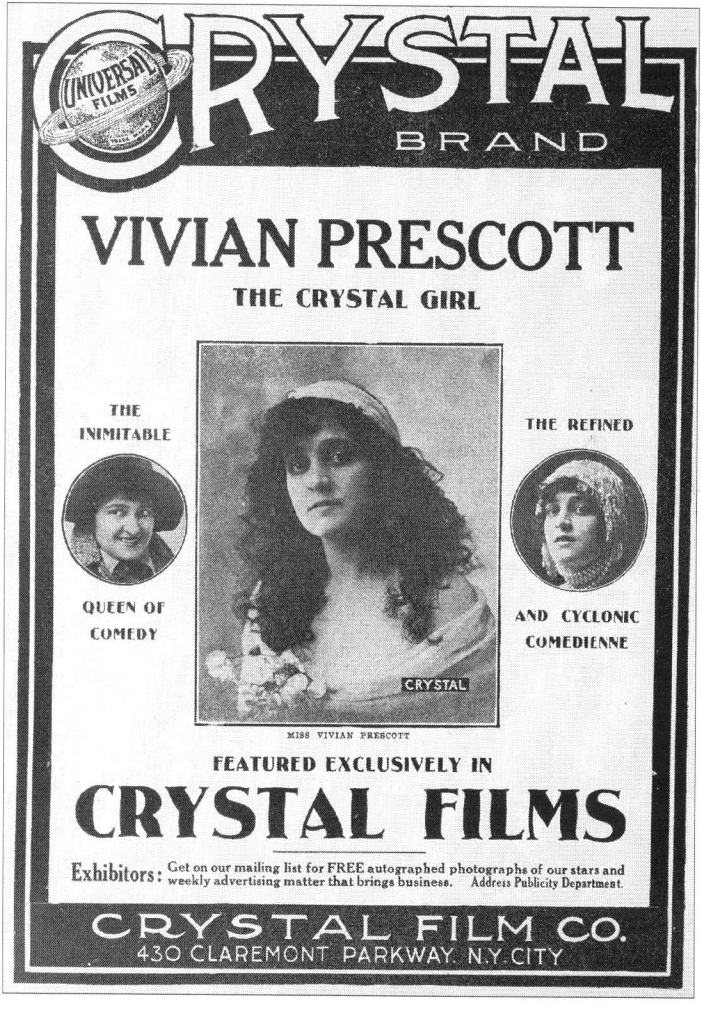

Vivian Prescott being "refined and cyclonic" in Crystal Comedies.

Peggy Prevost (Marjorie Prevost) (1904 – 1965)
Leading lady for Hank Mann and "Heinie" Conklin in 1917 Foxfilm Comedies such as *Suds of Love*, *His Final Blowout*, and *The Film Spoilers*, who was the younger sister of star Marie Prevost and began her career at Sennett and in some Hal Roach comedies like *Luke, Rank Impersonator* and *Luke's Fireworks Fizzle* (both 1916). After her work at Fox she appeared in Universal brands like L-Ko and Century for *Hello Trouble* (1918), *Hearts in Hock* (1919), *Uncle Tom's Caboose* (1920), and others, and then branched out into features. Before her film career ended in 1925 she supported Charles Ray in *The Old Swimmin' Hole* (1921) and Mildred Harris in *The Fog* (1923). She later worked on stage in Ziegfeld's *Palm Beach Follies*.

Peggy Prevost (sister of Marie) with Heinie Conklin (left) and unknown in the Charles Parrott-directed *His Merry Mix-Up* (1917). Courtesy of Robert S. Birchard.

Marie Prevost (1898 – 1937) **See Chapter Five**

Kate Price (1872 – 1943) **See Chapter Seven**

Edna Purviance (1895 – 1958) **See Chapter Eight**

Nena Quartaro (Gladys Quartaro) (1908 - 1985)
Black-haired and eyed ingénue of Mexican descent who began working in films at age fourteen for D. W. Griffith in New York. Hitting the west coast in 1928, she was "discovered" by director James Cruze and given the lead in his feature *The Red Mark* (1928). Renamed "Nena" by Cruze, in addition to bits in other features such as *The Redeeming*

Sin and *One Stolen Night* (both 1929) she became regular leading lady for Charley Chase in his late silents *All Parts* (1928), *Ruby Lips*, and *Loud Soup* (both 1929), plus his first talkie *The Big Squawk* (1929). Also on the Roach lot she appeared in *The Devil's Brother, Crook's Tour, Twin Screws, Sons of the Desert* (all 1933), and *Vagabond Lady* (1935). Her other work in the 1930s consisted of second leads in *The Monkey's Paw* (1933) and westerns such as *The Fighting Sheriff* (1931), *The Man from Monterey* (1933), and *The Cyclone Ranger* (1935). After working again with Charley Chase in his Columbia short *The Grand Hooter* (1937), she played small, uncredited bits in features like *Submarine D-1* (1937) and *Green Hell* (1940) until 1943.

Nena Quartaro tries to be nonchalant with Richard Tucker as Charley Chase hides under her bed in *Ruby Lips* (1929). Courtesy of Robert Arkus.

Queenie (?)

Horse which was a regular in early 1920s Century comedies, sharing the screen with human comics such as Charles Dorety, Lee Moran, Jimmie Adams, and Harry Sweet in opuses such as *A Dark Horse, Horse Tears, Me and My Mule* (all 1922), and *Game Hunters* (1923).

Florence Radinoff (?)

Radinoff was a skinny character actress who was part of the acting ensemble at Vitagraph. Starting in 1913 her films include *A Lady and her Maid, A Midget's Revenge*, and *He Fell in Love with His Mother-in-Law* (all 1913). Leaving films at the end of that year she returned to Vitagraph in 1916 for the features *The Chattel, The Blue Envelope* (both 1916), and *A Son of the Hills* (1917).

Marvel Rae (1901 – 1937) **See Chapter Eight**

Jobyna Ralston (1899 – 1967) **See Chapter Eight**

Caroline Rankin (1880 – 1953) **See Chapter Seven**

Jimmy Savo (left) mistakes Billy Engle's hand for that of Virginia Rappe's in the Lehrman First National Special *A Game Lady* (1921). Courtesy of Robert S. Birchard.

Virginia Rappe (1891 – 1921)
Comedy ingénue best-remembered for her role in, and subsequent death from the effects of a ruptured bladder after, the infamous 1921 Labor Day party thrown by Roscoe "Fatty" Arbuckle. For many years it was hard to determine fiction from fact in Ms. Rappe's story but it appears that she was born in New York City and after the death of her mother lived with relatives before she started a modeling career in 1908. Fairly successful, she traveled around the world modeling clothes and posing for photos before landing in Hollywood in the mid-teens. After getting her foot in the movie door in 1917 with the Fred Balshofer productions *Paradise Garden* and *Over the Rhine* (with Julian Eltinge, which was shelved but released in 1920 as *An Adventuress*, and then re-jiggered and released again in 1922 as *The Isle of Love*), she ended up in a relationship with comedy producer/director Henry "Pathé" Lehrman. Virginia appeared in a number of his shorts such as *Wild Women and Tame Lions* (1918), *His Musical Sneeze* (1919), *A Twilight Baby* (1920), *The Punch of the Irish*, and *A Game Lady* (both 1921). In her surviving films she's attractive and is an adequate straight women for the likes of Lloyd Hamilton, Jimmie Adams, Hugh Fay, Phil Dunham, and Frank J. Coleman. Sadly, it's hard to say if she'd be remembered if it wasn't for her sensationalized death.

Emma Ray (Emma Sherwood) (1971 – 1935)
Large Irish comedienne who with her long-time teammate and husband Johnny Ray were vaudeville favorites, and toured in shows such as *A Hot Old Time* (1900) and *King Casey* (1908). In 1916 they formed the Reserve Photoplay Company and made one-reelers in Jacksonville, Florida, Cliffside, New Jersey, and Cleveland, Ohio that chronicled their characters of "Casey and his wife." Johnny was little and wizened, while Emma was big and overpowering, and shorts like *A Laundry Mix-Up* and *Muggsy in Bad* came out through 1917. Johnny retired due to ill health and died in 1927, but Emma turned up in features such as *So Big* (1932) and W.C. Field's *The Old Fashioned Way* (1934) until her death in 1935.

Marjorie Ray, Dan Russell (center), and Harry Sweet (left) react to Leo's presence in *Lonesome Hearts and Loose Lions* (1919).

Marjorie Ray (Mrs. Dan Russell) (1890 – 1924)
Kansas-born actress, who started her career on stage around 1907 or 1908 as part of Dan Russell's touring vaudeville show *The Matinee Girl*. Eventually marrying Russell, the pair crisscrossed the country with their show until 1915, when Russell became one of the principal comics at L-Ko Comedies. Marjorie joined him at the studio in 1917, sometimes billed as Marjorie Ray and sometimes billed as Mrs. Dan Russell, for films such as *Spike's Busy Bike* (1917), *Lonesome Hearts and Loose Lions*, and *Siren of the Suds* (both 1919). Sadly none of her shorts are known to exist today, and besides her husband, she also worked with Billie Ritchie, Vin Moore, Harry Sweet, and The Century Lions. In late 1919 the Russells left films to return to the stage, and soon separated. Marjorie continued working on stage as a solo performer, but died of tetanus while performing in *The Suffragettes* at the Colonial Theatre in San Diego in July 1924.

Mildred Reardon (1900 – 1937)
Ziegfeld Follies girl who was leading lady in the Fatty Arbuckle shorts *The Sheriff* (1918) and *Camping Out* (1919), in addition to working at the fledgling Hal Roach Studio supporting Stan Laurel in *Just Rambling Along*, *Hoot Mon* (both 1918) *Hustling for Health* and *No Place Like Jail* (both 1919). She had a brief vogue in features such as *Number 17* (1920), and *Silk Husbands and Calico Wives* (1920), with her best-known film Cecil B. DeMille's *Male and Female* (1919), but her career petered out and her last appearance was in 1927's *His Rise to Fame*.

Teddy Reavis (?)
A poor man's Edna Marion who headlined in a number of the low-budget comedy shorts produced by the rock bottom impresario William Pizor in the 1920s. The hallmark of a Pizor short was non-existent gags, shoddy production values, and plodding direction. The one big name he used was Sid Smith, and the pretty blonde Ms. Reavis supported him, as well as Pizor's own "stars" Fred Parker and Lloyd Hamilton clone Art Hammond in titles such as *Hired and Fired* (1926), *Heave Ho*, and *Down on the Farm* (both 1927).

Emma Reed (1881 - ?)
Chubby black actress who appears to have been New York based in the teens as she turns up in Roscoe Arbuckle's *His Wedding Night* (1917), where she comes into "Fatty's" general store asking for make-up and he gives her charcoal, plus she's been spotted in the surviving rushes for the unfinished *Bert Williams Lime Kiln Club Field Day* feature that was shot by Biograph in 1913. Later locating to the west coast, she plays Farina's mother in three Our Gang shorts; *Saturday's Lesson* (1929), *The First Seven Years*, and *When the Wind Blows* (both 1930).

Emma Reed puzzled by Farina's industrious effort in *Saturday's Lesson* (1929). Courtesy of Cole Johnson.

Florence Reed (?)
Not the dramatic stage and movie star, but instead the wife of comedy director and character player Walter C. Reed. Before coming to films the Reeds had their own touring vaudeville company in which Roscoe Arbuckle and Minta Durfee got some of their early stage experience. Arbuckle brought Mr. Reed to films in 1915, and Florence came

along doing bits in the comedies, even appearing in the dramatic Fox feature *A Tale of Two Cities* (1917) when her husband was directing comedies on the lot. Her largest role is the battling and troublesome old lady train passenger in the Arbuckle-directed Al St John comedy *The Iron Mule* (1925).

Myrtle Reeves (1897 – 1983)
An Atlanta-born southern belle who began her career in 1915 for the Balboa Company, appearing in dramas and comedies, in addition to being cited in the trade magazines for her aquatic stunts. In 1917 she became an ingénue and bathing girl for Triangle comedies, playing in numerous shorts such as *A Good Elk* (1917), *First Aid, Mr. Miller's Economies,* and *Courts and Cabarets* (all 1918). Later she moved on to do support in features like *Playthings* (1918) and *Over the Garden Wall* (1919). She retired in 1920, and her main claim to cinema fame is as Oliver Hardy's second wife from 1921 to 1937.

Edna Reynolds (1888 -?)
Reynolds was a character comedienne who had a long career on stage in rep and stock companies, as well as four seasons at the New York Hippodrome. Her screen debut came in the early teens and she spent time at Thanhouser, Centaur, Crystal, Universal, and World. In 1915 she hooked with the team of Bobby Burns and Walter Stull (Pokes & Jabbs), starting with them at the Wizard Company in shorts like *Mashers and Splashers,* and continuing as they moved to Florida's Vim Comedy Film Company. Playing a succession of wives, mothers-in-laws, old maids, and widows she supported Burns & Stull in outings such as *The Midnight Prowlers, Mixed and Fixed* (both 1915), *A Bag of Trouble, Tangled Ties,* and *The Frame-Up* (all 1916). At the same time she supported Oliver Hardy and Billy Ruge in some of their Vim *Plump and Runt* opuses like *One Too Many* and *Hungry Hearts* (both 1916). The trail of her films seem to end in 1916, but she was married to stage and early film clown Frank "Spook" Hanson and in his *Variety* obituary it states that she did "strenuous and dangerous stunts" for Kalem Pictures, which brings up the possibility that at some point she may have been a stunt double for the likes of Helen Holmes or Helen Gibson.

Vera Reynolds (1899 – 1962)
Small and petite ingénue who spent the first six years of her career in slapstick shorts. Practically the minute she graduated from Polytechnic High School in Los Angeles she was busy in shorts for Rolin, L-Ko, and Sennett, which led to leading roles in one-reel Triangle Comedies such as *A Self-Made Hero, A Laundry Mix-Up, A Janitor's Vengeance,* and *Caught in the End* (all 1917). More shorts followed – Gayety Comedies like *Dry and Thirsty* and *Parked in the Park* (both 1920) with Billy Bletcher, a number of Al Haynes' *Atma Comedies,* a slew of Morris Schlank-produced *Broadway Comedies* released through Arrow that teamed her with Eddie Barry, and even a gig supporting Stan Laurel

in *The Pest* (1922). By 1923 she'd made the leap to features, making a splash in the drama *Icebound* (1924) although she still found time to work with Raymond Griffith in the comedies *The Night Club* (1925) and *Wedding Bill$* (1927). In the latter part of the 1920s she hooked up with Cecil B. DeMille and appeared in many comedy-dramas like *Sunny Side Up, Corporal Kate* (both 1926), and *The Main Event* (1927) for his production company. After making the transition to sound she worked in mostly low-budget features such as *The Monster Walks* and *Gorilla Ship* (both 1932) before leaving films in 1932.

Before graduating to features such as *Feet of Clay* (1924), Vera Reynolds started her career in shorts for Roach, L-Ko, Sennett, and Triangle. Courtesy of Cole Johnson.

Billie Rhodes (1894 – 1988) **See Chapter Four**

Irene Rich (1891 – 1988)
Statuesque brunette, who specialized in playing wives and mothers, and became a favorite foil of comedian Will Rogers. She had been married twice, had two daughters, worked as a real estate agent, and was twenty-seven when she entered movies as an extra in 1918. She quickly got supporting parts in dramatic features, but in 1920 she first worked with Will Rogers in *Water, Water, Everywhere*. Their easy-going chemistry led the comic to use her in other pictures such as *The Strange Boarder, Jes Call Me Jim* (both 1920), *Boys Will Be Boys* (1921), *The Ropin' Fool*, and *Fruits of Faith* (both 1922). Her other silent comedy appearances include *Rosita* (1923), *Lady Windermere's Fan* (1925), *Don't Tell the Wife* (1927), and *Beware of Married Men* (1928), plus she had her own starring dramas for Warner Brothers in 1926 – 1927.

In sound films she was back as Will Roger's spouse in *They Had to See Paris* (1929), *So This is London* (1930), and *Down to Earth* (1932), and continued with good supporting roles through *Fort Apache* and *Joan of Arc* in 1948. In addition to her films she also toured vaudeville with the act *Ask the Wife*, and appeared on Broadway with George M. Cohan in *Seven Keys to Baldpate* (1935) and the Bobby Clark show *As the Girls Go* (1948–1950). She also had a popular national radio show *Dear John* (also called *The Irene Rich Show*) which started in 1933 and continued for over a decade. After her Broadway run in *As the Girls Go* in 1950 she retired from show business.

Viola Richard (1904 – 1973) Richard was a very pretty and petite brunette who made many memorable appearances as a member of the Hal Roach Studio stock company in the late 1920s. Born in Ontario, Canada, her family relocated to America in 1910, but it's not known how Richard began working on the Roach lot. She began turning up in 1926 shorts such as *Why Girls Love Sailors* and *What Women Did for Me*. Very busy during her two years with the studio supporting Laurel & Hardy, Charley Chase, and Max Davidson, her many films include *Do Detectives Think?*, *Never the Dames Shall Meet* (both 1927), *Dumb Daddies*, *Blow by Blow* (both 1928), and especially *Limousine Love* (1928) where she ends up nude in the back of Charley Chase's limo as he drives to his wedding. Her last Roach picture appears to be *Should Married Men Go Home?* (1928), and it's thought that she, Edna Marion, and Dorothy Coburn were let go because of studio cutbacks. In 1928 she married a Fox Studio official in New York, and did one sound film there, *The Line-Up* (1929). She also appeared in the short-lived Broadway show *Geraniums in my Window* (1934) and may have had walk-on appearances in Our Gang's *Sprucin' Up* and Laurel & Hardy's *Tit for Tat* (both 1935). That appears to have been the end of her acting career and she passed away in California in 1973.

Viola Richard (left) and Martha Sleeper (right) behind the scenes on the Hal Roach lot. Courtesy of Cole Johnson.

Lucille Ricksen (1910 – 1925)
Blonde child actress, born in Chicago, whose mother got her started as a professional model from the time she could walk. Born as Ingeborg Myrtle Elizabeth Ericksen, after model work she appeared on stage, and at five began her film career as Baby Ericksen in the Essanay film *The Millionaire and the Baby* (1915). When her family moved to California she became the leading lady in a series of Goldwyn-produced two-reelers based on stories by Booth Tarkington. *The Adventures and Emotions of Edgar Pomeroy* lasted two years and Lucille was the love interest for hero Edgar played by Johnny Jones (Edward Peil Jr.). The series included the entries *Edgar's Hamlet*, *Edgar's Sunday Courtship* (both 1920), *Edgar's Country Cousin*, and *Edgar the Detective* (both 1921). When the series ended she played kids roles in features such as *The Married Flapper* (1922) with Marie

Prevost, and *The Stranger's Banquet* (1922), not to mention some Universal western shorts opposite Roy Stewart. At age fourteen she became a young leading lady in features such as Syd Chaplin's *The Galloping Fish*, *Vanity's Price* (both 1924), and *The Denial* (1925). Going from picture to picture she completed ten features in just seven months. Nervous exhaustion, leading to tuberculosis was said to have led to her death at age fifteen. Other sources claim it was a botched abortion, but her promising life and career came to a too early and tragic end in 1925.

Lucille Ricksen and Johnny Jones in the *Edgar* two-reeler *Edgar Takes the Cake* (1920). Courtesy of Sam Gill.

Margie Rieger (?)
Essanay ingénue who, along with Sade Carr, was under consideration to become Charlie Chaplin's leading lady in 1915 (the job went to Edna Purviance). Although briefly part of Chaplin's Essanay unit she made more appearances in the shorts directed by a young Hal Roach where he used idle Chaplin performers like Rieger, Bud Jamison, Harry "Snub" Pollard, James T. Kelly, and Jack Pollard in one-reelers such as *Street Fakers*, *A Countless Count*, *Off for a Ride*, and *Tale of a Tire* (all 1915).

Lorraine Rivero (1922 – 1974)
Child actress, daughter of actor Julian Rivero, who became a regular leading lady for Malcolm Sebastian in his Big Boy Comedies. Often playing a little rich girl who becomes the sweetheart of poor kid Sebastian, their adventures included *She's a Boy* (1927), *Navy Beans* (1928), and *Joy Tonic* (1929). As a child she also appeared in the features *Fourth Commandment* (1926) and *Chicago after Midnight* (1928) as well as later doing uncredited work in sound films such as *One Million BC* (1940) and *The Falcon in Mexico* (1944).

Lorraine Rivero with her constant screen companion Malcolm "Big Boy" Sebastian in *The Gloom Chaser* (1928). Courtesy of EYE Filmmuseum, Netherlands.

Edith Roberts (1899 – 1935)
Pretty blonde who paid her dues in comedy shorts in the teens to become a lead in dramatic features of the 1920s. She made her debut in Universal Imp shorts such as *When the Call Came* (1915), *The College Boomerang*, and *Toto of the Byways* (both 1916). In 1917 she moved on to other Universal brands such as Nestor and Victor, and became frequent support for the comedy team of Eddie Lyons and Lee Moran. *Taking their Medicine* (1917), *A Pigskin Hero*, *Give Her Gas* (both 1918), and *Penny Ante* (1919) are some of her Lyons & Moran titles, and she also worked for Universal with Jimmie Adams and at Christie before she switched to drama in 1920. Never appearing in any major films she was consistently busy in titles such as *A Front Page Story* (1922), *Backbone* (1923), *Roaring Rails* (1924), *Shattered Lives* (1925), and *Black Cargoes of the South Seas* (1928), until her retirement in 1929. Sadly she died in childbirth at age thirty-five in 1935.

Dora Rodgers (Fontaine La Rue) (1897 - 1976)
Dark-haired actress who specialized in exotic types in comedy shorts from 1915 through 1918. Born in Los Angeles, Rodgers attended Hollywood High and the New York School of the Dramatic Arts before working on stage, doing oriental and toe dancing. She's also said to have trained and kept snakes, which were sometimes used in films. A leg injury ended her dancing career and she turned up in 1915 in Keystone Comedies such as *The Home Breakers*, *Love, Loot and Crash*, *Mabel Lost and Won* (all 1915), *Stolen Magic*, *A Love Riot* (both 1916), *Dodging His Doom*, and *His Naughty Thought* (both 1917) where she vamped the likes of Chester Conklin and Mack Swain. 1918 saw her move over to Triangle one-reelers on the order of *Dimples and Dangers*, *An Ice Man's Bride*, and *Did She Do Wrong?* (all 1918). Besides an occasional comedy short such as *Cleopatsy* (1918), *A Prohibition Monkey* (1920), *The Two Twins* (1923), and *Who's Baby* (1929) where she supported the likes of Toto, Joe Martin the orangutan, Bull Montana, and Arthur Lake, she spent the 1920s in all kinds of features and shorts which included *A Blind Bargain* (1922), and *Love on the Rio Grande* (1925) as a character actress until she left films in 1929.

Laura Roessing (?)
Female member of Hal Roach's *Spat Family* Comedies, who spent the entirety of her film career at the studio. Along with Frank Butler and Sydney D'Albrook, Roessing was one third of the starring trio in two-reelers such as *Heavy Seas* (1923), *Hit the High* Spots

Laura Roessing along with Sydney D'Albrook (center) and Frank Butler (right) in the *Spat Family* comedy *Hot Stuff* (1924).
Courtesy of Karel Caslavsky.

(1924), and *Black Hand Blues* (1925) that chronicled the misadventures of Butler and Roessing as a quarreling husband and wife, with D'Albrook as her obnoxious brother. Although the series lasted from 1923 into 1925 it was one of the studio's rare misfires as the survivors aren't particularly funny and are irritating due to the characters constant bickering and battling. Besides the *Spats* Roessing also appeared in the Roach feature *Call of the Wild* (1923) and her final film is the comedy *Don Key (Son of Burro)* (1926), a problem short that was remade a couple of times, giving the impression that her appearance may be from left-over *Spat Family* material.

Dorothy Rogers (?)
Versatile stock and musical comedy actress from the stage who made her film debut in the 1915 Casino Star Comedy *Beauty in Distress* with comic Harry Vokes. She even wrote the short, but from here she abandoned comedy and appeared in dramatic films on and off until 1958.

Rena Rogers (1900 – 1966)
Blonde ingénue who started in Universal's Nestor and L-Ko comedies and was soon upgraded to leading roles in shorts made by the Crown City Film Manufacturing Co. and distributed by Kriterion. After a number of comedies such as *Sherlock Boob, Detective* and *Cousin Fluffy* (both 1915) she switched over to MinA Comedies, Balboa, National, and back to Universal, where she had a good role in the Lois Weber and Phillip Smalley dramatic feature *Where Are My Children?* (1916). In 1916 she became part of the ensemble in Vogue Comedies and worked with Ben Turpin, Rube Miller, and Paddy McQuire in entries like *Bungling Bill, Doctor, Delinquent Bridegrooms* (both 1916), and *A Vanquished Flirt* (1917). She then worked at Fox with Tom Mix in *Six Cylinder Love* and Hank Mann in *A Domestic Hound* (both 1917) before returning to Universal with her last known film being the early Stan Laurel comedy *Phoney Photos* (1918). For many years she was married to director Frank Borzage.

Rena Rogers shocks Hank Mann in his 1917 Fox Comedy *His Ticklish Job*. Courtesy of Cole Johnson.

Ruth Roland (1893-1937)
Roland was a leading lady who became an action serial star but began her career in comedy films. Born in San Francisco she made her stage debut at age four as "Baby Ruth" and

for fifteen years enjoyed a varied experience in vaudeville, stock, and big productions. She worked under Belasco and Morosco, and toured the Orpheum Circuit. She began her film career with the Kalem Company and by 1911 she was part of their regular ensemble appearing in westerns and in numerous comedies such as *The Dude Cowboy, Accidents will Happen*, and *Walk - You Walk!* (all 1912). She worked frequently with Marshall Neilan, John Brennan, and Marin Sais, keeping busy in outings like *Jones' Jonah Day, The Phony Singer* (both 1913), *Too Many Johnnies, The Family Skeleton*, and *Fleeing from the Fleas* (all 1914). She also appeared with Lloyd Hamilton and Bud Duncan in their early Ham and Bud comedies such as *Ham the Lineman, Bud, Bill and the Waiter*, and *Love, Oil and Grease* (all 1914). In 1915 she embarked on her action film career starring in the *Girl Detective* Series, and moved on to Balboa and even the Hal Roach Studio for movies such as *Ruth of the Rockies* (1920), *The Timber Queen* (1922), and *Ruth of the Range*. (1923). Her career slowed down after 1925, but she made a fortune as a real estate investor, as well as appeared in vaudeville. Her last film was the Edgar G Ulmer–directed *From Nine to Nine* (1935), and she died two years later of cancer.

Rosa Rosanova (1869 – 1944)
Russian-born character actress, who came from the stage and specialized in Jewish roles. Her early films were dramas such as *Blood and Sand, Hungry Hearts* (both 1922), *Cobra*, and *His People* (both 1925), but by the mid-1920s she began turning up in numerous comedies like *The Shamrock and the Rose, Jake the Plumber* (both 1927), and *Abie's Irish Rose* (1928), plus played "mama" to Max Davidson's "papa" in the feature *Pleasure Before Business* (1927). In sound films George Jessel sang *My Mother's Eyes* to her in *Lucky Boy* (1928) and she had a good part in Frank Capra's *The Younger Generation* (1929) before her career tapered off in the early 1930s.

Queenie Rosson (1889 – 1978)
Cute blonde who started her career at Universal appearing in Joker and Powers comedies such as *His Wife's Family, The Barnstormers* (both 1914), and *Skipper Simpson's Daughter* (1915), plus Rex dramas like *The Grind* (1915). Rosson joined the American Film Manufacturing Company in 1915, where her sister Helene and brother Dick worked as well, and turned up in numerous *Beauty* Comedies on the order of *A Trunk and Trouble, The Laird O'Knees*, and *All for Nuttin'* (all 1916) many with Oral Humphrey. Near the end of 1916 she gravitated to their dramas such as *The Quicksands of Deceit* and the feature *The Love Hermit* before leaving the screen.

Josie Sadler (1871 – 1927) **See Chapter Three**

Marin Sais (1890-1971)
Sais was an actress from a California Spanish family, born in, and named after, Marin County. With a background in opera, stock companies, and musical sketches on the Keith and Proctor circuit, she entered films in 1909 working for Vitagraph and Bison.

She quickly ended up with the Kalem Company, appearing in westerns like *The Ranger's Stratagem* (1911), comedies such as *He Who Laughs Last* (1911) and *Accidents Will Happen* (1912), or often a combination of the two on the order of *The Tenderfoot's Troubles* and *The Girl Bandit's Hoodoo* (both 1912). She also supported John Brennan and Ruth Roland in comedy one-reelers like *The Chaperon Gets a Ducking* (1912) and *The Scheme of Shiftless Sam Smith* (1913), and by 1915 she became a regular foil for the team of Ham & Bud, supporting the scuzzy ones in *Ham at the Garbage Gentleman's Ball*, *The Pollywog's Picnic*, and *The Phony Cannibal* (all 1915). The next few years saw her busy in Kalem serials often playing female detectives such as "special investigator Netty Walright" or "Frances Ballon House Detective." Following a stint supporting Sessue Hayakawa, she married cowboy star Jack Hoxie in 1920 and spent the bulk of the 1920s working with him. In the sound era she was busy in character roles in myriad "B" westerns until 1953.

Kalem Company actress Marin Sais. Author's collection.

Sally (?)

Sally was a chimpanzee which was part of the simian team of Napoleon and Sally in shorts for the E & R Jungle Film Company. Formed in 1914 by J.S. Edwards and John Rounan, Napoleon had been a stage favorite with an elephant named Hip, and after Hip died Napoleon was joined on screen by Sally. The monks' big heyday was 1916 when their adventures were directed by Louis W. Chaudet and they had support from Lillian Brown Leighton and Ralph McComas in comedies like *Stung*, *Father's Baby*, and *In Dutch* (all 1916). Their films stayed on the states' rights market for a number of years as they were re-released by Bulls Eye and Reelcraft at the end of the teens, and they even spawned rivals like the orangutan and chimp team of Mr. & Mrs. Joe Martin at Universal.

Thelma Salter (1908 – 1953)

Curly blonde who at five was the heroine in numerous *Keystone Kiddie* comedies such as *Just Kids*, *The Horse Thief* (both 1913), *Little Billy's Triumph*, *Kid Love*, and *A Back Yard Theatre* (all 1914). This fore-runner of *Our Gang* was started by Henry Lehrman and eventually morphed into the *Little Billy* series directed by Robert Thornby and starring

Paul Jacobs. She moved on to Majestic and then Triangle, making *In Slumberland* (1917) for the Fine Arts Company, as well as working for Thomas Ince who used her as support to William S. Hart in *The Disciple* (1915) and *Selfish Yates* (1917), in addition to starring her in *The Crab* (1917). After appearing in 1920 features such as *Huckleberry Finn* and *The Kentucky Colonel* she took a six-year break from pictures before returning as an extra in Sennett two-reelers like *Masked Mamas* (1926), *Should Sleepwalkers Marry?* (1927) and *The Campus Vamp* (1928). For producer Jack White she became leading lady for Lupino Lane in *Sword Points* and *Hectic Days* (both 1928). After marrying in 1928 she retired from the screen.

Teddy Sampson (1895 – 1970)
Dark-haired ingénue, who began working on the stage in 1910 at age fifteen, dancing in vaudeville in Gus Edward's *School Days* act. She also worked with Blanche Ring in *The Wall Street Girl* and returned to Gus Edwards to tour the Orpheum Circuit in his *Chorus Girl Revue*. In 1914, while appearing at the Palace Theatre in New York, she was introduced to D.W. Griffith and became a member of his Reliance/Majestic Company. Although working in dramas such as *The Life of General Villa*, and Griffith's *Home Sweet Home* (both 1914), she also spent much time in comedy shorts like *Hubby to the Rescue*, *Izzy the Operator* (both 1914), *Bobby's Bandit*, and *Bill Gives a Smoker* (both 1915) where she held her own with the likes of Fay Tincher, Max Davidson, and Bobby Ray. Her best known film at the time was *The Fox Woman* (1915) where she played a Japanese wife in a version of *Madame Butterfly*. In spite of later more serious features on the order of *Fighting for Gold* (1919) with Tom Mix, *Outcast* (1922), and *The Bad Man* (1923), she headlined in two-reelers for Nestor, Strand, "Smiling Bill" Parsons, Supreme Comedies, and Al Christie. Titles include the early Stan Laurel short *Hickory Hiram* (1917), *Dad's Knockout* (1918), *Don't Blame the Stork* (1920), and *Assault and Flattery* (1921), before she retired in 1923 after the Bobby Vernon comedy *A Perfect 36*. In 1914 she had married comedian Ford Sterling, and although they're reported to have had a rocky relationship, they remained married until his death in 1939.

Trade magazine portrait of actress, comedienne, and wife of Ford Sterling, Teddy Sampson.

Betty Schade (1894 – 1982)
Schade was a Berlin-born ingénue who spent much time in comedies as well as dramas. Raised in Chicago she started her career there at the Essanay Studio in 1911. Moving to California it's rumored that she spent a little time at Keystone before going on to American and Selig. Eventually she landed at Universal where she worked frequently with director Robert Z. Leonard in comedies such as *The Mud Bath Elopement* and *The Boob's Honeymoon* (both 1914), plus Joker shorts like *The Countless Count* and *How Father Won Out* (both 1914). She also appeared opposite future director Edward Sedgwick in *Married a Year* (1916) and did a slew of dramas that included Lois Weber's *The Dumb Girl of Portici* (1916). By 1917 she was primarily appearing in features with a return to an occasional short like *A Bum Bomb* (1918). After pictures such as *Flame of Youth* (1920) and *First Love* (1921) she retired in 1921. Although sometimes erroneously said to have been the daughter of Keystone comic Fritz Schade, she did marry fellow Universal comedian Ernest Shields in 1917.

Anne Schaefer (1870 – 1957)
Schaefer was a character actress who had a background of stock and road productions of Shakespeare and shows like *The Two Orphans* and *Lord Strathmore*. Her film career began when she joined Vitagraph in 1911, appearing in comedies such as *The Second Honeymoon* (1911), *Willie's Sister* (1912), and *Bedelia Becomes a Lady* (1913) in addition to their dramatic shorts. The aunt of Jane and Eva Novak, Ms. Schaefer got Jane started at Vitagraph and they appeared in many shorts together. Later moving to the western Vitagraph studio, she became one of their mainstays and did more comedies such as *What Did He Whisper?*, *A Scandal in Hickville* (both 1915), *Some Chicken*, and *The Cost of High Living* (both 1916). In 1917 she became support in features working with Mary Pickford in *The Little Princess* (1917), and *Johanna Enlists* (1918), and Mary Miles Minter for *Melissa of the Hills* (1917), and *The Ghost of Rosy Taylor* (1918). She continued working in small parts until 1938, along the way turning up in *Main Street* (1923), *The Goose Hangs High* (1925), *Smiling Irish Eyes* (1929), *Mr. Deeds Goes to Town*, and *Pennies from Heaven* (both 1936).

Doris Schroeder (1893 – 1981) **See Chapter Six**

Lois Scott (? - 1924)
Actress who as a child played in stock as well as New York productions of *The Bluebird* and *The Pied Piper* with DeWolf Hopper. At sixteen she became the ingénue in Johnny Ray Comedies, and after appearing in the *Ziegfeld Follies* she supported the likes of Clyde Cook, Jimmy Savo, and Harry Sweet in Fox comedies such as *The Toreador* (1921), *Hold the Line*, and *Off His Beat* (both 1922). Independent features *The White Panther* and *The Virgin* (both 1924) followed, but when her husband, well-known race driver Allen Mulford, was killed in an accident she died a few months later.

Lois Scott looks puzzled by the antics of Billy Armstrong (left), James C. Morton (center), Ford West (back right), and Leo Sulky (asleep) in *The Barnstormers* (1922). Courtesy of Robert S. Birchard.

Dorothy Seastrom (1903 – 1930)
Texas-born blonde and a former dancer at the Coconut Grove who was Lloyd Hamilton's leading lady in five shorts that included *Crushed* (1924) and *Hooked* (1925). Seastrom also appeared in Jack White Comedies such as *Oh, Teacher* (1924), as well as small roles in features like *It Must Be Love* (1926). The first wife of director/cameraman Francis Corby, she died of tuberculosis at twenty-six in 1930.

Dorothy Sebastian (Dorothy Sabiston) (1903 – 1957)
Alabama-born brunette, who ran away from home to New York, where she studied with musical comedy dancing master Ned Wayburn and joined the chorus of *George White's Scandals* in 1924. Thanks to her chorus work and connections she ended up with an MGM contract. Most of her work was in dramatic features such as *Our Dancing Daughters* and *A Woman of Affairs* (both 1928), but her comedies include early work in shorts with Lloyd Hamilton and Jimmie Adams like *Half a Hero* (1925) and *Beauty a la Mud* (1926). Her comedy features include *Bluebeard's Seven Wives* (1925) Raymond Griffith's *You'd Be Surprised* (1926) *The Demi-Bride* and *Tea for Three* (both 1927). She's best known today for her work as Buster Keaton's love interest in his last silent film *Spite Marriage* (1929), where she's a great foil for Buster and does the great "putting the wife to bed" sequence with him. Early sound saw her have a contract dispute with MGM, and her career hit hard times after numerous low budget films. By the 1940s she was appearing in uncredited walk-ons, and she left films in 1948.

Eileen Sedgwick (1898 – 1991)
One of the members of the family vaudeville team The Five Sedgwicks who entered films, along with her sister Josie and brother Edward, in 1914 and became a comedy ingénue at Lubin in shorts such as *All for Love, Love and Flames, The Belle of Breweryville* (all 1914), and *Green Backs and Red Skins* before moving over to Universal's Imp and Victor brands to appear opposite Victor Potel and Jane Bernoudy in one-reelers like *Hired, Tired and Fired* (1915), *Some Heroes, Ain't He Grand, The Gasoline Habit,* and *When Slim Picked a Peach* (all 1916). She also worked in numerous other Universal comedies with Lyons & Moran, Carter DeHaven, Harry Depp, and Ralph McComas into 1918, but at the same time became busy in western and action shorts, which took over her career after a hit in the serial *The Lure of the Circus* (1918) with Eddie Polo. The 1920s saw her in action mode in items such as *The Night Attack* (1922), *In the Days of Daniel Boone* (1923), *The Riddle Rider* (1924), and *Sagebrush Lady* (1925), but she reached a nadir when she did a series of shorts for the independent Tenneck Pictures with Lightning the Dog. In an attempt to get out of the action film grind she began working under the name Greta Yoltz and in 1927 had some nice supporting roles in features like *Hot Heels* (1927) and *Beautiful But Dumb* (1928), but she retired in 1930 after marrying. Her sister Josie appeared in a few Triangle comedies such as *The Poor Fish* and *Flapjacks* (both 1918) but predominantly starred in westerns.

Sybil Seely (1900 – 1984) **See Chapter Eight**

Gertrude Selby (1896 – 1975) **See Chapter Four**

Clarine Seymour (1898 – 1920)
Brunette ingénue remembered for her films with D.W. Griffith, who started her career in comedy shorts. In 1916 she began as an extra at the Thanhouser Studio in New Rochelle, New York and worked her way up to parts in shorts such as *It Happened to Adele* and *Pots and Pans Peggie* (both 1917). She also appeared in the Astra serial *The Mystery of the Double Cross* (1917) which was distributed by Pathé. Not long after Hal Roach was in New York at the Pathé offices looking for a new leading lady for his Toto the clown series. He was shown the serial and hired Ms. Seymour. After Toto shorts such as *Cleopatsy, An Enemy of Soap,* and *Check Your Baggage* (all 1918), she was discharged from

Before she worked with D. W. Griffith on *True Heart Susie* (1919) and *The Idol Dancer* (1920) Clarine Seymour worked with Toto, and at Christie with Bobby Vernon in *Pearls and a Peach* (1918). Courtesy of Cole Johnson.

the Roach lot for refusing to do stunts (contrary to some sources she did not appear as Stan Laurel's leading lady in 1918's *Just Rambling Along* – that was Mildred Reardon). Filing a suit against Roach she was ultimately awarded $1,325 in damages. In the meantime she had begun appearing in Christie Comedies like *Three Hours Late* (1918) with Bobby Vernon, and between film appearances did sketches and dancing acts in vaudeville. Her fortunes soon changed as she came to the attention of director D.W. Griffith and became part of his company, appearing in *The Girl Who Stayed at Home*, *True Heart Susie*, and *Scarlet Days* (all 1919). Griffith then starred her in *The Idol Dancer* (1920), but while shooting his *Way Down East* (1920) she became ill and underwent surgery for intestinal problems. She did not recover and died at only twenty-one, with Mary Hay taking over her role in *Way Down East*.

Peggy Shaw (1905 - ?)
Pittsburg-born beauty, who was a Ziegfeld girl appearing in the producer's *Nine O'Clock Frolic* and *Midnight Frolic* before entering films for Fox in 1919. She appeared as support in dramatic features like *Forbidden Love* (1921) and *Does It Pay?* (1925), as well as comedies on the order of *In Hollywood with Potash and Perlmutter* (1924) and *Subway Sadie* (1926). After a number of *Famous Melody* shorts for producer James A. Fitzpatrick, such as *Songs of Ireland* (1925) and *Songs of Central Europe* (1926), she headlined in the comedy series *Carrie of the Chorus*, the only live-action comedies made by famous animators Max and Dave Fleischer. Her supporting cast included Flora Finch, Joe Burke, and a young Ray Bolger in titles such as *"Morning Judge, The Berth Mark, The Chicken Coop,* and *Busting the Show* (all 1926). Shaw finished the 1920s in westerns, *Hoof Marks* (1927) and *The Little Buckaroo* (1928) are a couple of titles, before leaving films after the Walter Lantz-starring Bray two-reeler *Barnyard Rivals* (1928).

Pearl Shepard (Pearl Ginsberg) (?)
Beauty contest winner, who became a leading lady for Bobby Burns and Walter Stull in their *Pokes and Jabs* comedies for Wizard and Vim. In 1916 she began working for Thanhouser Films in New Rochelle, New York, and after the company went out of business she became part of a series of one-reel *Three C Comedies* produced by the Commonwealth Comedy Company. Commonwealth had taken over the Thanhouser plant, and Ms. Shepard was teamed with Lou Marks and Oom Paul for outings such as *His Watery Waterloo* and *A Hash House Romance* (both 1917) which "feature the laugh inspiring personality of Marks, the piquant beauty of Miss Shepard and the exclusive facial contortions of Paul." From this series she made more shorts for Jester and a group of *Merrytime Comedies* for Arnold Pictures distributed by Reelcraft. Moving into features for dramas such as *The Echo of Youth* (1919) and comedies on the order of *Bullin' the Bullsheviki* (1919), she later married Egyptian Prince Mohammed Ali Ibrahim and in 1923 retired from the screen.

Jane Sherman (Elva Jane Sherman) (1901 – 1983)
Dark-haired beauty who started her career in a 1918 Mack Sennett bathing beauty contest. After a small role in Eric von Stroheim and Rupert Julian's *Merry-Go-Round* (1923) she appeared in a run of 1925 Hal Roach comedies such as *What Price Goofy?*, *Innocent Husbands*, and *Cuckoo Love*, plus played a dance hall girl in Chaplin's *The Gold Rush* (1925). After the Wally Wales western feature *Vanishing Hoofs* (1926) she eventually got out of show business and became a chiropractor.

Rose Shirley (Rose Winona Jones) (?)
Shirley was an ingénue at Jack White Comedies in the mid-1920s who appeared in one-reel Cameo Comedies such as *What's Up* (1925) with Cliff Bowes. In addition to being a first cousin of Buster Keaton (her mother was Joe Keaton's sister), she married comedian Wallace Lupino in 1928 and left films before the family moved to England in 1930.

Gertrude Short (1902 – 1968)
Short was a little and slightly plump actress who specialized in playing offbeat friends of the leading lady. Born in a theatrical family she began appearing on stage as a child and often played boys, as she did in the popular 1909 production *A Man's World* opposite Mary Mannering. The gender switch continued in her first films such as the 1914 *The Little Angel of Canyon Creek* where she played a Norwegian orphan named Olaf. By 1920 there was no doubt that Gertie was definitely a girl, and she played bubbly characters all through the 1920s such as in the series *The Telephone Girl* as Alberta Vaughn's sidekick, not to mention features like *Leap Year* (1922), *Beggar on Horseback* (1925), *Ladies of Leisure* (1926), and *Tillie the Toiler* (1927) with Marion Davies. Married to comedy director Scott (a.k.a. Percy) Pembroke, Gertie's roles became uncredited walk-ons in the sound era, and she left the screen during World War II to work for the Lockheed Corporation, remaining there until she retired in 1967.

Gertrude Short (right) as sidekick to Alberta Vaughn (left) in the *Telephone Girl* comedy *The Square Sex* (1924). Courtesy of Karel Caslavsky.

Martha Sleeper (1910 – 1983) **See Chapter Seven**

Snooky the Human-Zee. (?) **See Chapter Five**

Eve Southern (1898 – 1972)
Southern was a Texas-born brunette who had a sultry screen presence and began her film career under D. W. Griffith. After a small bit in *Intolerance* (1914) she became a regular ingénue in *Triangle Comedy* one reelers such as *A Matrimonial Accident*, *Her Donkey Love*, and *A Modern Sherlock* (all 1917). Much of her later work was in dramatic features, but she did turn up in the comedies *Nice People* (1922), *The Dangerous Blonde* (1924) with Laura La Plante, *The Naughty Duchess*, and *The Haunted House* (both 1928). Beside an appearance with Laurel and Hardy in their two-reeler *With Love and Hisses* (1927), she worked for Charlie Chaplin, in the never-released film he produced in 1927 *A Woman of the Sea* (*The Seagull*) which was directed by Josef von Sternberg and starred Edna Purviance (see Chapter Eight). Her career in sound films was cut short by a broken back she received in a car accident. She later worked as a retoucher in a studio photography department.

Juanita Sponsler (?)
Part of the ensemble in Kalem comedies who supported stars such as Ruth Roland, John E. Brennan, Marshall Neilan, Ethel Teare, and Ham & Bud. From 1912 to the demise of the studio in 1917 she appeared in all kinds of shorts such as *Paying the Board Bill* (1912), *Parcel Post Johnnie*, *The Rube and the Boob* (both 1913), *Cupid Backs the Winner* (1914), *Ham the Diver* (1916), and *Politics in Pumpkin Center* (1917), not to mention some episodes of the 1916 serial *The Hazards of Helen*.

Trade magazine portrait of Kalem ingénue Juanita Sponsler.

Kathryn Stanley (1897 – 1978)
A Mack Sennett beauty from 1925 to 1933 who appeared in a large number of shorts over those years such as *The Soapsuds Lady* (1925), *Smith's Picnic* (1926), *The Girl from Everywhere* (1927), *Run, Girl, Run* (1928), *Calling Hubby's Bluff* (1929), *Radio Kisses* (1930), and *Dream House* (1932). After Sennett closed up shop in 1933 Stanley did uncredited bits in films and became a stand-in, first working for actresses like Jane Wyatt and Valarie Hobson, before becoming Irene Dunne's regular stand-in.

Vera Steadman (1900 – 1966) **See Chapter Eight**

Agnes Steele (1881 – 1949)
Heavy-set, Australian-born character actress who was a supporting player in numerous features and shorts, turning up as Laurel & Hardy's exasperated landlady in *You're Darn Tootin'* (1928) and as the terrified cook in Charley Bower's *There It Is* (1928). She continued working in mostly uncredited bit roles until 1949.

Merta Sterling (1883 – 1944) **See Chapter Seven**

Charlotte Stevens (1902 – 1946)
Chicago-born dancer who won a 1921 Operator's Ball beauty contest in that city which led to a Christie Comedies contract as Bobby Vernon's new leading lady. For the Christie organization she appeared in *A Hickory Hick, Choose Your Weapons, In Dutch* (all 1922), *Second Childhood, Take Your Chance* (both 1923), and *Ride 'Em Cowboy* (1924). She then moved into features where she worked in many dramas and westerns, such as *Riders Up* (1924), *Flying Hoofs* (1925), *The Heart of a Coward* (1926), and *The Coward* (1927) until 1928.

Jessie Stevens (1869 – 1922)
Stevens was a heavy character actress who was an important part of the acting ensemble in Edison comedies. Born into a theatrical family she started acting as a child and appeared in dramas and comedies such as *Faust* and *Richard the Third*, in addition to companies like The Schiller Comic Opera Co. and the vaudeville sketch *Fall of 63*. She entered films in 1909 with Essanay, and also spent time with Selig before joining Edison in 1913. Besides playing ten-year old Andy Clark's mother in the *Andy* series, she spent her screen time with William Wadsworth, Arthur Housman, Dan Mason, Elsie MacLeod, and Barry O'Moore in the studio's comedies. She moved on to features for Edison, and then mostly worked for Vitagraph until her death in 1922.

Josephine Stevens (1897 – 1966)
Dark-haired leading lady in three of Roscoe Arbuckle's Comique Comedies who came from a prestigious Philadelphian theatrical lineage – her father having been Benjamin D. Stevens, a longtime general manager for Klaw & Erlanger, and her mother actress Helen Beresford. She began her own stage career at age seventeen in *The Argyle Case*, and soon followed with other productions such as *Daddy Long Legs* with Henry Miller and *Captain Kidd Jr*. Her screen debut came

Josephine Stevens with Luke and Roscoe Arbuckle in *The Butcher Boy* (1917).

in 1917 with *The Butcher Boy*, and she continued with Fatty in *The Rough House* and *His Wedding Night* (both 1917). After the feature *Oh, You Women!* (1919) she disappeared from the screen, but returned to the stage and appeared in shows like 1923's *Go Go*.

Anita Stewart (1895 – 1961)
Stewart was a Brooklyn-born brunette who, like many of her contemporaries, began her career at her neighborhood Vitagraph Studio. Starting at age sixteen in 1911, during her

apprenticeship with the "Big V" she appeared in numerous comedies, which included *Billy's Pipe Dream* (1912), *Love Laughs at Locksmiths; or Love Finds a Way, Why Am I Here?* (both 1913), *Diana's Dress Reform* (1914) and *The Right Girl* (1915). Often teamed with actor Earle Williams in 1916 the studio moved her into features and she soon became a popular dramatic star with her own production company headed by Louis B. Mayer. *Virtuous Wives* (1918) was her first big hit, and continued on with titles like *In Old Kentucky* (1919), *Sowing the Wind* (1921) and *The Prince of Pilsen* (1926) until 1928. Having done well with her productions she retired as one of the wealthiest women in Hollywood.

Edith Storey (1892 – 1967)
Leading lady for Vitagraph, who had been a child actress on stage in productions of *The Little Princess*, *Mrs. Wiggs of the Cabbage Patch*, and *Rebecca of Sunnybrook Farm*. She joined Vitagraph in 1908, and outside of a brief stint with the American Melies company stayed with the "Big V" through 1917. Appearing in all types of pictures, she was very good in comedy, and while a leading lady she was a talented character actress. Outstanding in the feature *A Florida Enchantment* (1914), where she plays a woman who eats a magic seed that turns her into a man, she also did a re-occurring character named Jane, an awkward girl with freckles, pig-tails, and sometimes a missing tooth, that was more than a little based on Sis Hopkins played by Rose Melville (see Chapter Three). Very funny in the surviving *Jane's Bashful Hero* (1916), Jane also turned up in *Queen for an Hour*, *Jane Was Worth It* (both 1915), and *Jane's Husband* (1916). Other of Ms. Storey's many comedies include *An Aeroplane Elopement* (1911), *The Troublesome Step-Daughters*, *The Lovesick Maidens of Cuddleton* (both 1912), *A Regiment of Two*, and *Peggy's Burglar* (both 1913). In 1916 she moved into features for Vitagraph – paired with Antonio Moreno in titles like *The Shop Girl* (1916), *Captain of the Gray Horses*, and *Aladdin from Broadway* (both 1917), in addition to the serial *The Scarlet Runner* (1916). Finishing out her career in dramatic features for Metro and Hayworth such as *The Silent Woman* (1918), *As the Sun Went Down* (1919), *Moon Madness* (1920), and *The Greater Profit* (1921), she retired and lived the rest of her life in Long Island, New York.

Versatile actress Edith Storey in a Vitagraph photo postcard. Author's collection.

Dixie Stuart (1893 - ?)
Character comedienne from the stage who appeared in musical comedy, supported Elfie Fay in *The Belle of Avenue A*, and understudied Rose Melville for *Sis Hopkins*. In 1914 she made her film debut at Essanay where she supported the likes of Wallace Beery and Ruth

Stonehouse. Moving to the American Film Manufacturing Company she was busy in shorts such as *Uncle Heck, By Heck!* (1915), *Cooking His Goose, Cupid at Cohen's* and *Ima Knute Gets a Bite* (all 1916), and until 1916 was part of their comedy ensemble alongside John Steppling, Carol Holloway, Beatrice Van, and Orral Humphrey.

Anna Styers (Amma Styers) (?)
Brunette beauty who became a Jack White starlet in 1925 and spent the next few years appearing in Cameo, Mermaid, and Ideal comedies such as *Scratching Through* (1926) and *Sure Cure* (1927).

Janet Miller Sully (1866 - 1946)
Supporting actress, who began her stage career in 1885 and appeared in stock, vaudeville, and musical comedy, as well as shows such as *H.M.S. Pinafore* and *Human Hearts*, as a solo or with her husband W.J. Sully. She entered films in 1915 for producer David Horsley as support to comic George Ovey, first in MinA Comedies and then in Cub Comedies like *Jerry to the Rescue* (1915) and *Jerry's Big Haul* (1916). Today she's best known for her work supporting Charlie Chaplin in his Mutual comedies such as *Easy Street* (1917). Her later film work was intermittent, but she did support Hank Mann in his two-reel Sava Comedy *The Gold Brush* (1926).

Gloria Swanson and Bobby Vernon keep the train in repair in *Teddy at the Throttle* (1917).

Gloria Swanson (1899 – 1983)
Swanson was one of great divas of the silent screen, but got her start in slapstick comedies. Beginning her career as a teenager at the Chicago Essanay Studio, where she had small parts in shorts such as Charlie Chaplin's *His New Job*, *The Fable of Elvira and Farina*

and the Meal Ticket, and *Sweedie Goes to College* (all 1915) with her first husband Wallace Beery (a real-life comedy team if there ever was one). Swanson and Beery went west and soon were working for Mack Sennett, where Gloria was teamed with little Bobby Vernon for a series of romantic comedies that included *The Danger Girl, Haystacks and Steeples* (both 1916) and the famous *Teddy at the Throttle* (1917). The plots of their films were about young lovers embroiled in some kind of misunderstanding, often caused by vamps or problems with parents who didn't approve of their match. According to Swanson, when she found out that Mack Sennett had plans to make her the next Mabel Normand she refused, leaving Keystone and soon hooking up with Cecile B. DeMille for sly marital comedies on the order of *Male and Female* (1919), *Why Change Your Wife* (1920), and *Affairs of Anatol* (1921). Settling into more dramatic fare, she still occasionally returned to comedy for features like *Manhandled* (1924), *Stage Struck* (1925), and *Fine Manners* (1926).

Marion Swayne (1891 – 1973)
Leading lady for the Solax Company, who appeared in numerous comedies directed by Alice Guy Blache such as *Husbands Wanted* (1911), *Auto Suggestion* (1912), *A House Divided*, and *Matrimony's Speed Limit* (both 1913). Her leading men included Billy Quirk, Darwin Karr, and Fraunie Fraunholz. After Solax she spent her time in dramatic shorts and features until 1924.

Constance Talmadge (1898 – 1973) **See Chapter Five**

Norma Talmadge (1894 – 1957)
One of the great dramatic actresses of the silent screen, she started her career at age fourteen as a photographer's model for illustrated slides. Prodded along by an ambitious mother the next step was movies at the Vitagraph Studio – just a trolley ride from the family's Brooklyn home. Becoming part of the regular company in 1910, she was natural and charming in many comedies such as *The Lovesick Maidens of Cuddleton* (1912), *A Lady and her Maid* (1913), *Father's Hatband* (1913), and *The Peacemaker* (1914). As her career went on she found fame in drama and left the comedy to her sister Constance, but did occasionally return to lighter fare in *The Social Secretary* (1916) and *Kiki* (1926). After great successes like *Smilin' Through* (1922), *The Lady* (1925), and *Camille* (1926) she made only two talking pictures before retiring in 1930.

A young Norma Talmadge during her days at the Vitagraph Studio. Author's collection.

Eva Tanguay (1878 – 1947)
Eccentric star of vaudeville who was popular for her crazy antics and the song *I Don't Care*. Born in Marbleton, Canada, she appeared on stage as a child touring as the lead in *Little Lord Fauntleroy*. By 1903 she was starring in her own company and remained a star for the next twenty-five years. In 1916 she set up Eva Tanguay Films and made two pictures that were shot in Fort Lee, New Jersey – *Energetic Eva* (1916) and *The Wild Girl* (1917). Her career declined with the end of vaudeville, and she lived a reclusive life in her Hollywood home until her death in 1947.

Emma Tansey (1884 – 1942)
Former stage actress who specialized in sweet, little old ladies, and had a run playing Charley Chase's mother in a string of his early Roach one-reelers such as *Young Oldfield*, *The Fraidy Cat*, *Jeffries Jr.* and *A Ten-Minute Egg* (all 1924). In real-life she was the mother of two of the worst directors and performers involved in silent comedy – Robert and Sherry Tansey. Sound films found her continuing to perform, and her most memorable role is as the old lady that's "not able to wait much longer" in W.C. Field's *The Pharmacist* (1933). She worked in small bits up to 1941.

Rose Tapely (1881 – 1956)
A stage veteran and dramatic actress who joined the Vitagraph Company in 1912 and appeared in dramas and comedies such as *Ida's Christmas* (1912), *He Fell in Love with His Mother-in-Law* (1913), and *Nocturne in E-Flat* (1914). In 1915 she became a regular in the studio's *Jarr Family* comedy series playing Mrs. Jarr opposite star and director Harry Davenport. Based on stories by Roy McCardell, eighteen episodes were made which included *The Jarr Family Discovers Harlem*, *Mrs. Jarr and the Beauty Treatment*, and *Mr. Jarr and the Dachshund*. After the *Jarr* series she continued working for Vitagraph until 1916, and spent much of her time as a reformer, stumping for "clean pictures" and protecting young women from the lure of the movies. She also appeared in small parts in pictures such as *The Pony Express* (1925) and *It* (1927) into the 1930s.

Elsie Tarron (1903 – 1990)
British-born beauty who became a Mack Sennett girl in 1923 with shorts such as *Down to the Sea in Shoes* (1923) and *The Half-Back of Notre Dame* (1924). She worked regularly at Sennett until 1926 when she moved over to Universal's Bluebird Comedies where she was leading lady to Charles Puffy and Arthur Lake for numerous one-reelers like *Tight Cargo*, *Don't Be a Dummy*, *Not Guilty* (all 1926), *High and Dizzy*, *Meet the Husband*, and *The Party Man* (all 1927). After her run at Universal she returned to the Sennett fold and had larger roles in *Taxi Beauties* (1928) and *Caught in a Taxi* (1929), in addition to appearing in action and western features such as *Cyclone of the Range* and *Sky-High Saunders* (both 1927). Leaving films with the arrival of sound she married comic Andy Clyde in

1932. When Clyde passed away in 1967 she wed another Sennett veteran, George Gray, who died just a few months later, and Tarron shared an apartment with another former co-worker, Ruth Hiatt, before passing away at age eighty-seven.

Ruth Taylor (1908 – 1984)
Petite blonde, born in Grand Rapids, Michigan, who entered the theatre with the Red Lantern Stock Players. She began working in films as an extra at Universal in 1924 and by the next year she was an ingénue at the Mack Sennett Studio appearing in two-reelers with Billy Bevan and Ben Turpin such as *Butter Fingers*, *A Rainy Knight*, *The Window Dummy* (all 1925), *A Yankee Doodle Duke*, *Hesitating Horses*, *A Blonde's Revenge* (all 1926), *Broke in China*, *The College Kiddo*, and *For Sale, a Bungalow* (all 1927). In 1928 she was named a WAMPAS Baby Star, and after being spotted by Anita Loos dancing at the Cocoanut Grove, she starred as Lorelei Lee in Paramount's version of Loo's book *Gentlemen Prefer Blondes* (1928). This led to more films for Paramount like *College Coquette* and *This Thing Called Love* (both 1929) but she retired from the screen when she married New York stockbroker Paul Zuckerman in 1930. Later their son went by his first and middle name of Buck Henry and became a screenwriter famous for *The Graduate* (1967), *What's Up Doc?* (1973), and *Heaven Can Wait* (1978).

Ruth Taylor, Mack Sennett star and mother of Buck Henry. Author's collection.

Lyle Tayo (1889 – 1971)
Tayo was a heavy-set actress and one of the pillars of the Hal Roach stock company, regularly working at the studio from the early 1920s to the early 1930s. Born in Kansas, she appeared on stage in musical shows such as *The Girl of My Dreams* (1911) on Broadway and toured in others. Starting in films around 1921 she found a ready home on the Roach lot where she supported the likes of Harold Lloyd, Our Gang, Will Rogers, Jimmy Finlayson, Laurel & Hardy, and Charley Chase in classics such as *Jus Passin' Through* (1923), *Ask Grandma*, *His Wooden Wedding* (both 1925), *Don't Tell Everything* (1927), *Two Tars* (1928), *Below Zero* (1930), and *Readin' and Writin'* (1932). Cast frequently as society ladies, flirty wives, or one of the Our Gang kid's mothers, although synonymous with Roach comedies she turned up in shorts for other units like Christie, Paramount, and Universal. These appearances include *The Little Pest*, *Red Suspenders*, *No Publicity* (all 1927), *Behind the Counter*, *Lay on McDuff* (both 1928), and *Single Bliss* (1929), not to mention the feature *Paths to Paradise* (1925), where she brought her expertise in the service of Neely Edwards, Slim Summerville, Edward Everett Horton, Jack Duffy, and Raymond Griffith. She left films for family life in the early 1930s.

Betty Teare (?)
Sister of Ethel Teare, with whom she had a pre-movie vaudeville act, and both started their film careers together at Kalem in 1914. Betty played the young ingénue on her own in shorts like *Percy Pumpernickel, Soubrette* (1914), in addition to comedies on the order of *For the Love of Mike* (1914) and *Ham and the Experiment* (1915) with her sister and comic John E. Brennan, but left the screen in 1915.

Ethel Teare (1894 – 1959) **See Chapter Three**

Barbara Tennant (1892 – 1982)
Tennant was a British-born actress who began her career as a dancer on the English stage and soon began appearing in plays such as *Charley's Aunt* and *Romeo and Juliet*. Her acting work took her to touring Canada and eventually New York. In 1912 she ran into a friend who was acting in pictures, and she visited the Éclair American Studio in Fort Lee, New Jersey and was soon an integral part of their ensemble. From 1912 through 1914 she appeared in mostly dramatic shorts, although there were occasional comedies such as *The Actress Pulls the String* (1912), and *Tango Versus Poker* (1914). By 1914 she was starring in East-Coast made features such as *When Broadway was a Trail* (1914), *M'liss* (1915), and *The Closed Road* (1916) for studios like World, Paragon, and Shubert, but by the early 1920s she moved to Hollywood to work in pictures such as *Circus Days* (1923) and *Captain January* (1924). In 1926 she became a regular in Mack Sennett comedies appearing frequently with Billy Bevan as suspicious wives and snarling relatives in titles like *Fight Night* (1925), *Hubby's Quiet Little Game*, *The Divorce Dodger* (both 1926) and *Motor Boat Mammas* (1928). After her stint with Sennett she made a few uncredited appearances in sound films until 1931.

Gladys Tennyson (1894 – 1983)
Tennyson was a dark-haired, leading lady in Universal comedies who did time in their L-Ko, Nestor, and Victor brands. One of her earliest films is the Billie Ritchie two-reeler *Cold Hearts and Hot Flames* (1916), and she continued working with the likes of Max Asher, David Morris, and Rube Miller in shorts such as *In the Clutches of Milk*, *The Magic Jazz-Bo* (both 1917), *The Great Sea Scandal*, and *Maimed in the Hospital* (both 1918). She also became a regular in the one-reelers of Eddie Lyons and Lee Moran, supporting them in *The Tail of a Cat*, *The Guilty Egg*, *The One Horse Show*, *Berth Control*, *Hearts and Let Us*, and *Why Worry!* (all 1918). In addition to a couple of features like *Broadway Love* (1918), *Broadway After Dark*, and *The Last Man on Earth* (both 1924) she spent the 1920s as a Sennett Bathing Girl in two-reelers like *Down to the Sea in Shoes* (1923), *Picking Peaches*, *Little Robinson Corkscrew* (both 1924), and *Breaking the Ice* (1925).

Eva Thatcher (1862 – 1942) **See Chapter Seven**

Rosemary Theby (1892 – 1973)
Theby was a brunette beauty who co-starred in a long series of sophisticated domestic comedies with actor/director Harry Myers. Although trained for the stage Ms. Theby never appeared there professionally. Instead a friend took her to the Vitagraph Studio, where she worked from 1910 to 1913 in shorts such as *The Hand Bag* (1912) and *Billy's Baby* (1913), and from there appeared at the Reliance Film Co. In 1914 she and Myers became a team at Lubin in one and two-reel comedies. The couple moved over to Universal's Victor brand to continue their shorts, then jumped around quite a bit, going to Vim in 1916, then back to Universal and to Pathé in 1917. Sadly most of their films are impossible to see, but this quote from a 1917 exhibitor ad sums up their series nicely: "Refined comedy of a high order – the Myers-Theby Comedies. The humorous adventures of a newlywed couple are shown in each release. All who intend to be, are, have been or don't want to be married will enjoy them." Eventually the pair married but dissolved their screen partnership. They did both appear in *A Connecticut Yankee in King Arthur's Court* (1921), and Ms. Theby was busy as a supporting player in features like *The Eternal Flame* (1922), *Tea: With a Kick* (1923), *So Big* (1924), and *The Peacock Fan* (1929). Her career waned in sound, with her best-known appearance as W.C. Field's wife in *The Fatal Glass of Beer* (1933). She was working as an extra when Harry Myers died in 1938. After *One Million B.C.* (1940) she remarried and left Hollywood.

A 1913 portrait of Rosemary Theby during her stint at Vitagraph or Reliance. Author's collection.

Olive Thomas (1894 – 1920) **See Chapter Four**

Duane Thompson (Violet Joy) (1903 – 1970)
Pretty brunette who started her career in 1921 as Violet Joy teamed with Billy Fletcher (a.k.a. Billy Bletcher) in a series of *Spotlight Comedies* for the Arrow Company. From there, still as Joy, she became Vernon Dent's leading lady in his *Folly Comedies* for the Pacific Film Company, and then changed her name to Duane Thompson. As that, she appeared in Christie Comedies with Bobby Vernon and Walter Hiers, in addition to shorts with Sid Smith, Jimmie Adams, and Edward Everett Horton. After some late 1920s features for Universal and Tiffany, she left films but became popular on radio. Besides soap operas and commercials, she was the telephone operator who opened the hit show

Formal portrait of Duane Thompson. Author's collection.

Hollywood Hotel from 1934 to 1938. Her last movie was Warner Brother's 1937 film version of *Hollywood Hotel*, where she repeated her radio character.

Mollie Thompson (1878 – 1928)
Plump character actress who was a regular in Hal Roach shorts, specializing in mothers-in-law or society women. Working with everyone from Harold Lloyd to Snub Pollard to Paul Parrott, one of her most memorable roles was in the premiere *Our Gang* short *One Terrible Day* (1922) where she was the wealthy lady who brings the Gang to her country home for the fresh air and lives to regret it. She was also the casting director for the Roach Studio, a position she held at her death in 1928.

Mary Thurman (185 – 1925) **See Chapter Eight**

Fay Tincher (1884 – 1983) **See Chapter Six**

Lydia Yeamans Titus (1857 – 1929)
Titus was a second generation vaudeville performer, born in Australia, who began her solo stage career at eighteen working for impresario Tony Pastor. She later toured around the world with Frederick Titus, her accompanist, manager, and husband, and some of her best known songs included *Sally in Our Alley, I May,* and *Peggy Cline*. After making her film debut in 1915 she worked for Universal, Morosco, and Metro in numerous shorts and features, and by the 1920s she had the market cornered on not-so-sweet little old ladies in features such as *The Married Flapper* (1922), *The Rag Man* (1925), and *Irene* (1926), in addition to shorts like *Visitor's Welcome* (1928) with Johnny Arthur, and Charles Puffy's *The Prince and the Papa* (1928). She worked right up to her death, with her last film *Lummox* (1930) released posthumously.

Thelma Todd (1906 – 1935)
A popular star of the late twenties and early thirties, who's remembered today as much for her early and unsolved death as she is for her talent and beauty. Born in Lawrence, Massachusetts, while in college she was part of several beauty contests, and in 1925 was "Miss Massachusetts" in the Miss America pageant. Spotted by movie talent scouts she began appearing in shorts, some at the Hal Roach Studio, but in 1926 she was signed by Paramount and became part of their stable of future stars. At first an all-purpose leading lady in features such as *Nevada, Rubber Heels, The Gay Defender* (all 1927), and *The Noose* (1928), she gravitated to comedy support in *Vamping Venus, The Haunted House, Naughty Boy* (all 1928), and *Seven Footprints to Satan* (1929). After making her sound debut in the Roach Studio's first talkies *Unaccustomed As We Are*, and *Hurdy Gurdy* (both 1929) she was very busy on the lot working with Charley Chase, and then in her own starring series – first with Zasu Pitts and then Patsy Kelly – that chronicled the misadventures of two working girls in the depression era 1930s. Roach also loaned her out for all kinds of features with some of the more famous being *Monkey Business* (1931) and *Horse Feathers* (1932) with the Marx Brothers, *Hips, Hips Hooray*, and *Cockeyed*

Cavaliers (both 1934) opposite Wheeler & Woolsey, plus *Broadminded* (1931), *Speak Easily* (1932), and *Counsellor at Law* (1933). She was in the middle of shooting Laurel & Hardy's *The Bohemian Girl* (1936) when she was found dead in her Los Angeles garage of carbon monoxide poisoning. One of the great unsolved Hollywood deaths, she was only twenty-nine years old.

Thelma Todd and Charlie Murray cut a rug in *Vamping Venus* (1928). Courtesy of Robert Arkus.

Kate Toncray (1880 – 1927)
Supporting character actress, who after a varied stage career during which she worked for Nat Goodwin, Charles Frohman, David Belasco, and the Shuberts became part of the D.W. Griffith Company at Biograph, and moved along with the master to Reliance/Majestic and his own Fine Arts Company. Besides the Griffith films she appeared in many of the comedies directed by Mack Sennett, Del Henderson, and Edward Dillon such as *Tomboy Bessie* (1912), *Cinderella and the Boob* (1913), *Scenting a Terrible Crime* (1913), and continued supporting Fay Tincher in *Love's Getaway*, *A Calico Vampire*, and *The Lady Drummer* (all 1916). Her features include Douglas Fairbanks' *The Lamb* (1915), *Casey at the Bat* (1916), *Peppy Polly* (1919), and *Bobbed Hair* (1925).

Biograph portrait of character actress Kate Toncray. Author's collection.

Anna Townsend (1844 – 1923)
Character actress who made a memorable impression at age seventy-seven when she played Harold Lloyd's grandmother in his 1922 feature *Grandma's Boy*. After a long stage career she retired to Los Angeles, but the inactivity saw her ending up in films in

the early teens. She worked for Selig in shorts such as *The Hoyden's Awakening* (1913), and Tom Mix's western comedy *The Real Thing in Cowboys* (1914), and appeared in some John Ford western features like *A Marked Man* (1917) and *Three Mounted Men* (1918). After her success in *Grandma's Boy* her other movies included *Daddy* (1923) with Jackie Coogan, Harold Lloyd's *Dr. Jack* (1922) and *Safety Last!* (1923), before she passed away in September 1923.

Hazel Tranchell (1895 – 1980)
Short and tubby actress who lived near the Balboa Studio and appeared in numerous comedies made there in 1919 to 1921 for Comedyart and Special Pictures such as *An Uneven Match* (1920). She also supported Milburn Moranti, worked at the Romayne Studio with Monty Banks, told the Long Beach *Independent* in 1960 that "They'd hook me up in a horse harness connected to some piano wire and toss me over the nearest cliff," in reference to her silent comedy days, and lived to be ninety-five.

Martha Trick (?)
Tall and scrawny character actress who played maiden aunts and ugly wives in 1916 and 1917 Mack Sennett's Keystone shorts released through Triangle, and after he left the company she stayed on for comedies made by Triangle. Her films include *A Tugboat Romeo*, *Black Eyes and Blue* (both 1916), *A Royal Rogue*, *Dangers of a Bride*, and *All at Sea* (all 1917).

Little Hazel Tranchell with her gigantic bridegroom Ingram "Seven Foot" Pickett in *An Uneven Match* (1920). Courtesy of Sam Gill.

Maude Truax (1884 – 1939)
Truax was a rotund character actress who spent twenty-six years on the stage in stock and musical comedy. After making a few early film appearances for Biograph, her screen career really began in the 1920s with some appearances in Christie Comedies such as

Choose Your Weapons (1922) and *Shore Shy* (1926). Besides turning up in features like *Up in Mabel's Room* (1926) and *Ten Modern Commandments* (1927), she was a regular in Pathé's "Smitty Comedies," where she played the title character's mother in titles such as *No Picnic, Camping Out, No Children* (all 1928), *Puckered Success*, and *Uncle's Visit* (both 1929). In the sound era she continued with character bits in the features *Symphony of Six Million* (1932), *The Captain Hates the Sea* (1934), and *Dante's Inferno* (1935), plus shorts like *Fish Feathers, Jitters the Butler* (both 1932), and *Love and Hisses* (1934 as Fanny Bender), until 1935.

Bess True (1899 – 1947)
Vaudeville dancer who started in movie around 1918, and was a leading lady for comic Billy West in some of his independent comedies for Arrow release such as *The Nervous Reporter* and *Not Wanted* (both 1924). Her other films included the features *Heartbound* (1925) and *Sailor's Wives* (9128), plus the Weiss Brother's shorts *Movie Mania* and *Oh, Taxi* (both 1928).

Doreen Turtner (1918 -)
Turner was a child actress who made her film debut in 1920 at age two and a half. In addition to features such as *Through the Backdoor* (1921), *Rosita* (1923), and *The Rose of Paris* (1924), she was the regular female star of the 1921 – 1922 *Campbell Comedies*, a series produced and directed by William S. Campbell about kids and their animal friends. In 1925 she became Mary Jane in Century Comedies

Doreen Turner as Mary Jane with Arthur Trimble and Pete the pup in one of Universal's *Buster Brown Comedies*. Courtesy of Robert Arkus.

Buster Brown Comedies, opposite Arthur Trimble as Buster and Pete the pup as Tige. After numerous entries such as *Educating Buster* (1925), *Buster's Girl Friend* (1926), and *Buster's Frame-Up* (1927) she left the series and movies in early 1929.

Florence Turner (1885 – 1946) **See Chapter One**

Mabel Trunnelle (1879 – 1981)
Actress, born in Dwight, Illinois, who spent her early years on stage touring in stock in New Orleans, Syracuse, and Philadelphia in shows like *Polly of the Circus*. While touring she met and married fellow stage actor Herbert Prior and the pair entered films in 1909. At first working at Biograph, they quickly settled in at Edison and did a wide variety of films including the comedies *How Willie Raised Tobacco, Mary's Masquerade, Three of a*

Kind, and *Keeping Mabel Home* (all 1911). By 1912 they were headlining for the Majestic Company and made a year of mostly comedies such as *Spare the Rod, Petticoat Perfidy, The Unwilling Bigamist Buncoed*, and *The New Butler* (all 1912). After rejoining Edison in 1913 Trunnelle mostly appeared in dramas but still did occasional comedies on the order of *Jones Goes Shopping, Othello in Jonesville* (both 1913), *The Girl in the Middy*, and *The Lovely Senorita* (both 1915). Having jumped to Edison features with items like *Eugene Aram* (1915), *A Message to Garcia* (1916), and *Where Love Is* (1917), she finished her career with *Singed Wings* (1922) and *The Love Trap* (1923).

Irene Tyner (Irene Tiver) (1898 – 1950)
Blonde ingénue who spent two years working for the Rolin Film Company where she appeared in late Lonesome Luke and early "glass character" comedies of Harold Lloyd. Titles include *Lonesome Luke on Tin Can Alley, Lonesome Luke Loses Patients, The Lamb* (all 1917), *Hey There*, and *Look Pleasant, Please* (both 1918). Became a Sennett bathing girl in the early 1920s as Irene Tiver.

Irene Tyner, ingénue at the fledgling Hal Roach Studio and later Mack Sennett girl. Author's collection.

Beatrice Van (1890 – 1983) **See Chapter Six**

Polly Van (Polly Bailey) (1882 – 1952)
Plain supporting character who was a child performer and dancer in vaudeville before entering movies in the teens for Biograph, Universal, and Metro, where she worked with Francis X. Bushman and Beverly Bayne. In 1917 she joined the ensemble of Billy West's King Bee comedies and supported the comic alongside Oliver Hardy, Ethel Burton, Leo White, and Budd Ross in *Back Stage, The Hero, The Millionaire*, and *The Goat* (all 1917). Afterwards she only appeared sporadically in pictures like *Wedding Bells* (1921) with Constance Talmadge and *Tearin' Loose* (1925), but in the mid-1930s she returned to do countless uncredited character bits until her death in 1952.

Virginia Vance (1902 – 1942)
Pretty blonde who entered films in 1922 supporting Jimmie Adams and then Cliff Bowes in a huge

Virginia Vance does her best to support Al St John from the onslaught of Otto Fries and Eva Thatcher in *Hold Your Hat* (1926). Courtesy of Sam Gill.

amount of Jack White produced Cameo Comedies. In 1925, she graduated to two-reelers where she was leading lady to Al St John, Lupino Lane, Lloyd Hamilton, and Johnny Arthur in shorts like *Fair Warning* (1925), *The Fighting Dude* (1925), *Here Comes Charlie* (1926), and *My Stars* (1926). After a few features and changing allegiance to appear in Mack Sennett's late 1920s *Dan the Taxi Man* series opposite Jack Cooper, she married actor Bryant Washburn and left the screen in 1929.

Elinor Vanderveer (1887 – 1976) **See Chapter Seven**

Vanity Fair Girls
A bevy of beauties which was featured with comedian Eddie Boland in a series of 1920 – 1921 Hal Roach one-reelers like *Alias Aladdin* (1920) and *Prince Pistachio* (1921). The group consisted of Ethel Broadhurst, Jean Hope, Norma Nichols, Del Lorice, Lilymae Wilkinson, Nina Trask, Georgia Davy, and Julie Leonard. Broadhurst and Hope (who also married Eddie Boland) later alternated as Boland's leading lady, with Broadhurst going on to do a number of shorts with Paul Parrott. Del Lorice later went to Educational and appeared with Lloyd Hamilton, plus Julie Leonard worked with Stan Laurel and married Norman Taurog.

Gladys Varden (Gladys Roach) (1895 – 1964)
Varden was the sister of comedian Bert Roach, and became a regular ingénue in L-Ko Comedies, first as Gladys Roach, before changing her surname to Varden. She spent most of her time at L-Ko appearing opposite Dan Russell or her brother in shorts such as *Little Bo-Peep*, *A Surf Scandal*, and *Props, Drops, and Flops* (all 1917). After a few early 1920s shorts with boxer Jack Dempsey, she appeared in sporadic uncredited bits through the early 1960s.

Alberta Vaughn (1904 – 1992) **See Chapter Five**

Lupe Velez (1908 – 1944) **See Chapter Eight**

Dorothy Vernon (1875 – 1970) **See Chapter Seven**

Florence Vidor (1895 – 1977)
Memorable screen beauty who spent the early part of her career in drama, but in the late 1920s became the leading lady of choice for sophisticated comedy directors on the order of Ernst Lubitsch, Mal St Clair, and Harry d'Abbadie d'Arrast. Born Florence Arto in Houston, Texas, she began her film career thanks to her first husband King Vidor, who was making industrial films in Huston. After their 1915 marriage the pair settled in California where King became a scenarist and Florence landed small roles with the

Vitagraph Company. She soon moved to bigger roles at Fox and Paramount in features such as *A Tale of Two Cities* (1917) and *Old Wives for New* (1919), supported star Sessue Hayakawa in seven pictures, and even appeared with drag artist Julian Eltinge in his comedies *The Countess Charming* (1917) and *The Widow's Might* (1918).

In 1919 King Vidor set up his own production company and Florence had good roles in productions like *Poor Relations* (1919) and *The Jack-Knife Man* (1920) and moved on to stardom in mainstream Hollywood features such as *Hail the Woman* (1921), *Alice Adams*, and *Main Street* (both 1923). 1924 saw her as the lead in Lubitsch's hit farce *The Marriage Circle*, which put her in demand for other frothy concoctions like *Are Parents People?* (1925), *The Grand Duchess and the Waiter*, *The Popular Sin* (both 1926), *The World at her Feet* (1927), and *The Magnificent Flirt* (1928). The peak of her career was 1928's *The Patriot* opposite Emil Jannings, which was followed by her only talkie *Chinatown Nights* (1929). Said to have had her voice dubbed by another actress, and having recently married famous violinist Jascha Heifetz, she retired from the screen.

Lillian Walker (1887 – 1975) **See Chapter Four**

"Boots" Wall (Margaret Wall) (?)
Wall had been a stage actress and was the wife of actor David V. Wall. After early film work for Edison, Vitagraph, and Pathé, the pair joined the Powers Company in 1911, and by 1912 Dave Wall was in charge of his own comedy unit with his wife playing the female lead in shorts such as the surviving *Eph's Dream* (1913). "Boots" Wall later supported Mary Pickford in *Caprice* (1913) and played Topsy in World Film's 1914 version of *Uncle Tom's Cabin*.

May Wallace (May Maddox) (1877 – 1938)
Vaudeville veteran who hit films in the late teens and worked with Mr. & Mrs. Carter De Haven in shorts such as *My Lady Friends* (1921) and *Private – Keep Off* (1923). After playing in support in features like *Forsaking All Others* (1922), *Gimme* (1923), and Tom Mix's *Oh, You Tony* (1924), she took up residence on the Hal Roach lot in the late 1920s supporting Charley Chase and Our Gang in titles on the order of *The Lighter That Failed* (1927), *Limousine Love*, and *School Begins* (both 1928). She continued to work at the studio all through the 1930s until her death while filming *Zenobia* (released in 1939).

May Wallace (left) and Edna Marion (right) in the Hal Roach two-reeler *Aching Youth* (1928). Courtesy of EYE Filmmuseum, Netherlands.

Jane Waller (?)
Waller was a blonde comedienne who was the second lead in many shorts made by Al Christie for Nestor and his own company. Her film career began right out of high school when she joined Del Henderson's comedy company at Biograph. After several months there she moved over to Balboa and appeared in *His New Job* and *The Wooing of Sal* (both 1914) and others directed by Charles Hayden. Following the Rolfe Company feature *My Best Girl* (1915) with Max Figman she joined the comedy ensemble at Nestor and specialized in the second female lead in shorts like *Kids and Corsets*, *Almost a Knockout*, *When Three is a Crowd* (all 1915), *When the Losers Won*, and *Double Crossing the Dean* (both 1916). When Al Christie left Nestor and set up his own company Waller went along with him and continued in Christie and Cub shorts such as *Seminary Scandal*, *That Doggone Baby* (both 1916), *A Gay Deceiver*, and *Bride and Gloom* (both 1917) before leaving films.

Alice Ward (1891 – 1973)
Mack Sennett regular, who generally played suspicious wives or neighbors, with her best role being Harry Langdon's domineering wife in *Saturday Afternoon* (1926). She also henpecked Billy Bevan in *Hubby's Latest Alibi* (1928), *Pink Pajamas*, and *Button My Back* (both 1929), in addition to appearing in *Smith's Farm Days* and *The Campus Vamp* (both 1928). She continued in Sennett talkies such as *Half Holiday* (1931) and *Courting Trouble* (1932), plus features like *Skyline* (1931) and *Crossroads* (1942) before her career ended in the 1940s.

Carrie C. Ward (Carrie Clarke Ward) (1862 – 1926)
Short and round supporting player whose pop-eyes gave her a strong resemblance to a Pekingese. Her long stage career had begun with Helena Modjeska, and she traveled all over the country with stock and rep companies where she was known for Irish character parts. Married to director Sedley Brown, she entered films in 1911 for Edison and moved on to Majestic, Apollo, and Kalem where she specialized in irascible landladies and busybodies. She even supported Charlie Chaplin in some of his 1915 Essanay comedies such as *The Bank* and *A Night in the Show*, before branching out into features on the order of *Daddy-Long-Legs* (1919), *Miss Lulu Bett* (1921), and *The Eagle* (1925). She kept busy right up to her death in 1926.

Carrie Clark Ward (right) does some alterations in *Rose of the World* (1925). Courtesy of Bruce Calvert.

Lucille Ward (1880 – 1952)
Following a fifteen year stage career that included vaudeville, musical comedy, stock, and taking over the lead role in *Tillie's Nightmare* after Marie Dressler, this heavy-set character actress made her film debut in 1912 and worked at Imp, supported Peter Lang at Lubin in entries like *Auntie's Affinity* (1913), not to mention Ford Sterling at Sterling Pictures in *Snookie's Flirtation* (1914) and others. After finding a regular berth at Keystone and American, in *Beauty Comedies* such as *Art and Arthur* (1916), she spent the next thirty years doing all kind of bits and occasional nice parts in features like *Oh, Doctor!* (1925), and shorts until 1944.

Marion Warner (?)
Warner was an actress who began her career with the New York Motion Picture Corporation in 1912. By 1915 she had joined the company at Selig, where she appeared in comedies such as *The Strength of a Samson* and *Hartwey Merwin's Adventure* (both 1915), as well as many dramas like *Lonely Lovers* (1915) and *The Grinning Skull* (1916). Leaving Selig in 1917 she branched out into features and supported Baby Marie Osborne, playing her mother, in lighthearted titles such as *Captain Kiddo*, *The Little Patriot* (both 1917), *Daddy's Girl*, *A Daughter of the West* (both 1918), and *The Old Maid's Baby* (1919). Her last known work was appearing opposite Sammy Burns for a brief run of King Cole Comedies made in 1919 and early 1920.

Virginia Warwick (Virginia Dieppe) (?)
Pretty brunette, who was a Sennett bathing girl in 1918, and soon became a comedy ingénue in Fox and Century comedies such as *Wild Waves and Women* (1919), *Good Little Brownie*, and *The Jazzy Janitor* (both 1920). A major role in the hit *The Four Horsemen of the Apocalypse* (1921) moved her from shorts to features where she was leading lady to Richard Talmadge in *Speed King* (1923), and also appeared in many westerns like *Pioneer's Gold* (1924), *Roped by Radio* (1925), and *My Own Pal* (1926). She married film comic Jimmie Adams in 1924, but her career trailed off after 1926.

Alice Washburn (1861 – 1929) **See Chapter Seven**

Hannah Washington (1923 - ?) **See Chapter Seven**

Maude Wayne (1890 – 1983)
Blonde ingénue who joined *Triangle Comedies* in 1917 as a leading lady in shorts such as *Won by a Foot*, *Innocent Sinners*, *The Camera Cure* (all 1917), *His Punctured Reputation*, and *A Playwright's Wrong* (both 1918). After a few Triangle features she spent 1919 working at Fox Sunshine Comedies in two-reelers like *Back to Nature Girls* (1919). The bulk of the rest of her career was spent in supporting parts in dramatic features, although her few

comedies include *Fixed by George* (1920) with Lyons and Moran, *The Bachelor Daddy* (1922), and Fatty Arbuckle's *Leap Year*, which was shot in 1921, and although never released in the United States came out in Europe in 1924. She continued working in films until 1927.

Bessie Welsh (Betty Welsh) (1908 - ?) Sassy brunette ingénue, who spent some time in musical comedy in New York and was the daughter of Universal Pictures stock company actor William Welsh. She began her movie career at Century Comedies in 1922 and became the leader of the Century Follies Girls in shorts such as *Scared Stiff*, *Harem Follies* (both 1924), and *Tourists De Luxe* (1925), where she supported Al Alt, Harry McCoy, Bert Roach, Buddy Messinger, Hilliard Karr, and Henry Murdock. Later changing her name to Betty Welsh, some of her latter shorts include the Weiss Brother's *Circus Daze* (1928) with Poodles Hanneford and the Stern's *Mike and Ike* two-reeler *Take Your Pick* (1929), in addition to the western features *Rough Riding Red* (1928) and *Come and Get It* (1929).

Maude Wayne braves the current in the Mack Sennett promotional short *Keystone Girls Open Trout Season* (1917). Courtesy of Sam Gill.

May Wells (Mai Wells) (1862 – 1941)
All-purpose character actress, scrawny and plain, who specialized in spinsters, busybody neighbors, and country wives. Beginning her career at age five in her parent's theatrical company, she appeared in David Belasco productions like *First Born*, and was also an accomplished singer and dancer. Moving to films in the very early teens, she appeared all over the silent comedy map working for Powers, Biograph, Edison, Reliance, Frontier, Éclair and the Oz Company, where she played the witch Mombi in the features *His Majesty the Scarecrow of Oz* and *The New Wizard of Oz* (both 1914). Making a move to Sennett for numerous 1915 – 1917 Keystone-Triangle shorts, she can be seen in *Fatty's Tintype Tangle* (1915), *Fatty and Mabel Adrift* (1916), and *The Grab Bag Bride* (1917). Later she mostly turned up in small roles in features such as *The Breath of the Gods* (1920), *Excuse Me* (1925), and *Blondes by Choice* (1927), but she's best remembered as the non-stop talking mother of bratty Dinky Dean Riesner in Charlie Chaplin's *The Pilgrim* (1923).

Virginia Westbrook (?)
Westbrook was a stage actress who began her career in 1901 and toured the country in show such as *Hearts Aflame* and *Too Many Wives*. She entered films in 1912 for the Reliance/Majestic Company with films like *Johnny on the Spot*, and in 1913 appeared in some of the Florida-made *Punch Comedies* with midget comic Herbert Rice such as *Tracked to Florida* and *Master Cupid*. Other films included *Madcap of the Hills* (1913) and her last was the Hal Reid written and directed feature *Prohibition* (1915).

Winifred Westover (1899 – 1978)
Blonde ingénue who began her career at Triangle with D.W. Griffith's Fine Arts Company doing bits in *Intolerance*, *The Matrimaniac* (both 1916), and *Jim Bludso* (1917). In 1918 she became a comedy leading lady for Fox Sunshine Comedies opposite male comics like Billie Ritchie, Hugh Fay, and Jimmie Adams in shorts on the order of *The Son of a Gun*, *Are Married Policemen Safe?*, and *Her Husband's Wife* (all 1918). After playing "Fatty" Arbuckle's sweetheart in the surviving two-reeler *Love* (1919), she moved on to being a western heroine with William S. Hart, Buck Jones, and Harry Carey, plus worked her way to good supporting roles in films like *Is Life Worth Living?*, and *Anne of Little Smoky* (both 1921). That year she married cowboy star William S. Hart and retired from the screen, although she did return in 1930 with the lead role in Herbert Brenon's sound feature *Lummox*.

Blanche White (1892 – 1963)
White was an English-born actress, real name Ethel Caroline McCann, who was the wife of character comedian Leo White (that is until their 1931 divorce). At the end of 1915 she began working for the fledgling Hal Roach Company in their Lonesome Luke comedies, appearing in entries like *Luke and the Bomb Throwers* (1916). In addition to having roles in dramatic features such as *Honor Thy Name*, William S. Hart's *The Dawn Maker*, and *The Chalice of Sorrow* (all 1916), she appeared in numerous shorts with her husband such as Billy West's *The Chief Cook* (1917), and Bulls Eye comedies like *Help* (1919) with Gale Henry. Making an impression in *The Chief Cook*, the September 29, 1917 *Motion Picture News* said: "Blanche White as the slavey revealed herself as a comedienne who will bear watching as a future star. Her interpretations are strongly remindful of the work of Polly Moran." Her last known films were the series of *Pinnacle Comedies* that she and Leo co-starred in such as *Damfool Twins*, *Save a Sucker*, and *Don't Never Marry* (all 1920). Produced by the Independent Films Association the series lasted less than a year before expiring.

Pearl White (1889 – 1938) **See Chapter Four**

Vera White (1894 – 1956) **See Chapter Seven**

Marjorie Whiteis (Marjorie Gay) (1899 – 1943)
Statuesque brunette who was born in Missouri, and spent a couple of years as an attractive leading lady at the Hal Roach Studio for the likes of Glenn Tryon, James Finlayson, Tyler Brooke, and Charley Chase. After moving to California around 1921 she began her movie work as an extra in 1924 in features such as *Inez from Hollywood* (1924). Getting a berth at the Roach Studio she appeared in shorts like *What Price Goofy?*, *Thundering Landlords*, *Sherlock Sleuth*, *Papa Be Good* (all 1925), and *Don Key (Son of Burro)* (1926). On leaving Roach she changed her name to Marjorie Gay and had supporting roles in the features *Other Women's Husbands*, *Volcano*, and *Dangerous Friends* (all 1926). Her film career ended here, but she stayed in Los Angeles and later had her own shop as a material re-weaver in the clothing repair industry.

Wanda Wiley (1902 - 1987) **See Chapter Five**

Cora Williams (1870 – 1927)
All-purpose character actress, who after many years on stage in opera and stock companies around the country, joined the regular ensemble in comedies at the Edison Studio. Working with the likes of William Wadsworth, Arthur Housman, Alice Washburn, and Edward O'Connor, over four years she appeared in numerous shorts like *For Professional Services* (1912), *A Reluctant Cinderella*, *He Would Fix Things* (both 1913), *A Buxom Country Lass*, *A Tango Spree* (both 1914), and *One Way to Advertise* (1915). Later she appeared as support in features such as *Greater Than Fame* (1920), *Womanhandled* (1925), and *Lure of the Night Club* (1927) up to her death in 1927.

Margaret J. Winkler (1895 – 1990) **See Chapter Six**

Jane Winton (1905 – 1959)
Winton was a tall and statuesque brunette who had been a dancer with the Fokine Ballet, Ben Ali Dancers, and the *Ziegfeld Follies* before she came to films in 1924. Having started working in small walk-on bits, by 1926 she had worked her way up to featured roles in popular films like *Footloose Widows* and *Don Juan*. She spent the rest of the 1920s as the second female lead in comedies such as *Lonesome Ladies*, *The Poor Nut* (both 1927), *Bare Knees*, *Honeymoon Flats*, and *Nothing to Wear* (all 1928). She was very effective as a comic antagonist for Marion Davies in *The Fair Co-Ed* (1927) and *The Patsy* (1928), and while she made the transition to sound films her appearances dwindled as she focused on a singing career in opera. Her last film was in 1937, and besides being very busy singing on the stage and radio, she also painted and wrote two novels before her death in 1959.

Dorothea Wolbert (1874 – 1958)
Wolbert was a small and bird-like character comedienne who was a ubiquitous face in

comedies all through the silent era. Starting her stage career as an ingénue in *Charley's Aunt*, she spent many years on the boards working for producers such as Charles Frohman, and appearing with names like A.S. Willard in popular shows such as *The Masquerader, The Little Minister,* and *The Butterflies*. She made her film debut in 1916, and the next year became a member of the Hal Roach Stock Co. supporting Harold Lloyd in his Lonesome Luke and glasses character shorts. Also doing bits in features such as *Cupid Forecloses* (1919) and *La La Lucille* (1920), in 1920 Universal gave her her own series of starring Star Comedy one-reelers, which included *Shapes and Scrapes* (1920), *Fresh from the Country* (1921) and *A Model Made* (1921). After this she worked everywhere supporting the likes of Larry Semon, Our Gang, Beatrice Lillie, Pola Negri, Louise Fazenda, Laurel & Hardy, and A Ton of Fun in shorts such as *The Heavy Parade* (1926) and *Their Purple Moment* (1928), in addition to features like *A Woman of the World* (1925), *Exit Smiling* (1926), and *Anybody Here Seen Kelly?* (1928). She kept busy after the transition to sound, and worked steadily in bit parts until 1957.

Dorothea Wolbert puts the squeeze on Charles Dorety as Charles King looks on in *All for Uncle* (1927). Courtesy of Jim Kerkhoff.

Grace Woods (1885 – 1952)
Small, dark-haired actress, who played small roles in many westerns, as well as Hal Roach comedies. After a background in music and performing on stage, she began her film ca-

reer around 1918 and had bit roles in features like *Dangerous Hours* (1919), *The Courtship of Miles Standish* (1923), *The Flying U Ranch* (1927), and *Mr. Wong, Detective* (1938). Her shorts for Hal Roach include *Here Come the Girls* (1918), *Two Tars* (1928), and *Perfect Day* (1929), although her biggest and best role was as one of the two spinsters in *The Cake Eater* (1924) who are trying to catch ranch hand Will Rogers for a husband. She appeared in other shorts for Al Christie, Century Comedies, and Mack Sennett such as *Are Brides Happy?* (1920), *The Family Row* (1924), and *The Swim Princess* (1928), plus is also listed as working as a studio seamstress before retiring from performing around 1938.

Fay Wray (1907 – 2004)
One of the great "scream queens" of 1930s horror films such as *Doctor X*, *The Most Dangerous Game* (both 1932), *Mystery of the Wax Museum*, and of course *King Kong* (both 1933), the Canadian-born Ms. Wray's early career was as an ingénue at the Hal Roach Studio, where she worked her way up from walk-ons in *Just a Good Guy* (1924) and *Isn't Life Terrible* (1925) to the female lead in two-reelers like *Moonlight and Noses* (1925). Western shorts at Universal led her to be "discovered" by Erich von Stroheim and starring in his *The Wedding March* (1928). In the late 1920s she became a Paramount star, and in the early days of sound carved her niche in horror films. Mostly retiring in the 1940s, she returned to films and television in the 1950s, continuing to work until 1980.

Fay Wray (right) eyes Charley Chase and Lassie Lou Ahern in *Sweet Daddy* (1924). Courtesy of Cole Johnson.

Catherine Young (?)
Part of the L-Ko beauty ensemble alongside Gladys Varden and Eva Novak, Ms. Young appeared in two-reelers such as *Vamping Reuben's Millions*, *From Cactus to Kale* (both 1917), *The Torpedo Pirates*, and *A Rural Riot* (both 1918). After a featured role where she steals Charles Ray's watch in the feature *A Nine O'Clock Town* (1918) she disappeared from the screen.

Clara Kimball Young (1890 – 1960) **See Chapter Six**

Flora Zabelle (1880 – 1968)
Zabelle was a stage actress, born in Turkey, who was married to star comedian Raymond Hitchcock. After making her Broadway debut in the musical *San Toy* in 1900, she first appeared with Mr. Hitchcock in 1902's *King Dodo* and they married three years later. Other shows they did together include *The Yankee Consul*, *The Man Who Owns Broadway*, and *The Red Widow*. The pair appears to have made their film debut in 1913 in some shorts for the Kinemacolor Company, and in 1915 starred in the feature *The Ringtailed Rhinoceros* for Lubin. Hitchcock moved over to Keystone for a few titles, and Ms. Zabelle joined him in *A Village Scandal* (1915) where they shared the screen with Fatty Arbuckle and Al St John. The next year she repeated her stage role in the film version of *The Red Widow* (1916) but this time opposite a young John Barrymore instead of her husband. Her last movie was *A Perfect 36* (1918), one of the Goldwyn features of her good friend Mabel Normand. Retiring from performing in 1920, after Hitchcock's death in 1929 she became a designer and partner in Jacques Bodart, Inc., a firm that specialized in furniture and antiques.

Raymond Hitchcock defends Flora Zabelle from Roscoe Arbuckle and Al St John as Keystone riff-raff Grover Ligon, Frank Hayes, Pat Kelly, and Joe Bordeaux get an eyeful in *The Village Scandal* (1915).

BIBLIOGRAPHY

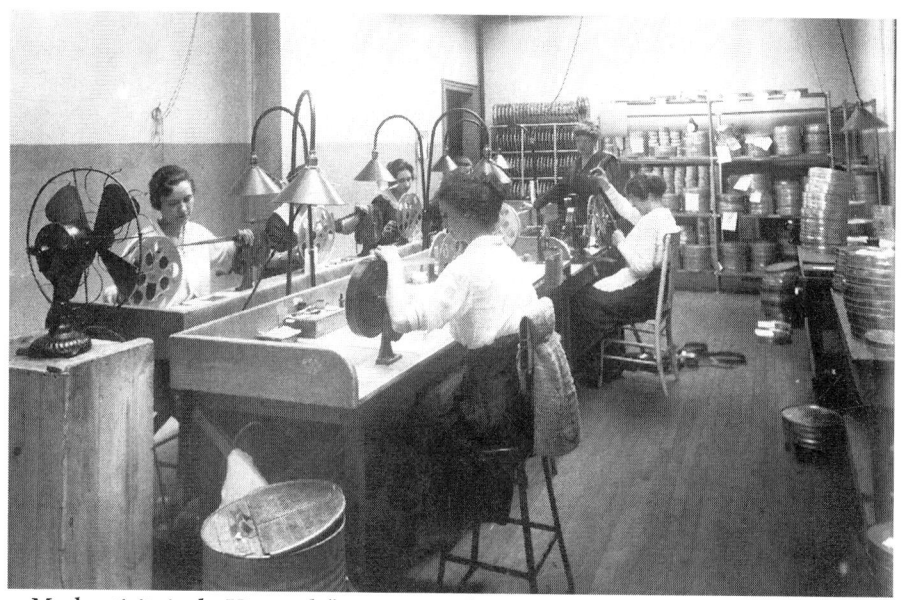

Much activity in the Vitagraph "joining room." Courtesy of Billy Rose Theatre Division, the New York Public Library for the Performing Arts.

Periodicals – Trade Publications
The Biograph, 1914 - 1915
Edison Kinetogram, 1911 – 1916
Educational Film Exchange Press Sheets, 1920 - 1930
Essanay News, 1915 – 1917
The Exhibitor, 1924 - 1927
Exhibitors Trade Review, 1922 – 1924
Film Daily, 1919 – 1930
Fox's Exhibitor Bulletin, 1915 - 1919
Kalem Kalendar, 1914 - 1915
Loew's Weekly, 1920 – 1931
The Lubin Bulletin, 1915 - 1916
Motion Picture News, 1913 – 1930
Motion Picture News Blue Book, 1929 - 1930
Motion Picture News Booking Guide, 1922 – 1927
Motography, 1911 – 1917

The Movie Home Journal, 1924 - 1927
Moving Picture World, 1910 – 1927
Paramount Pictures Press Books, 1918 - 1923
Pathé Bulletins, 1910 – 1916
The Pathé Messenger, 1920 - 1922
Pathé Press Sheets, 1925 - 1929
Photoplay, 1918 – 1930
The Photoplayer's Weekly, 1914 - 1917
Picture-Play, 1917 - 1920
Reel Life, 1914 – 1916
Selig Monthly Herald, 1915
The Triangle, 1916 -1917
Universal Weekly, 1913 – 1930
Variety, 1910 – 1930
Vitagraph Life Portrayals, 1910 – 1916

Periodicals –Articles

Bodeen, DeWitt. *Dorothy Gish*. Films in Review Vol. 19, #7, August – September 1968.

Caslavsky, Karel. *American Comedy Series: Filmographies 1914 – 1930*. Griffithiana # 51/52, 1994.

Doyle, Billy H. *Lost Players [Fay Tincher]*. Classic Images #165, March 1989.

_____. *Lost Players [Child Stars]*. Classic Images #174, December 1989.

Maltin, Leonard. *The Spice of the Program*. The Silent Picture #15, Summer 1972.

Massa, Steve. *Alice Howell and Gale Henry: Queens of Eccentric Comedy*. Griffithiana #73/74, 2004.

Randisi, Steve. *The Gal who Knew the Boys*. Filmfax #40, 1993.

Roberts, Richard M. *Their Gangs: A Look at the Our Gang Spinoff Comedies of the 1920s*. Classic Images #267, September 1997.

Slide, Anthony. *Madge Kennedy*. Films in Review Vol. 35, #3, March 1984.

_____. *Dorothy Devore: In an Interview with Anthony Slide*. The Silent Picture #15, Summer 1972.

_____. *Babe London: In an Interview with Anthony Slide*. The Silent Picture #15, Summer 1972.

Books

Blum, Daniel. *A Pictorial History of the Silent Screen*. New York: G.P. Putnam's Sons, 1953.

Braff, Richard E. *The Universal Silents*. Jefferson, North Carolina: McFarland & Co.,

1999.

Brownlow, Kevin. *Mary Pickford Rediscovered*. New York: Abrams, 1999.

Bruskin, David N. *The White Brothers: Jack, Jules and Sam White*. Hollywood: Scarecrow Press, 1990.

Cary, Diana Serra. *What Ever Happened to Baby Peggy?*. New York: St. Martin's Press, 1996.

Davies, Marion. *The Times We Had*. Indianapolis/New York: Bobbs-Merrill Co., 1975.

Foote, Lisle. *Buster Keaton's Crew*. North Carolina: McFarland & Co., 2014.

Fowler, Gene. *Father Goose*. New York: Covici Friede Publishers, 1934.

Gish, Lillian. *Dorothy and Lillian Gish*. New York: Charles Scribner's Sons, 1973.

Green, Stanley. *The Great Clowns of Broadway*. New York: Oxford University Press, 1984.

Jura, Jean-Jacques and Bardin II, Rodney Norman. *Balboa Films*. Jefferson, North Carolina and London: McFarland and Co., 1999.

Kennedy, Matthew. *Marie Dressler*. Jefferson, North Carolina: McFarland & Co., 1999.

Kerr, Walter. *The Silent Clowns*. New York: Alfred A. Knopf, 1975.

Kiehn, David. *Broncho Billy and the Essanay Company*. Berkley, California: Farwell Books, 2003.

Lahue, Kalton C. *World of Laughter: The Motion Picture Comedy Short*. Norman, Oklahoma: University of Oklahoma Press, 1966.

_____. *Mack Sennett's Keystone*. South Brunswick: A.S. Barnes, 1970.

_____., and Gill, Sam. *Clown Princes and Court Jesters*. South Brunswick: A.S. Barnes, 1970.

_____. *Dreams for Sale: The Rise and Fall of the Triangle Film Corporation*. South Brunswick: A.S. Barnes, 1971.

Lee, Betty. *Marie Dressler: The Unlikeliest Star*. Lexington, Kentucky: The University Press of Kentucky, 1997.

Loos, Anita. *A Girl Like I*. New York: Viking Press, 1966.

_____. *Cast of Thousands*. New York: Grosset and Dunlap, 1977.

_____. *The Talmadge Girls*. New York: Viking Press, 1978.

Louvish, Simon. *Keystone: The Life and Clowns of Mack Sennett*. London: Faber and Faber, 2003.

Maltin, Leonard. *The Great Movie Comedy Teams*. New York: Signet, 1970.

_____. *The Great Movie Shorts*. New York: Bonanza, 1972.

_____., and Bann, Richard. *The Little Rascals: The Life and Times of Our Gang*. New York: Crown, 1977

_____. *The Great Movie Comedians*. New York: Harmony Books, 1978.

Magliozzi, Ronald S. *Treasures from the Film Archives*. Metuchen, New Jersey: Scarecrow Press, 1988.

_____. *A Brief History of Winkler Pictures, Inc*. Unpublished manuscript.

Massa, Steve. *Lame Brains and Lunatics: The Good, The Bad, and The Forgotten of Silent Comedy*. Georgia: BearManor Media, 2013.

Mast, Gerald. *The Comic Mind*. Indianapolis, Indiana: Bobbs-Merrill, 1973.

Mitchell, Glenn. *A-Z of Silent Film Comedy*. London: Batsford, 1998.

Montgomery, John. *Comedy Films*. London: George Allen and Unwin, 1954.

Moore, Colleen. *Silent Star*. Garden City, New York: Doubleday, 1968.

Okuda, Ted, and Watz, Edward. *Columbia Comedy Shorts: Two Reel Hollywood Film Comedies 1933 – 1958*. Jefferson, North Carolina: McFarland & Co., 1986.

Robinson, David. *The Great Funnies*. London: Studio Vista/Dutton, 1969.

_____. *Chaplin: His Life and Art*. New York: McGraw-Hill, 1985.

Sennett, Mack, and Shipp, Cameron. *King of Comedy*. New York: Doubleday and Co., 1954.

Slide, Anthony. *Early American Cinema*. New York: Zwemmer/A.S. Barnes, 1970.

_____. *The Big V: A History of the Vitagraph Company*. Metuchen, New Jersey: Scarecrow Press, 1976.

_____. *Eccentrics of Comedy*. Lanham, Maryland: Scarecrow Press, 1998.

_____. *Alice Howell: An Imperfect History*. Unpublished monograph.

Stenn, David. *Clara Bow: Runnin' Wild*. New York: Doubleday, 1988.

Stone, Rob. *Laurel or Hardy*. Temecula, California: Split Reel Books, 1996.

Walker, Brent E. *Mack Sennett's Fun Factory*. Jefferson, North Carolina: McFarland & Co., 2010.

Watson Jr., Coy. *The Keystone Kid: Tales of Early Hollywood*. Santa Monica: Santa Monica Press, 2001.

White, Pearl. *Just Me*. New York: George H. Doran Company, 1919.

Other Sources

Dorward, William. *Interview with Alfred Santell*. November 1972.

Robinson Locke Collection of Theatrical Clippings 1870 – 1920. New York Public Library for the Performing Arts.

Nitrateville (nitrateville.com)

Silent Comedy Mafia (silentcomedymafia.com)

ABOUT THE AUTHOR

Steve Massa is the author of *Lame Brains and Lunatics: The Good, The Bad, and The Forgotten of Silent Comedy* and *Marcel Perez: The International Mirth-Maker*. He has organized and curated comedy film programs for the Museum of Modern Art, Library of Congress, The Museum of the Moving Image, the Smithsonian Institution, and the Pordenone Silent Film Festival. In addition to consulting with EYE Filmmuseum, Netherlands, the Cineteca di Bologna, the Royal Belgian Cinematheque, and other archives, plus contributing notes to the National Film Registry and the National Film Preservation Foundation, he is a founding member of Silent Cinema Presentations, which produces NYC's Silent Clown Film Series. Massa has also provided essays and commentary tracks to many comedy DVD and Blu-Ray collections, such as *The Forgotten Films of Roscoe "Fatty" Arbuckle*, *Harry Langdon: Lost and Found*, *Becoming Charley Chase*, Kino Video's *Buster Keaton: The Short Film Collection*, and *The Mack Sennett Collection*, Vol 1, as well as co-curated Undercrank Productions' *The Mishaps of Musty Suffer*, Volumes 1 &2, and the award-winning *Marcel Perez Collection*.

INDEX

Numbers in **bold** indicate photographs

Abbott, Gypsy 419, **419**
Aber Twins 420
Ackroyd, Jack 75, 297, 364
Acque Miracolose (Miracle Waters) 4
Adair, Josephine 420
Adams, Claire 420, **420**
Adams, Ernie **198**, 268
Adams, Jimmie 123, 277, 328, 331, 350, 362, 391, 393, 432, **449**, 456, 464, 473, 512, 538, 550, 552, 571, 572, 579, 585, 597, 602, 606, 608
Adams, Stella 111, 152, 421, **421**, **536**, 536
Adventurous Ambrose 351, 389
Ahern, Lassie Lou 421, 422, **493**
Ahern, Peggy 422
Aitken, Harry 39, 47, 63, 256
Alexander, Claire 422
Alice in Movieland 277
Allen, Alta 64, 317, 422
Allen, Irene 422
Allen, Phyllis 35, 250, 252, 423, 463
Allison, May 423, **423**
Amann, Bee 424
Anderson, Claire 424
Anderson, G.M. 220, 300, 443, 453, 546, 567
Anderson, Mary 424
Anthony and Cleopatra 94
Anything Once **65**, 65
Arbuckle, Roscoe "Fatty" vii, 30, 33, 37, 38, 40, 41, 42, 43, 45, 51, 55, 56, 68, 102, 154, 182, 202, 232, 247, 248, 270, 271, 276, 287, 304, 308, 310, 311, 329, 355, 358, 368, 389, **389**, 390, 391, 423, 431, **431**, 444, 459, 463, 466, 476, 482, 493-494, 498, 513, 516, 520, 535, 536, 546, 551, **552**, 552, 553, **553**, 563, 567, 572, 574-575, 590, **590**, 607, 608, 612, **612**
Ardell, Alice 206-207, **207**
Arly, Arby 425
Arnold, Cecile 73, **425**, 425
Arrival of Josie, The 69
Arthur, Jean 397-398, **397**

Asher, Max 72, 169, 249, 250, 252, 273, 492, 511, 563, **564**, 596
Ashton, Sylvia **426**, 426
Ask Grandma 323, 595
Asleep at the Switch 344
Astor, Gertrude 150, 187, 426-427, **427**
At Coney Island 30
Aunt Elsa's Visit 295, 420
Avery, Charles 34, 285, 286, 359
Aye, Marion 427
Ayres, Agnes 64, 427-428

Baby Early 492, 496
Baby Mine 166, 494
Baby Peggy **vi**, 172, 202-203, **202**, 313, 323, 343, 432, 497, 519, 526, 531
Baby's Birthday 282, 339
Bad Boy 332, 333, 441
Badger, Clarence 154, 184, 249
Baird, Leah 279, 428
Balfour, Betty 195-196, **195**
Balshofer, Fred **iii**, 392, 572
Bambrick, Gertrude 428
Baracchi, Nilde **6**, 6, **306**
Barnett, Chester 116, 263
Barney Oldfield's Race for a Life 30, **31**, 567
Baron, The 27
Barrett, Bonnie 429
Barrett, Judith see Dover, Nancy
Bataille, Lucien 3
Battle of the Century vii, 347, 415-416
Battle of the Sexes, The 236, 240, 243, 367, 431, 560, **560**
Be My Wife 317, 422, 459
Beans for Two 360
Beau Hunks 403
Beaudine, William 197, 345
Beauty a la Mud 393, 585
Beck, Billie 429
Becker, Bruno J. 250, 253, 254
Bedroom Blunder, A 297, 357, 359, 361, 531, 565
Beebe, Marjorie 370, 429-430, **429**

619

Beery, Wallace **72**, 102-103, **103**, **220**, 261, 405, 431, 436, 473, 591, 593
Belasco, Jay 137, **140**, 141, 388, 392, 459
Belcher, Alice 430
Bennett, Alma 322, 430, **430**
Bennett, Belle 430-431, 477, **560**
Bennett, Billie 431, **431**
Bennett, Catherine 431
Bent, Marion 432
Bernoudy, Jane 70, 313-315, **315**, **316**, 440, 549, 586
Bertha, the Buttonhole-Maker 387
Betty in Search of a Thrill 263, 264, **264**
Betty's Back Again 126
Bevan, Billy 84, 93, 205, **290**, **292**, 292, 307, 336, 344, **345**, 374, 399, 412, 485, 512, 514, 531, 556, 563, 568, 595, 596, 605
Biron, Lillian 432, **432**
Blache, Alice Guy 23, 33, 166, 210-211, **210**, 454, 593
Blackton, J. Stuart 23, 128, 129, 508
Blythe, Violet 433
Bogard, Delia 433
Boniface, Symona **346**, 433, **433**
Bonner, Priscilla 434
Boob and the Magician, The 387, 518
Boobley's Baby 212-213
Borden, Olive **77**, 434, **434**
Bosworth, Hobart 260, 263, 265, 266, 421, 509
Bow, Clara vii, viii, 193-195, **194**, 280, 469, 548
Boyce, St. Elmo 369
Boyd, Betty 435, **435**, 442
Boyd, Lois 435
Bradbury, Kitty 435
Bradbury, Robert 149
Bradley, Estelle 436, **436**
Brady, William A. 69, 164, 232, 241, 465
Breuil, Beta 277-279, **279**, 280
Brian, Mary 436
Bright Lights 207, 414, 483
Bringing Up Father **101**, 101, 186, 313, **411**, 412, 456, 558
Broadhurst, Ethel 386, 437, **437**, **486**, 603
Brockwell, Billie 437
Brody, Ann 437
Bronson, Betty 438
Brooks, Louise 358, 424, 438
Brown, Iva 438
Browne, Betty 282, **282**
Brownie the Wonder Dog 82, 201, 202, 292, 331, 343, 432, 552, 606
Bruce, Kate 438-439
Bryan, Leota 439

Buel, Kenean 408
Bunkered 214-215, **215**
Bunny Backslides 21, 69
Bunny, John 19, 20-21, **20**, 25, 26-27, 69, 102, 128, 129-130, **130**, 132, 278, 279, 303, 304, 327, 405, 424, 428, 541
Bunny's Dilemma 129
Bunny's Honeymoon 102, 513
Burglar's Bride, A 250, 256
Burke, Billie 44, 258, 439, 450
Burkett, Bartine 351-356, **352**, **354**, **355**
Burkhardt, Rose **440**, 440
Burnham, Bertha 440
Burns, Bobby 76, 384, 385, 441, 507, 551, 562, 575, 587
Burns, Evelyn 441
Burns, Harry 326
Burns, Neal 82, 111, 123, **124**, 125, 150, 152, 153, 186, 203, 253, 308, 325, 328, 350, 391, 392, 393, 429, 459, 466, 473, 476, 483, 487, 503, 512, 513, 525, 531,
Burns, Sammy 289, 297, 498, 605
Burton, Ethel 441, 487, 602
Busch, Mae 40, 441-442, **441**, 448
Byron, Marion 347, 414, 416-418, **416**, **417**

Cahill, Marie 19, 442, **442**
Caldwell, Betty 442
Callahans and the Murphys, The 101, 235, 411-412, 558, 560
Cameo the dog 338, 343-346, **344**, **345**, **533**
Campbell, Sadie 443
Campus Carmen, The 336-337, 398, 424, 479, 485, 568
Capra, Frank 206, 371, 375, 507, 581
Cards and Cupid 353
Carew, Ora 444
Carlisle, Lucille 443, **443**
Carlyle, Helen 444
Carmen, Jewell 444-445, **444**
Carpenter, Betty 445
Carr, Mary 445, **445**
Carruthers, Helen 446
Cartwright, Peggy 446, **446**
Carver, Louise 58, 306-308, **306**, **307**, 312, 502
Case, Lottie 447
Cassinelli, Dolores 447
Catto, Nema 447
Caught in the Act 97
Cavalier, Nita 447-448
Cecil, Nora 448, **448**

620

Champion, The 33, 455
Change in Complexion, A 316
Chaplin, Charlie vii, viii, 24, 33, 34-35, 36, 37, 45, 79, 81, 83, 100, 103-104, 107, 120, 231, 234, 270, 289, 297, 308, 319, 322, 327, 330, 376, **376**, 377-381, **378**, 403, 408, 423, 425, 427, 435, 439, 441, 447, 449, 454, 455, **455**, 474, 486, 490, 491, 495, 497-498, 501, 504, 512, 517, 525, 538, 545, 547, 552, 553, 563, 578, 588, 589, 592, 605, 607
Chaplin, Syd 103-104, 196, 423, 425, 434, 448, **503**, 578
Charming Mrs. Chase, The 215-216
Chase, Charley 13, **203**, 203, 253-254, **254**, 255, 275-276, 308, 331, 332, **332**, 334, 347, 385, 402, **403**, 403, 415, 416, 418, 421, 433, 434, 439, 448, **448**, 452, 456, 461, **461**, 469, 473, 475, 476, 488, 489, **493**, 493, 496, 506, 507, 509, 518, 522, 542, 554, 556, 567, 571, **571**, 577, 594, 595, 598, 604, 609
Chasing the Chaser 104-105, 517
Chene, Dixie 448, 463
Cherrill, Virginia 322, 449
Chicago 366, 478
Chop Suey Louie 146
Christie, Al 77, 104, 106, 110, 111, 125, 126, 127, 136, 137-138, 139-141, 143, 146, 148, 149-150, 152, 153, 184-186, 190, 196-198, **197**, 203, 205, 207, 208, 209, 244-245, 247, 253, 281, 307, 313, 324, 325, 327-328, 331, 342, 343, 350, 351, 359, 361, 389, 390, 391, 392, 393, 412, 414, 421, 429, 430, 449, 452, 456, 457, 459, 460, 461, 464, 466, 469, 470, 473, 476, 481, 483, 487, 488, 490, 498, 501, 504, 508, 512, 516, 523, 524, 525, 526, 531, 549, 556, 557, 579, 583, 587, 590, 595, 597, 600, 605, 611
Christy, Ann 449, **449**
Cinderella Cinders 83, 440
Clair, Ethlyne 450
Clark, Bessie 450
Clark, Trilby 450
Clark, Virginia 450
Clifton, Emma 174, 450-451
Cline, Eddie 93, 97, 99, 339, 371, 375
Close, Ivy 451, **451**, 551
Cloud, Margaret 452
Clyde, Andy 276, 313, **337**, 370, 375, 433, 536, **545**, 594-595
Coburn, Dorothy 204, 452, **452**, 577
Cody, Lew 48, 66-68, **67**, 172, 498

Cohens and the Kellys, The 305, **305**, 411
Colwell, Goldie 452
Comont, Mathilde **5**, 5-6
Compson, Betty 135, 148-154, **149**, **151**, **153**, **155**, 179, 207, 421
Conklin, Chester 1, 35, 75, 90, 93, 99, 207, 297, 309, 330, **334**, 357, 368, 413, 425, 426, 466, **492**, 553, 579
Conklin, Heinie 123, **187**, **248**, 249, **249**, 344, **365**, 401, 570, **570**
Conle, Lige **276**, 277, **298**, 298, 321, 328, 343, 362, 434, 436, 489, 497, 503, 512, 529, 558, **559**, 566
Connell, Grayce 453, 529, **529**
Connelly, Bobby 125-126, 410
Connor, Della 453
Contero, Norma 453
Convict's Happy Bride, A 84
Corbin, Virginia Lee 453-454, **454**, 468
Corby, Francis 246, 585
Cornwall, Anne 207-208, **208**
Cornwall, Blanche 211, 454
Courtney, Minerva 454-455, **455**
Cousin Kate 217, 218
Crazy Like a Fox 333
Crosthwaite, Ivy 455
Crowell, Josephine 455-456
Cruze, James 148, 154, 480, 570
Cullington, Margaret 246, 392, 393, 456, **456**
Cumberland, John 215, 216, **216**, 217
Cumpson, John 14-15, 17
Cunegonde de aime son maître (*Cunegonde in Love with her Master*) 4
Cupid Trims his Lordship 152
Cure for Pokeritis, A 20
Curses! 355
Curtis, Florence 456
Cutey and the Chorus Girls 21, 278

D'Avril, Yola 456-457
Dahlberg, Mae Charlotte see Laurel, Mae
Daisy Doodad's Dial 10-11
Dalton, Irene 457, **457**
Dalton, James H. 233, 235
Daly, Marcella 457-458
Dana, Viola 280, 382, 458, **458**, 480, 535, 540
Danger Game, The 168
Daniel, Viora 459
Daniels, Bebe vii, **183**, 183-184, 382, 384, 386, 430, 558
Daniels, Frank 296, 524, 535

621

Daniels, Mickey 323, 338, 340, 472, 513, 515, 544
Daniels, Phyllis 459
Daniels, Thelma 459
Daredevil Dan 222
Darling, Constance **460**, 460
Darling, Helen 460
Darling, Jean 340, 460-461
Darlington, Beth 461, **461**
Darmond, Grace 461-462
Daumery, Carrie 462
Davenport, Alice 30, 36, 37, 93, 99, **462**, 462-463
Davidson, Max 28, 58, **63**, 64, 65, 237, 239, 240, 256, 331, 334, 369, 416, **416**, 417, 430, 437, 475, **504**, 522, 540, 577, 581, 583
Davies, Marion vii, viii, 7, 13, 179, **191**, 191-192, **193**, 235, 258, 260, 369, **370**, 529, 551, 588, 609
Davis, Mildred 376, 381-383, **381**, **383**, 384, 386
Davis, Virginia 463
Davy, Horace 125, 139
Dawn, Charlotte 464
Dawn, Consuelo 464
Dawson, Doris 464
Day the Laughter Stopped, The 247
Day, Alice vii, 205-206, **205**, **307**, 322, 464, 488, 531, 556, 563
Day, Marceline 464, **465**, **548**
Day's Pleasure, A 327
De Foe, Annette 466
De Forest, Patsy 126, 467, **467**
De Haven, Flora Parker see De Haven, Mrs. Carter
De Haven, Mrs. Carter 86, 116, 143, 274, 467-468, **467**, 501, 524, 604
De Rue, Carmen 468
Deacon's Waterloo, The 151-152
Dean, Priscilla 64, 282, 340, 465
Deane, Doris 466, **466**, 482
Deane, Hazel 466
Deed, Andre 3
Del Ruth, Hampton 93, 99, 422, 444, 474
Delayed Proposals 228
DeMille, Cecil B. 114, 184, 269, 355, 366, 382, 426, 477, 478, 501, 513, 520, 574, 576, 593
Dennis, Amy 468
Depp, Harry 126, 359, 360, 535, 586
Deslys, Kay 331, 469
Detectress, The 252
Devore, Dorothy vii, 196-198, **197**, 298, 313, 328, 396, 434
Dillon, Edward 134, 237, 239, 256, 322, 428, 599
Dillon, Jack 138, 349, 350

Dimples, the Auto Salesgirl 131
Dines, Courtland 59-60, 68, 379
Dinner at Eight 235, 260, 404, 439
Distilled Love 84
Diving Girl, The 27, 30, 32, 322, 348
Dizzy Daisy **76**, 76
Doctor Bridget 102
Dolly's Vacation 176-177
Dooley, Billy 209, 313, 325, 342, **342**, 350, 391, 470, 473, 512, 554
Dooley, Ray 227, 469
Dore, Adrienne 469
Doree, Jean 470
Dorety, Charles 353, 371, **372**, 432, 450, 502, **519**, 526, 571, **610**
Dorothy Dares 221
Dover, Nancy 470
Dovey, Alice 470
Down Upon the Swanee River 358
Dressler, Marie vii, viii, 7, 37, 69, 70, 101-102, 108, 230-236, **231**, **232**, **233**, **234**, **236**, 259, 260, 324, 411-412, **411**, 491, 606
Drew, Dorothy see Daly, Marcella
Drew, Mr. and Mrs. Sidney 38, 116, 211-219, **212**, 274, 405, 427, 437, 493
Drew, Mrs. Sidney 38, 116, 210, 211-219, **212**, **213**, **215**, **218**, 255, 274, 405, 427, 437, 493
Drew, Sidney **20**, 38, 116, 211-219, **212**, 228, **229**, 274, 279, **302**, 303, 405, 424, 427, 437, 467, 493, 503, 541
Duffy, Jack 75, 106, 208, 253, 301, 313, 323, 325, 331, 393, 394, 476, 483, 525, 557, 595
Duhamel, Sarah 3
Dumb Daddies 369, 577
Duncan, Bud 88, 89, 90, 241, 272, **287**, 291, 369, 553, 581
Duncan, Rosetta 412, 473
Duncan, Vivian 412-413, **413**, 473
Dunham, Phil **83**, 84, 88, 94, 121, 292, 318, **320**, 436, **436**, 485, 504, 508, 537, 572
Durand, Gonda 470
Durfee, Minta 35, 48, 308-312, **309**, **311**, 574
Dwan, Allan 235, 357, 398
Dwan, Dorothy 471, **471**
Dwiggens, Jay 21
Dwight, Mabel 471
Dwyer, Ruth 471

Eames, Peggy 472
Earle, Dorothy 472, **472**
Eason, Lorraine **275**, 369, 472-473

Index

East, Henry 254-255
Eaton, Doris 473
Eddy, Lorraine 473-474, **473**
Edison, Thomas 1, 13, 14, 281, 294, 295, 296, 310, 315, 316, 420, 450, 458, 465, 471, 480, 507, 530, 534, 540, 544, 590, 601, 602, 604, 605, 607, 609
Education of a Prince (La Reine Liska Silistre) 381
Edwards, Gus 119, 127, 203, 453, 469, 493, 520, 583
Edwards, Mattie 474
Edwards, Neely 75, 86, 87, 143, 186, 207, 369, 392, 393, 481, 506, 529, 595
Edwards, Vivian **425**, 474, **474**
Egg-Crate Wallop, The 189
Eilers, Sally 336, 337, 475
Elephant on Their Hands, An 128, 303
Elliott, Lillian 475
Eltinge, Julian 104, **105**, 105-106, 483, 561, 572, 604
Emerson, Babe 475
Emerson, John 183, 256-259, 540
Emmett, Fern 476
Emory, May 476
Eskimobaby, Das 170
Ethel's Roof Party 237
Evans, Cecile 476
Evans, Muriel 476-477
Even Unto Death 288-289
Everett, Joseph T. 330
Every Other Inch a Lady 107
Exit Smiling **106**, 107-108, **108**, 526, 610
Extra Girl, The 58-59, **59**, 308, 364-365, 368, 502, 513, 545
Eyton, Bessie 477

Fair, Elinor 477
Fairbanks, Douglas 28, 182, 234, 239, 240, 256-258, 326, 379, 385, 402, 408, **444**, 445, 501, 526-527, **527**, 599
Fanny the Mule 477
Farley, Dot 19, 110, 123, 282-293, **283**, **284**, **286**, **287**, **290**, **292**, **293**, 297, 374, 399, 405, **405**, 406
Fatal Marriage, The 91, 120, 445
Father Was a Loafer 79-80, 120
Fay, Elfie 478, 591
Faye, Julia 366, 478, **478**
Fazenda, Louise vii, viii, 70, 72-77, **73**, **74**, **76**, **77**, 90, 92, 97, 107, 248, 249, 251, 277, 283, 297, 315, 330, 357, 364, 400, 417, 565, 610
Feed 'Em and Weep **416**, 417
Fellows, Edith 341

Feudists, The **20**, 129, **130**
Field, Elinor 145, 358-361, **359**, **360**
Field, Madalynne 479
Film Prima Donna, The 170
Finch, Flora 19-24, **19**, **20**, **22**, **23**, 25, 128, 129, **130**, 132, 187, 278, 282, **302**, 304, 405, 437, 493, 587
Finlayson, James 64, 82, 104, 329, **372**, 374, 393, **415**, 415, 424, 528, 595, 609
Fire Flingers, The 243
Fires of Youth 147
First Falsehood 309
Fischer, Margarita 273-274, 479-480, **479**
Fitzgerald, Cissy 1, **2**
Flaming Fathers 334, 522
Flapper, The 161-162, 260, 500
Floor Below, The 46-47, **46**, 382
Florence Turner Impersonates Film Favorites 11
Flowers, Bess 480
Flugrath, Edna 458, 480, 540
Folz, Artye 480
Footloose Widows 77, 609
Forde, Eugenie 109, **286**, 481
Forde, Victoria 109-114, **109**, **110**, **112**, **113**, 136, 137, 179, **286**, 286, 405, 406, 516
Foster, Helen 481, **481**
Foster, May 481-482
Fox, Harry 157
Fox, Virginia 371-373, **373**
Foy, Eddie 69, 98, 231, 262, 442
Francis, Christine 482, **482**, 505
Francisco, Betty 482, 483
Francisco, Evelyn 483
Franey, Billy 83, 93, 94, **248**, 249, **249**, 250, 314, 557, 563
Frascaroli, Valentina 3, **3**
Frazer, Nitra 131, 483
Fresh Start, A 362
Freuler, John R. 141
Frontier Twins Start Something, The 110, 286, 405-406
Fuller, Dale 483-484, **483**

Gaby's Gasoline Glide 121-122
Gail, Jane 281, 484
Gallagher, Toy **484**, 484-485
Gallant Gob, A 342, **342**
Garden, Mary 45, 168, **169**
Garson, Harry I. 227, 228-229
Garvin, Anita vii, 64, 66, 414-418, **415**, **416**, **417**
Gay Old Dog, A 215

Geezer of Berlin, The 351-352
Geraghty, Carmelita 485
Gerber, Neva 272, 419, 485-486
Gerdes, Emily **486**, 486
Gertie's Joy Ride 121, 124
Gibson, Ethelyn **440**, 486-487, **487**
Gibson, Margaret 487-488
Gilbert, Eugenia 488
Gilbert, Florence 488-489, **489**
Gill, Sam 247, 463
Gillstrom, Arvid E. 44, 147, 408, 441, 562
Gilmore, Helen 489, **489**
Girl from Everywhere, The 282, 336, 398, 568, 589
Gish, Dorothy vii, 163, **179**, 179-181, **181**, 256, 438, 537
Gish, Lillian 101, 179, 180, 192, 225, 313, 438
Giunchi, Lea 5
Glaum, Louise 490, 564
Goddard, Paulette 490
Godfrey, Ray 490-491, **490**
Going Gaga 417
Golden, Marta 491
Goldwyn, Samuel 45, 46, 47, 48, 49-50, 51, 52, 53, 55, 143, 165, 166, 168, 169, 190, 233, 234, 357, 390, 490, 532, 577, 612
Goodness Gracious, or, Movies as they Shouldn't Be 211, 228
Gore, Rosa 491, **492**
Gould, Bobbie 492
Goulding, Alf 336
Goulding, Edmund 266-267, 268
Graham, Betty Jane 492-493
Graham, Mrs. Samuel 367
Grant, Katherine **493**, 493
Graves, Ralph 58, **59**, 205, 206, 364-365, 470, 488, 514, 531, 556, 563
Gray, Betty 493-494
Green Stockings 132
Greenwood, Charlotte 494
Gregory, Ena 147, 494, **494**
Grey, Lita 379, 495, 497
Griffith, D.W. 14, 15, 19, 25, 27, 28, 29, 38, 110, 179-180, 182, 188, 225, 236-237, 240, 241, 244, 255, 256, 281, 322, 338, 367, 379, 387, 402, 413, 438, 439, 446, 453, 455, 468, 478, 498, 500, 504, 509, 526, 527, 529, 535, 543, 569, 570, 583, 586, 587, 589, 599, 608
Griffith, Julia 495
Griffith, Katherine **410**, **495**, 496
Griffith, Raymond 81, 154, **155**, 253, 272, 359, 394, 416, 436, 466, 554, 576, 585, 595

Guillame, Natale 5
Guiol, Clara 496
Gulliver, Dorothy 496-497, **496**

Ha Ha, Minnie 48, 57, 546, **546**
Hackett, Lillian 497
Hagar, Dorothy "Dot" 497
Hale, Georgia 348, 379, 469, 495, 497-498, **497**
Hallroom Girls, The 117-118
Ham at the Fair 88
Hamilton, Gilbert P. 285, 287, 288, 289-290, **405**, 406
Hamilton, Lillian 498
Hamilton, Lloyd 75, 88, **89**, 89, 90, 91, 202, 241, 272, 287, 291, 297, 298-299, 307, 313, 318, 320, 323, 328, 362, 371, 420, 422, 430, 435, 436, 438, 457, **457**, 469, 481, 485, 503, 508, 525, 526, 529, 533, 536, 537, 547, 549, 553, 559, 565, 572, 574, 581, 585, 603
Hammond, Harriet 498
Hampton, Raye 499, **499**
Hand Bag, The 21, 597
Handy Andy 390-391
Hanneford, Poodles 307, 390-391, 495, 607
Hansen, Juanita 358, 499, **499**
Hardwick, Lois 499-500
Hardy, Oliver 64, 66, 84, 104, 304, 313, 329, 338, 417, 429, 441, **452**, 471, **487**, 490, 504, 506, **510**, 516, 534, 551, 553, 562, 575, 602
Harlan, Marion 500
Harlow, Jean 235, 402-404
Harris, Marcia 500, **500**
Hart, Sunshine 206, 318, 321-322, **321**
Hasbrouck, Olive 501
Haver, Phyllis 58, 75, 297, 363-367, **363**, **365**, **367**, 524
Havey, Maie B. 239, 277, 280-281
Hawley, Wanda 501
Hayes, Frank 102, 103, **104**, 123, **612**
Hayward, Helen 501-502
Head Over Heels 49-50, **50**, 55
Hearst, William Randolph 191-192
Heart of Mary Ann, The 222
Heart Snatcher, The 361
Hearts and Flowers 75, 297, 364, 371, 498
Hearts and Masks 145, 360
He Did and He Didn't 42-43
Hello Mabel 36
Henderson, Del 25, 27, 256, 322-323, 324, 387, 426, 428, 457-458, 557, 599, 605
Henley, Connie 502

Henry, Gale vii, viii, 69, 72, 83, 111, 158, **207**, 247-255, **248**, **249**, **251**, **254**, 314, 343, 423, 557, 563, 608
Her Awakening 28
Her Dress Makers Bills 116
Her First Flame 252, 423
Her First Kiss 91-92, 159
Her Hero Maid 139
Her Ragged Knight 18
Her Rustic Romeo 142-143, 498
Hernandez, Anna 54, 58, 502
Herring, Aggie 502, **502**
Hervey, Wilna 503
Hey Doctor 81, 513
Hiatt, Ruth 205, 322, **327**, 339, 503, **503**, 595
Hicks, Mamie 503
Hicks, Tommie 321, **321**, 463, 503, **532**
High Sign, The 351, 352-353, **354**
Hill, Josephine 503-504
Hill, Thelma **iii**, **275**, 348, 368-371, **368**, **370**
His Birthday Jacket 220
His College Proxy 125
His Pajama Girl 146
His Wife's Husband 138
His Wooden Leg 139
His Wooden Wedding 253, 493, 595
Hitchcock, Raymond **38**, 38, 39, 612, **612**
Holderness, Fay 84, 504, **504**
Hole in the Wall, The 315, 516
Holloway, Carol 272, **426**, 504-505, **504**
Holly, Ruth 482, 505
Honeymoon Pact, The 131-132
Hooked 318, 585
Hope, Jean **437**, 505, 603
Horsley, David 123, 125, 270, 419, 431, 452, 463, 592
Hoskins, Edith 505
Hoskins, Jannie 505
Hotely, Mae 505-506, **506**, 551
How a Horseshoe Upset a Happy Family 295
Howard, Austin 353
Howard, Shemp 329, 337
Howell, Alice vii, viii, 72, 77-87, **78**, **79**, **80**, **82**, **83**, **85**, **86**, 92, 97, 107, 120, 158, 202, 251, 315, 333, 385, 417, 440, 504, 507, 513, 533, 566
Howell, Hazell 506
Howell, Helen 506-507
Howell, Yvonne 78, 87, 385, 507
Hula Honeymoon, A 328
Hulette, Gladys 507
Humor Risk 85, 385
Hunt, Jewell 508, **508**

Hurlock, Madeline 322, 369, 373-376, **375**
Hutton, Lucille 508, 508

Ich Mocht Kein Mann Sein (I Don't Want to be a Man) **171**, 171
Immigrant, The 378, 435
Imp, The 268, **269**
Ince, Ralph 14, 25, 26
Ince, Thomas H. 39, 43-44, 158, 160, 189, 237, 276-277, 439, 490, 542, 546, 583
Indiscretion 132
Inoculating Hubby 152-153
Ireland, Frederick J. 82-83, 440, 447, 517
Irwin, May **x**, 1
Ivers, Ann 509

Jackson, Mary Ann 205, 206, 338-341, **338**, **341**, 503, 509
Jackson, Peaches 338, 339, 509
Janis, Elsie 262-269, **262**, **264**, **265**, **267**, **269**
Jerome, Amy 466, 509
Jewish Prudence 334
Jones, F. Richard 44, 56, 58, 63, 64, 365, 402, 522
Josephine the Monkey 509-510, **510**
Joslin, Margaret **299**, 299-301, **301**, 547
Joy and the Dragon 172-173
Joy, Gloria **511**, 511, 516
Joy, Leatrice 487, 511-512
Joyce, Alice 25, 30, 217, **500**
Joyce, Natalie 512
June, Mildred **292**, 512-513, **512**
Jungle Goddess, The 360
Just Me 114

Keaton, Buster vii, viii, 13, 81, 125, 208, 232, 266, 276, 277, 298, **303**, 304, 308, 313, 329, 343-344, 351, 352-353, **354**, 354, 356, 371, **372**, 372, 395-396, **396**, 416, 418, 435, 458, 464, **465**, 466, 471, 475, 482, **482**, 494, 505, 509, 519, 551, 560, 568, 585, 588
Kelly, Dorothy 513
Kelly, Edith 513
Kelly, Fanny 513
Kennedy, Edgar 35, 75, 93, 285, 293, 297, 308, 361, 364, 403, 417, 556
Kennedy, Madge 45, 155, 163-170, **164**, **165**, **167**, **169**, 178, 215, 379
Kerrigan, J. Warren 135, 283, 284, **284**, 477
Kid-ing the Landlord 353
King, Henry 172, 173, 178, 419, 553
King, Judy 513-514

King, Priscilla see King, Judy
Kingston, Natalie 514, **514**
Kirby, Madge **386**, 387-389, **388**
Kirtley, Virginia 270-271, **270**
Kiss, The **x**, 1
Kleine, George 1, 453, 491
Klune, Raymond 413
Knight, Lillian 514
Knockout Buster 343, 500
Kohn, Marion H. 100, 547
Kornman, Mary 340, 460, **515**, 515, 544
Kornman, Mildred 515
Kovert, Fred 104-105

La Plante, Beatrice 199-200, **200**
La Plante, Laura 184-188, **185**, **186**, 246, 275, 589
La Verne, Jane 518
La Varnie, Laura 48, 51, 64, 99, 518-519, **518**
Lady and her Maid, The 278-279, 571, 593
Lady Baffles and Detective Duck **249**, 250, 557, 563, **564**
Laemmle, Carl 15, 17, 18, 81, 120, 122, 246, 270
Lake, Alice 515-516
Lake, Arthur 414, 464, 501, 513, **543**, 544, **548**, 548, 579, 594
Lamont, Dixie 516
Landis, Cullen 141, 172, 359
Langdon, Harry viii, 65, 94, 201, 205, 206, 261, 307, 313, 323, 344, 374, 375, 417, 426, 430, 434, 449, 464, 470, 482, 488, 497, 501, 514, 529, 537, **545**, 548, 605
Langley, Ramona 516
Latimer, Billie see Latimer, Villie
Latimer, Villie 517, **517**
Laughlin, Rhea Catto 447, 517
Laurel, Mae 518
Laurel and Hardy vii, viii, 24, 104, 196, 203, 208, 261, 309, 329, 331, 338, 347, 369, 375, 402, 403, 405, 415, 417, 418, 445, **452**, 456, 459, 469, 480, 496, 506, **510**, 528, 556, 568, 577, 589, 595, 599, 610
Laurel, Stan **5**, 6, 64, 104, 108, 207, 300, 313, 321, 327, 329, 330, 331, 351, 414-415, 427, 428, 431, **452**, 488, 489, 493, **510**, 518, 522, **523**, 547, 550, 552, 557, 574, 575, 580, 583, 587, 603
Lawrence, Florence 13-19, **14**, **16**, **17**, **18**, 24, 25, 109, 115, 278, 282
Leahy, Margaret 519, **519**
Leap Year 325, 358, 498, 588, 607
Leave It to Gerry 146-147
Lee, Florence (#1) 322-324, **323**, **324**

Lee, Florence (#2) 519-520, **519**
Lee, Frances 208-209, **209**
Lee, Gwen 520
Lee, Jane 406-411, **407**, **409**, **410**
Lee, Katherine 406-411, **407**, **409**, **410**
Lee, Lila 395, 520-521, **520**
Lehrman, Henry 79, 81, 99, 119-120, 122-123, 290, 292, 464, 552, 572, 582
Leighton, Lillian 521-522, **521**
Lend Me Your Wife 307, 454
Lentz, Irene 522
Leonard, Julie 522, **523**, 603
Leontine 4
Leslie, Lila 523, **523**
Lewis, Katherine 126, 524
Lewyn, Lewis 277
Liebes-ABC, Das 170
Lillie, Beatrice 106-108, **106**, **108**, 166, 610
Limb of Satan, A 223
Lincoln, Caryl 524
Lind, Myrtle 487, **524**, 524-525
Linder, Max 6, 317-318, 385, 422, 459, 536, 565
Little Annie Rooney 226, 344
Little Diplomat, The 154, 174-175
Little Fat Rascal, The 319, 508
Little Mother 340
Little Mouse, The 60-63, **61**
Littlefield, Emma 525
Live Agent, The 355, **355**
Lizzie's Dizzy Career 111
Lloyd, Ethel **302**, 525
Lloyd, Gayle 525, **525**
Lloyd, Harold vii, viii, 45, 107, 183, 184, 198, 199, 200, 226, 300, 301, 313, 330, 376, 381, **381**, 382-383, 384, 385, **385**, 386-387, 441, 446, 447, 449, 456, 485, 489, **489**, 502, 514, 538, 547, 550, 555, 595, 598, 599, 600, 602, 610
Lombard, Carole 336, 337, 398-399, **399**, 475, 479, 485
London, Babe 326-330, **327**, **329**
Loos, Anita 183, 237, 239-240, 255-259, **255**, 540, 595
Lopez, Aileen 526
Lorice, Del 526, 603
Lorraine, Louise 526, **526**
Lost in the Night 118
Love and Surgery 120
Love Hunger, The 134
Love, Bessie 274, 526-527, **527**
Love's Last Laugh 322
Lovejoy, Beatrice 527

Index

Lovesick Maidens of Cuddleton, The 129, 513, 591, 593
Loy, Myrna 399-402, **401**
Lubitsch, Ernst 170, 188, 194, 226, 379, 603, 604
Luddy, Barbara 527-528, **528**
Luther, Anna 528
Lynn, Elinor see Mack, Marion
Lynn, Sharon 528
Lyons, Eddie **110**, 111, 137, 150, 151, 196, 200, 207, 261, 270, 271, 315, 325, 326, 327, 351, 389, 391, 405, 421, 426, 430, 456, 461, 465, 486, 497, 516, 524, 539, 540, 549, 557, 579, 586, 596, 607

Mabel and Fatty's Married Life 29, 37
Mabel at the Wheel 34, 35
Mabel's Blunder 36, 446
Mabel's Dramatic Career 30-31, 270
Mabel's Strange Predicament 34-35
Mabery, Mary "Betty" 528
Mace, Fred 7, 29, 30, 32, **33**, 39, 69, 70, 285, 316, 491, 556
Mack, Marion 276-277, **276**, **278**, **324**, 396
Mackaill, Dorothy 529
MacLeod, Elsie 295, 534-535, **534**, 590
Madame Behave 106, 483
Madcap Marge 158, 502
Maid by Proxy, A 138
Maid of the Wild 172
Maison, Alice **296**, 531
Making a Living 35, 270
Malone, Molly 387, 389-391, **389**, **390**
Manley, Marie 535
Mann, Alice 535
Mann, Hank 35, 79, 277, 320, 325, **325**, 388, **388**, 505, 564, 567, 570, 580, **580**, 592
Manning, Mildred 535
Mansfield, Martha 536
Marcel, Marjorie 537
Marion, Edna 203-204, **203**,
Marion, Frances 161, 225, 233, 234, 235, 255, 259-260, **259**, 266, 411, 412
Marlowe, Helen 537
Marlowe, June 537
Marsh, Gene 537-538, **538**
Marsh, Veronica **23**, 24
Martin, Mrs. Joe 538-539, **539**, 582
Marvin, Grace 539-540
Marx Brothers 85, 94, 211, 385, 598
Mary Anne 58, 60
Mary of the Movies 277, **278**, 323, **324**
Mason, Shirley 253, 258, 458, 480, 540

Mass, Rose 540
Matchmaking Mama 337, 398
Maude the Mule 540
Maurice, Mary 541, **541**
Maxam, Louella 541
May, Betty 541
May, Doris 274, 541-542
McCarey, Leo 65, 66, 335, 555
McConnell, Gladys 529, **529**
McCoy, Gertrude 529-530, **530**
McCoy, Harry 35, 36, 93, 249, 355, 359, 390, **425**, 535, 607
McCoy, Ruby 530
McDonald, Marion 530-531
McDonnell, Inez 531
McGowan, Roxana 531
McGuire, Kathryn 395-397, **396**, 505
McIvor, Mary 532
McKenzie, Ella **207**, 532, **532**
McKenzie, Eva Heazlett 532, 533
McKenzie, Fay **532**, 533
McKenzie, Ida Mae 199, 533, **533**
McLaughlin, Florence 534
McPhail, Addie **536**, 536
McVey, Lucille see Drew, Mrs. Sidney
Mehaffey, Blanche 542, **542**
Melford, George 136-137
Melville, Rose 70-72, **71**, 591
Meredyth, Bess 260-262, **261**, 270
Merriam, Charlotte 75, 387, 391-395, **392**, **394**
Mersereau, Violet 543
Messinger, Buddy 332, 443, 461, 468, 483, 537, 544, 607
Messinger, Gertrude 468, **543**, 543-544,
Messinger, Marie 544
Mickey 44, 45, 47-48, **47**, 54, 55, 57, 64, 66, 310, 518, 546
Milford, Bliss 544
Miller, Patsy Ruth 401, 544-545
Mineau, Charlotte **545**, 545
Mingus, Anna 546
Mintz, Charles E. 230
Minzey, Frank 71
Miracle Man, The 148, 154
Miss Sticky-Moufie-Kiss 213
Mitchell, Belle 546-547
Mix, Tom 103, **112**, 112, 114, 123, 189, 301, 366, 397, 452, 481, 500, 512, 524, 540, 541, 555, 557, 580, 583, 600, 604
Mixed Nuts 371
Molly O 53-55, 57, 58, 368, 395

Monahan, Janethel 547
Monson, Bee 547
Montel, Mavis 547
Montgomery, Peggy 548
Montrose, Muriel **548**, 548
Moore, Colleen vii, viii, 179, 188-191, **190**, 193, 226, 269, 305, 313, 358, 366, 393, 395, 396, 403, 479, 486, 520
Moore, Eunice Murdock 548-549
Moore, Marcia 549
Moore, Marjorie 549
Moore, Mildred 391, 549
Moore, Owen 15, **17**, 18, 38, 55, 157, **265**, 266, 566
Moran, John Michael Joseph 100
Moran, Lee 76, **110**, 111, 137, 139, 150, 150, 151, 196, 200, 201, 202, 207, 261, 270, 313, 315, 326, 327, 351, 354, 389, 391, 405, 421, 426, 430, 441, 465, 486, 497, 503, 516, 524, 539-540, 541, 549, 557, 563, 571, 579, 586, 596, 607
Moran, Polly vii, 72, 90, 93, **94**, 95-102, **96**, **98**, **99**, **101**, 108, 235, **236**, 244, 324, 411, **411**, 608
Morano, Gigetta **4**, 4-5
Morris, Reggie 359, 392-393, 394, 456
Morrison, "Sunshine Sammy" 173-175, **175**, 176-177, 340, 423
Morrison, Ernest Frederick see Morrison, "Sunshine Sammy"
Morrow, Jane see McVey, Lucille
Mosquini, Marie 550, **550**
Mr. Bolter's Infatuation 128
Muddy Romance, A 31-32, 308, **309**
Mum's the Word 333, 351
Murphy, Edna 550
Murphy, Joe **245**, 246
Murray, Charles 73, **79**, 96, 97, 297, 305, **305**, 357, **358**, 363-364, **365**, 387, 424, 425, 437, 474, 537, 547, 553, **599**
Murray, Tom **306**, 306-307, 308
My Best Girl **226**, 226, 322, 399, 485, 605
My Valet **38**, 38, 39-40, 444
My Wife's Relations **303**, 304
Myers, Kathleen 550-551, **550**

Napoleon the Chimp 198-199, 250, 326, 466, 498, 521, 582
Nash, Alice and Edna 551
Navigator, The 395, 396, **396**
Ne Moyer, Frances 551
Nearly a Lady 263, 265, **265**
Neilan, Marshall 88, 190, 225, 428, 485, 486, 581, 589

Neilson, Agnes 551, **552**
Neilson, Lois 552
Nelson, Eva 552
Nelson, Evelyn 553
Nichols, George **47**, 48, 54, **57**, 57, 58
Nichols, Marguerite 553
Nichols, Norma 90, 172, 553-554, **553**, 603
Nielsen, Asta 170
Night on the Town, A 116
Night Out, A 22, 377, 502
Nip and Tuck 201, 344, **345**
Nixon, Marian 554, **554**
No-Account Count, The 87-88
Norman, Amber 554
Normand, Mabel vii, viii, 7, 11, 20, 25-68, **26**, **27**, **28**, **29**, **31**, **33**, **34**, **36**, **38**, **40**, **42**, **43**, **45**, **46**, **47**, **49**, **50**, **53**, **56**, **57**, **59**, **61**, **63**, **65**, **67**, **68**, 69, 72, 120, 138, 156, 166, 168, 190, 194, 199, 210, 237, 240, 275, 285, 297, 308, **309**, 309, 365, 368, 379, 422, 442, 450, 463, 481, 493, 502, 509, 519, 546, **546**, 565, 593, 612
Novak, Eva 280, 555, **555**, 584, 611
Novak, Jane 555, **555**, 584
Nuisance, The 353

O'Byrne, Patsy 556-557
O'Connor, Kathleen 557
O'Day, Molly see O'Neil, Sue "Bugs"
O'Dell, Georgia 557, **557**
O'Donnell, Spec 226, 230, 332, 338, 369, 463, 475, 548
O'Neal, Peg 558-559, **559**
O'Neal, Zelma **559**, 560
O'Neil, Sally 560, **560**
O'Neil, Sue "Bugs" 560
Oakland, Vivien 322, 555-556
Oakley, Laura 285, 556, **556**
Oderman, Stuart 136
Oh! Mabel Behave! 55
Oh, Sammy! 256
Ohnet, Dolly 557
Oliver, Edna May 557-558
Oliver, Violet 558
Olmstead, Gertrude **101**, 558
On His Wedding Day 285-286
On the Verge 284-285
One Mama Man, A 488, 253-254, **254**
Orth, Louise 561
Osborne, Baby Marie 154, 172-178, **173**, **174**, **175**, **177**, 273, 422, 511, 553, 606
Osterman, Kathryn 561

Index

Ostriche, Muriel 561-562, **562**
Oswalda, Ossi 170-171, **171**
Our Gang 229, 323, 324, 325, 330, 332, 340, 341, 342, 347, 415, 421, 422, 433, 446, 460-461, 463, 472, 475, 480, 489, 496, 505, 509, 515, 522, 537, 574, 577, 582, 595, 598, 604, 610
Our Wife 329

Paige, Mabel 562
Pair of Tights, A 347, 417-418, **417**
Palmer, Shirley 562
Papa's Night Out 393
Paperhanger's Revenge, The 291
Parquet, Corinne 563
Parr, Thelma 322, 563, **563**
Parrott, Charles see Chase, Charley
Parrott, James 385-386, 437, 461, 489, 512, 550, 598, 603
Parrott, Paul see Parrott, James
Parsons, William 143-145, **144**, 146, 182, 389, 431, 506, 532, 583
Pass the Gravy 334
Paths to Paradise 154, **155**, 347, 595
Payson, Blanche 147, 202, 277, 312-313, **312**, **314**, 361, 393, 460
Peacock, Lillian 249, 563, **564**
Pearce, Peggy 563-564, **564**
Peggy, Behave! 202, 343
Peggy's Burglar 360, 591
Pepper the Cat 565
Percy, Thelma 565
Perdue, Derelys 565
Perez, Marcel **6**, 6, 207, 307, 472, **472**, 534
Perfect Crime, A 398
Perry, Kathryn 565-566, **566**
Peterson, Delia 566
Phillips, Carmen 566-567
Phipps, Sally 567, **567**
Pickford, Jack 107, 155, 160, 162, 163, 390
Pickford, Mary 7, 19, 84, 155, 160, 162, 163, 169, 171, 196, **224**, 224-226, **226**, 234, 259, 260, 281, 304, 305, 322, 327, 344, 354, 379, 382, 408, 438, 463, 486, 488, 496, 502, 509, 511, 545, 554, 568, 584, 604
Picture Idol, The 228, 515, 541
Pierce, Barbara 567-568
Pitts, ZaSu 108, 277, 414, 568, **568**, 598
Play Ball 157
Pollard, Daphne **335**, 335-338, **337**, 399

Pollard, Snub 199, 300, 307, 322, 330, 336, 345, 382, 449, 459, 461, 479-480, **489**, 505, **538**, 542, 550, 578, 598
Pony Express, The 154, 594
Poor Fish **251**, 252, 586
Potel, Victor **85**, 123, 220, **299**, 300, **301**, 314, 481, 546, 586
Prescott, Vivian 118, 316, 569, **569**
Prevost, Marie vii, **187**, 188, **189**, 280, 282, 363, **363**, 366, 367, 401, 526, 557, 570, 578
Prevost, Peggy 570, **570**
Price, Kate 21, 128, 301-305, **302**, **303**, **305**, 383, 424, 508
Prodigal Bridegroom, A 369
Professional Scapegoat, The 212
Puppe, Die 171
Purviance, Edna 59-60, 376-381, **376**, **378**, **380**, 435, 441, 449, 547, 578, 589

Quartaro, Nena 570-571, **571**
Queen for a Day, A 102
Queenie the Horse 541, 571
Quirk, Billy **70**, 131, 182, 211, 225, 310, 385, 450, 454, 593

Radinoff, Florence 571
Raggedy Rose **63**, 64-65, 66, 275, 415, 422
Ralston, Jobyna 376, **384**, 384-387, **385**, 449
Rankin, Caroline 315-318, **317**
Rappe, Virginia 163, 350, **572**, 572
Rat's Knuckles, The 332-333
Ray, Emma 302, 573
Ray, Marjorie **573**, 573
Rea, Marvel 361-362, **362**
Reardon, Mildred 574, 587
Reavis, Teddy 574
Red Pepper 328, 514
Reed, Emma 574, **574**
Reed, Florence 574-575
Reeves, Myrtle 575
Regular Girl, A 267-268
Remodeling Her Husband 180
Revier, Harry 133
Reynolds, Edna 575
Reynolds, Vera **91**, 575-576, **576**
Rhodes, Billie 111, 135, 136-148, **136**, **138**, **140**, 142, **144**, **145**, 147, 150, 152, 179, 389, 421
Rich, Irene 537, 576
Richard, Viola 204, 452, 577, **577**
Ricksen, Lucille 577-578, **578**
Rieger, Margie 578

Ritchie, Billie 79, 80, 81, 91, 120-121, 122-123, 300, 445, 454, 508, 546, 552, 561, 573, 596, 608
Rivero, Lorraine 578, **578**
Roach, Bert 75, 86, 93, 186, 187, 246, 297, 364, 529, 603, 607
Roach, Hal 63, 64, 65, 66, 67, 87, 101, 104, 108, 172, 173, 184, 199, 200, 203, 204, 205, 229, 230, 253, 254, 275, 300, 301, 307, 313, 315, 320, 321, 325, 330, 331, 332, 333, 334, 338, 340, 342, 347, 369, 371, 375, 382, 383, 385, 386, 387, 400, 402, 403, 414, 415, 416, 417, 418, 421, 422, 427, 428, 433, 434, 435, 437, 441, 442, 447, 448, 449, 452, 461, 465, 469, 470, 475, 476, 478, 488, 489, 491, 493, 494, 495, 496, 497, 504, 505, 507, 509, 510, 513, 515, 517, 522, 526, 530, 538, 542, 544, 545, 547, 550, 553, 554, 555, 556, 557, 560, 562, 568, 570, 571, 574, 577, 578, 579, 580, 581, 586, 587, 588, 594, 595, 598, 603, 604, 608, 609, 610, 611
Roberts, Edith 281, 579
Rodgers, Dora 579
Rodolfi, Eleuterio 4
Roessing, Laura 579-580, **579**
Rogers, Dorothy 580
Rogers, Louis T. 410
Rogers, Rena 580, **580**
Rogers, Will 45, 166, 168, 181, **181**, 235, 390, 421, 434, 461, 481, 542, 550, 554, 556, 576, 595, 611
Roland, Ruth 172, 459, 553, 580-581, 582, 589
Rosanova, Rosa 581
Rosson, Queenie 440, 581
Rowdy Ann 244, 247, 488, 524
Run, Girl, Run 336, 398, 479, 568, 589
Rydzewski, Steve 375-376

Sadler, Josie **20**, 69-70, **70**, **128**, 129, **130**, **302**, 316
Sage-Brush League, The 319-320
Sais, Marin 581-582, **582**
Sally the Chimp 198-199, 326, 498, 521, **521**, 582
Salter, Thelma 582-583
Sammy's Scandalous Scheme 289, 297
Sampson, Teddy 126, 389, 583, **583**
Sandberg, Bob 100
Santell, Al 241, 242-243
Schade, Betty 584
Schaefer, Anne 343, 584
Schenck, Joseph 182, 183, 258, 413, 519
Schroeder, Doris 277, 279-280
Scott, Lois **92**, 584, **585**
Scrambled Brains 329

Scrambled Eggs 328, 537
Scrub Lady, The 233, 234
Seastrom, Dorothy 328, 585
Sebastian, Dorothy 585,
Sebastian, Malcolm 299, 323, 429, 578, **578**
Sedgwick, Eileen 281, 557, 586
Seely, Sybil 371, **372**
Selby, Gertrude 80, 119-127, **119**, **121**, **122**, **124**, 561
Selznick, Lewis 161, 182, 228, 241, 268, 566
Selznick, Myron 160-161, 266
Semon, Larry 60, 103, 105, 199, 298, 305, 312, 350, 388, 424, 427, 430, 443, **443**, 456, 467, 471, 485, 491, 506, 508, 535, 550, 554, 556, 565, 610
Sennett, Mack vii, 7, 25, 27, 28-30, 31, 32, 33, 35, 37, 38-40, 41, 42, 43, 44, 47, 48, 53-54, 55, 56, **56**, 57, 58-59, 60, 63, 72, 75, 76, 78-79, 90, 93, 94, 95, 96-97, 99, 100, 101, 102, 103, 110, 119, 120, 125, 137, 138, 185-186, 188, 201, 205, 206, 231, 237, 240, 243, 249, 270, 272, 277, 282, 285, 286, 287, 292, 297, 298, 305, 306, 307, 308, 310, 312, 313, 315, 316, 321, 322, 324, 328, 330, 336, 337, 338, 339, 343, 348, 349, 351, 356, 357, 359, 361, 363, 364, 365, 367, 368, 369, 370, 371, 373, 374, 376, 392, 395, 398-399, 408, 412, 413, 414, 420, 422, 423, 424, 425, 426, 427, 429-430, 432, 434, 435, 439, 442, 444, 448, 449, 452, 455, 457, 459, 463, 464, 466, 470, 472, 474, 475, 476, 478, 479, 482, 483-484, 485, 488, 495, 497, 498, 499, 502, 503, 504, 512, 513, 514, 516, 517, 518, 522, 525, 528, 530, 531, 536, 537, 541, 545, 548, 551, 552, 553, 556, 557, 563, 564, 565, 566, 568, 569, 570, 575, 583, 588, 589, 593, 594, 595, 596, 599, 600, 602, 603, 605, 606, 607, 611
Serenade by Proxy, A 295, 530
Seymour, Clarine 163, 586-587, **586**
Shanghaied Lovers 205-206
Shaw, Peggy 24, 587
She Cried 9
She Wrote a Play and Played It 249-250
Sheehan, John 272, **426**
Sheldon, James M. 359-360
Shepard, Pearl Sheppard, Pearl
Sherman, Jane 588
Sherman, Lowell 55
Shirley, Rose 588
Shiver, H.L. 178
Short, Gertrude 275, 588, **588**
Shot in the Excitement 79, 89

Index

Should Men Walk Home? 65-66, 495, 496
Sinclair, Johnny 371
Sis Hopkins 48, 70-72, **71**, 481, 551, 591
Sisterly Scheme, A 214, 215
Skirts 93, 100, 239, 422, 463, 487, 519
Slavey, The 252
Sleeper, Martha 331-335, **332**, **334**, **577**
Slim Princess, The 48, 221, 263
Smalley, Phillips 116, 263, 516, 580
Smile Please 201, 344
Smith, Dick 78, 81, 83, 84, 85, 86, 87, 385
Smith's Baby 322, 339
Smith's Candy Shop 339
Snooky the Human-Zee 93, **198**, 198-199, 326, 343, **533**
Solter, Harry 14, 15, 17, 18
Somebody's Widow 141-142
Southern, Eve 589
Spanking Age, The 340
Sponsler, Juanita 589, **589**
Spoor, George K. 219-220
Spoor, Gertrude 219-220
St Clair, Mal 259, 274, 379, **425**, 537, 603
St John, Al 40, 41, 42, 43, 79, 81, 103, 232, 299, 308, 309, 313, **327**, 328, 355, 357, 436, 438, 453, 457, **462**, 463, **466**, 482, 508, 536, **559**, 560, 575, **602**, 603, 612, **612**
St. Johns, Adela Rogers 51-53
Stanley, Kathryn 589
Steadman, Vera **197**, 349-351, **349**, **351**
Steele, Agnes 589
Stenographers Wanted 128-129, 303, 428
Steppling, John 220, 272, **426**, 504, 516, 592
Sterling, Ford 11, **28**, 29, 30, 31, **31**, 35, 37, 38, 55, 56, **56**, 73, 75, 119, 270, 285, 297, 298, **311**, 357, 364, 392, 451, 476, 492, 556, 563, 583, 606
Sterling, Merta 88, 94, 318-321, **319**, **320**, 508, 552
Stern, Abe and Julius 81, 82, 122, 202, 289, 342, 343, 421, 459, 464, 470, 499, 536, 537, 607
Stevens, George 87, 507
Stevens, Charlotte 590
Stevens, Jessie 294, 590
Stevens, Josephine 590, **590**
Stevens, Yvonne see Howell, Yvonne
Stewart, Anita 25, 277, 590-591
Stonehouse, Ruth 210, 219-224, **219**, **220**, **222**, **223**, 592
Storey, Edith 102, 591, **591**
Stranded 13, 253, 259
Street, Julian 215-216, 217
Stuart, Dixie 591-592

Styers, Anna 592
Subduing of Mrs. Nag, The 20, 26, 30
Suds 225
Sul-Te-Wan, Madame 530
Sully, Janet Miller 592
Summerville, Slim 87, 92, 93, 94, 97, 99, 187, 207, **296**, 445, 463, 477, 595
Sure–Mike! 333
Suzanna 55, 56-57, **57**, 58, 368, 546, **546**
Swain, Mack 35, 36, 73, 90, 91, 98, **258**, 297, 309, 322, 336, 351, 389, 398, 423, 490, 504, 541, 579
Swanson, Gloria 192, 207, 269, 357, 374, 438, 456, **592**, 592-593
Swat the Spy 408, 411
Swayne, Marion 211, 593
Sweeney's Christmas Bird 21
Sweet, Blanche 28, 44, 281, 424, 438

Tacky Sue's Romance 223
Talmadge, Constance 24, 127, 163, 179, 181-183, **182**, 207, **257**, 258, 259, 260, 437, 593, 602
Talmadge, Norma 69, 181, 205, 258, 278, 424, 437, 519, 593, **593**
Tanguay, Eva 594
Tansey, Emma 594
Tapely, Rose 594
Tarron, Elsie **348**, 594-595
Taurog, Norman 246, 328, 522, 603
Taylor, Ruth **258**, 369, 595, **595**
Taylor, William Desmond 55, 56, 58, 60, 68, 163, 247, 488
Tayo, Lyle 595
Teare, Betty 87, 596
Teare, Ethel 87-95, **87**, **89**, **91**, **92**, 318, 372, 463, 589, 596
Tennant, Barbara 596
Tennyson, Gladys 596
Thalberg, Irving 107, 235, 260, 411
That Little Band of Gold 37-38, 444, 476
Thatcher, Eva 75, **296**, 296-299, **298**, 357, **358**, 502, **602**
Theby, Rosemary 21, 277, 281, 405, 597, **597**
Their Quiet Honeymoon 150-151
Thicker than Water 338
Thomas, Olive 51, 155-163, **156**, **157**, **159**, **162**, 259, 260, 502
Thompson, Duane 597-598, **597**
Thompson, Mollie 598
Those Awful Hats 19
Those Primitive Days 153
Three Must-Get-Theres, The 317-318, 385

Three Wise Goofs 147
Thrilling Romance, A 204
Through the Keyhole 88
Thurman, Mary 356-358, **356**, **358**, 364
Tillie Wakes Up 232-233, 260, 448
Tillie's Nightmare 231, 233, 606
Tillie's Punctured Romance 37, 70, 230, 231, 329, 446
Tillie's Tomato Surprise 232
Times We Had, The 192
Tincher, Fay vii, 28, 69, 95, 125, 134, 199, 236-247, **236**, **238**, **240**, **242**, **245**, 256, 281, 333, 392, 488, 583, 599
Titus, Lydia Yeamans 222, 598
Todd, Harry **299**, 300, **301**, 301, 547
Todd, Thelma 108, 414, 430, 445, 448, 568, 598-599, **599**
Toncray, Kate 29, 599, **599**
Too Many Crooks **383**, 383, 482
Topsy and Eva 412, **413**, 413, 473
Totheroh, Rollie 379
Townsend, Anna 599-600
Tranchell, Hazel 600, **600**
Trask, Wayland 73, 243, 357, **358**
Trick, Martha 600
Trimble, Arthur 332, 343, 500, 601, **601**
Trimble, Lawrence 10, 11
Trouble Makers 406, 408
Troublesome Secretaries 26-27
Truax, Maude 600-601
True, Bess 601
Truex, Ernest 215, 258, 513
Trunnelle, Mabel 601-602
Tucker, George Loane 154, 484
Turner, Florence 7-13, **7**, **8**, **10**, **12**, **13**, 14, 19, 24, 109, 132, 228, 282
Turpin, Ben 90, 98, 104, **187**, 205, 277, 286, 289, 292, 300, **301**, 313, **331**, 331, 339, 344, 364, 369, 374, 375, 377, 395, 419, 430, 495, 498, 514, 536, 546, 548, 557, 563, 580, 595
Turtner, Doreen 601, **601**
Twas Ever Thus 263, 265-266
Twentieth Century Revue 94
Two Little Imps 408
Two O'Clock Train, The 239
Two Tars 369, 496, **510**, 595, 611
Tyner, Irene 602, **602**

Under a Spell 86
Up and Down the Ladder 9, 278

Vagabond Queen, The 196
Van, Beatrice 271-276, **273**, 592
Van, Polly 602
Van, Wally 21, 102, **128**, 129, **130**, 131, 132, 135, 437, 483
Vance, Virginia 323, 602-603, **602**
Vanderveer, Elinor **346**, 346-347
Vanity Fair Girls 348, 437, 497, 505, 522, 526, 553, 603
Varden, Gladys 603, 611
Vaughn, Alberta 94, 201-202, **201**, 588, **588**
Velez, Lupe 402, **403**
Vernon, Bobby 126, 186, 207, 209, 249, **249**, 313, 315, 328, **349**, 350, 351, 359, 391, 392, 414, 459, 470, 483, 500, 504, 525, 531, 532, 557, 583, **586**, 587, 590, **592**, 593, 597
Vernon, Dorothy 324-326, **325**, **432**
Vidor, Florence 603-604
Von Sternberg, Josef 380, 497, 589

Walker, Lillian 21, 127-135, **127**, **128**, **130**, **131**, **133**, 179
Wall, "Boots" 604
Wallace, May 604, **604**
Wallace, Richard 64
Waller, Jane 152, 605
Wallis, Hal 77
Waltzing Around 143
Wanted: A Leading Lady 150
Ward, Alice 605
Ward, Carrie C. 605, **605**
Ward, Hap 199, 250, **251**, 343, 344, 346
Ward, Lucille 272, 606
Warner, Marion 173, 606
War Prides 23
Warwick, Virginia 383, 606
Washburn, Alice **294**, 294-296, 534, 609
Washington, Hannah 338, 341-343, **342**
Watson Jr. Coy 321, 510
Wayne, Maude **91**, 606-607, **607**
Webb, Kenneth 164, 428
Webb, Roy 164
Weber, Lois 116, 263, 265, 298, 413, 539, 580, 584
Wedding Bells and Lunatics 125
Wells, May 299, 607
Welsh, Bessie 607
West, Billy 83, 85, 103, 146, 250, 308, 312, 317, 325, 430, **440**, 440, 441, 447, 450, 478, **486**, 486, **487**, 504, 512, 517, 525, 527, 533, 534, 536, 546, 550, 551, 601, 602, 608

West, George B. 85
Westbrook, Virginia 608
Westover, Winifred 608
What Happened to Rosa? 49
When Bess Got in Wrong 261
When Hubby Forgot 89-90
When Joe Went West 96
When Winter Went 393-394
Where's My Wandering Boy this Evening? 292, 374
Which Way Did He Go? 129-130
White, Blanche 608
White, Jack 75, **76**, 198, 203, 277, 298, 313, 315, 321, 325, 343, 361, 362, 391, 396, 397, 416, 429, 430, 434, 435, 436, 446, 458, 461, 469, 470, 476, 478, 481, 485, 497, 503, 508, 523, 526, 530, 536, 537, 547, 554, 557, 558, 559, 560, 583, 585, 588, 592, 603
White, Pearl 114-119, **115**, **117**, **118**, 179, 263
White, Vera 330-331, **331**
Whiteis, Marjorie 609
Whitewashing William 89
Who's Your Father? 103, **104**, 123, 530
Why Worry? 327, **385**, 386
Widow Jones, The 1
Wiggle Your Ears 340, **341**, 460

Wiley, Wanda 204, **204**, 459, **517**, 537
Williams, Cora 609
Wilson, Tom 106, 123, 327, 344, 401
Winkler, Margaret J. 229-230, **230**, 463
Winnie's Wild Wedding 360
Winton, Jane 609
Wolbert, Dorothea 108, 609-610, **610**
Woman Hater, The 114-115
Woman of Paris, A 379, 380
Woman of the Sea, A 380, 589
Won in a Closet 33-34
Woods, A.H. 60-61, 63
Woods, Grace 610-611
Wray, Fay 442, 611, **611**

Yallop, David 247
Young, Catherine 611
Young, Clara Kimball 22, 44, 126, 226-229, **227**, **229**, 266, 299, **302**, 303, 424, 469, 477
Young, James 44, 228, 266, 267, 268

Zabelle, Flora 39, 612, **612**
Zanuck, Darryl F. 372-373
Ziegfeld Jr., Florenz 156-157, 159, 160, 163, 414, 437, 438, 439, 549

Printed in Great Britain
by Amazon